Railroads of America

THOMAS B. BREWER
General Editor

RICHARD C. OVERTON
Consulting Editor

HISTORY OF THE MISSOURI PACIFIC
by Thomas B. Brewer and Allen Dickes

HISTORY OF THE
ATCHISON, TOPEKA AND SANTA FE
by Keith Bryant

HISTORY OF THE BALTIMORE AND OHIO
by William Catton

HISTORY OF THE LOUISVILLE & NASHVILLE
by Maury Klein

HISTORY OF THE CANADIAN PACIFIC
by W. Kaye Lamb

HISTORY OF THE NORTHERN PACIFIC
by Robert L. Peterson

HISTORY OF THE CANADIAN NATIONAL
by G. R. Stevens

HISTORY OF THE ILLINOIS CENTRAL
by John F. Stover

History of the
Canadian National Railways

HISTORY
OF THE
CANADIAN
NATIONAL
RAILWAYS

G. R. STEVENS

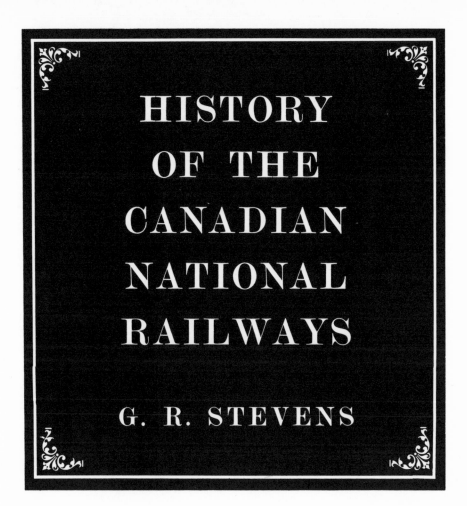

The Macmillan Company, New York, New York
Collier-Macmillan Publishers, London

Contents

1.

A Land in Its Beginnings   I

2.

The Portage Railways   8

3.

Promoters and Politicians   18

4.

Grand Trunk: The Trail of the Comet   34

5.

The Intercolonial: Monkeyshines in the Maritimes   75

6.

The First Canadian System   106

7.

The Confrontation of Systems   138

8.

The Tools of the Railway Trade   149

9.

Miracles Sometimes Happen   160

10.

Mackenzie and Mann: Amble to Jog Trot   171

11.

Consequences of a Bluff   189

12.

From Sea to Sea   208

13.

Mackenzie and Mann: Canter to Gallop   238

14.

Canadian Railways at War   265

15.
Mackenzie and Mann: Day of Reckoning   272

16.
The Grand Trunk Tragedy   281

17.
New Venture: Changed World   301

18.
Potentials and Perils   311

19.
The Summer of His Days   322

20.
The Lordly Buck and the Butcher's Dogs   345

21.
The Lean and Hungry Years   361

22.
At War Anew   379

23.
Shaping Up for the Future   395

24.
The Newfoundland Story   405

25.
Over the Hump   415

26.
Wider Still and Wider   448

APPENDIX   503

NOTES   513

BIBLIOGRAPHY   519

INDEX   525

Illustrations

NOTE: *Illustrations not otherwise credited appear through the courtesy of the Canadian National Railways.*

	PAGE
The *Dorchester*, first Canadian locomotive.	9
The first Canadian train.	11
The *Samson* and the *Albion*.	14
Replica of metal ticket used in 1847 on the Montreal & Lachine Railroad.	15
First "U" rail in Canada.	32
Toronto Station, 1857.	32
Milwaukee, which carried the Canadian defenders during the Fenian Raids.	58
Great Western Suspension Bridge over Niagara River, 1852.	63
Bonaventure Station, Montreal, 1871.	67
Horse and wagon ticket on the Nova Scotia Railway, 1864.	78
Sir Sandford Fleming.	85
High embankment, Intercolonial Railway, 1874.	93
Car ferry: Ontario-Michigan (Windsor-Detroit).	117
Great Western's *Oberon*, 1851.	117
Pileup on Central Vermont Railway, 1864.	134
What Sunday travel in Vermont was like in 1875.	135
Early trekkers to the prairies.	166
Early trekkers, three years later.	167
Memorial plaque to Sir Sandford Fleming, founder of World Standard Time System.	168

PAGE

Sir Donald Mann, partner of Mackenzie and Mann.   172

Sir William Mackenzie, partner of Mackenzie and Mann.   172

Winter survey crew, Mackenzie and Mann, 1904.   187

Sir Charles Rivers-Wilson.   190

Charles Melville Hays.   195

Early Canadian-built passenger car, 1860.   212

Central span of the Quebec Bridge collapses, 1916.   218

Grand Trunk Pacific location party in the Rockies, 1912.   220

Prairie construction on the Canadian Northern, 1905.   223

Mountain construction on the Grand Trunk Pacific, 1912.   230

"Swansie's Men," Grand Trunk Pacific tunnel crew, 1912.   231

Rafting supplies on the Upper Fraser, Grand Trunk Pacific, 1912.   233

Prince Rupert, where the National Transcontinental Railway
        reached the Pacific.   235

Locomotive abandoned in the bush after the Yukon gold rush, 1897. 249

Trestle goes out and in again: Mackenzie and Mann in northern
        Alberta, 1915.   255

Mackenzie and Mann tunnel on Hell's Gate, 1910.   261

Halifax disaster—the explosion of December 6, 1917.   266

The Grand Trunk Pier burning at Seattle in 1914.   267

William Howard Taft.   298

Sir Henry Worth Thornton.   309

Experimental road/rail car, 1930.   325

Canadian National Railways: Pioneer broadcasters, 1926.   327

Hudson Bay Railway construction.   328

Medical car, 1927.   330

School car, 1928.   331

The first aircraft: Stearman biplane, 1937.   368

The *Lady* line for Caribbean service.   373

The *Prince* line for Pacific coastal service.   373

Armored Diesel locomotive for service to Prince Rupert during
        World War II.   385

H.M.S. Prince David, converted during World War II into a landing
        craft carrier.   390

Early flying days—oxygen necessary for crossing the Rockies.   402

Newfoundland Railway—the "Newfie Bullet."   410

Central Vermont Railroad—White River Junction Station.   417

Donald Gordon.   426

Unit train of grain hoppers on the prairies.   428

	PAGE
Unit train of coal cars in the Rockies.	429
H.R.H. Princess Elizabeth clambers up to take the throttle during her 1951 tour of Canada.	430
H.R.H. Princess Elizabeth and her husband, the Duke of Edinburgh.	431
Car with mechanical temperature control for perishable freight.	432
Express container car.	432
Hopper for dry bulk freight.	433
Piggybacks.	433
Newsprint car.	434
Turbo train in Toronto yard.	435
"Super-Continental" fast passenger train crossing the Athabaska River.	437
Museum train with wood- and coal-burning locomotives, 1953.	438–39
The barren lands—the Canadian Arctic.	441
Intercolonial Railway: Causeway from Nova Scotia to Cape Breton Island, opened August 13, 1955.	443
Air Canada jetliner, 1970.	445
Montreal hump yards.	453
The last steam locomotive, 6218, retired in 1971.	463
Jasper Park Lodge from the Athabaska River.	465
Macdonald Hotel, Edmonton.	466
Queen Elizabeth Hotel, Montreal.	468
The Beaver Club: Donald Gordon in song.	470
Modern construction methods—lining up.	477
New methods—automatic spike driving.	478
Pine Point, Arctic mining town.	479
Electronic hump yard scale.	483
Current competitors: British 4472, Canadian steam 6218, Canadian Diesel 2302, Turbo Diesel 1970.	486–87
Canadian National Railways motion pictures: Buster Keaton in *The Railrodder*.	490
Canadian National Railways complex, Montreal.	493
Cartoon entitled "His Last Run" from *The Montreal Star*.	499

Maps

NOTE: *Maps prepared by the Canadian National Railways Drafting Department.*

	PAGE
The First Canadian Main Line, 1856	51
The Intercolonial Railway, 1876	91
The First Canadian System—The Grand Trunk Railway, Eastern Section, 1893	132
The First Canadian System—The Grand Trunk Railway, Western Section, 1893	133
Canadian National Railways System—Eastern Section, 1972	418
Canadian National Railways System—Western Section, 1972	419

Acknowledgments

I owe a deep debt of gratitude to the Canadian National Railways Company for permitting me not only to condense the first two volumes of their official history but also for allowing me to use some of the material assembled for their third volume, which will not be published for some years yet. In particular, I wish to thank Maurice Archer, senior vice-president, and Maynard Metcalf and E. A. Bromley, retired vice-presidents, for their kindness and helpfulness in the compilation of this book. Others who should not go unmentioned are K. H. Hand, chief of the Photographic Division, and Antony Clegg who designed the maps.

Since the period covered by this book comes up to 1970, it was inevitable that the historian would find fertile sources of information among the retired personnel of the company. Chief among these was S. W. Fairweather, indomitable and provocative, who was at the heart of activities for thirty-five years. Of almost equal assistance was G. H. Lash, director of public relations, who for two years after his retirement in 1964 worked intimately with the historian. Also there was Robert England, under whom the Department of Agriculture and Colonisation flourished during the depression of the 1930s, and F. J. Fusey, who had seen the Diesel engine out of its swaddling clothes into man's attire. Finally, last but far from least was Mrs. Henry James, formerly Lady Thornton, without whose wealth of information the chapters concerning her ill-fated husband would have lacked much of their drama and intimacy.

Among miscellaneous assistants I owe a great deal to Helen Duchief, librarian of the Canadian National Railways, and to M. Jean Coté, of her staff, who as local researcher constantly was running my errands. I also must record my gratitude to Mrs. Anne Desmarais and Mrs. Merlin Dobro of Montreal, and to Mrs. Emily Page of London and Mrs. N. McFeat of Glasgow, for typing and copying assistance.

It would be less than courteous to neglect similar acknowledgments to the aid and kindness of the publisher's readers, Dr. R. C. Overton of the University of Western Ontario and Dr. T. B. Brewer of the University of Toledo.

G. R. S.

History of the
Canadian National Railways

1

A Land in Its Beginnings

Three hundred years ago, when the map makers began to ink in details of the North American continent, there seemed no more unlikely place on the face of the earth to establish a new nation than the unwieldy land mass which is now Canada.

Its size was appalling—more than 3,000 miles from ocean to ocean, containing more than 3,000,000 square miles of emptiness. Its eastern expanses were furred with great forests whose removal would involve a labor of giants before food could be grown. The central plain was separated from the habitable east by 900 miles of rocky, boggy waste—a veritable land of Cain. Beyond the prairies a mountain range rose in midair, barring the way to the western ocean. Nothing seemed more certain than that when this vast, bleak area was occupied, its lines of communication would run up and down the continent. The northland would be no more than frontier to the fertile, inviting expanses of the south.

These geographical obstacles were reinforced by the vagaries of climate. In what is now Canada, there were brief in-between seasons of spring and autumn, a short fierce summer and a long winter in which forests, plains and mountains alike were locked in shackles of bitter, piercing cold. The land possessed but one redeeming feature—the great trench of the St. Lawrence and the huge bowls of lakes that fed that river. For approximately half of the year, these waterways constituted a navigable route through the eastern forests and past the wasteland to the edge of the central plains. Other rivers meandered across the prairies to the approaches to the Rockies. Amid that sea of mountains, deep valleys provided passages to the end of land and the pounding Pacific seas.

But even upon these waterways, in the best months of the year, traffic moved at the pace of the ox. There were rapids to bypass; portages, floods and swift currents to negotiate; storms to weather. Each spring the fur convoys left Montreal for the west. Should sailing ships weigh anchor in the St. Lawrence at the same hour that the *voyageurs* departed, the vessels might be 12,000 miles away, in the China ports, before the incoming and outgoing fur flotillas crossed in the Rainy river and lake chain, less than 1,200 miles to the west of Montreal. Little more than a century ago Sir George Simpson, with a crack canoe crew keeping fifty strokes to the minute for twelve hours each day, broke the record for the journey from Fort Churchill on Hudson Bay to Astoria on the Pacific coast. It took him eighty-four days.

The original land routes in Canada were immeasurably inferior to the water routes. They consisted of nothing more than Indian trails employed in hunting and in war. But in the course of two centuries of occupation, French Canadians had colonized a thin strip of territory on either bank of the St. Lawrence over a distance of 300 miles, from Maalbaie to Chateauguay. This area of settlement was seldom more than ten miles deep, but within this shallow zone there were three classes of roads. The main highway along the waterfront was the *chemin royal*; the short lateral roads from the back to the front of the zone of settlement were the *chemins des sorties et communications*; in the rear, along the fringe of unbroken forest, ran the *chemin de ceinture et de travois*. From 1780 onward a post chaise service operated over the 175 miles between Quebec and Montreal. The service had twenty-four staging posts and offered excellent accommodation; the trip was completed comfortably in two days, by two-wheeled *calèches* in summer, by *carrioles*, the *habitant* sleighs, in winter. Regular travelers preferred the winter, when they could use the ice of the river as their highway.

In what is now Ontario, the first governor, George Graves Simcoe, who held office from 1791 to 1795, found himself the ruler of sixty scattered settlements, with only one thing in common. They were all isolated, sealed from each other by the walls of the forest. Simcoe wished to see them coalesce, as in Britain, first into shires and thereafter into a kingdom. To this end he began to cut straight roads, in the Roman fashion, from the hub of his capital at York. Dundas Street ran west towards Michigan Territory; Yonge Street headed into the north, first to Lake Simcoe and

later to Georgian Bay. But by the end of the eighteenth century, the
United Empire Loyalists, men who stood in no awe of the land to which
their devotion to the Crown had exiled them, were thickening in the likelier
neighborhoods; by 1810 there were eighty thousand English-speaking
settlers in Upper Canada. They used water routes wherever feasible, and
the Great Lakes were feathered with their sailing craft; but they also built
roads on occasion, such as those which ran through the half-million acres
of the Talbot holdings along Lake Erie and across the lands of the
Canada Company beside Lake Huron.

As early as 1798, Asa Danforth undertook to cut a road along
Lake Ontario from York to Kingston, a distance of 175 miles. All these
early roads were abominable; in thaws and wet weather they became
morasses. Mrs. Simcoe, the governor's lady, had mired down in the course
of a moonlight canter along Dundas Street; a young officer reported that it
had taken him three hours to negotiate five miles on Yonge Street; William
Lyon Mackenzie, after one of his electioneering tours, declared the York-
Kingston road the worst that human foot had ever trod. Captain Basil
Hall, a seasoned traveler, in his diaries damned all Canadian roads alike;
a wayfarer in the Canada Company tract declared that he only encountered
one mudhole on the road. It extended from Walkerton to Kincardine.
These settlements were thirty miles apart.

Curiously enough, the Maritime Provinces—Nova Scotia, New Brunswick and Prince Edward Island—although blessed with sea-lanes on all
sides, would appear to have fared best in land communications. Well-built
roads linked the Nova Scotia settlements with those in New Brunswick;
the extensive Loyalist migration into the Saint John Valley had resulted in
perhaps the best road in all British North America. But by and large, all
Canadian settlers were prisoners of terrain and weather. Their isolation
was reflected in both their economy and their society. Their trade remained
almost exclusively in the hands of merchants in the ports, who sent orders
to London or Bristol by the first sailings each spring. The goods arrived
during the summer, often with a hundred items on a single bill of lading,
to be reparceled by the importers and forwarded to inland destinations by
bateaux or Durham boats—huge barges which were poled or tugged against
the current, unloaded at the rapids and carried on headstraps or men's
backs to the next stretch of navigable water. On receipt of the goods, the
local shopkeepers signed notes of hand at high rates of interest and dispatched such produce as ashes, peltry, woodware and grains by the outgoing flotilla. More than a year might pass before returns on these shipments were received.

Such commerce creaked with delays and bore heavy interest charges.

It restricted the settlers to a few imported staples and to lives of squalor. Habitation in a lean-to, reliance on wild foods, floods vying with drought, biting cold with scorching heat, furious storms, crop failures and unending unrequited labors reduced many settlers to subsistence on a brute level. The isolation, the silence and the immensity of the Canadian forest struck chill in many hearts; it brought the fear, and often the certainty, of being lost and forgotten.

The Great Awakening

Fortunately the times were on the march. There came that grim June day at Waterloo which wrote *finis* to the twenty years' struggle with Napoleon. Thereafter the British peoples were destined to learn that victory was scarcely less disastrous than defeat. The collapse of war-fostered industries led to acute distress; weavers' wages fell from twenty-five to five shillings a week; agricultural laborers fed on nettles; the homeless multiplied to a host and lived in the ditches. Revolution was in the air; Thistlewood's gang promised to parade the heads of cabinet ministers on pikes when a republic had been proclaimed. To millions the empty lands of the Empire called with no uncertain voices; an emigration pamphlet summed up their emotions in its boldfaced exhortation: "Seek a far place and go to it quickly lest a worse thing befall."

As soon as ships could be found, thousands were on the move. In the next twenty years, more than half a million British settlers arrived in Canada. Many were argicultural artisans whose livelihoods had been destroyed by the Enclosure Acts; this group included smiths, farriers, wheelwrights, ploughmakers, tanners, millers, weavers, cobblers, turners, thatchers, chairmakers, tinkers and masons. They had brought their tools with them, and having landed, they infiltrated into the forest in every direction. They made their way into Cape Breton and Prince Edward Island and through the rough New Brunswick forests into the lower townships of Quebec; they scouted the Lake Ontario shore and reached the fruitful Niagara peninsula; they followed Indian trails northward, scanning the river banks for sites for waterwheels; they reached the thinning hardwood forests where Galt, Guelph and Stratford now stand. Finally, in one place or another, in a sea of trees, they flung their packs to the ground, drew their axes and built lean-tos, slung their cooking pots over a blaze and told each other that here was as good as anywhere to make a start on a new home.

The newcomers on this second wave of migration were spared a great deal of the hardship and frustration of their predecessors. Of the one hundred thousand English-speaking settlers in Upper Canada, many had arrived from the United States, where they had tamed the wilderness in New England, upper New York State, Virginia and the Carolinas. They knew that the forest was not an enemy; for those compelled to live in its expanses, it had a great deal more to offer than did jungles, deserts or even open plains. With skill and determination, the first lean-to would soon give way to a log shanty. A few good seasons and a frame house would replace the shanty. The trim *habitant* farmhouses along the St. Lawrence, with their steep roofs, projecting eaves, dormer windows, outside chimneys and staircases, surrounding barns, root houses and bake ovens, all with scarcely an ounce of metal in their structures, showed what the forest could provide. Wood is the most docile of materials; a good pair of hands, an ax, a drawknife and a chisel could produce almost everything a settler required. He could make his own boards, spiles, slats, shingles and staves; he could build all essential furniture, tables, chairs, benches, beds, bins and shelves. He could equip himself with wooden carts and wagons, ploughs, drags, yokes, pumps, buckets and handles. He could provide his wife with churns, dippers, rolling pins, splint brooms, bowls and plates for the table.

There was no hunger in the forest. Crop failures sometimes put the early settlers on short commons of wheat, bread and vegetables, but on the other hand rye and corn usually ripened and of wild foods there was an abundance. Meat—venison, porcupine, black squirrel, bear, rabbit and beaver—was in plentiful supply. Turkeys up to forty pounds in weight, innumerable ducks and geese and wild pigeons, so large they broke the branches of the trees where they roosted for the night, could be shot and snared everywhere. The lakes and rivers teemed with magnificent food fishes; a month's supply could be speared in a day and amazing hauls trapped in the home-woven nets. Everywhere there were wild fruits and berries in abundance, maple sugar in which to preserve them, sumac leaves and hemlock for teas and tizanes, spruce bark for beers. There also was whisky galore, distilled with a pipe and a kettle from frosted or blighted grains that could not be milled.

Moreover the forest yielded cash crops. Ashes were carefully graded, fetching prices from a few pence to a shilling a bushel. If reduced to potash, they could command from nine to twenty-five shillings per hundredweight. During the Napoleonic wars, the supply of Baltic timber had been cut off and Britain had turned to Canada for her requirements. This demand transformed the backwoods. An early immigrant wrote, "The erection of a mill is the first event in the formation of a settlement in the bush. It induces others to come to the neighborhood since it offers the facilities of building timbers. Thereafter some bold man will erect a grist mill. A store is opened, a tavern is licensed and a village springs up in the heart of the forest."[1]

The growth of these forest industries provided an invaluable psychological stimulus. The winter no longer was a period of stagnation or frustration, of living on one's fat; it became a season in which neighbors drew together in such common employments as felling trees and swamping out trails along which oxen drew logs or squared timbers to the nearest stream, to be piled on the ice to await the spring breakup. The river drives, in which the logs were shepherded downstream into rafts or drams for conveyance to the St. Lawrence ports, brought movement and variety to the lives of the settlers. The forest ceased to be feared and came to house communities of increasing comfort and security.

The Emergence of Steam

It was at this juncture that boiling water began to transform the world. For more than half a century, steam had been employed in simple machines, such as pumps and hoists. Then in 1807 Robert Fulton had put a stationary engine into a ship, harnessed it to paddle wheels and had made ocean transport amenable to precise schedules, defiant of the winds and the waves. Seven years later George Stephenson gave the same engine land legs and drove the first locomotive over nine miles of tracks at Killingworth Colliery. Such events the Canadian settlers had watched from afar. Perhaps the first intimation of their personal interest came in the 1820s, when British mails were entrusted to trans-Atlantic steamships. Not only did such carriage cut the average time of transit by two-thirds and make for more regular deliveries, but it also reduced postal costs, particularly on newspapers, to a fraction of their former rate. Letters to or from Britain by horse post and sailing ship cost $1.12 in postage; by mail steamer and train, only forty-one cents. At this time Britain was at the point of adopting penny postage for local mails.

Steamships soon were a familiar sight on the St. Lawrence River and the Great Lakes. In 1809, John Molson of Montreal had built the *Accommodation*, a ship of forty tons' burden, eighty-five feet in length, with a six horsepower engine that turned twin paddle wheels. A rapid walker could almost keep up with it, for its maximum speed was five miles an hour in still water; spans of oxen stood by in the narrow channels to assist in upstream passages. Nevertheless, it was a nine-days' wonder, and its successor, the *Swiftsure,* built four years later, was ten times its size and carried one

hundred fifty passengers on its river runs. From then on, each generation of steamships was larger and more luxurious. By 1830 York, soon to
resume its original name of Toronto, had a scheduled steamship sailing for
every hour of the day. Vessels of 400 tons were common, and almost from
the beginning, lake and river travel aimed at luxury. The better ships had
stewards and stewardesses, staterooms with running water, ladies' drawing
rooms, flowers, oil paintings and chandeliers.

Finally, on Land

In 1830 British sappers undertook the construction of Quebec Citadel,
on the tip of the Cape Diamond promontory, which commanded both
reaches of the river. At first the great blocks of granite were brought up the
precipitous slopes on cable cars drawn by a windlass turned by horses.
General Durnford, however, who commanded the sappers, had been
longing for an opportunity to experiment. One morning the horses were
gone, and the cables were wound on a capstan driven by a pulley from a
snorting, belching steam engine in a nearby hut.

Less than a year later, the Mohawk and Hudson Railroad was opened
between Albany and Schenectady. It carried three hundred travelers
a day, and among its early passengers were Peter McGill, president of the
Bank of Montreal, and Jason B. Pierce, a New Englander who had been
captured in the War of 1812 and had remained in Canada to become the
leading citizen of St. John, a prosperous village on the Richelieu River sixteen miles across country from Montreal. They came, saw and were con-
quered. On February 25, 1832, Royal Assent was forthcoming on a bill that
had been presented at the previous session of the Lower Canada Legislative
Assembly. It was entitled "For Making a Railroad from Lake Champlain to
the River St. Lawrence" and constituted a formidable example of legal
draftsmanship. It included a preamble, fifty-one main clauses and a
sentence 1,453 words long. On its face the project meant nothing more
than a shortcut across country to interchange the traffic of the two river
systems. But Canadians saw it as the dawn of a new day.

2

The Portage Railways

It was some time before Canada's first railway project was given its name, but within two months of the passing of the act of authorization a group of Montreal business men, using the address of the Exchange Coffee House, were soliciting subscriptions for Canada's first railway. Results were disappointing. For the first but certainly not for the last time affluent Canadians, having cheered for a project with three-times-three, left their wallets at home when the hat was passed. Bad times were in the offing. Ship fever, the common name for Asiatic cholera, had struck the St. Lawrence ports twice in three years; in Montreal alone two thousand had died and shipping had fled from the river. A rebellious minority of settlers were demanding radical political reforms, and on a tide of wild words, parochial politicians were setting the scene for tragedy. A wet summer in 1835 was followed by an almost total crop failure in 1836; many of the poor families of the St. Lawrence settlements subsisted on frumenty, a porridge of frosted or blighted wheat. In May 1837, President Andrew "Old Hickory" Jackson's fiduciary aberrations sparked a panic in the United States; a week later all the banks in Lower Canada closed their doors. They remained shuttered for two years. In December of that year, extremists in both Upper and Lower Canada took the field in rebellion against the Crown.

Against such a background of events, Peter McGill, Jason Pierce and

John Molson (whose family had established Canada's first brewery forty years before) sought to keep the breath of life in the infant project. Pierce in particular made its cause his own; he was of the pioneer breed who saw nothing wrong in equating public service with private profit. The first estimates called for an outlay of £36,000, of which McGill and Molson found roughly half. In January 1835 the enterprise got under way. Two young American engineers surveyed a route from St. John to the nearest point on the St. Lawrence, which happened to be the hamlet of Laprairie, on the pool of the Lachine Rapids eight miles upstream from Montreal. The distance was 14.5 miles, the line was straight, the gradients impreceptible. The project was named the Champlain and St. Lawrence Railroad.

Twelve months later the committee of management reported that the project was nearing completion and that the shares of the company, which three years before had been peddled in friendship and sold by entreaty, now stood at a premium of £5 over par. The grading, the masonry, the bridges and a wharf at Laprairie stood ready, and the steam ferry to connect Montreal with that terminal was on the point of launching. A locomotive had been ordered from Britain, passenger coaches from the United States; flatcars and baggage wagons had been built in a Montreal foundry. Best of all, the costs of construction had been about 10 percent less than the estimate.

The tracks consisted of a wooden superstructure laid on the gradient without ballast. The rails were six-inch pine squares anchored to crossties by triangular blocks. These ties in turn rested on longitudinal supports. The rails were linked by iron splice plates. The upper surface of the rail

RIGHT: The *Dorchester,* first Canadian locomotive. From a drawing by John Loye, 1836.

was protected by an iron strap three inches in width and held in place by countersunk spikes. There was a certain amount of play at the rail junctions, and if the iron strapping broke, its jagged ends would slash up through the floor of the cars. As a consequence the rails were known as snakehead rails.

In June 1836, the *Dorchester*, the 127th locomotive built by Robert Stephenson and Company at its works at Newcastle-on-Tyne, in England, arrived at Molson's wharf in Montreal. It was thirteen feet six inches in length and had four driving wheels, each forty inches in diameter. Its high center of gravity and short wheel base impaired its performance and earned it the nickname of "Kitten" for its skittish behavior. It carried a puncheon that held eighty-four gallons of water; a cord of wood could be stowed in its tender. An indentured driver was supplied along with the locomotive, but as his contract was unenforceable in the colonies, he deserted soon after arrival. The *Dorchester's* unpredictable performances thereafter may have reflected the inexperience of his successors.

The Opening of the Line

On July 21, 1836, the Earl of Gosford, Governor-General of Lower Canada, led three hundred guests aboard the ferry *Princess Victoria*. On its main deck the band of the Thirty-second Regiment made music. A *Gazette* pressman proudly reported that all Canadian society, from lords to underlings, was represented. (Among the guests was Louis Joseph Papineau, destined in the following year to flee from Canada with a price on his head.) The admixture of such social extremes, to say nothing of their numbers, was almost too much for the ferry, which nearly capsized. Having regained its trim, however, it chugged its way upstream to Laprairie in fifty minutes.

There the locomotive chose to be contrary and balked at its load so that only two first-class coaches, carrying, thirty-two of the elite, were attached to it. The remaining coaches and some eight flatcars, on which sleighs and de-wheeled *calèches* had been lashed for seating, accommodated the remainder of the company, each car being hauled by a team of horses. In two hours everyone had reached St. John, where what was described as a "magnificent collation" was served in the brand-new railway station. There were toasts and testimonials, madeira and champagne galore. On the return trip, the *Dorchester* hauled four coaches, but the *Princess Victoria* was grounded for the night on a sandbar in the river, which in no degree diminished the conviviality of the occasion. Everyone was home for breakfast.

The first Canadian train. From a drawing by John Loye, 1836.

A Social Triumph

Three months before the opening of the line, a freight schedule, consisting of rates on barreled ashes, beef and pork, flour and meal, boards and timbers, had been issued. Shippers, however, found the railway to be expensive, and much of the produce continued to be borne from river to river by pack horses or sent by the roundabout water route. But if the freight yields were disappointing, the passenger traffic was astonishing. There were crowds of trippers from the start. Montreal families could not resist a combined ferry-railway outing which took up most of the day and only cost seven shillings and sixpence, with children at half price. Excursions became so numerous that the Operations Department complained that the trains ran late because of the clutter of picnickers who unpacked their luncheons on the line and sat on the rails eating. Everyone was intoxicated by the change from a five-miles-an-hour to a twenty-five-miles-an-hour world, and it became necessary to curb the carefree behavior of the passengers. No seats in the coaches might be occupied without a ticket secured on the ferry; no dogs were allowed in first-class compartments. Anyone who mounted the engine would pay a fine of ten shillings; the penalty for walking on top of the coaches while in motion was twenty-five shillings.

Travel for its own sake became the rage. The railway speedily reacted on the Lake Champlain shipping, which came down the Richelieu River and made St. John a port of call. Charles Dickens took a day off from his duties at the Bonsecours Theatre to ride the railway and then extravagantly praised the new facilities of travel. The fourteen miles of rickety tracks had wedded Lower Canada and New England in an exciting union. Unlike scores of others to follow, Canada's first railway prospered from the start. In its first fifteen years of operation it earned a steady 40 percent on turnover and paid dividends that averaged 16 percent per annum. Neither McGill's bank nor Molson's brewery did better.

Competition Springs Up

The success of the Montreal–St. John venture was like spark to tinder. The countryside began to spawn short lines regardless of necessity or utility. Within ten years, the original McGill-Pierce-Molson railway had been extended southward for twenty miles to the international boundary at Rouses Point, where it linked up with an American line that provided through connections to Boston and New York. But before this, James Ferrier had built a railway nine miles in length from the Recollet Gate of Montreal to the head of the Lachine Rapids. It crossed a swamp which gulped one day and swallowed a derailed locomotive. Alexander Miller, a Scot from Dundee, surveyed its route, built the line and managed it; on auspicious occasions he also acted as engine driver. When he was at the throttle, the train bounced along its unstable and undulating tracks as the Devil is said to have come through Athlone, in standing leaps. Once it was timed from gate to rapids at a mile a minute; its passengers, furious because their tall hats had been squashed against the roofs of the coaches, returned by post chaise. Although allegedly a portage railway, since it was built along the packers' trail, it would seem to have carried little else but passengers, and they mostly were Irish laborers on a spree (whose descendants to this day elect an independent member of Hibernian extraction to the Quebec Legislature for the constituency of Lachine) or Caughnawaga Indians from the reservation on the south side of the river. An interesting relic remains in the form of its metal tickets, which were about the size and shape of a half-dollar with a hole in the center, so that they could be strung by the conductor on a hoop of wire.

A True Portage Railway

There was one early portage railway, however, that lived up to its name. On the Ottawa River, twenty-seven miles west of its junction with the St. Lawrence at the upper end of Montreal Island, the Carillon and Grenville rapids made that waterway unnavigable for a distance of nearly twelve miles. British sappers had built a shallow canal around these chutes, but in 1848, after a number of false starts, work began on a railway. It was the first French-Canadian essay in railway promotion, and it was intended to form the central section of a line connecting Montreal with the Ottawa Valley. It likewise was the first recorded instance of community support of a railway; the city of Montreal, the towns along the route and the counties which it traversed underwrote the venture; but in the fashion of the times few of the promises were redeemed in cash. A contract was placed with James Sykes of Sheffield, and for the first time in Canada iron rails were specified. These raised the cost from £1,200 to £6,730 a mile. The portage section was opened on August 25, 1854, with one locomotive, two first-class coaches, four second-class coaches, two boxcars and four flatcars.

As it turned out, this beginning was the end of the project. James Sykes went to Britain to raise additional capital for the other sections of the line; he was bringing back £50,000 in cash when his ship was lost at sea with all hands. His brothers endeavored to persuade the Canadian subscribers to take up their allotments but without success. The Carillon and Grenville section was placed on the auction block and was bought by J. C. C. Abbott, a lawyer and railway speculator who in due course became Prime Minister of Canada. Those who had put up cash only retrieved 7 percent of their investment.

As a common carrier, this line was steadily in demand, chugging backwards and forwards over its well-built tracks. The years rolled on; other short lines disappeared, engulfed in systems; rolling stock changed its silhouette, locomotives grew larger, sleeker and faster; the forest thinned out along the Ottawa River; good roads criss-crossed the easy valley, settlements swelled into villages, villages into towns. Automobiles arrived with smoke and clatter; beside the Bras d'Or Lakes, the first Canadian aircraft lifted and flew. But in a world of change, the Carillon and Grenville seemed impervious to change; it just kept rolling along. After half a century, its original rolling stock was still in use. Many passengers took a trip in order to be able to tell their friends they had ridden on the last broad-gauge

(5′ 6″) railway in North America. Today six miles of its roadbed are still in use by Canadian National Railways.

Work Horse and Playboy

Another early short line that pulled its weight was the Albion Railway on the north shore of Nova Scotia. In 1818 good coal was found there, and the fuel was hauled along a tramway of horse-drawn carts to Pictou Harbour. In the 1820s, George IV gave these mines to his brother, the Duke of York, who in turn conveyed them to a London jeweler in payment of a debt. This Hatton Garden merchant shrewdly opened a number of new pits six miles inland from the original workings.

Whereupon Peter Crerar, who had never seen a railway, was commissioned to build one. He excavated more than 400,000 cubic yards of rock and soil to provide his gradients, built all bridges and culverts out of cut stone and equipped a shipping quay 1,500 feet in length. The railway was completed at a cost of £32,000 and went into service in 1838, with three British-built locomotives to haul the coal cars.

For more than fifty years this small bit of line continued in service. When the pits were worked out, the *Samson*, the sole survivor of the three original locomotives, teamed up with the *Albion*, a later arrival; in 1893 they found their way to the Chicago World's Fair. Thereafter for more than thirty years the locomotives continued in the entertainment business, rolling

The *Samson* (LEFT) and the *Albion*, early long-lived locomotives.

up great mileage as they chugged from state to state, playing the rounds of the fairs and exhibitions. In 1927, on the occasion of the Baltimore and Ohio centenary, they participated in a pageant of locomotives of all vintages. Thereafter they were presented to the province of Nova Scotia. The *Samson* is now on display at New Glasgow, the *Albion* at Stellarton.

Pleasure at the Helm

To conclude these instances of the impulsions which fostered and sustained the early Canadian short lines, there is the unique instance of the London and Port Stanley Railway, which was built exclusively for social purposes and which has outlived all its fellows. The town of London, beside another Thames in another County of Middlesex in the province of Upper Canada, had an almost feudal origin. Colonel Thomas Talbot, an eccentric, contentious soldier who held grants of upwards of half a million acres along Lake Erie, and who refused to have Dissenters, Scotsmen or half-pay officers among his tenants, had bestowed on one of his relatives a tract of fertile land along a winding river. Here the village of London was founded in 1826. Its early settlers, whose names still survive among the old families, were frugal, enterprising, hard-working and loyal; today the military services and big business are studded with their names. It was quite in the nature of things, therefore, that they should be among the first to want a railway. Their initial project, the London and Gore Railway, called

Centenary replica of metal ticket used in 1847 as
commuter fare on the Montreal & Lachine
Railroad.

for lines to be built eastward to Lake Ontario (80 miles), northward to Goderich on Lake Huron (60 miles) and westward to Michigan Territory (110 miles). Letters of incorporation took every conceivable contingency into account. They included the right of the Crown to take over the railway if after forty years the shareholders had received regular dividends of 12.5 percent annually. The proprietors would be empowered to collect double indemnity for any damage inflicted maliciously on their property; this stipulation probably reflected the Chartist unrest in Britain.

The capitalization was set at £200,000 in Halifax funds, which were at a discount of 10 percent on sterling. With the best will in the world, Canadians had no hope of finding any such sum and it was twenty years before this railway was built with British money as the Great Western Railroad. By then London had railways to the east, west and north, but nothing to the south, where twenty-four miles away lay the Lake Erie beaches. In January 1853, the original subscribers to the London and Gore Railroad—the Ridouts, the Leonards, the Hymans, the Carlings, the Peters and the Labatts—met and decided that a railway to Port Stanley would be justified. At the meeting there was some mention of bringing in coal from Ohio or Pennsylvania across Lake Erie and of the value of an independent line as a counterweight to the monopoly of the Great Western. There was also the circumstance that the old families owned most of the land between London and the lake, and as property owners they were not averse to increases in its value. But the main consideration remained, that they wanted a railway of their own.

A brisk canvass ensued and nearly £100,000 was pledged by London (Ontario) and the counties of Middlesex, Elgin and St. Thomas. The contract was placed at £135,000 and the line was opened for traffic on October 1, 1856, having cost £205,000; it afterward was discovered that some of the scions of the old families had not been averse to picking up a few perquisites. But no one seemed to mind; a three days' celebration brought trippers from Cleveland and Detroit; a press man reported that before the exhilaration of the champagne quaffed at Port Stanley had worn off the guests were tippling anew at London.

In due course the owners discovered (or perhaps they had known all along) that they had a railway and virtually no traffic to sustain it. No one seems to have been dismayed. When summer came, everyone adopted with enthusiasm the British custom of "a day at the seaside." The beach at Port Stanley was a pleasant rather than an exciting resort, but for twenty-five cents return fare the townsmen could be borne far from the hustle and bustle of the city into God's outdoors, where they might sport with Amaryllis in the shade, coming home in the evening pleasantly fatigued and with sand on their boots, conscious that they had attained metropolitan status.

In that first year, 1857, the "Port Stanley Picnic" became a staple entertainment not only for London but for the surrounding centers. There were Masonic picnics, Oddfellows' picnics, Grand Union Temperance picnics, Irish, English and Scottish picnics, Presbyterian, Anglican and Catholic picnics. On some days Londoners had as many as five outings to choose from. At first the picnickers rode on flatcars and in boxcars in which seats had been placed. There was always a rush to obtain a perch on the top of the boxcars where the absence of tickets might not be detected. Summer residences appeared on the beaches, and bit by bit Port Stanley began to profit from its visitors, by means of swings, merry-go-rounds, a coaster railway and a peep show.

The London and Port Stanley Railway never paid its way. Over the first twelve years its freight traffic only increased on the average of a few hundred tons a year and the operating surplus seldom equaled the interest on the outstanding bonds. It passed through many hands and eventually reverted to the control of the city of London, which probably regarded it as one of the municipality's pensioners, a good and faithful, if unprofitable, servant. In 1966, it became an element of Canadian National Railways, being swapped for the ground on which the old London car shops stood.

3

Promoters and Politicans

In the 1840s, railways came of age and became not only desirable but essential to Canadian amour-propre. Prior to that date, they had been adventures rather than ventures—the projects of the well-to-do or of voices crying in the wilderness. But in no time at all, a mystique had developed which proclaimed that mobility meant something more than mere movement. An admirable example of this inner implication could be seen in the Methodist circuit rider. All other priests, pastors and men of God were static; they remained with their parishes or congregations. But the American circuit rider, who passed through Canada in his annual peregrinations from the New England states to the Middle West, claimed a substantial following at the expense of the other faiths simply because he was not a fixture. He came riding over the horizon, gave his message and was gone; one day saw him in Capernaum and the next in Galilee. His mobility and impact magnified his mission.

Throughout the same decade, England was gripped by the remarkable outburst of railway promotion which became known as the Mania. An overwhelming desire not only to ride on railways but also to profit from them swept the City of London, then the unchallenged citadel of world finance. Above everything else, the railway became the symbol of keeping up with, or a little ahead of, the times. Bankers let it be known that they would always be interested in railway projects; they knew that some would be rewarding, some a speculation and some a dead loss; they therefore were prepared to back some themselves, arrange backing for others and even advise their clients to take gambles on the long shots, for they were certain that on the average enough railway investments would turn out well to justify a certain degree of speculation.

With bankers in this frame of mind, others cast caution to the winds. The dominating figure of the period was George "King" Hudson, a linen merchant who rushed into railway promotion and in a startlingly short time owned more than a quarter of the 5,000 miles of tracks in Great Britain. He inveigled all classes to back him with £30 million in his worldwide projects. Tales of his cunning and resource became tidbits in the gossip of the day. In thinly populated areas like the British North American provinces, the chief purveyors of such tidings were the nomads —the tinkers, the tailors and the cobblers, the quack doctors and the patent medicine salesmen, the old soldiers and the common tramps would drop in to earn their supper and breakfast, sleeping in the haymows and performing as few chores and indulging in as much blarney as the farmer and his wife would endure. In the long evenings, these floaters regaled the family with the topics of the moment, which often involved railways.

Thus the seed was sown. Railways became a prime subject at church doors after services, in the crossroads shops, in sewing circles and on market days, where the conversation inevitably led to the conclusion that the present lamentable state of the community was because of its lack of a railway. Local leaders would detect the mood and would add their voices and advice to the rising tide of discussion. Not everyone was moved by the same motives. There would be the honest, if confused, idealists who believed in the virtue of railways, just as the circuit rider believed in salvation. There would also be the material-minded who appreciated the increase of land values and the other perquisites which railways brought with them. And there would be the local politicians who came to realize that a railway presented the best of all bait for vote-catching. Perhaps most numerous of all would be the local patriots, who maintained that if one area possessed a railway its neighbors dare not go without one.

After the idea of building a railway had been accepted, a canvass would be followed by a community meeting. A committee would be formed and a petition drafted to the Legislative Assembly for the incorporation of a company. Such news would spread like wildfire, and ambitious citizens would identify themselves with the project. A small cash levy would be paid and a representative of the company would take off for England to sell bonds for the construction capital. Almost any bond could be placed if offered at a sufficient discount. Of all capital invested

in railways in Canada, not more than 10 percent of the cash was subscribed by Canadians. In the great majority of instances, the bondholders
never recovered more than that percentage of their investment.

The First Professional Promoter

Before the first sod had been turned on the first portage railway, a
New England evangelist had taken the field. John A. Poor was a Maine
man, hailing from Portland; his concern for Canadian railways arose
out of ambitions for his home town. In 1834 he had watched the first
train pull out of Boston Depot, and on that day he became a man with a
mission. He began to study the political, economic and social implications of railways. In due course he felt that he had an answer: the
transportation future of Portland and of Maine lay with Canada. From
Boston to Savannah the Atlantic ports had staked their claims in the
United States hinterland; the little railways were linking up, the systems
were thrusting their railheads westward, in anticipation of a breakout on
to the Great Central Plains. But because of Lake Champlain, Portland
was blocked from expansion to the west, whereas to the north, the St.
Lawrence Valley provided a natural route into the heart of the continent.
No Canadian ocean ports were as favorably situated as Portland, which
was half the distance from Montreal to Saint John and only a third of the
distance from Montreal to Halifax. In addition it was the American port
nearest to Europe. It therefore should be the natural *entrepôt* for Canada.

In 1844, Poor took to the stump, preaching the revelation of railways. He was a fine figure of a man with a rich flow of language.
"Within a matter of weeks," wrote Stuart Ball Holbrook, "Maine and
the province of Quebec were excited as never since the Revolution. He
roused the natives—then as now hardly a crowd to excite easily—to a
pitch bordering on delirium."[1] His first Canadian meeting was at Sher-
brooke. There his message, declared an irreverent observer, was like that
of the great light that shone on Saul on the road to Damascus.

To one listener in particular his message struck home. Alexander
Tilloch Galt, a shrewd, dour and indomitable Scot, was the local manager
of the Canada Company, which owned 747,000 acres of wild land in the
eastern townships of Canada East* along the international boundary.

---

* As a consequence of the Act of Union of 1841, which created the Province
of Canada, the names Upper Canada and Lower Canada were dropped, to be replaced temporarily by Canada East and Canada West, which in turn were superseded
by Quebec and Ontario.

Whatever else it accomplished, a railway was certain to raise the value of these lands. Poor's enthusiasms therefore fitted Galt's ambitions as a hand fits into a glove.

When Poor continued his Canadian tour, Galt was at his elbow. In Montreal he saw that the orator met the right people, including McGill, Molson and Pierce, who owned a small gold mine in the form of a portage railway. Poor presented the appealing prospects of transportation prosperity to them and their friends. The Montreal merchant community was with him to a man.

Boston Tries to Cut In

It has been noted previously that the British North American provinces did not love each other. The same was true of the states of the Union. When the prosperous Bostonians first heard of Poor's project, they treated it with derision; that Maine, that forlorn finger of rock and forest thrust into the middle of the British North American colonies, should attempt to sponsor an international enterprise was ludicrous. But to be on the safe side, the governor of Massachusetts approached the governors of Vermont and New Hampshire, requesting collaboration in either blocking or delaying the construction of a railway from Portland to Montreal. At the same time, a bill for a Boston-Montreal railway was rushed through the Massachusetts Legislature. In January 1845, a substantial delegation, said to have been headed by two citizens of distinction and consisting of three hundred fifty others certified by the mayor of Boston as being among the most wealthy capitalists of the city, journeyed to Montreal to reap what Poor had sown. Then came drama. Poor heard of the raid and he rushed a bill through the Maine Legislature; at the height of a February blizzard, he drove northward for three days, arriving at Montreal frostbitten and exhausted but in time to save the situation. On March 17, 1845, the Canadian Legislative Assembly granted a charter to the St. Lawrence and Atlantic Railroad to build from Montreal to the international boundary, where it would join its American twin, the Atlantic and St. Lawrence Railroad, to complete a line to Portland.

Lots of Enthusiasm; Little Hard Cash

While Canada and Maine thus put their hands to the plough publicly, New Englanders and Canadians alike kept their wallets in their pockets. The project required about $5 million for the construction and equipment of both lines. Beyond a minor grant by the city of Portland, virtually no support was forthcoming for the American section. Of £100,000 subscribed in Montreal less than one-tenth was paid up, and the Legislative Assembly refused to guarantee the bonds of the Canadian company. Indeed, the project had no other asset than Alexander Tilloch Galt, but he proved to be all that was needed. In the summer of 1845, he took off for England. There the Mania was at its height; in a single week that summer, eighty-nine new railways had been chartered with a combined capital of £84 million. But although it was easy to place the script against small down payments, Galt found it much more difficult to persuade subscribers to take up their allotments. He returned with only £35,000 in hand. However, he scraped together about £100,000 from one source or another, and an American contractor was hired who agreed to accept part payment in stock.

With the work under way, Galt returned to London in December for another try but had no success. The British government was at the point of terminating colonial preferences, which many construed as turning the overseas possessions loose to fend for themselves. In addition the "Fifty-Four Forty or Fight" controversy had been settled in a manner that left a bad taste in British mouths. Throgmorton Street was by no means sure that trouble with the United States was over.

Enter Francis Hincks

Galt therefore returned to seek official support as his last resort. For the next two years his land business ran itself while he turned his attentions to that emerging breed, the Canadian politician. Lord Elgin, the current Governor-General, was under pressure to install responsible government in the Province of Canada, and numerous ambitious men were anxious to serve their country and to enjoy the perquisites and opportunities that such service afforded. Among such candidates was an up-and-coming Irishman named Francis Hincks, who combined a flair for political maneuver with a first-class financial brain. He had founded a newspaper that propounded advanced views; he had been under the coverlets, if not between the sheets, with some fairly radical bedfellows. But this had not prevented a previous viceroy, Lord Sydenham, from appointing him Inspector-General in the first provincial administration, a position analogous to that of Minister of Finance today. As Galt's friend and sponsor in official circles, Hincks could scarcely have been bettered, for he had an ingratiating manner and an unfailing eye for the main chance.

Galt also had enlisted the aid of George Etienne Cartier, an eloquent French Canadian turned imperialist and Sir Allen MacNab, a redoubtable Tory, who had railway fish of his own to fry in Canada West. By the end of 1848, the first section of the St. Lawrence and Atlantic Railroad from Longueuil to Ste. Hyacinthe (thirty miles) had been completed and Galt was completely out of cash. The financial outlook, however, had brightened, for Hincks had been impressed by the example of the state of Massachusetts, which had invested $5 million in railways and stood to earn $400,000 annually from such loans. In April 1849, therefore, he sponsored the legislation that put the construction of railways in Canada on an official footing. His bill authorized Canada to guarantee, either to the Imperial government or to private enterprise, interest to a maximum of £20,000 annually on the bonds of "any reputable railway venture." The test of repute was the ownership of not less than seventy-five miles of line. In addition, should the Imperial government back any railway that linked the Canadian colonies, it would receive as security the title to all Crown lands for ten miles on either side of the right of way. The latter offer had strategic implications; if accepted, it would bind the Imperial authority to the defense of the North American colonies.

This legislation, however, did not arouse any particular enthusiasm in Whitehall, where with some justice the colonists were regarded as nuisances. At that time the "Little Englanders" and the Cobdenites, alike foes to colonial ties, were strong in the House of Commons, and Montreal merchants, in resentment against the abolition of colonial preferences, were circulating a petition inviting annexation by the United States. A year or more, therefore, passed in which Whitehall marked time. Galt, desperate for funds to extend his line from Ste. Hyacinthe to Richmond, which would give him seventy-five miles of tracks, mortgaged his land company, sold stock to Quebec religious orders and scraped the bottom of the barrel again and again to meet the monthly payrolls. By October 1851, he had won home; the line to Richmond was completed and so became eligible for a government guarantee on the funds for the last fifty miles to its junction with its American associate at Island Pond, eighteen miles south of the international boundary.

The Stern and Rockbound Coasts

With Hinck's Guarantee Act in operation, John A. Poor dropped out of the picture in Canada. Eloquence was small potatoes when money was in sight. But there remained the Maritime colonies of Nova Scotia, New Brunswick and Prince Edward Island. Might not these also be attracted into the Portland orbit? Poor felt that it might be worth a try.

Of the British North American possessions, Newfoundland, Prince Edward Island and Cape Breton were islands and Nova Scotia just missed being an island by seventeen miles—the width of the gut of Chignecto. New Brunswick was truly part of the continent, but as an appendage that hung down into mid-Atlantic. From its principal port, Saint John, to Montreal it was 500 miles by land and more than 1,500 miles by water, but land transport was from eight to twelve times more expensive than sea transport. In terms of ton-miles or the carriage of passengers or goods, almost any part of the Maritime Provinces was nearer to Britain or the West Indies than to Canada proper. The New England states, however, separated from the Maritimes only by narrow seas, were in a traffic sense just on the other side of the street. John A. Poor had marked these topographical factors. He thought he saw a way in which Portland might benefit from them.

At the dawn of the railway age, 1830, there were more than one hundred fifty thousand settlers in the Maritime Provinces. They were a very mixed bag, with quite a number of Acadians who had evaded expulsion in the Seven Years' War, a heavy count of Scots, some time-expired soldiers, some exiles from the Highlands, and substantial groups of United Empire Loyalists in the Saint John River Valley and southern Nova Scotia. There was also a colony of Germans, from His Majesty's domain of Hanover. Halifax, from which both the land and sea routes of the colonies radiated, had seen both high life and low during the incessant wars. There Prince William, a thoroughgoing royal tosspot, had openly paraded the Lieutenant-Governor's lady as his mistress; his brother, Prince Edward, Duke of Kent, had relinquished his lovely *Canadienne*, Julie de Montgent de St. Laurent, in order to breed an heir for the reigning house. (It turned out to be Queen Victoria.) But Waterloo put an end to these gaudy years, and thereafter Halifax might have been any garrison port on the seven seas. Its only man of mark was a young newspaper editor who deemed it his mission to proclaim whenever possible the shortcomings of the British colonial administration. He had a gift for harangue, an unabashed vocabulary and no awe of those set in authority over him. His name was Joseph Howe.

A port with the infinite highways of the sea at its doors could not be expected to raise a temperature over land transport, so it was among the United Empire Loyalists in New Brunswick that railways first received serious consideration. The Maine frontier was sketchy and there were clashes from time to time; eventually in 1839, Great Britain and the United States agreed to a firm demarcation. The Ashburton Award three years later almost cut the Maritimes off from the Canadas; whereupon the Imperial government offered to build a "military road" that would link up the all-but-severed colonies. Previous surveys had yielded no route acceptable to the Maritimers, and the other Canadians could not have cared less what happened to their fellow colonials. So nothing came of the offer.

In 1850 John A. Poor thought he discerned an opportunity. He proposed a railway that not only would bring New Brunswick and Nova Scotia into the Portland orbit but also would exalt his home town above its rivals and above Boston in particular. He arranged a conference at which the representatives of Maine and the Maritime colonies were implored, in floods of passionate oratory, to cooperate in a breath-taking project. The European and North American Railway would be built under three charters. The state of Maine and the provinces of Nova Scotia and New Brunswick would each be responsible for the mileage within their respective boundaries. But this was more than a local railway; it was designed to make Portland the headquarters and takeoff point for a transatlantic service. After traveling by rail to Halifax, passengers would take fast steamers to Galway, then a train to Holyhead, a ferry to Liverpool and a final train to London.

It was a quite mad scheme, although in years to come Sandford Fleming, greatest of the Canadian railway builders, favored something very like it. But Poor was fortunate enough to enlist the support of the one man willing to essay the impossible. In twenty years Joseph Howe had become the pride of Nova Scotia. He had won his battles with the Colonial Office; his newspaper, the *Nova Scotian*, had virtually the authority of Holy Writ among his countrymen. Moreover, he was now Provincial Secretary and more or less free to do as he pleased. A month after Poor's conference. Howe brought an excited Halifax audience to their feet. He endorsed the European and North American Railway and accepted a liability of $1 million as Nova Scotia's share of the cost. The province had no such sum available nor was it likely that it could borrow it at any reasonable rate of interest. An Imperial guarantee, however, would secure a loan. In November of that year Howe took ship for England.

In Whitehall no red carpets were out for him. The harassed colonial officials had had a bellyful of him over the previous two decades. But in a brilliant maneuver Howe bypassed them and made a direct appeal to the provinces and the City of London, both of which had a stake in the growth and prosperity of the overseas Empire. Addressing himself in a series of meetings and newspaper interviews to the bankers, manufacturers, merchants and shipowners, he painted a glowing picture of what the Canadian colonies might mean to the Britain of tomorrow in the form of homes for surplus population, food for hungry mouths, an ever-growing market for British manufactures, cargoes for British ships, employment for British capital. In his finale he swept to a vision of Imperial federation, with the Britain of the future the center of a worldwide hegemony. Thoughtful Englishmen, who remained unmoved by Howe's oratorical flights and supporting statistics in favor of the railroad, told themselves that such a dynamic policy might make Canada worth keeping. The government was moved to ask Howe what it was he really wanted. He could be as precise on paper as prolix on the platform:

> All our roads in Nova Scotia, made by the industry and resources of our people, are free to the people at this hour. Our railways should be built with the same ideal. If our government had sufficient means to build our railways and carry our people free we believe that it would be sound policy. Government ownership would keep down the rates and would save the people from the private greed which at this time is so manifest in the conduct of the English lines.[2]

By the end of February 1851, it was evident that Howe's presentations had caught the imagination of the business community and his proposals would not remain in a pigeonhole. On March 10 the Under-Secretary of State for the Colonies announced the willingness of Her Majesty's government to guarantee a sufficient loan to build a through railway to serve Nova Scotia, New Brunswick and the Province of Canada. Howe thus interpreted his victory:

> Great Britain virtually says to us by this offer "Here are seven millions of sovereigns, at half the price your neighbours pay in the markets of the world. Construct your railways, people your waste lands; organise and improve the boundless territory beneath your feet; learn to rely upon and to defend yourselves and God speed you in the formation of national character and of national institutions."[3]

In Howe's hour of triumph John A. Poor's transatlantic project and his high hopes for Portland went down the drain, for nothing was more certain than that Great Britain would under no circumstances support a railway that either took off from or ended in the United States. It soon became equally clear that not a golden sovereign would be forthcoming

until the Canadian provincials agreed in detail on what they wanted. A
quarter-century was destined to pass before any such agreement was
reached. By then both Howe and Poor were dead and before death Howe
was out of heart with the substance of his dream of the unity of the British
North American colonies.

The Great Western

It has been noted in an earlier chapter that the first essay into railways by the thriving city of London in Ontario was planned to have lines
to distant destinations, but ended up as a short pleasure route to nearby
Lake Erie. But if the seeds of the railway's founder's ambitions did not
ripen, neither did they die; in due course they brought forth abundance
in the shape of one of the most prosperous and best managed of all early
Canadian railways.

For this accomplishment almost the entire credit must go to Allan
MacNab. This Scottish Canadian, born at Niagara in 1798, had served
in battles both on land and on the Great Lakes before he was sixteen. He
was elected to the Legislative Assembly of Upper Canada in 1830, and
for more than twenty years thereafter he was never far from the center of
the political web, where he sometimes played the spider, sometimes the
fly. With the wide candor of the times, he made no bones about his special
pleading. Railways and politics were interchangeable terms to him.

He was concerned with the affairs of the London and Gore Railway
almost from the beginning, for he sat for Hamilton in the Legislative
Assembly, and that busy town, next to London, stood to profit most from
this venture. The preliminary survey for the railway had been carried
out by Elisha Johnson in the summer of 1836. Like the original charter of
this enterprise, his report was crammed to bursting with advice and
bestrewn with misinformation. It was padded with the opinions of those
who knew nothing at all about railways. That busy nomad novelist Mrs.
Anna Jameson assured Johnson that in the wake of the projected railways a new and superior social order would emerge. The Committee of
the House, however, took a more realistic and accurate view of the enterprise; it declared that its future lay in providing a short cut across
Canada for United States traffic to and from the Middle West. In place
of the lines radiating in all directions from London, as was proposed in
the original charter, the route finally chosen was much tidier. It consisted
of a railway 233 miles in length from Niagara Falls to Windsor by way
of Hamilton, Paris and London.

The immediate result of the acceptance of this route was a land boom in Hamilton, out of which Allan MacNab is said to have done exceedingly well. But then came panic in the United States, to be followed by rebellions in Canada. The end of 1837 found MacNab in the field in command of the Gore Loyalists, rounding up the rebels to the north of Toronto. It was not much of a war; a Canadian historian declares that "militarily both sides behaved in the best tradition of comic opera."[4] But because of hard times abroad and hard feelings at home, risk capital went to ground and for seven years Upper Canada stagnated.

Bit by bit the situation improved. In 1841 the Union of the two Canadas gave French- and English-speaking Canadians a stake in each other's welfare; in addition, British settlers of the post-Waterloo migration had found their feet and were making headway. In 1845 MacNab, now Sir Allan because of his services in the rebellion; Speaker of the Legislative Assembly by virtue of his wit and wisdom; and, as ever, member for Hamilton, decided that it was time to make railways a dominant issue. He had established contact with Andrew Tilloch Galt and Francis Hincks in Canada East, and he shared their view that whoever paid for Canadian railways, it would not be Canadians. So at the spring session of the Legislative Assembly that year the London and Gore Railway took on a new description as the Great Western Railroad.

That autumn MacNab followed Galt to London. There the mighty "King" Hudson himself agreed to back the project, taking up 90 percent of its common stock. But Glyn Mills and Company, bankers for the Province of Canada, were less eager to align themselves behind the venture. MacNab discovered, as had Galt, that the market did not regard Canadian issues as gilt-edged. Frustrated in the City of London, MacNab approached the Imperial government with a proposal to import settlers at public expense from the distressed areas of Ireland and the Scottish highlands, use them as railway labor and then settle them on land contiguous to the route. In addition he persuaded the Canadian Legislative Assembly to reinstate a loan of £200,000 that had been promised to the London and Gore Railroad eight years before. "Allan MacNab, Chairman of the Committee of the House, listened sympathetically to Allan MacNab, Chairman of the Great Western Railway," wrote O. D. Skelton in *The Railway Builders*. Finally, MacNab organized a force of door-to-door canvassers who took to the roads like peddlers and patent medicine salesmen, offering railway stock to all and sundry across the countryside.[5]

These campaigns, conducted with adroitness and energy, failed to provide more than negligible subscriptions. The times were out of joint;

the crest of the railway boom had passed, and throughout Europe and even in Britain there was distress with violence in its wake. The French monarchy fell and elsewhere in Europe mobs ran riot in the streets. Whereupon MacNab, whose thinking now was of one piece with that of Galt and Hincks, persevered with the last remaining prospect. He and Galt submitted concurrent and similar memorials, praying that the provincial government should guarantee interest on borrowed capital for railway construction. At first the Assembly refused to act, but in January 1849, when the petition was reintroduced, Francis Hincks took command. Three months later the Guarantee Act became law. There followed an ancillary measure that empowered other public bodies, such as counties and municipalities, to make loans or to invest in railway projects.

That the Guarantee Act required borrowers to have seventy-five miles of tracks in operation did not delay the launching of MacNab's project. On October 23, 1849, a mixture of top hats and moccasined feet gathered in a vacant lot in London to watch Colonel Thomas Talbot turn the first sod of Canada West's first railway. The lord of the Lake Erie marches was getting a bit long in the tooth, but at the banquet that evening he was more mellow than usual. He recalled that fifty-five years before, he had eaten a porcupine on the site of this flourishing town. He plainly regarded this to have been a happy augury of what was to come. It was his last public appearance.

Under the inspiration of such an occasion and beguiled by the glowing forecasts of Great Western prospects conjured up by Thomas Coltrin Keefer, whose *Philosophy of Railroads* was due off the presses in the following year, the counties, towns and even some of the villages to be served by the railway responded handsomely. MacNab had pulled it off, completing a triple mission. He had staked out what he had every right to believe to be an exclusive claim to the richest traffic area in Canada; he had arranged for partners to both the east and west and in the United States, and he had done exceedingly well for his own pocketbook. He lived to be Premier of Canada, but it seems possible that he may have regarded January 17, 1854, as the crest of his career. On that day, the first train of the Great Western Railroad ran from Niagara Falls to Windsor. That evening as darkness fell, the whistles of two locomotives shrilled amid the boom of guns along the Detroit River. The train, in two sections of six coaches each, swept into the Windsor station. Eight hundred Canadians piled out of the carriages and into the ferries; Detroit was *en fête*; seventeen hundred guests sat down to dine under a great banner that proclaimed: "NO LONGER COMBATANTS BUT COMPEERS." Queen

Victoria and Uncle Sam, said the orator of the evening, who was from Chicago, were pledging each other in right royal fashion on a momentous culmination.

A few days later a return excursion reached Hamilton. Sir Allan MacNab missed the fun; he was confined to bed, suffering from gout. A battery of militia artillery drove to his home at Dundurn Castle and discharged a celebration salvo under the windows of his bedchamber.

Toronto Makes a Start

A decade earlier, when a Montreal trio was giving the Canadian colonies their first railway, the sturdy British immigrants and Empire Loyalists of Upper Canada were engaging in their national habit of self-denigration. They were grumbling at the sloth and inertia of British North America in comparison with the vigor, initiative and progress of the communities to the south of the international boundary. Among the oft-repeated assertions of the broadsheets of the day was the declaration that the capital of Upper Canada had greatness at its door if it would only bestir itself and build a railway into the north that would intercept the ever-growing traffic of the inland tiers of counties, then in course of settlement.

Among those familiar with this complaint was Frederick Chase Capreol, a well-connected Englishman, and his friend Casimir Gzowski, a highly trained Polish engineer. York then constituted the terminus of a series of trails and portages that brought down a considerable volume of cross-country traffic from Georgian Bay on Lake Huron; such a route cut over a thousand miles from the all-water downstream passage from the Great Lakes into the St. Lawrence River. A railway would consolidate and perpetuate this *grand portage*. In addition York was growing rapidly, and with the nearby woodlands denuded, it was perennially short of firewood, which now had to be brought from considerable distances inland. For thirteen years a railway project had been under consideration but always had failed to get under way.

In May 1847, the small community of Barrie, on Lake Simcoe sixty miles north of Toronto, wearied of delay and addressed a petition to the Legislative Assembly seeking a subvention for railway connections with both Toronto and Georgian Bay. Capreol backed this project and rallied the citizens of Toronto behind it. It took shape in the articles of incorporation of the Toronto, Simcoe and Lake Huron Railway. The mayor of Toronto headed a list of eleven hundred petitioners who gave the company carte blanche to use steam or any other source of power that it might prefer. The financial proposals also were radical; construction would be financed by means of a lottery, with regular drawings and handsome prizes for the fortunate few. After some hesitation, this measure received Royal Assent, but then it was discovered that while the city fathers were quite prepared to invest £100,000 in tickets, the lottery was anathema in church circles. The virtuous declared that it would make Toronto another City of the Plain. After a vehement outcry from pulpit and press, the enabling by-law was defeated. Later in that year, however, Hincks' Guarantee Act ranged the Province of Canada behind railway construction. Upon passage of this act, Capreol, a man of independent means, hired Hezekiah K. Seymour, chief engineer and surveyor of New York State, to examine the project. After a thorough investigation, this consultant reported favorably and placed the cost of 110 miles of line to a still unchosen Georgian Bay terminus at $1,250,000. A New York contractor offered to build the railway at this figure, accepting stock to the par value of $600,000 in part payment. Whereupon Capreol set out to raise the balance locally. After two years' solicitation, the funds were in hand.

Capreol selected October 15, 1851, for the opening ceremony. There was some anxiety about the preparations; the occasion warranted vice-regal recognition, but the best circles were still a bit sniffish concerning railways; they were making the wrong people rich, and, as a sporting squire put it, they were tearing up the shires and frightening the foxes. The days passed without a response from Government House, and Jenny Lind, the "Swedish Nightingale," was imported as a standby. His Excellency, however, eventually consented to Lady Elgin's participation.

In the grand parade on that valiant autumn day, forty-six different Toronto organizations marched amid the blare of martial music and formed up on all sides of a square of turf on what is now Front Street, between Simcoe and John streets. There Her Ladyship, gracious and smiling, plied a silver spade and came up with a quite respectable sod, which she placed in an oaken wheelbarrow. His Worship the Mayor, "without even spitting on his hands," according to that scurrilous scribbler Thomas Storrow Brown, but in top hat, knee breeches, silk stockings, steelbuckled shoes and sword at thigh, wheeled it away. Thereafter young Sandford Fleming pounced upon it and preserved it for posterity.

The man who had created this auspicious occasion was not present. On the previous day, Capreol had been dismissed as general manager by a board of directors, whose total investment in the Toronto, Simcoe and

TOP: First "U" rail in Canada. Toronto, Simcoe and Lake Huron Railway, 1851.

BOTTOM: Toronto Station, 1857.

Lake Huron Railway, according to contemporary report, amounted to £37.10.0. He had never been forgiven by the righteous for his advocacy of a lottery, and the rumor ran that in some unspecified manner he was out to make a killing out of the promotion. This was completely false; he had spent $12,000 of his own money on the project, for which he never sought reimbursal. He was an honest man, perhaps a bit hoity-toity for the taste of some of the burgesses, who, fortunately perhaps, could not see what awaited them. For, as Capreol went out of the picture, Francis Hincks made his entrance.

The Inspector-General had a beagle's nose for the scent of easy money. The Toronto City Council had backed the railway with £50,000 in municipal debentures. There was some question as to the legality of this action, so it was decided confidentially to redeem them at par. The mayor of Toronto and the Inspector-General, who were privy to the decision, bought up the debentures at discounts that were alleged to have netted them approximately £10,000. Such a tidy perquisite led a distinguished Canadian historian to this description of Hincks:

> A clever little man, a typical sharp-eyed child of that unpleasantly prolific marriage between railways and responsible government. Hincks had gone about the business of furthering his own personal interests with the direct uncomplicated ingenuity of a precocious infant. He had presented the public with a scandal so simple, so instantly comprehensible, so wholly malodorous.[6]

The foregoing case histories are perhaps fair examples of the manner in which promoters and politicians capitalized on the romantic credulity that enveloped railways in the minds of pioneers to whom the twin streaks of steel and the scream of the locomotive whistle in its ponderous flight across the countryside promised an almost psychic release from the bondage of their isolation and loneliness.

4

Grand Trunk:

The Trail of the Comet

Francis Hincks' early essays in railway promotion, as already recorded, had been no more than trial gallops. This artful Irishman had placed himself in training for major occasions on which he hoped to help the British North American colonies (and himself) in even greater degree.

His Railway Guarantee Act of 1849 had brought him into intimate contact with Glyn Mills and Company, the London merchant bankers who were the financial agents of the Province of Canada and who occupied the same position toward that colony as the Bank of England toward the Chancellor of the Exchequer. During the Mania of the 1840s, these bankers had let it be known that they would be interested in railway inquiries and that their incursions in this field would be shared with Baring Brothers, who had provided millions for United States railways and who on the whole had done well out of such financing.

This was right up Hincks' alley. In casting about for a guideline to a railway policy, he remembered his history. The trunk road was an imperialistic device, a heritage of Rome. It sustained group interests in diverse and scattered communities; it buttressed a common citizenship, it fostered trade; but perhaps most important of all, it created on land something of the advantage that the Royal Navy enjoyed on the seas. The Imperial authorities had learned a great deal from the twenty years' struggle with Napoleon and no lesson better than that of mobility. The French had been prodigious marchers, covering great distances swiftly to strike at unwary foes. In the Spanish campaign they had met their match; Sir Arthur Wellesley, afterward the Duke of Wellington, a great quartermaster as well as battle commander, gave prime consideration to roads and waterways; he created the Army Service Corps and compelled his supply officers to think in terms of elapsed time in the movement of personnel and tonnage. When in due course the American invasions of Canada in the War of 1812 came under critical examination, the dearth of colonial communications was noted. There followed the building of canals that bypassed obstructions in the Canadian waterways, the slashing of snow roads through the hitherto unbroken forests, comprehensive surveys of the Canadian wilderness and the employment of British garrisons in roadmaking.

Then steam arrived, and it became obvious that while portage and other short railways were matters of local concern, the trunk lines must reflect imperial policy; and since it would be British and not Canadian money that would build them, the home government rather than the provincial legislatures would call the tune. At first the British authorities were lukewarm toward encouraging such expensive ventures in such faraway places, but Joseph Howe had proved that it was possible to stampede the British trading community and thus persuade Whitehall to change its mind. Francis Hincks therefore decided on a combined operation. He would sell the project of a trunk railway in the Canadian colonies to private interests, but he would endow it with the glamor of an imperial enterprise. The British government could scarcely fail to approve an undertaking that was costing it nothing, and such support would provide the essential incentive to private investors to risk their money.

The Lure of Chicago

Canada West (Ontario) selected itself as the territory to be served by the first Canadian Main Line. The post-Waterloo immigration combined with the area's fertile soil had led to a much higher rate of growth there than in either French or Maritime Canada; but, even as it surpassed its sister colonies, so it in turn was outstripped by the phenomenal development of Michigan Territory, beyond its western boundary. By midcentury, the American occupation of the Middle West was in full swing; thousands of wagon trains had debouched from the Appalachian mountain spine, heading for the central plains. Chicago, at the foot of Lake

Michigan, was the focal point of takeoff for the second stage of this trek, and this former frontier post already seemed destined to become one of the great cities of the New World. But even the most direct all-American line from the northern Atlantic seaboard to Chicago was several hundred miles longer than a route across Canada. There therefore emerged in Hincks' mind the vision of a Canadian Main Line that would begin at a New England port and end at Chicago. It would serve Canada, and at the same time it would wax fat on the transit traffic of the American Middle West.

Nor was this Chicago's only allure, both for Hincks and for the English merchant bankers. Sooner or later the Canadians, like their American cousins, would occupy the western prairies. At that time (1850), no one contemplated such an audacious project as a railway across a thousand miles of empty wasteland to the north of the Great Lakes. It was taken for granted that the Canadian route to the west must go through Michigan Territory. A railway to Chicago, therefore, would provide the first leg of the trans-Canadian trunk line of the future.

Thomas Baring, M. P., as the head of the great bank which bore his name, was on somewhat better than speaking terms with Sir Morton Peto, senior partner of Peto, Brassey, Jackson and Betts, the world's leading railway contractors, who had built one-third of Britain's total mileage as well as railways in France, Spain, Russia, Persia, Italy and India. Peto was thoroughly aware of the potential of a Canadian shorteut to Chicago, and it seems possible that he initiated the conversations that ensued. From Chicago to Portland, Maine, was 1,150 miles, of which 659 miles lay within the Province of Canada and hence would be eligible for government assistance under the Railway Guarantee Act. Yet with its principal sources of traffic in the United States, it would be immune to the parochial pressures and political flimflam that had hamstrung so many early Canadian railway ventures.

Hincks Sets the Stage

Both Baring and Peto realized that they must deal with some Canadian political figure. By reason of his earlier operations and his skill in maneuver, Hincks virtually nominated himself as their partner. In May 1852, he arrived in London, where, as aftermath to Howe's campaign, the plan for a Main Line from Halifax to the western extremity of Canada West still was on the Imperial agenda. Hincks immediately took steps to ditch this project by announcing that the Province of Canada was not interested in it any longer. It proposed to build its own trunk railway.

Hincks' statement was bald and terse to the point of discourtesy, but it appealed to the upper echelons of the Colonial Office; rarely had a project which promised little but trouble removed itself so easily into the closed files. That it constituted a betrayal of Nova Scotia and New Brunswick was regrettable, but Whitehall's skirts were clean. It was the spokesman of the Province of Canada who had reneged on his compatriots. On May 20 the Imperial guarantee on the proposed intercolonial railway was withdrawn, and Hincks sat down to dicker with Peto, Brassey, Jackson and Betts. His scheme was to persuade the contractors to buy existing railways or charters along the acceptable route from Portland to the Michigan boundary and thereafter to bridge the gaps. The Main Line thus acquired by the Province of Canada would be named the Grand Trunk Railway.

Viewed in retrospect, Hincks' success in selling pigs in pokes to contractors of worldwide experience seems almost incredible. The only property of any value on the projected route was the Great Western Railway, then nearing completion from Niagara Falls to Windsor, opposite Detroit; and, as this line already had substantial American backing and the promise of an alliance with the Michigan Central into Chicago, it had no reason to be enthusiastic over Hincks' proposals for it also had a charter for a line into the East, from Hamilton to Toronto (45 miles) that certainly would be more profitable to keep than to sell. Between Toronto and Montreal (345 miles) there was not a mile of track, but Alexander Tilloch Galt and his friends had sewed up this section by overlapping charters, leaving nothing to chance. They had opened the stock books of these incipient companies on the day of incorporation and within a matter of minutes had subscribed for all their shares. Between Montreal and Portland (292 miles) the contractors would also be dealing with Galt, who had assumed control of the two railways that John A. Poor had conceived and which would be willing (for the proper consideration, of course) to become elements in the Canadian Main Line.

Easy Money for Canadians

That the difficulties and expense of Hincks' project did not weigh unduly with Peto, Brassey, Jackson and Betts can best be explained by their conviction that the cost of the Canadian section did not really matter in comparison with the rewards of an entry into Chicago. At the end

of July 1852, Hincks returned to Canada. He was accompanied by
William Mather Jackson, a Peto partner, a jovial and easygoing Englishman whom the money-thirsty Canadians found to be a walking oasis. He
arranged the purchase of Galt's ramshackle and partially built lines
between Montreal and Portland for a reasonable figure, but he also took
over their indebtedness—a $400,000 loan from the city of Montreal;
$2 million in city of Portland bonds; a stock investment of $100,000 by
the Sulpician Order; and a long list of minor commitments ranging from
Galt's numerous notes of hand down to a pension of $40 a month for one
Sarah Jenkins. He bought up the three essential charters between Montreal and Hamilton, paying quite enough to the Great Western for the
Hamilton-Toronto rights, but through the nose—three times as much per
mile—for Alexander Tilloch Galt's charters. Jackson refused to commit
himself, however, on the construction of a railway bridge two miles in
length across the St. Lawrence at Montreal, and he got nowhere in his
approaches to the Great Western Railway, whose directors undoubtedly
reasoned that if he was prepared to pay such thumping sums for primitive
and nonexistent lines, he should be willing to shell out in right royal
fashion for a property that was within a few months of being in operation. The sum that the Great Western management had in mind appalled
even the ebullient promoter, so Jackson passed the ball back to Thomas
Baring, who undertook to bring the Great Western's London board to a
more accommodating frame of mind. The Great Western directors, however, stood fast, for they felt that Hincks as promoter eventually would
come to heel, since in the previous year as Inspector-General of the Province of Canada, had officially designated this railway as an element of
the Main Line.

Hincks Deserts the Maritimes

They were soon to learn how little a pledge by Hincks in one capacity mattered to him in another role. Alexander Tilloch Galt, having done
very well for himself on the eastern sections of the projected trunk line,
now discerned a fresh opportunity. His engineering subsidiary, Gzowski
and Company, had obtained a charter for a railway from Toronto to
Guelph, fifty miles to the west of the Ontario capital. Its construction had
begun in slow motion, while Galt roved the towns and counties along its
route in search of cash, either from stock sales or from subsidies. An
extension of this line for 122 miles beyond Guelph would bring it to the
Michigan boundary at Sarnia; such a route would be fifty miles shorter
to Chicago than the Great Western route by way of Hamilton. Moreover

Sarnia, on the St. Clair River at the foot of Lake Huron, was in a better position than Windsor to intercept the outward-bound traffic of three of the five Great Lakes. Finally, a railway was in course of construction from Port Huron, on the opposite bank of the St. Clair from Sarnia, into the southwest. At a pinch it might provide connections of a sort with Chicago.

Galt was quite willing to assist the Grand Trunk to Chicago (or to the moon) as long as there was a profit in it. But only Hincks could disqualify the Great Western as the chosen instrument of the Main Line in western Ontario. There are no records of the conversations that ensued; all that is known is that Hincks came into possession of £25,000 of Grand Trunk stock that he assuredly had never bought on the open market. On the grounds that Great Western recalcitrance had imperiled the completion of a quasi-official project, he announced that the route of the Main Line would be altered, with its western terminal at Sarnia instead of Windsor. For Galt as a promoter this was one of the great coups of his career. For Hincks as a colonial official it was a shady deal.

The Flotation

In the first months of 1853, the British Hotel on Jermyn Street in London and the chambers of Swift, Wagstaff and Company, Solicitors, in Great St. George Street of that city were the scenes of continuous activity. No one mentioned Chicago; all were dedicated to the launching of that Imperial structure, the Canadian Main Line. Its cost grew day by day. The bridge over the St. Lawrence was accepted as a matter of necessity, as was an extension along the river below Quebec City to a point of linkup with a railway from Halifax, if and when it should be built. Everywhere the colonials had a field day at the expense of their imperial associates. Alexander Tilloch Galt remembered just in time to include an additional £15,000 in his Montreal-Portland bill to cover interest charges to date on his two railways. The Province of Canada unloaded bonds to the value of £170,000 on the promoters; the bonds represented loans to the Ontario, Simcoe and Huron Union Railroad, which ran in the wrong direction to be of any immediate value to the Main Line. A host of new charters had been rushed through the Legislative Assembly by promoters who hoped to share in the pickings; of one of the railways thus chartered, the Grand Junction Railroad, from Belleville to Peterborough, Thomas Storrow Brown, the rebel journalist, wrote:

> Some one from Peterboro' timidly enquired how such a road would benefit that section. "Build you a loop line," briskly replied

Mr. Jackson, clapping his big hand over the map, thumb at Belleville, little finger at Port Hope, middle finger at Peterboro. People were charmed with this facility of construction. No one had ever heard of a loop line before.[1]

This as yet unborn orphan was allotted £400,000 as a christening gift. The final tally revealed that the Grand Trunk prior to incorporation had acquired in all 1,112 miles of railways and charters, in being or yet to be, involving expenditures, actual and estimated, of something in excess of £7 million—a sum which would represent more than $100 million today.

Components of the Main Line

Montreal-Portland	292 miles
Montreal-Toronto	345 miles
Toronto-Guelph-Sarnia	172 miles
St. Lawrence extension	253 miles
Belleville Loop Line	50 miles
Bridge allowance at Montreal	2 miles

On April 12, 1853, the English newspapers carried profuse details of the new comet in the railway sky. The purple passages of the prospectus writer were interlarded with assurances excerpted from the dispatch of the Earl of Elgin, Governor-General of the Province of Canada, to the Colonial Office. These assurances included statistical summaries that revealed the Canadian colonies to be pulsing with rude health. Meteorological reports were appended that proved that Canada had a climate in which Britons would thrive. Three days after the issue of the prospectus Alexander Tilloch Galt wrote exultantly to a friend. The Grand Trunk shares had been oversubscribed twenty times; they already had gone to a premium. Galt had every reason to be pleased. He and his friends were destined to make fortunes; the contractors and the English investors, to lose everything.

But this belonged to the morrow. For the moment the Grand Trunk's first birthday teemed with happy auguries. It was spring in the land and in men's hearts; the winter of dispute, of projects clashing with each other, seemed to be over. In London, then the financial capital of the world, the streets which held overseas interests buzzed with activity. British engineers were devising new installations, bankers were speculating on how they might venture, and still justify their risks, in the far parts of the earth. Commerce had taken on fresh dimensions. Of the score of opportunities that beckoned, none seemed more propitious than those from what had been the wilderness of Canada and the hour was ripe for those who would make their way along the great rivers, who would plunge into the depths of the forests, who would clamber over the high mountains.

It was on such a shining prospect that the Grand Trunk project was launched. No star ever had burned more brightly in the railway firmament. Never did what looked like a great occasion turn out to be more of a flop. As one writer put it, it was as though a ballerina, after a dazzling opening pirouette, had stubbed her toe and had fallen on her face. She might rise and limp through her performance, but the bruises of her mishap would remain.

Reams have been written and explanations by the score have been devised to account for this extraordinary reversal of fortune. The most common contention has little truth and less sense in it—that the fiasco occurred because the scheme had been formulated by those who knew little or nothing about Canada. For instance, O. D. Skelton, in his biography of Alexander Tilloch Galt, gives the impression that the misfortunes of Canadian railway promoters derived from the fact that the English investors took the projects out of their hands.[2] This is quite untrue. Canadians had neither the money nor the technicians to build the Main Line, yet of the sponsors of the Grand Trunk charters, twenty-two out of twenty-three were Canadians; they included the leading citizens of nine different Canadian communities. Twelve of the first twenty-six directors, including six cabinet ministers, were Canadians, although less than 2 percent of the stock of the company was held in Canada. The first president was a Canadian. Until Peto, Brassey, Jackson and Betts had completed the construction, a head office in London rather than in Canada constituted an advantage and not a handicap, since London was at the end of a twleve days' voyage from the favor-seekers who haunted the anterooms of the Canadian Legislative Assembly in search of handouts. Had Dean Skelton stated that the British promoters knew too little about expatriate Britons like Hincks and Galt, who found in Canada a fertile field for their talents, he would have been nearer to the truth.

The Bankers Resent Trickery

More than a century afterward it seems highly probable that the man who dreamed up the scheme in the first instance was the chief culprit in its collapse. Inspector-General Francis Hincks, having erected a lordly structure, pulled the props from under it by a last-minute (and typical) bit of maladroit chicanery. Neither Glyn Mills nor Barings had been impressed by the fanfare that had characterized the promotion. They had not been consulted over the prospectus and, when invited, they had refused to lend their names to it.

Nevertheless on April 9, four days before issuance, they discovered that their banks had been named as sponsors of the flotation. In surprise and anger, Thomas Baring wrote to John Ross, Solicitor-General of Canada and president-presumptive of the company-to-be. Baring pointed out that the invitation he had refused had come not from an official but from a private source and that he never recommended any stock to his clients without exhaustive examination. George Carr Glyn agreed with Baring in every particular; indeed, he went further. At this time, his bank held the accounts of 256 railways, of which 89 were overseas. He therefore knew something about the railway business, and he had watched the wastrel progress of Peto, Brassey, Jackson and Betts in Canada with dismay. As controller of Canadian credit, he believed that the first Main Line should have been no more than Canada could afford—a railway perhaps from Montreal to Hamilton, with extensions and feeders as warranted, with the province paying in full for the political extension downriver from Montreal to meet the Halifax line, and with Galt's shoddy properties and questionable charters bought up at auction for whatever they would fetch. Everything else should wait until the project had proved itself. In the meantime, all he was prepared to do was to advise his clients that the Grand Trunk was a risk venture; his suggestion would be that they buy a few shares, put them in a safe place and for the time being forget about them. More than six hundred Glyn Mills customers accepted this advice and bought small parcels of the stock.

Both banks took immediate steps to protect themselves, Canadian credit and the investing public. They insisted that the issue of common stock, which would have produced £3,601,000 should be halved. The contractors were stunned, but the bankers were adamant and spoke plainly. The project had ballooned until its estimated costs had tripled. The Mania, the era of easy railway money, was almost at an end. The period of stable colonial administration under Imperial authority also was drawing to a close; the Imperial administration was preparing the colonies for virtual independence; the local politicians would have to learn the ways of government, which usually proved an expensive item of education.*

---

* This suspicion was fully warranted. In the ensuing decade, there were ten different ministries in the Province of Canada, each a coalition of diverse splinter groups and each of which needed to make politics profitable for its supporters in order to stay in power.

Work Gets Under Way

For half the working capital to be lopped off at a banker's dictate was a body blow. Worse was to follow. By midsummer, work was under way on the three principal unbuilt sections—on the portion extending downriver to Trois Pistoles, the selected point of junction with the line from Halifax; on the key central section from Montreal to Toronto; and on the section from Guelph to Sarnia—696 miles in all. This construction required approximately twelve thousand unskilled laborers, whom the contractors expected to recruit in Canada. Earlier mass labor projects, such as the digging of canals, had been carried out in large part by gangs of imported Irish navvies—good workers but a rowdy, undisciplined lot, whose capers and antics on pay nights or when the drink was high in them did not commend them to God-fearing folk. They had given mass labor a bad name. To many Canadians, joining a railway gang was little more respectable than running away with a circus. Recruiting therefore was slow in Ontario and almost fruitless in Quebec, where the Church distrusted gregarious associations for its faithful. All too many *habitants* returned to their homes after a winter in a timber camp with the seeds of unrest sown in them. Thomas Brassey, who came to Canada when construction began, thought the work was too heavy for French Canadians. It seems more probable that the stymie lay in the priest's shepherding crook, ever extended to keep the sheep from straying.*

Soaring Costs

Equally serious was the miscalculation of the impact of the Canadian climate. Irish navvies had dug the canals under the supervision of sapper officers who set the daily tasks and would not be content with less; their established quotas did not vary greatly with the seasons. The railway contractors soon discovered that it was difficult to induce Canadians to work in winter at all; it was their custom to "hive up" in rough weather and only to turn out for the most essential tasks. They knew nothing about working frozen ground, and they were utterly disinclined to keep in step in team tasks, which was common practice in railway construction in that

* This conclusion is borne out by an examination of the operational payrolls of the Grand Trunk of a century and more ago. Virtually all the stationmasters, yardmen and gangers—that is to say, those of static employment whose work enabled them to be home at night, have French names; whereas those of train crews or other staff whose tasks compelled them to move about have English or Irish names.

day.* As the Canadian spring was little more accommodating than the winter, it quickly became manifest that for upwards of half the year, labor costs would soar high above the estimates and that it was quite impossible to expect a steady yield from Canadian workers. Nor was this all. Peto, Brassey, Jackson and Betts had based their labor costs on five shillings a day, which was the pay of imported navvies, who being indentured labor, could not demand as much as freemen. Hence, if only as a matter of status, the free worker demanded more.

Thomas Brassey on his return to Britain in the autumn of 1853 therefore presented a thoroughly discouraging report. The contractors were compelled to pay seven shillings and sixpence a day for unskilled labor that did considerably less work than the imported navvies did at five shillings a day.

Costs of construction had been estimated at an average of £8,000 per mile. It quickly became obvious that this was far too low—a serious matter in view of the curtailment of working capital imposed by the bankers. Furthermore, it was discovered that much more construction would be necessary than had been anticipated. Some of the railways purchased as operational were barefaced swindles. For instance, the Portland-Montreal trackage, which the Grand Trunk prospectus declared would show a surplus of £100,000 annually from the start, was simply thrown down—substructures spongy, rails unballasted, gradients abrupt, curves jug-handled, stations and fixed installations nonexistent. It required £850,000 to put these 292 miles of track in working order, and for years they were not safe enough for trains to operate on at night. Their net income paid less than one-third of the interest on their fixed charges. In the case of the charters along Lake Ontario, the right of way under contract had been bought because it was cheap rather than serviceable. At Kingston, Cobourg and Port Hope, it provided no access to the waterfront. At Toronto, the railway land was so isolated from the business section of the town and the waterfront that double terminal facilities, were required—two stations, two yards, two roundhouses. At Sarnia, it ended on the bank of the St. Clair River, with no provision made for wharfs or other waterfront facilities.

---

* In the Second World War, the Sappers and Miners of the Indian Army were still building railways, and very effectively, as team tasks. Every work job had its count of numbers and its prescribed drill movements. Standard gauge lines were built by engineering companies in this fashion in Western Desert at the rate of two miles daily.

The Impact of the Crimean War

On top of these problems of construction costs and the purchases of shoddy trackage and useless right of way, there came a serious extraneous embarrassment. In March 1854, the Crimean War broke out. Risk capital immediately disappeared and interest rates and commodity prices soared, with unhappy impacts on the cost of living. In little over a year, flour doubled in price to eight dollars a barrel, butter rose from between six and ten cents to between twenty-three and twenty-seven cents a pound, eggs from ten to sixty cents a dozen. Rents soared and craftsmen demanded higher pay. In the fashion of the times, Peto, Brassey, Jackson and Betts had agreed to accept more than half their contract prices either in Grand Trunk bonds, which could be sold to provide working capital as required, or in Grand Trunk common stock, which was expected to provide the profit on the jobs. By midsummer 1855, the contractors had spent upwards of £3 million, which represented all their cash in hand, including the receipts from the sales of the bonds; yet the line was far from ready for operation, and the common stock had fallen to half its par value. There seemed no choice except to throw up the contracts, to go bankrupt or to scamp the work.

Peto, Brassey, Jackson and Betts refused to consider any of these solutions. They were men of consequence, and they felt their personal honor to be at stake. The only possible solution to their difficulties lay in getting the line open for operation as soon as possible. To this end, work was suspended for sixty-nine miles east of Sarnia; a new route was surveyed and right of way contiguous to the waterfront was purchased at the principal towns between Montreal and Toronto. Finally—and this was the ultimate evidence of their courage and determination—they embarked without delay on the construction of the highly expensive bridge across the St. Lawrence River at Montreal.

Determination Reaps Its Reward

Their resolution paid off, for it rallied the London bankers to their aid. In the spring of 1855, Barings and Glyn Mills abandoned their aloofness and undertook to keep the work under way. In addition, they endorsed the petition of Peto, Brassey, Jackson and Betts to the Province of Canada for a loan of £900,000, against the pledge that with this sum available the key central section, from Montreal to Toronto, would be completed not later than the autumn of 1856. This loan was granted, subject to the stipulation that the contractors would find pound for pound of the loan and that the total proceeds would be devoted to the completion of this section. This promise was kept to the letter.

By the autumn of 1855, the Quebec City–Richmond section (100 miles) of the downriver extension and the Toronto-Hamilton section (45 miles) were open for operation. Construction was well-advanced on the Belleville-Montreal section (227 miles) and the Toronto-Stratford section (88 miles). The Montreal-Portland line had been relocated for twelve miles on the approaches to its ocean terminal. At Toronto, local interests were demanding their pound of flesh, and it was more than fifteen years before the Grand Trunk obtained satisfactory entries to the downtown section of the city and to the waterfront. These essential tasks cost a great deal more than their estimates, and by the spring of 1856, the contractors were out of money once more. At this juncture they had a stroke of luck. The Bank of Upper Canada now shared the Province of Canada account with the Bank of Montreal; its head, Thomas G. Ridout, had been one of the original sponsors of the Main Line project. He had close working arrangements with both Barings and Glyn Mills and when Peto, Brassey, Jackson and Betts gave notice that they were reaching the end of their resources, Ridout persuaded Thomas Baring and George Carr Glyn to accept seats on the Grand Trunk board, an arrangement which more or less postulated that in extremity the province would back the railway. Ridout also persuaded the government to regard an unsold debenture issue as security for such advances as were necessary to continue the construction.

Politics Intrudes

The Grand Trunk now was assured of a source of ready money, but it had paid for it with its independence; it was now officially sponsored and hence was eligible to become a political issue. The British system of government necessitated the existence of a Loyal Opposition, and its loyalty did not prevent it from opposing the government in any way that it saw fit. Political warfare in Canada in those days was of a catch-as-catch-can nature, with no holds barred. The Grand Trunk, in order to obtain money, had bought trouble, which began with that previously quiescent body, its shareholders. Until then they had not been unduly concerned. They had seen their shares soar to 70 percent premium and thereafter fall to 60 percent discount, but this was not unusual in railway flotations

of that day. The Province of Canada loans, however, were another matter; British investors had had more than one sad experience with colonial
administrations that had got their fingers into private enterprises. In 1856,
therefore, the Honorable William Napier came to Canada to present the
investors' views. He was by no means an ideal emissary; he prided himself on his plain speaking and he overstated his case to an almost dishonest
degree. He declared that British investors had backed the Grand Trunk
venture because of its quasi-official sponsorship, and he wanted to know
what the Province of Canada proposed to do to protect their interests.

He should have been told bluntly that he was talking nonsense; the
Grand Trunk was in every sense a private venture for which the Province
of Canada accepted no responsibility. But Thomas Cayley, then Inspector-
General, was no Hincks, and he weakly accepted Napier's contention. This
properly put the cat among the canaries both in Britain and in Canada,
where the official Oppositions had field days; the "Little Englanders" at
Westminster denounced the Grand Trunk project as a Canadian swindle,
and the House of Lords dwelt on Canadian malfeasances sanctimoniously.
In Canada the local patriots sprang to arms, with Joseph Howe, the
pride of Nova Scotia, and George Brown, the leading light of the Reform
Party, endeavoring to outshout each other on the grounds that a London
stockbroker's misstatements had gulled the simple Canadian innocents
into indiscretions. Hincks (now Sir Francis) had nothing to say. He had
left a few months before on appointment as Governor-in-Chief of Barbados and the Windward Islands.

The Origins of Distrust

This uproar had momentous consequences. From then until its dissolution more than sixty years later, the Grand Trunk remained a bone of
contention between Canadians and Britons. Re-echoes of this controversy
are heard this day. Any time an imperial power relinquishes authority, it
can never hope for gratitude; its former colonists cannot tolerate the
thought that freedom has been given to them; they must cherish the illusion that they have won it. In the same way, the one-time imperial power
is very apt to believe that its former subordinates were not ready for the
heady gifts of liberty, that they would have been better off had they
remained under imperial tutelage for a little longer.

There is a certain amount of truth in both these contentions. More
than one Canadian historian has pointed out that the alliance of railway
promoters and colonial politicians was injurious both to private enter-

prise and to its official sponsor. Perhaps the basic circumstance was that
the seeds of nationhood had been sown in Lord Durham's Report.* If
Canadians proved themselves both willing and able, self-government surely
would follow. How better could Canadians prove their worthiness than
by building railways? They were the badges of progress, the insignia of
achievement. So ran the arguments of a thousand orations, the recurrent
theme of countless dissertations in barrooms, pulpits and marketplaces.
The politicians, assembled in legislatures, could not choose but hear.
Unfortunately in all too many instances they were listening for other
reasons than to serve the public well. Temptation often proved too strong
for not too unwilling flesh.

A British View

The Trout brothers, the earliest Canadian railway historians, listed
fourteen different approaches by which public monies could be solicited
for railway ventures. With so many streams flowing, even those who did
not ply their dippers often managed to get mud on their boots. Sir
Edmund Grimani Hornby, a remarkable Englishman who at one time had
been a judge of the Consular Court of the Ottoman Empire, came to
Canada on Grand Trunk business. In his autobiography, he wrote:

> Some twenty-five members [of the Legislative Assembly], con-
> tractors, etc., were simply waiting to be squared either by promise of
> contracts or with money. £25,000 would have bought the lot, but
> I would rather that someone else had the job than myself. . . . Upon
> my word, I do not think there is much to be said for Canadians over
> Turks when contracts, places, free tickets on railways or even cash
> is concerned.
>
> Sir Edmund Head, the Governor-in-Chief, was as kind as ever,
> but he seemed in terrible fear that I had a purse in my pocket and
> was ready to shell out. . . . "I don't doubt your winning," he kept
> saying, "if you are prepared to spend money. But pray do not. It is
> not worthwhile soiling your fingers. If you fail now it is only a
> question of time until the colony will have to come to the assistance
> of the Company." I do not know if it ever did but it was quite
> clear to me that the colony was getting a good deal more out of the
> line than the shareholders were ever likely to get.[3]

---

* Governor-in-Chief of British North America, 1838-1840. His report, one of
the great state papers in the English language, led to the union of the Canadas and
prepared the way for responsible government.

Vindictive Newspapers

Such suspicions, tinged with dislike and contempt, were restricted to the few in Britain. A similar distrust was cherished by the generality in Canada. Newspapers then had a great deal more authority than now; editors had power to sway and to convert. The religious press in particular spoke in pregnant accents; to the faithful its views often were taken as a concordance of Holy Writ. It is recorded that the pages of *The Witness*, the chief Protestant periodical, seldom were used for wrapping up the school lunches or other homely tasks; they were kept intact and laid away reverently in the attic for generations to come. John Dougall, its editor, was a fanatical Calvinist whose thunders reverberated throughout the rural communities. He hated railways; they were Satan's snares. "The worship of material interests has prevailed. . . . They have founded a new idol in the Grand Trunk Railway. . . . Before this new Dagon the Governor-General, his responsible ministers and the whole Legislature has bowed." This sort of Machiavellian diatribe, half politically inspired and half minor prophecy, poured off Dougall's press each week and was received by many Canadians as almost a concordance on Holy Writ. George Brown, editor of the *Toronto Globe*, was another gross offender. As a parochial demagogue, he seldom took the trouble either to be accurate in his facts or fair in his conclusions. In at least one instance he shared in the spoils of a juicy railway rakeoff. A leading Canadian historian has written:

> Resistance to the Grand Trunk and its financial exactions became an integral part of the new liberalism which Brown and his associates were building up in Canada West. The railway was represented to the edified populace of Upper Canada as a malign creation of Montreal finance, which robbed the public treasury, debauched the country with the bribery of jobs and contracts and impoverished the poor patient farmers of Canada West with its exorbitant freight rates.[4]

The love-hate psychosis of Canadians toward their railways constituted a remarkable example of the mob impulse on an otherwise dour and unemotional people. When a railway project was in the egg, while it was still under the hen, it was the object of lyrical and almost hysterical anticipation. But once it was hatched and had begun to go about its business, feelings changed almost overnight. A glance at the rate sheets wrote *finis* to the infatuation; it apparently had never occurred to most Canadians that a railway was a profit-making enterprise; to charge for its services seemed next door to taxation without representation. So began the years of disillusion. But of all Canadian railways none was greeted with the same degree of abuse, contempt and hostility as the Grand Trunk. Its managers were shocked by the unreasoning malice of those whom it was intended to serve. It staggered them as much by its senselessness as by its injustice.

The Victoria Bridge

On July 1, 1856, the Toronto-Guelph section (forty-eight miles) opened for traffic. Less than four months later, on October 26, the great day came when the first train, with a wood-fed locomotive crowned by a vast sparkcatcher and hauling seven yellow passenger coaches at thirty miles an hour, completed the articulation of the Province of Canada by opening a through route from Quebec City to Windsor. For that day at least the jeers changed to cheers, and at the sixty-four way stations between Montreal and Toronto, the countryside had assembled to celebrate with addresses of welcome, bands blaring, impromptu orations and the women in their Sunday best scurrying between trestles heaped with their baking. Even *The Witness* and the *Globe* laid aside their bludgeons for a few issues. Five months later, sleeping cars were introduced. All marveled that it was possible to go to bed in Montreal and awaken in Toronto.

At Montreal further progress could be observed, for while the traveler to Quebec City still crossed the St. Lawrence in a small ferry, the great piers of Victoria Bridge continued to grow out of the bed of the river in serried order. From beginning to end, this project was a professional job that revealed that Peto, Brassey, Jackson and Betts, whatever their deficiencies as promoters, were worthy of their reputation as master builders. Many engineers held it to be lunacy to attempt to build a bridge more than two miles in length, at a height under which ocean steamships might pass, across a mighty stream given to heavy floods and violent ice jams. However, two eminent Canadian engineers, Casimir Gzowski and Thomas Coltrin Keefer, said that it could be done, and Robert Stephenson, whose father had built the first locomotive, designed another of his famous tubular structures. Peto, Brassey, Jackson and Betts fabricated it in their ironworks at Birkenhead with such accuracy that out of 1,540,000 rivet holes not one needed reaming or redrilling. Best of all, they got James Hodges, a brilliant young engineer, to erect the bridge. At the completion of his task, he wrote a dramatic narrative, illustrated by his own drawings.[5] Neither in Canada nor anywhere else has a great feat of

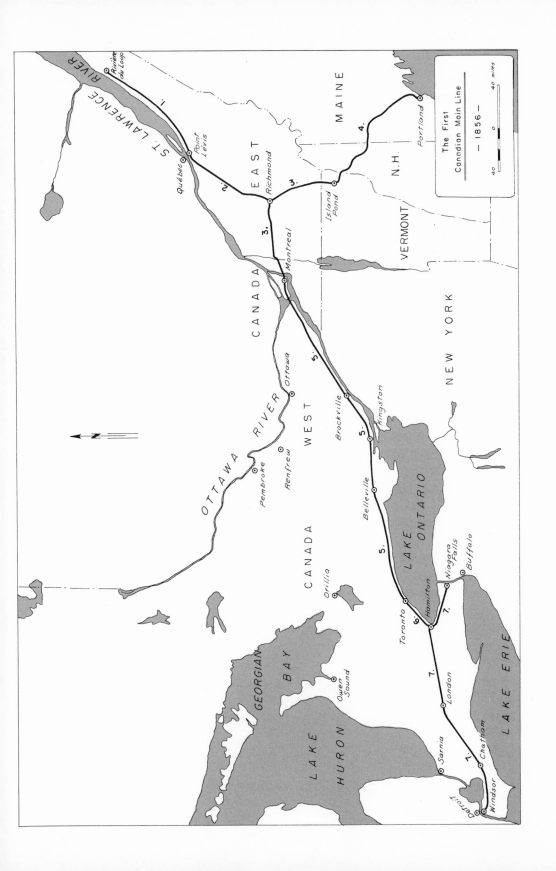

The First
Canadian Main Line
— 1856 —

ST. LAWRENCE RIVER

Rivière
du Loup

1

Point
Lévis

Québec

MAINE

Portland

4

N.H.

EAST

Richmond

3

2

3

Island
Pond

VERMONT

CANADA

Montreal

3

OTTAWA RIVER

Ottawa

5

WEST

Renfrew

Pembroke

Brockville

5

Kingston

NEW YORK

Belleville

5

LAKE
ONTARIO

CANADA

Orillia

5

Niagara
Falls

Buffalo

Toronto

Hamilton

7

GEORGIAN
BAY

Owen
Sound

London

7

LAKE
HURON

Sarnia

Chatham

7

Detroit

Windsor

LAKE ERIE

engineering been carried out more efficiently or been more amply documented.

Hodges was accompanied by several hundred craftsmen—finishing masons, master carpenters, blacksmiths and other specialists. They suffered greatly from the extremes of climate—frostbite and snow blindness in the winter, sunstroke in the fierce heat of midsummer. There was also an outbreak of the dreaded ship fever (the colloquial name for cholera). Yet these skilled workers stuck to their tasks manfully and quickly learned the ways of the country. Hodges himself had an early indication of unforeseen problems. He found suitable stone for his piers on the Caughnawaga Indian reserve, sixteen miles upriver from Montreal. But when he approached the local chiefs to obtain permission to open the requisite quarries, his youthful appearance frustrated him; he was told that he was much too young to participate in such an important powwow. It was only when he produced evidence that he was more than forty years of age that they consented to palaver.

A local attitude that caused him considerable trouble was the unwillingness of Canadian workmen to accept long-term contracts. Twice a year, on the opening of navigation and at harvest time, the increased demand for workers (after slack winter and summer seasons) impelled local labor to demand higher pay and to refuse further employment without considerable haggling. As previously reported, the colonists were reluctant at any time to accept the disciplines of group tasks; they resented being compelled to do their work in any other way than their own.

Such difficulties, however, both with imported craftsmen and local labor were no more than learning pains. The British craftsmen quickly adopted colonial practices, and the Canadians soon took pride in pulling in harness with their fellows. Throughout the five years it took to build the bridge, Hodges again and again reported instances in which the colonists and the home countrymen pooled their knowledge to common advantage. A typical instance was a primitive traveler, the ancestor of the rail-layers of the future. It moved along 1,300 feet of temporary tracks laid on gantrys; its sixty-foot boom hoisted the ten-ton blocks of stone from the river barges, stacked them and later conveyed them to the sites of the piers or retaining walls. Such a machine had been shipped out from England, but had proved useless and had been thrown aside. A subcontractor named Chaffey, described by Hodges as "an Englishman who had been in Canada sufficiently long to free his genius from the shackles riveted on him in early life," undertook its reconstruction. Thereafter it worked perfectly.

The piers had been designed with sharp cutwaters, as protection against the ice, and with substantial cribwork around them because of possible damage during the summer months from the great rafts of logs that it was impossible to steer between them. The first caisson was towed into position on the Queen's Birthday, May 24, 1854. The first pier took several months to build, but improved teamwork progressively reduced the period until the last pier was completed in forty-five days. In August 1857, the assembly of the superstructure began. It consisted of twenty-five tubular spans sixteen feet in width and eighteen feet in height; the sides were plate girder and the roofs were of timber covered with tin sheeting. The tubes were erected in pairs and were connected with expansion joints mounted on rollers. The total length of the tubular portion was 6,521 feet; of the entire bridge, 10,410 feet.

On December 15, 1859, the first train crossed; the contractors not only had kept within their time estimate but they had also delivered the bridge for $500,000 less than its estimated cost. On August 25, 1860, H. R. H. the Prince of Wales, the first member of the Royal Family to undertake an official tour of Canada, had driven the last rivet.

Grand Trunk Fortunes at Low Ebb

With the completion of this great structure, Peto, Brassey, Jackson and Betts disappear from the Grand Trunk history. It had been a costly experience for these contractors. The Imperial link served them ill; they were much more at home and had an easier time on their contracts in many foreign lands. Not only the climate, but the money markets and the politicians were against them; in Canada they were pioneers without the advantages that accrued to those who were making a beginning in a new country. They had to build to a scale far above the normal level. But even at that they had done a far better job for the Grand Trunk Railway than had its management. According to George Carr Glyn, the Victoria Bridge was the straw that broke the back of that company's credit. Grand Trunk debentures quoted at a discount of 25 percent in London in 1856 became unsalable in the following year, when a sudden panic struck the United States and fourteen hundred banks closed their doors. This made a third appeal to the Province of Canada inevitable; the Grand Trunk already owed it £3,111,500; when such indebtedness was reduced to the status of a secondary liability in order to foster the sales of the debentures, there was an immediate uproar in the Legislative Assembly. John A. Macdonald, the Kingston attorney whom Sir Edmund

Grimani Hornby had described as "an able man, with unlimited power of consuming champagne," was leader of the Liberal-Conservative coalition and he almost came to blows with George Brown on the floor of the House. The government concession failed to revive interest in the debentures, but loans totaling £160,000 were negotiated. It was amply apparent, however, that official patience and funds alike were running low and that the entire Grand Trunk project stood in danger of collapse.

The Blackwell Investigation

Confronted with this emergency, the Grand Trunk shareholders dispatched one of their number, E. T. Blackwell, with plenary powers and with the description of managing director. In September 1858, his report portrayed a tottering enterprise. Eleven million pounds had been spent, two-thirds of which had been found by British banks and shareholders; the company owed roughly the same amount in borrowings, interest, rentals and miscellaneous indebtedness. One thousand fifty-seven miles of tracks were in operation, and since the opening of the Montreal-Toronto section the traffic had doubled, but rising costs had kept pace with every increase in earnings and the operating ratio stood at a hazardous 91.4 percent. The Montreal-Portland line still was costing much more than it earned; on the whole, shippers along Lake Ontario had remained faithful to the slower but cheaper water routes. Owing to shortage of funds, the Grand Trunk had not been able to maintain construction up to their vaunted English standards.

Galt Does It Again

Blackwell, however, remained optimistic. Canada surely must grow and the Grand Trunk would grow with it. He therefore saw the present problems as temporary, and in such terms he discussed them with Andrew Tilloch Galt, who above all others had waxed fat on the original flotations and who now, by a quirk of politics, was Inspector-General of the Province and thus a man of political consequence. Once again this shrewd Scot's acquisitive instincts did not fail him. He pointed out that the Great Western was doing very well out of Chicago transit traffic. Would it not be possible to siphon off some of the Michigan Territory eastbound freights, diverting them to Portland and thus sustaining the fag end of the Grand Trunk, which chronically had cost more to operate than it earned?

How could this be arranged, asked Blackwell. Very simply, according to Galt. Build an extension from Port Huron, on the opposite site of the river from Sarnia, southward to Detroit and thereafter offer cut rates on eastbound exports. And what shall be used for construction funds, was the next query. Try the English bankers, was Galt's advice. They were first to recognize the potential of Michigan Territory. And who will build the line? All of Galt's advice had been designed to lead up to this key question.

In the spring of 1859, construction began on the Chicago, Detroit and Canada Grand Trunk Junction Railroad from Port Huron to Detroit. Gzowski and Company—Alexander Tilloch Galt under another name—had been given the contract; Baring Brothers had advanced a little more than half its cost estimated at £450,000; and the Grand Trunk had found the remainder. The contractors had agreed to accept a substantial portion of their payments in stock of the new line. In November 1859, this railway, sixty miles in length, was open for traffic. Then—and only then —was it revealed that Gzowski and Company owned the railway. It had paid off a sufficient proportion of the Baring advance to acquire a controlling interest. It was quite willing to lease the line to the Grand Trunk, but at the thumping figure of 50 percent of the gross receipts, with the railway company providing the rolling stock.

Alexander Tilloch Galt, the old master, had done it again. But by now the politicians, particularly those who comprised · Her Majesty's Loyal Opposition, to say nothing of the English shareholders, were sniffing on his trail. Could it be possible that as Inspector-General he had diverted public funds into Grand Trunk coffers in order to pay that company's share of the costs and incidentally to make a profit out of it for himself? There was no more than circumstantial evidence to support this speculation, but men have been hanged on less. What made the transaction so infuriating to the politicians was that this railway prospered from the start. By January 1860, it was booking substantial volumes of beef, pork and lard from Chicago to Liverpool at twelve cents a hundredweight, less than the standing rates from Chicago to New York City. In its first five years of operation its earnings increased four times more rapidly than those of the Grand Trunk as a whole. At times there was a queue of several hundred cars awaiting passage across the St. Clair River. Flour freights swiftly built up to thirty thousand barrels a week. In addition to the inadequate ferry service, the shortage of Grand Trunk rolling stock and the inconvenience of the change in gauge at the Michigan boundary retarded the growth of the traffic.

Chapman's Report

As far as Canadian politicians were concerned, the coincidence of the roles of Alexander Tilloch Galt as government official and as railway promoter soon was forgotten; it was a circumstance of comparatively common occurrence. The British shareholders were less amenable, and their wrath fell on Blackwell, who had been so neatly and openly gulled. In the summer of 1860, H. C. Chapman, a tough Lancashireman and substantial shareholder, invited himself to examine the affairs of the company on the spot. He returned to Britain in a snarling mood, and at the November meeting he accused Blackwell of connivance in the matter of the Gzowski contract and Walter Shanley, general manager and chief engineer of the company, of being the associate of a Canadian politician in an outright swindle. He gave chapter and verse for the latter accusation. In a Sarnia land deal, the Canadian government had authorized the sale of a certain property to the company for £165.10.0. In a series of sleight-of-hand transactions the property eventually arrived in the possession of the Grand Trunk at a round cost of £24,000. In Chapman's opinion the colonists were altogether too quick on the uptake for the virtuous railway officials, who kept their promises and treated their customers and suppliers as though they were all as decent and as honest as themselves. Whereas if you saw the Canadian colonists' without rose-tinted spectacles (and particularly cast eyes on their politicians), you could only decide that they were a breed that required watching, for one and all they deemed it not only their privilege but their duty to bilk the English investor.

Chapman's views, expressed in such language, were as good as meat and drink to George Brown and his Reform Party, now as always in a mortal feud with the Macdonald administration. Out of rude and bad-tempered exchanges in the Legislative Assembly there emerged a Committee of Enquiry. Its report, tabled in the spring of 1861, carefully skirted the points at issue and could be summarized in the not very original conclusion that the Grand Trunk would be a better railway if it offered better facilities. In other words, if money grew on trees, all would be well. It elicited a stinging reply from Walter Shanley, who, in a defense eighty pages in length, denied everything, ending with a masterpiece of Victorian circumlocution: "The Commissioners have used figures in a strikingly negligent manner to arrive at erroneous conclusions derived from false data; arithmetical blunders are stupidly added until imposing-looking tabulations contentiously prefaced can be shewn to contain little except dross."

The impact of Chapman's violent denunciations of his fellow shareholders, however, led to a petition by the Grand Trunk management, to the Canadian government, admitting a sorry state of affairs. The company, said its statement, was overwhelmed with debt, wholly destitute of credit and in ultimate danger of lapsing into utter insolvency and confusion. It acknowledged that it had no claim for public assistance except that its shareholders had sunk £11 million in it and now stood to lose everything. Its plea therefore was compassionate and its impact on the Macdonald administration negligible; a company that consistently provided the Opposition with ammunition was a poor candidate for official philanthropy. The party in power saw little reason to mourn its threatened dissolution.

A Fresh Start

Fortunately for the Grand Trunk, the British bankers were of a different mind. The company owed Barings and Glyn Mills more than £800,000, which was too much to lose without a struggle; moreover, George Carr Glyn was of the breed that, having put hands to the plough, does not look backward. He announced that he proposed to apply for a writ of seizure, not to satisfy his own claims but to forestall such action by less generously minded creditors. "We consider ourselves invested with a security and a trust," he declared, "which we will hold to the advantage of all. We will prevent, except under the most extraordinary and unexpected circumstances, the closing of the lines."

This generous undertaking spurred the Committee of Grand Trunk Shareholders and Bondholders to concrete proposals. In July 1861, it offered to raise £900,000 of new capital if the government would consent to the amortization, over a period of from twenty-five to thirty years, of the annual subventions for the carriage of the mails and of military personnel. Such a concession would permit the company to borrow approximately £1,200,000. Concurrently, the Committee made a clean sweep of the top management; President Alexander Mackenzie Ross, his board and principal officers resigned. Edward Watkin, a highly regarded figure in the British railway world, left at once for Canada to take charge and to effect a sweeping reorganization.

He arrived at a critical but, as it turned out, highly favorable moment. The first battles of the American Civil War had aroused the

Milwaukee, the locomotive that drew the mobile brigade of Canadian defenders during the Fenian Raids.

North to the implications of British sympathy for the Southern cause. Already some of the less restrained Union spokesmen were at fever heat; in July of that year, the *New York Herald* had pronounced the British North American colonies to be legitimate targets for reprisals and in due course logical prizes of victory. In November, when the packet *Trent* was intercepted and boarded by a Union patrol on the high seas, British anger led to the reinforcement of the sparse Imperial garrisons in the Canadas; within the next few months seven thousand regulars, including Guards battalions, gunners and services, were landed at New Brunswick ports and, in an extraordinary operation, marched or were sleighed for 400 miles across snowbound forests to man the Canadian boundaries. In a twinkling, therefore, railways assumed new and urgent importance.

The hour could not have bred a better man. Watkin was a tireless worker, an able technician, a fearless advocate. Soon after arrival, he declared in a letter to his wife, "The Grand Trunk is an organised mess— I might say, a sink of iniquity." He apparently was the first to realize that running a railway under Canadian winter conditions necessitated modifications of British equipment and practice. In the next months, laboring far into the nights, he hastened to convert lagging and scrambling routines into something resembling efficient operations. A Canadian railway historian has written:

> He discharged more than half the professional engineers, thus avoiding the expense of various experiments that an excess of these gentlemen is likely to cause. He completely reorganized the stores department and in the process discovered large stocks of parts which when equitably distributed over the system could be used for repairs and extensions. He simplified the work of the traffic department. In a personal letter to Glyn he called the freight manager an unmitigated scoundrel who set his own rates, audited his own accounts and fixed fares to suit the steamboats which he owned.[6]

While this housecleaning was in progress, Watkin wisely made no approach to the Canadian Legislative Assembly. In the spring of 1862, John A. Macdonald resigned after defeat in the House and was succeeded by another of his name, Sandfield Macdonald, who enjoyed strong French-Canadian support. By then American resentment had crystallized into unofficial action, with the Fenian and the Hunters Lodges extremists advocating an immediate invasion of Canada. The new administration therefore immediately announced that the first duty of all Canadians must be to prepare for war, and that above all else, steps must be taken to keep the railway in operation.

Watkin handled the situation admirably. One of his first moves was to create a brigade of militia out of railway employees; for many years afterward, the Grand Trunk regiments remained on the Official Gazette. In dealing with the government, he emphasized at every opportunity that his basic policy was to put an end to the annual appearance of the Grand Trunk before the Legislative Assembly, cap in hand in search of a dole.

As a result of his attitude, the Grand Trunk Arrangements Act, as passed on July 9, 1862, contained virtually everything he could have sought. Permission was granted to capitalize the postal and military subsidies, which gave the company a reserve fund of more than a million sterling. Additional preference stock was issued to liquidate outstanding indebtedness and authorization had been granted for £500,000 in Equipment Bonds. Thirteen priorities were established for the distribution of railway receipts over and above actual working expenses. Five out of twelve directors thereafter must be residents of the Canadas.

This measure, which eliminated the threat of seizure and provided working capital that was not at the mercy of the politicians, was a veritable blood transfusion. The anemia of the Grand Trunk disappeared overnight. Watkins, taking full advantage of the menaces in the air, had driven the bailiff from the doors. In brilliant expositions, he reported to the shareholders that Canada had a great future, far beyond its present bounds; that it was lunacy to think that a railway could be operated over vast distances as though it traversed the English shires. He persuaded C. J. Brydges, the young and successful managing director of the Great Western Railway, to join the Grand Trunk as general manager. Four eminent Canadians—none with active political affiliations—accepted seats on the board. Thereafter he made ready to withdraw, his mission accomplished, but the Grand Trunk shareholders would not hear of it. In October 1862, he became president.

A Vision of Canada's Future

He had brought to the company something even more valuable than his energy and eloquence—a vision of Canada's future. He had been in the United States on previous occasions in connection with the bankruptcy of the Erie Railroad, and he had marked the tide of American expansion, which by now had reached the shores of the Pacific. He was certain that unless Canada took immediate steps to stake her claims, American settlers soon would begin to filter northward into Ruperts Land, the vast stretches of prairie, bushlands and mountains under the administration of the Hudson's Bay Company. The ousting of that great trader from its Oregon holdings constituted fair warning that no chartered company would be able to hold empty territories against the encroachments of land-hungry pioneers. Britain, he urged, should take immediate steps to place the Hudson's Bay holdings under the jurisdiction of the Province of Canada, which should embark without delay on the establishment of communications from ocean to ocean.

Before leaving London, Watkin had discussed this situation with Glyn and Baring. They were impressed with his views and had arranged an appointment for him at the Colonial Office. There, too, his proposals found favor; as a result he had come to Canada not only in a private but also in an Imperial capacity. Immediately on arrival he had incorporated the Atlantic and Pacific Transit and Telegraph Company, to bridge the gap of 2,500 miles between the Canadas and British Columbia with a means of communication, as a tangible token of unity. But he had found little local support for such an undertaking; it was beyond the thought range of the Canadians. Moreover, it incurred the instant and outright hostility of the Hudson's Bay Company, which realized its significance. Under such circumstances the Colonial Secretary deemed the hour not to be ripe and quietly shelved the enterprise.

The honeymoon of the Grand Trunk and the politicians was quickly over. With a comprehensive force of eighteen thousand British troops bolstering the militia garrisons along the frontier and with the realization that the hostile demonstrations to the south of the border meant little more than noise and nuisance, the Macdonald-Sicotte administration recovered its nerve and began to regret the concessions it had made under the Grand Trunk Arrangements Act. When Watkin applied for the implementation of the capitalization of the postal and military subventions, he was asked for a quid pro quo under the table: he must agree to deliver the votes of the Grand Trunk employees at the next election. When he refused contemptuously to consider anything of the kind, Luther Holton, the new Inspector-General and a former partner of Andrew Tilloch Galt, instituted a witch hunt into the Grand Trunk past and managed to delay the fulfillment of its undertaking for more than three years.

Trouble with the Shareholders

Another embarrassment now confronted the Grand Trunk, with more serious implications than the ill will of the politicians. The Arrangements Act, which had repaired the fortunes of the Grand Trunk in one direction, threatened to ruin them in another. The thirteen priorities designated for revenues over and above working expenses dealt with the order of distribution of such surpluses to the proprietors of the company. Unfortunately the present-day shareholders were not the original investors who, as clients of Glyn Mills and Barings in easy circumstances, were prepared to take the long view. The shares of the original investors had been bought up by a very different breed, many of them tough Liverpool speculators, men who knew the value of the scurf on a penny and who were not interested in anything except milking the company of its uttermost farthing.

The Arrangements Act had given them their pound of flesh; if there was not enough money to satisfy their annual claims, they demanded that the management issue equivalent stock to them. In three years (1862–1864) the capitalization of the company rose from £12,243,470 to £17,209,070, and there was scarcely a shilling of new money in the lot. Watkin was obliged to battle desperately not only for the funds to make the modest improvements that the increasing traffic demanded, but also to maintain the present trackage and equipment. In the winter of 1862–1863, there had been eight thousand broken rails, and much of the rolling stock was falling apart. In addition, the company was taking a severe beating on its American earnings because of the wild fluctuations of exchange; in the last six months of 1864, a surplus of £167,696 of dollar earnings at par only realized £78,412 on conversion. An operating ratio of 57 percent on the American lines had worsened to 75 percent solely because of these circumstances. Canadian freight movements, however, increased rapidly in volume and promised to repair such losses speedily if funds were made available for the improvements of the lines and for the provision of new equipment. The shareholders, however, had wearied of accepting stock for their cash entitlements, and at every meeting their complaints were loud and long. That the Canadian provinces after many setbacks were at point of uniting into a dominion meant nothing to them. What they wanted were their legitimate apportionments and more of them.

A Cold Douche from Watkin

At the spring meeting of 1867, with the momentous political event of Confederation only weeks away, the shareholders arrived in their customary querulous mood, prepared to challenge even the most modest needs of the railway. They were destined for a rude awakening. Watkin, buttressed by Brydges, declared that a new day had dawned; Canada was at point of Confederation, of "dominion from sea to sea." This new nation would need first of all a Main Line; it was the destiny of the Grand Trunk to provide it. There therefore must be a complete reorganization, beginning with the merger of competitive lines and feeders, the shifting of emphasis from American to through Canadian traffic, the extension of the Grand Trunk as the Queens Highway from a Canadian Atlantic terminal to a port on the Pacific. The first step must be the reversal of the priorities and a ruthless pruning of the capital of the company.

The majority of shareholders gasped as they realized the trend and intent of Watkin's proposal. It involved the transformation of the Grand Trunk from a commercial to a political project and at the investors' expense. As his address concluded, a dozen speakers were on their feet. Each regarded it as his bounden duty to denounce the Watkin's proposals as little better than highway robbery. They had put their hard cash into a speculative venture which might or might not win home, but they never expected anything approximating confiscation. They felt that at the very least they were entitled to a run for their money. Anything less was a gross betrayal of their confidence.

Great Western Suspension Bridge over Niagara River, 1852.

Tyler's Report

In the free-for-all that ensued when the shareholders claimed the floor, Henry Whatley Tyler stood out. He had been an able officer of the Royal Engineers and was about to accept the appointment of Inspector-General of British Railways. He attacked Watkin and Brydges for what he termed their timidity. His flashing style carried the meeting, and he accepted a commission to examine the Grand Trunk and to make recommendations. He spent two months in Canada; at the December meeting, his detailed report brought little comfort either to management or shareholders. With reference to Watkin's imperial vision, he declared that there was not a ghost of a chance of the Grand Trunk being selected as the official instrument in a trans-Canada Main Line. It had blotted its copybook with all Canadian politicians alike.

The new federal authority had decided to complete the long-delayed linkup of Nova Scotia and New Brunswick with Ontario and Quebec at public expense and thereafter to retain it as a nationally owned property. The western railway, which would be designed as bait to draw the prairie territories and British Columbia into Confederation, also would be officially sponsored. There was no intention to invite Grand Trunk participation in either of these projects.

On other aspects of the future, Tyler agreed almost completely with Watkin. There was great promise in the present property but the shareholders would have to wait their hour. In 1864, the Buffalo and Lake Huron Railway, 160 miles of ramshackle trackage between Goderich and Fort Erie, had been unloaded on the Grand Trunk by its owners, who were the Liverpool speculators with the loudest voices at the company's annual meetings. It cut across Great Western traffic territory and as it stood it had little but nuisance value; but if the Niagara River were bridged and junction effected with competitors of the New York Central, it might easily claim more of the Michigan transit traffic. Tyler strongly recommended such a bridge. In addition he backed immediate expenditures on steel rails and new rolling stock at a cost of £900,000. He forebore to say where this money would be found, but it was obvious to all. The shareholders once more must forgo their perquisites.

Potter Takes Over

Tyler had pulled no rabbits out of hats. Instead, he had pointed out succinctly that the owners must tighten their belts if their property was to survive. To the speculators, who were calling the tune, such advice was monstrous. A scurrilous campaign immediately was launched against Watkin; it would have got nowhere if staged in the City of London but it would seem to have thrived in Liverpool. The result was an Extraordinary General Meeting on October 2, 1868, at which Tyler and Watkin alike were abused and accused; they had betrayed their principals and principles alike. Watkin pointed out that in his six years of office the Grand Trunk had earned £2.5 million over and above its working expenses; of this sum the shareholders had received £950,000. How much more, in decency, could they ask? He warned them that if they were left to the tender mercies of the Canadians, they would not get more than scrap iron value for their property. The shareholders, however, were in no mood to listen. On March 27, 1869, Watkin refused reappointment. Richard Potter was elected president in his stead.

Potter had been on the board of the Grand Trunk for more than six years as the nominee of the London bankers. He was of good family and in comfortable circumstances; he was the father of nine daughters, one of whom was Beatrice, destined to be the wife of Sydney Webb and in her own right a distinguished statistician and historian. In her autobiography, she makes it clear that her father did not seek the position; he stipulated that he be paid only a nominal salary and he seldom took the trouble to collect it. His sole desire was to keep the peace and to extricate the Grand Trunk from its predicaments.

Unfortunately he undertook to be sweetly reasonable with the ginger group that had hounded Watkin out of office, and consequently its members considered him to be subservient to their demands. He therefore was in trouble from the start. The replacement of virtually all the remaining original Grand Trunk rails was a first priority, and Alexander Tilloch Galt, who never missed a bet, had set up a rolling mill in Toronto and had persuaded the Canadian government to impose a duty on imported rails. With a monopoly established, the price of the local product naturally went sky high. In the summer of 1869, Barings and Glyn Mills for a second time secured a friendly writ of attachment to protect the property. At the autumn meeting, Potter, undoubtedly under orders of the bankers, switched from his former placatory approach to words of one syllable. He told shareholders that they knew nothing about the railway business in Canada, and unless they talked sense he proposed in future to ignore them. The whip was out. The pack withdrew sullenly, snarling.

Vigor and Progress

From then on, Potter's administration was characterized by energy and imagination. He persuaded the city of Montreal to contribute $150,000 for the purchase of right of way that would give the company access to the dock area and for a bridge across the Lachine Canal. He placed a contract of the value of $1.17 million for the bridging of the Niagara River at Buffalo, most of the cost being found out of the bonds and preference shares of the bridge company. He then turned to the costly and controversial problems of iron versus steel rails and declared wholeheartedly for steel; in 1870, he hoped to replace 157 miles of unsafe iron, and he declared that steel rails would effect a saving in maintenance of £150,000 per annum. On the other vexed question, that of gauge, he was less positive. There still were five different gauges in use in North America; if the government persevered with its program of railways on both the eastern and western extremities of the Grand Trunk and chose the favorite 4'8½" gauge, it probably could be persuaded to assist the company in the center in changeover. However, Potter was prepared to convert the former Buffalo and Lake Huron tracks to the narrower gauge immediately, since this line subsisted almost entirely on Michigan Territory traffic. The changeover on 215 miles was effected expeditiously in two days.

At the December 1871 meeting, Potter rendered a detailed account of his stewardship. He had spent several months in Canada that year and had been accompanied by James Allport, general manager of the Midland Railway, an officer of high repute. In his three years' tenure, Potter had more or less brought the recalcitrant shareholders to heel, and he now was backed solidly by Glyn Mills and Barings. The Niagara Bridge had proved an excellent investment; it had more than doubled the flow of American transit traffic. Steel rails, which had only cost £2.10.0 more than iron per long ton, had been a good buy; in the previous winter, there had been six thousand breakages of iron compared to only seven of steel rails.

Potter Cracks the Whip

When James Allport took the floor he declared that he had expected to find the Grand Trunk in rack and ruin; instead, he had inspected a property of growing efficiency and excellent prospects. He agreed with the majority of the recommendations that President Potter would lay before the meeting. These projected expenditures were the meat of the matter; everyone leaned forward to listen. Potter's list seemed endless. A further 862 miles of steel rails, the substitution of Nova Scotia coal for wood fuel, purchases of rolling stock which would end troublesome and expensive rentals, many miles of new sidings and spurs, scores of grain elevators and new stations. These improvements would cost £1.485 million; to pay for them it would be necessary to sell securities held by the Grand Trunk to the value of £410,000, to issue £600,000 of equipment bonds that would take precedence over existing indebtedness and to impound for three years all surplus revenues over and above actual costs of operation.

This was an even more drastic proposal than had overthrown Watkin. It was a measure of Potter's ascendancy that he did not hesitate to declare that this program would be carried out regardless of the shareholders' opinions. George Carr Glyn (now Lord Wolverton) and Thomas Baring had opposed the scope of his requirements, entreating him to keep faith with at least some classes of preference shareholders. In response Potter had invited them to meet him, had confronted them with the necessary sacrifices and had won their support without playing the ace that was up his sleeve. In the Grand Trunk Act of 1857, the Canadian government had relinquished its first mortgage charges on the company in favor of other creditors. This concession in effect constituted a gift of £3 million. But the act also specified that if ever the Grand Trunk ceased to provide the requisite services for which it was built, this debt might be reinstated and the property seized to satisfy it. Had the shareholders refused to support him, Potter proposed to tell them that the Grand Trunk no longer belonged to them.

A *Serious Error of Judgment*

In the elation of success, however, he made a serious mistake. He closed out his survey by sermonizing on a matter of little importance to the Grand Trunk but that touched a nerve both in Canadian politicians and in the growing Canadian communities. After the extravaganza of railway promotion in the 1840s and 1850s, there came a lull; in the 1860s, scarcely a new project was broached or a mile of new track laid. But

Bonaventure Station, Montreal, 1871.

under the impetus of growth and the consciousness of a promising future, the Canadian towns had begun to take in each other's washing; the countryside was switching from subsistence to cash crops and improving the quality of their foodstuffs. Canadians also were beginning to break into export markets. The first cheese factory in Ontario was opened in 1864, and eight years later, there were two hundred of them, with an increasing proportion of their output findings its way to Great Britain. There were growing incentives to improve communications, therefore, and in the early 1870s, there broke out a veritable rash of local railway projects, designed not as in the past for prestige purposes, but because of the more sensible consideration of expanding traffic. Promotional methods, however, were much the same as before. There would be a town meeting, a whip-around for immediate expenses, an incorporation and the dispatch of a promoter or a citizens' committee to London to place sufficient bonds to cover the costs of construction.

Many of these projects were unwarranted, and some were plain swindles, and Richard Potter took the occasion of his victory to warn his countrymen against them. Whatever the accuracy of his comments, they were ill timed; under the exhilaration of emancipation from colonial status, Canadians were less amenable to grandmotherly advice and more touchy concerning their status as a free people managing their own affairs. Although they were destined to remain colonials in all but name up to the First World War, it was never safe after 1870 to tell them so. Potter's warnings, therefore, were not well received. If Canadians wanted to build more railways than they needed, whose business was it but their own?

An Audacious Gamble

The Grand Trunk president did not improve matters insofar as his personal popularity in government circles was concerned when soon afterward he consented to a financial transaction as outlandish as anything attempted by small town promoters. On the strength of Watkin's and Potter's labors, Grand Trunk common stock, which had never paid a dividend, rose by some 40 percent from 17 to 24. Whereupon one Alexander M'Ewen, with rather obscure financial connections, sponsored an audacious speculation. At that time, the Grand Trunk common stock on issue had a par value of £3,488,590 against preferred stocks and other fixed capital charges of £18,300,000. M'Ewen's scheme was to peg the protected indebtedness at the latter figure and thereafter to float £10 million of Grand Trunk common stock at a discount of 81 percent. This would provide more than £2 million, which would be enough to pay for the program of improvements. It was an outright gamble, and Potter at first was inclined to ignore the offer; but he had forgotten the lure of a long shot for his countrymen. Grand Trunk common stock was widely distributed, and almost every shareholder was eager to reduce the cost of his holdings by buying some of the cheaper issue.

At the general meeting of March 1873, Potter presented the M'Ewen offer. Everyone enthusiastically endorsed it. It did not increase the standing debt; it lowered the overall cost of the common stock and made it a better speculation; it presented the company with money for steel rails, conversion to coal and much-needed new rolling stock, at little cost to anyone. Bondholders and shareholders alike stood on their chairs and waved papers; only a grumpy few sulked in their seats. The meeting enthusiastically endorsed the suspension of service on the Grand Trunk preferential issues for a period of three years and authorized without qualms a second parcel of equipment bonds.

Freebooting Years and Panic

This essay in high finance turned out better for the customer than for the speculators. About £7.5 million of the discounted stock was taken up, but although sold at 19, it never climbed above 25 and soon fell back to around half that figure. Nevertheless, it went a long way toward easing the company's most pressing problems, and had the times not been out of joint, it might have marked a turning point in Grand Trunk fortunes. Unluckily the United States economy in the years after the Civil War had become the happy hunting ground for predators on the grand scale. It was the era of the robber barons—of "Commodore" Vanderbilt, Jay Gould, Jim Fisk, the Credit Mobilier *camarilla* and other promotional freebooters who stopped at nothing; Gould and Fisk, for instance, with the aid of President Grant's son-in-law, tried to corner the gold supply of the United States Treasury. As so often before and afterward, unbridled license precipitated a downfall; on this occasion the crash came in September 1873, when Jay Cooke, the super salesman of Civil War bonds, admitted bankruptcy. There followed panic; banks, railways and a thousand other business ventures operating on precarious credits toppled into ruin. Prices and rates nose-dived; American currency sank to a heavy discount on sterling. The Grand Trunk took a beating anew on its transit traffic.

Nevertheless, either because the banking structure of Canada withstood the shock or because the M'Ewen "manna" had cushioned it, the company weathered the storm. In 1874, its revenue for the first time passed the £2 million mark, its operating ratio improved, 800 miles of main line were converted to standard gauge, and the management was reorganized to entrust wider powers to the men on the spot. Thereafter they need only consult the London board on questions of policy. The managing director, secretary-treasurer and traffic manager constituted an executive committee that was accorded almost complete control. On Thomas Brydges' retirement in 1874, it became a duumvirate of two exceptionally able officers: Joseph Hickson, who had been with the Grand Trunk in Canada for eleven years, was appointed managing director, with Lewis Seargeant, a highly qualified executive from the South Wales Railway, as his traffic manager.

Fatal Blunders

At this juncture, when the company appeared to be struggling out of the morass of the depression, Richard Potter again elected to speak out of turn and became embroiled in the controversy that ended his career. Sir John A. Macdonald, first Prime Minister of the Dominion of Canada, had a fractious cabinet; whether he rode his ministers on the curb or on the snaffle, they usually managed to fall at their fences. In 1874 scandalous revelations of under-the-counter dealings with Sir Hugh Allan, a Montreal promoter, led to his defeat at the polls. The incoming administration was headed by Alexander Mackenzie, a dour Scot of unquestioned integrity, tireless industry and unyielding prejudices. In his book, railways were dubious blessings; they made people restless, ambitious and venal; as for those who lived by them, from promoters to stationmasters, they were not the sort that he cared to know. He came into power hoping to evade the commitment to build a railway across the plains to British Columbia. A dirt road, he held, would be ample. His principal political colleague was George Brown, the Toronto editor who nursed an almost pathological hatred of the Grand Trunk. In addition Mackenzie, as an expatriate Briton, was a more ardent nationalist than the general run of the native-born. He took an early opportunity to appoint Edward Jenkins, another Scot, as the first Canadian Agent-General in London, in large part to symbolize emancipation from the leading strings of the Colonial Office.

At this time Sir Hugh Allan, after apprenticeships in counting houses, drygoods and steamships, was rather more than dabbling in railway promotion. He was one of the more dubious local patriots who had knelt to receive the Queen's accolade; as will be recounted in a subsequent chapter, he was the mastermind of perhaps the most impudent swindle ever perpetrated in Canadian railway history. It was a confidential file filched from his office that had assisted in the overthrow of the Macdonald government. Among his irons in the railway fire was the Montreal and Northern Colonization Railway, which sought to invade Grand Trunk traffic territory almost anywhere between Portland and the Michigan boundary. He had undertaken to float such a project in London, but there he found none of the portals of Lombard Street on the latch for him. Indeed, the financial editor of *The Times,* in paragraphs that braved the laws of libel, declared in almost as many words that anyone who would back Sir Hugh should have his head examined.

That gentleman, in no degree abashed, enlisted the Canadian Agent-General in his support. Jenkins replied to *The Times* strictures, implying that British lack of success in Canadian railway ventures was because the investors had neglected to hire Canadians to spend their money for them. This whopper was too much for Potter. He entered the fray, providing *The Times*, then a power in the land, with details of Canadian railway promotions and adding scathing comments on the *modus operandi* of Sir Hugh Allan and gentry of his ilk. Nine days after the financial editor had stated his views, the controversy reached the leader page of *The Times.* There the commentator found emphatically for Potter, quoting chapter and verse. British investors had sunk £38 million in Canadian railway ventures. Of this sum only £10 million had yielded any return whatsoever. The Grand Trunk had had £25 million of British money, four-fifths of which had never earned a farthing. The best that its first preference shares ever had yielded was a 2.5 percent dividend. Railway by railway, the writer recounted the sorry results. If there were worse investments abroad than Canadian railways, he did not know where they were to be found.

Prime Minister Mackenzie held no brief for Sir Hugh Allan. Nevertheless, the formidable *Times* attack had been touched off by Potter, and it behooved the Canadian head of state to protect the good name of his country in the principal money market of the world. It seems unlikely, however, that Mackenzie would have intervened had it not been for a further and flagrant intervention by the Grand Trunk spokesman. The North Shore Railway, an Allan promotion, had been subsidized by the province of Quebec through a substantial grant of wild lands. In a backstairs transaction, these lands were returned to the donor province for the substantial sum of $1.25 million at a time when not a sod had been turned on this railway.

It was a typical example of promotional sleight-of-hand, with little or no impact upon the Grand Trunk, but Potter chose to regard it as illicit support of a potential competitor. He hastened to put pen to paper and to write the two letters destined to destroy him. In his protest to the Prime Minister, he invoked the hoary and unprovable allegation that at the time of the flotation of the Grand Trunk that company, as the Main Line, was assured of the monopoly of traffic. He followed up with a request to Lord Carnarvon, Secretary of State for the Colonies, that the Imperial government should disallow any Canadian legislation which would validate the Allan transaction.

The representation to the Prime Minister was silly. The demand on Lord Carnarvon was folly; the Secretary of State promptly returned Potter's letter with the notation that as Canada now possessed responsible government, the Mother Country could not intervene in matters of local jurisdiction. Mackenzie was justly annoyed by such a *gaffe* by a man in Potter's position, but he had no wish to soil his fingers with railway intrigues; he asked Thomas Brydges, now in retirement, to give him a memorandum on the Grand Trunk contention. Brydges appears to have been nursing a grudge, for he burst into print with a farrago of nonsense over an alleged attempt to reimpose colonial servitude. In reply, Potter expertly tore this insinuation to ribbons and left the administration a sitting duck for the Opposition. Mackenzie therefore had no choice but to defend himself. He instructed Sir John Rose, who had replaced Jenkins in London, to complain to Glyn Mills and Barings that Potter was meddling in matters that were none of his concern.

If Thomas Baring and George Carr Glyn had been consulted, the matter probably would have gone no further. The Prime Minister would have received an assurance, Potter a slap on the wrist. But they had retired and their replacements were of less staunch stuff, accustomed to dealing with the emasculated London board, which now took little or no action except under pressure from its executive officers in Canada. Among its members Joseph Hickson was preeminent. As a born negotiator, he had been appalled by Potter's rashness. There therefore can be little doubt that he dictated the line that the shareholders accepted. Whatever their sympathy with Potter's view, the company should not support him should he fall out with the Canadian government. The banks, the board and the management would stand together. Potter would be regarded as expendable.

A New Approach

Potter had no inkling of this decision. His every thought was given to the affairs of the railway, which was in deep water once more. In the wake of the 1873 panic, railroading had become a cutthroat business, with any stratagem admissible that would steal traffic from competitors. Contracts or promises were not worth ink or breath; anyone would agree to anything, sign anything and then without qualms disown the transaction to save or make a dollar. While such conditions prevailed in the United States, it seemed impossible to reach agreements in Canada. Again and again Potter had approached the Great Western, his competitor for American transit traffic; again and again the boards of the two companies had met and had made commiserating noises; again and again the best of intentions were thwarted because of the alliance of the Great Western with the American railways. Finally, Potter had been approached by the Great Western Railway with an offer to lease his lines west of Toronto—a proposal that plainly bore the seal and superscription of Commodore Vanderbilt of the New York Central. Potter did not entirely reject it; he was willing to consider any plan, including partnership or amalgamation, that would restore rational relations. The offer, however, turned his thoughts in another direction. Vanderbilt was at sword's point with many of the other United States railroads; perhaps they would be sympathetic to an accommodation that would end this competition. He therefore approached the heads of the principal American companies operating on the Atlantic seaboard, dilating on the folly of continuously striving to bankrupt each other and proposing some degree of consultation and association in the future.

The Last Scenes

He was surprised and delighted with the warmth of the responses, which in a number of instances included invitations to take the lead in the matter, with assurances of full support. In August he reported to his London board that he proposed to proceed to Canada to inaugurate such negotiations. He then was astounded to learn that a substantial number of his directors, including the representatives of the bankers, objected to his action, on the grounds that he was persona non grata to the Canadian Prime Minister. (It afterwards transpired that in response to Mackenzie's complaints, the banks had undertaken to curb Potter's activities.) In his protest against this palpable snub, Potter offered to apologize to Mackenzie for overstepping the bounds of protocol but insisted that it was his duty to defend the company against any circumstance that threatened to damage it and to explore any prospect that would improve its fortunes. In reply, the Grand Trunk directors played their ace in the form of an impudent intimation from Hickson that he would resign if Potter pursued his mission of pacification with the American railroads. The Bank of Montreal, which now shared the Canadian government account with Glyn Mills and Company, naturally was well aware of what was happening and cabled a protest against the proposed conference.

Thus the Grand Trunk president was left naked to his enemies. There is no documentary evidence that Prime Minister Mackenzie could be listed as one of them. For the most part, he was an even-tempered and just man, and it is doubtful if beyond a momentary irritation he ever gave Potter's precipitancy a second thought. But the Grand Trunk president had been overzealous, and on challenge his supporters had panicked. He went down gallantly. On October 11 he presented a resolution to a directors' meeting, empowering him to proceed to Canada for the purpose of consultation with the heads of the leading American railroads. There was silence in the room and no seconder. He waited for a minute and then tabled his resignation.

When he returned to his Gloucestershire home, a host of letters awaited him from those who resented his treatment and wished him to reconsider his action. The London press almost unanimously declared that he had been sacrificed to appease a Canadian politician. For seven years he had given his skill, strength and courage without stint and not without avail. Years later, Potter's daughter Beatrice Webb, by then a national figure, declared in her diary that railroading was not a business in which gentlemanly behavior was rewarding.

Henry Whatley Tyler, now a knight, a member of Parliament and at point of retirement as Chief Inspector of Railways, had defended Potter and had endorsed his project of consultation. In late October he took the chair at an Extraordinary General Meeting. He was elected president without a single dissent. For the first time, the Grand Trunk Railway would be under command of professionals.

5

The Intercolonial:

Monkeyshines in the Maritimes

A preceding chapter records how Francis Hincks double-crossed Nova Scotia and New Brunswick in the matter of the Imperial Guarantee of 1851, whereby Great Britain undertook to provide finance for a railway to link her North American colonies. This act of treachery aroused deep resentment among Maritimers; it was more or less, they felt, what one must expect from Canadians, who tolerated the papists and had given equal rights to Britain's immemorial foes. Hincks made no bones about his views; while the negotiations over the Imperial Guarantee were in progress, he had stated bluntly, "There is not a single advocate of the Halifax Railway that believes that it will pay its way." In the 500 miles between the Nova Scotia capital and the St. Lawrence Valley, there was only one European inhabitant to every 300 acres adjoining the route. Of that population it is doubtful if one out of every three stood to gain anything from a railway to the Canadas.

Nova Scotia delegates on a mission to London admitted that they had no trade of any importance with their fellow colonials. On the other hand, they provided half the traffic that entered Boston harbor. Nor had the Maritimers any common policy on the extent and direction of the railways they required. Nova Scotia thought in terms of radiating short lines to feed the port and capital of Halifax; New Brunswick cherished plans to link up with the New England traffic area. Prince Edward Island was quite content with its dirt roads and had no particular desire for truck or trade with anyone.

Such parochial differences, however, meant less than nothing to Joseph Howe. He viewed everything through the spectacles of his cause. In the matter of railways, his views were rose-tinted; the twin streaks of steel were precursors of vast changes tomorrow. All living, he believed would be altered by the mobility that railways bestowed. He declared on one occasion that smiles and kisses and wedding bells should be entries on the balance sheets of railways. Love made babies, and each year's tally of births added from £20,000 to £30,000 to the potential railway revenues of Nova Scotia.

The withdrawal of the Imperial Guarantee for a Main Line therefore was more or less ignored by Howe. He immediately switched to a program of local short lines for Nova Scotia. New Brunswick with equal celerity prepared to push ahead with a cross-colony railway to the Maine boundary, where it would effect junction with lines leading to Portland and Boston. By 1853, both these projects were under way. Peto, Brassey, Jackson and Betts took the New Brunswick contract for 150 miles at $32,500 a mile, of which half would be paid in stock of the line. In Nova Scotia, the same contractors had offered to become partners of the government in order to build four short lines—Halifax to the New Brunswick boundary (145 miles), Truro to Pictou (70 miles), Windsor Junction to Annapolis (140 miles), Pictou to the Strait of Canso (81 miles). This offer was later withdrawn, and in March 1854, Howe introduced legislation whereby the foregoing projects would be vested in the Nova Scotia Railway Company, a completely publicly owned enterprise. He resigned as Provincial Secretary to take charge of it, with five fellow legislators as his executive assistants.

The Nova Scotia Short Lines

Contracts were placed immediately for short sections of a few miles in length. It was hoped that the experience gained on these experimental contracts would lead to better methods and more realistic estimates on those to follow. These first jobs priced roadbed at £3,527 per mile, with the government providing sleepers, rails, spikes, chairs and keys, the latter being the wooden wedges that pinioned the rails in the chairs. The broad gauge of 5'6" was adopted, with rails of sixty-three pounds a yard laid on sleepers ten feet in length, ten inches in width, three feet apart. The first sod was turned on January 13, 1854.

With Howe tirelessly supervising the construction, all at first went well. In the following year, he crossed to London and without difficulty sold £800,000 in railway debentures through Baring Brothers, who reserved a substantial proportion of the issue for their own account. Indeed, if Howe had stuck to his last, he might have proved the exceptional man who could transform dreams into reality. Unfortunately he became involved in a brawl with Irishmen at Gourlays Shanty and earned additional criticism as a self-appointed recruiting agent in the United States for Great Britain during the Crimean War. These misjudgments allowed his political enemies to gather head. He was challenged to an election by Charles Tupper, a dour little doctor who had replaced Howe as Colonial Secretary and who proved to be a genius at parochial politicizing. In 1855, Howe rashly took on this formidable antagonist in Tupper's home bailiwick of Cumberland County and was solidly defeated, losing his seat in the Legislative Assembly and his post as commissioner-in-chief of the Nova Scotia Railway Board.

It was as well for Howe's reputation that the electorate sacked him when it did. Political loyalties in that day were almost as deep-seated as religious convictions, but they required something more substantial than prayer to sustain them. A vote was an asset on which a voter expected to receive a dividend when his party was in power. The available perquisites in taxation, land deals, mail carriage and road building were small potatoes in comparison with the cream that could be skimmed from such massive projects as the construction of railways. Howe's supporters, perhaps unknown to him, already had pocketed substantial rakeoffs and their appetites had grown with eating.

One of Tupper's first moves when he became Colonial Secretary was to appoint James Laurie, an engineer, to sniff about and discover how Howe's original contracts were faring. On the whole he found that road-bed construction was satisfactory but that the Nova Scotia winter was altogether too much for the British-style superstructure. A single passing train would jar loose an inordinate number of the wedges that held the rails in place and had to be driven home anew before the line could be used again. The policy of placing contracts for short sections had proved disastrous. Any farmer with friends at court might be awarded a contract on which he would work spasmodically in whatever time could be spared from his farm. He would put in monstrous quantity claims and would throw up the contract if they were not paid. He gave scant attention to the surveyed route but would build the line through or as close as possible to his property, in order to enhance the value of his land. Sometimes five different groups would be quarreling over the route in the same locality and nothing would be done at all.

In the operation of the completed short sections, Laurie found little to praise, much to condemn. Maintenance of way upkeep had been farmed out to local contractors at five shillings per mile per day. This represented two-thirds of similar costs on the heavily operated British lines, three times the average United States costs on its rural railways. Virtually all these contractors were slipshod and neglectful. Insofar as the operation of trains was concerned, they ran at the crews' pleasure; timetables and schedules were nonexistent. Stationmasters and conductors pocketed a substantial portion of their take; shippers of the right political persuasion were extended unlimited credit.

As a result of such clownishness, the Nova Scotia short lines continued for months and even years to be no more than hodgepodges of isolated bits of tracks, sometimes completed and in operation but with unfinished gaps between them. The Pictou-Canso extension for Cape Breton never was placed in work. The first continuous section from Halifax to Truro (sixty-one miles) took fifty-four months to complete. By then construction was in an appalling mess. Everyone talked too much, did too little, resented authority, looked after himself first, haggled, disputed, cut corners, ignored or defied the rules of the job. It was confusion compounded.

Nova Scotia Railway: The origin of piggybacks—horse and wagon ticket, 1864.

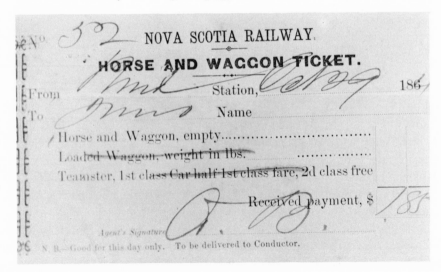

The Origins of Piggyback

There had been, however, one innovation of historical interest. Halifax, largely because of its British garrison, was a substantial market for produce. As its short lines progressed toward Windsor and Truro, more and more farmers came within its range of supply. Joseph Howe is said to have been responsible for the adoption of a device pioneered a half-century before by James Anderson of Edinburgh, whereby laden vehicles could be hoisted on and off flatcars. On September 19, 1855, *The Nova Scotian* reported that more and more farmers were using the railway for the last ten to fifteen miles of their weekly deliveries into Halifax. Their wagons were winched on to flatcars, and the horses were stabled in boxcars; there were separate charges for animals, vehicles and their loads; the carters traveled free. Eventually the stagecoaches came to use the railway in the same manner, since it cut from two to three hours from the last day of their journey. At first this method was used entirely for inward traffic, but its convenience soon converted many customers to return passages.

Beginnings in New Brunswick

Meanwhile in New Brunswick, John A. Poor's plan lived on in the name chosen by the provincial administration for the first of its short lines. Partly as a threat to the Canadas, partly as a promise to its own people, it was called the European and North American Railway. The first section, however, was not built toward the Maine boundary but eastward from Saint John for 107 miles to Shediac on Northumberland Strait. This line would constitute a short cut from the Bay of Fundy to the Gulf of St. Lawrence. On September 23, 1853, the first sod was turned by Lady Head, chatelaine of the Lieutenant-Governor. In the following year, however, Peto, Brassey, Jackson and Betts asked to be relieved of this contract, since the London money market would accept railway stock and debentures only at ruinous discounts. Baring Brothers then provided a loan, and the work continued under local management. The line was opened in August 1860 at a cost only 8 percent above the quotation of the British contractors. Unfortunately it failed in its main purpose; because of shallow seas and contrary winds the Admiralty refused to classify Shediac Harbour as a safe anchorage. But the construction of the railway solely by New Brunswickers had given them confidence, and from then onward they were more independent in their railway negotiations, both with the Imperial government and with the other colonies. They would cooperate if necessary, but they also were prepared to go it alone.

Nine years after Hincks had betrayed their interests, Nova Scotia and New Brunswick had only three short lines, in all totaling 288 miles, which did not in any sense integrate them or constitute a Main Line. Traffic was scanty since the heavy loads still moved by sea from outport to outport; there was no money in sight for improvements or extensions. At no time was there anything analagous to the outbursts of travel for its own sake that had sustained the early years of the Canadian short lines; life in the Maritimes was too serious a matter to be stimulated by speed; no one anticipated much pleasure this side of Heaven. Shortt and Doughty in their exhaustive study of the Canadian colonies thus described living conditions:

> The country was very sparsely peopled and the life of the inhabitants very primitive. Educational and religious privileges were few. A uniform method of thinking and of acting prevailed. It was almost an impropriety for one man to assume to be more learned, more religious or more polite than his neighbor. The older people were tenacious of the customs of their ancestors. Every man planted, sowed, ploughed, hoed and gathered in the crops as his grandfather had done before him. He salted down the same quantities of beef and pork, wore the same kind of stockings and said grace at the table with his wife and children in accordance with the traditions of many generations.[1]

Another Approach to Britain

In 1857, Charles Tupper, under the lash of Howe for failing to bring the Imperial government to heel, suddenly got a bright idea. He decided that, since Nova Scotia had never disowned the Imperial Guarantee of 1851, it still remained in force. Under this very thin pretext, he invited himself and the representatives of New Brunswick and the Canadas to form a delegation to London to insist on its implementation. But when there, they once again fell out among themselves and, as on their previous visit, they were told to go home and arrive at an agreement on what they really wanted. In their support, the Nova Scotia Legislative Assembly endeavored to put a pistol at the head of Great Britain in the form of a foolish memorial stating that if the Mother Country wanted an empire, it must be prepared to pay for its communications. Sir Edward Bulwer-Lytton, then Colonial Secretary, replied in blunter language than he was wont to use in his novels; he said that it would take a better case than the colonists had presented to date to loosen the Treasury purse strings. After this curt brushoff, the delegates sailed for home, but they left a certain amount of ferment behind them. The British colonies, until then pretty much the preserve of the missionaries and the soldiers, might turn out to be profitable properties after all. La Verendrye, who was the most traveled of Canadian explorers, had said it was a land fit only for otters, which slept cosily in their underground nests throughout the fearful winter and kept cool in the abundant streams during the fierce summers. But some of the knowing chaps in the City pointed out that La Verendrye, after all, was only a Frenchman and that he was certainly wrong about the otter, which does not hibernate. Perhaps he had overlooked something worthwhile in Ruperts Land or thereabouts. It was too soon to write off a wilderness.

Most of this fresh interest could be credited to the efforts of Edward Watkin, president of the Grand Trunk, who missed no opportunity to urge Imperial support of the integration of the Canadian colonies. He had founded the British North American Association, whose purpose was to see that Canadians in London met the right people and that they possessed at least the status of superior country cousins. On June 8, 1858, he presided at a well-attended meeting in the Thatched House Tavern to rally support for a Maritimes railway that would connect with the Grand Trunk in the St. Lawrence Valley below Quebec City. Out of this meeting came an invitation for yet another Canadian delegation to meet Benjamin Disraeli, the Chancellor of the Exchequer. Tupper again led the party, with Alexander Tilloch Galt and George Etienne Cartier, an eloquent French Canadian, as his colleagues. They got nowhere, although on this visit they presented a concrete proposal. They offered to assume responsibility for half of the interest charges on a sufficient sum to build the link-up railway. Disraeli was less terse than his brother novelist, but his reply came to the same thing. If the Canadian colonies wanted a Main Line, they must be prepared to pay for it.

Meanwhile events in the now Disunited States were making for tragedy. In April 1861 came the attack on Fort Sumter. Thereafter Britain's manifest sympathy with the South affected the security of her North American colonies. This tension lessened the aloofness of the Maritime colonies, and in September of that year agreement was reached for the dispatch of one more delegation to London. Joseph Howe of Nova Scotia, Leonard Tilley of New Brunswick and P. M. Vankoughnet of the Province of Canada crossed to discover that the Civil War, together with Watkin's assiduous efforts, had worked wonders. The delegates were not kept waiting in Colonial Office anterooms; within a week they had been received by the Prime Minister (Lord Palmerston), the Chancellor of the Exchequer, the president of the Board of Trade and other leading officers of the government. They no longer were regarded as squabbling, importunate colonials, for the strong voice of the War Office backed their demands. Military spokesmen declared that if the North had designs on the British North American colonies, the Union would wait until winter closed the St. Lawrence, interrupting sea traffic and isolating the Canadas. Under such circumstances, an intercolonial railway ceased to be a luxury and became a necessity.

While the Colonial Secretary was digesting these views, Howe took to the provinces once more. There his old magic prevailed; resolutions poured in endorsing the intercolonial project; the Associated British Chambers of Commerce voted £2,000 toward its further publicity. Then in November came the *Trent* affair; the St. Lawrence was frozen over, and it would take months to reinforce colonial garrisons. The Canadians had the ball at their feet; in the words of a most interested onlooker:

> The delegates put forward their case with great force, stating that the late startling events rendered their representations almost superfluous. The war against which they had desired security was imminent. Their frontier was unprotected and exposed to concentrations of hostile troops at the termini of seven railways of the United States. A hundred thousand men, they said, could be sent across the frontier with more ease than a single battery of artillery could be transported to Canada or a single barrel of flour carried from the seaboard.[2]

Thereafter the matter more or less arranged itself. The cabinet ruled that the Imperial Guarantee of 1851, won by Howe and spurned by Hincks, was still operative. Once the colonies had decided on the route, the project would march. On March 16, 1862, at a meeting in Quebec City, the terms of a joint submission to the British government were drafted. That autumn Howe and Tilley returned to London; the Canadian delegates were delayed. Nova Scotia and New Brunswick settled without difficulty the details of the size and management of the British loan, the surveying of a route, the supervision of construction. With everything snugly settled, Howe and Tilley returned home.

The Canadians still had not arrived. From this distance the delay would appear to have been deliberate. L. V. Sicotte and W. P. Howland, respectively Attorney General and Finance Minister of the Province of Canada, finally turned up in captious mood and inclined to haggle over everything. They resented the establishment of a sinking fund, saying that Canada's pledged word was all that was needed; but if a sinking fund was deemed essential, it must be invested in Canadian securities, in which it would earn twice what it would earn in Britain. (This was an impudent lie.) Although W. E. Gladstone, then Chancellor of the Exchequer, went to great pains to meet their wishes, it quickly became apparent that the Canadians had only one objective and that was to frustrate unanimity. By this time the *Trent* scare was over, and eighteen thousand British regulars were deployed along the Canadian frontier. With other arguments exhausted, Sicotte and Howland fell back on their dignity, which had not been particularly noticeable until then. After a series of thoroughly uncooperative sessions, they packed up and left, announcing that negotiations for the Halifax railway had been abandoned.

Thus for the second time in ten years the Canadians contemptuously had betrayed the Maritime colonies. At first, Nova Scotians and New Brunswickers refused to believe that they had been deserted at the post. But when George Brown gloated in *The Globe* over the breakdown (among other sage judgments, he declared that the Maritimes were not worth the £50,000 that the intercolonial railway would cost Canada annually), their anger knew no bounds. Howe, twice the victim of Canadian treachery, lost his faith in the efficacy of Confederation and never regained it. In New Brunswick, Tilley was thrown out of office by an avalanche of votes and replaced by a rapidly anti-Confederation administration. "No More Truck and Trade with Canada" became the slogan, and the New Brunswickers hastened to fulfill the original purpose of John A. Poor and to link their colony with the New England traffic area. A strong American group offered to provide the necessary funds for the entire railway from Halifax to Bangor.

Fortunately it finally dawned on the Canadians that the Maritimers were not suppliants seeking a dole but angry men prepared to take decisive action to obtain what they felt to be necessary. Alexander Tilloch Galt was perhaps first to recognize the danger; he called on Viscount Monck, the Canadian Governor-General, demanding his support. Monck was a plainspoken man, who on one occasion had declared that he had an equal contempt for all politicians. With the Queen's representative recognizing the needs of the Maritimers, the Canadian leaders resorted to excuses; they had been innocents abroad, misled by the circumlocution of the Queen's ministers. This got them nowhere; Monck did not hesitate to step beyond the bounds that hedged the neutrality of the Crown; he told the Canadians brusquely that they had played the fool. As a result, the Canadians offered to bear their share of the cost of survey of the inter-colonial route. Nova Scotia was willing to accept this offer, but Monck's frankness had set free Lieutenant-Governor Gordon of New Brunswick; he read the Canadians a stinging lecture on how gentlemen behave in the matter of ratified agreements. Throughout the winter of 1863–1864, the exchanges, now sniping and now heavy blasts, continued, until the Canadians realized that they had imperiled not only imperial relations but their own security. Bonding privileges on their goods in transit through the United States had been canceled, and the Americans had refused to renew the reciprocity agreement. The North now was certain of victory, and it might consider the takeover of the British North American colonies as a cleaning-up operation. Confederate sympathizers in Canada and the Fenian Brotherhood in the United States alike were intent on provoking a clash.

Canada Sees the Light

Confronted with such menaces, the Canadian attitude swiftly swung full circle. Early in 1864, the Legislative Assembly gave notice that it proposed to proceed independently with the survey of the Halifax railway, bearing all the costs. Furthermore, it invited Nova Scotia and New Brunswick to appoint representatives on a survey commission of which it would be a minority member, perhaps the only action that could have been taken to allay Maritime suspicions. There followed another gesture that more or less sealed the compact. Sandford Fleming, destined to become one of Canada's greatest engineers and social scientists, was at the beginning of his career serving on the Ontario, Simcoe and Huron Union Railroad, whose bonds, the reader may remember, were taken over by the Grand Trunk for no appreciable reason except to sweeten the flotation in the eyes of Canadian politicians. The province of Canada now nominated Fleming as its representative on the survey commission. Since New Brunswick and Nova Scotia could not possibly counter with anyone of his caliber, they also chose him, and automatically he became chief engineer of the railway-to-be.

He was a man of astonishing vigor, vivid imagination and great practical adaptability. He had a great deal of the Da Vinci approach to problems: he believed that it was possible to find a solution to anything. Even before he had seized and spirited away the first sod of Toronto's first railway he had been in the news; in 1849, when the Legislative Assembly in Montreal was burned by the mob, he dived into the flames and emerged with the portrait of Queen Victoria on his shoulders. Two years later he designed the first Canadian postage stamp. He preached unceasingly that ocean cables were destined to constitute the major bonds of the British Empire. He wrote books and pamphlets on such diverse subjects as telephone rates, forms of worship of the Presbyterian Church and the fostering of Canadian immigration; his subsequent book on the construction of the Intercolonial Railway remains a classic. Beyond everything else he is recognized today as the founder of a system of world time; he fathered the International Prime Meridian Conference at Washington, which established the longitudes for the changing of clocks to compensate for the earth's rotation.

Fleming received his appointment in February 1864. Defying the bitter winter weather, he completed his preliminary reconnaisance by spring. He exhibited almost unbelievable powers of physical endurance; on one occasion he drove a sleigh over forest trails from Shediac to Rimouski, a distance of 370 miles, in four days. As soon as spring arrived, he put four survey parties in the field. They investigated thirteen routes from the Nova Scotia boundary to the St. Lawrence valley. In midsummer Fleming rendered a report of one hundred sixty pages; he plainly favored the east coast route, as selected by British sapper officers thirty years before. His choice immediately elicited feverish rejoicings

Sir Sandford Fleming, greatest of Canadian railway engineers.

from the counties traversed, bitter resentment from the areas rejected. Every market town, it was said, had a paid hack who churned out arguments and unprovable statistics on behalf of parochial claimants and complainants. The rare unanimity of the colonies, as exemplified in their unanimous choice of Fleming, provided the Colonial Secretary with all that he needed. Without delay he accepted on behalf of the Imperial government a route that ran from Moncton to the Bay of Chaleur and thence by way of the Matapedia valley across the St. Lawrence escarpment to Rimouski, whence it followed the southern bank of that river to Trois Pistoles, the point of junction with the Grand Trunk Railway.

This involved in all 349 miles of new construction. Nova Scotia and New Brunswick, which under their individual policies had found no one anxious to undertake the junction of their short lines, besought the Colonial Secretary to include a link-up section between Moncton and Truro (124 miles) in the intercolonial project. He acceded to this request.

Railway Unanimity Breeds Political Union

Nor was this the end. Mutual trust among hitherto suspicious communities fostered fresh aspirations. In the autumn of 1864, Charles Tupper called a conference in Charlottetown, the capital of Prince Edward Island, to discuss ways and means for further cooperation of the Maritime colonies. This burying of hatchets and seeming devotion to common causes made a deep impression in the Canadas, where it was realized that that province thereafter might be confronted by a bloc too strong to ignore. The Canadian political leaders took quick counsel and cadged an invitation to Charlottetown, where they were not conspicuously welcomed but where they outnumbered and outtalked their hosts. They stimulated sufficient enthusiasm to arrange for a second session in Quebec City. There four out of the six colonies agreed to incorporation in a self-governing dominion. (Prince Edward Island stood out briefly, Newfoundland for more than eighty years.) Thus political union was born out of the problems attendant upon the construction of a railway; as Stephen Leacock said long afterward, Confederation was a cave to which all footprints led inward. John A. Macdonald is usually acclaimed as the George Washington of Canada, but it was Sandford Fleming, the railway builder, who planted the seeds that grew into a new nation.

Parochial Embellishments

Despite the brave acclaim, it was significant that neither Nova Scotia nor New Brunswick was content to put all its railway eggs in the Confederation basket. While the leaven of union was fermenting, they continued with their plans for local short lines. They reasoned that if they completed such projects, they would be able to embody them in the Main Line to their subsequent advantage, and if they failed, they would be able to dump them in the Confederation lap. The first of these projects to be placed in work was the intercolonial linkup from Moncton to Truro (124 miles). In August 1865, the International Contract Company undertook to build this line under an arrangement whereby each colony assumed responsibility for the portion within its own boundaries.

Immediately, the old obstacle of parochial ambition emerged, for the International Contract Company proved to be the creature of James Livesay, an ironmaster whose works on the slopes of the Cobequid mountains lay well to the west of the direct route and easy gradients that Fleming had staked for the Nova Scotia section. With the solid backing of the local politicians, the contractors altered the route so that it would pass through Livesay's property. Fleming refused to submit to this arrant nepotism, and for five years the battle raged. The International Contract Company disappeared to re-emerge under another name; in 1867, when the project became the concern of the new Dominion administration, the stormy encounters that had begun in the Executive Council chambers at Halifax continued in the committee rooms of the House of Commons at Ottawa. Fleming estimated that the meandering route demanded by the politicians would impose in perpetuity an extra shilling on every passenger fare and on every ton of freight carried. He damned such squalid intrigues by book, bell and candle. It was to no avail; the railway went where Livesay wanted it. "Thus arose Fleming" wrote, "the gigantic and conspicuous sweep which the traveller will observe on the southern flank of the Cobequids, where the line describes nearly a half-circle. The popular voice has applied to it the term 'The Grecian Bend.' "[3]

On the other side of the Missugash River (the Nova Scotia–New Brunswick boundary), Fleming had selected an equally economic and direct route toward a junction with the Saint John–Shediac line to the east of Moncton. But this too had one great defect—it bypassed the hamlet of Dorchester, once famed for its French inn, afterward for its penitentiary and finally as the home of Edward Barron Chandler, an influential member of the New Brunswick Legislative Assembly. On the latter count, the Livesay episode was re-enacted; no route was acceptable that ignored the claims of Dorchester, and Fleming resolutely refused to change his survey as a sop to a politician.

On July 1, 1867, the birth date of the Dominion of Canada, the New Brunswick Legislative Assembly instructed the contractors to submit all bills to the federal authority thereafter. Fleming, however, refused to certify them on the grounds that the contractors had altered the route without his authority. Immediately, the shillelaghs were out and there were wigs on the green; New Brunswickers screamed that they had been sold into Confederation at eighty cents a head and that they would build the Main Line where they wanted it. The first federal cabinet cringed before the provincial onslaught and left the choice of route to the newly appointed Intercolonial Railway Commissioners, one of whom was Edward Barron Chandler, whereupon the matter was settled expeditiously. The Dominion government would pay the whack, the railway would run, as it does to this day, under the walls of the penitentiary, and the Dorchester Diversion would join the Grecian Bend as characteristically parochial embellishments of the Main Line.

The Truro-Pictou Line

In 1853, when Joseph Howe undertook to provide Nova Scotia with railways in a hurry, the Truro-Pictou line (fifty-two miles) was one of the first to be put into work in short sections. Twelve years later, it was not only incomplete but in almost hopeless confusion because of the ignorance and perversity of the amateur contractors. In October 1865, Premier Tupper consulted Fleming, who had never built a railway but was willing to try. That he was consulting engineer on the Main Line and in deep water with the local politicians did not cause him to hesitate; in return for the promise of a free hand, he undertook to complete the Truro-Pictou line within the limits of its original estimate and to have it in operation before the tentative date of Confederation in mid-year 1867.

Never were his courage and resource better illustrated than in accepting a contract that for twelve years had been a hissing and a reproach and in his accepting a fixed price and guaranteeing a date of completion. He took over dilatory subcontracts personally and infused vigor into their routines; he gave praise and additional aid to satisfactory operations, erecting comfortable quarters for the workers, roofing over bridge sites, cuts and approaches to tunnels so that progress would not be impeded by the harsh Maritimes winter. He strung a telegraph wire along the line and kept in constant touch with all work in hand; he brought in steam excavators and opened quarries, doubling his force of masons and stonecutters. He devised a series of new bridge seats and drainage culverts and invented a scabbard rail joint to meet the exigencies of the Nova Scotia climate. His men marveled at his unceasing energy and caught his spirit, so that the line was completed well in advance of its guaranteed date and at a total cost, even with adequate rolling stock thrown in, of less than the estimate. It was by far the best-built line in the Maritimes. It is doubtful if Fleming made a penny out of it. He had been one of Kipling's men, who "worked for the joy of the working."

An Audacious Swindle

This short line was regarded as so valuable that it came to be used as a bargaining counter to entice others to undertake the promotion and construction of Nova Scotia short lines. In the late 1870s, the development of the coal measures along the north shore of that province and in Cape Breton put the provincial government into the railway business anew. The Nova Scotia government asked the Dominion government to return the Truro-Pictou line to the province, which would use it as bait to induce private interests to build the necessary North Shore–Cape Breton railway; it would provide an outlet and link-up with the Main Line for that otherwise isolated area.

Prime Minister Alexander Mackenzie at first refused to countenance what was plainly a political promoter hocus-pocus, but Sir Hugh Allan, having been awarded the contract, betook himself to Ottawa, where he knew the backstairs as well as anyone. He obtained a promise that after certain construction expenditures the Truro-Pictou line would be awarded to him. There followed a series of razzle-dazzle transactions whereby the contract was transferred to an Allan subsidiary of exactly the same name as one of his competitors. A subcontractor was gulled into building the Cape Breton line for 60 percent of what the provincial government was advancing, plus bonds bearing the name of not one but two companies and that had been issued by neither. There followed years of confusion compounded. Eventually in 1882, the Dominion government was persuaded to buy all the Nova Scotia short lines, including the Truro-Pictou trackage for a second time, and Allan, who had scarcely risked a cent of his own money in the venture, relinquished his interests for the tidy solatium of $1 million.

The Intercolonial Gets Under Way

But to return to Fleming's principal preoccupation. In March 1867, the British North America Act and its ancilliary measure, the Canadian Railway Loan Act, gave the Intercolonial a legal identity. The Dominion of Canada would pay for it, although as always seemed the case the money would be found by Great Britain. The Maritime Provinces, having been twice betrayed, were not taking any chances; their chief spokesman, S. L. Tilley, warned Prime Minister Macdonald that no Maritime colony would consider closer union with the Canadas without a firm promise of a connecting railway. It was a one-sided agreement; the new federal government in effect accepted responsibility for any railway ventures on which the Maritimers might embark. For fifty years thereafter it continued to rescue stray railway projects and to find stalls for them in the Intercolonial stable.

The ink was scarcely dry on the signatures of the Fathers of Confederation when Sandford Fleming, now engineer-in-chief, was at work. The terrain for eighty miles north of Moncton consisted of flat shore clad in light forest. Beyond the Miramachi River, the route ran in almost continuous tangent for forty-five miles across the base of the Tracadie Peninsula to the Bay of Chaleur, whose westering shore it skirted for seventy-five miles to the mouth of the Matapedia River. Then came the climb up the Matapedia Valley and over the escarpment for ninety-three miles to the St. Lawrence at Ste. Flavie (now Mont Joli). Thereafter the survey followed that great water highway upstream for eighty-three miles into the southwest to Riviere du Loup, which had replaced Trois Pistoles as point of junction with the Grand Trunk Railway.

Nine Years of Struggle and Strife

Sandford Fleming lived to a great age with his mind ever fresh and questing, his memory undimmed. In his later years, he often recalled with relish his first venture into railway building in Nova Scotia and his path-finding commissions for the Canadian Pacific in the Rockies. But he seldom spoke of the Intercolonial years; his book on this undertaking reveals that for a man of his talents the memory of them was that of an evil dream.

He could have built it in half the time had he not been thwarted and badgered to an almost intolerable degree. He was given a Board of Rail-

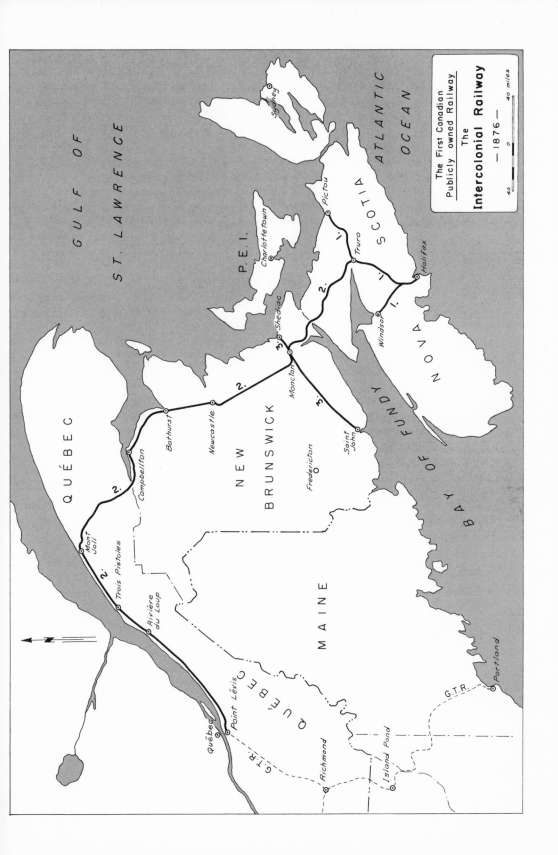

The First Canadian
Publicly owned Railway

The

Intercolonial Railway

— 1876 —

40   0   40 miles

GULF OF

ST. LAWRENCE

ATLANTIC

OCEAN

Sydney

Pictou

Charlottetown

P.E.I.

SCOTIA

Truro

Halifax

2.

Shediac

Windsor

NOVA

Moncton

BAY OF FUNDY

2.

Bathurst

Newcastle

NEW

Campbellton

BRUNSWICK

Saint John

2.

Fredericton

QUÉBEC

Mont Joli

2.

Trois Pistoles

MAINE

Rivière
du Loup

Portland

G.T.R.

QUÉBEC

Richmond

Island Pond

Québec

Point Lévis

G.T.R.

way Commissioners comprising representatives of the provinces. In all except one instance they were active politicians, and none of them knew anything about railway construction. Patronage was the breath of life to them, and one and all they were determined to breathe deeply. From the outset they sought to prove that they were the men who mattered in the Intercolonial project; Fleming was their obedient servant; they alone would appoint or dismiss and would rule on technical points at issue. Within four months of the opening of construction, they were interfering in such details as the assignment of inspecting engineers and the appointment of quantity estimators. In ignorance and arrogance, they set out to make sure that the primary objective of the Intercolonial project would be to serve political ends.

In the majority of instances, the appointments they foisted on Fleming were those of party heelers who had no ability to perform their allotted tasks nor any desire to do anything that would not yield personal gain. Marcus Smith, a widely-traveled engineer whose letterbooks (now in the Public Archives of Canada) are veritable mines of information, wrote of the subordinates posted to him on the Restigouche section:

> S———— has no intention of doing any work at all beyond the signing of pay sheets. H———— is behaving badly in many ways and has scarcely done any work. M———— refuses to hold either the rod or the picket, declaring that it would be derogatory to his dignity to do so. The Commissioners would save much time and thousands of dollars if they would give S———— a few months leave of absence and appoint a good man in his stead.[4]

In 1869, Fleming was notified that in future lump-sum tenders would be invited without allowances for extras and without preliminary estimates of quantities. The contractors would cross-section their own roadbed yardage and would classify it themselves as to rock, earth or other content. This was nothing less than an impudent attempt to allow the proper people to get both feet into the trough. Despite Fleming's angry protests, such regulations went into force. The results were apparent in the next bids for new subcontracts. In seven sections, they ran from $12,700 to $37,447 a mile for the same work. The lowest overall tender was $1,975,597; the highest, $6,029,150.

The alliance of politicians and contractors was seldom content with modest takes. Typical instances were heavy purchases at high prices from a firm of which a Canadian cabinet minister was a member; overmeasurements without orders; undermeasurements without refunds; bribes to inspectors and quantity surveyors; the delivery of materials (particularly lumber and sleepers) that made no pretense of being up to specification; the padding of pay lists, and arbitrary increases in contract prices. (In one instance Fleming was informed that he had no jurisdiction; the commissioners alone would rule on the task. Before completion its price was doubled.)

Some battles Fleming won. He carried his demand for iron instead of wooden bridges to the Prime Minister, who supported him. He fought for steel rails until he got them. Despite his vociferous objections the line was built in broad gauge, but before it was finished, the Grand Trunk had gone over to the standard gauge, and Fleming was allowed to conform.

High embankment, Intercolonial Railway, 1874.
(COURTESY OF THE PUBLIC ARCHIVES OF CANADA)

It was a happy day indeed when in 1873, as aftermath to railway scandals elsewhere, the Macdonald administration fell and Alexander Mackenzie became Canada's second Prime Minister. That austere Scot immediately sacked the Intercolonial commissioners and transferred control of the project to the Department of Public Works, a portfolio that he himself administered. But by then Fleming was nearing the end of the road. Much of the line was open in bits and pieces; in 1872 the Intercolonial had taken over the short lines of both Nova Scotia and New Brunswick, which transactions increased its trackage to 724 miles. On July 6, 1876, it was opened from Quebec City to Halifax.

Principal Construction Statistics

Stripping and grubbing right of way	5,162 acres
Earth excavation	14,546,218 cubic yards
Rock excavation	1,543,557 cubic yards
Masonry and concrete	249,467 cubic yards
Sleepers	1,250,000
Rails	48,000 tons
Bridges	15,240 lineal feet
Costs	
overall	$21,569,136
per mile	$43,180

The Prince Edward Island Railway

Until 1871, the ninety-odd thousand Prince Edward Islanders viewed the shenanigans that passed for progress on the mainland with feelings of superiority and even disdain. They had accepted a modicum of responsible government without any great enthusiasm for it; they were content with their status as a jewel, albeit of no great brilliance, in the Crown. They had no public debt and no illusions of grandeur. Although Confederation was born in their capital, they wanted no part of it; the only official welcome the Convention received was from Premier J. C. Pope, who went out in a rowboat to meet the ship. In 1870, the Legislative Assembly scotched a tentative inquiry as to the island's attitude by a resolution carried by nineteen votes to four that declared that Prince Edward Island was almost unanimously opposed to any change in the constitution of the colony.

Yet a year later, on April 3, 1871, another resolution praying that a railway be built "throughout the length of the island" was presented in the morning, committed to a drafting committee that afternoon, with the necessary legislation passed two days later. At the beginning of May, a chief engineer was appointed, a survey was instituted, and before the end of the month there was a call for tenders. The first sod was turned on October 5. In such expeditious fashion did a community given to airs and graces and content with yesterday hasten to catch up with the times.

No satisfactory explanation of this sudden reversal of attitude was ever forthcoming. Premier Pope's decision would appear to have been based on the circumstance that while dirt roads were sufficient for the colony's needs, the island was running out of gravel. It is of course possible that events in Nova Scotia and New Brunswick had awakened a desire for emulation. These colonies had begun to build their own railways, whereupon a federal authority had supervened and taken them over, saving the colonists a good deal of fuss and bother, to say nothing of hard cash. It was willing to do the same for Prince Edward Island; under such circumstances the locals could scarcely lose. If a railway proved a profitable property, it could be retained; if unprofitable, it could be unloaded (at a price) on the federal authority.

Haphazard Beginning

In the Prince Edward Island Railway Act, the length of its line was given as the length of the island, which was 120 miles. The cost was limited to £5,000 per mile, which must cover not only the trackage but the rolling stock and fixed installations. The route chosen, however, ignored the initial postulate; it began at Georgetown and ended at Alberton, which were only 84 miles apart; yet the railway between these terminals was 147 miles in length. The major meanders were the work of the politicians who, as one of them contended in the Legislative Assembly, did not see that an honorable member was asking anything out of the way in proposing a curve for the benefit of his constituents. The final survey was almost a continuous curve as the route wandered hither and yonder at the instance of interested parties. There were, of course, minor embarrassments; when, in 1872, the Pope administration was defeated, it was discovered that the line thereafter would benefit all the wrong people; so it was necessary more or less to resurvey it. In addition to such political necessities there were minor meanders to improve the profits of the contractors. The island is well named "the garden of Canada," and its easy contours made it possible to avoid nearly all rockwork and a good deal of the earthwork. The contracts were placed on a fixed price per mile irrespective of quantities.

But even such comprehensive perquisites, designed to reward as many as possible of the right people, were not always enough. The railway doubled, and in some instances quadrupled, the value of lands contiguous to it, but this was deemed no reason why right of way should become available at the government's offering price. The original estimate for such land was £35,000; as a result of incessant appeals for justice and generosity more than eight times that sum was disbursed. Private crossings took on significance as status symbols and few farmers were content to forego them; in all, 759 such crossings, or nearly 6 to the mile, were constructed outside the towns and villages. The local horses, cows, pigs and sheep, accustomed to a genteel old world atmosphere, believed that when they could see through a fence, they could go through it. The railways' wire fencing, therefore, had to be replaced again and again because its strands trailed around the fields on the necks of the animals.

Another Sudden Decision

In 1872, the work was proceeding in leisurely fashion and an additional fifty-two miles of line was added, as extensions at either end of the island. Then suddenly, out of nowhere, a crisis arose. It is the general opinion of historians that it was extraneously stimulated, perhaps by the new Dominion government, perhaps by the Imperial authority, both of whom wished to tidy up the map by compelling Prince Edward Island to enter Confederation. The railway contractors were being paid with debentures whose fixed charges were guaranteed by a small increase in the prevailing import duties. There were ample funds available to meet such charges, but a rumor gained credence that Sir John Rose, the Canadian Agent-General in London, had undertaken to spoil the market there for these securities. There was not the slightest truth in this canard, but the citizenry of the island behaved like children whose toy house had caught fire. Their parochial pride turned to panic; they sent an emissary dashing to Ottawa who confronted the Canadian Prime Minister with an irrefutable argument. If the Dominion government could afford to build a line 2,800 miles in length to British Columbia, it certainly should not cavil at the purchase of 120 miles of Prince Edward Island railway as the price of entering Confederation.

Sir John A. Macdonald concurred and made what he considered to be a fair offer. The islanders were affronted; did the Canadians really believe that they could be bought into union for a measly fifty dollars a head? (The price offered by Macdonald was roughly double that of the contractors' price for a completed line, and at this stage the railway was anything but complete.) A new provincial administration came into office with a mandate to deal sternly with the federal authority. On the strength of this attitude, a few face-saving concessions were wangled and the deal was closed. The Canadian Governor-General, Lord Dufferin, arrived to be greeted by an arch that proclaimed "Long Courted, Won at Last," a euphemistic transliteration of the fact that the lady had sold her favors for the ultimate farthing that they would fetch.

Opera Bouffe in the Takeover

Under the terms of the agreement, Prince Edward Island would enter Confederation on July 1, 1873, and the federal government would assume responsibility for its railway from the date of completion. This latter proviso was ignored; from the moment that the island entered Confederation, its politicians, press and citizenry alike denied all responsibility for the completion of the line. The failure to place it in operation immediately evoked vociferous criticism, and Prime Minister Mackenzie despatched Thomas Swinyard, chief engineer of the Department of Public Works, to see what could be done to stop the squalling of the infant province.

Swinyard was an able man but without a sense of humor. On arrival he was confronted with a thoroughly farcical situation. Neither the premier nor his officers nor the contractors would give him any information concerning the degree of completion of the line. He was, however, allowed to ride over those portions that were operable, and he was appalled by what he saw. He agreed in full with an earlier examiner that it was the worst-built railway ever seen in North America, and he reported that the only sensible course would be for the Dominion government to take it over as it stood, deciding thereafter whether to complete or rebuild it.

This decision did not find favor with any Prince Edward Island politicians. They decided to stand fast until the resentment of the citizenry at being denied the railway they believed the federal authority was withholding from them should reach gale velocity. Then it should be possible to extract further concessions from the Dominion government. When Swinyard attempted to make a detailed inspection of the line, no provincial officer would accompany him, and the premier refused to provide him with a locomotive and coach. The contractors went into hiding, the chief engineer took to his bed. Singlehanded, Swinyard began to investigate. In a week he unearthed unreceipted payments amounting to $100,567 and overpayments of $62,000 on accounts rendered. Whereupon the Prince Edward Island premier ordered this sniffing out to cease, the chief engineer recovered his health sufficiently to crawl from his bed and issue a certificate that the railway was complete in all respects. (He also announced that he proposed to leave for foreign parts immediately.) Confronted by such unreasoning perversity, the Dominion government decided to yield lest something worse befall. After a final protest for the records, Swinyard took over the railway as it stood. It cost several millions and a year's hard work to make it into an operable property.

In retrospect, the Prince Edward Island Railway would appear to have been a stupid project from the start. With the sea at every man's door, there was no particular need for it, nor was there the traffic to justify it. Its original estimates were ludicrously low, and they were inflated inordinately by the greed of the local politicians. In the ensuing forty-four years before its absorption into Canadian National Railways, it never managed to break even; it cost $1.44 to earn every dollar of revenue. It provided a classical illustration of an addlepated venture.

The Ordeal of a Publicly Owned Railway

It would be pleasant to record that the publicly owned railways of the Maritime Provinces, having come out of the tribulations of divided counsels, parochial prejudices and abysmal ignorance, found strength in unity, accord in policy, honesty in practice, and thereafter became good and faithful servants of the urge to progress. But this perhaps would have been asking too much. There was no magic impact to change the natures of those whom it served; the Nova Scotians, the New Brunswickers and Prince Edward Islanders remained more or less what they had been before—citizens of small, primitive communities intensely attached to their heritages, suspicious of all beyond the immediate bounds of their experience and convinced they were justified in profiting personally out of the lesser breeds beyond their familiar ambits. Their loyalties ran in a descending gamut, from the family through their blood kin to the churches and political parties and thence in ever-lessening intensity to their villages, counties and provinces. Their expectations were in reverse; the more distant a relationship, the greater the opportunity and justice of making a fat thing out of it. As an instance, a privately owned railway could not be expected to offer the opportunities of a provincially owned railway; and a nationally owned railway, virtually under absentee management and political control, seemed to provide a God-given invitation to the Maritimers to help themselves.

There is nothing that the average mind prefers more than to elevate or debase some simple fact into a myth or a legend. The Intercolonial Railway because of the manifestly arbitrary behavior of both its employees and its customers came to acquire an image that was shameful and hilarious. It provided the material for outrageous fictions, which, despite such evidence as the Pottinger papers, was much worse than the Maritimers deserved. But without question it provided an object lesson in the risks if not the folly of entrusting the management of a railway to a government. This conviction lived on after the Intercolonial had become a respectable institution and was destined to play a considerable role in the thinking of the generations to come. A great many Canadians still regard government intervention in business as inviting waste and venality. The Intercolonial had all the characteristics of a public spree, in which everyone first looked after himself and left the Devil to take the hindmost.

It already has been noted that when Alexander Mackenzie became Prime Minister in 1873, he made short work of the Intercolonial Railway Commissioners, who had been largely responsible for a horrible example of how not to build a railway. He acted on information provided by C. J. Brydges, whom he had commissioned to report prior to taking office. This able officer gave a shocking exposure of extravagance, mismanagement and venality. Mackenzie promptly appointed him General Superintendent of Government Railways. Within a matter of weeks, Brydges had got rid of a round dozen of the top officers of the Intercolonial and had reduced management costs by 25 percent. Unfortunately, in the course of this housecleaning he had fallen foul of Charles Tupper, the former Nova Scotia premier, who enjoyed at least friendly associations with a Halifax company that regularly received railway orders at prices up to 45 percent above those of other tenderers. (Brydges reported that the staff of this corporation consisted of a single clerk who had previously been employed in the sale of "mousetraps, oyster knives, spittoons and other notions.") In 1878, on Mackenzie's defeat at the polls, Tupper became Minister of Public Works at Ottawa, and Brydges instantly was given his walking papers. Curiously enough, his replacements also were honest men: Collingwood Schreiber, an able New Brunswicker as General Superintendent, had David Pottinger of Pictou as his chief assistant. The latter officer took the precaution to commit everything to paper, and it is from his voluminous records that the sorry story of Intercolonial mismanagement has been extracted.[5]

Railwaymen and Politicians

Any contact between railwaymen and politicians (to say nothing of closer relations) tended to bring out the worst in both of them. Either the railwaymen, administering a new and stimulating instrument of socio-economic advantage, corrupted the politicians; or the politicians, with their ability to secure privileges and priorities, corrupted the railway-men. The railwaymen in the case of the Intercolonial were in effect civil servants, and it was probably too much to expect honorable and honest dealings between them and their masters, the politicians. As has been previously noted in the narrative of the Grand Trunk, ministers of the Crown of that day did not hesitate to put a price on their favors by insisting that railwaymen should support the party in power. When the federal party in power was in Opposition in the provinces, this pressure doubled; railway employees not only were instructed how to vote but were also shepherded to the polls and told that their futures depended on the way they voted. The roster of call-outs of train crews was so arranged that the Rights would be at home on polling day and the Wrongs would be at the other end of the runs, where their names were not on the electoral lists.

Under the patronage system, officers of the Intercolonial were obliged to consult the local political leaders when there were perquisites available. Between Halifax and Riviere du Loup, the Intercolonial traversed eighteen constituencies; it therefore had eighteen advisors whom the store-keepers and the purchasing agents were obliged to inform and if neces-sary, to pacify. These officers had standing instructions to buy supplies normally only from recommended sources; but this was only the begin-ning of their restrictions. The local politicians down to village level felt entitled to interfere in the hiring and dismissal of personnel; on one occasion a New Brunswick member of Parliament bluntly informed Pot-tinger, "The parties that I have recommended for employment have not been given the proper recognition; officers of the Railway are attempting to please themselves in the matter of employment rather than accepting the advice of those holding the patronage of the several counties through which the railway runs."[6]

These purveyors of patronage directed a continuous stream of job-seekers to the Intercolonial management. Few of such nominees had the slightest qualifications for employment; most of them, in the words of Pottinger, "sought appointments in which they could do nothing all day long." Of nineteen candidates sponsored by one Nova Scotia member of Parliament, Pottinger reported that eleven refused the work offered them; one, after employment, declined to carry out his set tasks; one was dismissed for using his job as a cover for selling liquor and another for willful damage to railway property. Of thirty-eight members of the crews of two small railway coasting craft, thirty owed their employment to the demands of politicians. Legislative assemblymen and members of Parliament insisted on being consulted on the employment of personnel down to the level of dining car waiters, cooks and pantrymen.

These political advisors were quite as active in procuring the dismissal of political opponents as in securing employment for their own faithful followers. The charge usually advanced was that of "offensive political partisanship." In such instances no written proof was needed and there was no appeal; the accusation was in effect a conviction. Occasionally questions about such dismissals were tabled in Parliament, and for them Pottinger had a set form reply; action had been taken at the instance of local advisors. This was deemed sufficient. One conductor with a clean sheet lost his job because he had espoused the wrong side in a Mock Parliament. A cabinet member who within five years would be Prime Minister of Canada addressed the following letter to Pottinger concerning a malignant named Pushie:

> He is a section foreman, I believe, on the Eastern Extension Railway. When I went to run my election this man used to the sectionmen under him the most blackguardly language against the Government, myself, Sir Charles Tupper, Bishop Cameron and the Catholic clergy. . . . He is a most indolent and faithless officer, frequently sitting down for hours when all his sectionmen require to be at work. . . . I think he should be removed and that Donald McGillvray should be appointed in his place.[7]

Manipulation of Contracts

Railway contracts were a logical and almost indisputable perquisite. In January 1885, Pottinger was instructed that thereafter the packing of locomotive cylinder heads must be purchased from a specified senator. The previous cost had been $12 per engine; the senator's price was $233. A Halifax contractor on a firm quotation of $12,312 demanded $15,000 extra compensation; it was proved that he had disregarded the specification, but he was awarded $12,000. Local members battled bitterly for their share of the spoils even in piddling transactions; two members of Parliament insisted that a stationery order totaling $60.10 be split between their nominees; the member for Saint John blocked a purchase of rat traps valued at $190.60 until it was divided between three of his constituents. Before the Civil Service Commission, Collingwood Schreiber testified that one of his maintenance-of-way crews had taken a small quantity of sand from an unauthorized pit. Schreiber valued it at $5 and offered this sum; the owner of the pit, backed by the local politicians, demanded $70,000. In the end he obtained $16,000. The estimate for an extension from St. Charles Junction to Hadlow (fourteen miles) was $600,000. In a report to the *Journal of Political Economy*, Samuel O. Dunn wrote, "The property owners whose lands and buildings had been condemned (for right of way) appealed with such success to the local politicians and swore one for the other as to values so ably that the line finally cost $2,000,000."[8]

Special Privileges for the Right People

Many of the politicians behaved as though the Intercolonial was their private preserve. A former provincial premier laid police charges when a stationmaster refused him entry to a closed platform. A cabinet minister shipped his horse from Ottawa to Halifax under his official frank and insisted on special facilities for the animal. A federal member for Pictou County struggled to have the Tatamagouche post office moved into the railway station so that the stationmaster might draw two salaries. Another member tabled a question in the House of Commons because he was refused permission to erect private premises on the railway right of way. There were bitter complaints in Parliament when a special train for a Liberal picnic was charged the same amount as a similar train for a Conservative rally. A Prince Edward Island senator ordered a private car for his sessional conveyance to Ottawa; he carried eighteen relatives with him and protested vehemently about having to pay anything for their carriage on the Grand Trunk beyond the Intercolonial terminal at Riviere du Loup.

This belief in private privileges on a publicly owned property was not restricted to politicians. The Intercolonial customarily was regarded as a clan possession—the property of the party in power rather than of the people as a whole. A magistrate refused to convict a farmer accused of driving his team along the railway tracks. A construction company felt justified in sending out invitations to a bridge-opening ceremony with the intimation that the invitation card could be used as a railway pass with which to reach the scene of the ceremony. A New Brunswick town, in an endeavor to collect local taxes, seized the railway station as security; Pottinger, entering into the spirit of the thing, instructed his stationmaster to defend it, if necessary by force of arms. A local Restigouche doctor, suspecting smallpox, ordered a coach onto a siding where he held the passengers incommunicado for twenty-four hours. His suspicions had been aroused by a vaccination certificate in French, a language which he did not understand.

Sir Edmond Grimani Hornby already has been quoted on the noteworthy number of passengers who traveled on passes. Friends of politicians and relatives of railway employees considered themselves entitled to passes as a matter of course. Pottinger endeavored to bring the situation under control by ordering that every pass should be signed by its carrier; a member of Parliament flatly refused to submit to such indignity and laid charges against the general superintendent. Politicians requested passes by the dozen for any public event, from a christening to a funeral; post office inspectors issued passes to mail carriers; militia commanders, to all ranks proceeding to camp or rifle ranges. In March 1881, the general officer commanding at Halifax used his pass to transport fourteen officers and their ladies to Ottawa for a vice-regal ball. In December 1894, when Prime Minister Sir John Thompson died while a guest of Queen Victoria at Windsor Castle, the state funeral was held in Halifax. Among many others was a request from a staunch Tory in Antigonish for two hundred passes for the party members of that market town.

Special trains were a prized perquisite. Cabinet ministers, members of Parliament, senators and members of the provincial legislative assemblies got them free. In the first five months of 1891, fifty-six special trains were provided for such travelers. For such political occasions as rallies, picnics, conventions and elections, they were available at a flat rate of $10 per train regardless of distance.

Indiscipline, Loutish Behavior and Irresponsibility

The Intercolonial employees, particularly those in contact with the traveling public, fully lived up to the uncouth behavior and venal irresponsibility of the politicians and their followers.

When the railway was opened, the management specified that uniforms should be worn by the operational personnel who must be "neat and tidy, civil and courteous at all times." It took years to achieve even the appearance of such instructions. Canadians (like the Americans described by Charles Dickens in *Martin Chuzzlewit*) regarded themselves as freeborn sons of liberty and resented uniforms as a badge of servitude. A member of Parliament declared in the House of Commons that to insist on uniforms for Intercolonial employees was equivalent to equating them with jailbirds. Some employees refused to pay for their uniforms, or since they were their own property, wore them continuously, on and off duty. As for mannerly behavior, such instruction was regarded as presumptuous; one Canadian should be prepared to take another as he found him. In the first ten years of operation, 80 percent of the fines imposed were for uncouthness, such as too-free remarks to women passengers, cursing and blasphemy in their presence, insolence to superiors, fighting with fellow employees and spitting in the aisles of passenger coaches.

Drunkenness was the most serious of individual offenses. A railwayman, like a soldier, felt that the nature of his duties bestowed certain freedoms upon him, particularly when he was away from home. In the Maritimes the Calvinist conscience reigned; alcohol, like blasphemy, imperiled the soul. The intoxications of speed were intensified by the high-ethers of homemade Canadian whisky, available at twenty-five cents a gallon. On December 28, 1876, the mayor of Saint John led an angry delegation to report that they had been brought over the steep gradients and twisty curves of the Folly Mountain section in a train that bucked and bounced and swirled and only by God's grace had stayed on the tracks. One of the passengers, a British soldier, declared that he had felt safer in cavalry charges. The engineer admitted that he had taken a drink, but his offense was condoned because it had occurred on the day after Christmas.

A Baptist minister, in the course of a sermon, declared that he had seen Intercolonial engineers so drunk that they had to be carried to the cabs of their locomotives. A brakeman who was tried in Truro for a breach of the Scott (Temperance) Act, became so intoxicated in celebrating his acquittal that he provoked a small riot. On the question of sobriety, however, Pottinger won an early victory. In 1883, all Intercolonial operating personnel were compelled to take the pledge, with instant dismissal for backsliding. Two years later the same penalty was imposed on all other employees.

It was far from easy to inculcate responsibility in the execution of routine tasks. Railway employment carried a cachet and conferred status. A good many employees translated this social advancement into the right to do as they damn well pleased. They regarded rules as made to be broken, with a moronic disregard of the consequences. These Peck's Bad Boys were partly fools, partly knaves; they flourished on the Intercolonial long after they had disappeared from most other railways. They regarded it as good clean fun, when a roadway paralleled the tracks, to frighten horses out of their senses with monstrous blasts on the whistle. Being late on call was deemed almost a personal privilege, and trains often were delayed for hours until the missing man turned up. The early Intercolonial trains were equipped, in the British fashion, with bell-cords for use in emergencies; crew members often brought their trains to crashing halts for no better purpose than to obtain the time of day from the engineer or a chew of tobacco from the fireman. It was common practice to heave lumps or even sacks of coal out of the tender at chosen points where they would be picked up by friends or relatives. A serious accident occurred in May 1875 when a maintenance-of-way gang, under orders to replace sleepers singly, had seventeen of them out of the track when a special train came along. One section foreman used his gangers, in addition to their railway duties, to raze a church, to dig a well, to cut his winter fuel, to remove fencing from the right of way and re-erect it on private property. Another section foreman threatened his men with dismissal when they refused to endorse his notes of hand.

A New Day

If such arrant behavior could be traced to individual offenders, in many instances they were dismissed; but if they happened to be active supporters of a politician, the responsible Intercolonial official would be pressed to take them back. Sometimes he was threatened if he refused to do so. For upward of twenty years Pottinger and his fellow officers battled against every conceivable type of individual ineptitude, personal misbehavior, political interference and crass unconcern. Then in 1896 came a gleaming day. Sir Wilfred Laurier, perhaps the greatest of Canadian Prime Ministers, came to power with A. G. Blair, until then premier of New Brunswick, as his Minister of Railways and Canals. Blair was no more than in office when he dismissed a railway official whose announced offense was that he had put thirty or forty additional men on the payroll without the slightest authority or the slightest need of them, purely at the demand of local politicians and in order to secure and retain their influence and support.

The Parliamentary heavens shook, but Blair defied their thunders. The Intercolonial Railway never was quite the same again.

6

The First Canadian System

It may be remembered that when Henry Whatley Tyler returned from Canada in 1867, he reported that the new Dominion authority certainly would not consider the Grand Trunk Railway either as its instrument or as an element in the projected trans-Canadian railway system. Nine years later, when he became president of that company, he made no secret of his intention to convert the railway into an international system east of the Great Lakes.

As Tyler saw it, the intervening years had not changed the situation to any marked degree. A Canadian railway system that would stretch across the continent and pay its way seemed no more profitable a venture in 1876 than it had nine years earlier. If such a system were built, it would be because of political necessities. It therefore would be too much of a gamble to commit the Grand Trunk to building long lines to nowhere in order to buttress a rickety political structure. Kipling had not yet written *The Explorer,* but his vision of

A plant to feed a people—up and waiting for the power

was not Tyler's idea of how to make money in the railway business. According to the first Dominion census taken in 1876, of a total population of 3,485,761 Canadians, 2,812, 367, or 82 percent, lived in Ontario and Quebec. These provinces, therefore, were what mattered. If at some later date it was deemed expedient to expand, there were better prospects next door in the United States than in the vast empty territories of western Canada or in the sea-begirt Maritimes.

The Grand Trunk Leaders

Such views were neither new nor radical, but the great difference lay in the man who held them. In his technical qualifications, his intimate contacts in the City of London and with British political leaders, the new Grand Trunk president stood out from his predecessors. Sir Henry Tyler (his knighthood came from his conspicuous service as Chief Inspector of British Railways) was an outstanding man in any company. He had begun as a military engineer but he soon outgrew the modest requirements of such a career and when released from the forces he quickly proved his capabilities in a variety of assignments. He found himself in demand both in technical and financial enterprises and as a member of the Council of Foreign Bondholders he enjoyed special status in the City of London. He spoke and wrote fluently; he enjoyed debates, particularly when he encountered opponents dedicated to unalterable views. Then he would give his wit full play and the contest became that of a boxer against a slugger, in which verbal footwork counted. He brought gaiety and humanity to his employments and he could be as lucid on paper as on the platform. His courage and instinctive friendliness bred confidence in those who served him.

He could not have wished for any better partner than Joseph Hickson, who became his second self in the management of the Grand Trunk Railway. The two supplemented each other perfectly: Hickson had a lightning mind and an unsurpassed memory; he could provide his chief in a twinkling with a thesis or a policy to support any occasion. Once an issue had been broached, the two moved into double harness automatically. Hickson would provide the leads, Tyler would exploit them. Their teamwork moved their American contacts to undiluted admiration. Of Tyler it once was said that he wore conviction like a halo; another American railway president declared that whenever he was obliged to negotiate with Hickson, he took off his boots before he put his feet under the table with the Grand Trunk executive.

The Bad and the Good

Tyler had arrived on an uneasy scene. The first decade of Confederation had achieved little save the adherence of two additional provinces, Prince Edward Island and Manitoba. There had been virtually no leavening of parochial prejudices or local loyalties; the new Dominion remained a group of disparate and dissentient communities bound together less by good will than by common allegiance to the Crown. As an aftermath to the Civil War, American resentment of British support for the South had crystallized in the "Manifest Destiny" doctrine, which rephrased Benjamin Franklin's dictum that any political division of North America was unnatural and which provided the text for a continuation of interventionist activities. The key enterprise of Confederation, the trans-Canadian railway, had stalled at its outset and had come near to floundering, largely because that indefatigable artful dodger, Sir Hugh Allan, had taken a hand in its promotion. The United States panic of 1873 had continued for year after year to becloud the economic horizon. Grand Trunk traffic had steadily grown, the returns from it as steadily had diminished. When Tyler took charge, the earnings had fallen in four years from $1.44 to eighty cents per ton-mile.

Nevertheless, these discouraging developments did not fairly reflect the situation. Canada was still four-fifths rural and in the countryside there were many hopeful portents. With better facilities for cultivation, pioneer risks were diminishing, yields were increasing. The recession of the forest permitted better tillage and improved drainage; specialized implements had provided the farmer with mechanical hands that would do many times the work of his own; the first steam threshers were snorting beside the grain ricks. The transformation from subsistence to cash crops was under way, fostering new hopes and ambitions.

In the small towns and villages (at this time there were only nine cities with more than ten thousand inhabitants in Canada), the railway station had joined the church and the tavern as a community center. The event of the day was the arrival of the train. Everyone flocked to the station to see the monster lumber in, to watch the passengers descend, to stare through the windows at the lordly ones who were journeying on, to exchange gossip with the train crews. These daily visitations were melting the ice of rural isolation; they were giving the country folk ideas. They had been directly responsible for setting up the farmers' wives in business; "egg money" became a cherished perquisite, and year by year this kind of trade grew and came to include butter, cream, apples, chickens, berries, rabbits and garden truck, all of which were borne in ever-increasing quantities to the towns. Such earnings sooner or later caused the man of the house to ponder and to turn his thoughts from staple to diversified crops. Schools were founded to provide specialized know-how to the farmers' sons. Ontario Agricultural College, founded in 1874, was the first Canadian educational institution to earn international recognition. It was a godchild of the railway.

It was no longer necessary for the countryman to ride out in case of illness to intercept the neighborhood doctor on his rounds; the doctor could be reached more quickly and easily by train or telegraph. The small shops around the railway stations were compelled to recognize the farmer's wife as a customer and to stock some of the nonessential "notions" that bedecked Victorian homes. More and more salesmen dropped off the trains; mail order catalogues appeared and newspapers became a necessity. The railway had awakened and was stimulating the countryside.

Enter the Commodore

This socio-economic advancement through natural growth played a major role in Sir Henry Tyler's dilemma. Would Canada grow up before the Grand Trunk folded up? This time factor, perhaps more than any other element, was what led his eyes, in scanning the North American map, to linger on Chicago. The central United States had a good thirty years' start on Canada. In those years, the traffic and population of Chicago had multiplied sixtyfold, and yet the requirements and yields of the lands beyond the Mississippi were as nothing to what they would be tomorrow. Surely the soundest policy would be that enunciated by the English bankers at the birth of the Grand Trunk twenty years before—to assure Canadian development by association with the present-day growth of the United States.

Someone else now had become interested in Chicago but in a different context. His ambitions were not confined to anything so modest as a share; nothing less than control ever satisfied him. At the age of sixteen, Cornelius Vanderbilt had been the owner and operator of a tiny ferry from Staten Island to New York City. He parleyed this craft into one of the largest fleets of river and coastal steamships in the world. He became known as the Commodore, which was a title of discourtesy rather than courtesy, for his business methods were rough and tough, not unlike those of the prize ring, except that he tolerated no bell to end the rounds nor any referee to break the clinches.

It was more or less by accident that he came ashore; he was obliged to assume control, in his customary forthright fashion, of some short railways that were essential to the prosperity of his shipping. But having found his feet on dry land, he determined to make it as much his domain as were the rivers and the foreshore seas. Working less by book than by instinct (he had a rare nose for what might be profitable tomorrow), he quickly acquired a stranglehold on the rail traffic of certain areas. He became the classical exemplar of the dog-eat-dog, knock-'em-down-and-drag-'em-out school of unrestricted competition. He and his fellow magnates met with beaming faces and strong, warm handclasps; in their elegant private cars, champagne suppers and ten-inch cigars proclaimed their fellowship; but the slap on the shoulder as often as not was prelude to the stab in the back. The camaraderie afterwards exhibited by the Chicago gangsters who sent magnificent wreaths to the funerals of rivals whom they had executed may have derived from Cornelius Vanderbilt's concept of business relationships.

Having established a bridgehead overland to the Great Lakes through acquisition of the Hudson River and New York Central railroads, the Commodore is said to have increased his personal fortune in the following fifteen years by not less than $90 million. Admirers declared this to be a tribute to his daring and sagacity; enemies described it as the yields of extortion, blackmail and thievery. But by the middle 1870s, the calendar had caught up with him, and although he fought stubbornly against death, surrounding himself with charlatans—mesmerists, clairvoyants and faith healers—the clocks ticked him off the scene day by day. At the end, he became respectable, donating large sums to charities and such other good works as might find favor in the sight of God. It was all to no avail; in January 1877, he passed on, with his numerous children and grandchildren singing hymns around his bedside.

His heir, William, who inherited what was perhaps the greatest industrial fortune of the times, was astute and acquisitive, but he lacked the Commodore's audacity and impudence; his ambition was less to acquire his neighbor's herd than to build a secure paddock for his own cattle. By various transactions, his father had secured a foothold in Chicago, and William saw no reason why he should not fence in such a point of vantage against the intrusions of the lesser breeds. He was quite satisfied with his arrangement with the Great Western, which month by month delivered an ever-increasing volume of Michigan traffic to the New York Central at Niagara Falls. But what if some other Canadian line found its way to Chicago and offered equivalent advantages on Middle West freights moving to Atlantic ports other than New York?

This of course was exactly what Sir Henry Tyler had in mind. The Grand Trunk had paid proportionately more for its shambling Montreal-Portland lines than any other of its maladroit transactions; it had taken substantial outlays and the best part of twenty years to bring the lines up to the standard of other sections; the existing traffic was insufficient to recover such costs. His objective, therefore, was to use Michigan traffic to build up the Portland route.

The Vanderbilt Blockade

He made no secret of his plans, and Vanderbilt at once moved to counteract them. In 1878, the Canada Southern Railway, 150 miles of tracks that paralleled the Great Western for almost every furlong of its route, came on the market. Tyler bid for it, but was outbid. Vanderbilt followed up by offers to the Michigan Central, which that line, after some hesitation, accepted. This gave the American promoter control of both ends of the Great Western traffic. In what he apparently intended as the knockout blow, he bought the outstanding bonds and so obtained control of the Chicago and Northeastern Railroad, forty-seven miles from Flint to Lansing. This line was one of the central segments of the Chicago and Lake Huron Railroad, whose four constituents provided a route from Port Huron, on the opposite side of the St. Clair River from Sarnia, to Valparaiso, only fifty-six miles from Chicago. Beyond Valparaiso, trackage was available into Chicago by a variety of routes. Traffic other than Vanderbilt traffic was not permitted to traverse this section except at exorbitant rates. Preferential incentives were established for through freights over the Michigan Central–Canada Southern–New York Central route. Terminal charges at Detroit and Niagara Falls were so adjusted that Grand Trunk deliveries at these points were charged four times as much as those of the Vanderbilt carriers.

Preparation for Counterstroke

With these barriers erected, William Vanderbilt went into his "good fellow" routine. He visited Hamilton and Montreal and assured the heads of the Great Western and Grand Trunk of his warm regard for them. He trusted that in future any difficulties would be solved in a cooperative and generous fashion.

Sir Henry Tyler received his guest hospitably. He did not expect Vanderbilt to tell him the truth, nor did he deem it expedient to lie to him. He was not yet in position to take the field, for he had no ready money; but he knew where to get it. To approach his shareholders, the London bankers or the Dominion government for funds to fight his way into Chicago would have been folly, but downstream, along the south bank of the St. Lawrence, there ran the link-up line that had been built twenty years before to provide connections with the Intercolonial Railway. During these years, 125 miles of tracks below Quebec City had rusted in disuse, but when in 1876 the long-awaited junction with the Intercolonial occurred, this section immediately began to carry a substantial volume of traffic. The Intercolonial, of course, paid tolls to the Grand Trunk for the use of such trackage, and it seems highly probable that Tyler confidentially may have advanced the opinion that as a matter of both economy and prestige the Intercolonial should purchase this section, and that if it wished to do so, the Grand Trunk would not be grasping. As it would be the Canadian taxpayer, rather than the Maritime Provinces who would foot the bill, the Nova Scotians and New Brunswickers seized avidly on this suggestion, and their representatives at Ottawa presented telling arguments. In the summer of 1878, an offer was made and the deal was closed. Thereafter Tyler had $1.7 million in hand to prosecute his campaign in Michigan.

A Lesson in Gamesmanship

At the Grand Trunk semi-annual meeting in London in the spring of 1879, Tyler reported on William Vanderbilt's professions of friendship and the deeds that had accompanied them. He spoke neither in sorrow nor in anger, and he closed with the modest hope that in some manner or other the Grand Trunk might secure entry into Chicago. London and New York commentators chose to regard his statement as an admission of defeat and a saving of face. They could not have been more wrong. What Tyler had in mind was not fisticuffs but a sort of judo, in which an opponent might be overthrown as much by his clumsy strength and over-confidence as by the wiles of his adversary. William Vanderbilt tried to live up to his father's catch phrase: "The Public Be Damned." Tyler believed that it was getting a bit late in the day for this sort of thing. It might be easier and more efficacious to persuade competitors than to threaten them, to placate rather than to destroy them. The Commodore's brash brutality had not made friends for him; his competitors, strong and weak alike, might be expected to do more than stand on the sidelines and cheer if anyone went to the mat with his son.

But as it transpired, gamesmanship rather than alliances was destined to prove the decisive factor in the Grand Trunk campaign. Tyler had a lively and quite modern appreciation of what has come to be known as the corporate image. He felt that the inhabitants of Michigan might respond favorably to something more subtle and sociable than the customary clashes of competitors. In May 1879, he arrived in Detroit. He was accompanied by Sir Charles and Lady Young, who were well connected, charmingly mannered and convivially inclined. Although the Tyler special train had arrived in Detroit almost at midnight, Sir Charles before retiring received reporters in his suite and gave them headline stories for the morrow. The Grand Trunk party, he said, had come to examine no less than six available routes into Chicago.

For the next ten days Tyler and his companions kept open house in suites in the Russell Hotel. Michigan railwaymen crowded in; all had irons in the fire and all hoped to contribute to Vanderbilt's discomfiture. The Englishmen met them with drinks in their hands; a chummy atmosphere prevailed; the hosts listened to everyone, asked friendly questions, made sympathetic noises and refilled the glasses. Two other Grand Trunk directors, William Unwin Heygate and James Bold, turned up; they were hearty and full-blooded chaps who preferred to talk about everything but business; they were great admirers of Middle West Americans and were enjoying themselves hugely. None of the visitors made any promises and so left everyone in a pleasant turmoil of uncertainty; but they let it be known that they favored the Chicago and Lake Huron route, which William Vanderbilt had blocked by his acquisition of its central sector.

In Chicago in the following week, the Detroit performance was repeated. Modesty and charm characterized the visitors, but Sir Henry Tyler let it be known in an interview that he thought American railroad magnates, like the Vanderbilts, the Goulds and others, gave too much thought to milking the public and not enough to serving it. They would never get away with such practices in England, he said.

A Lightning Campaign

He was at the point of leaving for home when he staged the first counterstroke. The visitors had carefully concealed the purchase in the previous December of the bonds of the Port Huron and Lake Michigan Railroad, sixty-six miles of tracks from the St. Clair River to Flint. This railway was the eastern segment of the line to Chicago of which Vanderbilt held the center. On June 21, it went on the auction block and within a matter of minutes was purchased by a Grand Trunk representative for $300,000. When questioned, Tyler passed off this acquisition as a more or less routine transaction. At the end of the month he left for home; while he was on the high seas, it became known that Sir Charles Young and William Unwin Heygate had been exceedingly busy between their drinking sessions in Detroit and Chicago. They had bought up most of the bonds of the two railways beyond the Vanderbilt sector, the Peninsular Railway (Michigan), which ran one hundred miles from Lansing to the Indiana boundary, and the Peninsular Railway (Indiana), from the boundary for fifty-five miles to Valparaiso. They had paid as little as twelve cents on the dollar for them. Other unadvertised purchases followed, and before the end of August, William Vanderbilt's central section had no outlets save over Grand Trunk rails. It then became known that two years before, in a quiet transaction, Tyler had bought twenty-one miles of tracks between Twenty-sixth Street in Chicago and Elsdon. There therefore remained but two gaps to be bridged—forty-seven miles in the center to bypass the Vanderbilt holding and thirty miles from Valparaiso to Elsdon. Thereafter the Grand Trunk would have reached its goal, running over its own lines for every yard of the way.

On September 2, a contract was signed for construction of a line to bridge the western gap. Tyler now was in a hurry; the contractors were given ninety days to build the thirty miles of linkup. A similar contract was under negotiation in the center, where the Grand Trunk did not propose to parallel the Vanderbilt trackage; the replacement for the Vanderbilt line would swing into the north in a dog's leg to tap the Owosso coal fields. This line was never built, for William Vanderbilt belatedly realized that the game was up. He had been deeply hurt, he said, by Tyler's precipitancy. He offered his fenced-in railway to the Grand Trunk for $600,000, which he declared to be half what it had cost him. Tyler thought $450,000 was enough. They split the difference at $540,000. The linkup line was completed within its contract period, and at the Grand Trunk semi-annual meeting in April 1880, Tyler recounted the course of events:

> We are not indebted to anyone so much as to Mr. Vanderbilt for the cheap rate at which we have acquired this valuable property. You see, gentlemen, we do not profess to be clever or good at diplomacy. . . . We are perfectly plain, straightforward people. . . . Mr. Vanderbilt has assisted us in this way, that by buying the central

portion of the line to cut us off he cheapened the two ends for us to buy. Finding that we then were going to construct another line close to his own he became obliged to sell us his section in order to avoid the loss which he would have inevitably sustained.

Acclaim for the Giant-Killer

This swift and decisive rout of a formidable antagonist brought the Grand Trunk fame and prestige in the United States that it was destined never to know in Canada. David had felled Goliath with marksmanship equal to that of the best Kentucky rifleman and, as money went, with nothing more than pebbles in his pouch. At that time a generously minded female of glorious physical endowments was the toast of Chicago. One commentator declared that for some weeks she shared the affections of that city with the Grand Trunk Railway. The majority of local patriots regarded it less as a Canadian victory than as a rebuff for New York; then as ever, in Kipling's phrase, the cities "challenged each to each." The mercantile community was solidly arrayed behind any competitor of the Vanderbilts, and Tyler hastened to capitalize on this support by extending a concession long sought by the shippers and always refused by local railroads. Bulk shipments, such as grains, would not be dumped by the Grand Trunk into common carriers but would be transported as individual parcels, thus retaining their identity. The company also would issue combined rail and ocean bills of lading to foreign destinations at lower rates than those of the New York range of ports.

The rewards of victory were immediate. That autumn Tyler was able to address his shareholders in terms they had never heard before. Within four months of entry into Chicago, almost half the Grand Trunk's traffic originated in that city. The newcomer was accepted by the Joint Conference of Through Lines and substantial eastbound traffic allotted to it. When a congressional committee arraigned the Grand Trunk, on little more than rumor, for rate-cutting, the business community of Chicago vigorously intervened. When the Interstate Commerce Commission was established over the vehement protests of nearly all the American systems, Tyler welcomed it as a stabilizing influence, and he caught the headlines with the ironic comment that the presidents of American railways had not been noted for sacrificing their personal interests to those of the public. Curiously enough such interpolations seldom caused offense for there was a laugh in them. Tyler, Hickson and Lewis Seargeant (for the management now was a triumvirate) managed to retain the respect, and in some

instances even the friendship, of their competitors. If they could not tell
the truth, they kept silent, and it soon began to be known that their word
was their bond. In discussions and controversies, Tyler's humorous comments and leg-pulls, his ironic but always pertinent interpolations, more
often than not softened the acerbities of the disputants and made them
more accommodating. The Grand Trunk became known as the frank but
fair friend of both sides.

It therefore is not only generous but just that Canadian National
Railways should permit the name "Grand Trunk" to live on in the
description of its present-day properties in the state of Michigan.

Additional Acquisitions

Tyler had no wish or need for more than entry into Chicago, but in
course of time the Grand Trunk acquired additional properties along its
Michigan route. The Detroit, Grand Haven and Milwaukee Railway, 191
miles from Detroit to Grand Haven, with a car ferry operating across
Lake Michigan to Milwaukee, came with the takeover of the Great Western Railway, which had owned it since 1858. The Michigan Air Line
Railway had begun as little more than a spur 14 miles in length, running
into the southwest from the Port Huron–Detroit Line; bit by bit it was
extended to Pontiac and thereafter to Jackson, in all a distance of 106
miles. It was taken over from owners who were pleased to be quit of it.
The Cincinnati, Saginaw and Mackinaw Railway, fifty-six miles of tracks
from Durand to Bay City, was that unusual acquisition, a gift horse; the
Grand Trunk management looked long and earnestly into its mouth
before accepting it. It had been built by local industrialists, who felt the
need of a railway in the lumber trades and who, after examining all
Michigan railway companies, decided that they liked the Grand Trunk
best. They sent one of their number to London to offer it in return for the
service on $1.68 million in 5 percent bonds. The Toledo, Saginaw and Mus-
kegon Railway, ninety-six miles from Ashley to Muskegon, was an orphan
property that ran parallel to the Detroit, Grand Haven and Milwaukee
Railway; it had no eastern outlet, no money, no traffic and no prospects.
In the hands of a competitor, however, it might have had nuisance value.
Therefore Tyler arranged to take it over in return for a guarantee of
the interest on $1.56 million of its bonds. It secured an eastern outlet by
means of running rights over the Toledo, Ann Arbor and North Michigan
Railway between Ashley and Owosso.

TOP: Car ferry: Ontario-Michigan (Windsor-Detroit).

BOTTOM: Great Western locomotive *Oberon* with narrow-gauge sign on the cowcatcher, 1851.

The Next Objective—The Great Western

With Chicago secure and with Michigan transit traffic of paramount importance, Tyler deemed a final settlement with the Great Western to be his next objective. It was manifestly folly for two British-owned companies to continue to make and break agreements and to expend their resources in futile competition. After a precarious start, the Great Western had become one of the chief thoroughfares of industrial development in Western Ontario; such towns as London, Woodstock, Paris, Chatham and Windsor owed much of their rapid growth to its services. It had become known for its efficiency and integrity; a leading American engineer, voicing his admiration, declared that he doubted if its president, the Honorable H. E. C. Childers, had ever bought a judge in his life. By 1862, the Great Western was in position to bargain with the Grand Trunk for an amicable division of the traffic; the politicians, however, raised the cry of monopoly and the plan was abandoned. Thereafter, by virtue of its traffic exchanges with the Michigan Central and the New York Central, the Great Western became in effect an ally of, if not an element in, the Vanderbilt system.

As its traffic had grown, it had become necessary to expand. In addition to a loop line of 148 miles from Glencoe to Welland Junction that doubled its American trackage, the line had taken over the Wellington, Grey and Bruce Railway, including its Kincardine branch, acquiring in all 169 miles through the rich counties between Guelph and Georgian Bay. The Great Western also had built on its own account the London, Huron and Bruce Railway, sixty-nine miles of excellent construction between London and Wingham in the Huron Tract.

These Great Western feeders were invasions of Grand Trunk traffic territory, a fact that did not improve relationships between the two companies. The Great Western, being the first on the ground and the more prosperous, was not disposed to be accommodating, but the panic of 1873 and its aftermath affected its earnings more seriously than those of the Grand Trunk. There then developed the situation that always plagued the Canadian managements of British-owned railways: it seemed impossible to make the shareholders at home understand that increased traffic did not necessarily result in greater earnings. At Great Western annual meetings, the complaints became loud and long, and as the years passed, the shareholders grew increasingly unwilling to wait out the storm. The management, on the other hand, because of its Vanderbilt affiliations, was not prepared to consider offers from the Grand Trunk for a sensible apportionment of the Michigan and Western Ontario traffic.

The Takeover

Early in the 1880s, a fresh development impelled Tyler and Hickson to radical action. The Canadian Pacific Railway, the instrument of the federal government in redeeming the principal pledge of Confederation, gave warning that it proposed to expand in eastern Canada. The Great Western seemed certain to be one of its immediate objectives. At the semi-annual meeting of that company in April 1882, Colonel Francis D. Gray, who had replaced Childers as president, was unwise enough to express his elation at the prospect of a major competitor for the Grand Trunk in western Ontario. Tyler immediately took up the challenge and prepared a series of proposals, ranging from a pooling of operation costs and revenues to a lease in perpetuity or an outright takeover. When Gray, one of the bulldog breed, refused to consider any of these offers, Grand Trunk emissaries began to pick up Great Western proxies. With only £80,000 in hand, which was less than 1 percent of the total issue, Tyler demanded that the shareholders pass on his offer. The showdown came on June 29 only two months after Gray's blunder, at a special meeting in the City Terminals Hotel. The Great Western management bumbled and pled for delay; Tyler, waiting in a suite downstairs, cracked the whip, for the bankers were backing him. On August 12, the Great Western Railway, 852 miles of tracks, representing a capital investment of £11,534,671, became part of the Grand Trunk, which with this takeover rose into seventh position in mileage among all North American railway systems.

Move into the Midlands

While the fate of the Great Western hung in the balance, Tyler and Hickson had been investigating other areas where the growth of population and diversification in production were increasing the traffic potential. By the 1880s, there were few Ontario small towns that lacked at least one factory; the second generation of the post-Waterloo migrants were readapting their inherited skills at the benches and machines. After a smoking factory chimney the next compulsive need of a growing settlement was the shriek of a locomotive. Railway promotion became as infectious and far-reaching as it had been forty years before. But in this phase it was a lot more sensible; of the scores of short lines planned or built, virtually all had economic objectives. Nevertheless, local pride forebade them to consult with their neighbors; as a consequence, locally financed and built short lines ran hither and yon at random, as unintegrated as worm casts or animal paths, servants of purely local needs. But Joseph Hickson had marked them all down and had weighed them up, knowing that sooner or later either the Grand Trunk or a competitive system would find use for them. If any of their stocks or bonds were on offer, he was not averse to picking them up at bargain prices and tucking them in the Grand Trunk portfolio against the day of need.

In the midlands of Ontario, where the landscape is stippled with little lakes and the vistas of the countryside change in character from mile to mile, each small town was jealous of its identity. Irish, Scots, English, German and French settlers alike had found not only new homes but new ambitions there; they all wanted more roads and railways to create tributary territories. Toward the end of the eighteenth century, a group of American Loyalists, trekking along the Lake Ontario shore, had come upon a pleasant parkland, with hardwood stands interspersed with long grassy glades. They called it Hard Scrabble, but in 1831, in deference to the allegiance that had exiled them, it was renamed Cobourg, and was thus described by one of its citizens:

> A fine and flourishing village in which many half pay officers of H. M. Army and Navy have comfortably settled. It has stores in abundance, a postoffice, a printing office with a newspaper, churches, chapels, wharves, lawyers, inns and innkeepers, hatters, shoemakers and every other convenience that a wealthy, grain-growing, money-making generation could desire.[1]

Three years later, eight leading townsmen incorporated with all due formality the Cobourg Rail Road Company, for the purpose of building a plank road northward for eleven miles to Rice Lake. This project elicited little enthusiasm and less cash, but in 1852 the citizens made a second canvass and obtained promises of £125,000 for the transformation of the plank project into a real railway. To an exceptional extent, the guarantors paid up, and the line was built in leisurely fashion to Peterborough, a distance of twenty-three miles. Unfortunately its bridge across Rice Lake collapsed during the second winter of operation. In 1856, it borrowed £10,000 from the Canada West Marriage Licence Fund; its manager at that time was a relation of Francis Hincks (these were years when a man looked after his kin). The railway never accomplished very much either for Cobourg or for Peterborough, but it lived on and on, mostly by means of a series of more or less licit relationships with various local interests. Its one legitimate progeny, the Peterborough and Lake Chemong Extension, led an orphaned existence, until, in the late 1880s, it passed under Grand Trunk control.

The Midland—A Successful Venture

Port Hope, Cobourg's nearest but least affectionate neighbor, could not tolerate the thought of going without a railway while its rival had one. In 1854, its citizens embarked on the Port Hope, Lindsay and Beaverton Railway, which was envisaged as a line forty-six miles in length to an anchorage on Lake Simcoe. The municipalities along the route contributed generously with total subscriptions of £305,193, of which virtually all were paid up. (Undoubtedly this was a record.) A branch thirteen miles in length tapped the Peterborough area. The Port Hope, Lindsay and Beaverton Railway proved perhaps the most prosperous of all Canadian local promotions. It always seemed to have spare cash in hand for expansions, and in its best years it achieved an almost incredible operating ratio of under 50 percent. In 1869, in token of wider ambitions, it was renamed the Midland Railway of Canada and undertook fifty-nine miles of new construction westward to a terminal on Georgian Bay. Walter Shanley, whose name already has appeared in connection with a Grand Trunk investigation, accepted the contract at prices that greatly encouraged other local promotions. The substructure cost $6,200 a mile; rail-laying, $400 a mile; fencing, $0.75 a rod; road crossings, $105 each; sleepers, $0.18 each. Board and lodging was provided for workers at $0.43 a day.

The panic of 1873 halted the Midland in mid-career; its backers then were considering a still bolder project, in the form of a line northward into the Ottawa valley. Nevertheless, the company found the cash to complete its Georgian Bay extension and to change from broad to standard gauge and from iron to steel rails. The British bondholders were so impressed that for five years they forewent their interest, handing over their coupons to a trustee. Then George A. Cox, the mayor of Peterborough, who had graduated from telegraph operator into railway promoter, took command. He was on the best of terms with the Barings and Glyn Mills and through them with the Grand Trunk management; it seems possible that he may have been Tyler's man from the start. In unostentatious and almost benevolent fashion, he began to extend assistance to less fortunate short lines; every kindly deed sooner or later left him in possession. The Grand Junction Railway, that product of William Mather Jackson's manual dexterity and Peterborough's pride, although heavily endowed, had never managed to build more than its first section of forty-five miles from Peterborough to Belleville. There was a good deal of flimflam in its financing; its stocks and bonds were heavily watered, and the bailiffs were at the door when in 1881 the Midland absorbed it. By then it also included the Belleville and North Hastings Railway, a feckless venture represented by twenty-two miles of tracks built to serve a mineralized area in the second tier of Ontario townships.

The Nip and Tuck

Whitby, another pleasant lakeside town twenty-eight miles east of Toronto, was not to be outdone by its neighbors. As early as 1854, it financed a survey of its tributary territory, but it took a full twenty years to get under way. The charter of the Whitby and Port Perry Extension Railway in 1874 conferred rights to build to almost anywhere in North America. When reason regained its throne, this line eventually ran for forty-five miles into the north, to the market town of Lindsay. Its span of life, although brief, was not without incident. For the citizens of Whitby the "Nip and Tuck" was more than a railway; it was a personal possession. Its operators could do no wrong. Frequently they were out of money but inevitably a whip-around found enough local cash to keep the trains running. They were in trouble more often than out of it, but whatever the circumstances the management always seemed to meet the situation with a gesture. When the sheriff piled ties on the tracks in order to serve a writ, the engineer gave the old girl her head and charged; the locomotive stayed on the track and the ties were strewn over three acres. The last mile into Whitby ran down a sharp gradient; on more than one occasion, when the rails were wet, trains came within an ace of fetching up in Lake Ontario. In winter, they sometimes bogged down in the snowdrifts. Then, passengers and crew alike broached anything eatable in the baggage car and scoured the countryside for food until the spare locomotive buffeted the track open. Such happenings distressed no one; they were part of the game of owning their own railway. For ten years it jounced backward and forward over its twenty-two miles of track in its casual and devil-may-care fashion. In 1881, it succumbed to circumstance and became just another bit of line in the Midland merger.

The Victoria Railway

This short line did not originate in civic pride but in a rather ingenious colonization scheme. It affords the first recorded instance of assisted passages; immigrants would work out the costs of their transportation by laboring on the construction of the railway; thereafter they would be granted lands along its route that bore merchantable timber. The line would run northward from Lindsay for 163 miles to a point on the Mattawa River. It was a thoroughly logical and quite impractical project. It enjoyed imposing sponsorship, and the first sod was turned on August 5, 1874, with all due ceremony; the attorney general of Ontario was present and delivered an inspiring discourse. The only immigrants, however, who showed any interest in the scheme were a few Icelanders; the line was built by fits and starts and took six years to complete its first fifty-three miles to Haliburton. It went no further. It carried little freight and fewer passengers, and in the early 1880s, George A. Cox added it to his clutch of Midland refugee properties.

The Toronto and Nipissing Railway

An even more ambitious individual undertaking was the brainchild of William Gooderham, an eminent Toronto flour miller, distiller and church member. He believed that he knew not only how to build railways but also how to make them pay. No money must be borrowed, no investment must outmarch immediate earning power. He devised an inflexible construction manual that was almost as rigid as the old British Army drill, in which tracks were laid by word of command and count of numbers. He would tolerate no rule of thumb practices.

In the autumn of 1869, he began to build a narrow-gauge line from Scarboro, on the outskirts of Toronto, to Coboconk, on the Balsam–Mud Turtle portage, seventy-eight miles to the north. The railway was completed in under three years, and it immediately commanded substantial traffic; it might have gone further and have become a viable property if Gooderham had been less addicted to straitjackets. But he wished the management of the line to be as precise as the rule book could make it, and so he devised an operations manual that was even more exacting than that by which the railway had been built. Employees were classified, like souls in the Hindu religion, in constantly ascending and descending sequences according to merit; reclassification, fines and downgrading followed automatically for even the simplest offenses; reinstatements were few and far between. There was too much stick and not enough carrot in it for the average Canadian, who often expressed in suitably embroidered terms the hope that the owner would soon go back to his vats and millstones. In due course he got this message. In April 1881, after conversion to standard gauge, this rich man's plaything was absorbed by the Midland Railway. With it went its suckling, the Lake Simcoe Junction Railway, twenty-seven miles of tracks from Stouffville to Sutton.

The Midland Property

There still remained other bits and pieces, including an ambitious plan for a railway from Toronto to Ottawa and a Goderich-Peterborough line. These additional projects involved 325 miles of new construction. But by this time, either the persuasiveness or the ambition of George A. Cox was diminishing; or what appears to be more likely, Tyler and Hickson considered his acquisitions sufficient to block the advance of the Canadian Pacific into western Ontario. On February 1, 1884, therefore, the Midland Railway and its various engorgements, representing in all 469 miles of tracks, was taken over by the Grand Trunk by means of a lease that in 1895 was converted into ownership through an exchange of stock and a guarantee of service on the outstanding bonds of its constituent properties.

The Northern Group

In an earlier chapter there has been recorded, as one of the odder transactions of the Grand Trunk flotation, the assumption by that company of the bonded indebtedness of the Toronto, Simcoe and Lake Huron Union Railroad. These bonds were security for advances totaling £170,000 by the Province of Canada to finance the construction of the railway that Toronto had proudly proclaimed as its own. After base ingratitude to Frederick Chase Capreol and some profitable thimblerigging by Francis Hincks, the local sponsors engaged Frederick Cumberland, an exceedingly able British engineer, to build and manage their property. Like all other western Ontario promoters, they had great hopes of attracting American transit traffic, so the first necessity was the selection of a western terminal. Cumberland, together with Sandford Fleming and Alfred Brunel, a brother of the famous British engineer, cruised the Lake Huron waterfront and in January 1853 settled on a site in a cedar swamp at the

foot of Georgian Bay. They named it Collingwood. The line that connected it with Toronto (eighty-five miles) was built rapidly, and the first
train reached lakeside on June 2, 1855.

This railway, the nucleus of the Northern group and familiarly
known as the Oats, Straw and Hay, undoubtedly was at that time the
best-built and most completely equipped railway in Canada, if not in all
North America. Its tangent track, its easy gradients, its easemented curves,
its solidly built and excellently maintained roadbed, its tidy stations
with bright flower beds, its shining locomotives, its high speed (up to
forty-five miles an hour), its precise schedules and books of passenger
tickets, led a representative of the London bondholders to return and
report that it was the nearest thing to an English railway on the North
American continent. But Cumberland had not slavishly clung to established designs and routines; he equipped his locomotives with what were
perhaps the first snowplows ever to be devised, in the form of flat sheets
that could be lowered in front of their front trucks in order to clear the
tracks. Allowances were even made for the confusion in currency that prevailed in Canada, where sixteen different silver dollars and two sterlings
were in circulation. Travelers could pay in either currency or in combina-
tions of both.

Having seen the project off to a flying start, Cumberland resigned
and returned to private practice. It quickly became apparent that without him, the Oats, Straw and Hay was just another short line. The
lawyer-politician who took over its management soon began to lose money
as rapidly as Cumberland had earned it. In 1859, a reorganization
achieved little but a change of name; it became the Northern Railway,
with its ownership vested in the Province of Canada as the predominant
creditor. Cumberland was implored to resume management; he came
back, ruthlessly raised rates, instituted economies and restored disciplined
routines. His wrath fell on any slackness; it was alleged that he counted
the billets in every cord of fuel purchased. Within six months of his
return, the railway again was prospering. In 1863, it reached a record
low operational cost of 4.72 cents per engine mile, with forty-six miles
to the cord.

The Victorian Concept

After the promoters had skimmed off their cream, the stock of
Toronto's first railway fetched up in the possession of the old families of
the town, who were content to put it in a drawer and wait. But they did not

wait long, for Cumberland was their man and they gave him magnificent support. The letter books and other records are eloquent of the existence of a vanished tradition; if John Galsworthy had found them, he might have written another *Forsyte Saga* out of them. These men of property made no apology for their station, expected recognition of their standing and accepted its responsibilities without question. They felt that God had honored them, and in turn they honored Him. Any transaction that could not be mentioned in their prayers was deemed to be unworthy of them. They demanded that those beneath them should adhere to the code they set; indeed, they were the first group in Canada to define in specific terms how railway employees should behave toward the public. They took success or calamity in their stride, foregoing or accepting dividends without emotion; but if the winter was stark and firewood rationed, they brought in their cordwood and distributed it free of charge to those in need.

Steady Expansion

The high hopes of American transit traffic never materialized; the Northern offered a dog's leg route in comparison with the direct Great Western and the Grand Trunk services. Moreover, as the forests receded and timber freights fell off, they were replaced only in part by produce traffic. It therefore became necessary to follow the timber line into the north. The citizens of Grey and Bruce counties, as yet not served by railways, agitated strongly for such facilities; as a result, at the end of 1869, the Toronto, Simcoe and Muskoka Junction Railway came into being to build northward from Barrie to Orillia and later to a terminal on Lake Muskoka. This involved the construction of fifty-two miles of tracks. A year later the North Grey Railway was formed under more or less the same auspices to extend westward from Collingwood to Owen Sound, a distance of forty-two miles. The citizens of Grey County subscribed approximately half the cost of this latter line. As was ever the case with Toronto ventures, the bonds were placed easily in London. Both of these companies were absorbed by the Northern Railway in 1875.

The extensions immediately justified themselves; in 1876, gross receipts nearly doubled, with an operating ratio of 58.42 percent. Two years later, another Northern subsidiary, the North Simcoe Railway, was formed to build westward from Allandale to the prosperous settlement of Penetanguishene. This line, thirty-four miles in length, was opened in December 1878. It traversed a wide belt of merchantable timber; a number of short spurs known as tramways, in all totaling about forty miles of tracks, were built to facilitate lumbering operations.

A Competitor Appears

The citizens of Hamilton saw no reason why they should not emulate Toronto and profit out of the development of the Ontario hinterland. Twenty years before, they had backed a railway to link their city with Lake Erie, but the opening of the Great Western had stymied this project. In 1872, it was resuscitated, given a new name (the Hamilton and Northwestern Railway) and a route in the opposite direction. It proposed to parallel the Northern but to penetrate twice as far into the wilderness; its objective was Lake Nipissing, where it could effect junction with the Canadian Pacific transcontinental main line, if and when the latter was built.

Construction began in the autumn of 1874 but soon stalled for lack of funds. At the end of 1877, the Hamilton-Barrie section (sixty-five miles) was opened. A year later, trains were running into Collingwood. Upon this development the Toronto sponsors of the Northern and the Hamiltonians very sensibly got together and agreed to conjoint operation of the two railways and partnership in the extension to Lake Nipissing.

In 1884, a contract was placed for 111 miles through the bleak wasteland between Gravenhurst and Callendar, on the eastern arm of Lake Nipissing. This line was completed two years later, but the Canadian Pacific, for reasons of its own, refused to agree to an exchange of traffic. There were some wild thoughts of paralleling the transcontinental line for 250 miles westward to Sault Ste. Marie, and Parliament was asked for a subsidy of $20,000 a mile. A rumpus blew up in the House of Commons, and the project was dropped.

At this juncture, Joseph Hickson made his move. For over ten years, he had been picking up odd lots of the stocks and bonds of both the Northern and the Hamilton and Northwestern railways; he also held about a quarter of the preference shares of the subsidiary that had built the Gravenhurst-Callendar extension. In a series of quiet conversations with the old families of both cities, he convinced them of the folly of further expansion. In these talks, he obtained sufficient proxies to assume control. In February 1888, at the semi-annual meeting in London, the usually subdued Grand Trunk shareholders burst into cheers when Tyler announced the acquisition of 492 miles of tracks in return for an exchange of shares and the assumption of minor bonded indebtedness.

Bits and Pieces in Western Ontario

Admiral Vansittart, a doughty British sea dog, called his Canadian estate Town Plot. It lay on the Thames River to the east of Brantford. When settlement thickened, the estate took the more seemly name of Woodstock. Like all its neighbors, it wanted a railway of its own. Two Vansittarts were among the incorporators in 1848 of "A Track Iron or Wood Rail Road or Way" from the town to an unnamed port on Lake Erie. The project had little but local pride to sustain it, and it might have died in its sleep if Francis Hincks, by now Premier of the Province of Canada, had not been seized with the desire to set up in business one of his running mates of Great Western days, an astute, tenacious and unscrupulous Scot named Isaac Buchanan. There followed a dizzying series of financial manipulations that played a considerable role in the defeat of the administration and Hincks' departure for the Caribbean as a colonial governor. Thereafter for eighteen years the Woodstock, Lake Erie Railway and Harbor Company was in a state of suspended animation.

In 1872, the project was revived but like many others, in a different direction. In 1876, a line was opened for sixty-two miles from Woodstock to Stratford, where it joined forces with another local project, the Stratford and Huron Railway, and continued on toward Georgian Bay. By this time, this area was served by no less than seven railways bidding for the traffic of less than 7,000 square miles of territory. It therefore went no further than Listowel, forty-three miles beyond Stratford. In 1879, the Grand Trunk bought it for five cents on the dollar of its issued stock, together with an undertaking to remit one-quarter of its gross receipts to its former owner.

In similar fashion Guelph, an original Canada Company settlement that had grown into a prosperous community, was attacked by the railway virus. In March 1878, its citizens incorporated the Georgian Bay and Wellington Railway to build northward through the Huron Tract. They collected subsidies from a number of towns and reeveships along its route, but Joseph Hickson intervened, this time before much had been done. He took over the project and incensed the citizens of Guelph, which already was served by his main Grand Trunk line, by not building from there but from Palmerston north to Durham, a distance of twenty-five miles. After the amalgamation of the various Grand Trunk properties in this area, most of this trackage was abandoned.

The citizens of Brantford, proud of their navigable canal on the Grand River and the only Indian Royal Chapel in existence, spat blood when the Great Western Railway failed to build through their flourishing community, despite its traffic potential of 15 million feet of lumber and 400,000 bushels of grain annually. The citizens particularly wished a link with Buffalo, and as early as 1851, they had incorporated the Buffalo and Brantford Joint Stock Railroad. James Wadsworth, the mayor of the American city, became the leading figure in this promotion and visited England on several occasions to obtain support for it. The route ran from Fort Erie (more or less a Canadian suburb of Buffalo) through Brantford to Boderich on Lake Huron. It necessitated the construction of 162 miles of tracks.

At first, all went swimmingly, and the line from Fort Erie to Brantford (seventy-four miles) was opened on January 6, 1854. At the celebration, the Buffalo Fire Brigade, accoutered in brass helmets, brass breastplates and Wellington boots, stole the show. But beyond Brantford, the contractors ran into trouble and out of money; upwards of $300,000 disappeared without a trace, and a hitherto ignored clause in the London bondholders mortgage took on sinister significance—if the line was not open to Goderich by May 1856, the western section would be forfeit. Neither the Grand Trunk nor the Great Western was anxious to see the Goderich line completed, since it cut across their traffic areas.

At the end of 1855, when it became obvious that the line would not be open in time to avoid the bondholders' penalty, a reorganization occurred in which London and Liveprool financiers arranged an accommodation with the creditors. On June 18, 1858, the first train crawled into Goderich on temporary trestles. Only then, apparently, did the promoters learn that the lake was too shallow for ships of even moderate burden to come alongside and that all transfers of cargo must be effected in the fairway by means of lighters.

From then on, the Brantford and Goderich line was a dying duck. It was offered to the Great Western, which refused to consider it, since it would imperil connections with the New York Central at Niagara Falls. On July 7, 1864, after considerable bickering and a suit in Chancery, it became a Grand Trunk property.

At this time Brantford possessed two newspapers whose relationship well may have been modeled on the Eatanswill episode in Charles Dickens' *Pickwick Papers*. The support of *The Courier* automatically earned the enmity of *The Expositor*; when the pages of one rang with acclamation, the columns of the other shrilled abuse. The law of libel was ignored, and insults were the current coin of exchange. *The Expositor* was anti-railway, and an item in its issue of July 18, 1855, probably fairly represented its reportage: "Through the influence of brothers James and George hairy brother Bill is to be the station agent at Buffalo. California Charley is to be a conductor and Father is to have under his peculiar care the keeping of the spoils." In those days families hung or were hanged together.

Among the last of the waifs and strays to find shelter under the Grand Trunk wing was the Welland Railway. This line represented a belated admission by William Hamilton Merritt that in Canada water would freeze in winter. This distinguished soldier, parliamentarian and administrator had been, in the Chaucerian phrase, "the onlie begetter" of a continuous water route into the heart of the continent. During the 1820s, he had embarked on what has been described as "bringing ships down a mountainside" by means of the construction of the Welland Canal, which bypassed Niagara Falls. In the early days of railways, he had damned them vehemently; since God had given Canada majestic rivers and lakes, why should they be subordinated to snorting, stinking steam contraptions? But by mid-century, he had come to realize that a railway along the banks of a canal might have its uses in northern latitudes. He therefore undertook the construction, with his own funds, of a line twenty-five miles in length from Port Dalhousie on Lake Ontario to Port Colborne on Lake Erie. When he ran out of money, Baring Brothers backed him, and on June 27, 1859, a shuttle service opened. Only then, apparently, did Merritt make a discovery that seems obvious today; if the canal was frozen, so would be its lake approaches, and the transfer of any substantial volume of cargo would be impossible. In 1882, the Grand Trunk, undoubtedly under the nudging of the London bankers, bought the railway at a price that gave the first preference debenture holders thirty-seven cents on the dollar, the second preference holders twenty-five cents on the dollar and the common stock holders (of whom William Hamilton Merritt was chief) nothing at all.

Consolidation on the Eastern Flank

The Grand Trunk involvements in the New England states differed in considerable degree from the company's experiences in Michigan Territory. There was little of the frontier attitude and temper in New England; its communities had hardened into molds that reflected inherited traditions and the disciplines of manners, morals and religion. The New

England town meeting was in direct descent from the Anglo-Saxon moot; those who sought free play for their cunning and acquisitive instincts usually went elsewhere.

But every rule has its exception, and in Vermont there had prospered a family as rapacious and ruthless as any of the great buccaneers of American business. John Smith, a prosperous St. Albans farmer turned railway promoter, had little or nothing to learn from the Vanderbilts, the Goulds, the Fisks or the other celebrated freebooters. For thirty years he dedicated himself to guerrilla warfare in which no holds were barred and in which every conceivable gambit—bankruptcies, receiverships, loans and borrowings, transfers and retransfers of assets, abandonments and reclamations, political handouts, retainers to judges, transactions in which Peter was rooked to pay Paul who in turn had his pocket picked by Peter, statutory double talk, blackmail, bribery and thievery in transactions so complex as to be beyond unraveling—had been exploited to win ownership or control of fifteen railroads in New England and the Lower Townships of Quebec, with a total of 885 miles of trackage. But by 1875, the hounds were on his trail; Vermont had appointed its first railway commissioner, and there had been excited public protests against his depredations. No matter how alluring the opportunity, the innate repressions of the New England conscience sooner or later manifested themselves. New England legends might deal with wooden nutmegs and a wide range of traps for the unwary, but as a matter of record, the American flimflam community usually gave the New England states a wide berth, for there the pickings were slim and the magistrates were without humor. The renewed activity of the Smiths therefore can be attributed either to undue confidence or short memories.

The Grand Trunk line to Portland always had enjoyed amicable relations with the Smiths, who operated usually, but not always, under the description of the Central Vermont Railroad. As partners in a fast freight service to the American Middle West, the Vermonters usually were behindhand in their settlements, and from 1863 on, Hickson had been accepting Central Vermont stocks and bonds in lieu of cash. During the ensuing decade, the Grand Trunk became a substantial shareholder in some of the Smith enterprises.

The Central Vermont was hard hit by the panic of 1873; five years afterward a writer of the period described its constituents as a group of beggars huddling together to keep each other warm. But there always seemed to be cash available for unending lawsuits, and in 1883, the Supreme Court of Vermont went on strike. The chief justice declared

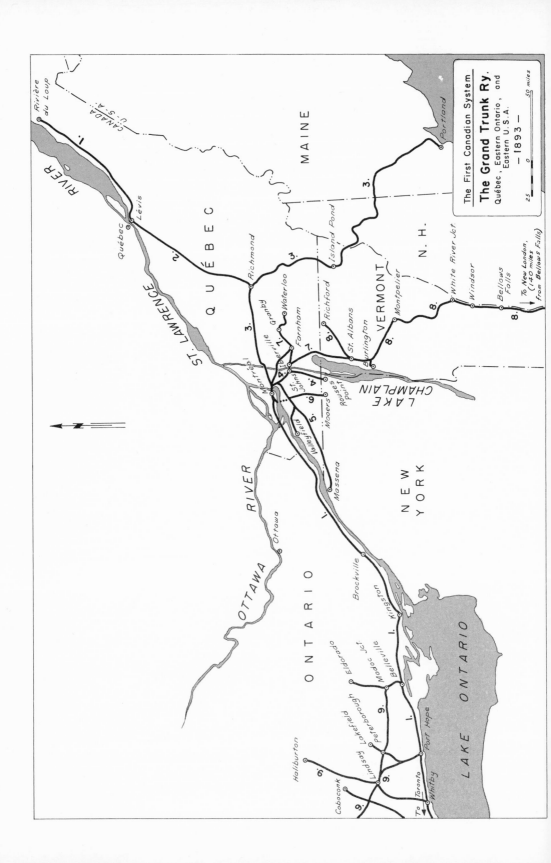

The First Canadian System.
The Grand Trunk Ry.
Québec, Eastern Ontario, and
Eastern U.S.A.
— 1893 —

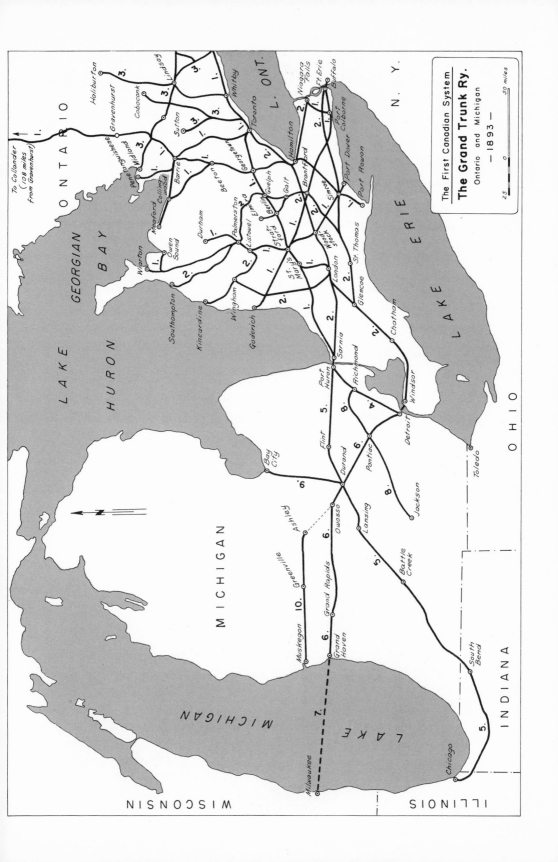

The First Canadian System
The Grand Trunk Ry.
Ontario and Michigan
— 1893 —

that he and his predecessors had been listening to the same rehash of accusations and entreaties for thirty years, and in future no more of the court's time would be wasted on legalizing the hatchetry of the Central Vermont disputants. A patched-up reorganization ensued, from which the Grand Trunk emerged as owner of half the paid-up stock of the Central Vermont Railroad. Full control however, was not achieved until 1898, when the following properties were taken over:

Grand Trunk Acquisitions in New England

Original Central Vermont trackage	178.0 miles
Absorbed short lines	91.0 miles
Canadian subsidiaries	43.0 miles
Leased lines	197.6 miles
Running rights	49.0 miles
	558.6 miles

Summary of the Grand Trunk Campaign

In these various expansion programs, the Grand Trunk had acquired a grid of branches and feeders that covered almost all the settled areas of Ontario, which secured a very valuable entry into Chicago and which assured substantial volumes of traffic to and from its eastern and western

Pileup on Central Vermont Railway, 1864.

What Sunday travel in Vermont, with compulsory religious service,
was like in 1875.

terminals. In the United States its popularity was no flash in the pan. On
the death of William Vanderbilt in 1885, Chauncey Depew, the famous
reconteur and *bon vivant*, became president of the New York Central
system. He hastened to establish friendly relationships with Tyler and
Hickson, and he made it plain that he would not countenance a continuation of the feud with the Grand Trunk. In a Senate hearing, the president
of the Chicago Board of Trade stated that that railway was rendering
better services to his city than any of its American competitors. At the
same hearing, a Boston spokesman declared roundly that New England
would not tolerate any restrictions on the activities of the Canadian railway.

The conversion of the Grand Trunk from a main line into a system
had involved the acquisition of forty-nine different railways, with a total
trackage of 2,763 miles. Including stock at par, these acquisitions had
cost the Grand Trunk £4,345,249. At an increase in capitalization of 12
percent it had achieved an increase of 120 percent in its trackage. The
capital charges per mile had been reduced from £17,000 in 1876 to

£8,376 in 1895. The good judgment exercised in the acquisition of these properties is demonstrated by the fact that three-quarters of this trackage is in use to this day.

Continuous Improvements

During the period of these takeovers, the Grand Trunk had continued to improve its fixed installations and its services. After the change in gauge and the replacement of iron by steel rails, maintenance expenditures remained on a high level because of the constant betterment of the roadbed, improvements in switching and handling services and the introduction of specialist rolling stock. An outstanding instance of this progressive attitude occurred in the frozen and chilled meats traffic. By the 1880s, this freight was rivaling grain and livestock tonnages. It required special care en route, including icing, and rapid delivery at its destinations. For some years the Grand Trunk monopolized this traffic between Chicago and the Atlantic seaboard, in 1885 handling 138,000 tons. Thereafter it had to battle for it, but despite occasional setbacks, it remained the predominant carrier of packing house products.

This traffic, perhaps more than any other consideration, led to the construction of a tunnel under the St. Clair River between Sarnia and Port Huron. Despite an efficient ferry system, traffic jams sometimes placed meat shipments in jeopardy. At the 1886 autumn meeting, Tyler informed the shareholders that he proposed to spend £400,000 on such a tunnel, of which 1,000 feet would be beneath the river and 5,000 feet would consist of deep cuts on the approaches to its portals. Joseph Hobson, then chief engineer of the Grand Trunk, took charge, designed and built the tunneling shields in Canada—testimony to Canadian progress in the manufacture of heavy equipment. The work proceeded smoothly; not even the discovery of quicksand and the necessity of laboring in double-density atmospheres delayed its completion. On August 30, 1890, the shields from either side of the river met in exact alignment. Three weeks later the first train passed through. The tunnel had a capacity of two thousand cars per day; it cut thirty minutes from the running time of through trains and saved £10,000 a year in ferry fees.

The double tracking of the Toronto-Montreal section began in 1887 and was completed in 1892 at a cost of over £1 million, all of which was found out of revenue. In that year also, the Grand Trunk was thrust somewhat unwillingly into the express business; it had served as carrier for the principal Canadian express company and was content to stay in such role. A series of lawsuits, however, made its position untenable unless it assumed full responsibility for the shipments. It therefore bought the express company. This transaction proved a windfall; in two years the Grand Trunk was netting 50 percent more than it had obtained as a carrier.

7

The Confrontation of Systems

Under Prime Minister Alexander Mackenzie's administration, the Grand Trunk had been mercifully free from political pressures; the quarrel with Potter had been an extraneous matter with little impact on the fortunes of the company. During the same period, that prime pledge of Confederation, the trans-Canadian railway, had all but foundered; it was much too hazardous to commend itself to the canny Scots Prime Minister. He endeavored to satisfy Manitoba and British Columbia with the promise of a dirt road; when this was indignantly rejected, he embarked on a peace offering in the form of local short lines. Three of these railways ran from nowhere to nowhere, but a fourth has a place in railway history as the catalyst that revived the trans-Canadian project. The line connected Winnipeg with Pembina in North Dakota and thus afforded entry into Minneapolis, head of navigation on the Mississippi River and railhead for a number of lines from Chicago and other parts of the eastern United States.

Thereafter, the story of the building of the Canadian Pacific Railway becomes the tale of two Scottish cousins, a Canadian-born American steamboat operator, an Illinois farm boy and the son of a Milwaukee policeman. Donald Smith and George Stephen had been born within the sound of the sea along Moray Forth. Both came to Canada before they were of age. Smith, who would die Lord Strathcona, was a Hudson's Bay

Company apprentice and Stephen, destined to become Lord Mountstephen, was a draper in the family woolen business in Quebec.

It took Stephen twenty-five years to reach the top as president of the Bank of Montreal, and it was thirty-two years before Smith became chief commissioner of the Hudson's Bay Company. The former institution, founded in 1817, was the first native Canadian bank; by the 1870s, it was a power in the land and not without influence in the United States, where it had established agencies and afterward branches in New York and Chicago. It was through these latter channels that Stephen met James J. Hill, born in Guelph of Scots-Irish parents and by the 1870s the proprietor of a successful steamship service on the Red River. Hill's heart, however, was in railways, and when in 1879 the St. Paul, Minneapolis and Manitoba Railroad got into difficulty, Hill approached Stephen to assist him in its purchase, as the nucleus of his dream of a railway from Minneapolis to the Pacific coast through western Canada or the northern tier of American states. The Bank of Montreal backed Hill with $700,000, and Stephen persuaded Donald Smith to take an interest in the project. By then Smith was a member of Parliament for the new province of Manitoba; he had broken with his party over the Sir Hugh Allan scandal and had led the assaults that resulted in the downfall of the Macdonald administration. At this time, he was one of the largest shareholders in the Bank of Montreal.

In 1878, Prime Minister Mackenzie, partly because of the hard times consequent on the 1873 panic, partially because he and his principal followers were too starry-eyed (and honest) to campaign in the Canadian fashion, was defeated, and Sir John A. Macdonald was returned to power. In his electioneering, Sir John had pledged his party to what was known as the National Policy, which in effect constituted high tariffs against American imports and the completion of the Canadian Pacific Railway. The latter project as espoused by Macdonald was more or less the policy of his predecessor; the western railway would be built in bits and pieces that eventually would be linked up into a Main Line.

It was this piecemeal program that deceived the Grand Trunk. Tyler and Hickson did not anticipate a threat to their system until the completion of an all-Canadian route, and they believed, as did virtually all other eminent transportation authorities of the period, in the physical impossibility and economic lunacy of a thousand miles of tracks across the empty and almost insuperable badlands between fertile Ontario and the beginnings of the prairies.

There was, however, one leading railroader who disagreed. William

Cornelius Van Horne had left the farm at the age of fourteen to become a telegraph operator on the Illinois Central Railway. By his early thirties, he was general superintendent of the Chicago, Milwaukee and St. Paul Railway. The circumstances of his first meeting with George Stephen are unknown, but it is part of the myth that on that occasion Van Horne declared that building a railway through the Canadian wasteland might be accomplished by hugging the shore of Lake Superior and constructing the line from the beaches, furlong by furlong.

Stephen never forgot this suggestion. Until then, he was prepared to back James J. Hill in his westering project if the line were built through Canada. Sandford Fleming was busily exploring routes through the Rockies and had found at least two negotiable passes—the Kicking Horse and the Yellowhead, respectively 125 miles and 300 miles to the north of the international boundary. There was urgency in the air; Donald Smith, with his unequaled knowledge of the 2 million square miles that constituted Canada west of the Great Lakes, was convinced that it was only a matter of time until the stream of American land-seekers would turn into the north and repeat the episode of the Oregon Country, with the eventual annexation of Canada's vast western territory.

It is a tribute to Smith's persuasive powers that Sir John A. Macdonald, who had read him out of the party as a traitor five years before, should have been brought to accept this view. George Stephen also supported it, for the Bank of Montreal, after its first dip into the railway grab bag, was eager for another. This interest was shared by its principal London connection, the merchant banking firm of Morton Rose and Company.*

Such were the circumstances that led to a reincarnation. On February 17, 1881, the Canadian Pacific Railway was incorporated with three Bank of Montreal nominees, James J. Hill and a partner of Morton Rose and Company as its original sponsors. On this occasion, the completion of the statutory requirements boded ill for the Grand Trunk, for the seal of the Crown was affixed on the incorporation documents by Charles Tupper. Since Tupper was a Minister of Railways and Canals, the Canadian Pacific now became the Nova Scotian's official responsibility, and as perhaps the least scrupulous of all Canadian politicians, he would have

---

* This view of the resuscitation of the Canadian Pacific is not shared by J. Murray Gibbon, who writes in *Steel of Empire* that "it was not easy to persuade Stephen to take over this white elephant, for the odour so far acquired by the Canadian Pacific Railway was not that of Araby." However, there is evidence that Van Horne did persuade Stephen of the feasibility of the all-Canadian route and that he in turn infused his Bank of Montreal colleagues and their British and American connections with his confidence.

been apostate to his past if he had not regarded this as a heaven-sent opportunity to benefit his party and confound his enemies.

The first estimates of the cost of the Canadian Pacific ran in the neighborhood of $100 million. Under an agreement signed on October 21, 1880, the Dominion government provided a subsidy of $25 million and a grant of 25 million acres of land, with a monopoly for twenty years in the territory between the route and the international boundary. In addition, the government accepted all responsibility for the costs of construction of the railway through the wasteland to the north of Lake Superior (1,000 miles) and for the Kamloops-Burrard Inlet section (225 miles) in the river canyons of the Rockies. The promoters subscribed for stock to the value of $6 million, and the Bank of Montreal and Morton Rose and Company undertook to place Canadian Pacific offers before United States and European financial houses. But even with such assistance, it was evident that the company must raise a large sum (perhaps $50 million) on its own recognizances, which meant that the ultimate fate of the venture depended on its reception in the City of London.

To London, therefore, George Stephen, Tupper (now Sir Charles) and two prospective directors of the Canadian Pacific journeyed in the summer of 1880. There they called on Sir Henry Tyler. There are two versions of the conversations that ensued. According to Tupper, the Grand Trunk was invited to build the transcontinental railway for the nation; Tyler replied that if it involved a route to the north of Lake Superior, his directors would throw the offer into the wastebasket. Tyler's version in his report to his board was that the Canadians called in company with a British cabinet minister. They showed him a map with the projected route, invited his comment but made no offer. Tyler commented that as the route did not touch the Grand Trunk traffic area at any point other than the dead-end line to Callendar, it did not concern his company.

Tyler's version seems the more likely. The Grand Trunk president did not believe that the Lake Superior route either could be built profitably or operated advantageously. By his own admission, George Stephen shared this view. Nor was the London money market more enthusiastic. At this time British foreign investments stood at a book value of £1,300,000,000, which was more than those of all the rest of the world combined. In the overall list, Canadian railways made a dismal showing; they earned less than one-quarter of the average of all British foreign investments. Morton Rose and Company was obliged to inform Stephen that there was no immediate market for Canadian Pacific offerings either in Britain or on the Continent.

In the following year, Stephen returned to London in an endeavor to raise money on the huge land grants that had been bestowed on the Canadian Pacific. Again he found the City disinterested. Sir Charles Tupper arrived as Canadian High Commissioner, and Stephen confided his anxieties to him. The Little Doctor immediately discerned a dastardly conspiracy on the part of the Grand Trunk and reported to the Prime Minister in such terms. Macdonald accepted Tupper's statements and vowed (unfortunately on paper) to make an end to Tyler. No one was particularly impressed by his outburst; Tupper was the Prime Minister's heir apparent and notoriously given to blustering; and Sir John, particularly if he was in his cups, was apt to say a good deal more than his prayers.

This tempest in a teapot, therefore, probably would have subsided with no great damage to anyone had not Cornelius Van Horne arrived in 1881 to take over management of the construction of the Canadian Pacific. He was a man of intense drive; he had never been in Canada before, and naturally he wanted to justify his appointment. He threw himself into the wrangle. He took the line that anything British should be open to suspicion and that the Grand Trunk in reality was a foreign company. (He did not know then that he would die a baronet.) On an early opportunity he purused this line of argument, declaring that wherever the Grand Trunk had gone, the Canadian Pacific would go, if only to show that the home-bred enterprise would give no ground to the interloper. The Credit Valley Railway, from Toronto to Woodstock, already was in his grasp and he made no secret of his intention to break the Grand Trunk monopoly in Southern Ontario. Day by day he made the headlines by such fulminations; the newspapers featured him, the citizens listened in awe. There is no patriot like the immigrant who has arrived on the day before yesterday.

At the Grand Trunk spring meeting of 1883, Tyler struck back. He said that Canadian Pacific spokesmen and Canadian politicians alike were denouncing the Grand Trunk as a foreign company that was endeavoring to hamstring the all-Canadian Main Line. Neither he nor his officers had ever afforded the slightest basis for such accusation. But there were twenty thousand British investors who held Grand Trunk stocks and securities, and he was going to advise them to take whatever steps were necessary to protect their property.

Stephen again was in London on a fruitless search for funds when Tyler's declaration caught the headlines. He immediately realized that if Tyler were to do what Macdonald, Tupper and Van Horne were saying he had been doing for some months past, the Canadian Pacific would be destroyed. On April 11, 1883, Stephen arranged an appointment with Tyler, whom he found in a calm but determined mood. That night a momentous cable signed by both of them sped to Montreal. It ordered an agreement to be drafted immediately for complete cooperation between the two systems, with the Canadian Pacific using Grand Trunk trackage everywhere, ceding to the latter company the short lines that it owned or controlled in eastern Canada. In addition, both companies would enter into a general undertaking to cooperate in every direction thereafter.

Here was a far-sighted solution that might have put Canada decades ahead of other nations in the provision of vital transportation facilities. Yet six days later, Tyler was advised that Stephen's associates had disowned it. No reason was ever given for their decision, and the historian can only speculate. The Prime Minister, weary and ill, undoubtedly ought to have welcomed such a sane accommodation; the Bank of Montreal executives were almost beside themselves with anxiety, for they were committed far beyond the margins of safety. Whatever his views, Van Horne was no more than a hired employee. Who remained? Only Charles Tupper, the Little Doctor of Cumberland County, now a Knight of the Realm and a baronet-to-be, yet ever an implacable antagonist.

Saved by the Bugles

From the date of this rejection, the Canadian Pacific and the Grand Trunk were at war with each other. True, it was only a war of words, but none the less stupid and damaging. "Shareholders were informed of the iniquities of the other company," wrote a Canadian historian. "Pamphlets poured out from the press, the newspapers took up the issue. The heads of both companies deluged the Prime Minister with statements, cajolements and threats."[1] On the whole, the Grand Trunk gained by this embroilment; its American friends rallied to its support, and at least some of its British shareholders went on the warpath in the City of London. The Canadian Liberal Party, which had never liked the transcontinental project (for little better reason than it had been conceived by the Conservatives), found manifold iniquities in it, and Macdonald's ministers began to waver. By the end of 1883, four of his cabinet wished to abandon the project, on which the work was continuing only because Stephen, Smith and a group of their Bank of Montreal friends had pledged their personal fortunes in notes of hand.

Then in the darkest hour, as by a miracle, came salvation. For the second time in fifteen years, Louis Riel took the field at the head of the

Metis* in rebellion. The Mounted Police were cut up at Duck Lake, there were massacres and withdrawals elsewhere, but by mid-May 1885, several thousand Canadian militiamen were deployed in the West, and every man of them had been carried there by the Canadian Pacific Railway. As in the case of the Intercolonial twenty years before, the threats of war overrode all other considerations. Money flowed like water into the coffers of the Canadian Pacific, and on November 7, 1885, its last spike was driven. Thereafter the Dominion of Canada by virtue of its Main Line, possessed the symbol of unity, as boasted on its crest, of "Dominion from Sea to Sea."

Verbal Battles

This triumphant culmination confirmed Van Horne, now general manager, in his certainty of victory over the rival system. In the late 1880s, tension mounted once more between Canada and the United States over the Bering Sea and North Atlantic fishing conventions. Then came the McKinley tariff, heavily penalizing the exports of Canadian produce to the United States. The Grand Trunk, with most of its through traffic of American origin, refused to be drawn into the political controversy. Van Horne was under no such restraint, and he took every opportunity to portray the Canadian Pacific as a national possession, the Grand Trunk as a foreign interloper. An outburst at the Canadian Pacific spring meeting in 1888 drew from Tyler one of his best-remembered retorts. He said that he had been very humble and had sought to placate his rival; apparently his offense was too great. Whatever his action, it would be twisted to place him in the role of the malignant animal that when attacked defends itself. But he remained in good heart:

> Mr. Van Horne still says that he intends to duplicate every line the Grand Trunk possesses. It is not merely the case of the wolf and the lamb but rather the case of Dr. Johnson and the eel. He recorded that he saw a fishmonger skinning an eel and he swore at it in a most abusive and horrible way because it wriggled. I think that is rather our position. We are being skinned—or rather they are trying to skin us—of our traffic and when we wriggle they swear at us for it. The more they try to skin us the more probably we shall wriggle. We have a great deal more power of protecting ourselves and I do not think they will get much skin off us after all.

* The Metis were of mixed French-Canadian and Indian descent and were the first nontribal settlers on the Canadian prairies. They were resentful of Canadian control and had gone into rebellion previously in 1869, when they were crushed by an expeditionary force of British regulars and Canadian militia.

Nevertheless, these unremitting assaults to some extent achieved their purpose by raising doubts in the minds of the Grand Trunk shareholders. Their company always seemed to be standing still or losing ground, the Canadian Pacific always ousting or outwitting it. In point of fact, these fears were largely illusion. In 1890, an analysis in detail by the authoritative *Financial Times* did not show a great deal of difference between the systems. The Grand Trunk had the edge in operational costs, with seventy-eight cents per train-mile as against eighty-two cents for the Canadian Pacific. This undoubtedly was because of the Grand Trunk's better trackage and superior fixed installations. The Canadian Pacific, however, showed higher earnings of $1.33 per train-mile as against $1.03 for the Grand Trunk. This advantage plainly was due to the monopoly enjoyed by that system in western Canada.

In 1890, Sir Joseph Hickson retired. With the team broken, Tyler never was quite the same man. Much of Hickson's financial adroitness was little short of wizardry; a long list of transactions proved him to be without a peer in obtaining what he wanted without sacrificing the friendship and esteem of those with whom he negotiated. After Sir John A. Macdonald's death, his papers revealed that he and Hickson had been intimate correspondents for many years. They gossiped like a pair of old ladies, sometimes cattily but never offensively. Macdonald made no secret of his desire to detach Hickson from Tyler and to enlist him in the Canadian Pacific service; Hickson in return told the Prime Minister that sooner or later Tupper would cut Sir John's political throat to succeed him. When that time came, Van Horne would be the power behind the throne, giving orders to everyone. These, however, were no more than domestic exchanges; the teakettle almost could be heard humming on the hob.

Hickson, however, was wrong in this prognosis, for in due course Van Horne's guerrilla tactics recoiled on him. Thomas Shaughnessy, the Milwaukee policeman's son, who had joined the Canadian Pacific in 1882 as purchasing agent, rose rapidly and within eight years was second only to Van Horne in authority. In temperament he was cool, calm and collected, and he realized that both in Canada and in Great Britain the witch hunt had begun to boomerang. George Stephen, who had relinquished the presidency to Van Horne in 1888, concurred in this view and the two took measures to limit the blackguarding and caterwauling. It is perhaps interesting to note that of the four chief architects of the Canadian Pacific, Stephen, Smith and Shaughnessy fetched up in the House of Lords, whereas Van Horne had to be content with a baronetcy.

Tyler's Downfall

However, neither the sane outlooks of Shaughnessy and Stephen nor the cosy confidences of Hickson and Macdonald were sufficient to save Tyler. The 1880s opened on a troubled scene. Canadians were torn between their emotions and what appeared to be their economic salvation; some called for unrestricted free trade with the United States at any cost, and almost as many hankered after closer Imperial ties and the retention of a British identity. At the end of 1890, Macdonald decided on a snap election; Tupper hurried back from London to manage it. The two railways were by far the largest employers of labor, and, as these were years in which gaffer usually voted as did squire, Sir Charles without delay sought out the heads of the two systems. There were no difficulties with the Canadian Pacific; it lived on east-west traffic. On February 22, Van Horne issued a rousing appeal to all his employees to vote Conservative, prophesying blue ruin for Canadians should the government be defeated.

Tyler was in England, and Tupper lost no time in informing Lewis Seargeant that he expected something similar to the Van Horne manifesto from the Grand Trunk. He stood no chance of getting it. It was not Seargeant's place to determine questions of high policy. Moreover, the Grand Trunk had pointedly refused such requests in the past. Furthermore, the prosperity of the company directly depended on American traffic, and it would be lunacy to issue anything that could be construed as anti-American bias when the bonding privileges on transit traffic were under attack in Washington.

Tupper, however, was determined to land his fish. He asked for a private appointment. Seargeant took precautions. A shorthand writer was concealed in position to record a verbatim report of the conversation. It opened as Seargeant had expected: Tupper was willing to forgive all the Grand Trunk shortcomings of the past and to load the system with favors if the management and the employees did the right thing on the polling day. He named some of the goodies that would drop into the Grand Trunk lap. A rebate of the duty on American coal would save the company $250,000 a year. There were even better things in the offing and all for the simple service of instructing all employees that a Conservative vote was expected of them.

With this unchallengeable record in his possession, Seargeant felt free to voice his honest opinion. He announced that he could not support Van Horne's views. He always had had fair treatment from the Americans, and he felt certain that whatever the decision of the electors, Canadians could rely on a friendly and fair-minded reception for their views in Washington. On March 5, the Conservatives were returned with a small majority; when secure in the saddle for another term, Tupper lost no time in giving voice to his anger. Five days later, in some of the crudest abuse ever spewed by a minister of the Crown, he denounced the "craven creatures" of the Grand Trunk as enemies of Canada and their railways system as nothing more than an attempt to block the legitimate aspirations of the Canadian Pacific.

Tyler dare not keep silent. In a letter to *The Times* he did not release the verbatim record of Tupper's interview with Seargeant, but he let it be known that the record existed, and he quoted with relish the comment of the *Toronto Globe* that it was typical of Tupper, that, having tried to bribe and having been repulsed, he should mistake honesty for treason. The Prime Minister unwisely came to the defense of his minister, and a battle of words raged across the Atlantic. There were some highlights in it; Tupper described Tyler as "a fish endeavouring to escape under an inky cloud" and the Grand Trunk shareholders as "ruined gamesters." Tyler replied that Tupper was a "poison bag," and in support of this description quoted Aristotle, Seneca and Ovid. It is safe to assume that if Hickson had still been about he would have limited Tyler's participation in these abusive exchanges. Few Canadians regarded it as unusual for a politician to offer bribes, but in Britain both bankers and shareholders knew that there were no dividends in abusing those in authority. Tyler had worked wonders for the Grand Trunk, but he was now sixty-four years of age. His ironical asides and irresistible good humor would appear to have deserted him. It might be time to consider a change.

Panic Strikes Again

The aftermaths of the panics of 1873 and 1883 had sapped the American economy for the remainder of those decades. The year 1893 opened with high hopes of the World's Fair at Chicago; of thirty-one railways serving that city only the Grand Trunk and New York Central were permitted to berth private cars in the grounds. But in June, a buildup of tensions began, out of labor troubles, fresh attempts to raid the United States Treasury and the continuing efforts of the railways to bankrupt each other. In midsummer, the Philadelphia and Reading Railroad was compelled to seek an accommodation with its creditors. This failure struck spark to tinder; call money leapt to 40 percent overnight, and banks by the score ceased payment. Sir Henry Tyler, on landing at New York, was met by Seargeant, who informed him that although the Grand Trunk had $150,000 on deposit in American banks, not a cent could be drawn to meet payrolls. Before the end of the year, 156 American railways, with a total trackage of 29,000 miles and capitalization of $2.5 million, had passed into receiverships. Strikes led to looting and burning of rolling stock in Chicago. For a time the Grand Trunk was forced to suspend its Michigan services. "Coxey's Army" of forty thousand unemployed began its march on Washington.

There was no sensible solution but to tighten belts and grin and bear it. But the Grand Trunk shareholders had never been distinguished for fortitude, and Tyler's great record was forgotten in a rising tumult of querulous questions. Why had he done this, or failed to do that; above all else, why had he not cut his payrolls? To this latter complaint he gave the answer that Sir Henry Thornton was destined to give nearly forty years afterwards: that in hard times he would not chuck men into the streets who had served the company faithfully and well. By the end of the year, rebellion against him had gained head under Duncan McIntyre, a member of the original syndicate that had formed the Canadian Pacific Railway. Investigations were instigated, each on a predetermined thesis. At the end of 1894, three hostile groups joined forces to put an end to the present administration. At the April 1895 meeting, Tyler staged his last stand. In eloquent terms he besought the shareholders to hold the fort until the economic siege was raised. They would not listen.

On May 5, Tyler and his board resigned. Sir Charles Rivers-Wilson, a distinguished civil servant with strong financial connections in the United States, took over. Joseph Price, a former president of the Great Western Railway, became his principal aide. The board was packed with the gentlemen of England, virtually all of them with fox-hunting names; but when it came to a general manager, Rivers-Wilson insisted on consulting his friend Pierpont Morgan. It was obviously in his mind that the best that Britain could provide was not good enough to deal with recently liberated colonials. Morgan strongly recommended Charles Melville Hays, at thirty-nine the virtual czar of the reorganized Wabash system. He became president of the Grand Trunk in January 1896, at a salary considerably higher than the emoluments that had so distressed shareholders in previous appointments.

The Tools of the Railway Trade

For railways, the first half of the nineteenth century was given over to experiment, the second half, to development. In both periods Great Britain and the United States led the way, with the diversity of their procedures reflecting their individual circumstances. Britain was a small island of short distances and dense population; the United States was a vast area, sparsely peopled. Canada, tied to Britain by her colonial status, naturally favored the findings of the Mother Country, but Canadian working conditions were akin to those of her great neighbor. Canada's railway practices and techniques, therefore, slowly but surely became a series of compromises, with the trend toward acceptance of American procedures.

In two particulars, however, Canada may be said to have gone her own way. The bountiful Canadian forests led to a greater use of wood in railway construction than in either of the other countries and remained the source of fuel long after both British and American locomotives had changed to coal. The intimacy of Imperial trade relations had given Canada a preferential entree in the City of London, which then was the fountainhead of world investment. In mid-century, Britain was building railways in every part of the globe and Canada had more than her share of such promotions. As has been noted previously, the isolation of the Canadian settlements, imprisoned by the walls of the forests and by the length

and severity of the winter season, had made railways in Canadian eyes
the keys of deliverance from solitude.

Choice of Sites

The selection of Canadian railways sites was governed by neither
economic nor technical common sense. Peto, Brassey, Jackson and Betts
built the Grand Trunk to high standards, but those who followed were
less concerned with the quality of roadbeds and the avoidance of excessive
curves and gradients than with prestige considerations and the enhancement of property values. After 1860, costs of construction and traffic
potential counted for more, but there continued to be a great deal of
undue optimism inspired by the ease with which railway bonds could be
marketed in London. To this day many areas in Canada have more trackage than they can employ economically and the percentage of mileage to
population remains among the highest in the world.

Roadbed and Substructure

The first railways in Great Britain were built on granite blocks, with
the rails held in place by chairs bolted to the stones. This type of structure
never reached Canada; the abundance of timber led in the first instance
to the employment of longitudinal stringers on which crossties were laid.
In the construction of early roadbeds, the Canadian winter received less
than due attention and each spring saw slides in the cuts, collapses in the
fills and confusion compounded. In the second half of the century, drainage facilities were improved to cope with the extremities of the climate
and "metaling"—the addition of broken stone to stiffen unstable soils—
became common practice. The advantages of tangent track, easemented
curves and the reduction of gradients were articles of faith with Sir Sandford Fleming, who was perhaps Canada's greatest railway builder. He
preached unceasingly on the impact of intelligent surveys on operational
charges. The vast and costly spiral tunnels introduced to modify gradients
in the Kicking Horse Canyon testified to conversion to his views.

The Rails

In rails, the Canadians took what the British and Americans gave
them. As has been noted in an earlier chapter, they began with wooden

rails, with which the Canadian winter played much the same havoc as with roadbeds. The original iron rails were flangeless, but in 1830, R. L. Stevens of the Camden and Amboy Railroad, while en route to Great Britain, whittled a model that turned out to be the T rail of today. Wrought iron, however, was scarcely more durable than wood under Canadian winter conditions, and each spring saw the replacement of thousands of broken rails. In 1856, the Bessemer process for direct production of steel from pig iron proved a godsend to railroaders; it produced rails that would bear three times their former weights with one-twentieth of the wear and tear. Experiments on the London and Northwestern Railway led the Grand Trunk to commit itself to steel rails, and only financial considerations prevented their adoption by all Canadian railways. The acceptable weight for a steel rail was roughly a pound per yard for every ton of the heaviest weights that it would be expected to bear. There followed the shrinking of steel tires on the wheels of rolling stock and the replacement of iron by steel in locomotive fireboxes, flues and boilers.

For fastening the rails to the ties, English-type chairs were tried in Canada but were soon discarded—in part because the wedges would not hold under extreme cold and in part because Canadian section gangs were too careless in their routine inspections. It was only after a series of experiments with iron bolts and splice bars that the fishplate, similar to that employed today, came into use in the 1860s. Modern frogs and switches evolved in similar fashion.

In Pompeii, the grooves worn by the chariots are still perceptible in the stones of the street and their distance apart is constant. George Stephenson chose this width of 4′8½″ as the gauge of his first locomotive, and it has endured to this day, but not without challenge. It was obvious that for certain purposes both broader and narrower gauges would have advantages; as a consequence, railways have been built in all widths from thirty inches to eight feet. In 1850, there were nine different gauges in use in the United States; these variations arose out of competitive rather than technical considerations. A different gauge was expected to ensure the fidelity of shippers, particularly those who possessed their own sidings. Canada never had more than two gauges. Both of its first main lines, the Great Western and the Grand Trunk, were built in the British broad 5′6″ gauge, and both were compelled on certain sections to install a third rail in order to permit exchanges of cars with the American railroads. At one time the retention of the broad gauge was defended as a security measure; in 1863, when relations with the United States were tense as a result of Civil War incidents, a Canadian writer maintained, "In case of invasion the enemy would be obliged to relay to his own gauge almost the whole of our railways before his rolling stock could be used."[1]

The last of the Canadian broad-gauge trackage disappeared in the 1880s.

Bridges and Culverts

The Roman arched viaduct has come down through the centuries as one of the best of all water crossings, and the early railway bridges conformed to this design. By 1850, however, many alternatives had been devised—truss and girder bridges of cast or wrought iron were common; the great tubular bridge at Montreal was composed of these materials. Wherever possible, however, the Canadians used timber, and trestle construction assumed new dimensions; while none equaled the Emperor Trajan's wooden bridge across the Danube (built in A.D. 104 and 4,000 feet in length), many of the Canadian trestles were too ambitious to be safe. The Desjardins disaster in 1857, which cost sixty lives, was the precursor of other tragedies to come. In a newer type of water crossing, Canada was well to the fore. The first suspension bridge, sustained by wrought iron chains, had been built in Wales in 1826. Ten years later the Select Committee of the Upper Canada Legislature authorized the construction of a similar railway bridge across the Niagara Gorge. It was not built until 1855, but even then it was among the first long-span suspension bridges in North America; it had so much sway that passengers were encouraged to detrain and walk across it, resuming their seats on the other side of the river. In similar fashion, the great Firth of Forth Bridge, which in 1889 introduced the cantilever principle, provided the inspiration for the ill-fated St. Lawrence Bridge at Quebec City.

In contradistinction to bridges, Canadian culvert construction and substructure drainage for many years lagged behind both British and American practice, with great resultant damage to roadbeds. There would appear to have been a fatalistic attitude toward the ravages of winter, almost as if frost, snow, ice and thaws were regarded as acts of God.

Rolling Stock—Locomotives

The stationary steam engine was a mechanical device of no particular social significance, but once it began to stalk about the countryside, breathing fire and jouncing bodies and goods across forests and fields at hitherto undreamed of velocities, it became a social as well as a technical phenomenon.

There probably has never been a single piece of machinery on which so much ingenuity and loving thought has been lavished. The immediate transformations—from a vertical to a horizontal boiler, from primitive to efficient compression systems, from individual to multiple power transmissions—created problems simple enough to engross everyone with a rudimentary knowledge of machinery. Everyone sought to fulfill some dream—of greater speed, or of more stability, or of lower operating costs; or else to comply with special circumstances—the length of haul, the range of gradients, the nature of the anticipated traffic.

During the period 1830–1860, there ensued a procession of locomotives of distinctive design, some foreshadowing changes that have existed until this day and some as fantastic as anything in science fiction. By the latter date, certain permanencies had emerged. Every locomotive must have its cab, its cowcatcher, its driving wheels, its trucks and its equalizing beams. But around these essentials there continued to weave patterns, with resultant diversities to which admirers swore allegiance as to a liege lord and to which their loyalty was unshakable.

The Canadians played little or no part in this quest for perfection but, like the cautious folk that they were, tried out nearly everything that was on offer. By 1860, they had accepted as their basic requirement the 4-4-0 locomotive, with a double set of driving wheels and with similar swivel trucks ahead of them. The engine that drew the Prince of Wales and his entourage throughout the Canadian colonies in that year was of this type and it was a typical blend of British and American practice; although built in England, it had been equipped in Canada with an American tender and with a bulbous spark-control smokestack. As locomotives grew larger, their center of balance shifted; more and more of them were equipped with bogie trucks in the rear of the driving wheels. By 1887, the Canadians were building their own locomotives, and they tended to follow American rather than British innovations. It was not until the 1920s that they got around to creating something of their own in the 6100 series, which incorporated changes to meet the long and heavy hauls, the bitter winter weather. The design was 4-8-4, and great burly brutes these locomotives were, with their overhanging feed-water heaters, all-weather cabs and twelve-wheel booster-fitted trailer trucks. One writer described them as "commanding, nay ferocious" and another as "beetle-browed." The offspring of this model was destined to see Canadian National Railways through to the end of the era of steam.

In one superficial particular, Canadian locomotives remained sturdily British. They refused to follow current American practice in the 1860–1870 period, when the latter flaunted their prowess through extravagant ornamentation, their sides gaudily painted with landscapes or with animals in wild career, or with scrolls or other decorative furbelows. Although disdaining such eye-appeal, the Canadian locomotives of that period were scrupulously clean, and their brass shone with every glow that elbow grease could extract from it. The difference drew the comment from a Chicago journalist that the Canadian locomotives looked like ladies, whereas their American counterparts resembled the ladies of the town. But then Chicago always had been partial to the Grand Trunk.

The early Canadian railways would seem to have required more loco-motives than American lines of similar mileage. In 1865, the Grand Trunk was third on the continent (after the New York Central and the Erie railroads) in its number of locomotives and first in the ratio of engines to other rolling stock.

Freight cars

Whatever its effect on locomotives, no amount of paint could make the freight car a thing of beauty. The English goods vans were unsuitable for Canada; their low capacity and their construction alike condemned them; North America was not the sort of place where merchandise could be left to look after itself on a siding, with only a tarpaulin to protect it. The adoption of American-type freight cars was expedited by the emer-gence of rental pools, which would supply whatever was required. Even such a strong company as the Grand Trunk relied upon them for its sea-sonal requirements. Rental cars were thrown together at a cost of approxi-mately $1,200 each; except for trucks, truss rods, couplers and minor fit-tings, they were built entirely of wood and were always in need of repairs. They were shambling, dissimilar vehicles of all shapes and sizes; a writer of the day gives an unprepossessing picture of them:

> A tortuous string of freight cars in motion is not what you would designate as a harmonious whole. It reminds you of elephants in baggy pants travelling trunk to tail . . . there are the tall and the short, the lame and the halt and the blind, with here and there a shiny aristocrat fresh from the shops. . . . They all receive awful treatment; they are side-tracked, knocked about, patched up and overburdened.[2]

At the Grand Trunk annual meeting in 1871, an auditor divulged that the rental pools were asking—and getting—$400 a year for these gim-crack wagons. The shareholders made a scene, and thereafter the company built its own stock in Canada, introducing steel frames and other improvements. Standardization eventually came out of the increased tractive power of locomotives. In the period 1880–1895, the capacity of the freight car increased from ten to thirty tons, and in the necessary exchanges of rolling stock between railways, no one willingly accepted the smaller cars.

A certain number of freight cars ended up as cabooses. In the first instance the only changes were windows set in the sides and doors cut in the ends. Thereafter platforms were built on both ends. In the 1870s, cupolas appeared for the first time. The only means of communication with the engine was by a swung lantern. It seems possible that the word *caboose* may have reached the United States through Canada. It apparently originated in the Dutch name for the temporary quarters on the main decks of slavers in which the crews lived during the Middle Passage, to escape the appalling stenches of the underdecks, which were packed with human cargo like sardines in a tin. It came to Canada as the name for the cabins erected on the huge rafts of logs that floated down the St. Lawrence to the loading ports. The word first appeared in the Master Car Builders List of railroad terms in 1879, forty years after it had been in use on the rivers and in the lumber camps of the Ottawa Valley.

Passenger Cars

The British compartmented passenger cars, offering three classes of accommodation in each car, did not thrive in the egalitarian air of Canada. The American coach, which seated sixty passengers and apparently had reversible seats from the start, quickly became standard Canadian equipment, with the addition of wood-burning stoves to mitigate the bitter winter weather. Sleeping cars, however, quickly improved, as engagingly related by an early Canadian railway historian:

When sleeping cars began to be talked about the superintendents of the Grand Trunk met in solemn conclave to consider the advisability of using them. There was a strong objection to their introduction, mainly because such cars, having recently been put on American railroads, had earned the reputation of being infested by bad characters. The matter was compromised by introducing benches and bunks along the whole length of the car without any curtains or divisions and with only a rug and a pillow for each passenger. When one entered one of these cars at midnight one saw a medley of dark, grotesque-looking objects with arms and legs sticking up in disorder, as if the passengers had been shovelled into the car. Improvements soon followed until the Pullman car made its appearance in all its glory. As each of these cars was in charge of a smart conductor the bugbear of their immorality was squashed and the traveller found himself as comfortable and as well protected as in a first class hotel.[3]

The Grand Trunk Pullmans, however, were handsomely beaten by a native product. The Great Western had introduced a superior type in 1867 on the run between Niagara Falls and Detroit. It was thus described:

> They had three tiers of berths and handsome draperies so that parties of three or six could curtain off a portion of the car for themselves. Each car was trimmed in black walnut. The beds had springs, hair mattresses, quilts and feather pillows. The charge was fifty cents per night in addition to the regular fare.[4]

Such outstanding accommodation was the result of considerable experiment, for this progressive railway had first put sleeping cars, built in Hamilton, in service ten years earlier. It also could lay claim to providing one of the first dining cars, in the form of a "hotel coach," which served snacks and beverages.

Brakes

The first trains had no brakes at all and were brought to shuddering halts by cutting off the steam. (On one early American railroad, slaves stood at stations to slow down the train to a pace at which stakes might be thrust between the spokes of the driving wheels.) When freight cars were equipped with hand brakes, it became necessary to extend the shanks and wheels above the roof of the car; each brake had to be set individually, and the brakeman perilously negotiated a narrow catwalk on the top of the swaying train. On steep gradients or when the rails were slippery, it often was impossible to set the brakes in time to prevent runaways; one of the ballads of the Canadian Pacific Railway describes how a heavy freight train passed through Field Station, on the "Big Hill" in the Kicking Horse Canyon, at ninety miles an hour. The Westinghouse airbrake was invented in 1867 but was not generally adopted in Canada until toward the close of the century—partly because of its cost and partly because of a lingering suspicion of the so-called vacuum process. The growth in the size of freight cars during the period 1880–1895 probably was the decisive factor in speeding up its introduction.

Couplings

Save for the steam cylinders of locomotives there was no railway item that evoked more experiment and resultant frustration than couplings. It was obvious that a coupling also must be a shock absorber, that there must be a certain amount of play in it, but that above all else, it must constitute an unfailing link between the units of a train. From the original chain couplings, generation after generation of alternatives emerged until in the 1860s the first automatic couplings were devised; but nearly all of them had some fault or other, and they were expensive to boot. Thus there are many alive today who can remember the old manual coupling, in which a moving car bore down on its stationery fellow, one with the pin poised above its slot, the other with the tongue of the link dangling, until at the last moment the yardsman flipped it upward into its aperture. Sometimes he lost his fingers in the process.

Signals

The invention of the semaphore by a French schoolboy in the eighteenth century gave railways their first signaling equipment. During the Napoleonic wars, this device was brought to perfection; it took only twenty-one seconds to dispatch messages from London to naval headquarters at Portsmouth, a distance of seventy miles. The invention in 1837 of the telegraph by Wheatstone in Britain and Morse in the United States provided the railways with an invaluable adjunct to the semaphore, and by 1860 all train orders were being sent by key. It was nearly thirty years, however, before a standard code was adopted; as in the case of gauges some railways insisted on their own code for little better reason than to ensure their singularity.

The telephone, when invented in 1876, seemed to be of little service to moving bodies, but in 1880 it was installed between engines and cabooses on the Northern Railway (Toronto to Barrie). This was perhaps its earliest application to trains.

Behavior of Railway Personnel

As servants of a new and exciting medium of transportation, early railwaymen enjoyed an aura of romance that all too often went to their heads. The English novelist Anthony Trollope, who visited Canada and the

United States for the express purpose of repairing the damage to Anglo-American relations done by his mother's outspoken book,* confessed to failure when it came to contacts with railwaymen. What he as an Englishman considered to be civility they interpreted as servility. In Canada, however, he found it next to impossible to draw any general conclusions. After the slovenliness and the insolence of train crews in the Maritime Provinces (which is commented upon in an earlier chapter), he found the behavior of railwaymen in Ontario to be decent, polite and orderly. He commented on the favorable features. Trains departed on time and kept to their schedules; the trainmen were in uniform, and there were flowers in the stationmasters' gardens.

Neither of these extremes was representative. The attitudes and behavior of railwaymen were dictated in almost every instance by local circumstances. The Irish navvy gangs that built the first Canadian railroads were a wild lot, given to drink and boisterous horseplay on pay nights; the English craftsmen who built the great Victoria Bridge at Montreal left behind them a lasting reputation for good conduct and community enterprise. (The great rock on which they carved a memorial to the victims of a cholera epidemic still stands on the approach to that bridge.) Operating personnel were equally unpredictable: some behaved correctly and reasonably, both on and off duty; others, succumbing to the incipient nomadism of their employments, worked and lived loosely. The early attitude of the Church in Quebec toward railways was based largely on the fact that operating personnel required beds at both ends of their runs. This put temptation in their way.

Canadian railways were fortunate in the number of former soldiers and sailors that they employed; those accustomed to taking orders usually found little difficulty in learning how to give them. This leavening of disciplined personnel made for responsible behavior and probably accounted for the establishment of craft unions at an early date. The Brotherhood of Locomotive Engineers and Conductors was formed in Canada in the 1860s; other unions, allied to the "Big Four" of the United States, soon followed. In their first years, these unions were more mutual insurance societies than bargaining agents, and they were dedicated less to obtaining higher pay than to improving working conditions. When they

---

* The book in question is *Domestic Manners of the Americans* by Frances Trollope, first published in 1832, republished by Alfred A. Knopf in New York in 1949. Mrs. Trollope visited frontier settlements, such as Cincinnati was in those days, and her comments were so candid that they were suppressed by the publisher in *Life on the Mississippi*, although Mark Twain had praised them openly.

took issue with management, their statements of case usually were moderately couched, and they inculcated a pride in their employments that endures to this day.

The Canadians began with British descriptions but soon began to adopt American usages. The principal differences and the present day Canadian preferences, are as follows:

Variation of Railway Terminology

BRITISH	AMERICAN	CANADIAN PREFERENCE
Wire	Telegram	Wire
Booking Office	Ticket Office	Ticket Office
Railway	Railroad	Railway
Line	Track	Track
Sleepers	Ties	Ties
Metals	Rails	Rails
Station	Depot	Station
Points	Switch	Switch
Engine	Locomotive	No preference
Tramcar	Trolley or Streetcar	No preference
Goods Train	Freight Train	Freight Train
Carriages or Coaches	Passenger Cars	No preference
Guard's Van	Baggage Car	Baggage Car
Brake Van	Caboose	Caboose
Goods Van or Wagon	Freight Car	Freight Car
Truck	Flatcar	Flatcar
Luggage	Baggage	Baggage
Invoice	Waybill	Waybill
Parcels	Express	Express
Trains Crossing	Trains Meeting	Meet
Seats, please	All Aboard	All Aboard or En voiture
Guard	Conductor	Conductor
Driver	Engineer	Engineer or Engineman
Stoker	Fireman	Fireman or Helper (Diesel)
Goods Manager	Freight Agent	Freight Agent
General Manager	Superintendent	Either—according to level
Timber	Lumber	Both—according to dimension

9

Miracles Sometimes Happen

The third decade (1887–1897) of Canadian nationhood threatened to be its last. For its first twenty years, Dominion unity had been little more than a pious wish. The political body of the new nation functioned like that of a puppet; its members were tied together by the strings of allegiance to the Crown, but it lacked native circulation of blood and nerves and had most of its activities governed by the jerkings of local strings. The provinces had found their way into the marriage bed before they had been much more than introduced to each other. As a result there had been a great deal more impotence than consummation.

The only evidence in this period of anything that resembled a wedding ring had been Sir John A. Macdonald's National Policy, which benefited the towns at the expense of the countryside. From the 1860s onward, there had been a discouraging erosion of agricultural revenues. Foodstuff prices declined until in 1890 they stood on an average of one-third less than thirty years before. On one occasion Prime Minister Macdonald (perhaps after tippling on more stimulating fluids) declared that under the National Policy, Canadian cows gave a quart more milk daily. His opponents naturally retorted that from that date the price of milk had fallen steadily.

The natural result of this disillusionment with cash crops had been the speeded-up migration of the oncoming generation from the farms to the towns; because the towns of the United States were larger and more resplendent than those of Canada, something of an exodus had ensued. According to the 1881 census, 717,157 residents of the United States were Canadian-born (approximately one-fifth of Canada's population at that time). In the preceding decade, 339,608 foreign and British-born immigrants had arrived in Canada, but by the end of that period there had been only an increase of 11,395 in total population. As someone put it, Canada was less a destination than a staging post. The local outlook was bleak, a national outlook was virtually nonexistent.

American Influence Grows

During this period, the residual animosity of Canadians toward Americans (that is to say, toward all Americans except New Englanders, who were regarded less as a different breed than as brethren who had strayed from the fold) diminished, due in part to improvements in communications media through American advances in printing, photography and lithography, and in part to the employment of American teachers trained in the Froebel techniques. Canadians, whether or not they liked it, had begun to realize that some sort of accommodation must be reached with their powerful neighbor. They did not particularly wish to become Americans, but they also did not particularly wish to cease to be North Americans. To many, closer ties seemed to be the only logical answer to the Canadian malaise, and in 1887 the premiers of five of the seven provinces supported, with full recognition of the eventual possibility of continental union, a policy of trade reciprocity with the United States. Naturally, the royalists sprang to arms, and the future of Canada became a political issue, with the Liberals supporting, the Conservatives opposing, continental ties. In 1890, the punitive McKinley tariff reduced the probability of such a consummation to no more than a remote possibility. Yet the hopes of the continentalists died hard, and only the clumsiness of Washington spokesmen, who insisted upon Canadian discrimination against Great Britain as the price of reciprocity, saved the day. As the Duke of Wellington was said to have said of the battle of Waterloo, it was a damned close-run thing. *The New York World* in a 1890 survey declared that $6 million judiciously distributed would be sufficient to secure the election of a Canadian parliament pledged to continental union.

Confederation a Grab Bag

To many thoughtful Canadians, it seemed as though the quarrels, the backbiting and the venality of the seven provinces had not been effaced by Confederation but merely had been concentrated in the federal capital at Ottawa. There was the same old hanky-panky, blather and handouts on the backstairs. All was for the party and none was for the state. After the death of Sir John A. Macdonald in 1891, there followed four undistinguished Prime Ministers in the next five years—a discredited railway promoter, a Grand Master of the ultra-loyalist Orange Order, and two former premiers of the province of Nova Scotia—all little more than timeservers with an incapacity either to inspire or to take command. The aftermath of the panic of 1893 seemed to be the last straw on the overladen camel of Confederation. A Canadian historian thus described the atmosphere:

> The provinces, divided by cultural antagonisms and economic jealousies, were quarreling among themselves and with the Federal government. The air was sullen and heavy with disillusionment, with disgust for the present and disbelief for the future.[1]

Turn of the Tide

Then suddenly, as out of nowhere, came transformation. It was not like Paul on the road to Damascus but rather like what occurs in a Canadian spring. On one day winter rages, confirmed in its reign; on the next a friendly sun stands in the sky and there is an instant stirring across the land, with new life moving in its womb. In retrospect, it seems certain that Canadians contributed little or nothing either to the origin or the immediacy of the change, but that it came out of the same awakening as that experienced by the rest of the Western World, as a result of the multiplication of communications and transportation devices. Within thirty years, ocean cables, telegraphs, telephones and phonographs had arrived to make mock of distances. An astounding proliferation of the printed word occurred when the sulphite process cut the cost of newsprint to a fifth of its previous figure and the development of the linotype machine halved composing costs. The mail order catalogue had arrived to break the isolation of the farms for thousands of lonely wives: the market reports turned farmers for the first time into business men. Periodicals opened windows on the world and so made an end to isolation. Typewriters and bicycles emancipated women by providing them with paid employment and mobility. On the railways, air brakes, refrigerator cars and faster locomotives had converted town and countryside into next-door neighbors. Nearly all these exciting developments forecast other changes to come, and they fostered ferment and restlessness, inviting explorations of the frontiers of experience. Immigration for the sake of movement became a hope and a vision in men's minds.

In the eastern United States, the growth of the towns and cities had raised the prices of land in contiguous rural areas. It therefore became profitable to sell out and to seek cheaper farms elsewhere. In Britain, millions awakened to the reality of what previously had been little more than an upper-class responsibility. Prior to the reign of Victoria, the British Empire had not taken concrete shape; it was just a collection accumulated, as someone has said, in moments of absentmindedness. The roving minority of Britishers whom the oceans drew to the ends of the earth came and went; they were nomads in search of a good thing and usually were prepared to take off for elsewhere if disappointed. But in the mid-1800s the fantastic expansion of the United States and the manner in which American pioneer groups found homes and occupations everywhere on a vast continent gave the British peoples a changed idea of their colonies and they began to move abroad in greater numbers, not only for the adventure of it or to make a quick killing, but also to start a new life in a new environment.

In the Limelight

In 1897, at the Diamond Jubilee of Queen Victoria, this greatest of imperial pageants was graced by the presence of a Canadian Prime Minister who stood out among his peers. Wilfrid Laurier, after twenty years of floundering in the morass of provincial politics, suddenly was transformed by reason of his eloquence, integrity and impeccable bearing into a national totem, an image in which every Canadian, whatever his politics, religion or origin, could take pride. Moreover, Laurier's cabinet contained some of the ablest administrators Canada has ever known. By the establishment of Imperial Preference and instant support of Great Britain in the South African War, Canada strode boldly into the forefront of the worldwide fraternity of the British Empire. Until then, the red-coated, Stetson-hatted Northwest Mounted Police was the only Canadian identity known to the generality of English-speaking peoples; thereafter individual Canadians began to be recognized around the world. Their twang was American, but their turn of speech was English, and on the whole they possessed the reputation of being slow and cautious but reliable and tenacious. Concurrently the British public discovered that Nova Scotia apples and British Columbia tinned salmon were quite as palatable as Ontario cheeses, and that Manitoba hard wheat flour was a quality product. Before the end of the century, Canada was selling more of her agricultural produce to Britain than to the rest of the world combined.

A Great Resolve

Laurier (Sir Wilfrid after the Jubilee) was resolved on some great gesture by which the emergent Dominion could break away from its provincial inheritances and assert unmistakable evidence of national identity. The proper setting for such a program would be the Canadian prairies, for until that gap had been closed, there could be no hope of unity from sea to sea. Laurier's first essential decision was not political but geophysical. Could this area provide a home for millions? It was generally believed that the southern prairies were too dry, the northern regions too cold, to attract and hold an agricultural population. However, those who knew the terrain best were of different mind—Sir Sandford Fleming, interested in everything; John Macoun, the botanist and soil chemist; the Tyrell brothers, geologists and surveyors, alike maintained that on the whole the prairies were habitable and arable.

Laurier decided to gamble on their judgment and to institute a campaign for settlers on a scale never before contemplated. As his instrument he chose Clifford Sifton, a young lawyer and Manitoba politician who had caught the gleam and who was convinced that he could turn the dream into reality. He demanded, and got, a free hand. His methods were those with which the common folk were familiar in all parts of the Western World—the ballyhoo of the carnival man, the fervent entreaties of the patent medicine salesman. There was nothing high-falutin about his approaches; after pilot campaigns in limited areas in Britain and the United States, he became the greatest barker of his time. He bestrewed the Western World with a profusion of broadsheet literature that embellished his slogan of "Free Homes for Millions." Four thousand rural newspapers in the United States carried his advertisements of a new frontier. (Editors and their families were brought to Canada to see for themselves.) He hired three thousand agents in Great Britain who toured the shires with magic lantern displays and samples of unequaled wheat for all to finger. (He was deeply impressed with the agility of mind and the persuasiveness of one of his Welsh employees, named David Lloyd George.) Europe was plastered with pictures that emphasized that on the Canadian plains there were no landlords and every man was lord of his own land. Educational classes and traveling clubs were founded and fostered. By a thousand ingenious devices, the message was driven home that those who were sufficiently courageous to aspire to a better way of life should pack up and trek without delay.

Success Abounding

The campaign succeeded beyond all expectations. As one writer put it, it inspired the greatest mass impulse to take to the roads since Peter the Hermit preached the First Crusade. For fourteen years (1898–1912), during which Sifton's successor was granted the first million-dollar advertising budget in history, the flow of settlers grew from year to year, until in 1911 the drive was climaxed by the entry of seven hundred thousand immigrants. During the same period, almost as many eastern Canadians took up homes on the prairies as immigrants arrived from abroad. There was a fivefold increase of land under crop and a tenfold increase in grain for processing in eastern Canada or for export.

This drive had no more than got under way when something akin to a miracle supervened. Thirty years earlier, in the 1870s, James Saunder, a British shoemaker and lay preacher with a love for gardens, began to breed varieties of flowers and plants hardy enough to defy the capricious Canadian climate. He bequeathed his hobby to his sons Charles and Percy; when Charles became Dominion cerealist, he persevered with crossbreeds of wheat. After countless experiments, he found a single head whose twelve grains constituted a promising variant. He chewed several to be assured of their milling quality. In course of time those that remained sired a crop of three hundred million bushels annually. By 1905, Marquis wheat, because of its sturdy sprouting and quick heading, had ousted the Arctic from a zone almost 200 miles in depth and had added at least 100 million acres to the cereal belt of Canada.

Trouble over Railways

This great discovery sparked a surge of settlers into prairie areas virtually devoid of railways. Only in Manitoba had there been any particular attempt to build northward from the zone served by the Canadian Pacific main line. The Manitobans, on entering Confederation, had lost no time in exhibiting their resentment at the Canadian Pacific monopoly, and after a decade of wild words in press and on platform, they took action. Although the issuance of railway charters was supposed to be a federal monopoly, Manitoba in 1881 sponsored three provincial charters and dared the federal authority to disallow them. One was deliberately provocative, since it ran south from Winnipeg across Canadian Pacific traffic territory. Rather than become involved in a political scrimmage, that company bought it but unwisely raised local rates to pay for it. There could have been no greater incitement. The settlers began to talk of taking the muskets down from over the fireplace, and the provincial government backed them with Wild West oratory. There were a few minor acts of violence, such as tearing out diamonds where Canadian Pacific and local lines intersected; the farmers built barricades of sleepers, the locomotive crews prepared to defend themselves with live steam. The federal government made indignant noises, and that redoubtable organ *The Manitoba Free Press,* spoke for nearly everyone in the West when it

Early trekkers to the prairies.
(COURTESY OF THE PUBLIC ARCHIVES OF CANADA)

declared that no one gave a damn what Ottawa thought or did: railways were purely a local issue. Thereafter the provincial legislatures issued railway charters to all and sundry, and that aggressive ex-patriot James J. Hill immediately set out to establish a grid of feeders to the north of the international boundary. However, his wings were clipped without delay by the Dakota and Minnesota grain growers, who enjoyed a differential of twelve to fifteen cents a bushel over Canadian Pacific rates to tidewater and who had no intention of allowing Canadian farmers to share such advantage.

The Stymie to a Program

In 1897, therefore, when the Sifton campaign for settlement of the prairies got under way, there were 2,841 miles of Canadian Pacific lines on the western plains, of which roughly half comprised branch lines or leased feeders. The agitation in Manitoba had resulted in 516 miles of independent short lines. The Canadian Pacific was thoroughly unpopular,

Early trekkers, three years later.
(COURTESY OF THE PUBLIC ARCHIVES OF CANADA)

THE BIRTHPLACE
OF
STANDARD TIME

On this site, in February of 1879, an address was given on time reckoning. His Excellency, the Marquis of Lorne, then Governor-General of Canada, sent out printed copies of the address to all governments.

The Czar of Russia called an International Time Convention which met at Rome, Italy, in the year 1882. This meeting was adjourned and met at Washington, D.C., in 1883. At the Washington conference, Standard Time was adopted by most countries of the world.

The originator of the idea of Standard Time was knighted by Her Majesty, Queen Victoria, and has since been known to his fellow Canadians as

SIR SANDFORD FLEMING.
1827-1915

Erected 1935 by the Canadian Jewelers' Association, Inc.

and no local politician would have dared suggest that it be entrusted with the construction or management of the vast grid of railways essential to a successful colonization of the plains. The earliest estimates of such trackage envisaged about 5,000 miles of new line at a cost of something like $300 million. The Province of Manitoba had no revenue that mattered, the territories of Assinaboia and Athabaska (afterwards to become the provinces of Alberta and Saskatchewan) had no revenue at all; in 1896, the consolidated federal revenue of all seven provinces (available to support all public services) amounted to only $36,618,501. Moreover, almost to a man the easterners objected to spending public monies on new railways beyond the Great Lakes. Nor was there any longer any hope of much direct support from the City of London. British investors, for the time being at least, had had a bellyful of Canadian railways.

The Breach in the Dike

Many Laurier supporters, therefore, accepted what appeared to be the inevitable formula. No money, no railways, no settlement of the West. Clifford Sifton, however, refused to countenance such resignation. He saw the prairie program as the salvation of Canadian nationhood; if it involved railways, the public purse in the last resort must pay for them. In 1897, he found the opportunity to demonstrate his determination. An American branch line was planning to push across the international boundary into promising mineralized districts of British Columbia. Basing his case on the necessity of forestalling such invasions, he persuaded his colleagues to grant a federal subsidy to the Canadian Pacific Railway for a line 330 miles in length through the Crows Nest Pass that would block such entry. In return the railway company would grant special rates on export grains and on some staple commodities from eastern Canada. There was a bit of Indian giving on both sides in this transaction, but there was at least a quid pro quo in it, which was more than could be said for many such deals.

There is nothing that brings more joy to the heart of a democratic community than an exception, since a rule once violated thereafter usually can be broken at will. Such was the achievement of the Crows Nest Pass

LEFT: Memorial plaque to Sir Sandford Fleming, founder of
World Standard Time system.

Agreement. It breached the dike of federal determination; whereupon promoters immediately got out the maps of western Canada and began to trace routes on them. Among them was a small-time operator who in twenty years had only done moderately well for himself. He possessed what was then known as "the gift of the gab," and he was confident of his ability to negotiate contracts whose fine print never would embarrass him. But his earlier ventures did not fairly represent the man; together with his low cunning he possessed a great fund of brute courage, abounding energy and pioneer adaptability. If there was any man competent to profit by exceptions to rules it was Donald Mann.

10

Mackenzie and Mann:
Amble to Jog Trot

Mann was born in 1853 in a log cabin on an Ontario farm. There is little evidence that his education amounted to much more than his mother's prayers. He soon quit routine labors on the land for the excitements of lumber camps, but in 1880 he managed to obtain a small subcontract on the Canadian Pacific main line to the west of Winnipeg. He broke into the news when, on Christmas Eve 1879, he dragged the first locomotive into Winnipeg across the frozen surface of the Red River.

In 1884, he got a similar subcontract on the final stretch of the Canadian Pacific in the difficult Kicking Horse Pass. Here he is said to have shortchanged a fellow subcontractor in a mules' deal. It was the best bit of horse trading that he ever did, for his victim became his friend and subsequent partner. William Mackenzie, another Ontario farm boy, the youngest of nine children of a Highland immigrant, after no more than a primary education and while still in his teens, became the virtual manager of the contracting business of his elder brothers. (Prior to that he had been employed as a storekeeper, a schoolteacher and a tie-cutter.) He was little more than of age when he obtained a subcontract on the Victoria Railway, that ambitious colonization project that has been described in an earlier chapter.* There Mackenzie met the man who would influence

* See Chapter 6, p. 123.

Sir Donald Mann, partner of
Mackenzie and Mann.
(COURTESY OF THE PUBLIC ARCHIVES
OF CANADA)

Sir William Mackenzie, partner of
Mackenzie and Mann.
(COURTESY OF THE PUBLIC ARCHIVES
OF CANADA)

his career in much the same manner as he himself was destined to influence that of Donald Mann. James Ross, a first-class Scottish engineer, had
emigrated to the United States in the late 1860s. Before he reached
Canada, he had gained ten years' experience in American methods of railway building. When he moved on to his next job, the Credit Valley
Railway, he took Mackenzie with him. In 1883 he was appointed chief
construction engineer on the 1,400 miles of Canadian Pacific tracks nearing completion between Winnipeg and Vancouver. Again he found a place
for Mackenzie, for he knew a good railroader when he saw one.

The Kicking Horse Canyon, the most difficult of all gateways to
the Pacific, put its stamp on the men who stormed its fastnesses. To Ross,
Mackenzie and Mann there now was added a fourth campanion of like
kidney—Herbert Holt, a young Irish engineer, of good family and well
educated, with a flair for brilliant solutions and an audacity bordering
on impudence. It was the greatest possible good fortune for these farmers'

sons, at the outset of their careers, to master their trades under such supervisors on a climactic section of the transcontinental railway.

On completion of the Kicking Horse section, the four found work together on the Canadian Pacific line across Maine, from Montreal to Saint John. Thereafter they returned to the West, to build the Qu'Appelle, Long Lake and Saskatchewan Railroad, a combined rail and steamship service between Regina and the navigable reaches of the Saskatchewan River. They also completed other short lines, but one of them, a first attempt to reach Hudson Bay, proved a dismal failure. They lost $80,000 on it, which suggests that they were becoming men of consequence in the contracting world. This fiasco had an aftermath, the first of many such, to give point to the common catch-phrase of later years, that if Mackenzie and Mann fell in a manure pile, they would emerge smelling of attar of roses.

These eight years with Ross and Holt were decisive in preparing the pair for what was to come. Mann developed into a remarkable master builder, with all the tricks of the trade at his fingertips and with the ability to inspire his subordinates to outstanding performances. Mackenzie acquired a rare sense of anticipation; admirers and competitors alike suspected him of second sight. His manipulative dexterity, both of men and of money, grew akin to wizardry. In after years, when they had become meteors in the railway sky, it was customary to declare that they had been born lucky. The fact was, they made their luck by shrewdness and courage and because they had had exceptional mentors. Holt became Sir Herbert and president of one of Canada's greatest banks. Ross rose to be one of the most eminent industrialists of his time.

Mann Waits for Something to Turn Up

In 1892, the four completed the last of the joint jobs in western Canada. William Mackenzie headed back to the farm, for he was intent on a political career. Mann, tough as nails and with an eagle eye for opportunities, decided to stay in the West. As he said long afterward, the frontier suited him.

In the early days of Confederation, the provinces seemed to give the federal authority trouble in inverse ratio to their size and population. Thus Manitoba, a postage-stamp province with only 18,995 inhabitants in 1871, was asserting itself as *primus inter, pares* almost from the day that it joined the Dominion. Railways, of course, were its prime concern, and immediately it was at odds with the federal authority over the right to issue charters. In true frontier fashion, the Manitobans condemned anything that limited their freedom of action, and Donald Mann, snugly ensconced in Winnipeg as a chummy convivial chap who knew everybody, was fairly certain that he soon would find scope for his talents.

Something turned up for him almost immediately. Two Ottawa contractors had come west with a modest job of building a railway from Portage la Prairie, 56 miles west of Winnipeg, to Lake Manitoba, a distance of 17 miles.* The easterners had obtained a land grant of 108,800 acres as endowment of this enterprise. But farther north, a colony of Icelanders cried out vehemently against their neglect, and the Manitoba legislators went to bat for them. Almost before the startled easterners knew it, their contract had been increased to 125 miles of tracks along the western forelands of Lake Winnipegosis. They had been endowed with an additional 691,200 acres of land grant, had been exempted from taxation, and their construction bonds had been guaranteed by the Province of Manitoba.

Mann Takes a Hand

Yet even with these goodies showered upon them, the eastern contractors failed to get under way. According to the legend, they and provincial government officers made a joint approach to Donald Mann. They found him ready and willing, but what he had in mind went far beyond a short line to serve a handful of scattered settlements. He still had a legal interest in the charter of the Hudson Bay Railway on which he, Ross and Mackenzie had lost a sizable sum. He was able to bring this project out of the closed files, for Manitobans never had been content with their first failure to establish their own ocean port. They had measured the distances on a globe and had discovered that their wheat by its conventional route must travel 418 miles from Winnipeg to Fort William by rail and thereafter 4,808 miles by lake and ocean to British ports. There was no comparable railway to Hudson Bay, but the calipers showed the land route to be little longer than to Fort William, while the water route was only 2,976 miles—little more than half that by way of the Great Lakes.† Why, asked the Manitobans in ringing terms, should they not have

---

* This was perhaps the last of the portage railways. Portage la Prairie stood on the site of Fort La Reine, built by La Verendrye in 1738. The route of the railway followed the old packers' trail to the edge of Lake Manitoba.
† The flaw in the Manitoba argument, of course, was that it was impossible to build a direct line from Winnipeg to Hudson Bay. The present route is 975 miles in length, or considerably more than twice that to Fort William, and rail transport is from eight to twelve times more costly than sea transport.

their own port of exportation instead of being at the mercy of the predatory easterners who set the rail and water rates?

In March 1895, the complaints of the Manitobans were loud enough to reach Ottawa, and it became apparent that there might be some unloosing of the federal purse strings. This was big news to Donald Mann. With two opportunities confronting him, why should he not combine them into a single project, with millions of acres of land grants and thousands of dollars of guaranteed working capital per mile? With such a prospect in mind, Mann realized that he would be confronted with reams of paper work, to say nothing of platoons of cross-examining lawyers, bankers and politicians. This was not his line of country, and he immediately bethought himself of William Mackenzie. The situation had need of him.

William Mackenzie—His First Jackpot

That embryonic politician had never reached his home hustings. In Toronto, he had fallen in with Americans intent on a takeover of the three horse-drawn tramways of that city and their replacement by an electric street railway. They were deeply impressed by Mackenzie's fertility of suggestion; one of them said long afterward that he shuffled money matters like a pack of cards and dealt himself whatever hand he desired. They asked him to join them; he agreed on condition that they include Ross. In the subsequent negotiations, the group made a killing (said to be in millions) in return for a piffling commitment (said to be $10,000.)

There seemed to be no reason why what had worked in Toronto should not be repeated elsewhere. Mackenzie and Ross took to the road and in the next three years executed similar coups in Montreal, Saint John and Birmingham, England. They were at point of leaving for Jamaica when a call came out of the West. Mann was hastening east with urgent business to discuss with Mackenzie.

It is permissible to speculate on the nature of that historic meeting. Donald Mann, all frontiersman, was tough as nails. Crammed with assurance, work in hand, political support assured, with the worldwide Sifton campaign for settlement of the prairies in full swing and with railways the unquestionable key to its success—their costs underwritten by public monies, and above all else, by huge land grants that made the railway builders the barons of the areas that they opened to the immigrants—he told a tale of unequaled opportunities. The trim figure of William Mackenzie sat across the table listening, his quick mind discerning a dozen secondary possibilities that never would have occurred to Mann. Throughout his career Mackenzie was destined to prove daring, quick, impetuous, dominating, always breasting waves, always sailing uncharted seas, and now an odyssey awaited him. Before they rose, the two men were partners, perhaps without even a preliminary handshake across the table.

Under Way in Manitoba

On March 5, 1895, the Railway Committee of the Privy Council recommended a loan of $2.5 million to the Winnipeg Great Northern Railway. This was a reincarnation of the earlier Hudson Bay project but by a more roundabout route. On January 26, 1896, Mackenzie and Mann, still without formal association, acquired the derelict charter of the Manitoba Railway and Canal Company and within a matter of minutes subscribed $195,000 in cash, let its construction contract to themselves and declared the lists of the company to be closed. Thereafter, in a bit of legislative flimflam, which, according to one writer, was "suggestive of the gently-smiling jaws into which Mann and his associates beguiled many a little fish in years to come" they transferred their Hudson Bay Railway interests to their new wholly owned property in such manner that there was little or nothing left for their associates in the earlier venture. They already had taken over the contract of the easterners, and so they had two separately subsidized railways that they intended to build as one, with its destination ostensibly the Pas, the terminus of an old trading route on the Saskatchewan River, 450 miles to the north of Winnipeg, whence the Hudson Bay Railway would take off to the east, if and when it should be built. But Mackenzie and Mann had not the slightest intention of building across intractable and uninhabitable terrain, nor did they propose to go as far as the Pas. No matter what the provincial and federal governments expected, they were using the line to the Icelandic settlements as a takeoff for entry into the black soil belts of the northern prairies beyond Manitoba's western boundary. They were betting their all on Clifford Sifton's campaign years before anyone had heard of Marquis wheat.

Hanna Joins Them

They had no more than settled into work when the partnership expanded into a triumvirate. David Blythe Hanna, a restless and irrepressible Scot, had been in the railway business for twenty years. On the evidence of his autobiography, one of the best of all Canadian railway books,[1] he had been searching for someone like Mackenzie and Mann from the beginning. He was indefatigable and indomitable; he carried their burdens, fought their battles and remained to defend them long after they had departed from the scene.

An Image Emerges

Within six weeks of receiving legislative authority, a railway was under construction from Gladstone, ninety-one miles west of Winnipeg, through the well-settled Dauphin area to the west of the Manitoba-Winnipegosis lake chain. By the end of the year, it was in operation for 123 miles to Winnipegosis. Day by day, as the scars of the shallow cuts and fills marched northward, the Mackenzie and Mann image emerged. It was the first truly Canadian-type enterprise of its kind. The Grand Trunk had been British to the core; in its routines, it conformed to established habits of mind and codes of conduct. The Canadian Pacific had been built with typical American drive and assurance; the "genial ruthlessness" which Ramsay Muir declared to be the overriding characteristic of the United States socio-economic system, could not have found a better exemplar than Cornelius Van Horne.

Mackenzie and Mann, by accident or design, were neither disciplined nor methodical, genial nor ruthless. British railway builders would have considered them haphazard; American contractors, slack and casual. They entered the countryside neither as intruders nor as lordly visitants from afar; instead they worked and behaved as though native to the scene. They bought what they needed locally and without fuss; if a farmer asked too much for his right of way and proved adamant, they would shift the route onto the land of a more accommodating neighbor. The actual construction had something of the air of a barn-raising about it; everyone was allowed to pitch in and do what he could. If farmers and their teams showed up, they earned a day's pay, just as though they were working on a roadway or on a school or on some other community venture. This casual labor soon became as skilled as the terriers and the gandy-dancers in the small specialist jobs, such as tidying up a gradient or setting a culvert.

From time to time, there was the equivalent of a village picnic, and every now and then, Mackenzie and Mann played squire. For instance, in the spring of 1897, they bought three thousand bushels of seed wheat in Winnipeg, cleaned it and distributed it free of charge in the Dauphin district. It was said to have been the first seed grain ever sown in that area. Farmers and their families rode on the work trains as a matter of course. "Service was our motto," wrote D. B. Hanna. "We had more stopping places to the ten miles, I think, than any other railway in the world."[2] The iron horses, when occasion required, performed as neighborhood work teams, and from such small services there grew the image of Mackenzie and Mann as friends and patrons. Much of their astonishing success in years to come was due to their sturdy support by parochial bodies—village councils, county committees and road boards whose members had had good tidings of them from other neighborhoods.

Their Second Venture

Before the Winnipegosis job was completed, Hanna was in charge of it and Mackenzie and Mann had begun to build another railway in an opposite direction. They had picked up a dormant charter for a line approximately one hundred miles in length, to be built into the southeast from Winnipeg to the Minnesota boundary at the Lake of the Woods. The Manitoba government had guaranteed its construction bonds. It seemed rather a pointless venture, as most of the route traversed either was unfit or nearly unfit for farming; nor did the American connections at the boundary promise much traffic. But it made sense in other ways: the charter carried a land grant of 680,320 acres, which could be taken up anywhere in Manitoba and which Mackenzie and Mann believed, with a little judicious wire-pulling, might be transferred to the North West Territories, where an abundance of rich farming land was available. The first forty miles of this line were open before the end of the year and had freight waiting for them; when the right-of-way crews slashed the line's passage through belts of light timber, they also cut and piled firewood. By autumn forty thousand cords were awaiting transport to Winnipeg. This small sideline produced enough revenue to pay the interest on the construction bonds for two years. The ability to turn such small items to account spread the fame of Mackenzie and Mann throughout the countryside. On one occasion, a locomotive killed a heifer. Instead of seeking out its owner and haggling over compensation, the animal was dressed on the spot, the meat sold to a construction camp cook and the hide to a tanner, with a consequent profit for both farmer and contractor.

The Breakout

In 1898, these two bits of Mackenzie and Mann line, amounting to 167 miles in all, earned gross revenues of $106,698, or a profit of approximately one hundred percent on operational costs. In that year, the first fruits of the Sifton campaign were to be observed in a substantial intake of American settlers, nearly all of whom sought free land; the zone of occupancy began to creep northward, and the partners realized that it was time for them to be seeking traffic beyond the bonds of Manitoba. A certain amount of statutory jugglery ensued that resulted in the North West Territories railway land grant being increased to 12,800 acres per mile; on January 13, 1899, two Manitoba charters died in giving birth to the one destined to represent Mackenzie and Mann thereafter—the Canadian Northern Railway.

Work already had begun on a line from a point on the Winnipegosis Railway to Prince Albert, a flourishing town on the North Saskatchewan River originally founded by a Scottish missionary and surrounded by mixed farming and timbering districts. This venture involved the construction of 250 miles of tracks across areas of low traffic potential, but, as if to demonstrate their audacity, the partners in the same year began work on a parallel railway heading for Saskatoon, then best known as the colonization project of an Ontario temperance society, most of whose early settlers took good care to live outside the municipal limits. These ventures into the blue constituted typical Mackenzie and Mann calculated risks. If railways preceded the anticipated influx of colonists, their land grants eventually would pay all costs of construction. Should Sifton succeed in his worldwide selling campaign, their fortunes would be made, but they could do with a little help from Mother Nature as well. If the newcomers were greeted by bad weather—late or early frosts, drought or blizzards— the quality of the soil would not be enough to stimulate settlement. But here the luck held. The meteorological records show more moderate and equable temperatures, rainfall and snowfall during this period than ever before or since.

Incredible Activity

In the five years surrounding the turn of the century, Mackenzie and Mann were virtually in a state of perpetual motion—here, there and everywhere. They had fingers in a score of pies and seemed able to pull out plums at will. They were thrusting not only across the western plains but also eastward from Winnipeg, completing the original firewood line to the international boundary, where they bought trackage rights from a Minneapolis lumber company to build through United States territory for forty-four miles to secure re-entry into Canada at Rainy River. The remaining 431 miles to Port Arthur were provided by two derelict and partially built railways on which the Manitoba government had bestowed handsome land grants and guarantees of construction bonds. The opening of this line to lakehead would break the Canadian Pacific monopoly—a consummation greatly to be desired by westerners. In a driving campaign, this ambitious project was completed in time for a New Year's Eve party at the end of 1902, when Mackenzie and Mann gathered fifteen hundred guests in the Northern Hotel at Port Arthur for such a celebration as lakeside had never seen before. In the following year more than six million bushels of grain moved over this route.

The Branch Line Coup

Concurrently, a second victory over the Canadian Pacific was in the making. The Northern Pacific owned 313 miles of tracks in the province, linking Winnipeg and Brandon with its system at the international boundary. These branches crossed the Canadian Pacific traffic area and that company was in the market for them. But William Mackenzie was very busy behind the scenes in a series of highly confidential conversations, and in January 1901, the fruits of his labors were revealed in a deal that rocked Manitoba. The provincial government leased the Northern Pacific lines and immediately conveyed them to the Canadian Northern but at anything but a giveaway price—a rental of $300,000 a year, control of rates by the province, an undertaking never to pool traffic with the Canadian Pacific and an immediate slash of 15 percent in the rates to lakehead.

On announcement of the Canadian Northern coup, Sir William Van Horne (on his knighthood he had ditched his more familiar given name) lost his temper and visited his wrath on iniquitous legislature and knavish competitors alike, to the intense delight of virtually every resident of Manitoba. From being merely popular, Mackenzie and Mann in a trice became revered figures. By then they were more or less honorary members of the Manitoba legislature, and thereafter applications for land grants or for guarantees of construction bonds became little more than a formality; nothing was withheld from them. With great rapidity, they built 133 miles of extensions and link-ups to improve the services of the leased line and to go after the grain trade in earnest. This single transaction, as someone put it, changed the Canadian Northern from a boy into a man. It was on the map to stay.

Although the stream of settlers was still little more than a trickle, it was growing at a sufficiently satisfactory rate to compel the Laurier administration to think in terms of a second transcontinental railway. After the branch lines coup in Manitoba, many took it for granted that the Canadian Northern would be the federal instrument in such program. Unfortunately Mackenzie was absent in Brazil, and when approached, Mann gave a cocky and ill-advised interview to an eastern newspaper; in effect he said that if the Canadian Northern wished to extend from sea to sea it could do so without cooperating with anyone. As if in furtherance of this independent attitude, the company during 1901 obtained charters for new railways that virtually spanned Canada—from Quebec City to the head of the Great Lakes, from northern Manitoba to the Pacific. Sir Wilfrid Laurier was offended by Mann's brashness, with results that will be related in a subsequent chapter.

Mackenzie in Foreign Parts

The absence of Mackenzie at a time when crucial developments were in train deserves explanation. His legerdemain in urban transportation problems had not been forgotten, and toward the end of the century S. F. Pearson, a widely-traveled American engineer, came seeking him. He had studied Mackenzie's procedures in the Toronto, Montreal, Saint John and Birmingham ventures, and he believed that an exceptional opportunity was offering in São Paulo, the principal coffee port and second city of Brazil. Mackenzie, incorrigibly adventurous, consented to examine it; the result was the incorporation of the first unit of what eventually grew into the great Brazilian Traction group. There is no evidence that Mackenzie ever put anything except perhaps his traveling expenses into this venture, but in after years he declared on one occasion that he had taken a million dollars out of Brazil in a single season, adding wryly that that was more than he had ever been able to do in Canada. There followed similar excursions to Mexico and Spain, out of which came the Mexican Light, Heat and Power Company and the Barcelona Traction Company. Both of these ventures, like that of São Paulo, were financed almost completely in the City of London. The records of Mackenzie's participation in these flotations are piecemeal, but there would seem to be little doubt that he not only conceived them but assisted at their births. Perhaps the best evidence of his role was to be found in the growing interest in the City of London in his various projects; from then onward, the investment bankers regarded him as a man whose fancies were worth backing. He was credited with a water diviner's talent—a magic tingle in the fingers when approaching treasure trove.

Major Enlistments

The recurrent absence of Mackenzie did not throw the full burden of major decisions on Mann and Hanna, for in addition to several brilliant engineers, Canadian Northern Railway had attracted into its services two of the ablest men of their time in the fields of law and finance. Zebulon Aiton Lash, Newfoundland-born, had served as Deputy Minister of Justice before returning to private practice, where he came to be known as the outstanding Canadian authority on commercial law. His preeminence in this field has not been challenged to this day. In Canada there never has existed the no-man's-land between state and federal authority that gave legal sharpshooters in the United States such opportunities, but the rigidity of British legal definition had almost the same effect in many Canadian contexts, making it almost impossible to frame legislation or to draft contracts to which no exceptions could be taken. In avoiding such gins and snares, Lash was supreme. "So exquisite was his appreciation of word values," wrote Hanna in his autobiography, "that although others might embody an intention in a series of paragraphs apparently beyond criticism, his mastery of precision and shade was such that he could clothe it in language that had the exactitude of a multiplication table and the clarity of a mirror."[3]

Numerous Canadian writers have dealt cynically or sanctimoniously with Mackenzie and Mann, declaring or implying that if all were known, they would be revealed as light-fingered operators, slick dealers never averse to greasing palms or to buying what they wanted if they could not get it any other way. In 1955, the Department of Research and Development of Canadian National Railways embarked on a statistical exploration of its constituents; all too little, it was felt, was known of the origins and subsequent involvements of the 221 railways that comprised the original content of that system. In the course of this task, hundreds of documents were examined and more than eight million words of record were compiled. *None was subjected to closer scrutiny than those that dealt with the Canadian Northern Railway; yet not in a single instance could it be confirmed that Mackenzie and Mann ever had stepped beyond the letter of the law.* This restraint was the measure of the achievement of Z. A. Lash, who after eight years in an advisory capacity became an officer of the company in 1904.

Concurrently an equally talented financial specialist joined its inner circle. Robert Montgomery Horne-Payne was born of a distinguished English legal family, his father having been chosen by the Emperor of Austria as advisor on the reconstitution of that nation's legislative structure. When little more than a boy, he had visited British Columbia, where, as a result of a chance meeting, he promoted the merger of a number of struggling electrical companies into the British Columbia Electric Railway group, of which he became chairman at the age of twenty-two. In 1902, although crippled by illness, he founded the British Empire Trust Company for the specific purpose of encouraging investment in Canada. In the following twelve years, he is said to have channeled $500 million into Canadian enterprises. He had an unfailing flair for presenting projects in inviting guises; it was said of him that he could conjure cash out of the very cobblestones of cathedral towns. Mackenzie and Mann were favorite clients from the start; in all he found about $200 million for them.

The Broad Strategy

By 1902, it became clear what Mackenzie and Mann were up to. Despite a confusion of charters for lines running in all directions, they were going to concentrate in the first instance on populated areas, where they were quite willing to take on whatever competition they might meet. From such bases they hoped to be able to discern the trends of settlement and to be first to reach the unserved areas. They had no intention of activating most of the charters that they had picked up out of statutory dustbins but they were keenly interested in such of them as carried land grants or other forms of assistance, which to date they had been able either to transfer or to alter to their profit. They therefore had set out to break the Canadian Pacific monopoly in Manitoba, for in that company's traffic territory, the land was richer, the population was denser and the rates to lakehead and eastern Canada lower than elsewhere in the West.

The Land Grants Campaign

Within three years of securing the former Northern Pacific lines, they had built nine feeders and branches, totaling 332 miles in all, in what previously had been Canadian Pacific territory. The Manitoba legislature with unconcealed satisfaction had guaranteed bonds up to $10,000 a mile on this new construction. Thereafter on the same terms they had built an additional nine branches (282 miles) in central Manitoba, on either side of and between the lake chains. They thus had established themselves as the predominant Manitoba carrier. At the same time they had managed, by one method or another, to transfer the bulk of their Manitoba land grants from that province to the virgin expanses of the North West Territories. Of the 100 million acres that the federal government had set aside in 1871 to finance a transcontinental railway, 32 million acres had been distributed before such grants had been rescinded (officially if not actually) in 1890. Of this great area* (which a learned observer declared to have been almost exactly what Richard III had offered for a horse at the battle of Bosworth Field), Mackenzie and Mann in one way or another had come into possession of 4,102,951 acres.

When the Sifton campaign first swelled the flow of settlers, Mackenzie and Mann were inclined to sell this land to all and sundry. It had cost them nothing, so its proceeds were clear profit. In 1903, an American land company bought 68,000 acres from them at $5 an acre and immediately began to sell it at double that price. Whereupon Mackenzie and Mann went into partnership with an English group, from whom they netted $9.50 an acre. But they soon realized that instead of endeavoring to guess where settlements would first thicken, it would be more profitable if the immigrants and the railway were to arrive together. They therefore went into the land business for themselves and did exceedingly well. When the surveyors' stakes went down, when the grubbing parties cut the swaths, when the teams and gangs moved up to shift the soil into a roadbed and when the track-layer, like a giant caterpillar, crawled forward, the set-

---

* "Great" perhaps by Canadian standards but small potatoes in comparison with some of the United States grants. The Peoples Pacific Railroad, promoted by the Boston peepshow proprietor Josiah Perham, was endowed by Congress with 47 million acres.

tlers would follow close behind, choosing their future homes. A writer in the *Queens University Quarterly* thus described the way it worked:

> North Battleford was ushered into existence in June 1905 with one house to its credit. Six months later it had a population of five hundred. Farm property at $6.00 an acre had become city lots at $10.00 a frontage foot. It now has shops of every kind, a large hotel and four churches. It is difficult to find a resident who does not believe that nearly the same ratio of increase in size and prosperity will not be maintained indefinitely. There are a hundred or more bustling little towns along the main line and the branches of the railway.[4]

The revenues from these land sales not only covered all immediate construction but also left Mackenzie and Mann with tidy balances in hand. Money breeds money, and Horne-Payne had no need to gild his lilies in his presentations to the merchant bankers in the City of London. The first issue of Canadian National Railways stock (£400,000 4 percent consolidated debentures) was snapped up; British investors bought parcels of wild lands freely at current prices. The house of Morgan in New York took $5 million of Canadian Northern bonds on exceptionally favorable terms. Finally, the Canadian government, now committed to a transcontinental railway, could scarcely do less for Mackenzie and Mann than for its protégé. In 1905, therefore, it backed construction bonds at $31,000 a mile for a long leap across the new provinces of Saskatchewan and Alberta —from Grandview in Manitoba to Edmonton, the former Hudson Bay Company trading post on the North Saskatchewan River, the gateway to the Arctic waterways and at that moment in high elation at having snatched the provincial capital from that pretentious cowtown, Calgary. This grant represented a total guarantee of $19.22 million.

The Crash Program

With money in the bank, settlers pouring in, and all portents being fair, Mackenzie and Mann decided that railhead must be in Edmonton by Christmas of that year. An all-out drive across plains, coulees and rivers seemed in keeping with the spirit of the hour. Before the frost was out of the ground in the spring of 1905, advance parties were running stadia and transit surveys, estimating the yields of cuts, the requirements of fills, scouting the river banks for bridge seats. Within days of the spring breakup, gangs were at work over a distance of fifty miles. The steel marched out of Grandview and had reached the Doukhobor settlement at Kamsack, seventy-one miles away, by the end of April. May was a banner month, and on the 31st the German-American settlement at Humboldt was *en fête*, the steel had reached it, 146 miles beyond Kamsack. Then came the big bridges over both branches of the Saskatchewan, one of them nearly half a mile in length. By October, the work trains were chugging in and out of Battleford, and the back of the job had been broken, with only 254 miles to go. On December 17, the first locomotive whistle out of the east was heard in Strathcona, the southern suburb of Edmonton, on the opposite bank of the Saskatchewan River. This rapidly growing town stood on the fringe of the great belt of bushland that stretched westward to the haunches of the Rockies, with the inviting gap of the Yellowhead Pass (which Sandford Fleming long before had declared to be the most economic route to the Pacific) a mere 130 miles away. But Mackenzie and Mann were not to be diverted by such temptation; grain does not grow on glaciers, nor do herds fatten above the snow line. They had serious business awaiting them in Saskatchewan, for there the Qu'Appelle, Long Lake and Saskatchewan Railroad was on the market. (It will be remembered that Mann had worked on its construction.) It was 249 miles in length, between Regina (whose original name was Pile of Bones because of the huge heaps of buffalo skeletons left there by the pemmican hunters) and Prince Albert, which had exchanged its Indian for a royal name when it became one of the earliest and most attractive of the European settlements. This line ran north and south and was a bit of a mess as railways went; from 1896 onward, the Canadian Pacific had operated it at cost for its British owners. On the other hand, it traversed a fertile area and it possessed a thumping land grant of 1,678,000 acres. At the turn of the century an American group bought half of its land at the absurd price of $1 per acre. Within two years this same land was selling for $12 an acre. Three thousand families were settled along its route, and its traffic was thickening week by week.

Nevertheless, its proprietors wished to dispose of it, but not of the remainder of the land grant. The Canadian Pacific then learned that there is no sentiment in business; despite its ten years of free service, it had neglected to file any legal claim or to make any arrangement with the line's owners. A minor offer was refused; whereafter, either in pique or in anger, the Canadian Pacific would not reconsider its bid. Mackenzie and Mann could scarcely understand this attitude, for its situation made the railway a perfect spine for short feeder ribs in central Saskatchewan. According to D. B. Hanna, they completely failed to live up to their reputation, for they visited Sir Thomas Shaughnessy, president of the Canadian Pacific, told him that they recognized his prior claim and would not make

Winter survey crew, Mackenzie and Mann, 1904.

an offer without his consent. James J. Hill, however, was not bound by any such gentlemanly weakness and gave them stiff competition; eventually, however the railroad was knocked down to the Canadian Northern partners for $3,739,000. It proved an invaluable branch; in its first year it provided 6 million bushels of grain for conveyance to lakehead.

By 1906, there were 132 villages and towns on the prairies that would not have been there had it not been for the Canadian Northern Railway. Donald Mann in an expansive moment said that they held sixty thousand inhabitants, with as many more in their contiguous areas. As always, his estimates must be received with caution, but it seems certain that the method of inducing settlement by building railways in advance played a predominant role in the colonization of the prairies. Whatever their private profit (and subsequently it was revealed that they never made the killings in Canada that they did abroad), they had served their nation well. The basic statistics of their first decade tell their story:

	1897	1907
Trackage (miles)	124	2,640
Rolling stock		
locomotives	3	190
cars	87	7,279
Gross operating revenue	$27,129	$8,350,108
Operating surplus	$10,243	$2,926,034
Share capital	$200,000	$37,750,000

In that period, they had borrowed $129,944,602.18 and had contracted other liabilities of $13,561,240.77. Of this indebtedness about one-third was covered by various government guarantees. The remainder consisted of twenty-nine different stock or bond issues, of which two-thirds had been marketed in London and the remainder by the indefatigable Horne-Payne in New York and various European capitals. In all instances, the prospectuses had been plain statements of fact to which Mackenzie and Mann adhered to the letter. In addition, like George Stephen, they had interested local capital in their enterprises; as early as 1899, the Canadian Bank of Commerce had loaned them $3 million and in quite unprofessional fashion had boasted about it to a newspaper reporter. It was destined to prove the luckiest transaction that Mackenzie and Mann ever made.*

* For details of this transaction, see Chapter 15, pp. 272–80.

11

Consequences of a Bluff

In an earlier chapter, it has been recorded how in fifteen years of constant struggle Sir Henry Tyler and his talented henchman Sir Joseph Hickson had converted the Grand Trunk Railway from a dubious local enterprise into a compact system, handling substantial traffic between the American Middle West and the Atlantic seaboard. And how, when the United States economy collapsed, Tyler was shown the door and replaced by Sir Charles Rivers-Wilson, with Joseph Price, an able British railwayman, as his second-in-command. The London board of the Grand Trunk, having concluded that Canadians were ceasing to be British in their habits and were adopting American behavior and sentiments, also had decided to place their property under American management. To this end, Charles Melville Hays had been selected as general manager. He was given one rigid instruction—his job was not to aim at either a bigger or a better system but to earn dividends with the means at his command.

Rivers-Wilson had no railway background, but he was a wise and experienced administrator, of the type that was beginning to be recognized as the mainspring of the vast British colonial empire. He could be trusted to mind his own business and to see that his subordinates did the same. He was a product of the gentlemanly tradition who deemed it his duty to tell the truth as he saw it and to take full responsibility for his subordinates, defending them when necessary, sacrificing himself for them in extremity.

Sir Charles Rivers-Wilson,
chairman of the Grand Trunk
Railway, 1895–1909.

Such an attitude might have invited some degree of reciprocity. There is no evidence that he ever got it, either from Price or Hays.

Many Changes

In the first years of the new regime, neither of these officers was much more than a compliant executive. Rivers-Wilson stood in no awe of his London directors; not only could he outargue them, but he also could outstare them. He therefore spent much of his time in Canada putting many things to rights. The clouds attendant on the 1893 panic had begun to disperse, and a new and vigorous Canadian administration promised to make an end to the shoddy and makeshift accommodations that had masqueraded as government policy in the past. Change was in the air; Rivers-Wilson listened to advice, measured its value and acted without delay.

He began by instituting major innovations in operational routines. American-type rolling stock, such as thirty-ton freight cars, replaced the ten-ton Grand Trunk wagons. Larger and more powerful locomotives to haul heavier trains were ordered, with a consequent saving in double tracking. Air brakes were made compulsory. A number of projects designed to provide facilities for short-haul passenger traffic were canceled: electric tramways were bobbing up everywhere, and there were ten thousand bicycles on the streets of Toronto. On the other hand, both the Niagara Bridge and the Victoria Bridge at Montreal were double-tracked; leases of running rights over these structures soon earned more than $500,000 a year. The shrunken traffic consequent upon the panic of 1893 had driven all railways in the state of Michigan into cutthroat competition. By means of foreclosures, Rivers-Wilson executed a drastic financial organization of the seven Grand Trunk properties in that state, combining them into the Grand Trunk Western Railroad. Extensive improvements were placed in work on the Portland docks and on the Central Vermont Railroad; that group of lines then became in law what it had been in fact for many years—an element in the Grand Trunk system.

Rivers-Wilson Exalts Hays

The company immediately profited from these changes, which were aided by the rising tide of prosperity. In 1900, after thirteen years, the Grand Trunk paid dividends on its preference stocks. Since the change in management, Grand Trunk shares had risen in value by $65 million. Nevertheless, when the shareholders asked for common stock payments, they met with a blunt refusal. Nothing more would be paid, said Rivers-Wilson, until all current necessities had been satisfied.

He had a strong sense of public relations; he wished the Grand Trunk to acquire an identity and a personality. To this end he claimed nothing for himself but made much of his subordinate. He apparently had been impressed by Van Horne's vault into the public eye and he was prepared to fight fire with fire, confronting American with American, if the Canadians wanted it that way. He was not going to play it safe, to insist on British tactics and strategy if the Canadian Pacific had found a better way. Rivers-Wilson always made light of his own contributions. Every now and then he toured the system in style, but on such occasions he presented himself as a reigning monarch who never failed to remind his subjects that his prime minister was the man who mattered. These official visits, however, were not devoid of profit; after a week as guest of Philip D. Armour in Chicago, the Grand Trunk dressed-meat traffic increased by more than 46,000 tons in the following year.

Unfortunately Rivers-Wilson and Hays had little in common. In thought and in deed, as in intelligence and in behavior, they were as unlike as chalk and cheese. The Englishman was given to oblique approaches and well-calculated interventions; Hays prided himself on his ability to take a running broad jump into any situation and overwhelm the opposition. In his first essays in Grand Trunk management, he did not distinguish himself. The industrialization of Ontario was in full swing; at a semi-annual meeting, Rivers-Wilson had reported that during the previous year, 151 industries, ranging from coffins to pickles, had established factories beside Grand Trunk tracks. This traffic, however welcome, led to many prickly disputes; every plant manager was intent on obtaining preferential treatment for his raw material and his product. When it came to negotiating with such customers, Hays proved heavy-handed; on one occasion, he denounced the unreasonableness of Canadian shippers in an interview with a New York reporter. His lack of give-and-take on another occasion resulted in a court action, which the Grand Trunk lost—to the unconcealed joy of Ontarians. The honeymoon with the Grand Trunk, in any case, may have been nearly over, but Hays assuredly speeded its passing.

A Bluff Fails

In one particular, however, the president and his general manager saw eye to eye. Both realized that the new century had brought change and challenge in its train, that these were not years for holding one's own but for reaching beyond the horizon. The Grand Trunk had done well; it now carried about one-sixth of the general eastbound traffic of the American Middle West, including about one-fifth of the remunerative chilled-meats freight. But competitors were not standing still; reports of new routines, faster services, superior handling facilities, were coming in regularly. The overriding necessity was to search further afield, since without more long-haul traffic, increasing volumes would not compensate for higher costs of improved services.

To present any proposal for expansion to the London board would be asking for trouble. The company policy—Not Growth but Dividends—was unalterable. Hays therefore decided to lay a false trail in order to wring a concession from the Canadian Pacific Railway. In the spring of 1900, he dispatched survey crews and right-of-way buyers into Northern Wisconsin, where they ostensibly engaged on preliminaries for the extension of the Grand Trunk lines from Chicago into Manitoba. When these activities had been sufficiently advertised, Hays approached the Canadian Pacific and offered to exchange running rights over all Grand Trunk lines in eastern Canada for reciprocal privileges over the thousand miles of Canadian Pacific tracks that crossed the empty wilderness to the north of Lake Superior.

Thomas Shaughnessy, who had recently replaced Van Horne as president of the Canadian Pacific, was too cagey to be caught on such bait. He summarily rejected the offer. The London board was deeply shocked by Hays' action; Canadian Pacific acceptance would have represented a reversal of policy. Why, its members asked angrily, had they not been consulted? They believed that they had scotched this insane policy of plowing every cent of earnings into the growth of the system instead of rewarding the long-suffering shareholders. After weary years of waiting, dividends had been restored and nothing must be allowed to interfere with their continuance. Hays, therefore, was rapped sharply over the knuckles both for laying a false trail beyond Chicago and for his approach to the Canadian Pacific. He was told to stick to his knitting and to leave questions of high policy to the directors. As a result of this reprimand, in August of that year he resigned and took off into the United States.

Friendship at the Top

Such summary action shook the board. Its members had never dreamed that their general manager would take a difference of opinion so much to heart. Curiously enough, Rivers-Wilson remained relatively undisturbed; he saw Hays, whom he had so often lauded, off the premises with no more than perfunctory expressions of regret. There is considerable evidence that he did not expect his manager's departure to be permanent; no successor was appointed, and Rivers-Wilson spent the ensuing eighteen months establishing excellent relations with the Canadian Prime Minister. He and Laurier were birds of a feather, both with a good deal of the *grand seigneur* about them. The Prime Minister, in the eyes of the Englishman, was that rare bird in Canadian politics, an honest man and a gentleman. Laurier, for his part, saw Rivers-Wilson as a distinguished servant of the Empire, several cuts above such pushing and importunate fellows as Mackenzie and Mann. They became firm friends, and there seems little doubt that from then onwards they were much in each other's confidence. Rivers-Wilson emphasized that the Grand Trunk dare not neglect the West, and Laurier came to see that company as his favorite instrument in providing the second transcontinental service that the enlarged cereal belt demanded.

In 1902, Hays resumed office as general manager almost as abruptly as he had left eighteen months before. His return signified the success of Rivers-Wilson's labors; the board, impressed by their president's manifest intimacy with the Canadian Prime Minister, had agreed to a policy of expansion. During Hays' absence, Rivers-Wilson also had met Mackenzie and Mann. Unlike Laurier, he had been impressed by them; as a colonial official he knew how little accents and attitudes mattered when there was work to be done. This pair had the ball at their feet; why not play with them? They were seeking capital; Rivers-Wilson knew that he could help them to get it. By so doing, they could arrive at collaboration and perhaps in due course at association. He therefore instructed Hays to keep on friendly terms with them as prelude to future developments.

The Pranks of Fate

There now ensued an extraordinary series of mishaps, such as sometimes bedevil human aspirations on this unpredictable planet. During his previous incumbency, Hays had had no dealings with Laurier; there is no evidence that they even had met. But after Hays' return, Rivers-Wilson felt that he could entrust official negotiations to his general manager. At the first meeting with Hays, Laurier welcomed plans that seemed to be in harmony with his own; when he and Hays began to discuss developments on the prairies, the Prime Minister divulged that he had no great opinion of Mackenzie and Mann. This was entirely in keeping with Hays' line of thought; he wanted the Grand Trunk to go it alone. He therefore reported to Rivers-Wilson that the Canadian Northern partners were *personae non gratae* at Ottawa, that they were no more than promoters and contractors and that there would be little purpose in treating with them.

Shortly afterward, Hays encountered George A. Cox, who already has appeared in this narrative in connection with the takeover by the Grand Trunk of the Midland group of short lines.* He was now president of the Canadian Bank of Commerce, which, as also has been noted, had made substantial loans to the Canadian Northern. He therefore had a foot in both railway camps and his advice to Hays regarding Mackenzie and Mann was characteristic; he said, "Bluff them." The Grand Trunk should proceed as though already committed to a transcontinental railway; when the Canadian Northern partners realized that they would have to meet the competition of another system in what they regarded as peculiarly their own domain, they would hasten to come to terms. Such strategy appealed to Hays, and he recommended it to Rivers-Wilson.

The Grand Trunk president was loath to dampen his subordinate's enthusiasm, but he had grave doubts of the wisdom of attempting to play poker with Mackenzie and Mann. He felt they were more apt to mislead than to be misled. He asked Hays for details of what "the bluff" entailed.

* See Chapter 6, pp. 121–22.

Charles Melville Hays,
president, Grand Trunk Railway,
1905–12.

It proved to be nothing less than a plan for a complete transcontinental railway. It would take off from the Grand Trunk terminal at Callendar in northern Ontario and would traverse the Lake Superior wilderness about a hundred miles to the north of the Canadian Pacific, through an area that had been erroneously described as the Clay Belt; except for the first hundred miles there was no clay, and nowhere was there a belt. Thereafter, the route would descend into Winnipeg from the north and would cross the praries, following an original Sandford Fleming survey along what was then the northern fringe of the cereal zone. Beyond Edmonton, it would pass through the Yellowhead gap and continue across the British Columbia interior plateau to a Pacific terminus at Port Simpson, at the entrance to the Portland Canal.* This would bring Chinese and Japanese ports several hundred miles closer to Canada than the route through Vancouver, from which the Canadian Pacific operated its highly successful *Empress* liners to the Orient.

* Portland Canal is not a canal. It is a long, deep fjord that provides the boundary between British Columbia and Alaska.

"The Bluff" in Operation

On October 23, 1902, Hays called on the Prime Minister to advise him that the Grand Trunk board had approved his recommendations. Sir Wilfrid was delighted, for it afforded him an opportunity to escape from an embarrassing provincial commitment. For many years, there had been agitation by Colonel Church, an American geographer turned British imperialist, for a railway to be built across the high latitudes of Canada as part of an All-Red Route, a British encirclement of the globe. It was a lunatic project but it received considerable support from Quebec nationalists who viewed it as an enterprise that would serve both God and Mammon: the Church would carry the Cross and the tongue to whoever lived in those deep solitudes, and prospectors would be aided in their searches for the suspected but as yet unrevealed mineral wealth of the pre-Cambrian shield. Laurier, in the throes of organizing railway facilities for hordes of immigrants, could scarcely refuse his own province and his French-Canadian compatriots some share of the federal largesse, and so in 1900, he had consented to a subsidy for the Trans-Canada Railway, to be built from Roberval, 187 miles north of Quebec City, across bleak and uninhabited terrain for 400 miles to the foot of James Bay. It was the hope of the promoters that some miracle would supervene so that the line might be continued on to the Pacific coast. It had no traffic prospects whatsoever, and there was an immediate outcry (from beyond Quebec Province) at such wanton waste of public funds. Laurier, therefore saw the Grand Trunk in a rescue role. He would endeavor to persuade it to shift its eastern terminus from Callendar to Quebec City. This would increase the length of the Grand Trunk by 400 miles, but it would reduce the Trans-Canada subsidy and would be less liable to evoke criticism from the provinces. The Prime Minister, of course, had no inkling that the Grand Trunk proposals at this stage were no more than a false front to impress Mackenzie and Mann.

A Suggested Role for the Prime Minister

Rivers-Wilson, however, was conscious that his bluff might be called, and he anxiously asked Hays to give him an approximate cost of the project. Since for more than two-thirds of the projected route land grants would be virtually valueless, Hays reported that a federal subsidy of $16,000 a mile would be required, or upwards of $50 million in all. This was a

startling figure; suppose the government refused to play? Rivers-Wilson
had consented to the attempt to bluff Mackenzie and Mann, but he had
never dreamed of gambling with such a vast sum. Nor had he any particular wish to pit his wits against those of the Canadian Northern partners.
Again and again he urged Hays to cultivate them. When his general manager's counterarguments were no better than excuses, he did not hesitate
to tell him so. He finally hit upon a promising line of approach, and on
February 3, 1905, he wrote to Hays, "I think that Sir Wilfrid Laurier
would be well-advised if he undertook the part of intermediary between
the Grand Trunk and Messrs. Mann and Mackenzie. . . . The moment
seems opportune for the handling of the matter by Sir Wilfrid as the 'honest broker.' "

Laurier and George A. Cox therefore, were of like mind, and
although there is no documentary proof, it seems highly probable that the
latter conveyed the Prime Minister's views to the Canadian Northern
partners. They would seem to have had effect, for in mid-February of that
year, William Mackenzie arrived in London unheralded and immediately
called at Grand Trunk headquarters in Dashwood House. He had come
prepared to negotiate, and he bore letters from prominent politicians,
promising that he would receive the same measure of federal aid as the
Grand Trunk in any transcontinental venture. Certainly no government
would be mad enough to subsidize two railways to build thousands of
miles of parallel trackage in order that they might fight each other.

Then blind chance intervened again. Rivers-Wilson had not been
advised of the impending visit and was on holiday on the Riviera. Mackenzie was not prepared to deal with anyone else, nor would he impart
any details of his mission. Indeed, it is difficult to escape the conclusion
that he was simply going through the motions of an approach to the
Grand Trunk in order to satisfy the Prime Minister. As Rivers-Wilson
said afterward, he would have been back by special train overnight had
he known that Mackenzie was in London. As it was, that gentleman
returned to Canada empty-handed after what he later described as "a
week of waiting."

Complete Impasse

Immediately on Mackenzie's return to Canada the Prime Minister
summoned him to make a report. Once again, there is no documentary
record, but it seems certain that Mackenzie gave Laurier the impression

that his approaches to Rivers-Wilson and the London board had been fruitless. The Prime Minister refused to accept this as conclusive and demanded that negotiations be resumed. Whereupon Mackenzie, Mann and Lash called on Hays in Montreal. They were sure of themselves; the most that they were prepared to offer was participation in a holding company for the construction of the transcontinental railway. As Hays correctly reported to Rivers-Wilson, their offer meant nothing at all.

Sir Wilfrid would not be denied and insisted on further discussions. Mann and Hays met on several occasions, each of which degenerated into a snarling session; the two, so much alike, loathed each other. Mann said he was prepared to sell the Canadian Northern to the Grand Trunk for $30,000 a mile, which was about twice what it had cost to build; his only other proposal was that the Canadian Northern would stay out of the East if the Grand Trunk would stay out of the West. It was a "thank-you-for-nothing" offer.

Laurier Grows Critical

These fruitless exchanges served to damage the Grand Trunk in the eyes of the Prime Minister. It seems probable that from one source or another he learned that that company's first offer was insincere and that he had been used as a stalking horse. Although he and Rivers-Wilson remained on friendly terms, he no longer distinguished between him and other railwaymen when it came to business. He was sick of all of them. They had got him into serious trouble not only with his province but also with his party. No sooner had the Grand Trunk accepted the switch of its eastern terminal from Callendar to Quebec City than the New Brunswickers gave tongue. They demanded that the new transcontinental railway should erase the infamy of the Intercolonial, which they claimed had been built by a roundabout route. This was complete nonsense; the new line that the New Brunswickers sought across the provincial diagonal was only 22 miles shorter than the Intercolonial, and for 125 miles the two railways were destined to run almost within sight of each other. Sir Wilfrid Laurier, exalted as no other Canadian Prime Minister either before or since by his personal triumphs through the Diamond Jubilee, the institution of Imperial Preference and Canadian participation in the South African War, certainly was in a position to ignore such a crass manifestation of sectionism, but it constituted a characteristic example of an attitude that is to be found in Canada to this day.

Divided Counsels

There was no mention, however, of the New Brunswick demands when on March 31, 1903, the enabling bill for the transcontinental railway was introduced in the House of Commons. In its seven years of office, the Liberal Party had never been so divided. No one liked the terms of partnership with the Grand Trunk, and at least half of Laurier's cabinet objected to the principle of it; the project, they maintained, was monstrously distended by the extension to Quebec City and would require so much official aid that it would be wiser to go the whole hog and build it as a government-owned system. But others, remembering the horrible example of the Intercolonial Railway, wished the administration to take no responsibility for it beyond the initial and inevitable subsidy. There was one cabinet member, however, who dissented from both these views. Clifford Sifton, whose outstanding achievements in attracting settlers had made the railway necessary, declared that the government should compel the Grand Trunk and the Canadian Northern to associate. Treat their principals like quarrelsome children, he urged; knock their heads together, lock them in a room on bread and water until they came to their senses and agreed to pull together for the good of the nation.

Meanwhile, Rivers-Wilson was enduring the full consequences of his consent to the bluff. At Ottawa, Hays was completely out of hand, making promises and accepting government proposals as though he owned the Grand Trunk. In London, however, the board of directors was furious at having been enticed into what they regarded as an unpredictable project. They bade Rivers-Wilson hasten to Ottawa and do what he could to redeem the situation. On arrival in the Canadian capital, the Grand Trunk president was told bluntly by the chairman of the Select Committee of the House of Commons that it was intolerable for Hays to give an assurance in Ottawa and promptly to have it denied in London. The company must make up its mind. Either it must consent to partnership with the government on agreed terms or it must abandon the venture.

The Grand Trunk Offer

When a gentleman is caught bluffing, he does not upset the card table; he plays on and accepts the consequences of his action. Rivers-Wilson therefore sat down with Hays to work out a detailed offer. On May 26, it was placed before the Prime Minister. For the Quebec City–

Winnipeg section (1,350 miles), the Grand Trunk would require a subsidy of $6,400 a mile together with the guarantee of construction bonds
to a maximum of $20,000 a mile. On the Winnipeg-Edmonton section
(793 miles), it would expect the same subsidies or other aid as might be
extended to Mackenzie and Mann or other competitors. From Edmonton
to a Pacific terminal (approximately 950 miles), the subsidy must be
increased to $10,000 a mile and the construction bonds guarantee to
$25,000 a mile.

Acceptance of this proposal would bring the official commitment to
a maximum of between $75 million and $100 million for the new
transcontinental railway. This was more or less what the Canadian Pacific
had cost, a circumstance that sparked a new uproar. The Canadian
Pacific had been built to bring British Columbia into Confederation; was
a similar investment necessary to ensure the loyalty of Clifford Sifton's
hordes of immigrants? Or was this just another instance of big ideas in
the West, with the easterners paying for them?

Harsh Terms

As the split in the Liberal Party widened, Laurier realized that he
could save the situation only by cracking the whip, not only over his
disgruntled supporters but over the Grand Trunk. On May 29, he tabled
an entirely different proposal. The Grand Trunk Pacific Railway Company would be formed as a wholly owned subsidiary of the parent company. It would build the Eastern Division (Moncton-Winnipeg, 2,019
miles) on behalf of the Dominion government, from whom it would lease
the line for operation. It would build the Western Division (Winnipeg-
Pacific terminal, 1,743 miles) on its own account. The two divisions
would constitute the National Transcontinental Railway.

Under this plan, the Dominion government would be the dominant
partner. Its conditions of association were severe. The Grand Trunk would
be required to deposit $5 million as surety against breach of contract
and also would undertake to subscribe $25 million in the shares of its
subsidiary, giving an undertaking not to dispose of such stock. (The first
of these stipulations afterward was withdrawn.) There would be no
federal cash subsidies for the Western Division, and its guarantees on
construction bonds would be restricted to a maximum of $9,750 on the
prairies and $22,500 in the mountain sections. The company must under-
take not to route any of its eastbound traffic over its New England lines
to Portland unless the shippers specified this route. Finally, the Grand

Trunk Pacific would build the Eastern Division under the supervision of four federal government commissioners. If Rivers-Wilson had read Sandford Fleming's book on his experiences with such gentry in the construction of the Intercolonial Railway, his blood must have run cold on encountering this proviso.*

On presentation of these terms confusion reigned. Everyone was at sixes and sevens. The Prime Minister had set out to beat down the rising tide of revolt among his followers and to reconcile the divergent views of his ministers, his party, his province and the remainder of Canada. His most vehement critics, curiously enough, were Quebec and New Brunswick politicians whose insistence on 900 miles of unnecessary construction had fouled up the project almost beyond rescue. With illogic indistinguishable from impudence, they insisted that the Grand Trunk had diddled the people of Canada into paying for the Eastern Division.

In London, Rivers-Wilson was thunderstruck by what he could only regard as savage terms. He immediately instructed Hays to report in detail on what protection the Grand Trunk might expect in event of failure to meet such onerous conditions. It was a fair question to which he never was able to obtain a straight answer. Hays was determined that the Grand Trunk would undertake the transcontinental project, whatever its costs and risk; he also knew that Laurier was under extreme political pressure and as a consequence would not be in an accommodating mood. He therefore replied to Rivers-Wilson's repeated inquiries extemporaneously, bidding him be of good cheer and stand fast by the project; he also warned him that Mackenzie and Mann were in Ottawa, waiting to pounce should the Grand Trunk falter. The latter statement was untrue. Laurier and his ministers regarded the Canadian Northern partners as no more than new boys on the make, lacking the stature to demand or obtain anything of more than local importance.

The Moment of Truth

Rivers-Wilson's decision therefore resolved into two bald and brutal alternatives. Should he behave like a business man or a gentleman? He felt in his bones that the new government terms would place the Grand Trunk in jeopardy; they introduced too many intermediate and unpredictable factors. Moreover, they riveted anew the irons of official cooperation and political interference, which had hobbled the company in its

* See Chapter 5, pp. 90–94.

first quarter-century. Every instinct urged him to a flat refusal of Laurier's terms. But to withdraw would be to disown Hays, to whom he had entrusted the negotiations. Worse still, it would betray the Prime Minister, who had chosen the Grand Trunk as his instrument. On July 24, he cabled a reluctantly worded acceptance of the government's proposals.

A week later the National Transcontinental Railway Company Bill was tabled. To Laurier's astonishment, the concessions he had imposed upon the Grand Trunk were not exacting enough to satisfy substantial sections either of the Opposition or of his own supporters. Both sides of the House considered the undertaking to be too much of a gamble and too expensive; they would have preferred either to delay or reduce its scope. R. L. Borden, the leader of the Opposition, presented a plan that re-echoed Sifton's advice to compel the Grand Trunk and the Canadian Northern to cooperate. The Intercolonial could be extended westward from Montreal to the Great Lakes; the Canadian Pacific would be expropriated for a thousand miles across the head of Lake Superior, and running rights over its tracks would be leased to all railways on the prairies and in British Columbia, the Grand Trunk and the Canadian Northern would divide the territory and arrange for the use of each other's trackage. It was a sensible but probably unworkable proposal.

Laurier, in defense of the measure, fell far below his usual standard. He dragged out some hoary chestnuts, such as Andrew Carnegie's campaign to compel Canada to drop Imperial Preference. He doubted whether the agreement with the Grand Trunk would cost the taxpayer more than a few million. In the debate that followed, the ties of party loyalty were badly frayed, but on September 2 the act became law by the hairline majority of six votes.

Why Did They Do It?

Two questions demand answers. Why did Laurier, a parliamentarian of unstained character, suddenly impose such harsh terms? Why did Rivers-Wilson, an exceptionally able administrator, accept them?

In the first case, the overall answer is that Laurier was not the man he had been at the inception of the negotiations. Joseph Schull puts it very well in his biography:

> [The Prime Minister] was not seen at his desk in the House so often and each time he appeared he was a greyer, more harried man. The doubts of Rivers-Wilson, the blustering and conniving of Hays, the still unresting manoeuvres of Mackenzie and Mann, all had

descended on him in a thick smother of feuds and competing interests. He emerged from it three months later with little left as intended and everything left to explain.[1]

In those months, Laurier undoubtedly had succumbed to two illusions. He believed that to save his administration he must reunite his party, divided between those who believed in public ownership and those who considered railways as much a curse to politicians as politicians were to railways. He was too honest to realize that if it came to a crunch, such an issue would weigh little in comparison with the desire to stay in power; indeed, only one member of his party felt impelled to resign as a protest against the Grand Trunk contract. Laurier likewise was in error in forgetting that, as head of a federal administration, he constantly would be subjected to sectional pressures on such a major item as railways and that it would be almost impossible to avoid compromises and exactions. As a man of great integrity he was obliged to resort to gross and harsh expedients to satisfy his followers, and as a great Imperial figure he set the largest single British overseas investment on the road to ruin.

As for Rivers-Wilson, the Grand Trunk president made a fatal error in allowing Hays any latitude in his negotiations with the Canadian government. The general manager, a first-class operating railwayman, was entirely out of his depth in matters of high finance and in administering a partnership between a privately owned corporation and an official authority.

He undoubtedly believed that he could capitalize on the shortcomings of both parties—Canadian politicians' ignorance of railways, British businessmen's ignorance of Canadian politicians. He had succumbed to the enthusiasm and aspirations of a new era; he considered that Rivers-Wilson and his board were living in the past and that for Canadian politicians the sky was the limit. He was wrong on both counts, but he felt justified in feeding soothing syrup to both parties, even if it involved misrepresentations and at times deliberate falsehoods. Nor was he unmindful of his personal interests; out of a very similar Canadian railway project, two fellow Americans had emerged, one with a knighthood and the other in the House of Lords. He therefore had everything to gain by reconciling by any available means the divergent attitudes of the London fuddyduddies and the Canadian Jacks-in-office. So his thoughts may have run.

A month after the National Transcontinental Act had passed, Rivers-Wilson faced an angry shareholders' meeting. He made no attempt to defend himself; he admitted that he had far exceeded the wishes of the board. He plainly clung to the hope that sooner or later there would occur some conjunction of the interests of the Grand Trunk and of Mackenzie and Mann and that a joint approach would secure some amelioration of the exacting terms of contract with the federal government.

He was soon to be disillusioned. In November, Laurier, still smarting over the rebellion in his ranks and under the outspoken protests of prominent easterners (who saw no sense and a lot of expense in a second transcontinental railway), sent for Hays and told him that now that the act was on the statute books, there must be no more dallying or attempts at circumvention. The Grand Trunk must accept the law to its last comma or else drop the project forthwith. On receipt of this ultimatum the London board to a man was in favor of telling the Canadian Prime Minister what he could do with his legislation. But again Rivers-Wilson met them head on, invoking the sahib's code: Laurier and his government, soon to face the electorate, must not be deserted in their hour of need. His directors sullenly accepted his view and agreed to await the results of the election.

The Triumph of Hays

Meanwhile Hays had benefited from the advice of Lewis Seargeant, who emerged from retirement to assure the general manager that Canadian governments seldom meant what they said or said what they meant. He thought that a rupture of relations should be avoided and that Hays should adopt a nibbling policy, seeking small concessions that if refused should be followed up by other requests. At this juncture William Mackenzie made a major miscue. He deemed the moment auspicious to call on the Prime Minister and inform him that powerful British banking interests would support the Canadian Northern in preference to the Grand Trunk. At this attempt to knife a competitor, Laurier lost his temper and all but threw Mackenzie down the stairs, declaring that he and his partner already had all they would ever get from the government, whatever the results of the Grand Trunk negotiations.

This rebuff brought fresh hope to the London board. Hays was summoned hastily and instructed to draft a memorandum for submission to the Canadian Prime Minister. Because of what it tells of Hays, the first paragraph deserves to be quoted:

> You must regard the Grand Trunk and the Grand Trunk Pacific as one and the same "sandy-haired boy" for purposes of finance. Yet

the Grand Trunk is made to take a back seat all along the line. . . .
Our backs by conceivable circumstance may be broken. . . . In
point of fact the [Canadian] Government is carrying on their shoulders
none of the risks and are playing with us the game of "Heads-I-Win-
Tails-You-Lose." Sir Wilfrid Laurier must be made to understand
that we must go to our shareholders with an agreement which on the
face of it can be justified. We cannot go to them and say "Here is an
agreement which may be the death of us if the other party to it does
not give a reprieve."[2]

This homespun appreciation of the situation, with its deliberate accusation of sharp practice, certainly would have put an end to the negotiations if laid before the Prime Minister. The Grand Trunk board again
was in favor of writing *finis* to what it regarded as a thoroughly bad
transaction, but again Rivers-Wilson dissuaded it from immediate action.
Instead, Hays was invited to address the shareholders at the impending
annual meeting. On March 8, 1904, he faced a large and stony-faced
gathering. Rivers-Wilson opened the proceedings with a stalwart defense
of Hays' role in the negotiations. The general manager then took the floor.

The English outlook is a strange amalgam of pragmatism ("taking
a bash at it") and of sentimentality. It grumbles at prosperity and
rejoices in adversity, but if something invokes the lyric strain, almost
anything may happen. Hays spoke at length, in the terms and idiom of
his undelivered memorandum. It was a simple down-to-earth appeal. He
declared that, whether they liked it or not, the proprietors of the Grand
Trunk had no option but to press on with the transcontinental project in
partnership with the Canadian government. He ended with a skillfully
juxtaposed summary: "The question is not what is going to happen to you
if you adopt this enterprise," he said. "It is what is going to happen to
you if you do not adopt it."

The shareholders reacted as to a bugle call. Dozens clamored for
the floor, each with some variety of the demand "We go on." One member
was cheered to the echo when he declared that if the Grand Trunk
management had been what it should have been, it would have built a
transcontinental railway before the Canadian Pacific got around to it.
A fighting spark had been blown into a flame, and in an hour Hays subordinate had become Hays dominant. The shareholders would follow wherever he led them.

The Partnership as an Election Issue

The ensuing election was certain to center around the railway issue. At the spring session, Laurie introduced a revised contract with the Grand Trunk under the description of the National Transcontinental Bill. Brickbats immediately began to fly; the majority of blows were below the belt: A new low in defamation was achieved by a member of Parliament when he compared Rivers-Wilson, who had risked everything in a quixotic determination to keep faith, with Whitaker Wright, a swindler who had committed suicide in the dock on conviction at the Old Bailey. The aim of virtually all spokesmen in the debate was to record in Hansard views that would serve as ammunition on the stump. After a spate of speeches that probably sounded no better than they read, the railway bill became law in July by a substantial majority. Whereafter the House adjourned, and both parties whetted their knives for the in fighting of the autumn campaign.

The Conspiracy

There then ensued the extraordinary incident that has passed into Canadian political folklore under the description of the Election Conspiracy. A group of wealthy and influential easterners, perhaps under the leadership of Hugh Graham, the dynamic founder of the *Montreal Daily Star,* had agreed to cooperate, not quite as a secret society and not quite as a private club, in matters of common interest. They had progressed to the stage where they held midnight meetings, had adopted passwords and had assumed code names. For reasons of their own, they had decided that the defeat of the Laurier government would be desirable, and in anticipation of this event, they had formulated their own railway policy. It included the official purchase of all independent short lines in the Maritime Provinces and their absorption by the Intercolonial Railway. There would follow the similar acquisition of the Canadian Northern lines in the West. Both properties thereafter would be leased to the Canadian Pacific for management. The basic purpose, therefore, would seem to have been to keep both the Grand Trunk and the Canadian government out of the transcontinental railway business.

The active plot called for certain newspapers that normally supported the Liberal Party to declare on the eve of the election that they could no longer identify themselves with the government program. Their editors would issue manifestos to the effect that they were ratting on the party in the interest of the nation. This summary action was expected to stampede the electors.

It was a madcap scheme that never has been explained convincingly. It seems unlikely that either Thomas Shaughnessy, president of the Canadian Pacific, or R. L. Borden, leader of the Canadian Opposition, was privy to it. If it had any effect at all, it was in the opposite direction to what was intended, for the Liberals were returned with an increased majority, and the National Transcontinental Railway was under way. But before a sod had been turned, its future had been compromised by the legacy of mistrust that had accumulated during the protracted negotiations. The course of events had been something like the buildup of a Greek tragedy. Two honest men who stood above the crowd had attempted to deal justly with each other, but their efforts had been distorted and thwarted by the ignorance and malice of their followers.

From Sea to Sea

By any criterion, the building of the National Transcontinental Railway was a remarkable undertaking. With the exception of the Panama Canal, it was the greatest construction project of its time. It was sponsored by a partnership between the federal government and private enterprise, which, in the unfortunate context of Canadian politics, meant partnership with the party in power. As it could not be built within the lifetime of a single parliament, there was always the possibility that it would be inherited by those who previously had been duty bound to oppose it. In addition, it traversed seven of the nine of the Canadian provinces, all of which had railway programs of their own, which might conflict with those of the federal authority. There were manifest opportunities, therefore, for the project to stumble and thereafter to remain prostrate.

Organizational Difficulties

These general risks were augmented by many specific difficulties. It had been found impossible to adhere to the simplicity of the initial plan, wherein the Grand Trunk Pacific would build the Eastern Division for the Canadian government and thereafter lease it from its proprietors for operation, concurrently building the Western Division on its own account.

The final terms of partnership were anything but simple; indeed, they almost completely reversed the roles of the partners on the two divisions. In the East, the lease agreement would be based on the cost of the railway; it was therefore in the interests of the Grand Trunk Pacific as constructors to build the best possible line at the lowest possible price. But the federal government decided that it dare not put its fate in the hands of a private company by a partnership without recourse, and so it appointed a board of four commissioners as an overriding authority for management of the project. It had only been thirty years since Sandford Fleming had been bedeviled almost beyond endurance by similar appointments in the construction of the Intercolonial Railway; the ignorance, the political bias and the venality faithfully recorded in his history of that venture should have served as a warning to Sir Wilfrid Laurier. Unfortunately, the sad degeneration of the Prime Minister was revealed in his appointment of commissioners who faithfully reflected the same attitudes as those encountered by Fleming three decades before. A discredited ex-premier of Quebec, a banker, a manufacturer, and a grain dealer were selected as the final court of appeal in a vast technical project about which none of them knew anything.

Concurrently, there blew up a storm in Parliament against entrusting the entire construction of the Eastern Division to the Grand Trunk Pacific. That company undoubtedly would subcontract the work, but there was no assurance that it would choose the right people. It therefore was decided that the company would continue as chief supervisor, as in the terms of the original partnership, but that it would be compelled to tender in competition with other contractors for any sections that it wished to build. The awards of such contracts would be the duty of the Railway Commissioners. No one would appear to have given a thought to what might happen if the Grand Trunk Pacific as supervisor felt obliged to take action against itself as contractor.

Official Complications

Even before the survey parties went out, two extraneous circumstances added additional complications. Sir Wilfrid Laurier in the debate on the National Transcontinental Railway Bill had been foolish enough to quote estimates on the costs of the Eastern Division, of which approximately half traversed uncharted wilderness. It was obvious that his figures at best were no more than bad guesses, and his Minister of Railways hastened to correct them in calculations that virtually quintupled them.

As the operational lease by the Grand Trunk Pacific was to be based on 3 percent of the completed cost of the Eastern Division, Hays quite sensibly pointed out his concern at these divergent estimates and suggested that the supervisory authority of the Grand Trunk Pacific should be widened to cover the survey of the routes as well as standards of construction. He was promptly told in almost as many words to mind his own business. Such matters were the exclusive concern of the Railway Commissioners.

A further unsettling circumstance was the selection of Frank W. Morse as general manager of the Grand Trunk Pacific. He was a tough two-fisted American who had begun his railway career as a master mechanic. He never got much beyond that level of capacity. His policy was to get things done and damn the consequences. He knew nothing about negotiations nor Canadians nor politicians. He was another Hays, only more so. Laurier and most of the government figures who were compelled to deal with him found him odious.

The Surveys

On the Eastern Division, the terrain divided between the known and the unknown. Of the thirty-four survey parties who took to the field in the spring of 1905, those on the New Brunswick diagonal were the most fortunate. They managed to stake a direct route on a high specification (0.4 percent eastbound, 0.6 percent westbound maximum gradients, four degrees maximum curve) before the local politicians realized what was happening. "Up in heaven," said someone, "Sandford Fleming smiled."* As has been previously noted, the new railway ran parallel to the Intercolonial for 125 miles along the south bank of the St. Lawrence River. At Quebec, it crossed that great stream and headed in a dog's leg into the northwest, to La Tuque in the St. Maurice Valley. Thereafter it made its way through 300 miles of empty but accommodating countryside before plunging into monstrous terrain, empty wasteland as savage as any on the planet, where rocky ribs burst through the scanty soil as in a decayed skeleton and the intervening hollows held muskeg swamps which gulped down yardages of fill before providing firm footing for a roadbed. Thereafter, the morasses gave way to the great stony extrusions that barricaded the passage between Lake Superior and Hudson Bay. Finally, fertile ground and healthy growth heralded approaches to the prairies and offered a fair countryside into the line's terminal at Winnipeg.

* The speaker was anticipating events. Sir Sandford Fleming still was very much alive. He died in 1915.

Hazardous Passages

In all, there were 240 rivers to cross, as well as countless lakes
to be evaded. From the settled areas, the survey parties worked their way
up swift rivers to the prescribed latitude and began to run their traverses
to east and west. To keep to specification usually meant the intimate
examination of a zone of wilderness perhaps fifty miles in width. Thereafter, when a tentative location had been made, it usually proved to be
miles out of bearing with those of its neighbors, and to obtain linkups
required thrice-done work to be done once more. On one section of 358
miles, it took eighteen months and 9,156 miles of survey to reach a final
determination; between the Manitoba boundary and Lake Nipigon (112
miles), the survey alone cost $335,000 before an acceptable route had
been staked.

In the spring, the freshets took their toll of the supply canoes, which
were tracked by hand lines up swollen streams. If a party came to disaster,
no one might know of it for days or even weeks. Sometimes the pack
parties deserted, declaring the passage to be too dangerous. On such occasions, the survey groups lived as best they could on the sparse yields of
their areas until supplies reached them. In summer, bush fires blocked the
groups' advance and destroyed their food caches. There were plagues of
black flies and giant "bulldogs" (moose flies), which ate flesh and drank
blood, and such a smother of mosquitoes that it was necessary to work
with hands and faces coated with a mixture of tar and bacon grease.
There were no medical services: if a worker became seriously ill, the
rigors of his evacuation often were enough to kill him.

Yet the mind of man is such a strange amalgam that in the surveyors'
records and diaries no more than passing references are to be found to
such discomforts and dangers. Instead, the field notes are interspersed with
small intimate descriptions, not of a lonely and dangerous land, but of
wilderness that in due season could be tamed into a place of abode. Even
in the winter, when the crews worked in temperatures far below zero, in
snow six feet deep with no carrying crust, the rigors of the land and of the
season were taken as a challenge. Few quailed before them.

Trickery in the Tenders

In the spring of 1906, the sections on which determinative surveys
had been completed were put to tender. It then became unmistakably

Early Canadian-built passenger car, 1860.

apparent that the commissioners had been busily rounding up the right
people and charting the course to the contracts. They had ruled, even over
the protest of the Minister of Finance, that the cash deposits that accompanied the tenders should be sufficiently high to limit the competition.
Thus on nine of the twenty-two contracts, the commissioners had the right,
if they chose, to demand deposits of a million dollars or more. This
threat, which was never exercised against any of the right people, kept
the small fry from underfoot. As a result, six of the big contractors
received nine-tenths of the mileage; nine little fellows split up the
remainder between them. The Grand Trunk Pacific, which had tendered
on sixteen sections, was awarded five of them. On nine contracts, only
five firms tendered; on eleven, there were only two bidders, and only a
single firm put in a price on one contract. The tendering, therefore, represented a travesty of competition.

From this takeoff, the looting of the public purse proceeded apace.
The main contractors for the most part were no more than middlemen;
they subcontracted virtually everything at from 10 to 30 percent below
their tender prices. The subcontractors were allowed to estimate their own
quantities and to distribute unit prices to their own advantage. Thus on
Contract 18, the principal item was the removal of 655,400 cubic yards

of moss, enough to cover every yard of the contract to a depth of two feet over a width of twenty feet. The actual existing volume of moss proved to be 15,000 cubic yards, which meant that the unit price was paid on forty-four times the amount of the material removed. Similar tactics were followed on all classifications of material, and fortunes were made on borderline differentiations. Loose rock was entered as solid rock at three times the price to which it should have been entitled. Specifications were purposely indefinite; in one contract indurated clay was described as soil in which "a team of six good horses hauling a ten-inch plow could complete a furrow." There was no definition of what constituted "good horses" or a "ten-inch plow" or a "furrow." Another item that yielded fat profits was "overbreak"—rock that must be cleared away to obtain the prescribed face and slope of cuttings. Traditionally it represented about a 20 percent extra on contract rock work, but on the Eastern Division it frequently mounted to a 50 percent extra.

Many of the administrative officers and engineers of the Department of Railways and Canals were honest men and protested against this flagrant picking of the public pocket. On behalf of the Grand Trunk Pacific, Hays also protested, but not too much, for his company as subcontractor was behaving neither better nor worse than its fellows. In 1909, the Chief Government Engineer resigned, declaring that he could not countenance any longer the utter disregard of departmental regulations. By 1910, the greed and defiance of the contractors had mounted into an open scandal, and in the following year, when the Laurier government was obliged to seek re-election, the affairs of the National Transcontinental received full ventilation on the hustings. The Liberals were defeated, and the incoming Conservatives, under Prime Minister R. L. Borden, hastened to expose the iniquities of their predecessors. The former Board of Railway Commissioners disappeared overnight, and a Royal Commission was given the task of investigating and reporting on their malfeasances.

The Commission's Findings

In this investigation, the affairs of the Eastern Division for the first time came under neutral technical examination, for Colonel R. W. Leonard, who headed the investigation, was a well-known railway and hydroelectric authority. In addition, none of the members of the Royal Commission had either political affiliations or aspirations. The ensuing investigation continued for over two years, and seldom in Canadian affairs has a final report presented a more damning indictment. The cost of the project to the Canadian taxpayer, given by Laurier at its inception as $13 million, had been increased by his Minister of Finance prior to tendering to $68,007,192. By 1908, this estimate had been written up to $114 million. In September 1911, with the line virtually complete, the actual cost was $161.3 million. In the opinion of the Royal Commissioners, approximately 43 percent, or nearly $70 million had been wasted or stolen. The stupid duplication of the New Brunswick section had cost $35 million; among thirty-three other documented instances of extravagance and unwarranted or dishonest practices, the restriction of tenders to the favored few, had resulted in an $8 million handout. Defective surveys cost another $8.6 million and improper classification of materials amounting to $3.6 million were other shameless jobberies. In inaccessible sections where road-building allowances had been made, such roads seldom were built. The contractor simply delayed completion until the steel had reached his section from one end or the other. On twenty-one contracts covering 1,804 miles, the accepted tenders had averaged $33,073 per mile. The completed cost had averaged $55,030 per mile.

The Superior Junction—Winnipeg Imbroglio

Long before completion, the Grand Trunk Pacific was paying a heavy price for its involvement in the construction of the Eastern Division. Hays and Laurier, to say nothing of their subordinates, were at daggers drawn. To do him justice, the Grand Trunk general manager knew how to build railways, and he did his best to exercise the supervisory capacity entrusted to him under the terms of the partnership. In reviewing his controversies with government officials, the Royal Commissioners described Hays' submissions as "absolutely unanswerable." When he offered to take over dilatory sections and complete them at prices far below the tender rates, he was told that such contracts were unalterable.

The most serious individual revelation of cross purposes, double dealing and open enmity concerned Contract 14, awarded to the Grand Trunk Pacific for 200 miles of branch line between Fort William at the head of Lake Superior and the main line at Superior Junction. This contract had been awarded to the Grand Trunk Pacific before it had been realized that it would allow that system to ship grain from western Canada to Atlantic export ports before the National Transcontinental line had been completed. This oversight was remedied in high-handed fashion by the cancellation of the Grand Trunk Pacific contract and a fresh call for tenders on terms that a Royal Commission described as a prize example of skullduggery. The second tender left 48 out of 101 items blank to be filled in at pleasure and thus effectively retarded the completion of the branch.

This so infuriated Frank W. Morse that he forgot his manners and protocol and addressed a blunt letter to the Prime Minister, virtually accusing him of participation in a swindle. This approach cost the Grand Trunk Pacific whatever friends it may have retained in official circles, but the offense had been too blatant for even such a distinguished diplomat as Sir Charles Rivers-Wilson to overlook; he spoke his mind at the Grand Trunk annual meeting in the autumn of 1909 in unmistakable terms: "During the last three or four years we have built some 1,200 miles of road, yet during this period the 245 miles that we need so badly has remained unfinished. . . . I saw Sir Wilfrid Laurier and told him that he had been badly served. That is absolutely the case." It seems possible that Rivers-Wilson's frank and angry comment, so unlike his usual courtesy, may have been the Prime Minister's first intimation of the shabby maneuver that had blocked the route of the Grand Trunk Pacific to the Great Lake ports. Undoubtedly because of Laurier's intervention and unmistakable demands the contractors in November of that year dispatched ten cars of wheat over an unballasted roadbed from Winnipeg to Superior Junction. On the strength of this shipment, Laurier announced in the House that this key section was in operation. It was nothing of the sort; in the following year the Government Engineer reported that the line still needed 300,000 cubic yards of fill and 100,000 cubic yards of ballast to bring it up to specification. Even when, in August of that year, the line was accepted as complete, various impediments (including a Mackenzie and Mann attempt to block entry into Winnipeg) prevented its use for regular operation until April 1911.

It is only fair to record, however, that, when in his last months in power, Sir Wilfrid Laurier learned that his officers were attempting to hold the Grand Trunk Pacific to ransom to compel it to take over the Eastern Division before it was ready for operation, he refused pointblank to countenance such shabby malpractices.

Summary of the Achievement

By the end of 1913, the Eastern Division, except for the bridging of the St. Lawrence at Quebec City, was complete.

Details of Construction

Rock removal	37,394,000 cubic yards
Common excavation	20,568,100 cubic yards
Train-hauled filling	32,633,500 cubic yards
Track ballast	6,229,200 cubic yards
Concrete masonry	691,000 cubic yards
Rail laying	252,000 tons
Bridging	61,000 tons
Ties (number)	5,400,000

During the summer of 1908, twenty-one thousand workers were engaged on construction, some in hospitable areas of easy access and others in the depths of the silent northland. To obtain access to many of the sections was in itself a costly and arduous task, involving the slashing of hundreds of miles of bush trails; the employment of fleets of small steamers, launches and canoes; the building of light railways around the portages and a narrow gauge line eighteen miles in length to bypass the rapids on the Nipigon River. In one section, a primitive monorail was employed, its platform tracks riding on central wheels, with its equilibrium maintained by attachments to horse or oxen yokes on either side. In the great, empty wilderness, no one could foresee what the next mile held or what the next day might bring. William Hard, writing in *Everybody's Magazine*, declared:

> It is a land where nature started to say something and stuttered a thousand times, an extraordinary region where there is one small landscape constantly shifting. . . . The workers are forever filing across shallow hollows, dodging lakes, jumping streams amid a glint of birch and poplar, through gloom of spruce and balsam, crossing the resilient moss of the muskeg on saplings or going through its surface up to the ankle and occasionally to the thigh.[1]

These workers were spared the knowledge they were in training for a deadlier ordeal. Before five years had passed, many of them were in France, again shifting materials on the 300 miles of battlefront from the Swiss border to the North Sea. The profusion of fire power had driven the combatants underground, and the First World War had resolved into a vast earth-moving operation in order to kill or to oust handfuls of enemies. In such a task, the Canadians came into their own, in some part at least because of the hard apprenticeships that they had served in their conquests of an obdurate wilderness.

The Drama of Two Great Bridges

Although the Eastern Division was complete save for less than 2,000 yards, five years would pass before this gap would be closed. In all, it took fourteen years to build a railway bridge across the St. Lawrence River. Its story is the tragedy of Theodore Cooper, a distinguished American engineering consultant who had dreamed a dream and would not be wakened from it. A cantilever bridge is a beautiful, sensitive structure in which the ends counterbalance the center. Cooper was obsessed by the belief that the British, who had been the principal bridge builders during the nineteenth century, put more weight into their bridges than was necessary. He never ceased to vent his scorn on the Firth of Forth Bridge, the first of the great cantilevers, declaring it had twice the steel in it that was necessary and that it had cost far too much to erect.

In 1898, the Railway Committee of the Privy Council had authorized the construction of a cantilever-type bridge across the St. Lawrence five miles upstream from Quebec City. A local company was formed, and Cooper was hired as consultant. He recommended a bridge that could be double-tracked to accommodate both trains and trams, as well as afford footpaths and driveways for walkers and horsed vehicles. The center or counterbalance span would be 1,800 feet in length, 90 feet longer than the main span of the Forth Bridge and about 60 percent lighter than that design.

In 1904, an order was placed with a Pennsylvania company that previously never had built such a structure. Cooper, who staked his professional reputation on this design, remained as consultant at a nominal fee—a concession that made it difficult to challenge his judgment. When the specification was circulated, a leading British engineer criticized it severely and the Chief Canadian Government Engineer asked for its re-examination. But Cooper chose to regard such doubts as reflections on his professional qualifications, and he was allowed to have his way.

Disaster upon Disaster

For three ensuing summers, construction continued uneventfully, and by August 1907, the work was well advanced on the central span. Some of Cooper's staff were far from happy over this portion of the structure, and their doubts were shared by the Caughnawaga Indian workmen, whose phenomenal sense of balance on high structures obtains them technical employment to this day. On August 27, Cooper refused an appeal from the resident engineer to suspend operations pending an investigation. Two days later, when a locomotive, a traveling crane and a load of steel were perched on the tip of the span, it collapsed. Seventy-four workers perished in the crash.

A Royal Commission, with perhaps justifiable compassion, let Cooper off lightly, although charges of criminal negligence were mooted. The Dominion government took over the project, and a committee composed of distinguished British, American and Canadian engineers agreed on a new design almost double the weight of the former bridge and employing nickeled steel for the first time in such structures. Work began in the spring of 1910 and continued for seven months in the year over the next six years. By May 1916, the approaches were complete and there remained only the emplacement of the central span that would link the cantilever arms. This span was 640 feet in length, weighed 4,701 tons, and had been assembled on shore and mounted on pontoons for towing into the central gap, where it would be raised into position by powerful jacks set in hoisting frames on the cantilever arms. On September 11, all roads led to the bridge site and a vast crowd gathered to witness the final scene. When the central structure was thirty feet above the water, a cruciform casting in a hoisting frame split, dropping the southwest corner of the span. In the words of an eyewitness, "the mass twisted on its side as though in pain and plunged to the bottom in a great cloud of spray. . . . Bodies were shaken down like apples from a tree, to fall splashing into

Central span of the Quebec Bridge collapses on September 11, 1916.

the river. One man fell from a great height like a mannikin or wooden doll."[2] Most of the workers were rescued, but ten men perished.

In that same September, the Canadian Corps had been committed to bloody fighting in the battle of the Somme. The mood of the country was grim, and the accident was accepted as a casualty to be replaced. The Dominion government ordered a duplicate span to the same specification to be built without delay. On September 17, 1917, it was hoisted into place without incident. Four weeks later the first train crossed and the Eastern Division of the National Transcontinental Railway at long last was complete.

Foreshadow of the Future

The Eastern Division represented an outlay of $169,090,125.55, which was more than twice the estimate on which the Grand Trunk Pacific had agreed to lease it at 3 percent per annum on its cost. Even though seven years' grace was allowed before the rental became compulsory, it was obvious that in the foreseeable future, this section of the National Transcontinental Railway could not earn enough to meet such a fee. In June 1915, therefore, Canadian Government Railways was organized under official auspices to operate the Eastern Division in conjunction with the Intercolonial Railway, which had picked up nearly a thousand miles of branch lines over the years. The Dominion government, therefore, controlled 4,500 miles of tracks in eastern Canada—approximately the same mileage as that operated by the Grand Trunk Railway both in Canada and the United States and considerably more than the trackage of either the Canadian Pacific or the Canadian Northern systems. Whether Canadians liked it or not, they were in the railway business and were destined to stay in it. From this nucleus Canadian National Railways was born.

Prospects in the West

Whatever arrangements were reached by the government and the Grand Trunk Pacific in dissolving their partnership on the Eastern Division, it remained amply apparent that the earnings of the new system must be drawn in large part from the 900 miles of the Western Division on the prairies. There, two rival systems already were in operation—the Canadian Pacific, with its traffic area along the international boundary, and the Canadian Northern, whose main line traversed the prairies on a parallel

Grand Trunk Pacific location party in the Rockies, 1912.

bearing 250 miles farther north. Intensive settlement promised to create sufficient traffic to warrant a third main line halfway between these systems, and this circumstance presented the Grand Trunk Pacific with a ready-made route. From Winnipeg to the western limits of the prairies at Wolf Creek, it might have been drawn with a ruler. For nearly all of this distance, it traversed what had been the northern fringe of the cereal zone before the development of Marquis wheat. It was a rich and fertile expanse, much of which might have been described as parkland rather than as bare prairie. Beyond a few rivers there were no obstacles. As a site for a railway, it assuredly was equal, if not superior, to the lands controlled by its rivals on either side.

The Takeoff

On August 29, 1905, at six o'clock in the morning, the first sod of the Western Division was turned near Carberry, 110 miles west of Winnipeg. Unlike the Mackenzie and Mann operations, there was virtually no improvisation or make-do in the Grand Trunk Pacific routines. They were highly organized by people who thoroughly knew their jobs. There were only four contractors on the entire 1,804 miles of route, and government intervention was restricted to ratification of standards of construction. Whereas the Canadian Northern had been in effect a colonization railway, and hence a fluid operation that created its own traffic by engaging in settlement schemes, improving its tracks and other fixed installations as funds became available, The Grand Trunk Pacific had only one immediate objective, which was to build a line up to the highest possible standards. There is considerable point to the story of a Canadian Pacific official who was dispatched to spy out the nature of the impending competition. On his return he was alleged to have reported, "The Canadian Northern has lots of traffic and no railway. The Grand Trunk has a good railway and no traffic. God help us if they ever get together."

Orderly Construction

Of the ten contracts, seven, which represented four-fifths of the total mileage, were awarded to a company that was a recognized master of its trade. The Foley brothers from Minnesota were well known in Canada by reason of their Canadian Pacific contracts. They now were joined by "Paddy" Welch of Spokane, an equally familiar figure in the Pacific Northwest, and by J. W. (Jack) Stewart, of whom more will be heard hereafter. Their work force was organized into units consisting of 120 men, each of which constituted a small mobile village, entrusted with the construction of a six mile subdivision on the prairies and lesser trackage in the bushland and in the mountains. These groups were self-contained, each with their own tools, vehicles and draft animals, and their routines were remarkable for their elimination of wasted effort. Their scraper teams, slowly moving in an unending circle, would cut a gash in a hump to build up a welt in an adjoining hollow. The graders would follow along to smooth and trim the roadbed. The culvert men would be far ahead, roofing over the runlets and the drainage ditches; the trestle gangs, with their wagons laden with timbers, would be still further in front, at work on temporary bridges over the streams and ravines. Following up, a work engine would chug forward, hauling a string of flatcars piled high with ties,* rails and fishplates, and pushing an extraordinary looking contraption whose high projecting booms gave it the profile of a praying mantis. This was the rail-layer, and its booms were served by two

* The British name of "sleepers" for ties has been retained in British Columbia.

troughs, which brought forward the ties and the rails—ties to be arranged in order across the roadbed, the rails dropped in succession and pinned down by holding spikes prior to fitting with fishplates, which were tightened by giant wrenches. Thereafter, the ties received the attention of the shovel gangs, who pried the ballast from under them until they snuggled firmly into it. To the onlooker, this last process seemed primitive, but nothing had been devised to improve it. In a ten-hour day of such routines, railhead would advance by at least two miles.

By the spring of 1906, the roadbed was far ahead of the superstructure because of shortage of labor and tardy deliveries of rails and ties. But by the end of 1907, railhead was nearing Saskatoon, where the Canadian Northern already had arrived. Morse had proposed to bypass the town, but local pressures compelled him to enter it in a rather roundabout fashion. A year later, the line reached Alberta, where the greatest of the bridges, fifty-four spans over the Battle River, was ready and waiting. Once again the tardy delivery of rails held up the advance, and it was not until the close of 1910 that the line was opened for traffic from Winnipeg to Wolf Creek, where the roadbed had been waiting for the steel for upwards of three years. The first Grand Trunk Pacific service from Edmonton to Winnipeg cut four hours from the running time of the Canadian Northern, an early intimation of its competitive ability.

An Outstanding Achievement

On the completion of the prairie section, Hays proclaimed with pride that it was the best-built long railway in North America.

The same locomotive therefore could haul three times the load on the Grand Trunk Pacific as on comparable American railroads and six times the load as on the Canadian Pacific.*

Despite the line's excellences, the cost of the prairie section did not greatly exceed estimates. The construction total came to $27,801,988, or $30,514 per mile. This was less than 20 percent above its anticipated cost five years before, although Hays had spent an extra million dollars equipping it with eighty-five-pound instead of sixty-five-pound rails.

---

* It is only fair to record that after the construction of the spiral tunnels on the Kicking Horse Pass, the Canadian Pacific improved its tractive capacity greatly, although not sufficiently to match that of the Grand Trunk Pacific.

Statistical Comparison of Leading North American Railroads

RAILWAYS	MAXIMUM GRADES (FEET PER MILE)		TRACTIVE RESISTANCE (POUNDS PER TON)	LOCOMOTIVE TRACTIVE CAPACITY (TONS)
	EASTBOUND	WESTBOUND		
Grand Trunk Pacific	21	26	16	1876
Great Northern (U.S.)	116	116	50	572
Northern Pacific (U.S.)	116	116	50	572
Union Pacific (U.S.)	116	105	50	572
Santa Fe (U.S.)	175	185	76	376
Canadian Pacific	237	116	96	298

Prairie construction on the Canadian Northern, 1905.

The Colonization Formula

The Canadian Pacific Railway as its christening gift had received 25 million acres of land in western Canada. Mackenzie and Mann by their clever, if devious, methods had come into possession of about 5 million acres. The Western Division of the Grand Trunk Pacific never received an acre of free land, but in 1906 Hays drove across the prairies by horse and buggy for 750 miles to gain a first-hand impression of the potential of the areas contiguous to the route of his railway. He forwarded an enthusiastic report to London, and in November of that year, the Grand Trunk Pacific Town and Development Company was incorporated. Its policy was the reverse of that of Mackenzie and Mann. It was not interested in bringing in farmers but in establishing along the railway towns and villages that would grow with the settlement of the countryside. For this purpose the railway bought eighty-six townsites at costs of from $12 to $15 an acre. They were laid out in a standard pattern, at distances of not under seven miles or over fifteen miles apart. They were named, in rather unenterprising fashion, in accordance with the sequence of the alphabet, from Atwater to Zelma, Allan to Zumbro, Bloom to Zenata. A newspaper, under the heading "Towns Made to Order," thus described their beginnings:

> "We will put down a town here," said the engineer in charge. The man who held the map put a spot on the sheet. Other men made marks on the ground. There was no ceremony—no one was there to applaud, no residents came out to shout, for there were no residents. These towns-to-be would grow up straight and orderly according to explicit instructions, just as babies are raised nowadays according to formula instead of by the old pot-luck methods of other days. Before the first settler arrived the streets were marked out and the parks were labeled, the stables put in a certain section, the market place determined upon. . . . The main street always runs down to the railway station. It is 80 feet wide and no building costing less than a $1000 can be erected on certain parts of it.[3]

Reasons for Success

In such positive and unromatic fashion did the Grand Trunk Pacific thumb its nose at the frontier tradition and insist on law and order from the start. The plan succeeded handsomely and for two reasons. Many immigrants, particularly those of British descent, preferred an address for their relatives at home to an unidentifiable location in the wilds. The elevator companies, who then were scouting the West for sites, also preferred a town with a name, even if it had nothing else, to a bare siding. Those structures, towering above the plains, proclaimed to settlers for many miles around that they were part of a community. Thus, before the countryside had built up the towns, the townsites were helping to populate it.

None of these made-to-measure settlements ever grew to greatness, but many of them flourished. As an example, Wainwright, nationally known today for its military training establishments and for its nearby bison park, was a spot on the sheet in 1906. But within two years it had some 450 inhabitants. Its main street was lined with shops; it boasted three churches, a weekly newspaper, a restaurant, a pool room, a quadrille club, a bowling league and a hockey team.

These new-born settlements obtained their share of the footloose fraternity that followed the frontier, those who were ready to pull up stakes and try their luck in a new stand at any rumor's beckon. Among them would be the respectables—clerks who had invested their savings in small stocks in order to set up in business for themselves, boarding-house keepers with twice as much space for guests to sleep on the floor as in beds, medical and law students looking for somewhere to hang out their first shingles, agricultural implement and insurance salesmen who had worn out their welcomes elsewhere with their pitches, God's shepherds hoping to round up new flocks. Almost matching them in numbers were the roustabouts, men of no trade or stock in trade, willing to try their hands at anything or to settle down and exhaust their credit while waiting for something to turn up. This mixture of true and debased human currency made these little communities fluid and unstable but there was life and laughter and generous good fellowship in them, which gave rise to the legend, long cherished by the panhandlers and floaters, that the easiest touch in all North America was the citizenry of the Canadian prairie towns.

The Branch Lines

As aftermath to the Grand Trunk Pacific's successful campaign to establish towns and villages along its route, a comprehensive plan of branch lines was authorized. On November 30, 1906, a company was formed with authority to build a total of 7,509 miles of feeders and secondary railways, or more than four times the total length of the main line. Its parent, the Grand Trunk Railway, subscribed $5 million as its capital. It envisaged the invasion of Canadian Pacific traffic territory in southern Manitoba, thirty-one different branch lines in Alberta and Saskatchewan, together with substantial ancilliary projects in eastern Canada and British Columbia.

This move to catch up with its competitors came too late. In Manitoba and British Columbia, the proposed charters were received by the provincial authorities with studied indifference and nothing came of them. In Alberta and Saskatchewan, thirteen branches, totaling 992 miles of tracks, were opened for operation during the period 1911–1917. Most of them provided entry into centers already served by the other main lines— Calgary, Prince Albert, Regina, Moose Jaw and Brandon. The proposed extensions in the Maritime Provinces and in Quebec were never built.

In September 1909, Sir Charles Rivers-Wilson addressed the Grand Trunk shareholders for the last time. For that brief afternoon his fears were forgotten. He had toured the prairies that summer, and he believed that whatever the fate of the Grand Trunk, it had well and truly served Canada. He recalled his old days in Egypt; the bounty of the Nile, he said, could yield nothing half so rich and rewarding as what he had seen in the Canadian West. He had taken the occasion of conversing with many of the settlers. He found them to be staunch and earnest folk, absorbed in the task of awakening a new land to its greatness.

Double Trouble

It was saddening that a project so superbly executed and so potentially promising should have failed to earn the esteem of those whom it served. To this mistrust and dislike almost everybody contributed, except the parent Grand Trunk Company, which had invested five times the amount of its original liability in an enterprise which it had entered reluctantly. The basis of the trouble lay in the march of the times. On September 1, 1905, the North West Territories of Assinaboia and Athabaska disappeared, to be replaced by the provinces of Alberta and Saskatchewan. Thereby the federal government relinquished control in many fields of authority to provincial legislative assemblies. The elected members of these bodies were as anxious as their neighbors in Manitoba and British Columbia to justify themselves to their constituents, and their federal members of Parliament to a considerable extent were competing with them for the favor of the electors. Thus was set the stage for triangular confrontations between the railway and the provincial and the federal governments.

In the last years of the long Liberal administration, when the Conservative Opposition with victory in view was whooping it up, Sir Wilfrid Laurier had so far departed from his previous integrity that on occasion he besought Hays to alter his location surveys to serve Liberal politicians. This was the sort of thing that the Grand Trunk general manager understood and appreciated. He was too brash and certain of himself to heed the sage conclusion voiced by Sir Henry Tyler some thirty years before, when Sir John A. Macdonald had behaved in a similar fashion. "In arguments with a government," said the Grand Trunk president, "private enterprise cannot win." Hays' appointment of Frank W. Morse proved an unmitigated disaster. This hard-driving American had much the same standards of conduct in the great open spaces as is shown to this day in Hollywood westerns. Hays scarcely could have been expected to choose as his chief subordinate anyone of higher caliber and finesse than himself. Tragedy, however, lay in his choice of F. W. Morse, who would seem to have behaved abominably on every conceivable occasion. Whatever the shortcomings of Canadians, they had inherited respect for contracts; as Bob Edwards once put it, "We like to do our cheating before we sign on the dotted line."* Morse and his principal officers made no reservations; contract or no contract, from date of arrival they outraged railwaymen and government officials alike. They refused to obey basic regulations, they disdained general orders and they denied mutual undertakings. The Canadian prairie was simply a Wilder West to them, where they suited their own convenience. They knew how to build railways and they scorned the people for whom they built them.

The Origin of Hostility

Morse and his underlings apparently expected prairie communities established before the advent of the railway to accept whatever the Grand Trunk Pacific chose to give them and not to argue the point. As a consequence, they did as they pleased, without reference to anyone. Despite an undertaking not to build within thirty miles of any existing main line,

* The *Calgary Eye Opener* and its editor Bob Edwards were famous in the early decades of this century. His raffish but acute comments were probably more repeated than any others; yet it cannot be determined which of those that remain were ex his columns or simply extempore. There is no copy or record of his files in Canada. Occasionally the *Eye Opener* came out blank, carrying the single comment "The editor is drunk this week." He and his sayings are a myth in Canada.

the Grand Trunk Pacific tracks ran virtually beside the Canadian Pacific right of way from Winnipeg to Portage la Prairie (fifty-five miles). At Fort William, the new railway masked the waterfront with a spur line, and community protests were ignored until legal action was taken. At Miniota, the highway was diverted without permission, and Morse refused to bridge a high cut on the approaches to that town. At Saskatoon, it established a cab rank monopoly and kept others at a distance from its station. In Alberta, eighty highways were crossed without obtaining the requisite permission, and at Edmonton, the Fort Saskatchewan Trail, one of the main exits of the city, was closed by the contractors. It took three years of protest and summary federal action to reopen it.

In view of such arrogant and provocative behavior, the prairie communities, remembering the easygoing and accommodating methods of Mackenzie and Mann, came to regard the Grand Trunk Pacific as a foreign interloper, contemptuous of the rights of local populations. In the federal election of 1908, these stupid, strong-arm incidents received a good deal of publicity, and Hays and Morse were foolish enough to make counteraccusations. The Liberals were returned to power but R. L. Borden, leader of the Conservative Opposition, took an early occasion after the election to announce that his party thereafter must regard the Grand Trunk Pacific as hostile, and the line would be treated accordingly when the Conservatives came into power. He had only three years to wait.

The British Columbia Section—Change of Terminal

As noted previously, Fort Simpson had been selected as the Pacific terminal of the railway. In 1903, however, a commission was appointed to adjudicate on disputed territory along the boundary between Alaska and British Columbia. The British member of the commission supported the American claims. His action aroused intense resentment in Canada and much more was said than was meant; but President Theodore Roosevelt, who recently had charged up San Juan Hill at the head of his Rough Riders, was not taking any nonsense from his neighbors, and he threatened to send an occupation force unless the Canadians ceased to clamor. As Fort Simpson was almost within cannonshot of the disputed territory, Sir Wilfrid Laurier, acting perhaps on the advice of the British Admiralty, ordered that the Grand Trunk Pacific terminal be moved to a more defensible location. An excellent harbor was found in the lee of an island twenty miles north of the mouth of the Skeena River. A competition gave it the name of Prince Rupert, which proved suitable, for that romantic figure had been an indefatigable adherent of lost causes.

Construction Begins from the West

In the autumn of 1908, in deference to the wishes of the premier of British Columbia, construction began eastward from the Pacific waterfront. For eighty-nine miles, the route followed the tidal flats of the Skeena until the estuary firmed up against the "Hole in the Wall" in the Coast Range that marked the beginning of the river's canyon. It was terrain as difficult as any in the world for railway builders obliged to keep within specifications. To follow the bed of the stream involved an endless series of sharp curves: to mount the hillsides created a succession of uneconomic up-and-down gradients. The surveyors ran 12,000 miles of line, the equivalent of seventy complete routes. In the canyon there was little earthwork; the roadbed was blasted out of almost solid rock, with more than 2 million charges of high explosive employed to clear the way. The rock drillers were lowered down the cliff sides on scaffoldings to drive holes, tamp down the dynamite, light the fuses and hurriedly scramble up the rock faces ahead the blasts. On the tidal section of the estuary, it was necessary to dyke long sections with cribbing and to bring in earth for its backing.

In the canyon, it took as much labor to build a work road as a roadbed. A small fleet of shallow draft paddlewheelers were brought down from the Bulkley River to distribute supplies on this section. There scarcely could have been a more hazardous passage; the river, pent in its gorge and fed by seasonal stormwater, gained pace until it cascaded through the "Hole in the Wall" at fifteen miles an hour. On many reaches it was necessary not only to winch these small steamers upstream with hawsers attached to iron shackles cemented into the cliffsides but also to control their return downstream by paying them out on cables. They covered the eighty-eight miles downstream in fourteen hours; it sometimes took them eight days to complete an upstream passage.

On the first hundred miles east of Prince Rupert, it was necessary to shift 12 million tons of earth and to blast away 4 million tons of cubic rock to shape a roadbed. The heroes of this epic task were the station men,* who perhaps for the last time asserted the domination of muscles over machines. In tight little groups, they took jobs of piece work that

---

* In the United States these station men were known as "tarriers," as in the folklore song "Drill, Ye Tarriers, Drill." This undoubtedly was a corruption of "terriers," whose habit of making the dirt fly around rabbit or woodchuck holes afforded some similarity to the labors of the stone-drillers. It was not a term in general use in Canada.

Mountain construction on the Grand Trunk Pacific, 1912.

might take a week or a month to complete and on which they might earn a modest pittance or nothing at all. William Hard in "Spiking Down an Empire" thus described a subcontractor's impressions of a typical crew headed by Swansie the Tireless Swede:

> I have a contract to do five miles of the road. I can hire men to work for me. Can I make them work? Yes, I can. But can I kill them? I cannot. I can try but they won't let me. The only man a man will let kill him is himself. Hence the station man.
>
> The station man goes and gets a bunch of fellows as dippy as himself and they make a gang, all equal partners. They come to me and say: "We will chew the rock out of this hill and chuck it into this mighty river for so many cents a cubic yard." I say: "Very well; get

busy." And do they? My dear old chap, ten station men will take out more rock in a month than twenty men, yes, sometimes more than thirty men, working for wages.

You see them working sometimes in the dark with banjo lamps, making you think the forest is on fire. And you always see them working all the time when it is light, from half-past two and three in the morning till nine and ten o'clock in the evening.

All the requisitions this particular fellow Swansie and his bunch ever made on the contractor for food supplies were for meat. Just meat. Why, just meat? "Got to work," says Swansie. No time to boil porridge or make bread. No time to suck water with a carrot or tomato flavour, which is all a vegetable is. Give him meat, every ounce the solid, right stuff. Dried meat, brined meat, smoked meat, canned meat, and if it comes fresh and raw, just gulp it like a dog. Total elapsed time preparing dinner—three minutes. Total elapsed time eating dinner, nothing. Eat it while driving the stone boat. "Got to work," says Swansie.

"Swansie's Men," Grand Trunk Pacific tunnel crew, 1912.
(COURTESY OF THE PUBLIC ARCHIVES OF CANADA)

After a few months when Swansie and his friends had red sores all over their legs and their feet are swollen up and there is blood in their eyes the contractor sends them down a barrel of lime juice (its the one best bet for scurvy). And says if they don't drink it he will take the job away from them.

And now the whole job is done. The cut is cut all the way through the hill. The contractor settles with them. He charges them so much and so much for all the dynamite and all the horses and all the hay and all the supplies of every kind which they have ordered from him, including the lime juice which they did not order. On the other hand, he credits them with so much per cubic yard for all the rock they have taken out.

How much does Swansie and his gang get? Twenty-four hundred dollars apiece, net, clear cash. Two of the fellows bought 160 acres apiece of Saskatchewan farmland. Fixed for life. Quitters. But not the rest of them. And particularly not Swansie. He is a railway builder. "Got to work."[4]

Such Herculean performances completed the Skeena section at a cost of $80,000 a mile. Today, despite all the machinery available, it is doubtful if it could be built for treble that price. By midsummer 1910, the steel had been laid for the first seventy miles. By autumn, it had reached the Kitselas Tunnel, but there it halted, for it took more than two years to pierce a granite casement 2,200 feet in thickness along the "Hole in the Wall." Beyond the tunnel the roadbed was ready, and sixty-three miles of tracks were laid in the Skeena canyon in sixty-four days. Construction through the Bulkley valley involved lessening hazards, but the work continued to be a pitched battle against obdurate terrain. Difficulties were encountered in bridging at Skeena Crossing (Mile 174) and Sealey Gulch (Mile 185), but by the end of 1912, the roadbed awaited the steel at Finnemore, the selected point of junction with the Rockies section, 416 miles east of Prince Rupert. This job should live in railway history.

The Route Through the Rockies

Both of the mountain sections were built by Foley, Welch and Stewart, and the failure of the eastern section to keep pace and to arrive at Finnemore on its due date could be attributed to circumstances beyond the contractors' control. Construction westward from Wolf Creek was held up in the first instance when Mackenzie and Mann, on the strength of an ancient charter, undertook to prevent the Grand Trunk Pacific from building through the Yellowhead Pass. This claim had no merit, but it

Rafting supplies on the Upper Fraser, Grand Trunk Pacific, 1912.

had to be settled before work could begin. Long trestles on the first hundred miles delayed completion of this section for fourteen months. Beyond the bushlands and on the approaches to the Athabaska River Valley, it became necessary to build a wagon road that continued for 200 miles through the pass to Tete Jaune Cache on the upper Fraser River. This supply line proved a difficult and expensive undertaking. It involved sling ferries over numerous rivers, corduroy roads over many miles of muskeg and the blasting of innumerable rocky obstacles. Along this trail, fifty construction camps were erected; in the first year of operation, 30,000 tons of provisions, tools and timbers were distributed. On the approach to the pass, the packers charged five cents a pound, irrespective of distance. In the pass and beyond it, however, their rate rose to $1 per ton per mile.

Despite the contractors' wide experience, they encountered unique problems on the approaches to the pass. At Brulé Lake, they were obliged to become gardeners: a fill of 117,000 cubic yards adjoined a cut of 87,000 cubic yards. The soil was friable, and the prevailing winds frolicked with it, blowing the fill into the cut and the cut into the fill at regular intervals. There was no nearby rock for surfacing, and so grass seed was bountifully sprinkled and watered until it rooted and provided protective sodding.

Near Jasper, beavers took strong exception to the emptying of a backwater that hampered construction of the roadbed. Whenever their dam was broken, they repaired it before the following dawn, and by the next noon, the water level had risen sufficiently to handicap the workers. Whereupon chivalry and not brute force prevailed: the route was relocated and the beavers remained as victors of the field.

In the Miette Canyon within the pass, sliding hillsides of greasy shales were almost impossible to stabilize except by long stretches of timbering and revetting. Nevertheless, by the end of 1912, the steel was approaching Tete Jaune Cache and the men of the camps on the completed sections were being transferred for 180 miles westward to the Prince George district. At that town the Fraser River became useful. It was unsafe for steamboats, but the camps were replenished by fleets of scows steered by long sweeps at bow and stern and afterward "tracked" back upstream by groups of rivermen harnessed to the tracking line by body slings. On this portion of the route, there were no less than thirty-two bridges across the Fraser. On the last of them at Prince George, the British Columbia government intervened, ostensibly to protect navigation, and a temporary structure was installed to get the rail layer across. The final fifty miles to junction with the western section at Finnemore were completed in a month. On April 7, 1914, the National Transcontinental Railway, nine years in the making, was open for traffic.

Prince Rupert—A Comedy

There only remained the construction of an ocean terminal. Prince Rupert lay on a group of tiny islands contiguous to the mainland. The only similarly situated city was Venice, which it did not resemble in the slightest. One early visitor described it as a mountainside that had slid piecemeal into the ocean. The provincial government offered 10,000 acres of shore to the railway company at $1 an acre, but most of this land was worthless. The Indian reserve, consisting of 13,519 acres that occupied most of the remainder of the group of islands, was purchased from the Dominion government at $2.50 an acre, but the provincial government

Prince Rupert, where the National Transcontinental Railway reached the Pacific.
(COURTESY OF THE PUBLIC ARCHIVES OF CANADA)

insisted that one-quarter of this land be reconveyed to it free of cost, apparently as a token of local sovereignty.

Company gangs arrived to clear the forest from the waterfront. As fast as the trees were felled, the land was grabbed by settlers who paid nothing for it nor acknowledged any prior claims to it. A Grand Trunk representative, who happened to be an American citizen, arrived and told the settlers that they were "squatters," a description that has none of the polite connotations in North America that it possesses in Australia. Whereupon a British Columbia politician known as "Fighting Joe" Martin arrived to rebuke the insolent Yankee and to incite the settlers to resistance. In addition John Houston, a notorious newspaper man from the Kootenay country, rolled into town to defend his compatriots. As the railway company was in effective occupation, Houston did not dare prosecute his campaign against it except from ground owned by the provincial government. He printed *The Empire* in a tent set in the middle of Center Street, kept his type in the provincial police station, stored his ink and paper in a private warehouse and wrote his copy in the bedroom of the provincial telegraph operator. Every issue breathed unshaking loyalty to the Crown and stern enmity to the British company that was endeavoring to oust honest Canadians from their native haunts.

The squatters, however, were dealt with summarily when settlement was launched by a well-publicized auction. *The Montreal Star* unkindly said that the map of Prince Rupert, which showed parks, plazas, boulevards, terraces and lovers lanes, belonged to the far, far distant future; that nothing short of magic would transform the stumpy clearings, the gullies, the rocky outcrops and the sinkholes into fit places to live. Any visitor, it went on to say, should come equipped with high watertight boots and be prepared to leg it untiringly over 3,000 acres of unkempt clearings.

This discouraging advice did not prevent the real estate fraternity from turning up in force. A representative of the Rothschilds was said to be present, and the bidding for town lots swiftly mounted into the thousands. The sale realized $1,140,060, and subsequent auctions at Vancouver and Victoria greatly increased this figure. The dream of tomorrow had bidden common sense begone.

Whereupon the ex-squatters, who still comprised the local citizenry apart from Grand Trunk Pacific employees, swiftly organized the Municipality of Prince Rupert and took the proceeds of the sales of town lots as basis for a municipal assessment roll of $15,330,166. They then presented the Grand Trunk Pacific with a bill for $100,000 for local taxes. There was scarcely one of them in legal occupation, but the railway company deemed it wise to tempt the town council with an offer of $15,000, which was instantly accepted.

Meanwhile, the port engineers had concentrated on the problem of shaping the natural features of the site into decent service. Long before the railway was open, quays, warehouses and shipyards were ready, with a drydock, a fish processing and a cold storage plant as the beginning of seaboard industries. All that was needed to add Prince Rupert to Vancouver, Seattle and San Francisco as a port of consequence on the North Pacific range was traffic. It never came. The average freighter could make three more trans-Pacific crossings in the year from Prince Rupert than from Vancouver, five more than from San Francisco. On the other hand, the land freight rates to eastern destinations were unfavorable, since Vancouver was 271 miles or 18 percent closer to Winnipeg. Prince Rupert's insuperable disadvantage, however, was that, as the northernmost harbor of the Pacific range of ports little or no outward cargo existed and it was a distant and expensive port of call. British shipping, which had formerly dominated the North Pacific, was in the process of being ousted by Japanese bottoms, which had little interest in shorter routes to and from Canada to the Orient.

The Grand Trunk Pacific, on the strength of a subsidy for carriage of mails to Queen Charlotte Islands, installed a coastal service that is still in existence but that handles little but casual traffic. Half a century later, Prince Rupert remains another outport and not the harbor crowded by stately steamers that its sponsors hoped it would be.

13

Mackenzie and Mann:
Canter to Gallop

In an earlier chapter,* it has been recorded that those brash and unabashed westerners William Mackenzie and Donald Mann had seized time by the forelock, and by a mixture of courage, chicanery, foresight and good salesmanship, had created in ten years a substantial railway property and had acquired an enviable rating in the principal money markets of the world. They had proved that they could build railways cheaply and expeditiously; they could command government support when they needed it; in legal and financial matters they were superbly served. They were meteors in the railway sky, and their first ten years seemed to forecast greater things to come.

Despite their apparent willingness to try anything, anywhere, they usually had been guided by certain basic reservations. They did not wish to embark on expansion beyond the prairies until they had consolidated their interests in that area. They were convinced that there they could meet their rivals on better than even terms, and, as a consequence, they would not hesitate to invade both Canadian Pacific and Grand Trunk Pacific traffic territories. They had estimated the 5,000 miles of lines which they controlled in Manitoba, Saskatchewan and Alberta to be an earning

* See Chapter 8, pp. 149–59.

nucleus that would warrant expansion to east and west and that eventually would create a transcontinental system.

In their first ten years, they had acquired 2,607 miles of tracks. It therefore would be necessary for them to double their prairie mileage or else abandon their target. As the years passed, it became obvious that although it might involve risks, they must stake out claims in other parts of Canada before their position on the prairies could be regarded as impregnable. The bulk traffic of Canada manifestly must remain in raw materials for many years to come, and the prairie area, despite its remarkable growth during the first decade of the century, could not support three competitors on the single bulk freight of grain. These central provinces could only provide one-way cargo, and no railway could prosper unless it had traffic in both directions. The only incoming bulk cargo to the prairies was lumber, which originated largely in British Columbia. This circumstance dictated a speeding up in Mackenzie and Mann's construction program, particularly toward the Pacific coast.

Growth of Canadian Wood Products Traffic

Around the turn of the century, there had been a substantial revival of demand for Canadian forest products. During the Napoleonic wars, when the Baltic was closed to British shipping, England had turned to Canada as a source of timber. Each spring, huge rafts, often many acres in extent, came down the St. Lawrence to be loaded for overseas destinations. This particular trade was of little account to the railways, for such timbers were too cumbersome for the handling facilities then available. But in the 1880s, the development of the sulphite process had cut the cost of newsprint and other rough papers to a quarter of its former figure, and there had ensued a vast outpouring of printed matter stimulated by the new techniques of advertising. Thereafter, pulp and paper became substantial freights, as did a wide range of secondary wood products. There therefore were traffic opportunities in this field, not only in the West but in eastern Canada, which Mackenzie and Mann were compelled to consider.

Mineral Prospects

An even more potent incentive to ignore caution and to embark on nationwide expansion without awaiting the insurance of prairie earning power came from a source to which Mackenzie and Mann never failed to cock listening ears. In the 1890s, the Canadian Government Geological

Survey had been reorganized and had attracted many able officers. Chief among them, perhaps, was Charles Camsell, who spent upwards of twenty years in exploring and reporting upon the mineral potentials of unsettled areas. Autumn by autumn, he returned from the wilderness with details of traces, and often more than traces, of the presence of merchantable minerals in the great empty expanses of the pre-Cambrian shield and elsewhere in the Canadian Arctic areas.

To Donald Mann in particular Camsell's reports were as good as wine; with the brilliant geologist Charles Price-Green at his elbow as comrade and advisor the railway builder saw Ophirs and Colcondas. He was incorrigibly optimistic; he believed that what did not come to him today would be waiting for him tomorrow. In most enterprises he was Mackenzie's faithful adjutant, but when it came to minerals he was a law unto himself and his partner became his subordinate. Both always were willing to listen to prospectors, to grub-stake them and to exploit any vestage of hope in finding the mother lodes that would make them rich men overnight. Not all their ventures are liquidated to this day; a firm in Toronto still keeps some of their speculations alive in the hope that they may yet pay off. No more ardent and unwearying fishermen in the bottomless sea of the land have ever existed, and neither their catches nor the ones that got away mitigated their passion for more and more quests. They made a few strikes, missed a few important discoveries by an eyelash and wasted a great deal of money on worthless holes in the ground. Their mineral gambles were their love affairs, in which every bad guess created the urge for another try and in which nothing was final.

William Mackenzie's interest in minerals centerd around those that promised heavy freights. He had no part in Mann's harebrained scheme to build a railway into the Yukon at the time of the Klondike gold rush, but he agreed to the opening of a gypsum property on Lake Manitoba which continues to supply tonnage to the Oak Point branch of Canadian National Railways to this day. In 1905, again on the strength of Camsell's reports, the partners formed a company to extract iron ore at Atikokan in northern Ontario, whence it could be shipped to Port Arthur for smelting. Here they missed fantastic fortunes by a hairbreadth, for the great Steep Rock ore body was proved within two miles of their original claims.

First Move in the East

The first real breach in the "Prairies First" policy occurred in 1902, when the James Bay Railway charter was picked up for a song because of its handsome endowments—$710,000 in cash, 875,000 acres of Crown lands. In 1905, it was transformed into the Canadian Northern Ontario Railway and its direction altered (by some deft legal footwork) from Hudson Bay to the Sudbury district, where a great find of nickel had been proved. This line was opened from Toronto in November 1906; when further strikes were made in the same area, short feeders were built to serve individual properties, and arrangements were placed in train for a port terminal on Georgian Bay. The project in all amounted to 335 miles of new trackage.

Prairie Attitudes Alter

Year by year, as the prairies filled up, the railways began to pay the price of individual, instead of collective, planning. With three competitors in the field, some flourishing areas were overserved, others were neglected. Moreover, the day was past when railways need only to ask and it would be given. Provincial subsidies and construction bond guarantees now were doled out sparingly and on fairly rigorous terms. The settlers now wanted more than trackage out of their railways; they demanded better services and lower rates, particularly on their grain. They had organized to get what they wanted and they made themselves heard. Bob Edwards, the homespun philosopher of the *Calgary Eye Opener,* declared that out of every hundred prairie boards of trade, ninety-nine had been organized to bedevil the railways.

William Mackenzie in later life stated that after 1905 he never built a branch line unless subjected to acute political pressures. The provinces saw no incongruity in their continuous pleas for more trackage and additional railway expenditures and their coincident complaints to the federal administration at Ottawa concerning the high costs of transportation. Under such circumstances the Mackenzie and Mann honeymoon with the prairie farmers had ended.

Impact of the 1907 Panic

While the frontier spirit was evaporating and the railway image was changing for the worse, there came the 1907 panic. Speculative stocks collapsed, and blue chip issues took a beating. For a full year the survival of Mackenzie and Mann could be attributed solely to the wizardry of R. M. Horne-Payne in London. His principals had borrowed or had accepted liabilities on acquired properties for a total of almost $150 million.

Their lines in operation were not earning nearly enough to meet the interest charges on such sums, and less than a third of their construction outlays were covered by the provincial bond guarantees. They had sold twenty-nine different bond or stock issues and had given them almost as many different names to evade priority problems—mortgage bonds, gold mortgage bonds, land grant bonds, income bonds, prior lien bonds, sinking fund gold bonds, consolidated debenture bonds, mortgage debenture stock, perpetual debenture stock, perpetual consolidated debenture stock. Yet in the City of London or in Zurich or in Amsterdam, when this incredible array was recited in accusation, Horne-Payne never failed to persuade the grumpy creditors to stand fast and to await the morrow. It is doubtful if any other man could have done as much.

By one device or another, Mackenzie and Mann weathered the depression. They stopped work on virtually all projects but managed to keep their programs intact, at times expending substantial sums out of their private pockets.* A Royal Commission, enrolled to report on the western grain trade, received no change at all from their spokesman, D. B. Hanna, who declared that intake and output always must govern a private enterprise. He quoted figures to show that the operational ratio on the prairies was steadily worsening; the Canadian Northern, he said, would be more than pleased to place all branch lines under provincial control if their records would be accepted as constituting proof of whether or not fresh construction or lower freight rates were most needed. Naturally everyone continued to grumble but shied away from such a forthright invitation.

The Emergence of the Grand Design

Fortunately the slump that followed the panic was of short duration. By the middle of 1909, the clamor was rising anew for more railways, and Horne-Payne reported that London and European markets were sanguine and receptive. Canadian Northern stocks, as well as bonds, would be marketable. Whereupon Mackenzie and Mann, feeling their hour to be upon them, launched their nationwide program. They would embark on projects from the Atlantic to the Pacific, all of which in due course would be cemented into the Canadian Northern mosaic. In 1910, they marketed fourteen issues of a total value of $129,617,187, or almost as much as they had borrowed in their first ten years of partnership. Of this great

---

* To an extraordinary extent Mackenzie and Mann lacked any sense of self-preservation in their financial affairs. They never adopted simple legal devices to protect their personal fortunes or the revenues of their prosperous properties against the inroads of their speculative ventures. It was all Canadian Northern money as far as they were concerned.

sum more than half consisted of stock issues, which meant that they were turning successfully from the bankers to the general public for their support. This daring gamble succeeded: in four years (1906–1910) the stock register of the Canadian Northern Railway increased from two thousand to thirty-six thousand shareholders.

This speedup from a canter to a gallop rose out of the realization that the Mackenzie and Mann entries in the railway stakes were turning the corner for the home stretch. It was now or never. It was typical of the partners that they gave no hint of desperation but that they mobilized every possible source of support for their entries. They knew exactly what they wanted. First of all, a transcontinental main line that could command its proportion of the long-haul, heavy-volume traffic that was the only sure source of continuous revenues. Secondly, they would attack their competitors by invading their most prosperous traffic areas. The common instrument in such invasions would be the loop line, which would take off and return to the same main line. Thirdly, they would exploit mineral areas to the hilt. In this field, coal held pride of place, for unless the earth's axis tilted, Canadians had to be kept warm for at least half the year; moreover coal was still the supreme source of power. Then they must never forget the northlands, for those vast areas soon must attract explorers and settlers and in due course become prime sources of traffic. Finally, they must find ways to break into the densely settled areas of Canada, which were still closed to them, for if they were to establish a Dominion-wide system, they could not afford to allow their competitors to monopolize any of the areas that constituted the present sources of heavy traffic.

The Maritime Provinces

Nothing could be more characteristic of Mackenzie and Mann than that at the turn of the century, when they apparently were engrossed in creating a favorable climate for their projects in Manitoba, they also should be engaged in a series of similar enterprises 2,200 miles to the east, along the stern and rock-bound coasts of Nova Scotia.

The story of the Intercolonial Railway, the fame and the shame of it, has been told in a previous chapter.* In such a rewarding field as railways, political and financial skullduggery was not restricted to the major enterprises; in the Maritime Provinces there were scores of subsidiary ventures, some almost honest in inception and some which in due course

* See Chapter 5, pp. 75–105.

might achieve economic stability. Confederation had created a source of financial manna which might fructify almost any project, however bleak its economic or social prospects, as long as it promised a commensurate yield on election day. At Ottawa there had been created a national cow which many Canadians believed to have bulging udders.

Nova Scotia Short Lines

By 1901, there were no fewer than fifteen different short lines in operation in various sections of Nova Scotia. In the words of the old British music hall catch, they were all dressed up with nowhere to go. Some were remnants of earlier attempts at grandeur; some had never expected more than local employment and support; some were snippets of trackage that would appear to have been built in moments of exuberance.

In 1898, while the Mackenzie and Mann partnership was in swaddling clothes, local, provincial and federal support had been enlisted for a railway along the north shore of Cape Breton, where extensive coal and gypsum measures existed. There Donald Mann in his personal capacity had obtained a contract for a line sixty miles in length, from the Strait of Canso to Inverness, the site of the coal mines, with the anticipation of extending it for another thirty miles to Cheticamp, where the gypsum lay. It was opened on June 1, 1901, and at the price of a small investment in the coal mines, the railway became a Mackenzie and Mann property. For six years it prospered and thereafter fell into disuse. Legally it came to be regarded not as a railway but as a coal mine. As a consequence it did not enter the Canadian National Railways stable until 1929, long after the liquidation of other Mackenzie and Mann interests.

In western Nova Scotia, there were more than a dozen railways sustained by little but local pride. Few of them had reached the destinations authorized by their charters. Some of them had been hardy perennials for over a quarter of a century in the matter of renewals of charters or appeals for provincial aid. There was really little necessity for any of them, for they all either began, ended at, or ran along the coast line, where small craft served the communities just as well and much more cheaply. However, for provincial governments of that day, a railway was like a jewel worn by a beautiful woman: it enhanced, and was enhanced by, its location. In 1901, the Nova Scotia Legislative Assembly, wearying of the annual parade of suppliants, offered to make financial advances to anyone who would undertake to link up these orphan lines. If the contractor afterward would buy them, the Legislative Assembly would loan the money for their purchase.

This was the sort of transaction Mackenzie and Mann never could resist—a customer willing to provide not only the eggs but the incubator. The provincial government loaned them $13,500 a mile either to build or to buy or both. The project involved the construction of three link-up lines totaling 246 miles and the purchase of four short lines (three in operation) with a combined 99 miles of tracks. The deal was completed early in 1907, and everyone would appear to have been satisfied. The outports kept their railways and Mackenzie and Mann profited sufficiently out of their operation to do something that they never did elsewhere at any time. They repaid in full the provincial advances.

No Offers in New Brunswick

No such luck, however, attended them in New Brunswick. It will be remembered from an earlier chapter* that in that province one of the first railways had been built by New Brunswickers themselves; thereafter they proved independent cattle in their dealings with promoters. Short lines multiplied until that province was cobwebbed with them; none of them ever made a profit, and few of them earned more than half their costs of operation. But in some manner or other, they were kept off the bargain counter, and eventually when they came on offer, they always were absorbed by the Intercolonial Railway, which was given no option but to accept them. Thus one lame dog after another was brought into the federal kennel, and gentlemen on the make like Mackenzie and Mann found no bargains.

The Intercolonial Disappointment

The New Brunswick short lines, however, were not a main objective. The Canadian Northern partners were intent on an ice-free Atlantic port terminal, such as their transcontinental competitors possessed. Mackenzie and Mann also were well versed in the rowdy and sinful history of the Intercolonial Railway, and they felt that they could anticipate unqualified support from other parts of Canada if they offered to take it over. But when they began to make inquiries, they discovered they were several years too late. The untiring labors of David Pottinger and Collingwood Schreiber together with the steadfast support of the Honorable A. G. Blair (whose initial housecleaning as Minister of Railways and Canals has been reported in an earlier chapter†) had made an end to

* See Chapter 3, pp. 18–33.
† See Chapter 5, pp. 75–105.

the traditional nepotism, patronage, political handouts and mismanagement. The Intercolonial now was being operated in proper fashion; passengers, whatever their political persuasion or family connections, paid their fares; local politicans carried no weight with the management. Indeed, to the astonishment of nearly everyone, the Intercolonial, as railways go, was a reformed character and a complete vindication of public ownership.

Nor was this all. When Sir Wilfrid Laurier began to think in terms of another transcontinental railway, he was told by many of his prominent supporters (as by virtually every newspaper in the Maritime Provinces) that already he had the beginnings of its eastern division in the Intercolonial. All that was needed was to extend that railway for 600 miles beyond Montreal to the Great Lakes. As early as 1902, when it had reported surpluses for the third successive year, Blair as the officer responsible tried to persuade the Prime Minister to purchase the Canada Atlantic Railway, 394 miles of tracks between the international boundary at Lake Champlain and Lake Huron, a well-built property that traversed a traffic area as rich as any in Canada. It crossed the St. Lawrence at Coteau Landing, only thirty-nine miles west of the Intercolonial terminus in Montreal, and it would have provided that railway with access to the Great Lakes.

Canadians, however, are canny folk. A great many of them simply did not believe in the apparent reformation that had overtaken the Intercolonial. Ontario and Quebec suspicions remained sufficiently strong to make this extension a political risk, so Laurier persevered with his northern "escape" project, which added 1,000 miles of tracks with little or no traffic potential to the Eastern Division of the National Transcontinental. Mackenzie and Mann, therefore, kept sniffing around the Intercolonial. When Blair resigned as Minister of Railways and Canals after a fracas over the Grand Trunk Pacific, the Maritimes system lost its stoutest defender; but year by year, as the railway fever mounted, it became evident that unbridled private enterprise did not promise to prove any more rewarding than circumscribed public ownership. The leaders of the Conservative Party, anticipating office after more than ten years in the wilderness of Opposition, began to consider the Intercolonial to be a property worth keeping. This opinion grew when the failure of the Eastern Division of the National Transcontinental to attract traffic left only two available solutions to its problem—public ownership or abandonment. In 1908, therefore, R. L. Borden, leader of the Opposition, pledged his party to the retention of the Intercolonial, and in the same year Laurier was warned by his leading supporters that any attempt to dispose of it would be politically disastrous. Thus, after Mackenzie and Mann had been on the spoor for ten years, the scent died out, and they were obliged to admit to one of their rare failures.

Shopping in Quebec

From the time they began to think of an eastern extension, Mackenzie and Mann had not been oblivious to opportunities in Quebec. For more than a century after its conquest, Quebec City, which originally had been a fortress, preserved a good many characteristics of such a structure in its social and commercial constituents. The Old Families, both French and English—the Langeliers, the Thibideaus, the Babys, the Rosses and the Prices and their various collaterals—continued to behave like a garrison, intent on the common purpose of safeguarding each other's interests and of keeping the lesser breeds (notably those pushing Montrealers) out of their preserves. Thus when railways became the vogue, they built their own line in their own fashion. It ran northward into a forested area and thence was built with wooden rails; moreover, no citizen was able to buy shares unless he burned ten cords of firewood annually. The shares were peddled from door to door for $10 each, and there was a bonus of a cord of wood to every purchaser from the mills that would provide the rails and ties. In all, 1,241 citizens subscribed for shares, and those who did not pay for them in full were hailed into court as delinquent debtors.

Enter a Promoter

On November 26, 1870, the first twenty-five miles of tracks were opened. The roadbed had been built at a cost of approximately $3,000 a mile, and the subscribers were in clover, for the Canadian government, some of whose members were on first-name terms with the Old Families, had provided a cash grant of approximately two-thirds of this amount. For the first three years, the railway went swimmingly, but the hard winter of 1874 virtually destroyed every vestige of its superstructure. The Old Families tut-tutted over their liqueurs and tisanes, and there the matter might have ended if an Elijah had not arrived in the person of Charles Newhouse Armstrong. He was the son of a gentleman of the Southern states, and it may have been his courtly manners that arranged his entree into the closed circle of the Old Families. He was a complete railwayman; in a typical transaction, Promoter Armstrong would present the project, would persuade the locals to entrust the fund raising to Financier Armstrong, who would place the contract with Builder Armstrong, who would hire Manager Armstrong to operate the railway when completed. For more than twenty years he provided Quebec City with whatever a railway needed.

One of his typical moonstruck promotions was a railway over 500 miles in length, from Ottawa to the Kingdom of the Saguenay, the gracious, easy highlands that surround the great pool of Lake St. John, about 150 miles north of Quebec City. This project, however, did not commend itself to the Old Families. Their wooden railway had been headed in that direction, and although it no longer existed, it had made their intentions plain. It was part of their preserve. There followed cozy dinners with conversations afterward; Armstrong was told to go and build a railway somewhere else. The Old Families, with no help from anyone, would take care of the connections with the Kingdom of the Saguenay.

The Northering Venture

They immediately formed the Quebec and Lake St. John Railway to rebuild the old firewood line and to extend it for 125 miles to the northern farming districts. They had money in abundance, including cash grants from both the federal and the provincial legislatures and Crown land grants totaling 1,871,950 acres. They sold the common stock more or less in the same fashion as in the earlier venture, from door to door. British bankers underwrote the construction bonds. Despite heavy rock work, the line was built expeditiously by local contractors and was opened to its destination in the midsummer of 1888. There followed colonization of the intervening area and the establishment of the Laurentian National Park, with its summer colonies, hunting and fishing lodges.

In every respect but one the project had been a noteworthy success. Unfortunately, it cost a great deal more than the countryside it traversed could earn. Its British bondholders, with $1,450,000 invested in it, were long suffering, but it led a hand-to-mouth existence until Mackenzie and Mann spotted a new use for it. In 1906, the construction of the Eastern Division of the National Transcontinental Railway had begun to the north of the St. Lawrence, through trackless lake and forest districts where supply routes took almost as much building as railways. At one point, however, the Quebec and Lake St. John Railway was only about forty miles distant across country from La Tuque, a divisional point on the National Transcontinental project in the upper St. Maurice Valley. The Canadian

Locomotive abandoned in the bush after the Yukon gold rush, 1897.
(COURTESY OF THE PUBLIC ARCHIVES OF CANADA,
FROM P. E. ALLEN'S ALBUM "YUKON VIEWS")

Northern partners therefore quietly bought up the bonds of the Quebec and Lake St. John Railway and built a supply line from Linton Junction, seventy-five miles north of Quebec City, to the isolated National Transcontinental construction sections. Within a year, this feeder was handling heavy tonnages. When the Old Families learned to their astonishment that they no longer controlled their property, they accepted a stock exchange, and thus the Quebec and Lake St. John Railway became a Canadian Northern subsidiary.

A Typical Armstrong Venture

Charles Newhouse Armstrong, although frustrated on the Lake St. John project, still retained the confidence of his Quebec City cronies, and when he embarked on the Great Northern Railway of Canada, a line about 400 miles in length between the Ottawa and the St. Maurice rivers, he took a fairly substantial local investment with him. In a campaign unique in Canadian railway annals, he made virtually every mile of this project pay for itself. He divided it into small sections and borrowed its costs from individuals, towns and counties along its line of route. In all, he solicited and obtained $1,570,125 in eighteen sections, with bond guarantees to the amount of $1,559,979 on five sections and land grants totaling 319,000 acres on four sections. This land was returnable to the province of Quebec at seventy cents an acre. It took him sixteen years to complete this railway, and at no time was it more than a few strides ahead of the bailiff. When opened for traffic in 1900, it represented expenditures of approximately $5 million, and it had outstanding indebtedness of rather more than that amount. It had four branch lines or feeders, including an entry into Montreal, but whatever hopes it had of survival were dashed by the construction of the Eastern Division of the National Transcontinental Railway, which ran roughly parallel to it and took the bread out of its mouth. Its financial affairs were in such a fantastic tangle that no one really knew who owned it, and it therefore was a sitting bird for Mackenzie and Mann. In April 1903, they swooped, securing half its capital stock (of a par value of $5 million) for $100,000 in cash. By shrewd bargaining, they settled its debts for a few cents on the dollar, redeeming its stocks and bonds at a fraction of their face value with Canadian Northern debentures.

Entry into Montreal

The Great Northern branch line that provided an entry into Montreal crossed the St. Lawrence by way of the Bout de l'Ile viaduct at the eastern end of the island. Local interests opposed this project, for the business section of the city was a thin intestine stretched between the heights of Mount Royal and the waterfront, with bulging bowels on either side. This narrow passage already carried the tracks of the Grand Trunk and the Canadian Pacific as well as the local tramways. The Great Northern terminal was on Moreau Street, well to the east of the main business section, and Mackenzie and Mann had no intention of being content with it. They had been particularly adept at making their way into cities in all sorts of guises, as well as holding to ransom rivals who sought entry. At an instance, it had taken several millions of extra expenditure to get the National Transcontinental into Winnipeg over the obstacles that they progressively introduced. At Montreal they were seized by the splendor of a simple solution. As there was no room to enter around Mount Royal, they would go through it. This involved approximately three miles of tunnel, and the exit would be in the center of the business section, where there would be no room for yards or other installations. But it would be something that no one else had ever attempted, and this counted for a good deal with Mackenzie and Mann.

For more than five years, they continued to use the Moreau Street station without a hint of change, but every now and then, a farm or apple orchard in the rear of Mount Royal passed into their possession, or a business site on Dorchester street or along the crest of the St. Lawrence escarpment would change hands. By midsummer 1911, they owned 14 acres in the center of the city and 4,800 acres, admirably suited for conversion into suburbs, in the rear of Mount Royal. On October 20 of that year, letters patent were issued to the Montreal Tunnel and Terminal Company. The work was entrusted to S. T. Brown, a distinguished American engineer. In little more than two years, a double-tracked tunnel 16,315 feet in length had been driven through the mountain, and the stately homes of Westmount (it was estimated that at that time their occupants owned two-thirds of the total wealth of Canada) never felt a tremor. The cost had been $12,346,791 and the land sales from the new subdivisions behind Mount Royal eventually more than met this bill.

In Full Career

On the Honours List for 1911 there were two new Knights of the Bath—Sir Donald Mann and Sir William Mackenzie. These adventurers had come into their kingdom, and there were not enough hours in the day to administer their affairs. The boom to outboom all booms was under way. Canadian real estate, as long as it was not under water or on the mountain peaks, could be relied upon to increase in paper value from week to week. Immigrants were flocking in, the bulk of them no longer penniless peasants seeking free land, but bringing substantial sums with them from the sales of their former properties. The growth of Canada seemed as inevitable as the divisions on the calendar. Week by week, month by month, the intake grew. This, said the optimists, would be Canada's century.*

---

* In their enthusiasm in welcoming immigrants, the Canadians usually forgot to count their emigrants—the native-born who went to live abroad, usually in the United States. Thus in the first decade of this century, while 1,782,000 new Canadians arrived, 1,066,000 espied greener pastures elsewhere, so that the net increase for the period, counting the native births, only came to 1,836,000.

Linkup of East and West

Mackenzie and Mann's transcontinental project now was in full career. Their disappointment over failure to acquire the Intercolonial Railway was mitigated by the generosity of the Dominion government in the matter of the construction of a main line which would link their holdings in the East with those on the prairies. On May 1911, they were granted a federal guarantee on construction bonds to a maximum of $35,000 a mile for 1,050 miles between Montreal and Port Arthur, at the head of the Great Lakes, where they would meet the most easterly of their prairie lines. Work began at the close of that year from both ends. For three-quarters of the distance the route lay within easy reach of one or the other of their transcontinental rivals so that few difficulties of supply were encountered. Costs, however, far outran estimates, for an inflationary cycle was in full swing. There were 109 rivers and streams to be bridged, and because the Canadian Pacific and the National Transcontinental had prior choices of route, there was a great deal of relocation, with consequent delays. The last spike in this linkup was driven in January 1914, but the railway was not really fit for operation until it had been under construction for more than four years.

Ontario Short Lines

While this main line was in work, Mackenzie and Mann had not neglected Ontario, where short lines originally sponsored by ambitious towns and cities now realized the necessity of integration in one or another of the three Canadian systems. In bidding for such properties, particularly against the Grand Trunk, the westerners had indifferent success. They had great hopes of securing the Booth group of short lines, amounting to about 450 miles of tracks between the Ottawa Valley and the international boundary, but over the years, the feud between the Booths and the Canadian Pacific had edged this valuable property toward the Grand Trunk camp. However, they picked up a number of short lines, of which two already have received notice in this narrative. The Nipissing Central Railway, built by a Toronto distiller in a queer fashion all his own, had been extended by two Americans under the description of the Irondale and Bancroft Railway into the Ottawa Valley, and its 200 miles of tracks afforded connections of a sort with western Ontario. Economically it never amounted to very much, but it remained a sort of congenial personal property which derived its custom from tourists, hunters, fishermen, winter sportsmen and traveling salesmen. It created its own legends, such as its willingness to stop on request beside a mountain spring whose waters were credited with magical regenerative properties. No one knew why Mackenize and Mann bought it, for they never did anything with it.

They also acquired two groups of properties in which it almost might have been said that they had residuary interests, since both had developed out of the early promotions of William Mackenzie who, it will be remembered, was engrossed at one stage of his career with tramlines. In the Niagara peninsula, seven electrical railways with a total of sixty miles trackage were integrated as a Mackenzie and Mann property. In addition William Mackenzie had always retained a minor interest in his original Toronto suburban promotion. In 1911, he used it as a takeoff for an extension to Guelph, an addition of fifty-five miles of tracks.

Northward in Manitoba

By 1910, Manitoba was riddled with the short lines of the three systems. The only empty lands lay to the north of the lake chains, where the muskeg encroached on the arable prairie. But Mackenzie and Mann, ears ever to the ground, heard the first faint rumblings of the resurrection of a long-dormant but still-cherished enterprise in which they had had an interest fifteen years before—the construction of a railway to Hudson Bay. The story of this venture will be told in due course, but it was characteristic of the partners that even with work in hand over a front of more than 3,000 miles, they still could spend time and money on anticipating a project still in the womb. If a railway ever was to be built to Hudson Bay ports, its point of takeoff would have to be The Pas, on the Saskatchewan River 470 miles north of Winnipeg, a point of assembly and dispersal for fur traders for over two centuries. The intervening territory between it and the northernmost of the Mackenzie and Mann lines had nothing to offer in the way of traffic, but it was one of those gateways which never failed to intrigue the partners. In 1907, they built northward from their Swan River–Melfort line for eighty-eight miles across the wasteland. Their foresight was rewarded, for they had no more than started to build when government-sponsored survey parties took off, working eastward from The Pas, on the preliminary examination of a route to a Hudson Bay port.

The Mackenzie and Mann holdings in Manitoba were completed by the construction of 124 miles of short lines which largely comprised extensions of existing branches or feeders.

Overbuilding in Saskatchewan

In the central prairie province, the struggle of the three systems rose to a frenzy of overbuilding, as if they deliberately had set out to bankrupt each other. In this province, branch lines ran anywhere and everywhere, providing an outstanding example of senseless competition. The Canadian Northern grid consisted of six parallel lines, which sprouted subbranches in profusion. At one time Mackenzie and Mann had more than thirty different projects in work in that province. In less than five years, 1,349 miles of new tracks were laid and a further 850 miles were placed in work.

Sane Growth in Alberta

In comparison with this frenetic campaign in Saskatchewan, the Mackenzie and Mann operations in Alberta were restrained and sensible. They had one main objective, which was to open up the excellent coal fields along the line of the eastern upthrust of the Rockies. The Drumheller mines in the upper Red Deer Valley already were in production, and the additional Canadian Northern trackage to serve them, amounting in all to 480 miles, was warranted, for there was no alternative fuel to mitigate the long and bitter winters on the priairies. The Brazeau field, 150 miles to the northwest of Drumheller, also appeared to offer good prospects. R. M. Horne-Payne found considerable capital, mostly in Germany, for its development, and Mackenzie and Mann, having obtained federal support for a railway into this area, in their opportunist fashion hastened to transfer this subsidy to another project and built into the Brazeau field from Warden in the east instead of from their main line to the north. This branch, 154 miles in length, proved to be one of their most profitable ventures.

The Arctic Calls

In Alberta as in Manitoba, the partners succumbed to the lure of the unknown. A series of great rivers—the Peace, the Slave, the Mackenzie and their tributaries—provided waterways which drained more than 1 million square miles of Arctic wilderness. These rivers were navigable only for four months in midsummer and then only for incoming traffic.

Tremendous asphalt deposits covering a surface area of approxi-

1915: A trestle goes out (TOP); forty days later it is in again (BOTTOM).

mately 2,000 square miles had been demarcated along the lower Atha-baska, as had natural gas fields on the Mackenzie. There were evidences of substantial mineral occurrences around Great Slave Lake and in other Arctic areas.

Such virgin prospects drew Mackenzie and Mann like trout to the lure. Their first move was quick and easy. They swiftly built a branch line seventy-four miles in length northward from Edmonton to Athabaska Landing, the head of the sub-Arctic traffic on the river of that name. There Indian tracking teams, at the end of their long upstream haul, heard the whistle of a locomotive for the first time. This line, completed in August 1912, immediately inherited heavy freights but only during the brief season in which the rivers were open. To the west, however, beyond Lesser Slave Lake, there existed a huge belt (estimated at 50 million acres) of excellent farming land, well-watered and, despite its high lati-tude, possessing a climate no more severe than that of the open prairies. In this area, known as the Peace River Block, settlers were arriving in substantial number by means of roundabout dirt roads. Mackenzie and Mann decided to stake the first claim on this promising area. Their branch from Edmonton, destined to be the first element of Northern Alberta Railways, ignoring the muskeg swamps and huge rivers in its path, headed due west to Grande Prairie in the center of the block, a distance of approximately 250 miles. Should the tide of settlement continue to advance, they would extend this line, perhaps even to the Pacific coast. Its construction began in 1914.

Thus Mackenzie and Mann, after a campaign of fifteen years unequaled in the history of railway promotion, entered the home stretch. All they now needed was for the boom not to burst and for governments and private investors to continue to be compliant in the provision of capital. With such aids, their foresight, skill, audacity and occasional chicanery would win them leadership in the Canadian railway field. In confident mood, therefore, they faced the last lap, involving the comple-tion of their system to a Pacific terminal.

British Columbia—Something Different

Ethnic geography receives less attention than it deserves. If mobility is the prime determinant of change, topography and climate follow close behind. Put a cockney or a Dutchman in the sun and the character of his offspring will alter, perhaps even in the first generation, as witness the Australian and the Afrikaner; the "dark, little mountainy men who live in the glen" will sire a different brood wherever the peaks stand against the sky. Travelers in the Russia of today return to report that it will take more than cities built on permafrost to transform Siberians into good Communists. Their climate, not their philosophy, dictates their course of development.

With the great rampart of the Rockies at his back and with the sea at his doors, the British Columbian never has been a particularly good Canadian. Instead, he is much nearer to being a Pacific colonial, akin to his American neighbors in his habits of both body and mind. Nearly a century ago, he sold himself into Confederation, but he has remained essentially a nonconformist, with an individual viewpoint and attitudes.

The early history of that province revealed a lack of dourness, a liveliness and an affection for shibboleths found nowhere else in Canada. The first provincial governments were comprised largely of British-born, but they were markedly un-English and unstable. They conducted their public affairs in such uninhabited fashion that there were fifteen changes of administration in the first thrity years of Confederation. The climax came at the turn of the century when the lieutenant governor of British Columbia dismissed two successive ministries as unworthy of his confidence and he himself was dismissed by the Governor-General of Canada. Out of this hurly-burly there emerged a native son well trained in the verbal judo that passed for controversy in those days. After a short period in Opposition, Richard McBride in 1903 clobbered his enemies and became premier. He ruled for twelve years. The story of railway expansion in British Columbia is very largely the narrative of his policies and their application.

McBride Turns Tough

On taking office, McBride found Mackenzie and Mann camped on his doorstep. They had been toying with one British Columbia project after another without coming to terms with any of them. Under an earlier administration they had agreed to continue their prairie main line from Edmonton through the Yellowhead Pass to a terminal on Vancouver Island, whose citizens felt they had been defrauded when the Canadian Pacific chose to stop at Vancouver. This enterprise succumbed when the provincial and federal administrations, the one Conservative, the other Liberal, failed to come to terms on the proportion of aid that each would provide. On accession to power, McBride made no secret of his railway policy. In joint projects he expected the federal government to pay most of the bill. Railway promoters would not be allowed to batten on the province. They would have to accept his terms or stay out.

This policy had been put to a test in the case of the Grand Trunk Pacific Railway. The British Columbia section of that line cost the province next to nothing, but McBride had imposed stipulations that enabled his fellow provincials to make a fat thing out of it. The colonization of areas contiguous to that railway was reserved for the local real estate promoters, and in one instance the premier insisted on a costly diversion of the route to satisfy them. The Grand Trunk obligingly had made itself unpopular by endeavoring to obtain permission to import Oriental labor, as had the Canadian Pacific thirty years before. British Columbians, who had staged riots in 1907 against the importation of time-expired Sikh soldiers, had attempted to loot Chinatown; whereupon there had emerged line after line of Japanese, veterans of the Yalu, each with a broken bottle in either hand. They drove the mob in a wild scramble before them. Naturally white men wanted no more of that sort of thing.

Harsh Terms

When McBride felt that he had put the Grand Trunk Pacific sufficiently in its place, he let it be known that he was willing to talk business with Mackenzie and Mann. In April 1910, the requisite legislation was introduced. The premier, in a flowery introduction, declared that he had awaited the hour when he could employ an all-Canadian company to give British Columbia its third transcontinental railway. This ardent nationalism, in addition to being a back-handed slap at the Grand Trunk Pacific, was an expression of self-congratulation, for by then he had brought the Canadian Northern as completely to heel as its British-owned competitor. He had demanded and obtained its construction in British Columbia by a subsidiary company completely under his jurisdiction; he had selected its route; although guaranteeing its construction bonds to a maximum of $35,000 a mile for 600 miles, he had insisted that the proceeds of such bonds should not be handed over to Mackenzie and Mann but should be disbursed by the provincial treasury against certificates of completed trackage. Both passenger and freight rates would be subject to provincial control without the right of appeal to the federal authorities. Finally, penalities were imposed against the railway company for any failures to complete the line within the limits of a prescribed period.

The acceptance of such shackling terms was perhaps the first solid intimation that Mackenzie and Mann had overreached themselves and had prejudiced their freedom of action. Such rigorous stipulations were the subject of unflattering comment in the London financial press, evoking the view that if a substantial borrower was compelled to finance his projects in such humiliating fashion, it behooved British investors to examine Mackenzie and Mann offerings more carefully in the future. Horne-Payne's explanation that his principals were dealing with Wild Western-ers and that the contract gave no cause for alarm was received politely but with reserve.

Edmonton to the Yellowhead Pass

The Canadian Northern, with its western railhead at Edmonton, had 250 miles of Alberta bushlands to traverse before it reached the gateway to the Rockies. This section had virtually no local traffic to sustain it. As has been noted, the Brazeau coal fields might have supported it, but this source of traffic had been tapped from another direction. The Grand Trunk Pacific already was under construction through this area, and its London board would have acceded joyously to any proposal for sharing its trackage with its rival, since it was sick with anxiety over the liabilities that this western venture had imposed. But Mackenzie and Mann had determined to play singlehanded, come what may. They persuaded the Dominion government to give them a cash grant of $12,000 a mile and a bond guarantee of $35,000 a mile over this section, and in 1911, they began to build a line, in every respect a duplicate of the Grand Trunk Pacific, for 318 miles from Edmonton to Lucerne, at the western portals of the Rockies. Thus the Canadian taxpayer was footing two bills for a single project. For the sake of appearances, the Canadian Northern route kept out of sight of its rival, now to its north, now to its south, as it traversed the bushlands; but on approaches to the Yellowhead Pass there could be no concealment, and for the last 140 miles the tracks of two railways ran side by side.

Signs of Strain

This construction, which occupied most of 1911–1912, afforded additional evidence that Mackenzie and Mann were losing the adaptabil-ity and resource that had carried them over so many hurdles in their earlier years. They were now conscious of a race against time: with vast borrowings coming due, it was necessary to force the pace, whatever the cost. When they embarked on the first British Columbia section, 258 miles between Lucerne and Kamloops, they had the North Thompson River valley entirely to themselves, and· for the most part, the terrain was accommodating; yet costs grew from mile to mile. From Kamloops to tidewater (approximately 250 miles) they were confined in the Thompson and Fraser canyons, where the Canadian Pacific had been in occupancy for upwards of thirty years and was in no mood to assist a competitor that would break its monopoly of the Vancouver–Puget Sound traffic. On this final section, Mackenzie and Mann would appear to have lost their heads. Instead of getting through quickly and improving their trackage afterward out of operational earnings, they elected to build to an even higher specification than that of the Canadian Pacific. Sometimes they had no option for many miles but to blast a continuous niche in the walls of the canyon; costs sometimes mounted to as much as $300,000 a mile. The British Columbia government was persuaded to raise its guarantee on the construction bonds of this section to $45,000 a mile, but this only added to the mountainous indebtedness that must be confronted on the completion of the line.

A serious by-product of the Fraser Canyon construction was its interference with the salmon run. These fish in enormous numbers fought their way up this swift river to their traditional spawning grounds. It was necessary for them to rest en route and recruit their strength in small bays and backwaters. These havens in many instances were destroyed by the enormous quantities of rock and spoil dumped into the river, and the fish, denied recuperation, were compelled to continue to breast the swift currents unceasingly. Many thousands, utterly exhausted, were washed ashore, to perish on the sand bars.

Trouble with Labor

Labor at this time represented about 70 percent of the total costs of railway construction. In British Columbia, Mackenzie and Mann discovered that what was good enough elsewhere was not the answer there. Previously their labor force had given them little trouble. It had been ruled in traditional fashion by the straw bosses, who issued the orders and enforced them, when necessary, with fists or ax handles and who discharged instantly any worker who gave them trouble. The new century, however, had brought a new outlook, particularly in western America, where the Industrial Workers of the World and other similar associations had encouraged resistance to the absolute authority of employers, presenting collective representations in cases of complaints or disputes. In some of the western states, bloody clashes had ensued between workers and company police. On the prairies, there had been no trouble, for anyone who did not like his job could quit and take up a homestead or find employment without difficulty in the many small towns. In the mountains this was impossible; labor was scarce and knew it and did not hesitate

Mackenzie and Mann tunnel on Hell's Gate, 1910.

on occasion to set its own terms for continuing on the job. There were strikes and abstentions in abundance, with a footloose, shiftless minority imposing its will on occasion and impeding the progress of the work. On some sections, therefore, costs rose alarmingly above estimates, and there was little that the contractors could do about it.

The situation was embittered by the refusal of British Columbia to recognize the authority of the Royal North West Mounted Police. This splendid body was confined to the prairies, where, in their traditional fashion, they had made law and order a watchword. The British Columbia provincial police in many instances had no mandate to act beyond their immediate areas, and large stretches of countryside were without supervision. Each railway contractor had authority in the immediate area of his contract and for three miles on either side, but beyond these limits there was virtually no authority. As a result there sprang up along the construction route the "end of steel" villages, whose squalid shacks housed itinerant entertainers—liquor vendors, prostitutes and gamblers—as well as peddlers and cheap-jack storekeepers, all eager to persuade the railway worker to spend next month's paycheck before he had earned it. These shanty towns, immune to regulation, fostered restlessness, discontent and disorder and contributed their full quota to the delays and unnecessary expenses of construction.

The Pacific Terminals

In the matter of a Pacific terminal, Mackenzie and Mann proved to be their shrewd, surprising selves. As at Montreal, they pulled an unexpected rabbit out of the hat. In their earliest negotiations, it had been taken for granted that the terminal of their line would be situated on Vancouver Island, since it seemed impossible that they would be able to break into Vancouver, where the Canadian Pacific owned almost the entire waterfront. But under modern conditions, a port that was sustained by a train ferry would have been a dubious venture, and after a certain amount of window dressing, Mackenzie and Mann undertook to compensate Vancouver Island with three branch lines, totaling 120 miles. Thereafter an area was purchased on the eastern bank of the Fraser River, about twelve miles upstream from its mouth and about fifteen miles across country from Vancouver. It was named Port Mann, and the Canadian National partners announced that either the Fraser would be dredged to accommodate ocean carriers or a port would be built at the mouth of the river, on the site of the fishing village of Steveston.

Neither of these projects was sensible, and there can be little doubt that Mackenzie and Mann intended them as a cover plan under which they would make their way into Vancouver. A further obstacle to such entry, however, existed in the form of a subsidiary of the Great Northern, a United States railway, which crossed the Fraser below the site of Port Mann and threaded its way over the rolling ridges to a terminal of False Creek, a minor inlet in the center of Vancouver that at low tide left a large area of mud flats between the downtown and the residential sections. Mackenzie and Mann, therefore, were cut off from the waterfront not only from the west but from the east, and no more difficult hurdle ever had confronted them. They were well aware that there was little or no possibility of navigation on the Fraser, and as a consequence, their outgoing freights would have to be carted for fifteen miles to Canadian Pacific docks in Vancouver; eastbound freights, largely consisting of lumber which would have to be brought in from mills on ocean waterfronts beyond that city. Their terminal, therefore, would be at an overwhelming disadvantage in competition with the Canadian Pacific, which could unload timber cargoes from the coastal ships on to its flatcars on the Vancouver docks.

A Dazzling Coup

Neither in government reports nor in the minutes of the Vancouver City Council is the campaign of Mackenzie and Mann fully spelled out, but it undoubtedly originated in the eagle eye of Z. A. Lash. He discerned certain omissions in the terms of purchase by the Great Northern of its terminal property at the head of False Creek. Riparian rights were something that Canadians had not troubled to think about for themselves; they had taken over English laws as they stood, and such statutes ruled that any damage to beach or river bank rights must be specifically identified in contracts of purchase or sale. This the Great Northern had failed to do, apparently regarding the tidal intake and outlet of False Creek as an unalterable fact of nature and consequently a freeway for all time to come. Mackenzie and Mann's plan traded on this ignorance and possessed the simplicity of genius. They offered to dam False Creek, thus recovering 164 acres of land in the very heart of the city. (How the real estate dealers must have gnashed their teeth. According to the Vancouver Yearbook of 1913, there were 1,053 land salesmen licenced in the city as against only 325 grocers.) Of this reclamation, Mackenzie and Mann would return 35 acres to the city free of charge and would buy the other

129 acres for a dollar an acre. But this was only the beginning of their offer. They would drive a double-tracked, electrically operated tunnel through seven miles of ridges intervening between the Fraser Valley and the city; they would build a modern hotel in Vancouver within five years and would establish a trans-Pacific steamship service within eight years.

Success in Sight

Who could have resisted such a luring array of goodies? The Vancouver citizens, with the exception of the real estate fraternity, threw their hats in the air. The British Columbia Legislative Assembly rushed through a bill guaranteeing construction bonds for the terminals to a value of $10 million.

The wonder-workers had done it again. To the east of the Rockies, their transcontinental service had been opened on January 1, 1914. There rail services had been complemented during construction by a leased steamship line from the St. Lawrence to British ports. Mackenzie and Mann also had taken over a thriving express company and multiplied its services; they were at the point of buying the Canadian wires of an American telegraph company that served all of eastern Canada and also the prairies. They had invested $11 million in the Dunsmuir coal properties on Vancouver Island, which were perhaps the finest source of this fuel in all Canada. They already were thinking in terms of a shorter line to eastern Canada via the Crow's Nest Pass and had embarked on its first leg, from Kamloops Junction to Kelowna (131 miles). A host of other projects were in train, awaiting their hour. They included one branch in Quebec of 175 miles, two new lines in Ontario totaling 195 miles, one in Manitoba of 40 miles, six new projects in Saskatchewan totaling 670 miles, and no less than 1,070 miles of new lines in Alberta—a tidy addition of 2,100 miles to be added to the 9,000 miles of lines already under operation.

What could halt, or even embarrass, such a far-flung operation, carried out with such courage and resource? What indeed? Only the moving finger of Fate, which

> having writ,
> Moves on, nor all thy Piety and Wit
> Shall Lure it back to cancel half a line,
> Nor all thy tears wash out a word of it.[1]

14

Canadian Railways at War

It is perhaps permissible to interpolate a short account of the Canadian railways during the First World War, not only in commemoration of their splendid services but also because that catastrophe was destined to prove a catalytic factor in the events that were to follow.

As a self-governing colony and not yet an independent state, Canada was bound by the British Government's declaration of war on Germany. Her loyalty to the Crown, however, far outran statutory responsibilities, and her official offer of an expeditionary force went forward on August 2, 1914. But even before that date, railway personnel were aware of what was about to come. The station agent at Provost, an Alberta hamlet, had reported in the preceding week that on a hot, stilly afternoon, a man had presented himself at the wicket. He was drunk and singing; the song was *La Brabanconne*, the Belgian national anthem; he had received his call-up papers and was demanding a ticket to Antwerp. He never came back. From Walhachin, in the Thompson River Valley below Kamloops, the telegrapher reported that by the outbreak of war there was scarcely anyone left. The fruit farmers in that district were nearly all Royal Navy reservists; they had left their fruit to rot on the trees, had given their poultry and livestock to whoever would have it, had locked their doors and had taken train for the east. In every railway construction camp,

Halifax disaster—the explosion of December 6, 1917.

men presented themselves, asking to be paid off. A complete survey party from the Canadian Northern extension into the Peace River Block walked in for forty miles to railhead. They had heard the first call for men, and they all wanted to go.

In a thousand hamlets, the telegraphers became the men of the hour. Security was less prized then than now, and the wires were humming with military information. Every evening, groups assembled at the station, and the telegrapher turned Morse into English as the stories came through. These sessions often became recruiting meetings; many a bereft mother would remember to her dying day the night her son, barely of age, came home from the station and said "Mum, I've got to go." As troops began to assemble at Valcartier near Quebec City from all parts of Canada, the townspeople and the villagers along the lines felt in duty bound to honor them; they flocked to the stations with cigarettes and cakes and cups of tea and in the larger towns with brass bands. No one was more at war than the railways.

The Canadians took the railway idea to the battlefront with them. They conformed to the establishment of the British Army, which had only two methods of transport—shanks' mare, which were men's feet, and horses proper. Motor vehicles were virtually unknown, and in the prewar discussions, the French spokesmen had assured the British War Office that they would be able to provide whatever railways were needed. On the outbreak of war, therefore, the British Army had only two railway companies available, both for operational employment.

In September-October 1914, the Battle of the Marne, followed by the advance to the Aisne, carried the Allied fighting front eighty miles ahead of its railheads. When confusion and transport difficulties arose, the War Office dispatched Sir Percy Girouard, a Canadian who had distinguished himself in railway construction during the South African and Sudanese campaigns, to report on the situation. He immediately recommended that the Imperial forces should organize their own railway construction and operational cadres as quickly as possible. The Canadian government at once offered to provide such specialists, adding with perhaps more truth than diplomacy, "Canada can supply the want better than any other country." Early in 1915, recruiting for the Canadian Railways Overseas Corps began. The first units proceeded to Britain in June of that year, arriving in France two months later. They were employed solely on the repair and extension of standard-gauge lines.

By then the profusion of fire power had driven both adversaries underground, and the war had become a great earth-moving operation, in which millions of tons of soil were displaced by shell fire in order to kill or oust enemies from trenches or dugouts. This static warfare necessitated the daily transport of thousands of tons of supplies from railheads

The Grand Trunk Pier burning at Seattle in 1914.

far enough behind the lines to be out of range of the heaviest artillery. Scores of horse-drawn supply columns plodded slowly forward in full view of enemy observers in balloons, and heavy losses became inevitable, with consequent interruptions of food and ammunition supplies that might lead to disaster in event of enemy attacks.

Submarine Warfare Impels a Change

By the beginning of 1916, submarine warfare had emerged as perhaps the chief menace of the Western Alliance. It took a heavy toll of merchant shipping, and it became necessary to ration tonnage to meet the necessities of the British civilian population. One of the chief military uses of shipping space was to fetch forage to France for the horse transport; the estimate for 1916 was no less than 780,000 tons. This circumstance, perhaps more than any other, led the British authorities to give greater consideration to light railways, which could carry heavier loads and were less vulnerable than horse transport. Another advantage of railways was that they could deliver supplies under cover of darkness. First plans called for no more than six pounds per yard-rails, which would support flat trucks horse-drawn or propelled by hand, but through the ingenuity of a British engineering firm, the first rails were scarcely laid than they were replaced by heavier tracks; a tiny locomotive had come to hand that would draw a string of five or six trucks. Other improvements followed rapidly, as light railways went down everywhere. In May 1916, the War Office approached Canada, asking that specialist railway units, both of constructors and of operators, should be recruited as rapidly as possible.

"Jack" Stewart Becomes a Legend

The First Battalion, Overseas Railway Construction Corps, was organized at once under command of Lieutenant-Colonel J. W. Stewart, a dynamic partner of the contracting firm of Foley, Welch and Stewart. He was not permitted however, to take his unit overseas; before it was ready he was summoned to the United Kingdom, promoted and named Deputy Director of Light Railways in France.

About Stewart the legends have gathered with the years. His utter personal fearlessness, his tendency to adopt unconventional and audacious solutions, his informality and his outspoken aversion to anything of an official nature that hampered his freedom of action made him an Empire figure in a matter of months. Even official documents described him as "Jack" Stewart. He was alleged to have ordered two officers to accompany every requisition to the Army dumps, one of whom would hold the officer in charge in talk while the other stole what he wanted. He did not like inspections by distinguished personages; they wasted his time and might even draw fire. On one such occasion, when he was informed that a visiting foreign royalty had been pleased to bestow a decoration upon him, he instructed his servant to sew its ribbon on the seat of his pants. According to the legend, the award was the Order of Chastity, Second Class.

From then onward, a continuous stream of construction and operating battalions were raised, usually under the patronage of well-known railwaymen. By the following year (1917), there were seventeen such battalions in France; Jack Stewart was a major-general, and the Canadians were completely in charge of the construction and maintenance of all light and standard gauge lines on the British sector of the battlefront. The Canadian Corps had its own railway cadres; in the great battles of Vimy Ridge and Third Ypres, the tracks ran virtually into the front lines; there were at least three alternate routes to every sector as guard against interruption of supplies by enemy action. Long and arduous approach marches were a thing of the past; the troops rode forward by night on open trucks almost to the entrances of the communications' trenches.

The railwaymen took great pride in being classed as forward troops; they were of the same category as combatants, for they were exposed, often continuously, to enemy fire. As an illustration, Tenth Battalion Canadian Railway Troops spent five unbroken months in 1917 in the Ypres salient, never being out of observation of the enemy or of the range of his artillery. They paid the price: in the last nineteen months of the war Canadian Railway formations sustained 1,977 casualties.

Meanwhile in Canada

In Canada, railwaymen bore their full share of the civilian burden. The growth of war industries in many centers overtaxed the existing services; war priorities retarded the replacement of worn-out rolling stock. On the credit side, the war wrote *finis* to the branch line boom, which had expanded to senseless proportions. It also made a positive contribution to the railway economy in a number of instances in which parallel lines were merged in order that half the rails might be raised for dispatch to France. The most striking instance of this consolidation occurred on the

Grand Trunk Pacific and Canadian Northern lines from Edmonton westward to the entry to Yellowhead Pass. By July 1917, the Canadian Northern had lost 206 miles of rails and was operating over Grand Trunk Pacific trackage on most of this section.

The Intercolonial Role

However, it was on the other side of Canada that the Canadian railways made their greatest single contribution to the war effort. The British Admiralty preferred to route its ships through open seas rather than enclosed waters, which gave German U-boats greater opportunities. As a result, as much military traffic as possible was shifted from St. Lawrence ports to Halifax and Saint John, and, as United States neutrality regulations prevented the use of the Canadian Pacific line across Maine, the whole burden of transporting men, machines and munitions fell on the Intercolonial, which, it may be remembered, originally had been proposed as a "military railway." Thus Halifax became the marshaling yard of the North Atlantic. There the convoys assembled, picked up their loads and their protectors—the great battleships, the swift cruisers, the swerving destroyers.

The statistics of Intercolonial service constitute a proud page. During three years of war, it handled 1,081 troop trains, carrying 691,262 men of all ranks. The war almost doubled its freight traffic, whose volume rose to 8,177,862 tons in 1918. Among its many unusual commissions were the "fish trains," the code name for the carriers of British gold reserves to secret Canadian destinations, in order that they might be used as collateral against dollar loans. A typical shipment, carried by a single closely guarded train, and with its coaches linked by telephones, was valued at $67 million. During a period of nine months in 1917–1918, the "silk trains" bore 47,708 Annamites, Indo-Chinese coolies on their way from their homeland to France, where they served as laborers behind the lines.

In these duties, Intercolonial employees were on their toes. They were as much at war as the 2,200 of the staff who had enlisted and now were on the battlefields. An American journalist thus wrote of them:

> One cannot but marvel at the part the Canadian railwaymen have played in the war programme and the deep-seated spirit of loyalty that actuates them. . . . The tightening of the jaw or the breaking of the voices as they speak of friends and relatives in the trenches, are

surface indications of the determined spirit that lies behind the present operations. So far as improved methods are concerned there is little that is new. The splendid results that are being obtained under abnormal traffic conditions are due rather to an intensive application and development of practices that were in effect on most progressive roads before the war; the new element is the really remarkable spirit that dominates the employees.[1]

The Halifax Disaster

That spirit so highly praised was destined to be put to as cruel a test at home as ever on the battlefield. On December 6, 1917 a French vessel lying in Bedford Basin and laden with 4,000 tons of high explosives, caught fire. Its crew panicked and deserted the ship, which drifted down the fairway on to the docks in the center of the city. There it blew up, destroying all of downtown Halifax and much of the residental sections. More than two thousand civilians were killed, more than eight thousand were injured and twenty-five thousand were left homeless. Among the dead were fifty-eight Intercolonial employees, including a telegraph operator who stayed at his key stopping all incoming traffic until his station was blown to bits. The waterfront was razed; among the wreckage were 550 pieces of Intercolonial rolling stock.

The tremors of the blast scarcely had died away when an Intercolonial emergency force went into operation, opening the torn and twisted lines to traffic. Relief trains were arriving at improvised halts within twenty-four hours. In four days, normal services were resumed. Thereafter, by official request, the Intercolonial wrecking force undertook the restoration of the naval dockyards.

Out of such occasions enduring fellowships are born. By the end of the war, the Intercolonial Railway functioned like a good regiment, taking emergencies in its stride, smoothly and unostentatiously. On the morning of July 19, 1919, HMT *Olympic*, greatest of troop carriers, docked at Halifax. Within four hours, eleven trains carrying 5,430 returning soldiers were dispatched—a record performance that made a good many people decide that it really does not matter whether a railway is owned by a government or by private enterprise. It is the morale of its employees that determines its value to the communities it serves.

15

Mackenzie and Mann:

Day of Reckoning

To many it seemed a cruel jest of circumstance that Mackenzie and Mann should have been stricken down by the advent of the First World War when within sight of their goal. Another $100 million on top of the $400 million they already had spent and they would have been home. In reality, however, their fate had been in brew from their high-water mark in 1911, and it had taken shape in that year with the change of government. The new Borden administration contained three tough-minded men who had viewed the extravaganza of railway construction with highly critical eyes. Francis Cochrane, Minister of Railways and Canals, Thomas White, Minister of Finance, and Henry Lumley Drayton, chairman of the Board of Canadian Railway Commissioners, were determined to amend or to end an era that promised to give Canada 30,000 miles of lines, a mile for every two hundred fifty inhabitants, against four hundred in the United States, two thousand in Great Britain and four thousand in Russia. Roughly half of the cost of this trackage had been met by the taxpayer and the Canadian Northern had been by far the greatest beneficiary of the public purse. Mackenzie and Mann, therefore, virtually chose themselves as the horrible example.

Their first break in their hitherto unblemished record for meeting their commitments had occurred, significantly enough, within a few weeks of the 1911 election. The amount was insignificant, but the Dominion government was obliged to meet the service on a small parcel of debenture stock. This was all Mackenzie and Mann's critics needed as a talking point. But White was thorough and visited London in the spring of 1912 to make inquiries on the spot. There he discovered that Horne-Payne had been obliged to switch to the Continent because of the disinterest of British investors in a parcel of $4 million of Canadian Northern bonds. The maximum allowable guaranteed bonded indebtedness had been reached on virtually all Mackenzie and Mann's enterprises, and it was only by resorting to expensive short-term loans in the New York market that the partners managed to scrape together $37,280,083 during that year to sustain their voracious enterprises. By the spring of 1913, there was no other source of money available than the federal government, and Mackenzie directed his steps to Ottawa in full knowledge that no warm welcome awaited him.

Harsh Terms

There he had a surprise. The Conservative Party, long the bulwark of private enterprises, had undergone a change of heart insofar as railways were concerned. Cochrane, now Minister of Railways, examined the Intercolonial meticulously and had found it a thoroughly desirable property. It thereafter is possible that he regarded it as a government-owned stable in which other Canadian railways, should they come to distress, might find stalls. His policy—not necessarily that of his party—would be based not only on the possibility but on the probability of such takeovers, and the federal authority, in return for future aid, must be given an equity. As a result, Cochrane met Mackenzie with cash in hand. He offered a subsidy of $15,040,000 on 1,420 miles then under construction, but in return he demanded the transfer to the government of Canadian Northern stock to the nominal value of $7 million. Mackenzie had no choice but to accept the offer at the expense of his highly prized independence of action. His walls for the first time had been breached, and his citadel no longer was secure.

Month by month, Canadian Northern traffic increased and a satisfactory operational ratio had been achieved. But by now the burden of interest charges had mounted beyond any anticipated earning power. In the spring of 1914, Mackenzie was obliged to approach the Canadian government anew. In his appeal to Sir Robert Borden, he stated that it would cost $96 million to complete all the tasks in hand. Of this sum he would undertake to raise $54 million from private sources if the Dominion government would guarantee construction bonds to the value of $45 million. The Prime Minister's response was brisk and clear and brutal. Such guarantee would be forthcoming only after Mackenzie and Mann had merged all their subsidiary properties—their land companies, their mines, their timber limits, their shipping, telegraph and express companies, in a single holding company, the Canadian Northern Railway, leaving nothing outside this enveloping body. In addition, Mackenzie and Mann must transfer another parcel of its stock, of a nominal value of $33 million, to the federal treasury.

The Ultimate Catastrophe

The terms thus had grown appreciably harsher in the space of a single year. Yet Mackenzie and Mann did not hesitate. They were prepared to do anything to keep their enterprises afloat. The enabling measure of this transaction passed the House of Commons after vicious in-fighting between a minority that considered that the Canadian Northern principals deserved better terms and a strong faction who were all in favor of putting an end to them when an opportunity offered.

In mid-July, Sir William Mackenzie joined Horne-Payne in London, in quest of the $54 million that would permit them to meet the federal terms. There was a curious air of disinterest in the City; small groups coalesced but not to talk business; they seemed to be waiting for something. Lazard Frères were persuaded to take $3 million of guaranteed bonds, but the tensions manifestly were mounting, with the intransigence of Austria, the wild clamor for war in the streets of Germany, the mobilization of Russia, the frantic inquiries from France as to whether Britain would stand beside her. The violation of Belgian neutrality settled the matter. Sir Edward Grey, Foreign Secretary of the Imperial government, rose on a dying afternoon to tell a hushed House of Commons that before midnight Great Britain and her Empire would be at war with Germany. The Royal Navy faded to battle stations in the mists of the North Sea, the British Army disappeared down long canvas chutes at ports of embarkation and reappeared in Belgium, fighting magnificently. But this high drama spelled ruin for the Canadian Northern partners, for two days after the declaration of war the export of capital from Britain was banned.

Concurrent Investigations

Nevertheless Mackenzie fought on. He rushed to New York, where loans were available, but they were sporadic and expensive, representing no more than 60 percent of the face value of deposited securities. Costs of construction mounted, fixed charges alone increasing by nearly $2 million in 1915. A hitherto ignored clause in the Dominion government subsidy contracts, whereby certain services in emergency were to be performed by the railways without charge, was invoked in connection with military movements, at considerable expense to the Canadian railways. After the Battle of the Marne, Wall Street became more receptive; the magnificent stand of the First Canadian Division in the Second Battle of Ypres and the intensification of submarine warfare brought home to many Americans that a Canadian cause was of some pertinence to them. In the autumn of 1915, therefore, a group of prominent American bankers agreed to come to the assistance of Mackenzie and Mann if an examination of their properties warranted it. Coverdale and Colpitts, prominent United States consultants, were commissioned to undertake a detailed survey of all Canadian Northern enterprises and to report on their prospects and viability.

Meanwhile, the Dominion government made sufficient advances to keep the railway in operation and its construction under way. Sir Robert Borden, however, felt it his duty to ascertain at the source what the Wall Street support involved. He journeyed to New York, where he learned that the bankers considered that they would be entitled to an *en bloc* government guarantee on any loans that they might make on the strength of the Coverdale and Colpitts reports. In other words, the taxpayer constituted the Canadian Northern's sole hope of delivery. Borden immediately denied any such compulsion and returned home resolved to settle railway involvements once and for all. He empowered a Royal Commission to advise what steps should be taken, in view of both the Canadian Northern and the Grand Trunk Pacific defaults.

In July 1916, this body convened under the chairmanship of A. H. Smith, vice-president of the New York Central Railroad, with Sir Henry Drayton and Sir George Paish, a well-known British economist, as its other members.The presence of Sir Henry Drayton on a supposedly judicial board of inquiry was ominous, as was the wording of the instructions "to ascertain the approximate physical value of the entire systems of the Canadian Northern and Grand Trunk Pacific railways." Such determination was exactly what Drayton, Cochrane and White required to support their radical demands. Drayton's influence on the Royal Commission increased perceptibly when Sir George Paish found it impossible to serve and was replaced by W. H. Ackworth, a railway statistician of considerably more modest reputation and attainments.

The Reports of the Investigators

These concurrent investigations effectively prevented Mackenzie and Mann from renewing their quest for funds, since no investor would consider their offerings until both the consultants and the Royal Commission had rendered their reports. In this period the Canadian Northern became virtually the retainer of the federal government. The Coverdale and Colpitts findings, however, as completed in March 1917, proved a heartening document. It declared the Mackenzie and Mann structure to be sound and that it could be brought to a warranted completion by the investment of a further $86 million over a period of five years. A net operational surplus of $4,615,000 might be anticipated in the first year after completion, with gross revenue rising to $80,320,000 in the sixth year.

The Royal Commission's report was destined to be tabled five weeks later. This intervening period haunted Mackenzie and Mann for the rest of their lives. Coverdale and Colpitts had revived their hopes; if the Royal Commission saw their affairs in anything like the same light, Wall Street might move to the rescue. Traffic had increased by 40 percent in volume during 1916; there seemed every reason to anticipate commensurate improvements as the unfinished sections of the system came into operation. The property therefore retained a potential for growth that might in due course allow it to meet all its liabilities.

In this interval of waiting, however, another extraneous development provided fresh complications. On April 17, the United States entered the war. The American economy immediately was stimulated by the prospects of huge government expenditures, which meant free money, which in turn meant higher prices and wages. The New York bankers who had commissioned Coverdale and Colpitts immediately let it be known that even if their terms concerning government guarantees should be met, they would be compelled for the time being at least to limit their advances to Mackenzie and Mann.

Findings of the Royal Commission

In its preamble and general conclusions, the Royal Commission's report ran roughly parallel to that of Coverdale and Colpitts. Mackenzie and Mann had been overoptimistic in their grand plan, which had been formulated when four hundred thousand settlers were arriving annually and when export grain tonnage was mounting by many million bushels at

every harvest. There was no evidence that the Canadian Northern principals had diverted any funds to enterprises for which they had not been
borrowed, or that they had profited personally out of cash or land subsidies or from guaranteed construction bonds. On the other hand, $218,-
215,409, or more than half of the vast outlay on Mackenzie and Mann
projects, had been contributed or guaranteed by official bodies: such aid
came to $20,505 in cash and more than 600 acres of land grants for every
mile. It therefore was obvious that Canadian taxpayers were the principal
creditors of Mackenzie and Mann enterprises, and as such they had the
right to determine the form that the disposition of the property should
take.

On this key determination, the Royal Commission could not arrive at
a unanimous recommendation. There were a number of solutions available. Mackenzie and Mann had lost their equity in the Canadian Northern,
and the Canadian government must assume their liabilities. On the other
hand, the Borden government at that moment was demanding that the
Grand Trunk Pacific should live up to its commitment and take over the
Eastern Division of the National Transcontinental; it therefore could
scarcely ask the taxpayer to assume a new railway burden at the moment
when it was endeavoring to divest him of another. A receivership would
not suffice, for it manifestly could not be granted authority to tear up
branch lines or restrict services. A partnership with the Canadian Pacific
seemed the easiest way out except for one factor: the people of the four
western provinces would not tolerate a railway monopoly under any circumstances. It was equally impossible to consider sale to United States
railway interests, even if an investor lunatic enough to put up half a billion
dollars could be found.

These impossible alternatives reduced the choice to a single solution.
During the war and even before it, Great Britain had led the way in entrusting authority to quasi-independent bodies empowered to secure two
factors greatly to be desired—management by experts and freedom from
political pressures. The majority report of the Royal Commission therefore recommended that the Canadian Northern properties be taken under
government control by means of a presumably independent Crown corporation. But it took pains not to define the degree of such independence,
for it was an axiom of democracy that those who paid the piper called
the tune.

To this solution, the chairman and the only trained railwayman on
the Royal Commission vigorously dissented. A. H. Smith held that the
Coverdale and Colpitts report faithfully reflected the condition of the

Canadian Northern and that its restoration as a profit-earning property was only a matter of time. He therefore urged that the present crisis be regarded as a temporary mishap caused by the war and that it could be satisfied by an agreement whereby the two distressed systems should pool their services under Grand Trunk Pacific management in the East, Canadian Northern management in the West. Such cooperation should continue until the participants had regained solvency.

The End Comes

Curiously enough, this territorial allocation of management was virtually the policy urged by the Prime Minister fourteen years before when, as leader of the Opposition, he had opposed the construction of the National Transcontinental Railway. There is no reason to believe that by 1917 he had forgotten such views or had changed his mind; the certainty that confronted him was that the times had changed. In the last six months of 1916, the inconclusive battles on the Somme had mauled the flower of the British Empire forces, to the extent of six hundred thousand casualties. The Verdun battles in the early months of 1917 had inflicted even more grievous losses on the French armies, which were threatened with collapse. The Russian armies already were a rabble; the Americans had entered the war, but it would be at least a year before their military strength could be deployed; in the meantime, the British Empire forces must carry virtually the entire burden of the struggle against the Central Powers. In such an emergency, decided the Prime Minister, Canada could not afford a costly and indeterminate railway policy. His decision was best conveyed in his own words:

> Sir William Mackenzie, the dominant partner of the firm of Mackenzie and Mann, was possessed of brilliant initiative, immense resourcefulness and unflinching courage. His conception of constructing and operating a transcontinental railway was almost a dream; and yet it was a dream that in all probability would have become a reality had it not been for the outbreak of war.
>
> On July 14, 1917, I had an interview with Sir William and I definitely informed him that the Government could not grant further aid and must take over the Canadian Northern in its entirety. Sir William was a man of iron nerve and this was one of the only two occasions on which I saw his self-control desert him. Knowing that my decision was final he was silent for a moment and then completely broke down with audible sobs which were most distressing.[1]

The Valuation Proceedings

Had the Royal Commission stuck to its guns, the Prime Minister's decision would have been the end of the matter. It had decided that the shares of the Canadian Northern were worthless; the Canadian government already held 40 percent of them; the way, therefore, was clear for a creditors' takeover. But there was a snag in this straightforward process, for the Canadian Bank of Commerce, which held a lien on the remaining 510,000 shares, stood to lose $10 million under the commission's determination. In Canada, banks are sacrosanct; their failures (until recently) have been regarded as national calamities. It therefore became necessary to set a price for this stock that would get the bank off the hook. It was agreed that the price would be determined by arbitration and that it would not involve the Dominion government in an outlay of more than the amount of the bank's reimbursal. In a letter to Sir George Perley, the Prime Minister admitted that the sole purpose of the valuation was the rescue of the bank.

As a result, such proceedings were sheer hypocrisy, and their only interest to the historian derives from the fact that they gave Mackenzie and Mann one last chance to appeal for a reprieve. If by the arbitrary ruling of the government the outstanding shares of the Canadian Northern might be worth up to ten cents on the dollar of nominal value in order to satisfy the Canadian Bank of Commerce claim, every cent of increase on this figure would add roughly a million dollars to the assets of the Canadian Northern, whose principal officers had maintained without ceasing that such assets had been ludicrously undervalued, both by Coverdale and Colpitts and by the Royal Commission.

The board of arbitration was headed by Sir William Meredith, chief justice of Ontario. Its proceedings ran to 6,393 pages of record and occupied more than three months. The Canadian Northern was represented by a brilliant team led by D. B. Hanna, undoubtedly the ablest Canadian railroad operator of his time, who gave no ground and refuted the charges of insolvency by quoting the contributions that Mackenzie and Mann had made to western Canada—551 towns and villages founded on the naked prairies. These partners had been servants of the provincial and federal governments in every phase of colonization and expansion. All Canadian grain elevators stood beside Canadian Northern tracks, more than nine-tenths of the total population of the prairies was served by that system. Hanna described as inexcusable the omissions of certain Mackenzie and

Mann assets from the Royal Commission's balance sheet, and he declared that, but for the impact of the war, there would have been no shortage of capital nor any crisis over earnings. Z. A. Lash's evidence was a brilliant juridical assault on the conduct of the arbitration that involved him, perhaps unwisely, in sharp personal exchanges with Sir William Meredith. The Canadian Northern spokesman was adept in controversy, knowing when to ply the bludgeon, when to rely on the rapier; some of his deadly ripostes are remembered to this day. No one ever fought more bitterly or better. He was ably seconded by F. H. Phippen, a Minnesota lawyer who gave details of Canadian Northern assets to the value of $65 million that had been omitted by the evaluators. The rival arguments hung in large part over what became known as "replacement costs," which Sir William Meredith was loath to accept, and appraisal of the claims that the provinces hastened to enter in the hope of sharing in the pickings of the corpse. The Canadian Northern case undoubtedly was prejudiced by the failure of its principals to live up to their reputations. Sir Donald Mann proved a bumbling witness, and Sir William Mackenzie did not give evidence.

On May 25, Sir William Meredith delivered judgment. With "replacement costs" accepted as basis of valuation, the $85 million claimed by Canadian Northern advocates as the surplus of its assets over liabilities had been cut down to $25 million, which represented $10.8 million for the outstanding stock. This was the equivalent of $18.00 a share, but this figure was cut to $16.66 to meet the government stipulation of its maximum liability. Mackenzie and Mann were allowed to retain one hundred shares each as souvenirs of twenty laborious years.

On September 6, they and all their principal officers resigned. A new board, headed by a permanent civil servant, took over. On December 20, 1917, an Order-in-Council placed all government-owned railways, including the Eastern Division of the National Transcontinental Railway, the Intercolonial Railway, the Prince Edward Island and eight New Brunswick short lines, a total of 4,205 miles, under management of the Canadian Northern Railway Company, which in future would be known as "Canadian National Railways." Such was the origin of the name that endures to this day. At the outset, it represented 13,610 miles of tracks.

Like spent fireworks, Mackenzie and Mann dropped out of sight, over the public horizon. Mackenzie died in 1923 and Mann at the ripe age of eighty-one in 1934.

16

The Grand Trunk Tragedy

The outbreak of the First World War had come like a thunderclap to both of the new Canadian transcontinental railway systems. They had been under construction for upwards of ten years, and they were still well short of completion; in that period they had become priority enterprises in the growth of Canada. Now as in a twinkling they had been relegated to secondary importance. Thereafter their needs and indeed their futures would be subservient to the requirements of the Canadian war effort.

For both the Grand Trunk Railway, as the parent of the Grand Trunk Pacific, and for the Mackenzie and Mann enterprises, the immediate embargo on the export of British capital was a knockdown blow. But it fell on the Grand Trunk Pacific with particular severity, for its parent had subsisted almost entirely on private British investment, whereas Mackenzie and Mann had relied mostly on Canadian government support. The breakdown figures for August 1914 are not available, but those for June 30, 1916, are indicative of the differing situations confronting the two systems:

RAILWAY	PUBLIC FUNDS		PRIVATE INVESTMENT	
Canadian Northern	$298,253,263	60.3%	$196,509,226	39.7%
Grand Trunk	$28,145,693	6.6%	$396,025,617	93.4%

The Grand Trunk a Viable Property

The Grand Trunk Railway, which had embarked on its transcontinental partnership with the federal government unwillingly, was a strong and growing company. In the first decade of the new century, it had doubled its freight tonnage, its passenger traffic and its gross receipts; it had consolidated its position in the New England, eastern Canadian and Michigan traffic areas; it had established a profitable operational ratio of outlays to earnings. The haulage capacity of its lines had been doubled, and it had acquired some valuable branches and feeders, notably those of the Booth and Rathbun groups in Ontario. Since 1896, its common stock had risen from 5 to 23 and its preferred and protected issues in commensurate degree. It had no outstanding indebtedness of importance except its investment in the Grand Trunk Pacific.

Hays Runs Wild

This investment ($25 million) did not constitute a dangerous liability. It is difficult, however, to acquit the London board of appalling short-sightedness in relinquishing almost complete control of their property to Charles M. Hays. As a dynamic operator, he had aided Rivers-Wilson adequately in the restoration of prosperity, but there was nothing in his history or background to suggest that he was competent to decide issues of high policy. He had enjoyed marked success in his first appearance before the Grand Trunk shareholders, but there was a great deal of difference between stampeding a meeting and negotiating with a government. When in 1909 he replaced Rivers-Wilson as president, Alfred M. Smithers, a static and rather passive Englishman with a financial background became general manager, a position for which he had few qualifications. E. J. Chamberlin took over as head of the Grand Trunk Pacific, relieving F. W. Morse, who had blotted his copybook with everybody.

By and large, this team was not up to the tasks that confronted it. The Bank of Montreal, no friend of the Grand Trunk but recognizing the needs of the times, endeavored, through its British connections, to have Lord Milner succeed Rivers-Wilson. It is interesting to speculate on how that efficient and hard-bitten nobleman would have teamed up with Hays. He certainly would not have allowed him to run wild.

The story of Hays' administration when left to his own resources is one of mounting tragedy. He deeply antagonized the leaders of the Conservative Party, which sooner or later must come into power, and he alienated Laurier and his ministers in almost equal degree by his high-handed behavior. He knew that the contract for the management of the Eastern Division could never be consummated in its present form because the government could not escape responsibility for the delays, waste and venality attendant on its construction. His reasoning apparently ran that if the government could do as it liked, he too was freed from restraint. So instead of adopting a cooperative attitude, he allowed himself to become embroiled in a series of incidents that left Laurier and his ministers in considerable doubt not only of his good sense but also of his good faith.

Acts of Folly

The first of such occasions was the railway strike of 1910. It arose out of the time-honored claim of international unions for the same rates of pay in Canada as in the United States. The Canadian Pacific settled it without difficulty but Hays decided to dig in his heels. This brought him into conflict with Laurier's Minister of Labour, William Lyon Mackenzie King, the most devious politician that Canada has ever known. When Hays was compelled to surrender, he vented his spleen on the strike leaders by refusing to take them back. This stupidity led to an ultimatum from the Prime Minister that advances to the Grand Trunk Pacific would cease until such time as the men were reinstated. Hays never should have invited such a stinging rebuff.

Under terms of the Grand Trunk–Dominion government partnership in the National Transcontinental, it had been laid down that the Grand Trunk Pacific would route as much of its export traffic as possible to Canadian ports. Hays apparently never accepted the prospects of diminishing use on his New England lines; Indeed, it would seem that he saw the Grand Trunk as an American system whose main value lay in its short cut across Canada. Soon after the turn of the century, he proposed an all-American route from Michigan to New England by means of the purchase of a railway along the south shores of Lake Erie and Lake Ontario. He was roundly rebuked by Rivers-Wilson for considering such a project.

Now that Hays was confirmed in control, he returned to another of his castles in the air. It took the form of the extension of the Central Vermont to a terminal in New York City. He was too wise to submit any such proposal to his London board; instead, he represented his project as being of purely local significance—a line seventy-six miles in length to

Providence. The Rhode Island legislature rose to this lure and granted him $10 million for his terminals, whereupon Hays proceeded to lease two small steamships for an interim service to ply southward in the coastal trade.

When construction of this extension began, the banking house of Morgan, which, as the residuary legatee of the Vanderbilt railroad empire, controlled the New York, New Haven and Hartford Railroad, asked their London correspondents to ascertain if the Grand Trunk board knew what their man was up to. As soon as the directors realized that they were challenging a well-established and heavily financed competitor, they immediately vetoed the extension. But at Ottawa, both parties interpreted this enterprise as an attempt to evade a National Transcontinental commitment, for Hays had been stupid enough to admit that he hoped to divert a considerable volume of Canadian grain exports to American ports. This act of folly may have cost the Grand Trunk its last friends at Ottawa.

A Crowning Mercy

Although the parent company was doing well, it had been overtaken by the inflationary spiral attendant on the real estate boom, and from 1911 onward, everything under its Grand Trunk Pacific commitment—wages, maintenance, rolling stock, permanent installations and hotels—was costing far more than the original estimates. At some time in the winter of 1911–1912, Hays began to dream of a masterstroke. He would get rid of the Grand Trunk Pacific by foisting it on the government, after the fashion of the Eastern Division. He then would build into western Canada by way of Chicago. He prepared to place this proposal before the London board, but he was spared rejection and perhaps dismissal when he sailed on the ill-fated *Titanic*. His body never was found. His personal tragedy represented a close parallel to his business career. The Grand Trunk was a lordly property when he took it over—one of the greatest British investments abroad. Hays was an excellent administrator in fair weather but he had little circumspection and poor judgment as a navigator when the fogs came down over tricky channels. Then he began to guess and to falter. Without a background of behavior to guide and to warn him, he piled his ship on the rocks.

If the appointment of Hays to succeed Rivers-Wilson was a mistake, the selection of his successor was a catastrophe. Edson J. Chamberlin was a New Englander of limited education, having entered railway service in his teens; he had no right to be in the same ring with such tough and able adversaries as confronted him in the Borden cabinet, which had come into power the previous year. These ministers were determined not only that largesse to railways must cease but also that the recipients must account for what they had received from the previous administration. Their policy became plain within a few months of taking office, when the government formally requested the Grand Trunk Pacific to take over management of the Eastern Division as in terms of the 1904 agreement. As has been noted previously, this contract called for a rental of 3 percent per annum on construction costs, which by then were triple the original estimates and which made it utterly impossible for that division, with two-thirds of its mileage traversing trafficless terrain, to earn any such fee. Chamberlin was able to sidestep this request by pointing out that the Grand Trunk Pacific contract stipulated that such lease became operative only with the completion of the Eastern Division, which was still far from complete; but the request revealed the stern attitude of the new administration.

An Escape Refused

In January 1912, the Lynch-Staunton-Gutelius Royal Commission was given menacing terms of reference. Although directed primarily at the highly publicized scandals of the Eastern Division, its authority covered the Grand Trunk Pacific as well. It alarmed the London board, which brought Smithers from Canada and appointed him chairman, instructing him to advise Prime Minister Borden privately that it would be quite impossible for the Grand Trunk Pacific to undertake the management of the Eastern Division under the existing agreement.

Borden received this intimation calmly but replied that in that case, the government would be obliged to take over the Grand Trunk Pacific Western Division, as there could be no dismemberment of the National Transcontinental project. Here was a heaven-sent opportunity to escape, and Smithers should have immediately asked the government's terms for such a takeover. The Grand Trunk Pacific had cost its parent and the government approximately the same amount (roughly $100 million) and in the event of a takeover, the company would only lose what it had put into it. The Grand Trunk board, however, refused to comtemplate a humiliating ending to its dream of a system from sea to sea.

The Royal Commission Report

During 1912–1913, the Canadian boom was mounting to its climax, and the Grand Trunk shared in the prosperity of the day. In the spring of 1913, it borrowed £3 million in London without difficulty. In August of that year, Chamberlin, elated by rising returns, gave a foolish interview to the effect that everything was proceeding splendidly and that the Grand Trunk expected to undertake the management of the Eastern Division under the terms of the original agreement. As this was in direct contradiction to Smithers' representations to the Prime Minister, it left the impression that either the Grand Trunk management did not know its own mind or else it was playing a deep game. In either case, the announcement was a silly and unwarranted admission.

When the official report was released, it proved on the whole to be comforting to Grand Trunk supporters. Its tenor may be gleaned from the following general statement:

> The Grand Trunk proper has received much less official assistance than either of the two other great companies with which it is in competition. It began as long ago as 1851, before the Dominion of Canada came into existence and before the modern policies of subsidies and guarantees had been introduced. In the main it has had to rely throughout its history on its own resources and it had had for many years to compete with heavily subsidized rivals. While it was pioneer in giving Canada railway services its shareholders have never had more than moderate dividends. We have felt that this should be borne in mind when dealing with the question of the Grand Trunk Pacific and it has had some influence on the recommendations which we will make later on this subject.[1]

The report also praised Hays' attempts to limit the looting of the the Grand Trunk Pacific project by dishonest contractors and politicans. Here was the material for an immediate approach to the Dominion government, demanding a revision of the terms of partnership of the National Transcontinental project. The company had an unanswerable case; that it did not present it was due in part to Chamberlin's and Smithers' fumbling leadership, in part to a bad conscience over the behavior of Morse and the Grand Trunk Pacific officials in the construction of the Western Division. In addition, there was the danger that the government might require of the Grand Trunk the same terms it had imposed on the Canadian Northern—the provision of parcels of stock in return for cash advances, in which case the shareholders and debenture holders would be instantly in rebellion.

The Pressure Mounts

In January 1915, the Minister of Railways and Canals repeated his request that the Grand Trunk Pacific should respect its responsibilities and take over the management of the Eastern Division. Chamberlain replied with a detailed report, which gave chapter and verse for his contention that as a workable property this section of the National Transcontinental Railway was a dead duck. Its gross earnings were little more than half its operational costs, to say nothing of the interest on its $153 million of debt. The Grand Trunk Pacific would have to find at least $6 million a year to keep it in operation, and that railway was barely breaking even on its own traffic.

When Borden laid this challenging statement before his cabinet, a split ensued. Many of his ministers realized that the difficulties of the Grand Trunk arose from the pressures that Laurier's government had exerted in setting the terms of the original National Transcontinental agreement. Borden himself had declared that the Grand Trunk had been "dragooned" into acceptance; as a consequence, allowances should be made for its present plight. But Cochrane and White, dedicated to their vendetta, had been reinforced by two other cabinet members, both of whom in the course of time were destined to be prime ministers of Canada. Arthur Meighen, a western lawyer of outstanding debating ability, speedily established himself as Borden's heir apparent. Richard Bedford Bennett of Calgary, who in his strange emotional involvements reconciled sentimental imperialism with hard-shell Canadian nationalism, had intimate connections with the Canadian Pacific Railway, and his crusade against the Canadian Northern and Grand Trunk Pacific did him little credit.

The Borden Plan

Cabinet arguments waxed and waned; public controversy mounted. Borden was in a quandary, but he had no intention of making the Grand Trunk pay for honoring a disastrous agreement with a former Canadian government. In a letter of November 27, 1912, to Sir George Perley, the Canadian High Commissioner in London, he revealed that no matter how worthless the shares of the Mackenzie and Mann properties, they must be redeemed at a certain price, "on account of our concern for the stability and reputation of a large financial institution." (This, of course, was the Canadian Bank of Commerce.) The key instruction came in his final paragraph:

> It is important to have it appear that we are willing to stand by the Grand Trunk Pacific in the same way as we propose to stand by the Canadian Northern Railway. . . . I hope in conferring with Mr. Smithers you will see to it that some such clause as that which I have suggested to embodied in his letter to me so that it can be used in Parliament if necessary.

In other words, whatever the financial conditions of the Grand Trunk as a result of its Grand Trunk Pacific venture, it could rely on official support either by transfers of its stock as security against government advances or an evaluation of its stock to be determined by arbitration.

At this juncture the Grand Trunk Pacific indebtedness stood as follows:

Distribution of Grand Trunk Indebtedness

To the Dominion government	$100,027,897
To provincial governments	13,864,774
To the Grand Trunk Railway	106,871,929
Total	$220,764,600

A Lunatic Refusal

The Prime Minister's proposal was sane and generous. He would undertake to keep the distressed systems in operation throughout the war and give them a breathing space thereafter in which to pay off or compound their indebtedness; in return they would give the Canadian taxpayer a measure of assurance and security such as any creditor had a right to expect. It is difficult at this distance to regard its immediate rejection by the London board as other than lunatic. In Smithers' reply, he demanded that the Dominion government take over the Grand Trunk Pacific in entirety and refund Grand Trunk advances in full. This would have cut the Grand Trunk loss to $25 million. Smithers had no case either in equity or in law for such a request, which represented a second refusal by his company to honor the 1904 partnership agreement, this time with far less reason than in the case of the Eastern Division. No

Canadian government could have tolerated such a surrender of its entitlements. In the midst of a war for survival, a fair-minded Prime Minister had been treated as though he could not add or subtract. In this almost incomprehensible stupidity the fate of the Grand Trunk Railway was sealed.

Another Royal Commission

Yet when, on May 8, 1916, the Minister of Finance rose in the House of Commons to discuss the railway situation, the way still seemed open for a reasonable and equitable settlement. White announced that the government would provide a sufficient accountable advance to keep the systems in operation until a Royal Commission could advise on their disposition. Thus the Smith-Drayton-Ackworth Commission, with which the reader already has become acquainted, came into being.

On November 30 of that year, the Grand Trunk was asked to present its case for release from its Grand Trunk Pacific commitment. Here was a superb opportunity for the Grand Trunk to admit its misjudgment in partnership with that of the Canadian government, to state its sound grounds for failing to undertake its Eastern Division commitment, to present in detail the cycle of rising costs on the Western Division and the deliberate blockade that prevented it from benefiting from the traffic of three successive harvests. In conclusion, it could have enumerated the disastrous impacts of the war on its efforts to honor its Grand Trunk Pacific commitments, which had cost four times their original estimates, and it could have ended with an expression of willingness to meet the government wishes in any plan that would preserve its equity and identity.

The Crowning Blunder

It is possible to imagine the conviction and the eloquence with which Sir Henry Tyler or Sir Charles Rivers-Wilson would have driven home such an incontrovertible presentation. But instead, the Grand Trunk spokesmen not only fumbled the ball, they virtually gave away the game. In his main statement of case, Chamberlin made a complete ass of himself. He accused the federal government of having supported a competitor —something that it had not only the right but the duty to do. He threatened it with discredit in the financial capitals of the world. His evidence well deserved the Royal Commission's rebuke:

"Confiscation," "crime," "repudiation of legitimate indebtedness" are grave words to be used by the president of a great company in an official communication referring to the action of the Government. The matter could not rest there. A serious situation was created and one which in our opinion could not rest on mere affirmation or unsupported opinion. We accordingly arranged to hold a *viva voce* examination.[2]

Under expert questioning, Chamberlin gave a pitiful display. He admitted that Grand Trunk policy was to get rid of the Grand Trunk Pacific by any means, at any price. An even more fatal admission was made by Smithers, that current earnings, instead of being employed to meet maintenance charges, had been used to pay interest on certain classes of company securities. This started a witch hunt among Grand Trunk Pacific records. Other instances were unearthed in which that company had manipulated accounts to divert funds to meet its private obligations without commensurate treatment of government advances. Each discovery drove a new nail in the Grand Trunk coffin. These accusations might have been countered in part by Great Britain's recruitment at this time of every available dollar to support her war effort, but neither Chamberlin nor Smithers had the wit to think of such a rejoinder.

Trivial Arguments

The Royal Commissioners met these utterly inept performances by the Grand Trunk spokesmen with the rebuttals they deserved, but they went on to more controversial findings. One of their principal arguments in support of a takeover of the Grand Trunk was that as its head office was in London, it could not properly manage a Canadian enterprise. This was absolute balderdash. The 1916 copy of *Bradshaw's Railway Manual, Shareholders Guide and Directory* showed that 113 railways in twenty-nine different countries were owned by British investors and managed from British head offices. Indeed, as has been pointed out previously, there was a distinct advantage of a Canadian enterprise having a London head office, in that this arrangement kept greedy politicians and other parasites out of the company's waiting rooms.

Another Royal Commission recommendation cannot be described as other than flagrantly unjust. The commissioners refused to recommend a catalogue and valuation of Grand Trunk assets as prelude to expropriation. It would not appraise capital resources, replacement costs and normal peacetime earning potential, although in the examination of the

Canadian Northern, it had been forced to consider each of these factors. Instead, it contented itself with generalities and such futile comparisons as "The Canadian Northern had been economically constructed and moderately capitalized. The same cannot be said of the Grand Trunk and the Grand Trunk Pacific." Yet the commissioners knew that the Canadian Northern in the first instance had been a "colonization railway," not so much built as thrown down whereas the Grand Trunk Pacific had been constructed to the highest specifications; it took traffic from the Canadian Northern from the day it opened for operation. For over fifty years, the Grand Trunk had been built as railways should be built, and in 1917 it showed gross earnings per mile of tracks of more than 50 percent above those of its Canadian competitors. For the Royal Commissioners to make fish of one system, fowl of another, was a shameful procedure, unworthy of the Canadian people.

A Nation Emerges

The mention of "the Canadian people" is deliberate. They had never been a people before. A good case can be made for the emergence of Canadian nationhood, not at Confederation but a full half-century later on the battlefields of Flanders. They had responded magnificently to the call of the Mother Country; a half-million Canadians had seen service in the field. At the end of the war, one out of every five members of the Royal Air Force was Canadian; Billy Bishop of Toronto had shot down more enemy planes than any other Allied airman; Roy Brown of Edmonton was credited with the kill of Baron Richtofen, the greatest German ace. The immediate acceptance by Canadians of mature roles in the Imperial structure of the British Empire gave them authority and created a national identity. The Statute of Westminster in 1926 did no more than legitimatize something already attained: Canada had become a nation.

The first fruit of freedom usually is folly, and this truism the Canadians hastened to demonstrate in their treatment of the Grand Trunk Railway. It was one of the largest Imperial investments, with upward of $400 million of British money in it. This great sum was distributed over nearly one hundred thousand shareholders and debenture holders, the same people who had been steadfast comrades throughout four bloody years of war, those form of government, whose arts and skills, were Canadian prides and inheritances. Yet these ties and obligations were deemed to have ceased to count beside the exhilarating stimulus of coming of age. The truthful Canadian case concerning the Grand Trunk

Railway, whether elevated to its highest common factor or reduced to its lowest common denominator, should have been put in some such form as this:

"We have been obliged to take over the Canadian Northern system, with its indebtedness of upward of a half-billion dollars. It has only piddling connections outside the prairies. It cannot possibly pay its way without a complementary system in eastern Canada. What are we to do? Spend another half-billion in building its eastern division—trackage that we don't need in the slightest? Or take over the Grand Trunk, which has given us our opportunity by letting us down in our partnership in the National Transcontinental?"

Possible Solutions

There was a rough logic in this argument that did not make its implementation any less unjust. It is highly doubtful if the people of Canada would have tolerated an expropriation so close to confiscation if someone whom they respected had replied with equal logic and directness:

"We were your partners in a transaction, the National Transcontinental Railway, which turned out badly for both of us. You yourselves have admitted that part at least of our difficulties have derived from the scandalous behavior of your officers and your politicians in the construction of the Eastern Division of that railway. We built our Western Division in a manner in which we take pride but at a cost, largely because of the war, incommensurate with its earning power. You now wish, without instituting an examination of what we are worth, to take over our parent company, which is prosperous and valuable, for no better reason than that you have been obliged to make a costly deal with another system. This is unfair and you know it. It is not your way or our way of settling such matters."

There was another way out, which Grand Trunk spokesmen, for reasons that are beyond conjecture, failed to exploit. On the outbreak of the war in 1914, the British government took control of all railways for the duration of the conflict, guaranteeing the same returns to their shareholders as they had received in the last year of peace. After American entry into the war, the United States government had acted in similar fashion. There was no reason why Canada should not have done this also, except that it would involve an increase in rates, which a prosperous economy could well afford but which rural Canada would oppose as a matter of principle. But by 1917, the course of the war had introduced another factor that complicated the situation. The volunteer system had run its course, and throughout that year, five Canadian soldiers had fallen in battle for every new enlistment. The Prime Minister, therefore, was negotiating with the Opposition for a coalition administration for the purpose of introducing conscription. French Canada was in rebellion against such a measure, and Borden feared that a rate increase at such a time might cost him the support of the western farmers in his efforts to form a union government.

The Last Opportunity

In August 1917, Chamberlin resigned. He was replaced by Howard Kelly, chief engineer of the company. With its existence at stake, the wonder grows that the board did not seize the opportunity to appoint some outstanding figure competent to array its case in proper context and background. In many parts of the world, the tide was turning against private ownership of communications and transportation media; they were coming to be regarded as essential to national security. In Germany, Hungary, Austria and Russia, railways had been nationalized; in Australia, New Zealand, South Africa and India, they had been taken over for the duration of the war, and the general tendency was to retain them as Crown corporations on the coming of peace. In Canada, the Canadian Council of Agriculture, an influential organization, openly backed nationalization.

The coalition government, as installed in November 1917, therefore, was in a strong negotiating position, and in the following January, Borden reopened correspondence with Smithers, warning him that a settlement with the Grand Trunk could not be delayed. His principal supporters were even more precipitate: White announced that the Grand Trunk was bankrupt and must take whatever the government offered it. He advised Borden to allow the company to default and take the consequences. Meighen declared in the House of Commons, "I think it is quite clear that our negotiations have their cause and starting point in the financial position of the Company and not in any desire on our part to acquire their property."[3] This statement at best was arrant hypocrisy; at worst, utterly untrue.

A month later Meighen as Attorney-General shaped an offer for the lease of the Grand Trunk for 999 years at a rental rising in the ninth year to $5.6 million. Smithers was shocked by this offer, which would only meet the dividends on the priority preference stock (approximately $84 million) and leave nothing for the remainder (approximately $150 million). Sir George Perley, who submitted this offer on behalf of the Canadian government, sympathized with Smithers and thought that it should be improved. But any hope of better terms was dashed by another monumental blunder. The Grand Trunk semi-annual meeting in April resolved into an outright attack upon the Canadian proposals, with the dual role of Sir Henry Drayton assailed by speaker after speaker. As Chief Commissioner of Railways he had no right, they argued, to be appointed to the supposedly judicial Royal Commission. Whatever the substance of this accusation, it was far too late to do anything about it. The London financial press viewed the shareholders' irruption as a call to arms; Borden and his ministers interpreted it as more than a personal insult: it was a reflection on Canadian status, an attempt to treat Canada as if she were still a colony. Aghast at this reaction, Smithers denied the board's responsibility, but the damage had been done.

The Government's Move

In June the Prime Minister, accompanied by Meighen, crossed to London for a showdown. He found the Grand Trunk directors at sixes and sevens; about the only belief they shared was that the Canadian government, having set a valuation on Canadian Northern shares, would never move against the Grand Trunk without a similar valuation; that sort of thing might be done in banana republics but not in a British dominion. Smithers declared that he could raise £3 million in a morning if Canada would guarantee the bonds; he was told abruptly that the day for that sort of thing was past. By the end of July, the Grand Trunk chairman was convinced that the Canadians would stop at nothing to secure control of his property, and he began to dicker on terms. He demanded an annuity of £1,163,000. The Canadian offer amounted to £719,000.

The difference between offer and demand therefore was slightly more than $2 million a year on a property valued conservatively at $400 million. Again it seems incredible that no effort was made to bridge this comparatively minor gap. The British apparently held to the belief that the Canadians were bluffing and if pressed sufficiently would agree to a favorable valuation of Grand Trunk shares; if granted the same treatment as the Canadian Northern, its $115 million of common stock would be worth approximately half that sum. The Canadians for their part had been incensed by what they regarded as the under-the-counter tactics of the Grand Trunk management and were unwilling to make any concessions. They knew that negotiations had begun with the Canadian Pacific Railway for the acquisition of the Grand Trunk's American properties, which the London board believed (foolishly) to be out of reach of the rapacious Canadians.

The End of the Dicing

The end of the war in November 1918 in effect ended the efforts of the Prime Minister to obtain adequate compensation for the Grand Trunk. Borden was a spent man, and Sir Thomas White thereafter dealt with railway matters with very little reference to his chief. Early in 1919, there was an unsatisfactory exchange of proposals, and at the end of February, Kelly announced that services on the Grand Trunk Pacific would terminate on March 10. White immediately put that company into receivership and obtained a court order to compel the parent company to liquidate its commitments. Kelly refused to take this demand seriously and announced that he was hiring a distinguished firm of accountants to recommend terms on which he might reopen negotiations on the annuity offer. He received a reply—postponed for two months because a substantial element of the Union government did not like White's highhanded methods—to the effect that the government offer had expired and would not be renewed.

Once again it seems incredible that the Grand Trunk board should not have foreseen such a move, which effectively shackled it. Unless the parent company could arrange a settlement of Grand Trunk Pacific liabilities, it was finished. It had no case in law for avoiding its responsibilities, and its strong claim for compassionate consideration was of no account under a receivership. When the Grand Trunk Pacific debenture stocks became due in September, the government met their service as the de facto proprietors of that railway and introduced legislation in the House of Commons with which to determine the liability of its parent. This measure had a rough passage through both the House and the Senate, not because of any particular sympathy for the Grand Trunk but lest the arbitrators might feel justified in placing an undue value on its shares. A last-minute rider limited the maximum award to $5 million, which was more or less what the Grand Trunk had sought as an annuity.

The Grand Trunk Acquisition Act passed on November 5, after an all-night sitting, by the sparse margin of four votes. At noon that day, Arthur Meighen appeared before the Canadian Club of Montreal to sell the deal to the public. There was now no high-minded nonsense of rescuing the railway from itself; Canada must possess the Grand Trunk in order to make the Canadian Northern pay. This shameless avowal of expediency led to interruptions and heckling (almost unheard of previously at Canadian Club luncheons): one gentleman was reported as having risen in his place, shouted "Naboth's Vineyard," and walked out. Its reception by the Grand Trunk annual meeting was more decorous, although one critic, a gentleman of the cloth, interpolated that its shareholders got what they deserved for building a railway in a country that had no morals whatsoever.

On May 21, 1920, the government of Canada took formal possession of 7,957 miles of tracks of the Grand Trunk and Grand Trunk Pacific railways, including 1,614 miles in the United States. A board of arbitration was set up to determine the current value (if any) of the $629,950,532 in securities sunk in the parent company and its offspring. It was headed by Sir Walter Cassels, Chief Justice of the Exchequer Court of Canada, with Sir Thomas White, no longer a cabinet minister, as the representative of the government of Canada. William Howard Taft, formerly President of the United States and a lawyer of outstanding distinction, appeared for the Grand Trunk.

The Arbitration Proceedings

There was neither good will nor good manners in the initial contacts of the adversaries. Proceedings were delayed until February 7, 1921, ostensibly because employees of the Grand Trunk refused to aid the government officers in their examination of company records. At this juncture, strong-arm tactics were introduced and the government threatened to cancel the arbitration proceedings and to defy the Grand Trunk in any attempts to regain its property. Under this threat of forcible dispossession, the Grand Trunk employees became more accommodating. In April, the head office was transferred to Canada and arbitration was reauthorized.

On May 26, an all-Canadian board of directors headed by Sir Joseph Flavelle took charge. The arbitration proceedings continued throughout the summer but with a foregone conclusion. White and Taft were barely on speaking terms. White's case dealt almost entirely with ancient history and the Canadian public had the edification of hearing a

Liberal Prime Minister defended by a Tory of the Tories; the conniving Rivers-Wilson had hypnotized the simple, honest Laurier into the National Transcontinental catastrophe. It was Morse and Hayes and not those free companions of railwaydom, Mackenzie and Mann, who had been responsible for the overbuilding of branch lines on the prairies; it was the Grand Trunk who did not know how to operate railways. And so on. Knowledgeable officers must have listened with amazement as the government spokesman got the venom out of his system.

Sir Walter Cassels, on the other hand, behaved as a judge should. He weighed the evidence carefully, and in large part he convicted the Grand Trunk out of the mouths of its officers. After the departure of Rivers-Wilson, expediency had been the hallmark of Grand Trunk administration. Hays and Smithers alike had condoned devious and sometimes outright dishonest methods to achieve their twin necessities of meeting the commitments inherent in the partnership with the government in the National Transcontinental Railway and in keeping the London board and shareholders from asking too many questions. In many instances, they had deceived no one but themselves, for they were hounded remorselessly by the calendar. By 1917, interest charges on the Grand Trunk Pacific were increasing by $21 a minute; the mounds of unproductive indebtedness swelled into hills, the hills into mountains. Cassels' inexorable conclusion was that the situation of the Grand Trunk had passed the point of no return and that there was not the slightest hope of any shareholder in the unprotected issues of that company ever receiving a cent on his investment.

In rebuttal, William Howard Taft fought magnificently. He took off the gloves where White was concerned; he recited as many malfeasances by government officers as White had found among Grand Trunk executives. He believed that an independent authority should have been entrusted to make a valuation, and he refused to believe a railway company that over the years 1910–1917 had achieved a steadily increasing volume of traffic and had maintained an average operational ratio of 74.05 percent could be dismissed as insolvent and without value, whatever its extraneous commitments. All it needed was time; with peace restored, a breathing space should be granted it. He estimated that by 1926, the operational surplus of the Grand Trunk would be in the neighborhood of $22.5 million, which would permit a distribution of $3 million to its shareholders; this sum, if capitalized on the ordinary basis of 5 percent, would give the unprotected Grand Trunk stocks and bonds an overall value of $64 million.

William Howard Taft,
former President of the
United States who led the
defense of the Grand Trunk
Railway in the expropriation
proceedings.
(COURTESY OF THE PUBLIC
ARCHIVES OF CANADA)

Taft warned Canada of the long-distance impact of what was, in effect, an act of confiscation. The government was in considerable part responsible for the Grand Trunk plight; it had accorded the Canadian Northern a more favorable basis of valuation than it was prepared to extend to the Grand Trunk; it had refused to accept American valuations for the Grand Trunk lines in the United States, which earned more than half its gross revenues; in other words, the government actions were arbitrary even if within the letter of the law. For a country that would be in need of foreign investment for a long time to come, there was every advantage in generosity and corresponding danger in demanding its pound of flesh. Here Taft was repeating Borden's warnings as given on more than one occasion. He might have added that Canadians had established a shining name for themselves in the First World War and it ill behoved them to tarnish it by taking advantage of kinsmen whose blood had commingled with their own on a score of battlefields.

However, the views of the two Canadians on the arbitration board prevailed, and unprotected Grand Trunk shares to the par value of $180,422,381 became waste paper. It was perhaps the greatest single overseas loss sustained during the war, when British foreign investments fell from $22 billion to little more than half that figure. But the majority of such losses—the buying ring that cooperated to take over British branch factories at next to nothing in the United States, the forced sales imposed on British-owned properties in South America—were accepted willingly as part of the price of survival; whereas the forced expropriation without compensation of a railway that had served a British dominion faithfully and well since colonial days and had fallen on evil times through little fault of its own left a bad taste in British mouths that never has been entirely eradicated.* It might have been far wiser of the Canadians to have allowed normal bankruptcy proceedings to have taken their course.

Bob Edwards, the scapegrace editor of the *Calgary Eye Opener* who had the knack of packing wisdom into a nutshell of words, summarized accurately the denouement of the episode. "The Grand Trunk got a shabby deal," was his comment. "It had asked for it."

An immediate Grand Trunk appeal against the award was rejected by the Privy Council, on the grounds that it lacked jurisdiction. A shareholders' petition besought review of the decision on the grounds of morality and equity. This approach was referred to a committee of Canadian civil servants, who took eighteen months to deal with it. While this request was under review, a shareholders' committee operated on another tack, apparently to impress on Canadians that good manners are not necessarily a sign of weakness; it condemned the Grand Trunk proceedings as basically a "Stand-and-Deliver" operation, the equivalent of highway robbery. This approach was rejected out of hand and it also undermined the compassionate plea. In the months that followed, both sides talked a lot of nonsense, with their eyes on newspaper headlines. In 1923, when William Lyon Mackenzie King, the new Prime Minister, was about to leave for an Imperial Conference, to cushion his reception he issued a pamphlet in which he appealed to British sporting instincts, inviting the hundred thousand shareholders to take their losses like gentlemen, hoping for better luck next time. Had he ended there, with perhaps an expression of sympathy, no one would have thought him either better or worse than the general run of politician. But he continued with a carefully scaled denigration of the Grand Trunk in which there was scarcely a word of truth. That railway he maintained, never had been a Canadian property;

---

* The writer, in the course of fifteen years in the Canadian foreign service, occupied posts in the Caribbean, in Africa and in Australia. He seldom visited any part of the Commonwealth in which he was not reproached, sometimes in bitter terms. The kin of the Grand Trunk's hundred thousand shareholders and debenture holders were far-flung; at best they considered its takeover as arbitrary, at worst, as thievery.

it had been mismanaged from London; it had failed to keep up, with the times and so had come to an untimely end. There was scarcely an item in this elaborate distortion that did not invite those who knew the history of the venture to strike fists on the table and say "That's a damned lie." The Prime Minister's sorry inventions were a shocking example of political expediency, and had it not been for the proud name that Canadians had won on the battlefields of Flanders, his pamphlet might have done incalculable damage to the relations with Great Britain.

The harassing campaign continued, and in 1923, George P. Graham, then Minister of Railways and Canals, was given a rough reception in London. He lost his temper. Action was taken in Ontario courts against the Crown for illegal expropriation. It ran through Trial Court, Court of Appeal and on to the Privy Council, where their Lordships ruled as before that they lacked jurisdiction.

In 1934, the former shareholders attempted to persuade the British government to sell Newfoundland, then a Crown colony, to Canada for enough to satisfy their claims. The authorities naturally rejected such a harebrained suggestion and the agitation gradually became a lost cause, but not without leaving its scars.

17

New Venture: Changed World

In September 1917, when the government of Canada took over the Mackenzie and Mann properties, it also acquired, almost as a matter of course, David Blythe Hanna. He was the outstanding Canadian railway executive, a man of few illusions and unparalleled experience. He knew that the only hope of success in the operation of publicly owned properties lay in their insulation from politicians of all ranks and cadres, from aldermen to prime ministers. Before accepting the post, he made it quite clear to Sir Robert Borden that an official pronouncement to this effect must precede his appointment as general manager of Canadian National Railways.

In September 1917, J. D. Reid, Minister of Railways and Canals, provided the requisite assurance. In a letter to Hanna he wrote, "Your Board must operate without any interference from anyone connected with this Department or outside of it. The future of government ownership of railways depends entirely on their operation being carried on free from any political or other influence." On March 16, 1918, the Prime Minister underlined this assurance in a speech in the House of Commons: "We shall use every means available to the Government (and if necessary we shall come to Parliament for that purpose) in order that anything like political influence, political patronage or political interference shall be eliminated from the administration of the railroad." Such forthright declarations carried extra weight since they were announced as the policy of a union government and so became the pledges of both political parties.

Hanna naturally enough chose the majority of his staff from his Canadian Northern associates, since that company had contributed more than two-thirds of the 14,360 miles of tracks of the new system. Z. A. Lash remained as senior counsel and R. M. Horne-Payne continued as financial representative in London. Among others retained Gerard Ruel, S. J. Hungerford and R. C. Vaughan were destined for long and honorable service. The system was reorganized into eastern and western regions, with seven divisions in all. Hanna's first concern was rehabilitation, for due to the exigencies of war, everything was in a thoroughly dilapidated condition. In April 1918, a vote of $50 million provided for 70 locomotives, 6,400 cars and coaches, 300,000 tons of rails and 2.5 million ties. Terminal facilities, marshaling yards and repair shops also received attention.

Cost of the McAdoo Award

This heavy program was no more than in train when labor troubles intervened. The United States government, on taking over all railroads for the duration of the war, immediately was confronted with a host of wage demands, in part justifiable because of galloping inflation, but also because in the American tradition any government was regarded as a fount of largesse. At the end of April 1918, the McAdoo Award gave United States railwaymen more cream than they had hoped for; in the ensuing twenty months the American Treasury disbursed $2,587,810,000 over and above the gross earnings of the railroads. Canadian railwaymen, as brethren of the same international unions, sought equal treatment, and because the war had reached its critical stage, they got it; in some instances Canadian wage rates quintupled. In 1914, labor costs on Canadian lines amounted to $2,717 per annum per mile. In 1919, the corresponding figure was $5,372.

On a November forenoon, the war ended, and immediately the east bound trains began to disgorge hundreds of westerners at Ottawa to demand that branch line construction, which had been halted for four years, be resumed without delay. During the last two years of the war, the "Feed Britain" campaign had sent grain prices soaring and land values with them; ordinary farm land had tripled in cost. Virtually everyone believed that millions of Britons and Europeans, freed from the shackles of privation and danger, would turn to Canada with yearning eyes, seeking new homes and opportunities.

Signs Patent of a New World

It did not work out that way. The fearful toll of the First World War made only one thing certain—that things never would be the same again on this planet. For fifty years, subconscious urges had been fermenting in the Western World, and four years of conflict had detonated them. As always in history, the instruments of change were mobility media—the devices of communication and transportation. The shrinking of the earth that began with the utilization of steam continued with the employment of electricity in instantaneous communications and with an extraordinary proliferation of the printed word. The two devices that outranked all others in their impacts on human behavior arrived with the twentieth century. The motion picture brought the whole world into individual ambit, and the motor car made every man his own engine driver and thus freed him from the confines of distance. These enlargements of human experience presaged revolutionary developments in habits of mind and ways of life.

During the Victorian era, while communications devices, such as the telegraph, the telephone, the phonograph and ever-increasing advertising media, were preparing the way for a worldwide expansion of human awareness and intimacy, the transportation industries had failed to keep pace with them. Railways were not greatly different at the end of the reign of the Good Queen than at its beginning, sixty-odd years before. The only new transportation device of this period, the bicycle, was useful only for short distances on good roads. Together with the typewriter, it played some role in the emancipation of women, but, on the whole, it was of local importance. But in 1885, Gottlieb Daimler managed to harness explosions in cylinders and persuaded them to drive pistons. In Michigan, Henry Ford heard of this and decided to apply it to a stationary engine that would become a man-of-all-work on his father's farm. It was only when he got a job in town that he realized that he had hit upon something that would enable workmen to get to and from their daily employments more quickly and easily. From the Chicago slaughterhouses (which got it from a British admiral of the seventeenth century, who cranked a circular platform through a ship's oven to cook his sea biscuits) he learned of the workings of an assembly line. He began to produce horseless carriages almost as fast as he could sell them, with their costs steadily falling; in fifteen years the Model T came down from $780 to $290. There were no frills and furbelows about it; as Ford put it, his customers could have a car of any color they liked as long as it was black.

The Magic of the Motor Car

Then came the First World War, which made the United States the richest nation in the world. In those years, the automobile became a social symbol; according to the Middletown Survey of that period, one in every six of the population of a typical American community owned a motor car, although eight out of every ten still had no bathrooms.

At the end of the war, automobiles took Canada by storm. The returning troops wanted to forget dead comrades and the bonds of discipline; to be behind the wheel of a car satisfied their needs. The Canadian newspapers of the early 1920s seldom went to press without some mention of them. Some extolled them, some damned them; they were represented as symbols of joyous living and also as mobile bedrooms into which no virtuous woman would allow herself to be enticed. They revolutionized leisure and increased the annual travel mileage of the average Canadian by more than twentyfold; they made the streets and roads more dangerous and led to unheard-of-expenditures on thoroughfares and highways. They contributed to crime and accidents, and they infuriated farmers whose horses they frightened and whose sheep they killed. The Quebec legislature in 1923 introduced a measure making it compulsory for herdsmen on roads to carry a red light with their animals in hours of darkness; on the other hand, a Montreal magistrate described traffic signs as a Yankee desecration of decent streets and gave a driver two months in jail for a parking offense. At the end of that year, there were eight hundred blacklisted drivers in the province and the legislature was confronted with concurrent demands for heavier penalties for traffic offenses and equally strident appeals for increases in the speed limits. Only one thing was certain. Automobiles had come to stay.

A Change of Direction

The first impact of motor cars on railways was oblique but unmistakable. It changed the axis of travel of Canadians, which previously, either for business or for pleasure, had been east-west. In the pre-automobile years there were no north-south roads of much consequence and only nine railway crossings of the international boundary on a frontier of 3,000 miles. But by the early nineteen-twenties there were hundreds of roads linking Canada and the United States, each of which to some degree intensified Canadian sectionalism. The British Columbian became more of a Pacific coaster, the prairie folk felt closer to Montana and the Dakotas than to Ontario and Quebec; these latter provinces had neighbors near at hand who were more to their taste than their kin farther away.

The First World War had eroded provincialism, but the motor car reinstated it. Thereafter, Canadians on Armistice Day were old soldiers, on Victoria Day they were citizens of the Empire, but on Dominion Day they played baseball. If a national canvass in search of a Canadian identity had been made at this time it would have found the Maritimers to feel neglected, the *Québeçois* rejected; the prairie dwellers believed that they existed to be milked by the easterners, the British Columbians that they were too few and too far away to count in Canadian affairs. What the citizens of this straggling line of provinces needed above all else was to see more of each other and to get to know each other better, but the traffic lanes now had begun to run in the wrong direction, eroding the ties that the railways had created so sedulously and expensively.

In January 1920, the takeover of the Grand Trunk properties began. Other absorptions followed; by the end of the year, Canadian National Railways was probably the largest system in the world.* It had originated in 221 different railway ventures, some of which had no sensible reason for being, but all of which had to be maintained and sustained, for no Canadian constituency would relinquish a mile of track willingly. Traffic was growing and the system earned operational surpluses but never nearly enough to satisfy the requirements of its bonded indebtedness. When the postwar boom began, the costs of operations soared. Hanna was obliged to admit that the original government grant fell far short of his requirements; in a single year operational costs had risen from $61,054,588 to $84,265,268. The operational deficit in 1920 reached $36,842,070, and when interest charges were added, it rose to $67,505,059. The colonization campaign had been an almost utter failure; in 1920, the sales of farm land on the prairies only amounted to 17,032 acres. Wages remained at double their prewar level, and taxation had increased fivefold since 1914.

Public Discontent

Such results could not go unnoticed, and it began to dawn on the Canadian public that in their railways they had inherited not a lordly craft but a leaky ship. When in 1921 the results were no better, complaints

---

* The Russian Railways, if regarded as one system, probably was larger.

began to be heard. The Maritime Provinces spokesmen, who had always resented the inclusion of the Intercolonial in the national system, wanted their property back. Outcries in the House of Commons elicited the customary soothing syrup in the form of an inquiry by a select standing committee. Five weeks and 499 pages of fine print later, this body adjourned with the only result, according to a cynical observer, that the committee members had learned enough about railway operations to make nuisances of themselves on future occasions. But the situation did impel two prominent Canadians to proffer suggestions. Sir Joseph Flavelle, interim chairman of the Board of Canadian National Railways, approached Prime Minister Meighen with a tentative plan for reorganization, which involved in some instances autonomous powers to eastern and western divisions, with 4,600 miles of western branch lines to be abandoned and with government loans and advances to a total of $353 million to be written off, since it was manifestly impossible for the system ever to earn interest on them.

Lord Shaughnessy, president of the Canadian Pacific Railway, suggested something different. He believed that expert management was what the situation required. He agreed with Flavelle on the necessity of abandoning a considerable mileage of unproductive short lines; after such action, the Canadian Pacific should be hired to manage what remained. He felt that it should be possible to reach an operational ratio that would meet all charges, including debt redemption. On the whole, Canadians doubted Flavelle and distrusted Lord Shaughnessy, and the proposal to abandon unprofitable branch lines all but brought the muskets down from over the fireplaces.

Hanna's Clash with Mackenzie King

Canadians, therefore, were sharply divided on railway issues when the December 1921 election ousted Meighen and replaced him with William Lyon Mackenzie King, who had been hanging around the portals of power for a decade. This extraordinary man, an able but untrustworthy negotiator who still nourished the feud with Great Britain that had sent his grandfather into rebellion in 1837, who believed himself to be in communion in the spirit world, not only with his mother but also with his dog, yet who possessed an unncanny comprehension of Canadian trends of thought and of how to exploit them to his own advantage, had no intention of allowing any Crown corporation to exercise any degree of independence, as promised by his predecessor. He immediately clashed with

Hanna, who had dismissed three railway employees for flagrant violations of his order against participating in the election campaign. The general manager, when compelled to reinstate these men, made no secret of his displeasure; he declared quite openly that when ministers of the Crown instructed him to keep Canadian National Railways free of political influences, he had been naive enough to believe that they meant it. There followed a heated hearing of the Public Accounts Committee, which undertook to compel the railway to divulge the prices that it had paid for certain commodities; Hanna said bluntly that such information was none of its business and that he was well aware that the request was designed to assist the right people to get the next order. When Hanna ruled that no employee could accept nomination for any political post and continue in the service, the Prime Minister immediately telegraphed a Manitoba railwayman who proposed to stand in a provincial election to disregard such instruction, whereupon Hanna put on his coat, took his hat off the rack and walked out.

Search for a Successor

There manifestly was no Canadian of the caliber to succeed him, and Sir Joseph Flavelle let it be known that he wished to be relieved as chairman of the board as soon as possible. If it meant importing a manager, the likeliest coverts to draw were those of the United States, which already had provided Canada with such outstanding railwaymen as Shaughnessy, Van Horne and Hays. A number of leading executives, including the president of the Southern Pacific, were approached; some came, looked, listened and expressed regrets; it is doubtful it they found Canadian political attitudes reassuring. Then out of nowhere a new name was heard. It was that of Sir Henry Worth Thornton.

First of all, he was Anglo-American and these were years in which Canadians were still proud of their British heritages and respected those whom the Crown had honored. He was born in Indiana and was a university graduate when he joined the Pennsylvania Railroad in 1894. He was among the first of the educated railroaders, and he found no difficulty in competing with those who had learned their trades in the hard school of experience. By 1901, he was a divisional superintendant, and when the Long Island Railroad, the first of the great New York commuter services, was inaugurated, he became assistant to its president. Conventionally trained railway executives had a lot to learn about short-haul passenger traffic; it was a much more intimate business than other types of railroading. Thornton had taken to it like a duck to water; he concealed his energy and adaptability behind a genial and easygoing exterior. His conceptions of management centered around the thesis that subordinates should be made to feel that they counted and that they were essential elements in the processes of transportation; also, he believed that commuter traffic was something more than handling human cargo. Morning and evening customers deserved something similar to what passengers got on ocean liners. They were not only travelers but also guests of those who carried them.

At that time, the largest commuter system in the world was the Great Eastern Railway, which served the southern suburbs of London. Lord Claude Hamilton, chairman of its board, having heard rumors, dispatched directors to report on the Long Island setup. As a result, in February 1914, Thornton was offered the post of general manager of the Great Eastern Railway.

It was a plum, and naturally he took it. Barring a few die-hards who deemed the intrusion of an American a blot of the British escutcheon, he was received warmly and by none more so than the rank and file of railwaymen, whose hearts he won by the reception of their delegation at a directors meeting soon after his arrival in London. He insisted on their being seated and he addressed them as "gentlemen." Thereafter he could do no wrong. He became a firm friend and boon companion of their leader, the irrepressible J. H. ("Jimmy") Thomas, with results that will be reported in due course.

Then came August of that year and the end of an era, when the British peoples drew themselves together to fight for the survival of their ways of life. Thornton only had been in London for five months, but he had been gauged and immediately had been recruited as an advisor to the War Office on transportation problems. There he broke the ice immediately by the sort of apt comparison that a seagoing people would appreciate. The Royal Navy, he said, had been renowned across the centuries because of its mobility; it could go anywhere, do anything, because its lines of communication were assured. Railways could circumvent the problems of distances for the footsoldier, giving him the same degree of mobility. Such bold thinking, coupled with his friendly disposition and powers of persuasion, caused the War Office to claim him, first for a local appointment and afterward for service in France as Inspector-General of Transportation. There he met the Canadian railway troops under Jack Stewart, whose service is descirbed in an earlier chapter; he did not fail to honor such valuable auxiliaries. He became known for his courteous treat-

ment of all ranks, which contrasted with that of many senior officers of
that day, and he rose to the rank of major-general. In March 1919, only
five years after arrival in Britain, he became Sir Henry Thornton. He
bore his honors modestly and engagingly as he settled back into harness at
Great Eastern Railway headquarters.

The Call to Canada

The postwar years in Great Britain were in sad contrast to the
orderly, prosperous scene that had greeted Thornton in 1914. With
nearly a million dead, half her vast overseas investments liquidated, with
disillusion challenging her traditions and Imperial relationships weakened,
British postwar reconstruction promised to be long and laborious. Among
Thornton's personal friends was Sir Henry Wilson, an eccentric but far-
sighted Ulsterman who had served notably as chief of the Imperial General Staff. On a morning in June 1922, at Thornton's invitation, he had
unveiled a memorial to the war dead of the Great Eastern Railway, under
the glass dome of Liverpool Street Station. An hour later he died on the
steps of his home, sword in hand, under the pistols of Irish assassins.

Thornton was deeply shocked; murder in the heart of perhaps the
safest city in the world may have brought to a head his own difficulties
and discouragements in repairing the ravages of the war on the Great
Eastern Railway. Now for the first time he showed the lack of toughness
in an emergency that was destined to haunt him throughout his days. He
apparently consulted Jimmy Thomas, who drew to his attention that the

Sir Henry Worth Thornton,
president, Canadian National
Railways, 1922–32.
(COURTESY OF UNDERWOOD &
UNDERWOOD, WASHINGTON, D.C.)

Canadian government was searching for a successor to D. B. Hanna. Thornton immediately was interested. He told Thomas that he had met many Canadians in France; that they were a hard-bitten lot who endured rather than enjoyed life; but, like the British, when they made a promise they kept it. He was destined to learn that there were exceptions to that rule.

It seems possible that Thomas also made it his business to see that the Canadians were apprised of Thornton's willingness to make a change. In the summer of 1922, the High Commissioner of Canada in London received instructions to render a confidential report on him. It was favorable, and Thornton was invited to visit Canada. No time was wasted; he arrived in Ottawa on September 17, and that evening Prime Minister King introduced him as "the man who is going to head Canadian National Railways." His appointment dated from December 1, at a salary far beyond the range of civil service emoluments of that time.

His decision to leave England evoked newspaper headlines in all parts of the British Isles, with widespread expressions of regret. "He was a Right Sort of Bloke" and "England to Lose Superman" were typical headlines in the London press. He had not been Anglicized, but he was what nearly every Englishman in his secret heart would have liked to be— a good chap at his job but not chained to the rule book, able to sustain the dignity of his position without being stuffy about it. Honors crowded in on him; His Majesty the King invited him to stay at Windsor Castle, and perhaps most significant of all, he received the first membership badge in a railway union ever to be awarded to an executive officer.

On his first interview in Canada, Thornton paid a tribute to Hanna and declared that he proposed to pick up the task of integrating the constituent properties of Canadian National Railways where his predecessor had dropped it. He nailed his flag to the mast with his final declaration: "I intend to make it as clear as I possibly can that there is not going to be any government interference in the management of Canadian Government Railways. My Board, I feel sure, hopes to administer this great property in the interest of no section but of all Canadians."[1]

He thus repeated the assurance that Prime Minister Borden had given Hanna four years ago and whose dishonor by Mackenzie King had caused that able officer to depart. In other words, Thornton was prepared, if necessary, to carry his case of independence for a Crown corporation past the politicians to the people. It was probably then, before he had taken office, that the first knives were loosened in their sheaths. Elephants have nothing like as long memories as Canadian politicians.

18

Potentials and Perils

The physical property with which Thornton had been entrusted included the residual assets of 221 different railway companies, with 22,110 miles of tracks of which 1,300 miles lay in the United States. As of January 1923, its staff consisted of 99,169 employees, which made it by far the largest private employer of labor in Canada.

If the new president had been impelled to reduce his problems as head of Canadian National Railways to their lowest common denominators, his tabulation might have been set out as something like this:

Major Problems and Solutions

PROBLEM	CURE
1. Inherited debt	More long-haul traffic
2. Canadian Pacific hostility	Competitive services
3. Political interference	Insistence on independence

Converted into concrete objectives, these solutions might have emerged as follows:

PROBLEM	SOLUTION
1. Inherited debt	Traffic development by a new and vigorous Sifton-type campaign for the colonization of western Canada

2. Canadian Pacific Railway competition	The expansion of Canadian National Railways from a railway system into a transportation complex, offering the same attraction and conveniences as its rival
3. Political involvements	The creation of a national property that possessed an image too valuable to be subject to parochial pressures or to be at the mercy of the strategy and tactics of party politics

The Menace of the Political Factor

The high ideals of the Union government, which had sponsored Canadian National Railways because of the exigencies of the First World War, soon evaporated in the heat of the hustings. Canada was no sooner at peace abroad than the political parties were at war at home, with railway policy a major bone of contention. In the debate on the Speech from the Throne in the spring of 1922, the Liberals had appealed for fair play for the new system. The Conservatives had replied with a prognosis of disaster. Parliamentary critics overlooked nothing in their search for accusations; one speaker based his charges on the claim that a recently appointed director formerly had been a notorious bootlegger. The humorist Stephen Leacock, then the Will Rogers of Canada, pronounced the nationally owned system to be an intolerable burden and suggested that it be given to China. This sort of buffoonery gained a wider audience than it deserved, and when postmortems on the First World War revealed that victory had been only slightly less costly and inconclusive than defeat, disillusionment became the fashionable mood of the moment. There is an old Spanish proverb that declares that no man is a hero to his horse. At this time, a substantial proportion of the thinking public of all free nations was suspicious of the efficacy of their institutions; prominent figures were apt to evoke cynicism rather than admiration. Canada, which had left more dead on the battlefields than the United States, which had twelve times its population, was far from immune to this spirit of skepticism, and Sir Henry Thornton, hailed as a wonder-worker, was confronted on arrival with questions rather than handshakes. Canadians did not want to be told. They wanted to be shown.

On the evening of September 22, the elite of the business world of Canada gathered at the Windsor Hotel in Montreal for the official welcome to Thornton. There were the customary bouquets, but even on this first occasion, some roses bared their thorns. The guests on the whole were far from welcoming government ownership of railways. In his first official address, Thornton chose to be somewhat less than ebullient, pitching his response to the words of welcome in a moderate yet confident key. Soon afterward he set off on a nationwide tour of the system. He was received cautiously in Nova Scotia, where Ottawa appointments were still suspect, but in Ontario he fell into a carefully laid trap when he expressed interest in electrical transportation, which was a provincial monopoly; that true-blue and ultra-Tory newspaper *The Toronto Telegram* (from then onward classified him as an intruder when not as a menace. In the West he fared better, for there railways were objects of desire, and eastern Canadians were regarded as parasites who sucked the honest farmers dry. Anyone whom the East did not like could expect some sort of a welcome on the prairies.

From the first, however, Thornton managed to make friends. Many people liked him as soon as they saw him. Among others was Sir Joseph Flavelle, whose role in the formation of the merger has been noted. During the First World War, Flavelle's bacon, according to Canadian troops, had been no more than salt pig, but for civilians his sterling public services had placed him on a high plateau of opinion. After his first meeting with Thornton, he wrote to J. A. Dafoe, the brilliant but militantly nationalist editor of *The Manitoba Free Press:*

> He is very simple and unassuming, speaks little of himself but stresses the value of team-play. Nor does he attempt to create a favourable opinion of what he may do in the future by finding fault with the present system. . . . He is an excellent mixer and has quite won the hearts of all who have met him. If he is as good in action as on dress-parade the Government has made a wise choice.[1]

The Dead Weight of Opposition

From this view, Arthur Meighen, leader of the Conservative Party and recently ousted as Prime Minister, emphatically dissented. This dour Tory has been perhaps the only Canadian political leader to date with any pretensions to intellectual attainments. He took an early occasion to put on record his dislike both of the Canadian National Railways as a Crown corporation and of Thornton as an imported administrator. Guided by instinct rather than by logic, he began to marshal the hard-shell clans in opposition. At the 1922 autumn session of the House of Commons, battle was joined. It raged for five months. The principal bone of contention was a Thornton inheritance from the previous regime, in the form of a bill to build twenty-six additional branch lines, all but one of which were in western Canada. The Senate eventually threw out the measure, and opposition spokesmen saw to it that Thornton, who had no more than technical responsibility for it, was plentifully bespattered in the debate.

In these first confrontations with his political masters, he came to realize his lonely eminence. No one shared his staggering responsibility to transform Canadian National Railways into a viable property. In 1922, its operating expenses ($231,172,303) were within 1.3 percent of its gross earnings ($234,059,025), leaving virtually nothing for the service of $1,311,448,713 of inherited debt. In order to meet the annual charges on this sum, Canadian National Railways would have to increase its earnings by 24.8 percent with no increase in operating expenses—an impossible undertaking.

Thornton's plans for the property, therefore, had to start from well behind scratch. Arrayed against him stood the powerful Canadian Conservative party, the City of London (where the confiscated $200 million of Grand Trunk stocks were destined to haunt Canadian borrowers for years to come) and the Canadian Pacific Railway, whose tidy system of 13,342 miles of tracks, together with great hotels and lordly liners on the seas, were in marked contrast to the crazy patchwork structure of its government-owned rival.

No Help from the Board of Directors

Nor did government ownership confer any favors on the new system except insofar as it prevented foreclosure by creditors. Thornton adhered to the letter of the undertaking of his predecessor Hanna that he would seek no political aid nor would he grant any politically inspired privileges. The Government, acting on behalf of the Canadian people, therefore nominated his board of directors. Thornton had every right to expect that he would be given the best business brains of the nation to support him in his administration of a vast and difficult property. He got nothing of the sort. Among the first directors appointed was the Deputy-Minister of Railways and Canals, a civil servant directly under orders of his political chieftain. The others were chosen on a geographical basis, and as a consequence could be expected to espouse sectional rather than national interests. Some of the board members were superannuated political hacks, one being a thrice-defeated member of Parliament who had obtained employment in a government department at a salary of $2,500 per annum, where he had remained for twelve years with no increase before his elevation to the board of Canadian National Railways. Another, a Quebec director, refused to interest himself in anything except the protection of the French language and jobs for his fellow provincials.

The "Whisper of Death" Attack

In the summer of 1923, there ensued an extraordinary campaign in which a Canadian newspaper proprietor undertook, in the fashion of the Fat Boy in *Pickwick Papers*, to make Canadian flesh creep with details of Canada's crushing burden of public debt, to which Canadian National Railways was, of course, a prime contributor. Hugh Graham had come out of the Eastern Townships of Quebec to found the *Montreal Daily Star* and to build it into a great newspaper. He was addicted to Causes, which he either espoused or spurned passionately in order to increase the readability of his columns. He was much more flamboyant in his crusade than his competitor, *The Montreal Gazette*, which had been founded in the eighteenth century and which has remained to this day unalterably attached to a single principle, that it is wicked for governments to spend money since they must tax citizens to get it. (Its cartoon image of "Mr. Uno," the little man stripped of his trousers and forced to wear a beer barrel because of the exactions of the tax collector, is the prized possession of generation after generation of its cartoonists.)

In midsummer 1923, Mr. E. W. Beatty of the Canadian Pacific, at a luncheon given him by the Bank of England in London, expressed the pious hope that the harsh treatment accorded the common stock of the Grand Trunk Railway would not prejudice British investors against future Canadian offerings. This plea provided Graham, now Lord Atholstan, with the spark for a Cause, and his newspaper embarked on what came to be known as the "Whisper of Death" campaign—a series of front-page articles bedecked with such typographical garnishments as multicolumn headlines heavily slugged and bold-faced funereal type interspersed with subcaptions of solemn warnings. The writing lived up to its format; its style might perhaps have been described as Perpendicular Gothic.

The following awful warning, from the issue of July 21, was typical:

THE UNSPEAKABLE THING that threatens the life of our nation is that although the War has been over for nearly five years our national debt is still rising by the hundred millions and our railways, built to serve twenty million people, are tying up deficits at the same ruinous rate. . . . We are willing to pay for the War but we are not willing to imperil the very existence of our country by piling up these deficits to feed a veritable devil-fish of bankrupt railways. . . . If we had to begin *de nova* and provide for our eight million people scattered over Canada today, there are a lot of lines that we would not build. But they are built and we are in debt for them. It is a terrible condition and not a theory that confronts us.*

In this Cause, as in all his preceding ones, Atholstan called for prompt and drastic action—no nostrums, but the surgeon's knife. Sir Henry Thornton, who recently had been unwise enough to announce an operational surplus on the first six months of the year, received due attention; he was accused of overoptimism and was warned of the doom of the inherited debt. It is doubtful if anyone lost much sleep over these exaggerated irruptions; Bob Edwards, the irreverent chronicler of the *Calgary Eye Opener*, declared that Lord Atholstan had identified Canadian National Railways as the modern-day Whore of Babylon. After more than two months, the diatribes ceased abruptly, and through Montreal business circles the story ran that the passionate peer's right hand had forgotten what his left was doing. He had invested heavily in real estate in the rear of Mount Royal; the Canadian National Railways tunnel through that mountain was essential to the growth of this area. Should that company succumb to an austerity program such as he had advocated, it might cost him dear. It had never been his intention to lose money on any of his Causes.

Relations of the Canadian Pacific

During the first years of the Thornton regime, the Canadian Pacific system was prepared to wait out events, confident that time was on its side. When it did complain, it based its grumbles on the thesis that it was unjust to tax private enterprise to support a publicly owned competitor. From the beginning, Thornton sought an accommodation with his rival whereby frictions might be ironed out without official intervention, and in February 1924, an agreement for cooperation was reached. It was found almost impossible, however, to make it work. There could be no better example of the difficulties confronting the rival systems than their branch line programs. In order to reach a balanced competitive position, either the Canadian National must abandon some of its branches or the Canadian Pacific must build additional trackage; yet the shifting volumes of traffic

* The "Whisper of Death" series ran, with intermissions, from July 12 to September 26, 1923.

made it difficult to designate areas as the exclusive preserve of either of the railways. Parochical and political pressures had made it next to impossible ever to abandon Canadian branch lines; whether or not they were used was a secondary matter. Canadians regarded them as their birthright. The Canadian National, therefore, was always in the position of being unable to achieve economic advantage by reducing superfluous trackage, and the Canadian Pacific correspondingly was under the necessity of incurring unwarranted expenditures in order to maintain its competitive position.

Thornton's Popularity a Great Asset

In the bickerings that ensued between the two systems, the Canadian Pacific usually had a fair share of the argument; but when the issue came before the public, its spokesmen on most occasions were thwarted by the personal popularity of Sir Henry Thornton. Within a matter of months, he had built an almost unassailable position for himself among his hundred thousand employees. The Canadian National railwaymen were far less homogenous, far more sectionally minded than those of the Great Eastern Railway; nevertheless Thornton repeated his British triumph, and his workers became his men to a man. Like all good leaders, he evoked the simpler symbols of fellowship. He seldom failed to draw attention to the union medallion on his watch chain. He would be photographed with yardmen who had fifty years' service and would see that it was captioned as the oldest and youngest employees of the system. He would inquire about children's birthdays and say something appropriate to wives whenever he met them. He insisted on shaking hands no matter how grimy or greasy the workers' fingers. In a private letter from Montreal, he described one of the many occasions that contributed to the legend that had begun to grow almost from the day of his arrival:

> Last night, after dinner, I visited all the Montreal yards as I never get a chance to see the men who work at night. I took about three hours and visited all offices and engine houses. I found everything in good shape and the men on the alert. It was rather a shock to them as railway presidents have been rare visitors, but they obviously were delighted to see me. I understand that it is all over the road by now and that it is exciting a good deal of comment and good feeling. So perhaps it was an evening well-spent.[2]

Outstanding Officers

Thornton reciprocated this goodwill to the full. On another occasion he wrote, "I don't think any railway president ever had such a damn good lot about him as I have and when I look back and see what the team was made up of originally, with all the trials and troubles that they have come through, I marvel at the result."[3]

If the management echelons were less responsive than the rank and file to Thornton's charm and courtesy, it perhaps was because such officers had more to forget. Many of them retained traces (and sometimes more than traces) of their former loyalties—to Mackenzie and Mann, to the Grand Trunk or to the Intercolonial systems. From being bitter rivals they had been conscripted into the same team. Not all of them found it easy to accept subordinate status under those who previously had been their equals. But here also Thornton was equal to the occasion, and the weeding out and transplanting necessary to transform the management garden was accomplished with apparent ease and with very little residual resentment.

Sir Henry had the good fortune to find a number of outstanding officers available. In many instances, they served on long after he was gone, and Canadian National Railways owes an incalculable debt to them. There was Walter Thompson, a buoyant Scot with a newspaper background. He become Thornton's master of ceremonies, his director of intelligence and indeed his very eyes and ears. Thompson raised the craft of press-agency to a level that has never been equaled in Canada either before or since.

As a sieve to filter the vast accumulation of routine in search of those key items that require specific attention, R. A. C. Henry came from the Department of Railways and Canals to head Thornton's Bureau of Economics. His duty was to eliminate guess work and to run interference for his chief with the politically minded, with the local patriots and with the agile gentry who had made a good thing out of the railways in the past. From the same source came Starr W. Fairweather, one of the outstanding Canadian railwaymen to date. A university graduate and a born researcher, he had great gifts in the preparation and presentation of cases. As a controversalist, he seldom faltered or was found wanting under fire. Completing this valuable inner circle was C. E. (Ned) Brooks, chief of motive power and car development, who carried the burden of technological progress on his capacious shoulders and who could be trusted to be abreast, if not ahead, of contemporary practice. This outstanding engineer was a dreamer of dreams, and he could fashion them into reality with the same skill and assurance that a master sculptor exhibits when he liberates the shapes in his mind from the native stone.

The Personal Entourage

There will always remain a question as to whether Thornton might not have served himself better in Canadian National Railways if he had relied in his break-in years solely on the advice and assistance of this group of outstanding executives. Unfortunately there were gaps in this inner circle, and one missing member was what Thornton needed most—a tough-minded, down-to-earth financial advisor. He had had little experience of railway finance either in the United States or Britain, and in coming to Canada he had accepted the management of a vast enterprise that had been born with a black caul in the form of a monstrous load of debt. Unfortunately much of this debt was not institutional but was owed to the people of Canada, and there naturally was an abundance of financial critics and political sharpshooters who would make it their business to see that this loss of approximately $50 million a year continued to represent two strikes against the principle of a government-owned transportation system. With no sturdy sentinel to guard it as Walter Thompson guarded public relations, as Starr Fairweather watched over company policy and as Ned Brooks supervised technological developments, the financial organization remained exposed and vulnerable, and its lack of defenses was destined to haunt Thornton throughout his Canadian career.

On certain previous occasions, both in Britain and in the United States, he had found it rewarding to avoid embarrassing situations by recourse to informal negotiations with the aid of personal rather than official agents or officers. There was nothing questionable in such methods; from time immemorial those in authority have found it expedient and profitable to attain their ends by leapfrogging obstacles or by deviation from routine procedures. After some such missions had proved successful, Thornton had rewarded his agents with such generosity that they remained part of his personal entourage, on call as required. Perhaps the best instance was L. V. Hummell, who had been on the outskirts of Thornton's affairs since his service with the Pennsylvania Railroad. He was a thin, shrunken little man with a tart vocabulary who described himself as "Sir Henry's Chief Cook and Bottle-washer" and whom an Englishman once declared "Comes out of the woodwork whenever Thornton needs him." He had been of great service to his chief during the First World War, when he had acted as what is known today as an "expediter"; if Sir Henry, as Inspector-General of Transportation Services in France, wanted anything in a hurry, Hummel saw that he got it, and questions seldom were asked as to his methods or their cost. Soon after Thornton's arrival in Canada, Hummel turned up rather the worse for wear. He was employed by Thornton in a quasi-personal capacity—he was not on Canadian National Railways payroll, and on those occasions when he assumed that he was, his master was quick to disillusion him. He was an excellent informal negotiator, and he lived for no other purpose than to serve his chief faithfully. His methods on occasion, however, were too free and easy for ventilation before a stuffy and prejudiced Parliamentary committee.

Another former camp follower was less tolerable. Arnold Aronivici, said to have been Rumanian by birth, had rendered certain services in connection with the administration of the Great Eastern Railway. They manifestly had been of an undercover nature, for this operator would never have passed muster in the City of London. He manifestly was a promoter and quick-money man. He arrived in Canada even before Hummel, with a project that was entirely within the scope of Thornton's ambitions, and very unwisely he was placed on the payroll at once. In a matter of months he cost the company $38,041.46. As will be related in due course, his impact on Thornton's personal affairs was catastrophic.

At a later date, George W. Gaston was introduced as an unofficial financial advisor. He was a capable and honest American business man, but by then the suspicions about Hummel and the certainties concerning Aronivici had fouled the nest of Sir Henry's personal cortege, and his unofficial assistants came to be regarded as birds of a feather. Gaston's arrival evoked floods of rumors, most of them either libelous or scandalous, which discounted his services before he had a chance to render them.

Summary

By the end of 1923, Thornton could be said to be well launched, with the wind in his sails and set on a fair course. He had successfully evaded the shoals of political sponsorship. In an early speech, he defined his position in terms that appealed to all but hopelessly prejudiced partisans:

> I regard the Canadian National Railways as a child brought into the world by one government and fostered by another. As far as I am concerned I am merely the nurse of this child. I am quite indifferent

as to its parentage. Success or failure of this system must not be the sport of politicians or the football of special interests. It belongs to the people as a whole and not to the party in power.[4]

He had become well aware of his principal dangers—the intense parochialism of Canadians, the never-ceasing attempts to involve him in politically inspired byplay, the subdued but far from dormant hostility of the Canadian Pacific and the still active resentment engendered by the imposed Grand Trunk expropriation. On the other hand, he had come to believe there was a place for Canadian National Railways in the nation of the future and that strong elements, particularly in western Canada and in the Maritimes, would oppose fiercely anything that suggested a railway monopoly. But above all else, he had won a great victory with his employees, a triumph that not only gave him a personal following but also bestowed additional significance on Canadian National Railways from ocean to ocean. In 1923, his first full year of office, the operational surplus had sextupled from slightly over $3 million to more than $18 million. He saw this as a portent of change, and rather unwisely prophesied that in the ensuing year it would reach $30 million, which would take care of three-fifths of the annual increment of interest charges on the inherited debt. All in all, it was fair to say that he had made a good start.

19

The Summer of His Days

It has been noted previously that Thornton's design for the development of a viable railway system out of the wreckages he had inherited arose from the belief that after the First World War it would be possible to resume emigration to Canada on the grand scale and that Canadian National Railways should participate fully in such enterprise.

The federal government willingly relinquished its existing machinery for recruitment of emigrants, and Thornton hastened to improve on it. After four years of the devastation and turmoils of war, it seemed certain that there would be thousands, if not millions, of Britons and Europeans who would respond to the lures of a last frontier where there was land and peace and plenty for all.

Thornton had detected in W. A. Black, Deputy Minister of Agriculture in the provincial government of Manitoba, the qualities he required to manage the organization he had in mind. This able officer consented to head the newly formed Department of Agriculture and Colonisation of Canadian National Railways. A ten-point program was drafted, and ample funds for the exploitation of such objectives were provided.

Thornton gave the project his personal attention and inspired all ranks with its prospects. Offices were opened in the principal European and British centers, and a wide array of publicity projects was placed in train. The messages spoke to the young of new beginnings, to the war-weary of safety and security. They told of a great grid of branch railways that made the lonely expanses habitable, of engineering parties that were investigating the possibility of supplementing the standard gauge lines with narrow-gauge light railways of the Decauville type, so that virtually every farmer would have a locomotive of sorts snorting on the selvages of his fields. Recruiting campaigns were inaugurated to populate pasture areas with ranchers. Nor would assistance cease, as in the Sifton campaigns, when the settler was installed on his land. Auxiliary social and economic services would be established to improve the prospects of the colonist and to create community atmospheres that would make life in the Canadian countryside not only profitable but pleasurable.

The Reason for Failure

A score of such projects was launched with energy and skill. Virtually all of them failed to get off the ground. The fault was not in the stars or even in the underlings; as will be revealed in the subsequent chapter, the Agriculture and Colonisation Department was destined to make a tremendous contribution to Canadian rural communities in the years to come. But in the 1920s, the migratory urge was in eclipse. The First World War had transformed the socio-economic climate of the Western nations almost beyond recognition; the fascinations of the new devices of transportation and communication had cast a spell that could not be broken. The motor car now was a compulsive factor in living; for every inquirer at the Agriculture and Colonisation recruiting offices abroad who asked about the nature of the soil, there were ten who wanted to know about the state of the roads. They could not envisage rural life without an automobile.

Socio-Economic Impact of a New Industry

This vehicle had overrun the Canadian countryside. By 1923, motor car capital and operational expenditures in Ontario had mounted to $129 million, or more than half the total value of all field crops in that province. It had become the ruling factor in the Full Life: it impinged on every activity. The library of the *Montreal Daily Star* in that year contained more than eighty different motor car index cards, on which were classified its impacts on manners, morals, crime, family life, behavior of minors, home construction, road construction, taxation, the sprawl of cities, its incidence on various income brackets, the deflowerment of the countryside, accident analyses, policing, Sunday observance and the growth of nomadism. The social prestige of the motor car vastly outweighed its economic importance; it dominated the activities of those feverish years, when, together with the motion picture, jazz and a host of new pleasures that varied from the simply silly to the utterly insane, it created the Mauve Decade, whose characteristic figure was Noël Coward's Dancing Lady:

> Youth is fleeting to the rhythms beating in her mind,
> Though obsessed with second best no rest she'll ever find.

It was as corollary to this mood of a world released from death and destruction and anxious to make up for lost time that Thornton's dreams of a huge migration to western Canada foundered.

The Value of Personal Popularity

Nothing except his great personal popularity enabled him to survive this serious setback, on which he had staked the future of Canadian National Railways. In 1924, a minor slip-up revealed the strength of his position. The continental boom then was in full career, and the view expressed by the head of General Motors Corporation, that God intended that every American should be rich, convinced a substantial number of Canadians that He might tolerate a certain overflow of largesse onto that nation's northern neighbor. When Canadian National Railways results for 1923 were published, they flatly contradicted Thornton's forecast and showed not a conspicuous gain but a noticeable falling off in earnings, whereupon the chorus of his political critics rang out, eager to create the image of a fallen idol. E. W. Beatty deemed the moment propitious to revive his campaign against the iniquity of compelling a private enterprise to compete with public ownership. He went so far as to suggest that Canadian Pacific employees should organize themselves into something like a medieval guild in order to deal with each other as much as possible and so to withhold comfort from the lesser breeds about them. This rather silly suggestion to take in each other's washing aroused a certain amount of hilarity in the columns of the press, and the Canadian Pacific board of directors, a serious-minded lot, ordered their president to explain his thinking to Thornton in words of one syllable. Whereupon, on a fine summer's morning, Beatty wended his way down to Canadian National Railway headquarters on McGill Street. There it was agreed that it was

Experimental road/rail car, 1930.

nobody's business but their own where and how railway employees spent their earnings.

As far as the hundred thousand Canadian National workers were concerned, they were Thornton's men, no matter what anyone might say or think. His concern for their welfare never faltered. In 1924, he put into operation the Shopcrafts Cooperative Plan, which assured that non-operating staff, particularly in the repair shops and maintenance-of-way establishments, should enjoy more regular employment and improved incomes. The success of this innovation was immediate; within a matter of months, employees and the company alike were profiting out of higher earnings, reductions in unit costs, savings in labor turnover and better service to the public. In 1925, before a standing committee of the House of Commons, Thornton declared that when employees had given their lives to a service, it was not less than their due that they should earn special consideration when their working years were over. He tabled pension proposals that staggered the parliamentarians of that day but all of which came into effect in due course. Despite such radical tendencies, the government did not hesitate to renew his contract, and on September 5 of that year, Prime Minister Mackenzie King, who seldom made a direct statement if a circuitous pronouncement would suffice, declared, "I think it will be generally considered that we have the right man in the right place."

Canadian Broadcasting—A Great Success

By a curious freak of fate, these intoxicated years, which frustrated Thornton's hopes of abounding traffic for his railways, were destined to provide him with perhaps his greatest personal triumph. In the last years of the First World War, he undoubtedly had observed behind the fighting lines the experiments of those eager enthusiasts of the Royal Corps of Signals, each of whom bore his own Christmas tree of aerials and who vied with the flash-spotters and the Oscillographers (who located enemy artillery position by triangulation and sound measurement) as harbingers of the new age. From its beginning, radio broadcasting far outstripped all other means of communication in the dissemination of news and entertainment, and Thornton quickly reacted when experiments proved the possibility of radio reception on moving trains. On July 1, 1923, the Canadian National Railways Radio Department was formed. In the following month, a party of American tourists en route across Canada received a program especially prepared for 'them. Before the end of that year, Canadian National Railways were the outstanding broadcasters of Canada: parlor cars sold tickets for special events. The first network went into operation in December 1923; a year later Canadian National Railways possessed three broadcasting stations and eleven outlets in addition to its train services. In March 1924, it inaugurated a program that endures to this day—Hockey Night in Canada. Early in 1925, its Moncton station broadcast the first program from Canada to Great Britain. On this occasion both Canadian and American stations gave Canadian National Railways a monopoly of the air.

Thornton had arranged for all Canadian National employees to obtain radio sets on extended terms of credit, a concession whose significance was not lost upon them. In 1926, the development of the carrier current device, whereby a number of messages could be carried over the same wire simultaneously, enabled Canadian National Railways to extend its broadcasting services from the Atlantic to the Pacific. In the following year, special transmissions to Britain became regular features; more than 19,000 miles of telegraph, telephone and cable lines were employed.

By this time, transmissions for railway use were a minor element in the company's broadcasting services; without conscious desire or effort it found itself deeply involved in radio programing, with its studios

Canadian National Railways: Pioneer broadcasters, 1926.

Hudson Bay Railway: (TOP) Pick and shovel crew; (BOTTOM) the basic line before the roadbed was put down.

producing for all and sundry. It was first to provide opportunities for local talent and also it led the way in selling Canadian programs abroad. It was obvious, however, that sooner or later this industry must have an identity of its own, and in October 1932, the Canadian Radio Broadcasting Corporation, a separate public authority, took over the staff and broadcasting commitments of Canadian National Railways, which thus became the parent of the publicly owned services of today.

Widening Activities

Thornton was determined to convey to the general public the image of Canadian National Railways as something more than a common carrier. He wanted it to serve Canadian communities in other capacities. In 1926, he introduced school cars, by which the children of sparsely populated areas could receive primary education. These cars operated out of selected centers on an established round. In addition to school room equipment, they provided living quarters for teachers. Next came Red Cross cars equipped for first aid services in areas where doctors and nurses were not immediately available. The Agriculture and Colonisation branch of the company also provided an array of extracurricular assistance that will be enumerated in detail in a subsequent chapter.

These community services, all established at moderate expense, succeeded bountifully in their purpose. Canadians of all political persuasions began to reject the prevailing image of Canadian National Railways as a bankrupt, politician-ridden structure and to replace it by the concept of an organization dedicated to the welfare of Canadians at all times and places. This change of attitude was particularly noticeable in western Canada, where its auxiliary services were most appreciated. At an early date, the leading newspapers of the prairie provinces pounced on the Canadian National Railways burden of inherited debt and denounced its iniquity. Throughout 1926, a chorus of editors demanded that the federal government should revise the capitalization of the system, lowering it to a realistic figure and liberating it from the stigma of inevitable deficits. Unfortunately the hour was not ripe at Ottawa for anything so radical; public ownership still was haunted by the specter of socialism. Yet Thornton's achievements were too pronounced to be denied official recognition. In the autumn of that year, the Right Honorable J. H. Thomas, Under-Secretary of State for the Colonies of the United Kingdom and life-long leader of British railway unions, declared after a trip across Canada that one of the most refreshing memories of his tour had been the high spirit and outstanding teamwork of the Canadian National Railways employees.

Expansion, Improvements, Innovations

The western provinces had additional reasons for being pleased with Thornton. At this time the Liberal administration at Ottawa was a minority government, sustained in power by a bloc of prairie members who called themselves the Progressive Party and who prosecuted to the utmost their sectional interests. Under unceasing lobbying, their pet project, the Hudson Bay Railway (whose history will be related in due course) got a new lease on life and moved toward completion. The Peace River area in northwestern Alberta was served by two ramshackle railways owned by the provincial government, which had leased them to the Canadian Pacific

Medical car, 1927.

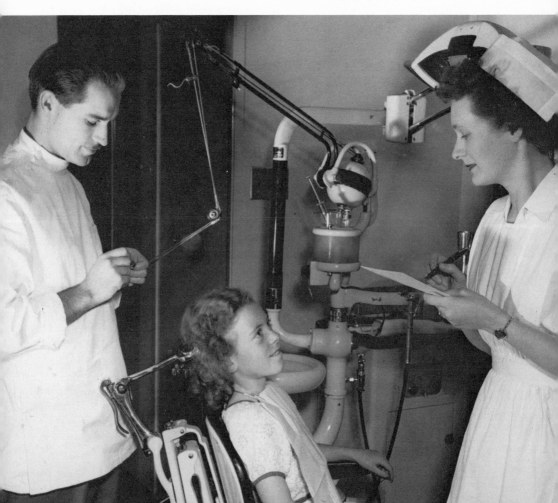

School car, 1928.

Railway for operation. By 1926, this company had had its fill of them, whereupon the Progressives intensified their pressures at Ottawa; Canadian National Railways took them over, merged them and thus added 490 miles to its operational trackage.

The carrier current device, previously noted in connection with radio, had come into general use, and in 1927, a service was inaugurated that carried ten Morse code cyphers and two telephone messages over the same wire at the same time. This was said to have been the first occasion on which these forms of communication were combined. In the summer of that year, three deluxe passenger services employing luxurious coaches, which for the first time equaled or surpassed Canadian Pacific rolling stock, were placed on the Toronto-Vancouver, Toronto-Chicago, and Montreal-Halifax runs. In that year also, the 6100 series of locomotives, the last and largest of the coal burners, went into service; each engine weighed 326 tons and developed 3,200 horsepower. At the same time, Thornton and Brooks were keeping close watch on Diesel developments. They had visited Sweden and Russia to inspect such locomotives; their advantages on long hauls were obvious because of their power and economy of operation. It was necessary, however, to take many factors into consideration before pensioning off that old and faithful servitor, Steam. Nevertheless, in 1929 Canadian National Railways led the way by putting No. 9000, the first Diesel locomotive in North America, into trial. It consisted of two cabs, each powered by twin engines of Scottish manufacture.

That year also witnessed the completion of the Toronto terminals, which had been built in the heart of the city on land adjoining the lake front. In the previous seventy years, a full score of little railways had managed in one fashion or another to wriggle into the Ontario capital; the task of consolidating their stations, trackage and operational installations had been in progress for more than four years. On August 6, 1927, the Prince of Wales officially opened the imposing Union Station in the presence of guests, including the Prime Ministers of Canada and of Great Britain. Six weeks later, Thornton announced that federal authority would be sought to effect a similar consolidation in Montreal and that forty acres in the heart of the city, contiguous to the southern portal of the tunnel that ran beneath Mount Royal, would be available for development. This would give Canadian National Railways terminal facilities almost beside and equal to those of the Canadian Pacific, eliminate three metropolitan stations, and involve extensive rerouting within the Montreal area. It also played hob with a variety of private interests, which promptly gave tongue. But Thornton now was in the saddle, and his choices were unchallengeable.

The American Properties

The story of the origin and growth of the Central Vermont group of railways has been told in an earlier chapter.* In 1927, it represented 560 miles of main lines. That autumn, torrential rain set the rivers swirling out of their channels, with immense destruction of property and with great damage to railways and highways. For several weeks all traffic was suspended. In December, Canadian National Railways petitioned for a friendly receivership on the grounds that it would be necessary to rebuild some thirty miles of line in entirety and that such outlays were beyond the resources of the Central Vermont group. This plea was granted;

* For details of the origins of American components of Canadian National Railways, see Chapter 6, pp. 112–16, 130–34.

repairs and renewals were placed in work immediately; a strong force was dispatched from Canada, and the Central Vermont was the first railway in the state to resume operations. The governor of Vermont took the occasion of the reopening of the line to express his warm appreciation of the generosity and expedition of the aid proffered by the Canadian National Railways.

Concurrently, the Michigan Trustees and Public Utilities Commission permitted the consolidation of the Canadian-owned railways in that state. They comprised 830 miles of tracks, including a main line from Port Huron to Chicago and the Grand Haven–Milwaukee car ferry across Lake Michigan. The consolidation was effected through the creation of a holding company; in view of the great popularity of the original owners of these lines, it was named the Grand Trunk Western Railroad.

The Prairies' Own Railway at Last

The construction of an ocean outlet on Hudson Bay had been the dream of prairie folk from the years of first settlement. Water freight seldom costs more than one-tenth of land freight per ton-mile, and for producers who must sell at least three-quarters of their crop overseas, the 1,400 miles haul either to Montreal or Vancouver was deemed to represent the difference between penury and prosperity.

The project first had been mooted in 1885, when the province of Manitoba sold guaranteed bonds to the value of $1 million as a first contribution toward a railway from Winnipeg to a Hudson Bay port. This start owed less to its feasibility, which had not been investigated, than to its role as a thumbing of western noses at the Canadian Pacific Railway, which enjoyed a monopoly in Manitoba, and at eastern Canada in general, which already enjoyed the reputation of bleeding the far frontiers in the interest of Montreal and Toronto bankers. This first million was expended on no more than forty miles of line northward from Winnipeg; whereafter Manitoba, in the manner of provinces, switched from accusations to supplications that Ottawa, in the fashion of the federal authority, ignored completely. But already the Dominion statute books prescribed a subsidy of $3,200 a mile for any Canadian railway, to be built anywhere, as long as it satisfied the vague purpose of being "of general advantage to Canada." In 1890, when an election was imminent, this legislation was invoked on behalf of the Hudson Bay project and put into effect in order to help the right people to be elected in Manitoba.

Political Shenanigans

Thereafter the enterprise got under way in rather desultory and floundering fashion. It attracted the attention of those long-shot promoters Mackenzie and Mann, as well as "Fighting Joe" Martin, afterward premier of British Columbia and subsequently a member of the Imperial House of Commons. A certain amount of British support was obtained for the venture, and with another election in the offing, the federal government was induced to provide a subvention of $80,000 a year for the prospective carriage of mails, police and Indian supplies over the proposed railway. By a combination of continuous nagging and backstairs negotiations, the Canadian government eventually was coerced into a loan of $2.5 million to whoever built this line. Before this could be claimed, another change of government occurred. In 1896, Sir Wilfrid Laurier came into power, and he was a bird of quite different feather to the general run of Canadian Prime Ministers. One of his first moves was to ask the British Admiralty to conduct a survey of the Hudson Bay passage and report on its feasibility as a trade route. The naval technicians were discouraging. They regarded Hudson Strait, the outlet to Hudson Bay, to be a fairway for merchant shipping for no more than four months in the year.

Largely because of this adverse finding, the Hudson Bay Railway file remained closed thereafter for almost ten years. But in 1905, two new provinces, Alberta and Saskatchewan, were born out of the North West Territories, and their accouchement rekindled the clamor for a railway that the prairies could regard as their own and that would be immune to the greed of the eastern Canadians. By then Mackenzie and Mann, who were the men of the hour, had embarked on a score of railway enterprises. They promptly offered to build the Hudson Bay Railway, taking off from their transcontinental line at Prairie River in northern Manitoba. It would traverse 538 miles of savage and empty terrain. As subsidy they asked for 2.7 million acres of Crown lands, which they would be allowed to choose in any part of Canada. Their arithmetic, however, seldom had been known to err in the public interest, and so their offer was declined, but on the prairies the clamor grew. As the 1908 election approached, Laurier was besought by his western followers to do something that might save their seats. He therefore undertook to embody the Hudson Bay project in the National Transcontinental Railway scheme, whose surveys ran through The Pas, eighty-eight miles to the north of the

Mackenzie and Mann transcontinental line. He authorized a subsidy to these promoters for a link-up to serve as a supply route between Prairie River and The Pas and accepted the construction of the Hudson Bay Railway from The Pas to a salt water terminal as a national responsibility.

The McLachlin Saga

No sooner was the election won than survey parties took the field for a rough determination of the route. The West was elated and the event went to some distinguished heads; in 1910 Governor General Earl Grey led a party down the Nelson River in canoes and afterward coasted along the shores of Hudson Bay, returning to describe that body of water without a blush as the "Mediterranean of Canada." By the following year, the scheme had caught the public fancy sufficiently for the incoming Conservative administration to adopt without question the Liberal baby. Prime Minister Sir Robert Borden undertook to complete the Hudson Bay Railway "without a single day's unnecessary delay." A contract was placed with a Winnipeg firm, which was given five years to finish the project.

There then ensued a strange, hilarious, yet perhaps sensible usurpation of authority. Donald W. McLachlin, chief designing engineer of the Department of Railways and Canals, arrived in Hudson Bay on one of the first supply ships. Thereafter he became monarch of all he surveyed. He was a law unto himself; there was little about the project that he liked, but he refused to return to Ottawa, and his relationship with his official superiors deteriorated until, on one occasion, they ordered him to be brought back in irons. Above all else, he abhorred the choice of Port Nelson as a terminal. He would appear to have been the first to realize that the kinetic energy engendered by the tides in a narrowing estuary would gouge new channels daily, filling up the old ones with countless tons of silt. McLachlin decided that the only way to make the location serviceable would be to build an artificial island in the estuary, together with huge breakwaters; a bridge seventeen spans in length would connect them with railhead on the northern shore of the river. Even such elaborate construction left him unhappy; without advising his minister, he called in a distinguished marine consultant who agreed with him in every particular. Thereafter McLachlin bombarded Ottawa with pleas intermingled with threats. As a result, in 1915 he was summarily dismissed.

He paid no more attention to his discharge than to other departmental instructions. No one turned up to replace him, and so he worked on. In 1927, the Minister of Railways and Canals informed him that for twelve years he had been drawing pay without requisite authority. In birth, in adolescence and until maturity, the Hudson Bay Railway remained his baby.

The Arctic Takes Its Toll

In this, the first incursion of railway builders into the Arctic, a heavy toll was paid for the ignorance of the habits and temper of a savage land. Two ships laden with supplies were lost in Hudson Bay. Along the ice-bound rivers and across the frozen muskeg, railhead advanced at a snail's pace. If Hudson Bay was open for only four months of the year, these months would also comprise the only effective construction season. In the winter of 1916–1917, the project was examined in detail by a parliamentary committee of inquiry, which damned it in almost every particular. In December of that year, when the head of steel reached Kettle Rapids, 333 miles east of The Pas, work halted, whereupon the westerners howled with rage, *The Manitoba Free Press* outshouting all others. "Malevolent eastern interests," it snarled, "may delay but they cannot defeat this great national project, designed to free the western producer from the exactions of his eastern financial master."[1]

Bit by bit, the handicaps and dangers imposed by isolation, biting cold, unstable muskeg and bleak tundra yielded to McLachlin and his dedicated band of engineers. In the summer of 1918, a Senate committee again examined the project. Among those who gave evidence were explorers, missionaries, police officers, navigators and others who knew the North—authorities who certainly should have been consulted at an earlier stage of proceedings. Among them was Vilhjalmur Stefansson, already famous for such Arctic exploits as spending a winter on an icefloe and living in comfort by aid of hooks and a spear; also on hand were the Tyrell brothers, first to recognize the permafrost as a stable foundation for heavy manmade structures. In the course of this investigation, McLachlin's expensive attempts to create artificial terminal facilities at Port Nelson received critical attention, and the Senate committee recommended investigation of alternate port sites.

In December 1921, Prime Minister Mackenzie King barely squeezed back into power through his alliance with the Progressive Party, which consisted almost entirely of western farmers who backed the Hudson Bay

Railway to the last man. As soon as the new Parliament assembled, this project became a principal bone of contention. An American historian wrote:

> The proponents of the Bay route adopted the technique of in-jecting the subject into every debate, regardless of its pertinency. It was dragged into discussions of immigration, minor budget items, the tariff and even into a debate concerning the regulation of water levels for the Lake of the Woods.[2]

In 1924, fifteen hundred delegates, from all parts of the prairies and also from adjoining American states, met in Winnipeg to organize an "On to the Bay Association" and to undertake to ginger up the Progressive Party members of Parliament for their flagging pressure on Prime Minis-ter Mackenzie King. That astute politician, after a stupid fracas with the Governor-General, had emerged from an unscheduled election with even slimmer support than before, and the Progressive Party immediately put its pistol to his head. The price of their support must be the comple-tion of the Hudson Bay Railway without delay. C. A. Dunning, Minister of Railways and Canals, hastened to provide the requisite assurance. Alfred Palmer, one of the world's greatest authorities on ports, soon was on his way from England to advise the government on the site of an ocean terminal.

A fortnight after arrival, Palmer and Dunning reached Port Nelson. The Englishman sat on his shooting stick and surveyed the costly attempts to foil the buffeting tidal bores of the estuary. "You Canadians constantly use two words as if they were one," he said. "Port and harbor. A port is the facilities you build to work ships. If you have any damn sense you put them in a harbor."*

Thus Port Nelson was discarded at first sight. Palmer went on to Fort Churchill, reported a good harbor there and worked out costs that cut the expenses of building an ocean terminal by something over $12 million. That winter the new route was surveyed. Within a year, three thousand workers were engaged on a type of construction that the Russians would make famous in years to come. A rough corduroy of brush was laid on the winter ice or snow; the ties and the rails went on top of it. When the spring thaw came, this trackage was hoisted as much as ten feet in the air; the work trains gingerly negotiated it, dropping thousands of tons of fill, which sank through the thawing muskeg to the primal ice, a foundation as firm as solid rock. In some places the gravel fills were astonishingly

* The late C. A. Dunning gave this anecdote to the historian.

thin, elsewhere it took twenty to thirty cubic yards of material per yard of surface to bring the roadbed up to its requisite height.

The Churchill River entered the harbor twelve miles from its headlands. In 1928, the construction of the port began. Channels, quays, a town site, streets, warehouses, elevators and all other essential structures were provided. On September 1, 1931, the harbor was opened to world trade by a British ship bearing out the first cargo of grain.

Thus the western farmers were appeased. A quarter-century later, they shipped perhaps 5 percent of their overseas exports by this route. Return cargoes were minimal. But modern facilities have lessened the perils of the Arctic route, and it has now become apparent that sooner or later, Canada must occupy and utilize more and more of its northern wasteland. The Russians have set them an excellent example; Soviet geneticists have bred vegetables—even such salad truck as tomatoes and lettuce —that will ripen in the short Arctic summers several hundred miles farther north than the Canadian verges of cultivation. In due course, this example may be followed on the North American side of the Pole, and the Hudson Bay Railway then will have justified itself.

Tributes at the Anniversary

At the Canadian anniversary celebrations of 1927, Thornton was much to the fore. In his five years in office, he had won the same degree of admiration from the Canadian public that he enjoyed from his employees. His many public addresses were eloquent yet homely. He never ceased to stress the ideal of service.

> It must be our first endeavour not to operate this publicly-owned railway for profit but to benefit the communities we serve. . . . Every individual in this railway is its loyal servant. I use the fine old English word "servant" in its highest sense because all of us are its servants. I am a servant and you are a servant and there is something very fine in the quality of being a good servant. One of the essentials of being a good servant is not only in loyalty to the organisation and jealous pride in its reputation but likewise in the loyalty of every officer and man to each other and the jealous regard for the reputations of all who are our neighbours.[3]

During this period, Thornton was fortunate in serving under an able, aggressive and loyal Minister of Railways and Canals. At the age of seventeen, Charles Avery Dunning had arrived in Canada as an immigrant farm hand. Twenty years later, he was premier of Saskatchewan. In 1926, he was lured into the federal arena to take the controversial portfolio of Railways and Canals. For the next four years he exhibited a freshness of mind and a vigor of action that dovetailed perfectly with Thornton's programs. The boom years were rising to their climax, bringing in their train a willingness to embark on risk ventures. It was on this mood that Thornton capitalized, with Dunning invariably his staunch supporter.

Trouble with the Canadian Pacific

He had need for such a political chieftain, for almost every move that he made to increase the stature of Canadian National Railways reawakened the suspicions and often the hostility of his Canadian Pacific rivals. In some cases, this was not the fault of either system. For instance, the Canadian Pacific operated well-patronized and lucrative ocean services on both Atlantic and Pacific routes. It therefore was inevitable that its principal North Atlantic competitors, the White Star and Cunard lines, should seek an accommodation with Canadian National Railways for the issuance of through bills of lading and passenger tickets for combined land-sea travel. When Canadian National Railways formed a Marine Department, it also was natural for the federal government to transfer to it the management of those sea services that had been created because of the exigencies of the First World War. When Thornton took over the Canadian Government Merchant Marine, he soon discovered that the operation of a number of the older ships was a waste of money and that he must seek, in the natural course of events, to replace them. This circumstance, willy-nilly, compelled Canadian National Railways to become an ocean carrier and consequently a competitor of the Canadian Pacific in that field of operation.

In another instance also, both systems were victims of circumstance. The Canadian Pacific operated a string of magnificent hotels across Canada, which paid handsome dividends not only in hard cash but also in prestige. Canadian National Railways had inherited a few similar hosteleries in the Grand Trunk and Canadian Northern estates, but they offered no direct competition with the Canadian Pacific. In Halifax, the latter company sought entry by acquiring running rights over Canadian National tracks; concurrently it undertook to invest in a Halifax hotel. Canadian National Railways also was asked to subscribe to this project, but as it needed a new station and terminals, Thornton decided that he would prefer to build a combined hotel and station. The cry immediately went up that he had double-crossed the Canadian Pacific project and that he was expending public funds in an extravagant and uncooperative manner. There was no substance to this charge, but it provided a talking point for his critics.

As readers may remember from an earlier chapter,* Mackenzie and Mann had made extravagant promises to reach the waterfront of the port of Vancouver. Among their undertakings were offers to build an electrically operated tunnel to connect with the Fraser Valley, a dam to drain the tidal flats in the center of the city, the inauguration of a trans-Pacific shipping service and the construction of a modern hotel. Canadian National Railways had inherited these commitments but they were still awaiting their hour when, early in 1927, the city of Vancouver lost its patience and threatened to close the port to that railway unless immediate action was forthcoming. To carry out these enterprises would have cost many millions, and the passage of time had destroyed the validity of some of the Mackenzie and Mann promises: for instance, the mud flats had been drained, the tunnel to the Fraser Valley had been recognized as uneconomic and the day of British flag shipping on the North Pacific was passing. But the Vancouver town council dug in their heels and would give no ground on the matter of the promised hotel. It was not really needed, for the Hotel Vancouver (a Canadian Pacific property) was acclaimed around the world for its quality and atmosphere; but unless Canadian National Railways provided the promised hotel, it might be obliged to sacrifice its ocean terminals. Thornton therefore considered it a lesser evil to accept the Vancouver ultimatum. Naturally enough, his action was bruited far and wide as an illustration of his extravagance.

Clash in Saskatchewan

Hotels were minor matters. The clash of the systems in Saskatchewan proved a more serious confrontation. In the 1880s, when the Canadian Pacific built Canada's first transcontinental railway, there were two reasons why its route clung to the international boundary. The Canadian climate was deemed to be too harsh and capricious to warrant more than a shallow cereal zone, extending for not more than 150 miles to the north of the boundary line. In addition, it was deemed necessary to seal off the Canadian frontier against the intrusion of American branch lines, which would claim a portion of the Canadian traffic from

* See Chapter 13, pp. 263–64.

its normal east-west axis. Early in the century, however, the development
of Marquis wheat completely changed the picture. Its early-ripening and
frost-resistant abilities more than doubled the depth of the Canadian
cereal zone and provided 100 million additional acres of virgin soil for
cultivation. This great expansion of arable prairie provided the opportunity for the entry of two new transcontinental systems. Both the Grand
Trunk Pacific and the Canadian Northern railways, therefore, possessed
as much acreage suitable for settlement as their predecessor, the Canadian Pacific Railway.

These newcomers immediately invaded Canadian Pacific traffic territory, particularly in the rich, well-settled districts of southern Manitoba.
The Canadian Pacific, however, made few attempts to strike back, perhaps
relying on the widely held belief that neither the Grand Trunk Pacific
nor the Canadian Northern would ever earn their keep and that in due
course both would end up in the Canadian Pacific stable. But in the
second decade of the new century, something unforeseen occurred. The
northern wastes began to yield minerals. Some of the finds were of astonishing value. It then became apparent that this vast sub-Arctic area no
longer could be dismissed as uninhabitable, fit for nothing but wild
animals and nomadic aboriginies.

These mineral discoveries touched the Canadian Pacific closely, for
in 1898 it had bought a small smelter in southern British Columbia,
which extracted the minerals from the abundant but complex ores of that
neighborhood. After a quarter-century of unremarkable performance,
however, there came a development as revolutionary in its way as Marquis
wheat: new methods were devised to treat the complex ores and to extract
a mighty fund of valuable metals from them. As a result, the Canadian
Pacific found itself the owner of one of the great mineral properties of
the world. Two of the contemporary wisecracks had a considerable
amount of truth in them. It was said that the Canadian Pacific had
become a mineral company with a railway as a sideline. It was also said
that if it could give away its railways, it would be able to pay dividends
in perpetuity.

As a consequence of this great mineral holding, the Canadian
Pacific dare not acquiesce in the Canadian National Railways monopoly
of the approaches to the Arctic. The Hudson Bay Railway, destined to
become an element of Canadian National Railways, was on point of completion, and already plans were in train for a number of its feeders to be
built northward to serve promising mineral areas. In 1928, therefore, a
Canadian Pacific spokesman let it be known that his company was con-

sidering a large-scale invasion of Canadian National Railways traffic territory in northern Saskatchewan. Some 1,200 miles of branch lines were envisaged, with connections with the Hudson Bay Railway.

On learning of these proposals, the Minister of Railways and Canals summoned Beatty and Thornton to Ottawa and cautioned them against duplicate construction. They would be better served, he urged, by mutual accommodations in running rights over each other's lines. Beatty, however, strongly protested against any reduction of his program. Any area, he declared, was better served by competition than by monopoly. Moreover, there must be need for expanded services in these sub-Arctic areas or Canadian National Railways would not be preparing to build some 700 miles of new branches along the fringes of the deep north.

Thornton was prepared to be reasonable. During that year, the two systems had agreed to a joint purchase of the Alberta government railways serving the Peace River Block. They were renamed Northern Alberta Railways, which remains jointly owned to this day. Thornton was quite willing to consider other transactions of the same nature, but on his announcement, the citizens of Saskatchewan instantly were up in arms. They did not want any agreement between the systems; they clamored for more railways and more competition, the more cutthroat the better. The fact that the current Minister of Railways and Canals was a former premier of their province was not overlooked, and Ottawa was overwhelmed by a spate of appeals, demands and threats. Everyone—legislative assemblymen, town councils, boards of trade, farmers' associations, church organizations and even fraternal societies—was brought into the act, in support of the sacred right to possess as many railways as could be obtained without paying for them.

Get them they did, almost in entirety; only by a feat of departmental dexterity was the Canadian Pacific blocked from connections with the Hudson Bay Railway. Eastern Canada naturally took a dim view of these expensive shenanigans. The feeling grew, particularly in financial circles, that Thornton might have taken a tougher line with both his competitors and his minister.

The Socio-Economic Transformation

As the 1920s wore away in abounding prosperity, social considerations more and more encroached on economic realities. The motor car, the motion picture, the radio, the floods of advertising, called the tune in creating what became known as the North American Way of Life. Traditional outlooks were discarded; the whim, the fad and the circumstances of the moment claimed an authority far beyond anything known in the past. The citadels of ethical disciplines—manners, morals and religion—crumbled before the continuous onslaughts of the New Thing, in almost every case devised to embody and exploit for profit social urges born out of the new devices of mobility and communication. As a Canadian writer put it:

> The age of the flapper girls, human flies, dare-devils, flag-pole sitters, stunt men, jazz bands, joy-rides and liquor in cars, Princess Eugenie and porridge pot hats, rolled down hose, singing telegrams, dancing marathons, revealing bathing suits, flat-chested figures, waistless dresses, boyish bobs and shingles, airplane antics, women smokers and drivers, prohibition, votes for females, descended on a topsy-turvy society with all the bombast and ballyhoo of a bombshell.[4]

With the United States as the chief purveyor of these accessories of fuller living, Canadians inevitably caught the current contagion, which meant that thereafter necessities would receive a smaller share of the consumer's dollar. In the face of ever-mounting demands, money lost some of its purchasing power and so decreased the real value of earnings. Inflation, that seldom-absent virus in the blood of free economies, naturally bred demands for higher wages, and here the Canadian railwaymen had a ready-made case. Their unions were branches of American unions; they performed more or less the same duties on either side of the international boundary, yet the Canadians were paid considerably less for their services. A clamor arose for equality of treatment, and with improving fortunes, Canadian National Railways was in a position to offer modest increases. In the arbitration proceedings of 1927, however, Thornton sturdily denied that there should be any compulsion to meet the American rates of pay; the situation must be judged not by comparison with neighbors, but by local circumstances. The Canadian increases were no sooner in effect than the American railwaymen made further demands; what was good enough for their Canadian brethren was not good enough for them. Thus out of social incentives began the escalation that has made Canada a socio-economic satrapy of the United States—a process that continues to this day.

The Crest of the Wave

In 1928, the operational surplus reached $58 million—an eighteen-fold increase in seven years. Thornton had turned out to be a miracle man, and out of the wreckages he had inherited he had built a viable property.

On every hand, there was evidence of growth and progress. Six short lines in Eastern Canada, totaling 638 miles of tracks, had been added to Canadian National Railways. That company also had bought the Western Union Telegraph Company with 6,670 miles of wires and 188 offices in Eastern Canada. Arrangements had been perfected, for the first time in any part of the world, for two-way telephony for moving trains.

Early in 1929, a new wing had been added to the Chateau Laurier Hotel in Ottawa, doubling its accommodations. Jasper Park had proved a most profitable venture; of it a visitor wrote:

> It is far less pretentious in its conception than rival resorts. The simple log cabins, with every comfort laid on, grouped around the lake and the main lodge, are far more in keeping with the magnificent wild country than the elaborate European type hotels. Every effort has been made to protect the natural features; the bears teaching their cubs to swim in the lake, the deer wandering fearlessly among the cottages, beavers busily building their dams, the proximity of other wild life in the park, add enormously to the pleasure of the guests.[5]

The Thornton concept of courtesy and service had permeated to every level of the system. A squaw resident on the outskirts of an Ontario village had been told that the wires of the "long-talk" carried things. She walked into the nearest Canadian National Railways station with a geranium in a tomato can and asked that it be delivered to her daughter, then a patient in a distant hospital. The agent took a small sum from her and telegraphed a florist to deliver one geranium (in a tomato can) without delay. There were many other similar instances of alertness and outstanding service to be found in the records of these years. James Malcolm, Minister of Trade and Commerce, tersely summed up the impact of such performances when he declared, "Sir Henry first sold Canadian National Railways to its employees. Now they have sold it to the businessmen of Canada."[6]

20

The Lordly Buck
and the Butcher's Dogs

No man is an island, entire of itself.

So wrote John Donne three centuries before motor cars and aircraft
made mock of distances and before telephone, phonographs, radio and
advertising created worldwide communities. It therefore was inevitable
that Canada should have become the junior partner of the United States in
the speculative delirium that swept the latter nation during the 1920s.
Canadians were more cautious than their neighbors, but they were equally
impervious to warnings; the Jazz Age, with its thrills and lunacies, was
too persuasive for resistance on either side of the international boundary.
Thus it came about that Canadians bought town lots in Florida before
the alligators had been ousted from them; in 1926, when that bubble burst
and the bank clearings of the Sunshine State in the following three years
fell by over a billion dollars, Canadians were among the victims. This setback unfortunately was of short duration. Wall Street was bolstered by
new supplies of gambling money, and the upward march of the stock
markets began anew; they went forward, according to one widely quoted
observer, "Like the phalanxes of Cyrus, parasang upon parasang upon
parasang." (No one knew who Cyrus or what a parasang was, but it
sounded wonderful.) In the autumn of 1929, in the most monumental
money crash of all time, a mass panic snuffed out the raptures. Everyone

lost confidence and courage in a matter of hours; paper millionaires yesterday became bankrupts in the dawn of the morrow. The suicide rate rose sharply, and a vast deflation began.

At this juncture, the personal fortunes of Sir Henry Thornton and of Canadian National Railways were abruptly reversed. For Thornton, it was not a matter of stock market losses, although according to his biographer, Arnold Aronivici arrived soon after the crash demanding (and obtaining) large sums from Sir Henry in liquidation of old commitments. It was rather that the general malaise attendant on the sudden advent of a depression left Canadians licking their wounds and out of heart with the images that they had cherished in the halycon days of prosperity. In the main, however, Thornton's embarrassments arose out of sheer bad luck. A federal election was due in 1930, and the abrupt and disastrous end of the boom provided the Conservative Party (in Opposition) with the ammunition that it needed to harass the government. In the spring of that year, the brickbats began to fly. Charges and countercharges engrossed the front pages of the press from coast to coast, revealing the inherent dishonesty of a free people accustomed to construe government actions in terms of palliatives or personal aggrandizement. Both parties promised that if elected they would reinstate prosperity without delay; each knew that it lacked the ability to do anything of the kind. The Canadian voters, naturally enough, decided on a change. In July of that year, the Conservatives came into power with a healthy majority.

Bennett and Thornton

The fact that while in Opposition the new administration had been critical of Canadian National Railways had less bearing on what was to transpire than the personality of the new Prime Minister. Richard Bedford Bennett was a western Canadian millionaire with positive ideas on how to mend the national fortunes. Sound money was his solution. No Canadian bank, trust company or insurance company would be allowed to succumb to the difficulties that were closing the doors of hundreds of such institutions in the United States. Bennett also was a sentimental Imperialist, and he saw the survival of the British Empire and Commonwealth in terms of closer trade relations, which he proposed to bring about by greatly expanded preferential tariffs. With regard to Canadian National Railways, his law firm had been solicitors in western Canada for the Canadian Pacific Railway for many years, but as a politician he knew it to be dangerous to take sides openly. In his electioneering, he had coined a slogan for his railway policy: "Competition—Ever. Amalgamation—Never." On more than one occasion, he had declared that he had severed all his relationships with the Canadian Pacific. This was not quite true. He had retained his connections with the Montreal and Toronto investment houses, to whom private enterprise was sacrosanct.

From the Prime Minister's point of view, Thornton, rather than Canadian National Railways, constituted a challenge. Bob Edwards of the *Calgary Eye Opener,* who, despite his frontier rowdiness came from an upper-class Scottish family, had launched his barbs mercilessly at Bennett while retaining a considerable personal affection for him. "R. B. [Bennett]," he is alleged to have said on one occasion, is a tough guy who wants to be kissed." There could have been no more accurate description. The new Prime Minister desired above all else to possess a popular appeal, an insinuating address, a gracious personality. These qualities he lacked and always would lack; yet they were those that had made Sir Henry Thornton outstanding. Furthermore, Bennett's basic policy in dispelling the depression was to instill a rigid sense of economy—to persuade Canadians to think twice and to turn over every coin before they parted with it. One of the chief charges against Thornton by the Conservative Party while in Opposition had been his extravagant expenditures. Under these circumsntances the Prime Minister saw the. head of Canadian National Railways as all too popular to be his associate in the major task of enforcing austerity upon a disillusioned nation.

Shabby Treatment

The rank and file of Bennett's party espoused a simpler and more primitive attitude. They saw Thornton as the creature of the former government and hence eligible for the ax as soon as an occasion offered. The choice of Dr. R. J. Manion as Minister of Railways and Canals was in keeping with this intent. This politician, glib rather than honest on platforms as on paper, struck the first blow and set the standard for the behavior of the government thereafter. The former Lady Thornton has written:

> Our job in those days was quasi-diplomatic. There never was a week when we were in Montreal when the Prime Minister did not ask us to look after some distinguished visitor whom he wanted suitably entertained. In 1929 the Board of Directors authorized us to negotiate for the purchase of our house which we had been renting since 1926 and which was now on the market. It was to be the prop-

erty of the Company, designed as the official residence of the President
—present and future. This was done with the full knowledge and approval of the then Minister of Railways, Mr. Dunning, and of the
Prime Minister, Mr. Mackenzie King.

The Directors furthermore had authorised me to furnish the
house in a manner appropriate for the residence of a president. As
Montreal in those days did not enjoy the fine speciality shops it has
today it was decided that I was to go to London for such things as
were not available at home. I sailed for England in the latter part of
September 1930. When I had contracted for most of the work and the
furnishings I was horrified to learn that the new Minister [Dr. Manion]
had reneged; that the purchase of the house would not be sanctioned
by the new Government and it would not pay for the furniture or
even certain alterations to the house previously authorised and
practically completed.

We therefore were placed in the impossible position of having
contracted to buy a house which we could not pay for ourselves and
which the Company could not assume without an Order-in-Council
which the Government would not sanction. It was at this time that
Sir Henry became convinced of a concerted plot to ruin his personal
reputation and the C.N.R. He clearly foresaw the difficulties of main-
taining public confidence and in the face of the growing depression
there was no bold panacea to offer. We could only cut expenses and
try to hold the helm steady.[1]

It was not until a year later that this disreputable repudiation received
an airing. By then Thornton's fate had been sealed.

Impact of the Depression

In 1930, Canadian National Railways caught the first impact of the
depression. Earnings fell by $46,249,000, or 17 percent, with a worsen-
ing of the operating ratio from 82.53 percent to 88.05 percent. Thornton
met the losses in large part by cutting operating expenses. He abandoned
some of the more glaring branch lines and services that were costing from
six to twelve times as much as they earned. He also suspended the luxury
passenger services, and he slashed the salaries of all railway employees
(including his own) by 10 percent. That the unions accepted this reduction without remonstrance was a tribute to his popularity. On the other
hand, he resisted the general industrial and commercial tendency to cut his
staff. He believed it to be the duty of employers under all circumstances
to see that their workers should not be thrown into the streets. In his New
Year's message for 1930 he declared:

The year that takes its departure has been filled with many problems from which none of us has been spared. I deeply sympathise with all the brave men and women on our railway in this troublous time through which we are passing. I would like you to feel that I speak from the heart but after all no problems are solved by tears, no battles are won by fear. It is your job and mine to meet the future with courage and confidence.[2]

The Attitude of the Canadian Pacific

E. W. Beatty, as spokesman for the Canadian Pacific, saw the difficulties of the Canadian National system as his opportunity. Friends now were in power at Ottawa, and while they were not addressed directly, they were expected to keep their ears open. The text of Beatty's complaint was unchanged; the burden and injustice of compelling private enterprise to meet official competition was paraded in a dozen different guises. One journalist described Beatty's utterances as "Variations on a single theme." Canada was on short commons, in the grip of a depression. In each year the government was obliged to tax its sorely stricken electors to find funds to support an unnecessary and bankrupt railway system.

The Hunt Is Up

Although the first exchanges between Thornton and the new administration had been correct, there soon came evidence that a strong group of Tory back-benchers were out to make an end to him. Their opening attack came in connection with the carryover of unfinished business from the former administration. The plans for the new Montreal terminals, although designed by one of the ablest railway consultants in the United States, had not found favor with the municipal authorities; after years of altercations and accusations, the new government declared its intention to enforce an immediate settlement. But it was an expensive project and manifestly should have been laid aside until the economic horizon brightened. The easiest way for the politicians to reconcile these diverse necessities was to attack the management of Canadian National Railways for what it had failed to accomplish under the previous administration. Early in 1931, John Hackett, a Quebec member, was allotted this task. At the spring session of Parliament, he rendered a report in thoroughly partisan terms. He made Thornton the chief culprit in the delays that had ensued. It was an utterly unjust and unwarranted determination.

His report was still the subject of current comment when, on June 5, the Railway Committee of the House of Commons opened its review of the events of the preceding year. This committee was bipartisan, but it naturally contained a government majority. Its members were supposed to be versed in railway matters. Canadian National Railways affairs would be discussed, reports rendered and thereafter recommendations would be submitted to the Minister of Railways and Canals.

In the past, this committee had followed the usages of directors' meetings of private companies. Witnesses would be given notice of controversial questions and would be allowed to decide whether or not it was in the interests of the company to reply in detail, in general terms or not at all. On this occasion, Thornton's opening submission was a statement of the frustrations of the depression. He doubted if much could be done except to wait and hope for the financial skies to clear. In conclusion he strongly defended his refusal to reduce his staff simply to save money. "You cannot turn people loose and merely transfer the burden of their maintenance from the railway company to the city or to the province or to the federal government," he said.[3]

Not an Inquiry but an Inquisition

As soon as the members of the Sessional Committee began to question Thornton, personal bias emerged. The proceedings ran to 505 pages of record, and with few exceptions they consisted of veiled or open attacks on the Canadian National Railways president. As an example, on the second day of the hearings, the question of railway wages arose. A member declared that he had been told that thirty-five officers of Canadian National Railways were paid higher salaries than the Prime Minister of Canada. There was not a jot of truth in this allegation; it was no more than a bid for a headline. The salary paid to any employee was available on request. Peter McGibbon M.P., chief of the rumormongers, frankly admitted that he had not a tittle of evidence to support his statement but that the general public "believed that the C. N. R. was a fertile field for graft." Here was a newsworthy item indeed, and the press wires instantly were hot with it. The more decent members compelled this unsupported charge to be withdrawn, but the damage had been done.

At this juncture, the Minister of Railways and Canals took a hand in the baiting by bringing up the subject of Thornton's salary. The rumor was abroad, Dr. Manion said, that the president of Canadian National Railways received various additional fees and allowances that raised his annual salary of $50,000 to something in the neighborhood of $300,000. He thought it would be well for Sir Henry to clear the air by a frank statement. This request was a trap. On his appointment, Thornton had been granted salaries by the American subsidiaries of Canadian National Railways on the understanding that he would not divulge them. They amounted to something under $25,000 in all. The minister's question therefore placed Sir Henry in the position that either he must refuse the information or break his promise. As a gentleman, he kept silence. This too made the headlines.*

In a series of unsupported insinuations, baseless charges and malicious innuendoes the Sessional hearing swiftly degenerated into an inquisition. Some members indignantly protested the trend of the questioning, but it was plainly in the minds of the die-hard group that in discrediting Thornton they were scoring over the Liberal Opposition. The years of his tenure were searched for possible clues to mismanagement and corruption; such hoary patronage perquisites as tie contracts were dragged out to confirm political intervention in the affairs of the system. Even Thornton's parentage was held to account for the employment of too many American-born by the company; in point of fact they were less than .05 percent of the total. Thornton's biographer thus summarized the inquisition;

> The best traditions of political piracy were being observed. Sir Henry fought losing battles for the defence of his administration. Hour after hour he answered first one question, then another. Over him hung the sword that Dr. McGibbon's accusation had placed there. Stories of personal extravagance were capped by the accusation of graft in the organisation that he controlled. Successive charges, proven or not proven, concerning building contracts, hotel and ship construction, operation of a merchant marine incapable of profitable enterprise and of ships built to implement a treaty—these huge expenditures of an earlier period assumed the proportion of an overwhelming indictment.[4]

Sir Henry Fails to Fight Back

In this savage assault, something happened to Sir Henry Thornton. The charges launched against him manifestly were politically inspired; his alleged defects were paraded principally for their impact on the political

* This agreement, which was made soon after Thornton's appointment, had been accepted by the contemporary Minister of Railways and Canals.

party that had sponsored his appointment. He did not lack defenders; even his archrival, E. W. Beatty, was so appalled by the injustice and viciousness of the attacks that he extended sympathy and advice. Had Thornton struck back with anything like the vigor and exactitude of Donald Gordon in similar circumstances two decades later, hosts of Canadians would have rallied to his cause. Had he thrown an ink bottle, had he called one of his enemies a damned liar, the general public would have backed him to the hilt. But in almost incomprehensible fashion, he failed to fight. Long afterward, one of the Canadian National officials present declared that his mind seemed to be on other things.

On conclusion of the hearing, he asked permission to make a formal statement. It lacked vigor and incisiveness; it wandered and it wavered. The gist was that an independent tribunal should be appointed to examine the overall transportation situation in Canada and submit recommendations. For him to make such a request after such an onslaught represented surrender, an admission of guilt. It left him in the power of his enemies. Whatever the findings of such tribunal, it assuredly meant the end of the road for Thornton in Canada.

The Duff Commission

The Government snatched at his suggestion. Here was an opportunity for a free hand to reconstitute the publicly owned transportation system nearer to its heart's desire. The Prime Minister in particular was pleased. He saw himself as Pathfinder out of the Slought of Despond of the depression. He determined that there would be no politicizing about the personnel of such a tribunal. It must be above suspicion—the best available brains in the world. He also decided that the government would not be compelled to accept its recommendations.

In November Thornton's suggestion materialized in a Royal Commission headed by Mr. Justice Lyman Duff of the Supreme Court of Canada, a jurist of high intellectual qualifications. Lord Ashfield came from England; he had begun his career on American railways as a penniless immigrant and had risen to the management of London's great network of underground lines. L. F. Loree, president of the Delaware and Hudson Railroad, was a tough individualist and successful executive. Of the Canadian members of the commission, Sir Joseph Flavelle had been connected with Canadian National Railways from its beginnings. His associates were Charles Murray, president of the University of Saskatchewan, and Dr. J. C. Webster, a brilliant Maritimer. No member of the commission

could be accused either of political bias or of lack of intimate knowledge
of transportation problems.

A Ray of Hope

As 1931 wore away, it seemed as though the fates were smiling on
Thornton. Canadian National Railway revenues continued to fall but in a
slower ratio than almost every other railway in Canada or the United
States. An operational surplus was in sight; for that year it reached the
substantial figure of $7,505,700. The Hudson Bay Railway, forty years in
the making and over 500 miles in length, had been opened, and the first
bulk cargoes had been dispatched from its terminal port that year. Canadian National Railways had made its first tentative entry into aviation in
association with the Canadian Pacific. A twenty-four channel carrier current system with a maximum transmission of 20,000 words an hour, said
to have been the first of its kind in the world, had been installed between
Toronto and Winnipeg. Each of these developments had received acclaim
in the press. They constituted ammunition for pro-Thornton adherents
and for the considerable body of Canadian opinion that was convinced
that the Duff Commission was nothing more than a false front for the destruction of Canadian National Railways.

In this critical hour, therefore, Sir Henry did not stand alone. A substantial proportion of the nation believed in him. Almost daily *The
Manitoba Free Press*, speaking for the western provinces, thundered that
a railway monopoly would not be tolerated at any price. Unless there were
two systems competing for the prairie grain exports, this immense freight
would be diverted to the south, in part at least, and would find its way to
the sea over the American systems. With such determined supporters, all
that seemed necessary was for Thornton to come out of his corner fighting. Even if Canada was split by the controversy, he could prove to be the
man of the hour.

The Battle Opens

The first witness to appear before the Royal Commission was the
Minister of Railways and Canals, Doctor R. J. Manion, who provided the
opening for a deadly riposte. The theme of his preachment was Economy
Above Everything. His views on the main issue, that of one or two railway systems, were unworthy of a man in his position. He chose to attack

Thornton's management on grounds of extravagance. In his autobiography, he thus sums up the substance of his submissions:

> The more spent on passenger traffic, the heavier the deficit. Ridiculous waste had occurred in the building of these magnificently-appointed hotels and in the purchase of vast and splendidly-equipped passenger steamships, in the building of huge and costly terminals; and in such other matters as radio operations and large expenditures on advertising in the United States. . . . He [Thornton] seemed to have no appreciation of economic necessities or of money values. He seriously proposed and urged on me the purchase for $17,000,000 of a passenger travel agency—a proposal too ridiculous even in good times to be submitted by me to the Cabinet.[5]

In such an attack, he gave Thornton everything needed for a counter-stroke. The minister was living in yesterday and was thinking of Canadian National Railways as a neat little patronage-riddled property. He professed to be totally unaware of the potential of the new devices of mobility; he was prepared to throw in his hand on passenger traffic at a time when tourism was worth $300 million annually in Canada; it was the next most valuable source of income to agriculture, and it was increasing every year. As for the purchase that Manion said he dare not put before the cabinet, it was that of Thomas Cook and Son, with its network of travel agencies in every corner of the earth. Subsequent events proved that this company would have been cheap at twice the price at which it had been offered to Thornton.

E. W. Beatty followed the minister with a cogent statement of case. As always, he built his argument around the injustice of confronting his company, an original constituent of the compact of confederation, with a government-supported agglomerate of bankrupt railways. To illustrate the fatuity of expecting Canadian National Railways ever to become a viable property, he urged the commissioners to see for themselves. Early in December, its members entrained for the Pacific coast. They crossed a thousand miles of empty wasteland at the head of the Great Lakes, terrain that would never support one main line, to say nothing of two. Thence the train wound across the prairies, unnecessarily overbuilt with branch lines because of the insensate rivalry of the systems that now comprised Canadian National Railways. Finally, in the Thompson and Fraser valleys of British Columbia, the original Canadian Pacific main line had been duplicated at vast cost mile by mile, bridge by bridge, tunnel by tunnel, often within a few yards of its predecessor. Because of this unnatural contiguity of competing properties, the people of Canada not only were shackled with a permanent debt that ran into billions but were also increasing their liability annually in the form of new ventures, such as hotels, ships and pleasure parks, in an endeavor to attract east-west traffic from the railway that had originated it. Such was the picture that Beatty spread before the commissioners' eyes.

When Thornton faced the commission, therefore, he had an easy mark in the Minister of Railways and Canals, a tough opponent in Beatty. By any of the rules of debate, he should have concentrated his attack on his weaker adversary, whose statements he could have refuted with ease. Why he did not do so must remain a mystery. Instead, he chose to deliver what can best be described as an historical summary. It was defensive in tone, begging for time to complete a task that had been overtaken by misfortunes not of its own making. It was anything but a fighting rejoinder, almost fatalistic in its acceptance of the difficulties for which he was being held to account. Thousands of Canadians who read his statement in the press the following morning scarcely could believe that this was the Thornton—the man of color, candor and courage—that they had once known.

Fairweather's Great Stand

What cruelly accentuated his failure were the sturdy, hardhitting submissions of those officers of Canadian National Railways who were examined by the commission. Gerard Ruel, head of the Legal Department, S. J. Hungerford, in charge of Operations, and Starr Fairweather, of the Bureau of Economics, gave no ground and in more than one instance slashed Beatty's arguments into ribbons. Ruel favored the retention of independence but the utmost cooperation between the two Canadian systems. Hungerford gave chapter and verse to prove that there was far less duplication of service than Beatty had intimated. His statistics effectively disposed of the Canadian Pacific claim of a saving of $75 million per annum under amalgamation.

Fairweather, who proved the outstanding witness, took the offensive from the start. He denied that profits should be accepted as the prime proof of value; contributions to the community should be the true test. As a result, the criteria of expenditure must be its socio-economic yield, which consisted of the real wealth it created. The expenditure by both railways on the prairies had amounted to $1,075,000,000, but it had increased the value of that area by $6,000,000,000. Item by item, he examined the projects sponsored by Thornton and declared that in virtually every instance their cost had been money well spent. The much-criticized Jasper Park venture, on which $2,576,000 had been expended, had increased the value of that area by more than $4 million.

He followed up with a slashing attack on the Canadian Pacific contention that the Canadian National Railways had wasted huge sums by over-building on the prairies. He produced charts to prove that the Canadian Pacific more often had invaded Canadian National territory than vice versa. In statistical summaries, he analyzed the consequences of amalgamation of the two systems and declared roundly that such a union would prove an economic catastrophe. Canada, with 3 million square miles of territory and a population of four to the square mile, required competition in everything and not least of all in its transportation facilities. Beatty and the Minister of Railways and Canals, he said, had presented Canada as a static economy. Thornton, more correctly, saw it as a country on the march, in which prearrangements must be made for social as well as economic progress.

This masterly presentation, with its wealth of data, restored the situation for Canadian National Railways. Fairweather's basic thesis might be challenged but not his wealth of statistical evidence. The commissioners decided to recall Thornton since, if Fairweather's contentions should be accepted, the head of Canadian National Railways would be responsible for their implementation.

A Lost Opportunity

Here was an opportunity to retrieve everything. Thornton always had been an optimist; he could demand almost anything from his hundred thousand employees; all that was needed was to reassert his former determination to make tomorrow a better day and to show how he proposed to do it. But on January 2, 1932, when he faced the commissioners anew, he was still obsessed by difficulties. As commanding officer he did not exhort his men to plunge into the fray, but only to make adjustments in their battle order. A reconstituted board of directors, more pooling of traffic, the consolidation of the hotel and shipping interests of the two systems, yet another plea for the reduction of the dead debt of Canadian National Railways—such were the best expedients that he could muster on this, his last chance. He was questioned by Mr. Justice Duff and Lord Ashfield in kindly but shrewd fashion in an endeavor to discover his basic thinking. Was he going the whole way with Fairweather? Or was he prepared to consent to some accommodation with the Canadian Pacific? The commissioners quickly discovered that he had not thought out the details of his proposals. "I merely present what best occurs to my feeble mind," he said. This was in jest, but there was more than a vestige of truth in it.

He no more than had completed his evidence before the commissioners than he was summoned anew to appear before the annual session of the Railway Committee of the House of Commons. After such a performance before the Duff experts, anyone except politicians intent on party gain might have been merciful, since it was obvious that Thornton was through. But his tormenters picked up where they had left off a year before. Their approach to facts was akin to that of Kipling's Tomlinson of Berkeley Square:

"Oh, this I have read in a book," he said "and this was told to me
And this I have thought that another man thought of a Prince in Muscovy."

A lot of people, said Peter McGibbon, were wondering if Canadian National Railways expense accounts were not padded. On the strength of no stronger evidence than this rumor, he demanded the production of all such accounts over the ten years of Thornton's management. When examined, the inquisitors made great play of the discovery of entertainment items, most of which (as in the terms of Lady Thornton's statement) had incurred at the former prime minister's request. They also managed to drag out a bill for the taxidermy of a moosehead. This was too much for the Liberal members of the committee to stomach, and they retorted in kind, pointing out that Prime Minister Bennett had had a special suite prepared for him at the Chateau Laurier in Ottawa at railway expense.

The End Comes

In this battle over trivia, the career of Sir Henry Worth Thornton, begun so gallantly, continued so rewardingly, came to its end. While the committee still was in session, one of his chief inquisitors, in a shocking breach of confidence, told a journalist that Thornton was about to be dismissed. On July 19, Dr. Manion announced with arrant hypocrisy that the president of Canadian National Railways, feeling that he had lost the confidence of the Canadian people, had resigned. In a personal letter, Thornton gave this statement the lie direct. "I resigned because I was asked to do so by the Minister of Railways and Canals, speaking for the Government," he wrote.[6]

There always may be a continuing mystery about this capitulation. Thornton was still in the prime of life; in the United States, Britain and notably in Canada, he had proved energetic, resourceful, adaptable and courageous. His standing with his employees could not have been higher, and if he had fought, the Canadian public and press, accustomed to political vendettas, undoubtedly would have rallied behind him. The rules of political encounter, on this continent at least, usually have been distinguished by their absence, and if Thornton had responded to the taunts and innuendoes of the Sessional Committee by daring its members to make a public issue out of them, there probably never would have been a Duff Commission. Or if, when before such a commission, he had battled for his cause with the forthrightness and courage of Ruel, Hungerford and Fairweather, there can be little doubt that he would have survived as an outstanding public figure. Two years later, the Canadian voters showed what they thought of the campaign of calumny that had been mounted against him. Every member of the Sessional Committee who had distinguished himself by badgering Thornton was defeated for re-election.

Why, then, did he not stand up and fight? Did he not have the instinct for battle in his blood? Or was misfortune so rare an experience that he could not counter it? These remain open questions. In the Canadian press, the expressions of sympathy often were tinged with shame; many editors regarded him as an innocent victim. The *Toronto Star* parodied Shakespeare for a telling epitaph: "Now hath the butcher's dog pulled down the lordliest buck in England." *The Manitoba Free Press,* in a moving farewell, declared that he was the victim of circumstances and had surrendered to political importunities and economic adversity but that "This country is in his debt for services of value not to be estimated which it is doubtful if any other man could have rendered."[7]

The British Take a Hand

Not all Thornton's friends accepted his persecution tolerantly. In April 1932, the *Toronto Star* received a blistering letter from J. Bromley, general secretary of the Associated Societies of Locomotive Engineers and Firemen of the United Kingdom, protesting in angry terms against the harassment and indignities to which Thornton had been subjected. It declared that his old employees retained their faith in him and affection for him, and should the British railways, as in terms of the current agitation, be nationalized, it was hoped that he would return as their first administrator.

Canadian behavior toward a Canadian public servant was, of course, no business of any British organization, but there came about another extraordinary reaction from the same source. Prime Minister Bennett, after a number of ineffectual attempts to break the grip of the depression, had decided to embark on his grand design, which was to turn the British Commonwealth and Empire into an exclusive trading bloc by means of towering tariff walls around all British possessions, with compensating preferences to those within the enclosure. In the summer of 1932, therefore, he invited the governments of all the dominions and self-governing colonies to confer at Ottawa as prelude to trade agreements that would put such plans into effect.

Great Britain then was under a combined Conservative-Liberal-Labour government, so the three-man British delegation to Ottawa included J. H. Thomas, leader of the British railway unions and an old and firm friend of Thornton. All the British delegates regarded Bennett's proposals as unworkable, and Thomas lost no time in giving his personal opinion on them. Before the conference opened, he described the Canadian proposals as "Umbug." (He only dropped his h's for effect.) This was surprising language from the fountainhead of Empire, but Thomas, soon after arrival in Ottawa, gave tongue in a metaphor that is not forgotten to this day: "These 'ere Dominions don't only want to milk the Old Cow dry; they want to bite off 'er teats as well." It was fair comment, for the only way the scheme could succeed would be if Britain, as a low-tariff country, paid the bill for everyone. But this was not exactly the language of felicitous exchange, and during the conference, scarcely a day passed without barbed quips in the same vein from the ex-engine driver. Little was accomplished, and it would be too much to credit Thomas with more than a fair share in the discomfiture of Bennett; but years afterward, when he was out of politics, he was asked at a luncheon why he had behaved so obstreperously at Ottawa. He paused with a forkful of More-combe prawns halfway to his lips. "Look at what they did to Thornton," he said*

The Duff Commission Report, as tabled in October of that year, was a mild and innocuous document. The survival of Canadian National Railways was confirmed, but no Canadian politician with any sense of self-preservation would have dreamed of any other decision. The commissioners emitted murmurs of sympathy for the problems of inherited indebtedness and for the annual ordeals of the principal officers of Canadian

---

* The historian was present at this luncheon.

National Railways before parliamentary committees. The two rival systems were adjured to avoid unprofitable competition and to take in each other's washing whenever possible. It was obvious that the members of the commission often had been of different minds and that their solutions, as embodied in their final report, represented compromises.

The Closing Scenes

The commissioners were extremely noncommital in their findings on Thornton. They regarded the Fairweather thesis as a formidable defense for his alleged extravagance. This did not suit the ginger group of the Conservative Party, which felt that as a matter of self-protection they should continue to hound him. He had been a director of a large Canadian bank, which had urged him to continue on its board. According to Thornton's biographer, it was obliged under pressure from Ottawa to eat its words and to ask him not to stand for re-election. Sir Herbert Samuels, the representative of the British Liberal Party at the conference, had approached Thornton in connection with the reorganization of the Indian railways. He believed him to be the best man available for this task. But when the appointment was delayed, it transpired that the India Office had asked the Canadian government for a report on him and that the reply had been in such terms that it was deemed unwise to proceed with the appointment.

In February 1933, Thornton visited Cuba on behalf of a financial group that was interested in the British-owned railways of that island. He was back in mid-March, and the employees of Canadian National Railways planned a dinner and reception for him, to be attended by the top labor leaders of both Canada and the United States. He was destined never to receive this unique tribute. At the end of February, he returned from Cuba suffering from a previously undiagnosed but advanced cancer. He died in a New York hospital on March 14, 1933.

21

The Lean and Hungry Years

Thornton's personal tragedy was enacted against a background of mounting disillusion and distress. The depression now was in its fourth year, with no relief in sight. "The Brave New World," "The Land Fit for Heroes to Live in" had deteriorated to shabby towns filled with hungry people and a countryside with no markets for its produce. One of every two Canadian males of adult age was unemployed. In Ontario and Quebec, with fairly well-balanced economies, the majority of the population could make do by scraping the bowl and licking the spoon, but only from day to day. The nation was in pawn; in the three years after that disastrous October 1929, thirty-five Canadian blue chip stocks had fallen by over $5 billion. Daily, the average town dweller saw the picture thus described by a Canadian writer:

> There was almost no starvation in the depression as the coroner would define starvation. A much greater tragedy was demoralisation— the demoralisation of able and willing men standing on street corners selling apples for a nickel, of sad, terrified girls on other street corners selling themselves for two dollars, a dollar and fifty cents, for anything; of an unending procession of 'hobos' knocking on the back doors at friendly restaurants for the scraps left on luckier people's plates. Hitting the rods, knocking at the back doors of the next town, hitting the rods again; of children going to school without shoes or proper

books; the demoralisation even of those not faced with hardship, but unable to face its spectre; the demoralisation of a nation fast losing its anchors and assurance.[1]

On the whole, Quebec and Ontario were prosperous in comparison with the rest of Canada. The Maritime Provinces, heavily dependent on their exports of fish and wood products, found their customers in far-away markets to be as grievously stricken as themselves, with the same closed doors and shuttered shops. British Columbia was in like case, and, in addition, its streets were encumbered by the hungry and homeless from other parts of Canada; those who had no place to go, who shifted aimlessly in search of work or charity, usually chose to remain in the milder climate of the Pacific province. The freight trains carried many times more nonpaying travelers than the passenger trains could command. These nomads arrived in such swarms that the local authorities could not cope with them.

Nowhere did the depression strike with such ferocity as on the prairies. Manitoba, Saskatchewan and Alberta lived on cereal crops, which had to be sold in overseas markets; even if the farmers stuffed themselves with no other food, these provinces could have consumed no more than a tithe of their annual production, which in a normal year amounted to upward of 500 million bushels of grain. Most of it was high-priced wheat sold in the quality markets; as a consequence, it was first to feel the pinch of failing demand. In 1928, Canada had exported 407 million bushels at an average yield to the farmer of $1.60 per bushel. By 1932, the total crop had fallen to 160 million bushels; on December 16 of that year, the price of the highest grade wheat on Winnipeg's grain exchange was thirty-eight cents a bushel. When the cost of harvesting, twine and haulage had been subtracted, the grower sometimes was left with no more than a cent a bushel for his toil and upkeep for the year.

Yet this economic catastrophe was but the first of the afflictions of the prairies. In 1929, there came a drought that persisted in whole or in part for upward of seven years. In that period, many areas were denuded of their topsoil, which blew away in vast clouds of dust, leaving no life-giving earth to cover the rock or gravel. There followed huge swarms of grasshoppers searching for whatever growth remained and an invasion of Russian thistles that choked out the sprouting grain.

Thornton's Successor

It, therefore, was upon a scene of distress and devastation, such as never has been known in Canada before or since, that Sir Henry Thornton's resignation in July 1932 was accepted. Samuel James Hungerford ostensibly replaced him. The qualification is warranted; the new appointment was not confirmed for eighteen months, and even then it was little more than a paper description; Hungerford was not even given the title of his office: his official designation was chief operating officer. On May 25, 1933, an Act of Parliament revealed how Canadian National Railways would be managed in future. The existing board of directors would be replaced by three trustees who would hold office at the government's pleasure. The Conservative Party, ever the critic of Canadian National Railways, now enfolded it in its coils and began the squeeze. "Economy at any Cost" was the watchword. Fifty posts in Head Office were abolished and their duties foisted on those who remained. Eleven of Thornton's chief officers resigned. Work studies were still a thing of the future, but a weeding-out process began without delay. In three years the staff was cut from 111,389 to 70,525, or by almost 40 percent. It is true that the situation was desperate; in the same three years the gross earnings of Canadian National Railways had fallen by $94 million or 36 percent. Every time the trustees looked at Saskatchewan they must have shuddered. It was reckoned that a Canadian railway needed a population of five hundred per mile to sustain it. In Saskatchewan, there were only one hundred and seven to the mile, and of that number forty were on relief, which meant no more than $10 a month and a ninety-eight-pound bag of flour for a family of five. As the numbers who "rode the rods" multiplied, the paying passengers proportionately declined, decreasing from 17,553,631 in 1928 to 9,434,812 in 1933.

Under such circumstances the trustees—an estimable judge as chairman, two undistinguished party adherents as his associates—failed to do more than to hold the fort and to pray for improvement. The minutes of their sessions reveal a sad lack of decision and of positive outlook. Prime Minister Bennett had bidden all Canadians to "bite on the bullet," to endure and to hope. About the only way that the trustees could find to obey such adjurations was to reduce all processes of management to their lowest common denominator, to make an end to as many auxilliary functions as possible and to pig it out on rock bottom until a brighter day dawned.

The Nation Stands Up to It

For the most part, these trustees appeared to be in a blue funk, and their morale seemed to be considerably lower than that of the nation as a whole. Most Canadians still had streaks of pioneer blood in them, and they were an adaptable lot; in hard times they were prepared not only to look after themselves but also each other. The early inadequate official relief measures soon were supplemented by private philanthropies on a massive scale; communities drew together, took the shock and having organized local welfare hastened to extend a helping hand to neighbors. Ineffectiveness of government action at such a distressing time began to stimulate many minds toward political change. When everything was going well and political beliefs did not greatly matter, the main difference between a Liberal and a Conservative was that one side was in and the other out of power. But in the time of adversity, the commonality expected their leaders to do something about it. On the prairies, hard times bred hard thinking and with it a quest for something better than soothing syrup. In Manitoba and Saskatchewan, the Co-Operative Commonwealth Federation had absorbed a number of quasi-socialist organizations under the leadership of J. S. Woodsworth, an able crusader, and it prepared to present candidates at the next election. In Alberta, something new and strange emerged: William Aberhart of the Prophetic Bible Institute came up with Social Credit, which was partly Old Testament interpretations and partly broad deductions from the monetary heresies of John Maynard Keynes and of one of his disciples, Major C. H. Douglas. This doctrine, preached with revivalist intensity, decked with emotional catch-phrases and proliferated by radio, took that province by storm. It was estimated that its Sunday evening radio audience ran to two hundred fifty thousand listeners, which put Aberhart well ahead of Jack Benny and his violin in the ratings. Social Credit remains a political gospel of Alberta to this day.

The Morale Restorers

Amid this political ferment, one department of Canadian National Railways served the devastated prairies staunchly and well. There were only occasional trains, and most of the motor cars had been converted into "Bennett buggies," which meant that, as their owners no longer could afford fuel, the cars had been fitted with shafts and were drawn by farm horses. But lack of freight and passengers meant little to the Colonisation and Agriculture Branch of Canadian National Railways, which as has been recorded at the beginning of the previous chapter, had two main functions—to recruit farmer immigrants and to assist them during their break-in years in Canada. During the depression it had failed in its first mission, for immigration had ground to a halt, but under the inspiring leadership of Dr. W. A. Black, it gave itself with redoubled vigor to the task of making life endurable in the prairie countryside during the lean and hungry years.

In the last normal year (1928), AG and COL, as the branch was familiarly described, had assisted 2,582 families in the occupancy of 471,544 acres. Its services included lecturers, land advisers, demonstration trains and credit for the purchases of bloodstock. But it was not content only to render technical assistance; it moved into the social sphere as well, organizing Boys and Girls clubs and farm competitions, whose principal prizes were free trips to the Canadian agricultural fairs. When the drought became general, the AG and COL officers increased their efforts, doubling their imports of bloodstock and distributing seed grains. The trustees, however, detected these outlays and put an end to them; whereupon these devoted Samaritans switched to other services, including artificial insemination and development of expanded poultry and dairy production. (Among the poultry imports, there came by some error a few capercaillies. These prime game birds, being arboreal by nature, promptly sailed off in search of forests. Every now and then, one of them still is spotted in the bushlands.)

In 1933, control of Canadian national resources, including Crown lands, was transferred by the federal government to the provincial authorities. This might have proved an opportunity to dispense with AG and COL services, but fortunately it was overlooked. Two years later, its devoted officers were working harder than ever, veering more and more to social services. A community progress competition had been organized for non–English-speaking communities and was serving one hundred fifty thousand settlers, not only with various agricultural aids but with improved methods of marketing. These officers also had embarked on enterprises designed to preserve native folklore, folk art and folk music for the many settlements of Central Europeans. The Boys and Girls clubs had spread into eastern Canada, and by 1933 had twenty thousand members. The swine competition had become a nationwide event. A Tenancy Campaign was organized for the temporary establishment of displaced farmers on developed lands that had been abandoned by their owners.

Thus the AG and COL officers, by virtue of their incessant endeavors, became something like the English institution of Universal Aunts to the stricken countryside. Whenever an innovation became successful, its sponsors endeavored to turn it over to local management in order to embark on something new. As a result, these well-remembered officers have become part of the legend of the years and the source of many a song and story. Perhaps as representative as any is the tale of how a group of dwellers at a whistle stop yearned for a rink, for they had the makings of a hockey team in their midst. The AG and COL man came along, listened, found an unused acre of railway land and arranged for the railway tank to flood it. The local storekeeper rallied to the cause and ordered hockey sticks and pucks; he was alleged to have declared that they must be paid for when wheat again reached a dollar a bushel. The womenfolk got busy on uniforms, and in a short time, the team was ready to take to the ice, except that the goal-keeper had no pads. An unpadded goal-keeper in hockey is apt to hear the angels sing. So when the AG and COL man dropped in to see how everything was getting on he collected all the old newspapers in the hamlet and persuaded a housewife to make him a flour paste. Within a few hours, the requisite armor was hardening into shape, and one more community had found something to reduce the tedium of its days. AG and COL was not really railroading. But it was well worthwhile.

Voice over the Frontier

In the first years of the depression, there had been a tendency among Canadians to treat it rather as an act of God—a cataclysm for which no one in particular could be held responsible and whose impact in due course would pass. But as the years rolled by with no relief in sight, many minds began to speculate and to find reasons for what had happened. Having diagnosed the disease, they began to search for a cure. In this quest they were greatly aided by a voice over the frontier. In the presidential election of November 1932, Franklin Delano Roosevelt had carried forty-two of the forty-eight states of the Union. Even prior to his nomination, he had begun to assemble a plan and personnel for a radical intervention in the American Society and economy. In his inaugural speech in March 1933, his keynote had been "We have nothing to fear but fear itself." In his fireside chats over the radio, he had found a method of influencing the masses of the American people to an almost unparalleled degree. He put his plans for the recovery of the United States in train in the knowledge that whatever the politicians and the bankers thought of them, Americans as a whole would be solidly behind them. Roosevelt attitudes and maxims spilled over into Canada. They undermined every thesis by which the Canadian Prime Minister sought to buttress his "Stand Fast" policy. Bennett advocated scrimping, Roosevelt demanded spending; instead of a return to yesterday, Roosevelt planned a march into the future. A clamor arose across Canada, and with rebellion in his ranks, Prime Minister Bennett reversed his field. Like Paul on the road to Damascus, a great light shone upon him. He would out-Roosevelt Roosevelt. This change of heart seemed justifiably suspicious to most Canadians, and in the election of 1935, they deserted him, leaving him with only a handful of followers in the House of Commons.

Mr. Mackenzie King, on resumption of power, was as devious and uncommitted as ever, but he had brought with him at least one forthright supporter who did not wait for changes to occur. Charles Decatur Howe, American by birth, a consulting engineer of international reputation, was named as the first Minister of Transport, an appointment that brought railways, highways, air and water communications for the first time under one portfolio. The new minister immediately abolished the existing board of trustees of Canadian National Railways and replaced it with a directorate of Canadians distinguished in their fields and with few if any political axes to grind. It included a well-known consulting engineer, a director of the Western Canada Wheat Pool, the head of a transport union, a prominent industrialist and two leading lawyers. Howe revealed the direction of the policy of the new management by a bold statement concerning the capitalization of Canadian National Railways. He declared that its $1,500,000,000 of inherited debt should be written off and that it was nonsense to add annual deficits to capital account.

Beatty's Last Campaigns

The Canadian financial citadels were appalled by such unorthodoxy, and Mr. E. W. Beatty of the Canadian Pacific deemed the hour to be right to renew his attack on the rival system. Canadian railway traffic now was at its lowest ebb; grain cargoes in 1935, for instance, were only one-eighth of what they had been in 1928. On the luncheon club circuits, Beatty proclaimed that it was madness for two railways to destroy each other in battling for a volume of traffic that could not make either system prosperous. Public ownership, he declared, had cost the Canadian people

$3 billion; that was half of the value of all urban property in Canada and represented a tax on Canadian citizens of $3 a minute from the beginning of the Christian era. The only hope was to wipe the slate clean and start over again—with the Canadian Pacific in charge, of course.

Such views immediately came under challenge. Minister of Transport C. D. Howe was of tougher metal than Thornton, and he dispatched a team of speakers, led by the redoubtable S. W. Fairweather, on Beatty's trail. The Canadian National Railways thesis remained unchanged: mobility was a far too important socio-economic necessity to be left entirely to transportation managers. In the case of Canada, a railway monopoly would not be unifying but disruptive, with each of the principal segments—British Columbia, the prairies, Ontario-Quebec and the Maritime Provinces—determined to obtain advantages at the expense of the others.

This dispute was not continuous, but from time to time its embers were blown into flame. The small communities rang with the rival arguments, but for the Canadian Pacific it was a losing campaign; even the political stalwarts who had bedeviled Canadian National Railways during the Bennett regime now withheld their support from Beatty. Eventually, a Senate committee was given the unwelcome task of arbitrating the issue. Its findings were beautifully innocuous, splendidly null. Its

The first aircraft—Stearman biplane, 1937.
(COURTESY OF AIR CANADA, LTD.)

report declared that much could be said on both sides. Thereafter the integration of private and publicly owned railway systems never became a serious issue.

The Impact of Road Transport

During the years of the depression, the competition of road transport grew by leaps and bounds. Motor vehicles enjoyed no basic advantage; in cost per mile, they sometimes ran from two to four times the cost of transport over the same distances by rail; except for very short haul, road deliveries neither were more rapid nor more reliable. Other factors, however, established almost unchallengeable advantages for the truckers. Their right-of-way costs—the taxation on them for the upkeep of the highways—were only a fraction of the cost of a railway roadbed, since there were eight times as many private as commercial vehicles on the roads. There were no pick-up and delivery costs by the truckers nor any extra charges for less than carload lots. Lighter and cheaper packaging was acceptable on goods shipped by road. Finally, the unceasing clamor of the motorist for better surfaces on the highways provided the truckers with ever-expanding areas of operation.

As the growth of road transport coincided in considerable degree with the intensification of the depression, it is difficult to determine how much of the railways' losses should be attributable to either factor. In the last normal year (1928), Canadian National Railways freight traffic amounted to 23,064,790,500 ton-miles. Seven years later, it had been reduced by nearly half to 12,933,405,964 ton-miles. A Canadian National Railways review estimated that in that period, traffic to the value of $54 million had been lost to highway carriers, which would mean that they had taken about 4 billion ton-miles from the railways. An Ontario official summary, however, put the figure much lower, with total road transport tonnage not more than 7 percent of all traffic.

As road transport facilities multiplied, many of the branch lines began to feel the pinch, and the railways let it be known that should the trend continue, it might be necessary to close them. As always, this threat caused an outcry, and great play was made of the principal railway advantage; its trains continued to run on schedule both summer and winter, whereas in the winter the highways at any time might be rendered impassable. Some of the provinces, therefore, took steps to assist the railways by limiting the advantages of road transport, either by the imposition of taxes, by the classifying of highways as to permissible traffic or by limiting the sizes of trucks or of the weights carried on them.

Such legislation, however, did little to check the growing losses of the railways, nor did early experiments in road-rail devices, which by means of duplicate sets of wheels could operate both on roads and on tracks, offer any solution. No conventional innovation could counteract the natural advantages of the truckers, so the railways had no option but to offer similar services. In March 1933, Canadian National Railways began to hire local carters to pick up and deliver its less than carload lots of freight. The experiment was successful, and within a year it was in operation over much of the system. Where local facilities were not available, Canadian National Railways installed their own trucks and so edged into the road transport field. In a report in September 1935, the railway officer who supervised this service reported a gain of 8 million pounds of less than carload lot freights in the first three months of that year. This substantial volume of traffic had been reclaimed from the road transport services.

Once Canadian National Railways had obtained a foot in the door, it was not denied complete entry. The breakthrough came in 1932 on the Central Vermont lines, where permission was obtained to operate both buses and trucks in connection with train services. In Canada, however, it was some years before the principle was established that if the truckers had the right to compete with the railways, the railways had an equal right to compete with the truckers.

The Passenger Problem

As elsewhere in the world, the motor car had taken a heavy toll of railway passenger traffic. During the 1920s, the number of automobiles in use in Canada (as distinct from trucks and buses), had quadrupled to more than a million vehicles. The depression had restricted their increase in the countryside rather than in the towns and cities. Yet by 1935, the count of cars on the roads was only about 6 percent less than in 1928. In the same period, the consumption of motor fuels had increased by 20 percent, and expenditures on improvement of roadways had almost doubled; like the railway before it, the possession of a surfaced road inspired emulation, often for no better reason than local pride or prestige. Furthermore, the first multilane highways had been completed in the United States. What the Americans have today, the Canadians are bound to demand before too long.

The Beginnings of Air Travel

It was impossible at such a juncture to consider offering improved passenger facilities on the railways, either in the form of faster or more frequent services or through luxury accommodations. As a result, passenger traffic continued to decline throughout the years of the depression; bus services in some instances accentuated this decrease, but for the most part, the private motor car, regardless of expense, became the principal carrier of short-haul passenger traffic.

An equal challenge for long-haul passenger traffic was in the making. During the First World War, Canada had no air forces of its own, but twenty-two thousand Canadians had found their way into the Royal Flying Corps and its successor, the Royal Air Force. Many of these officers and men had returned to private life not only with the training but also the ambition to continue in the infant aviation industries. The great expanses of the Canadian northland provided inviting opportunities for experiment, and there the "bush pilots" soon found themselves promoted from occasional flights to regular runs. Such services, often operating between nowhere and nowhere, but providing invaluable facilities to isolated enterprises or communities, increased from year to year. By 1930, their operations had mounted to 6,114,997 air miles flown and 3,903,908 pounds of freight transported in that year.

By then, numerous airlines were in operation in the United States, and certain American companies wished to extend their services northward to Canadian terminals. Had this occurred, the aircraft would have joined the motor car in diverting traffic from Canada's normal eastwest axis. In 1930, therefore, Sir Henry Thornton and E. W. Beatty of the Canadian Pacific decided that the Canadian railways must protect themselves by stimulating the growth of airways as an element in the Canadian transportation structure. To this end they induced six small airlines in eastern Canada to merge and to link up with a local service in western Canada. Both railway companies bought substantial holdings in this merger, which was named Canadian Airways Limited.

For the early years of the depression this venture seemed becalmed; there was no rising wind of traffic to propel it. But during this same period, both provincial and federal governments had been compelled to provide extensive aid for the 4 million unemployed Canadians; by a happy circumstance, one of the projects placed in work was the construction of airfields for the principal towns and cities. By 1936, over a hundred such airports had been completed, equipped with the necessary airdromes and other buildings, as well as with lighting, radio and meteorological facilities. On his advent to office Minister of Transport C. D. Howe asked Canadian Airways why no trans-Canadian services had been established. He was not satisfied with the reply and made a formal offer of federal support for such a venture. He invited the private airlines and the two railways systems to cooperate in the establishment of a trans-Canadian air route which, in due course, would expand into a worldwide air system. In December of that year, he announced to the House of Commons that the federal government was in the air business to stay and that it would welcome the participation of private carriers in future ventures.

Neither Canadian Airways nor the Canadian Pacific Railway had any liking for such an arrangement, since it promised to subordinate them to Canadian National Railways. Howe, therefore, was obliged to go it alone. In March 1937, he presented the bill for the incorporation of Trans-Canada Airlines Limited. The organization of this venture was entrusted to Canadian National Railways, which would hold 51 percent of the stock on behalf of the federal government. The remainder would be on offer to any private air companies that wished to share in the venture.

Philip G. Johnson, a highly trained American, assumed the management of Trans-Canada Airlines, and over the next two years, step by step, a nationwide service was established. The first passenger flights began on the short Vancouver-Seattle run in September 1937. In the following year, mail and air express services were installed on the prairies and were linked up with eastern Canada. In 1939, services became fully operative on more than 2,500 miles between Vancouver, Toronto and Montreal. In the following spring, an extension to Moncton fulfilled the commitment to link Canada by air from sea to sea.

The Ocean Services

Canadian National Railways went into aviation of its own free will. It was dragged into the steamship business. Early in this century, as Canadians became conscious of the value of the preferential tariffs existing between countries in the British Imperial system, there arose a demand for government assistance to shipping lines operating to various parts of the Empire. Subsidies were provided for services from Canada to the West Indies, to South Africa and to the Antipodes. During the First

TOP: A ship of the *Lady* line for Caribbean service.

BOTTOM: A ship of the *Prince* line for Pacific coastal service.

World War, as a result of heavy losses of shipping, it was found necessary to withdraw the British vessels operating on some of these subsidized
routes, whereupon Canada, her shipbuilding industries revived by the
exigencies of the conflict, undertook to continue such services with her
own vessels.

A shortage of shipping continued after the end of the war, and the
Canadian Government Merchant Marine, built and owned as a public
enterprise, grew into a substantial property. In 1921, it was operating
fifty-four vessels of 302,597 gross tons. On the formation of Canadian
National Railways, the management of this fleet was entrusted to it, and
the new system, like its Canadian Pacific competitor, was in the shipping
business. There was no similarity, however, between the situations of the
two railways. The Canadian Pacific had well-established services, with
ships built specifically for certain routes; Canadian National Railways
had inherited a heterogeneous array of tonnage, thrown together under
the impact of war necessities and by now aging rapidly.

In 1920, as a result of the signing of the Canada–West Indies Trade
Agreement, the Canadian government became responsible for the provision of two shipping services to the Caribbean area. The Canadian
Government Merchant Marine ships were not suitable for tropical routes,
and immediately there arose an outcry when West Indian shippers, whose
exports to Canada consisted in considerable part of tropical fruits and
vegetables, discovered that their goods spoiled in transit because of the
lack of proper ventilation and refrigeration facilities. Thornton considered such complaints to be warranted, and in 1925, he persuaded the
federal government to build ships designed for this particular service.

Thus originated the *Lady* fleet, five excellent vessels, each named
after the wife of a famous British admiral. They carried both passengers
and freight. They were given their own statutory identity, but they
remained, like Trans-Canada Airlines, a residual constituent of Canadian
National Railways.

These ships met every claim upon them, and their success emboldened
Thornton to attempt another essay in a different direction. Prince Rupert,
the northwestern Pacific terminal of Canadian National Railways, had no
local or coastal trade to sustain it; although it saved a full day's steaming
to the Orient in comparison with Vancouver, the trans-Pacific services
would not consider it as a port of call. Canadian Pacific liners were the
queens of the north Pacific, and this situation may have contributed
to Thornton's determination to place Canadian National ships in operation
in those waters. He planned to begin with coastal services, extending from

Alaska to San Francisco, with the emphasis on tourist trades in summer and with the eventual aim of a service to the Orient. He ordered three ships of size and type that best can be described as miniature liners; they were luxuriously appointed and capable of high speeds, and they were built in the same British yards that had constructed the *Lady* ships. They were named after not very distinguished princes of the British royal line, and they were delivered during 1930, with the *Prince Henry* allotted to the Alaska service, the *Prince David* to the Seattle-Victoria-Vancouver triangular run and the *Prince Robert* given the task of beating up coastal traffic.

These ships, whose overall cost was $8,532,389, proved a disastrous investment. There were few tourists who wanted to visit Alaska, and the *Prince Henry* was not competent to deal with the ice floes that blocked the approaches to the northern harbors. On the triangular Puget Sound run, aircraft already were skimming the cream of the passenger traffic. Coasting trade for liners did not exist, nor was there any incentive to create it.

In addition, there had been a serious error in the construction of the *Prince* ships. They had been built to an Admiralty specification, in order that they might be taken over as ships of war in emergency. As a result they were hopelessly overpowered for their size, and far from comfortable, even in moderate seas.

In addition to the *Lady* and *Prince* ships, Canadian National Railways was saddled with the liquidation of the Canadian Government Merchant Marine, whose war-built holdovers rapidly deteriorated toward the end of the 1920s. Thornton wished to replace them, but the government refused; one by one they either were sold to last-resort flag services or to the ship-breakers. In 1936, the final nine of them were taken over by private interests, and their account was closed. In seventeen years, they had cost the Canadian taxpayer $82,176,699.

The Tide Turns

For the Canadian National Railways, the tide of the depression turned with the 1934 election. This change of government ended a management that had acted more or less as administrators of an estate in bankruptcy; it was replaced by stouthearted and nonpolitical directors; such a change was as good as wine to many hard-working and dedicated railwaymen. In an early directive under the new program, President Hungerford reflected the feeling in the air when he called for every department to file, without delay, a report on what it found to be wrong and to recommend what could be done to repair it. The senior officers sprang to such tasks; they had been waiting for years for just such an opportunity. Among radical suggestions that were put into effect without delay was that of the Express Department, which insisted upon highway carriers to handle its traffic at both ends of train journeys. The Bureau of Statistics recommended that specialists should be hired as advisors in planning the future of the company and that a merit system should implement seniority considerations in the promotion of employees. This too was done. The Investigation Department presented a strong case for training programs for all management cadres, and this suggestion afterward took shape in the Railways Staff College. These and many other proposals of like nature revealed that the company was flexing its muscles and coming to life once more as a dynamic community after its release from the shackles of the depression.

Such changes undoubtedly were aided by extraneous circumstances, for by 1935, the times were on the mend, and the hard climb back to normalcy had begun. In 1936, revenues once more equaled operating costs; the situation was sufficiently encouraging for the Minister of Transport to embark on a project that had been in his mind from the day of his appointment—the alleviation, in part at least, of Canadian National Railways vast burden of unproductive debt. As of December 31, 1936, it stood at $2,435,400,000, of which roughly half was owed to the Dominion government. It manifestly was good tactics to deal with this portion of the debt first, for $675.6 million of it consisted of advances made in the fourteen years since the organization of the system, and it included, among other items, the amortization as capital of $461.5 million of interest charges—a procedure which, as previously reported, the Minister of Transport had denounced vigorously. Another item was $262,424,927 as the par value of the common stocks of the Grand Trunk and Canadian Northern Railways—stocks that officially had been pronounced worthless twenty years before, at the time of the takeover of these systems. This long-overdue transaction, as completed in March 1938, relieved Canadian National Railways of $1,174,000,000 of its government debt and left only the private indebtedness of $1,184,600,000 to be dealt with on some future occasion.

Canadian National Railways was by no means out of its dark tunnel, but there was daylight ahead; on the national economy the sun was shining. Slowly the fright revenues rose, particularly on the long hauls; the short-haul traffic that had been lost steadily to road transport began to sort out. As for passengers, at least a third of that business had been lost forever, but there still remained a sizable volume that might be held. The responsible officers began to seek solutions.

The Challenge of the Future

The economic atmosphere, therefore, was clearing but as the depression ended, an even more sinister situation was in the making. After Japan's seizure of Manchuria in 1931, there followed similar defiances of the rule of law—the occupation of the Rhineland and the conquest of Abyssinia. Year by year, the aggressor nations grew bolder and their threats more formidable to all free peoples. In 1935, Britain began to rearm, and two years later, for the first time in her history, that nation introduced conscription in peacetime. The Canadian government, at great pains to say one thing and do another in the interests of national unity, was well aware that if it came to a crunch, the mass of Canadians would insist on standing beside Britain and the Commonwealth; so Canada also began to take certain precautions, which were not misunderstood and which had beneficial effects on the economy.

In 1938, Germany's annexation of Austria and seizure of Czechoslovakia should have settled the matter, but the free nations needed more time to make ready. Hitler's first moves against Poland in the following spring, however, brought an immediate notice that Britain and France would take the field against him. The die had been cast; it was just a matter of time. Its first impact upon Canadian National Railways was the loan of its vice-president of purchasing and stores, R. C. Vaughan, for the organization of similar military services. In response to a demand from President Hungerford, the Bureau of Railway Economics prepared a report on the readiness of Canadian National Railways to assume additional burdens imposed by a state of war. In comparison with 1914, its progress was unmistakable:

Equipment in Two World Wars		
ITEM	1914	1939
Weight of rails (per yard)	80-85 pounds	100-130 pounds
Average locomotive tractive power	52,000 pounds	90,000 pounds
Train haul, (average weight)	350 tons	550 tons
Locomotive fuel (per power unit)	330 pounds	240 pounds
Toronto-Vancouver (average time)	11 days	7 days

The Royal Visit

Month by month the tensions grew; the insults and the blatant arrogance of the aggressor nations bred a slow, deep anger, even as far away as Canada. It was in such an atmosphere that in June 1939 Their Majesties King George VI and his consort arrived for their first state tour of Canada. The royal train consisted of twelve special coaches provided by the two systems, and it bore the distinguished visitors on a long leisurely tour of the Dominion. A huge pack—170 in all—of newspaper correspondents traveled with the royal party. Walter Thompson, as public relations officer of Canadian National Railways, acted as master of ceremonies and made himself indispensable. In the words of His Majesty, as transmitted by his secretary in a letter of farewell, "Your work called for a combination of the qualities of a successful ambassador, a firm yet just father of a large family and at other times as an efficient lion tamer."

In the first days of autumn, the confrontation came. Germany invaded Poland. On September 10, for the first time as a wholly independent nation, Canada declared war on the German Reich.

22

At War Anew

The Second World War opened with none of the fireworks and imminence of decision that had characterized the encounter of Germany and her foes in 1914. The land clash was restricted to the eastern front, where it was manifestly impossible for France and Britain to aid Poland; at sea and in the air, the immediate impacts were minor and without special significance. For Canada the declaration meant little more than preparations—the raising of a token division for immediate dispatch to Britain, the institution of escorted convoys for Atlantic shipping, hasty preparations for the construction of aircraft and the training of air crews. But even these preliminaries created additional traffic for Canadian National Railways; during 1939, freight shipments of manufactured goods increased by one-third, with a corresponding improvement in revenues of 12 percent. In that year, the system earned a surplus, but not enough, of course, to satisfy the service of $60 million interest on the inherited debt.

Poland fell; Russia and Germany, alike predatory, divided its lands. Early in 1940, a German courier was captured who carried details of re-enactment of the Schlieffen Plan of 1914, which involved the violation of Belgium and Holland by a gigantic swing around the right flank of the British-French deployments. The Low Countries rejected this evidence as inspired to force their alliance with the West; the French, who had little stomach for battle à outrance, continued to insist on the invulnerability of the Maginot Line. Thus six months passed in which the enemies, except on the seas, sat and stared at each other. Then the Royal Navy precipitated action by violating the territorial waters of Norway, which had been serving as a protected route for massive German imports of Swedish ore. Early in April, Hitler, in a brilliant stroke, seized Norway and Denmark, and the land forces of the antagonists met for the first time when British troops endeavored to win back the ports that gave the enemy an additional thousand miles of coastline as cover for the German submarine operations. In not very clever fighting, the Allies were worsted; with the Scandinavian flank secure, there followed massive German attacks on the western front. Thirty thousand civilians died in a brutal bombardment of Amsterdam; two German armies thrust through Belgium toward the unprotected northern frontier of France. The French Ninth Army broke up like a rotten pumpkin under massed panzer attacks in the Ardennes, and disaster faced the Allies. The British Expeditionary Force, few but full of fight, gave as good as it got in a masterly withdrawal toward the Channel ports. There, in an amphibious operation unequaled in history, a thousand craft, ranging from Thames barges to pleasure launches, rescued and bore away to England 338,125 fighting men—the nucleus of the forces that would retrieve the situation in the aftermath of a disastrous defeat.

Great Britain and her Commonwealth—indeed all the English-speaking world—responded to this derring-do with a spontaneous outburst of dedication to a cause that was all but lost. The British found a voice in Winston Churchill and shared his forthright intention to fight to the end, whatever befell. In phrases that will outlive the years, he solidified determination to be exterminated rather than to yield; amid his eloquence, he scattered everyday phrases that all could understand. Under the sway of his oratory, the British peoples closed ranks as never before.

The Treasure Episode

With the capitulation of France, Hitler turned without delay to the invasion of Britain. He proposed to land sixteen divisions on the eighty miles of English Channel between Ramsgate and Selsey Bill; but first he must put paid to the Royal Air Force, which had fought on the Continent with skill and resolution. Since he considered cities and civilians to be fair targets, there ensued an enterprise that gave Canadian National Railways its first taste of war service. The City of London, long the financial capital of the world, held great masses of gold and negotiable securities. It manifestly was impossible to leave such treasure in such a prime target, and it was decided to transfer it to Canada, where the United Kingdom government would seek sanctuary in event of the British Isles being overrun. Two repositories were selected—the vaults of the Sun Life Assurance Company in Montreal and those of the Bank of Canada in Ottawa.

Because of the submarine menace, the treasure ships would deliver their cargoes at Halifax and Saint John rather than in St. Lawrence ports. Thus Canadian National Railways became the carriers of these precious consignments for over 840 miles to Montreal, 957 miles to Ottawa.

George A. Shea, superintendant of the Investigation Branch and G. E. Bellerose, head of the express services, were entrusted with the entrainment and delivery of these shipments. Escorts were provided by the Royal Canadian Mounted Police. Ten baggage or express cars, with their windows sealed and papered over, would constitute a train, and each car would carry two hundred boxes of bullion, each box containing 110 pounds of gold. An exact drill was improvised for the takeover by Canadian National Railways on the wharves and for delivery to the repositories.

On July 1 HMS *Emerald*, a fast cruiser, which had outfooted her destroyer escort in rough seas, docked at Halifax. She carried bullion and securities to the value of $586 million. On the following evening, the streets of Montreal between the Canadian National station and the Sun Life Building were cleared and picketed, and the delivery was completed without incident. There followed a treasure flotilla consisting of a battleship, a cruiser and three merchant ships, which, after an anxious crossing due to bad weather and engine defects in two recently liberated Polish liners, landed shipments valued at $1,989,000,000 at Halifax and Saint John. Throughout the summer, other ships without loss brought the remainder of the British reserves. As they docked, a police line formed from the gangway to a table on the wharf, where the requisite exchange of documents was completed. The trains divided at a secret siding before reaching Montreal, and a certain number of cars continued on to Ottawa, where similar precautions were taken to avoid knowledge of the arrivals of the treasure. The task was completed without incident save for the flooding of the Sun Life vaults during an exceptional storm. Canadian National Railways contributed two miles of steel rails for the reconstruction of the walls of the vaults, and the Dominion government increased the deposits of $278,045,685, covering the purchase of the outstanding stocks and bonds of the Grand Trunk Railway that had remained in British hands. The transfers in all came to a value of $7.5 billion.

The Weeks of Decision

During this movement, the Battle of Britain opened, with heavy air assaults intended to clear the way for the infantry landings. The first attacks were directed against the airfields of southeastern England, and the defenders were heavily outnumbered. The day was saved in almost miraculous fashion by the foresight of a man and woman who had no prior inkling of the roles their private ventures would play. Lady Houston, an eccentric widow, provided £60,000 for a young designer who believed it was possible to build an aircraft with wings that would provide an eight-gun fire platform. Such was the origin of the Spitfire fighter plane, which took a deadly toll of its German adversaries. Robin Watson Watt, nursing his hobby of radio experiments, with toy balloons on weekends at the seaside, provided the beginnings of radar, by which the enemy air fleets could be detected in time to mass the defenders on their lines of approach.

When the assaults on the British airfields became too costly, the enemy switched his attacks to the British cities, bombing them by night, ruthlessly and at random. In this phase of the battle, British losses were sustained that might have become intolerable had it not been for the exuberant morale of the civilian population, which reacted to wholesale death and destruction in a manner that evoked the admiration of the free world. The English, the Scots and the Welsh mobilized swiftly to fight, in the terms of Churchill's exhortations, to the last man. Even the smallest villages mined their approaches and dug trenches in their gardens; the men made "sticky bombs" to destroy marauding armor, their wives bottled Molotov cocktails to drench in flames the supporting infantry. It was a time when all walked proudly, consecrated to taking toll of the invader; there was a debonair spirit that inspired such slogans as "You can always take one with you" and "We are in the Final and it will be played on the home grounds." Foreign correspondents told of comportment which might have come out of the Arthurian legends, when courage and faith ruled the minds of every man and every woman and the hearts of a nation rose indomitably to the challenges to survival.

Nowhere did this outpouring of the spirit strike with greater impact than in Canada. There, groups—social, economic and political—closed ranks to prepare for whatever might befall. And nowhere did British behavior kindle greater emotions than in the ninety thousand employees of Canadian National Railways. The war became part of the substance of their days. As will be related subsequently, the ships already had been in

action; two thousand of their fellow workers had disappeared into the
Canadian land forces; fifty-three of the company's senior officers had been
claimed by the federal authorities for war duties. Military priorities were
accepted as a matter of course; already a number of company shops were
under conversion into munition or armament factories. Despite the swiftly
rising traffic attendant upon the war effort, the railway's needs were de-
moted to low priority; it became next to impossible to obtain more than a
minimum of new rolling stock, fixed installations or track equipment. In
the face of these shortages, the native adaptability of the employees received full opportunity; many of them had grown up on the farms and
were conversant with "make-do" improvisations. For more than five years
of war, their ingenuity was tested again and again; the trains seldom failed
to fulfill their missions. In the autumn of 1940, there came a heavy movement of troops to Atlantic ports (the Canadian Expeditionary Force had
been expanded to five divisions) and a reciprocal delivery of British women
and children refugees to inland destinations. At this juncture, Colonel J. L.
Ralston, a fine soldier now in the cabinet, paid an eloquent tribute to the
dedication of Canadian railway personnel to the war effort.

On June 22, 1941, there came the startling news that the Nazis had
violated what always had been a cardinal German military precept; by a
treacherous attack on Russia they now were fighting concurrently on two
fronts. The British Commonwealth immediately moved to the assistance
of the Soviet forces; no Churchillian quip was more widely quoted than
his statement that even if the Communists had been the Devil himself, he
would have sought the opportunity to make a favorable reference to
Satan in the House of Commons. More railway shops immediately were
requisitioned for the satisfaction of the needs of the underequipped Russian armies.

On July 19, 1941, President Hungerford, feeling the weight of years,
was replaced by R. C. Vaughan, previously vice-president of purchases
and stores, who returned to railway service from loan to the Dominion
government on military account. Walter Thompson, who had organized
the Canadian censorship section on the outbreak of war, afterward became Dominion government Director of Information; when compelled to
retire because of illness, he was succeeded by G. H. Lash, his colleague in
the Public Relations Section of Canadian National Railways.

The second year of war (1941) saw the long-awaited emancipation
of Canadian National Railways from dependence on the public purse. With
revenues of over $300 million, the company showed sufficient surplus to
meet its heavy inherited interest charges, to hire 6,705 additional employ-

ees and to provide a cost of living bonus and unemployment insurance for all ranks. In addition, it was found possible to consider some essential capital expenditures, and orders were placed for four thousand boxcars and smaller numbers of specialized rolling stock.

The Pacific Campaign Opens

The war had spread into other theaters. In June 1940, for no better reason than a desire to share in the spoils of what appeared to be a certain German victory, Italy had declared war on Great Britain and had dispatched substantial forces to invade Egypt. In December of that year, the Italians had suffered a crushing defeat in their first advance toward the Suez Canal; a superbly handled British force of less than one-fifth of the Italian strength took one hundred fifteen thousand prisoners. To save his ally's face, Hitler was obliged to dispatch an armored corps to its aid. The Germans were driving deep into southeastern Russia, and the grand plan emerged of an advance over the Caucasus into the Middle East that would link up at the Suez Canal with Axis forces thrusting across North Africa. An equally sinister development in the Orient saw the Japanese convinced that the moment for a monstrous grab had arrived; they planned a grand coup in which they would drive the white man back to Suez and so bring all Pacific and Asian areas under their sway. On December 7, 1941, an unheralded attack on Pearl Harbor, the American naval base in Hawaii, opened the assault on American, British and Dutch possessions in Asia.

The excellence of Japanese organization and the fanaticism of their fighting men at first promised to sweep everything before them. One of their early objectives was the conquest of the Aleutian island chain, with the manifest intention of advance to Alaska and northern British Columbia. This prospect was countered by the creation of the Pacific Command for the defense of the threatened areas, a development that brought Canadian National Railways into a war zone, for its terminal at Prince Rupert was only a few miles below the southernmost tip of Alaska, and the line offered the only transportation facilities into the great empty expanses of the British Columbia northland.

Early in 1942, Canadian National Railways, reinforced by military sapper sections, began the construction of trunk lines for telegraph, telephone and carrier current circuits in the huge wilderness that stretched northward to Alaska. The task was speeded by the urgency of the hour; 2,000 miles of line were built in a few months over mountains, along brawling streams and through forests. The line was equipped with repeater and radio sta-

Armored Diesel locomotive for service to Prince Rupert during
World War II.

tions whose crews were trained by Canadian National Railways. The isolation of upward of half a million square miles of terrain was broken.

When American forces moved to the defense of Alaska, they found Prince Rupert to be a convenient base. It was several hundred miles closer to the threatened areas than any American port, and it lay at the southern extremity of a sheltered and easily defensible water route northward. In April 1942, American detachments arrived to construct the essential camps, warehouses and staging facilities. At the same time, other groups passed through to the north to build the Alaska Highway, 1,671 miles in length between the end of Canadian National Railways steel at Dawson Creek and Fairbanks in central Alaska. This road, which traversed hitherto trackless terrain, was built at great speed and to a considerable extent out of imported materials. It was estimated that United States military precautions at Prince Rupert and in the construction of the Alaska Highway provided Canadian National Railways with at least 1 million tons of additional traffic.

Pressure in the Maritimes

On any morning at Halifax or Saint John, a convoy of thirty or
more heavily laden merchant ships might be found on what had been
empty docking berths on the previous evening, all demanding "quickliest"
clearance. The railway from Halifax to Moncton was single track, 189
miles in length, and every ship required from twenty to thirty trains to
move its complete cargo. For the clearance of a convoy, it was necessary
that seven hundred freight cars should arrive and leave the port of entry
each day. Nothing but Centralized Traffic Control could have handled such
movements; sometimes there were as many as twenty-two trains operating concurrently on forty-eight miles of single track. The problem was
aggravated by the necessity of providing up to four hundred cars whenever
a bauxite ship arrived from British Guiana. The giant refineries at Arvida,
swollen with war orders, no longer dare risk the St. Lawrence passage,
and the incoming ores traveled for their last 900 miles over Canadian
National Railways.

The Search for Replacement Minerals

In yet another direction, the war effort made heavy demands on
Canadian National Railways. Many prime sources of essential minerals, such
as Italian mercury, Burmese tungsten and Malayan tin, had been cut off
by enemy action. It therefore was necessary that, regardless of cost, additional sources of supply of these metals be brought into production. There
followed many searches, particularly along the Arctic fringe; when a find
was reported, transportation facilities immediately were demanded, irrespective of economic feasibility. As a consequence, Canada became an
important supplier of mercury, producing six times its own needs; finds of
tin, tungsten, molybdenum, mica and chrome, as well as such alloy elements as vanadium, tantalum and indium, were exploited, and each contributed its quota to the war work of Canadian National Railways.

In the shipment of motor vehicles to the battlefronts, the company
contributed more than their inland carriage. Ocean convoys, because of
the importunities of war, were irregularly spaced; nor was it feasible to
hold a fleet of ships in harbor to await arrival of their cargoes. Canadian
National Railways therefore established six storage depots sufficiently contiguous to Maritime ocean ports to feed a steady flow to ships at dock. On
an average, several hundred carloads of motor vehicles, representing more
than twenty-five thousand units in all, were held in these depots. In similar

fashion, re-icing points were established for cars that carried foodstuffs or other items that required refrigeration.

General Effects of the War

Canadian National Railways contribution to the war effort can be gauged by a comparision of a boom year of the 1920s with that of a mid-war year. In 1928 and 1942, the system had more or less the same count of rolling stock—eighty thousand freight cars, three thousand passenger cars and twenty-five hundred locomotives. Yet in the latter year, it carried 44 percent more freight with 8.6 percent less staff in 25.9 percent fewer freight cars and twice as many passengers in 14.2 percent fewer passenger cars and with 6 percent fewer locomotives. Yet the war years brought no inflation; revenues per ton-mile were less at its end than at its beginning.

The conflict had led to a heavy movement of population from the countryside into the towns. The rural areas, however, had grown prosperous, with a considerable consolidation of holdings. A wide range of power machinery had been introduced, together with a striking increase in roadways, which opened up the countryside; rural electrification had become general. Canadian National Railways, whose many branch lines formerly had sustained steady losses, now showed up on the right side of the ledger. Heavier movements of crop and reciprocal increases in local demands for farming equipment and for the refurbishing of farm households had effected the favorable changes.

The Situation in 1943

In July 1943, the Battle of Europe opened with the Sicilian landings, with Canadian troops in action in numbers for the first time. By then, the movement of military personnel had become almost a separate passenger service, with commissary cars, "long-table diners," and a wide range of hospital cars. During that year, there was a constant exchange of distinguished personages who inevitably were shepherded by Walter Thompson; they included Winston Churchill once more, President Roosevelt on a state visit to Ottawa, Madame Chiang Kai-shek as representative of her husband at an Allied conference. Indeed, the railway had become one of the most important Canadian partners in the business of war, and although far from any front, its involvements in the conflict now could be noted on every hand. Women had replaced men in many railway capacities; they served in the workshops as oilers, crane operators and even as black-smiths' helpers. At long last it had become possible to open the Montreal terminals; as significant of its need, thirty-five hundred trains and 6.5 million passengers were dispatched from the new station in its first year of operation.

The entry of the United States into the war had an immediate impact upon Canadian wages scales, which, like fares and rates, had been frozen from the beginning of the conflict. No such policy was adopted to the south of the border: within a matter of months the wages on Canadian National American subsidiaries such as the Central Vermont and the Grand Trunk Western groups, had increased by $7.5 million a year. It manifestly was impossible, in the face of such increases, to maintain the Canadian freeze, and in 1944, a number of Canadian unions applied for wage increases. The management was more than willing, although it was carrying its traffic at prewar rates and costs of operation had increased substantially. There was no desire, however, to match American figures, and the increases in both wages and rates were modest and reflected preoccupation with the thing that really mattered—the winning of the war.

Out-of-Office War Work

Determination infused Canadian railwaymen not only in their working time but also in their leisure hours. A high proportion of them had joined one or another of the unofficial service groups that supported the war effort—the Red Cross and other community organizations. These groups provided mobile canteens, parcels and community letters for the troops in the field, and particularly they showed to advantage in the anti-waste campaigns, in which millions of pounds of paper and metals were recovered for reuse. They also participated in the successive Victory Loan campaigns, to which the company and its employees subscribed no less than $177 million during the war. With 85 percent of all personnel as subscribers, local railway leaders reminded the recalcitrant of their duty, as witness the report in the *Canadian National Magazine*, in connection with the Fifth Victory Loan:

> Our Pacific Coast shipyards yielded 100% support. A youth who had decilined to buy a $200.00 bond was taken in hand by a pal who proved so persuasive that within a couple of hours the lad had made a cash purchase of $1,500.00 in bonds. In the same shipyard a woman worker whose husband was in the Air Force, signed a payroll deduction for the whole of her wages for the next six months. On the prairies a section foreman sold his summer house to put the money into war bonds; a stenographer did the same with the money that she

received from the sale of her home. Cases of parents investing the assigned pay of sons or daughters in uniform were common.[1]

With such dedication in the ranks, President Vaughan, appearing before the standing committee of the House of Commons in March 1944, could speak proudly:

> We have a tremendous property to operate. Our Canadian National family of railways, steamships, air lines, telegraphs, express companies and hotels contains approximately thirty active separate companies. Measured by territories served and route mileage operated we are the largest railway on the North American continent. We have over 100,000 employees and our present payroll is approximately $200,000,000 a year. With respect to the general officers under whose directions these operations are conducted I think it fair to state that [during the war] there has been practically no increase in their number and their scale of compensation is lower than that paid by other railways to officers with comparable responsibilities.[2]

At the end of that year, a detailed statement showed Canadian National Railways to be by far the largest single industry in Canada. Since the outbreak of war its trains had covered 330 million miles, carrying more than 433 million tons of cargo and more than 132 million passengers; 5,540 special military trains had transported more than 4 million soldiers, sailors and airmen; 21,168 employees had served in the armed forces, of whom 582 had given their lives to their cause; more than 100 former employees had received decorations for gallantry or devotion to duty.

The Saga of the Railway Ships

For six months after its outbreak, the Second World War stagnated on land, but at sea it began on its first evening, when the Donaldson liner *Athenia* on the Montreal run was torpedoed without warning. Prior to declaration of war, German surface craft and submarines had been dispatched to all oceans to begin harassment of Allied shipping without delay. Great Britain countered with the immediate mobilization of naval auxiliaries and with the organization of convoys for merchant ships. Among the first craft to be requisitioned for naval duties were the *Prince* ships of Canadian National Railways, which then were precariously justifying their existence on free routes in the Caribbean area.

The *Prince Robert*, *Prince Henry* and *Prince David* were fitted out with an assortment of weapons as armed merchantmen. It was nearly a year after the declaration of war that they embarked on their first tours of duty, which concerned the presence of enemy supply ships in neutral

HMS *Prince David,* converted during World War II into a landing craft carrier.

harbors. *Prince Robert* scored a kill amost immediately when, in September 1940, it intercepted the German vessel *Weser* as it endeavored to slip out of Manzanillo harbor on the west coast of Mexico. It was captured intact, renamed *Vancouver Island* and placed in British service without delay. The enemy did not make the same mistake twice. *Prince Henry,* having identified two enemy ships in Callao Harbor, lay over the horizon until advised of their departure and then closed on them at top speed, whereupon their crews immediately cast off in lifeboats and the ships burst into flames. They had been mined against the eventuality of capture.

In January 1941, *Prince Robert* was transferred to the Antipodes to escort shiploads of Australians and New Zealanders to Canada to train under the Commonwealth Air Plan. She afterward accompanied a Canadian garrison to Hong Kong, and in December, by a narrow margin, escaped when, after Pearl Harbor, Japanese naval craft swarmed into the Pacific. In midsummer 1942, she joined her sister ships as elements in the Aleutian expedition, a mixed Canadian-American force dispatched to expel the Japanese from those islands. In the bleak Arctic sea, the weather was the principal foe, and in November, without contact with the enemy, the three ships were withdrawn. The *Prince Robert* and the *Prince David* were allotted routine patrols in British Columbia waters, and the *Prince Henry* became depot ship of the Newfoundland Escort Forces.

At the end of that year came radical changes. The buildup was beginning for the invasion of Europe, and the Admiralty ordered the *Prince* ships to be converted for specialist employments—the *Prince Robert* as an antiaircraft cruiser and the *Prince Henry* and *Prince David* as landing craft carriers—mother ships of the small blunt-nosed launches which would put the men, tanks and guns ashore on the hostile beaches.

On their emergence after this second conversion, they were changed beyond recognition. The *Prince Robert* had been converted into a great fire platform crammed with weapons. The *Prince David* and the *Prince Henry* had been shorn of their superstructures, and heavy davits were set in their hulls to raise and lower the twenty-ton landing craft.

On recommission, these ships went their several ways. In October 1943, *Prince Robert* arrived off Gibraltar as an element in the escort force of a large convoy, consisting of more than sixty vessels, which in cruising formation covered fourteen square miles of ocean. Battle was joined almost immediately, the enemy attacking with heavy bombs, glider bombs and torpedoes. The *Prince Robert* had an exciting day, the scene thus being described by the Canadian official historian:

> Upwards of a hundred Allied vessels were dancing in a diabolic ballet with destruction, amid constant pillars of bomb misses. Above them, rising and falling in cadence and darting among the ink spots of flak, were the specks of the enemy planes. The merchantmen on their zigzag courses executed stately and measured emergency turns, with every now and then a ship twisting unrhythmically out of line to evade a glider bomb.[3]

There followed twenty months of such escort duty for *Prince Robert*. In September 1944, she entered a shipyard for refitment. In July 1945, she sailed for Australia. En route she was diverted to the Far East to participate in the disarming of the enemy garrisons in Hong Kong. In December of that year she was paid off as a ship of war.

The end of 1943 saw *Prince David* and *Prince Henry* in British yards, making final preparations for employment in the Normandy landings. On June 2, 1944, embarked their assault infantry, which in both instances happened to be Canadians. On D Day, June 6, amid the thunderous cacophony of the greatest amphibious operation in the history of the world, they had varying fortunes. *Prince David* lost five of her troop carriers en route to the beaches, whereas all of *Prince Henry's* boats landed safely.

Their next mission took them to the Mediterranean, where they participated in the landings of Seventh U.S. Army in southern France. Thereafter they were sent to Greece, where a civil war raged and where they might come under fire at any anchorage. By February 1945, they were back in Britain. *Prince Henry* was selected as Royal Navy Headquarters ship at Wilhelmshaven, and *Prince David* returned to Vancouver for refitment prior to service in the Pacific.

The surrender of Germany and Japan ended their vagabondages. *Prince Henry* continued as a ship of all work for the Royal Navy for another fifteen years, but *Prince David* and *Prince Robert* were sold to a Greek firm, which placed them on the Australian run. In 1951, *Prince David*, was scrapped, but her sister ships continued in miscellaneous employments for another ten years, before they met for the last time in an Italian shipbreaker's yard.

The Lady Ships

The *Lady* ships were less suitable for naval duties, but in October 1940, *Lady Somers* was claimed by the Admiralty as a communications ship. She was sunk on July 15, 1941. Six months later, *Lady Hawkins*, still on passenger service, was torpedoed off the New England coast, with the loss of 241 lives. The *Lady Nelson* also was torpedoed while lying at a St. Lucia anchorage; after being patched up, she was converted into a hospital ship. She survived the war, having logged 136,407 miles in the delivery of 15,067 wounded and convalescent servicemen.

On May 4, 1942, *Lady Drake* was torpedoed while still on passenger service, with the loss of twelve lives. In the following month, *Lady Rodney* became a Canadian troopship. She survived the war. The *Cornwallis,* a Canadian National charter, had the least luck of all. After being torpedoed in Bridgetown, Barbados, harbor, she was repaired and plied her routes until December 4, 1944, when she was sunk by enemy action off the coast of Maine. There were only five survivors. Another Canadian National charter, *Canatco* was sunk off Labrador on October 21, 1942, fortunately without loss of life.

Despite these casualties, the Canadian National Caribbean services were maintained throughout the war, handling at all 5,839,177 tons of cargo in that period. In addition, other Canadian National ships operated on special assignments to every corner of the world. They had many adventures, but in the great majority of instances they won through. One of these tramps returned with forty-eight shellholes patched over in her sides.

In the Air

The infant Canadian air service could only participate in the war effort indirectly. One of its first losses was that of Philip G. Johnson, who had been responsible for its operation in its swaddling years; he returned to the United States to reassume the presidency of the Boeing Aircraft Company. The quickening of Canadian industry as war orders began to arrive gave an immediate impetus to air travel; in 1940, lines that had subsisted previously on mail and express showed healthy passenger earnings. New services quickly developed: on December 31, 1941, Trans-Canada Airlines were operating over 4,024 miles of regular route, with flights of 18,764 miles daily—an increase of 60 percent over the preceding year. Services already were established to various United States centers, and in 1942, they were extended to Newfoundland. By then the airline had a variety of war jobs in hand. It had placed its Winnipeg shops at the service of the Royal Canadian Air Force, and it had provided a number of instructors for the Commonwealth Air Training Plan. H. J. Symington, who in July 1941 succeeded S. J. Hungerford as president, reported that in 1942 the publicly owned airlines had carried 63 percent more airmail, 28 percent more air express and 24 percent more passengers than in the preceding year. Operating revenues were up by 20 percent and net surplus by nearly 40 percent over 1941.

This progress did not go unmarked in high places. On April 2, 1943, Prime Minister Mackenzie King, speaking in the House of Commons, declared that Trans-Canada Airlines would remain the sole instrument of the Dominion government in air transport, both inside Canada and on foreign and overseas routes. In November of that year, on a pathfinder flight, a Trans-Canada aircraft set a new trans-Atlantic record of eleven hours, thirty-eight minutes.

Not all of his supporters agreed with the Prime Minister in his decision to integrate the railways and air services. Among the dissentients was C. D. Howe, Minister of Transport and, because of his war services in that portfolio, perhaps the outstanding member of the cabinet. On March 17, he announced to a surprised House of Commons that legislation would be introduced to throw the air open to everyone and to restrict the railways, the steamship companies and the highway transport companies to their native elements. In short, he foresaw air services as an independent medium that would progress in competition rather than in cooperation with other transportation media.

In pursuance of this policy, an Air Transport Board was appointed that year. Prime Minister King, however, had not changed his mind; he still wished the public interest to be safeguarded in the air by Trans-Canada Airlines in association with Canadian National Railways. The fangs of Air Transport Board legislation, therefore, had been deftly drawn, and the measure, which passed the House of Commons, teemed with escape clauses. For all practical purposes, the situation remained unchanged.

The natural tendency in the growth of Trans-Canada Airlines (afterward Air Canada) was toward formal rather than intimate association with Canadian National Railways. It soon began to take over some of the administrative functions that as a matter of convenience had been entrusted to its parent. However, the ownership remained unchanged and the directorates continued to be interlocking; but today, after all the auxiliary services once performed by Canadian National Railways for its air associate, there remains no more than a formal association.

At the end of the war, Trans-Canada Airlines was eight years of age. It had established itself on 8,329 miles of route; its aircraft flew a million miles monthly. Its staff had grown to eight thousand employees, of whom many had seen service in the armed forces of the Commonwealth.

A Proud Record

The war did not end for Canadian National Railways with the surrender of the enemies of the Western Alliance. It still had the other half of the job to do—to repatriate upward of half a million men, to see them re-established in their civilian avocations, to assist whenever possible in the transformation from a wartime to a peacetime economy and society. Such duties however should not be allowed to dwarf or diminish the contributions that had helped to turn Canadians, for the second time in a generation, into first-class fighting men. Of all the praise and bays that were consequent on victory, perhaps the remarks of the Honorable Lionel Chevrier at Strathroy in October 1945 provide the most fitting tribute:

> The railways have been the backbone of this country's war effort. They have nobly upheld the best tradition of railroading. For five and a half years they have proven themselves to be one of the most important lines of defense and offense in a global war. . . . Much criticism was levelled at our railways in the pre-war years, particularly in regard to excessive mileage. These critics would have reduced overhead costs by curtailing the mileage in operation. Had this advice been acted upon it would have been impossible for Canada to have played such an important part in this war. Our railwaymen, whether chief executive, engineer or section hand, have played marvellous roles in keeping supplies moving to factories and to seaboard.

23

Shaping Up for the Future

Any period of exceptional stress leaves legacies in its train. Just as the First World War brought the motor car into its own and bestowed enormous mobility on the individual, so a quarter-century later another global conflict intensified the impact of communications media. The proliferation of radio, television, and the printed word, particularly in the form of advertising, established intimacies contemptuous of national totems and continental boundaries. Thereafter all peoples, wherever they lived and whatever their state of development, drank at the same fountain.

Among the earliest results of this monstrous spread of information (if not of knowledge) was the liquidation of Britain's worldwide empire; no imperial advantage thereafter could cancel the consciousness of inferior status. Another result of this overwhelming social development was the elevation of the United States into the rank of super-power and principal mentor of Western civilization.

Such developments touched Canada closely. As has been noted in earlier chapters, an East-West axis—political, economic and social—was the prime essential of Canadian nationhood. As long as the British Empire remained a world force, this axis extended beyond the seas and girdled the globe, creating ties abroad and helping to mold a Canadian identity at home. But when the United States emerged as the fountainhead of inspiration by virtue of its predominating role in world communications, the main Canadian axis of physical and intellectual activity changed direction. Thereafter more and more Canadian roads led to the south. Continental aspirations and inclinations began to dominate the Canadian outlook.

Paramount Social Pressures

Canadian National Railways could not hope to escape the impact of such trends. In order to survive, Canadian railways must conform more and more to American standards and usages. That was to say, they constantly must improve services and so provide the wherewithal to offer something different—something that would lend itself to the importunities of advertising. This was to become known as the Exploitation of the New Thing, in which a modicum of economic advantage might or might not supplement the major selling power of social attractiveness. Just as political authority had been obliged in this century to defer to economic considerations, so in turn the New Order compelled the economy to submit in ever-increasing degree to social pressures.

Translated into terms of transportation necessities, railways became the prisoner in the box, with customers as the jury. They might remain the most economic and reliable of common carriers, but they would need more frills and furbelows in order to attract their customers, particularly in the passenger traffic. By 1945, nine-tenths of the short-haul passenger movement had been lost to motor cars and buses. Commuter trains still were faster, cheaper and in many ways more convenient, but who wanted to wait for—or to miss—a train at a railway station when a motor car stood in the driveway? A train was a service. A motor car was a servant. The servant got the nod almost every time.

The Necessity of Renewals

In the autumn of 1945, Canadian National Railways was providing as many as fifty troop trains each week to convey military personnel from ports of debarkation to their demobilization centers. As this temporary traffic began to diminish, railway executives found time for a long, hard look at what lay ahead. In September, before a federal committee, S. W. Fairweather gave details of the expenditures that he deemed necessary if Canadian National Railways were to carry out its postwar responsibilities to the Canadian people. His total of $632,290,000 was staggering; it was far in excess either of what the system could earn or what Parliament would authorize. Other experts corroborated his findings. In November, D. C. Coleman of the Canadian Pacific Railway spoke for both systems when he declared that while the railways had held the line in rates throughout a depression and a world war, the costs of nearly everything they used had soared, elevating operating expenses to unforeseen levels. In the autumn of 1946, the Railway Association of Canada, speaking on behalf of its twenty-one members, gave the percentages of increases over the war period on major requirements as in terms of the following tabulation:

ITEM	INCREASE % (1946 OVER 1939)
Ties	94
Coal	63
Lumber	53
Unskilled Labor (per man-hour)	42
Miscellaneous materials (average)	42

Transformation of Labor Relations

The same source declared that an overall increase of 30 percent in railway rates would do no more than make good the losses that had been sustained. In addition, all other costs of operation were secondary to the imminent demands of labor. Throughout the 1930s, the depression had pinned down wages; during the war, patriotic considerations enforced the standstill. But after fifteen years of restraint, railway employees had begun to feel that in an economic sense they had become forgotten men. During that period, their duties had grown enormously; by 1945, Canadian National Railways was carrying 80 percent more freight and passengers than before the war.

Yet such was the strength of tradition that it was not until 1947 that a confrontation occurred. In that year, railway demands for rate increases evoked a counter pay claim from all ranks of employees. This relationship of company requirements to labor claims inaugurated a new era in employee relations, as afterward described by G. H. Lash, director of public relations, Canadian National Railways:

> Instead of bargaining with each group of unions more or less separately as had been the custom in the past, the railways now found themselves faced with an overall demand which took little account of

differences in skill or geographical location. The duties of a train dis-
patcher and those of a dining car waiter were greatly dissimilar and
the employees in Nova Scotia enjoyed a lower cost of living than those
in Toronto or Vancouver. But these things now ceased to matter. In
place of the paternalistic labor negotiator who bargained with management on a first-name basis, there now appeared for the first time on
the Canadian railway scene the new United States type in the person
of Frank Hall—affable but aloof, capable and dedicated to his cause,
surrounded by a well-organized staff of economists, statisticians and
lawyers.*

This professional type of negotiation paid off for the employees.
However recalcitrant the attitude of management and whatever the difficulties in meeting labor demands, the final authority in future no longer
remained an officially appointed conciliation board; intensified labor
pressures on the American model thereafter would prove a factor in how
one hundred thousand railway employees would vote in future. Politicians now were given a stake in wage negotiations, and those in power
were apt to become subconsciously sympathetic to the workers. No matter
how honest a member of Parliament might be, he could not afford to forget the effect of his attitude upon his career and upon his party on election day.

The first major claims under the new order occurred in June 1948.
It consisted of a cross-the-board demand for thirty-five cents per hour
increase. The railway executives stood their ground, the subsequent conciliation board dithered and a general strike was only hours away when
Prime Minister Mackenzie King intervened. He summoned the labor and
company negotiators separately to Ottawa and in effect told them that
they would take an award of seventeen cents an hour and like it. This
increase imposed an added charge of $126 million annually on Canadian
National Railways, which then showed an operating surplus but not
nearly enough to satisfy its service charges on existing indebtedness. As
a result the wage increases came directly from the taxpayers' pockets.
But in the brave new day that was dawning, the treasury had been marked
down as a target that would never shoot back.

---

* Excerpt from a letter to the historian. In one respect, Mr. Lash's description
may be misleading. Mr. Hall conformed to the British rather than to the American
tradition of labor negotiator. A soft-voiced East Anglian, he was tough in argument
but usually amenable to compromise.

Service Improvements

Despite its financial difficulties, Canadian National Railways on the whole managed to keep up with the times. Each year witnessed expanding services and improved equipment. Locomotives were a conspicuous illustration; after more than twenty years, the Diesel had come into its own. Mechanical defects in mountings and in controls, rather than in the engine proper, had restricted its use for at least a decade to auxiliary services, such as switching and similar local employments. In 1941, however, General Motors had produced a Diesel of 1,000 horsepower, whose reliability fitted it for heavy duty on long hauls. Scheduled services were adjusted accordingly, and by 1947 Diesels had begun to thrust steam locomotives into the background.

The boxcar, the flatcar and the tank car no longer were sufficient to serve all classes of freight. Nearly every bulk product required a carrier designed to meet its peculiar needs. Among the first special cars to appear were automobile carriers, which soon gave way to the multilevel open-sided transporters. Despite the discouraging trends of the passenger traffic, the company was prepared to fight for it, so new deluxe day coaches, sleeping cars, dining and parlor cars appeared, together with experiments in buffet-lounge cars. The company laboratories seldom had less than a dozen experiments in hand, seeking to provide better rather than cheaper services. Aside from rolling stock, a considerable sum had been allocated to the construction of a new headquarters building in Montreal, which would house everyone scattered about the city because of the lack of room in the old Grand Trunk buildings on McGill Street. A new freight terminal also was planned for Montreal, which would cover seven blocks in that city, and the electrification of lines in urban areas came under investigation with a view to smoke abatement and the general tidying-up of terminal operations.

Backlash on Motor Cars

The rapid expansion of motor car traffic, together with concurrent proliferation of widened highways, viaducts, complex crossings and a host of ancillary enterprises essential to the upkeep of automobiles, had begun to give the provinces, which must foot the bill for road improvements second thoughts on the supercession of railways. Doubts began to arise concerning the value to the community of a vehicle that made every man his own engine-driver. S. W. Fairweather, in an address to the Engineering Institute of Canada, declared that a three-lane motor highway cost as much to build as a double-track railway, yet the railway had sixteen times the carrying capacity of the highway and at remarkably lower costs to its users. The thesis that he had stated so eloquently in the defense of Sir Henry Thornton still held good. The value of railway service should be appraised on its contribution to the community rather than on its profitability. In a speech at the Canadian National Exhibition in Toronto in September 1948, President R. C. Vaughan supported the Fairweather contention with a down-to-earth illustration:

> Last year the railways of Canada hauled for each of you, although you may not have received or shipped a single package, an average of about twelve tons of freight over a distance of something like 400 miles. That tonnage was made up of your food, your clothes, your fuel, and the thousand other things which you needed. The Canadian railways hauled it for you at the lowest freight rates in the world.

John C. Noel, in *Canadian National Magazine*, put the railway case from a slightly different angle:

> $300.00 a minute is a lot of money in any nation's coin. That's what it costs to provide the inward and outward needs of the Canadian National system. Last year it placed 264,000 orders with 10,000 Canadian firms. Fuels topped the list; the annual outlay for coal, coke, oils, charcoal and wood approximated $60,000,000. It would take a single train of 140,000 carloads, stretching from Montreal to Winnipeg, to transport the 7,000,000 tons of coal consumed. That is enough to last the average Canadian householder for a million years.[1]

In 1948, Canadian National Railways earnings for the first time approached the half-billion mark ($491,296,150). Except for disastrous floods in western Canada, which immobilized sections of the main line for weeks at a time, it might have surpassed this figure and even might have achieved an overall surplus. It hauled 86 million tons of freight, carried nearly 21 million passengers, handled 22 million express shipments and transmitted 12 million telegrams. Its purchases in Canada ran to $213 million, its payroll to $315 million. Such achievements did not go unmarked. At a banquet in New York, Maynard Metcalf, on behalf of Canadian National Railways, received the *Financial World* award for the best in its class of North American Annual Reports in 1947. Early in the following year, five prominent executives, including President Vaughan and former President Hungerford, were recipients of orders of chivalry at an investiture at Government House in Ottawa.

Restoration of the Ocean Service

Early steps had been taken to replace war losses in the sea services, particularly in the Caribbean area, where Canada had contracted with the British colonies to provide regular sailings on specified routes. To replace the *Lady* ships destroyed by enemy action, orders for three new ships, each of 7,600 tons, primarily for freight but with ample passenger and refrigeration facilities, were placed with Canadian shipyards. Five smaller vessels, designed to provide general dry cargo services and to put an end to the last of the Canadian Government Merchant Marine bottoms, were acquired for Caribbean employments. The three *Prince* ships taken over by the Royal Navy were not replaced, and of the two remaining company vessels on the Pacific, *Prince George* was destroyed by fire in an Alaskan port in the autumn of 1945. In its place an excellent liner was launched under the same name and went in service three years later. In 1946, the company fleet had been augmented by SS *Abegweit*, a unique combination of icebreaker and car ferry, said to be the largest of its type in the world. It provided the main connection between Prince Edward Island and New Brunswick.

Rapid Expansion in the Air

The Second World War had done more for aviation than twenty years of peace. Bomber fleets of vast striking power had become, in the public eye, the essential tools of victory. It was discovered later that their principal contribution had been the slaughter of noncombatants, but because of their reported performances, civilian aviation marched from strength to strength. In 1946, Trans-Canada Airlines mileage was virtually double that of the previous year. It included the thousandth crossing of the Atlantic by a Canadian passenger aircraft. Year by year the services multiplied, and Canadian manufacturers were busy devising air equipment to counter extremes of climates and distance. In 1948, the Canadian-built *North Star* took to the air for the first time. Powered by Rolls-Royce engines, it carried forty passengers at a cruising speed of 325 miles an hour, and it remained the principal Canadian air carrier for a decade. In that year also, Trans-Canada Airlines inaugurated its

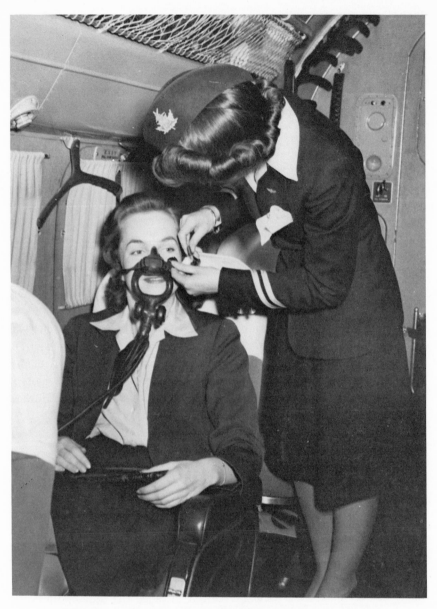

Early flying days—oxygen necessary for crossing the Rockies.
(COURTESY OF AIR CANADA, LTD.)

all-freight service to British and American destinations, covering, in all, 11,000 miles of routes. In every respect, therefore, Trans-Canada Airlines had emerged from the fledgling stage and was exhibiting world standards of performance.

Perilous Developments

Long before the detritus of depression and conflict had been cleared away, profound economic and social changes made it all too evident that life on a minor planet with an oxygenated atmosphere never would be the same again. The speedup induced by an extraordinary range of new or improved machinery created a fetish of mobility for its own sake rather than for its intrinsic advantages. An enormous diversification of production had ensued that compelled the manufacturer to concentrate as never before on his customers and on convincing them that the new article was an improvement they could not afford to forgo. Salesmanship had become the prime incentive to change and advertising the chief method of effecting changes. As Marshall McLuhan afterward put it, the medium had become the message.

Transportation media soon discovered that they must learn without delay the same lesson as other industries. It was not enough to repair the ravages of fifteen years of depression and conflict and re-equip with prewar routines; the railways must be prepared, if they wished to hold or regain or increase their business, to go out and fight for it immediately. They could not afford the gradual span of recovery; their competitors, with no heavy capital backlog to hamper them, already were on their heels. Survival therefore depended on taking chances and anticipating events. As a railway writer put it:

> The modern corporation must focus its attention as never before on the consumer, on what he wants and is willing to pay for. Concentration on any accepted way of doing things or on a traditional product now must be viewed as on the high road to oblivion; it must be demonstrated that the existing product is what the customer wants and will continue to want and that the existing technology is competitive with its newer alternatives. This way of viewing the corporation in relation to customers is known as the Marketing Approach. It recognizes the ultimate will power of the buyer in a free economy and that the quality and efficiency of a process is irrelevant if there are no purchasers. The problems imposed on a railway corporation by these circumstances are enormous. The successful industrial enterprise must make more and more choices of material and processes, for the discretionary income of consumers is increasing until it has become more difficult to determine what is a fad and what is a real change in a style of living.[2]

Two Menacing Developments

It was while President Vaughan and his executives struggled with the implications of such changes that two developments, both beyond the possibility of escape or amelioration, threatened Canadian National Railways with future rather than immediate involvements. There had ensued as one of the aftermaths of the Second World War a revival of interest in the St. Lawrence Deep Waterway project, whereby all impediments to navigation would be circumvented on the St. Lawrence–Great Lakes system, which thereafter would be opened for oceangoing shipping for 1,500 miles into the heart of the continent. By 1949, Canadian opinion, spurred by westerners who foresaw a huge saving on export grain rates, was veering toward approval of this project, either with or without the support of the United States. Its completion undoubtedly would divert a huge tonnage of wheat to ocean bottoms at lakehead with a corresponding loss of the main eastbound bulk cargo to the railways.

The second involvement was immediate, and it promised nuisance rather than serious effects. Out of the ferments of the Second World War there had arisen in Newfoundland a public controversy concerning the future of that island. Should it continue as a self-governing British colony or should it appeal for admission as the tenth province of the Canadian Confederation? It seems probable that a newspaper editor who afterward became premier of the province decided the issue. One of the irrevocable conditions of union was that the Newfoundland Railway, which had been a bone of contention and an expense to the colony for sixty years, must be taken over, holus bolus, as a charge on the Dominion. This of course meant that Canadian National Railways would inherit it. That system already had more than sufficient problems on its plate without taking over a detached property of questionable value. But time does not stand still, and with a new set of growing pains imminent, the addition of another railway, whatever its condition, would neither make nor break the fortunes of the company.

The Newfoundland Story

Newfoundlanders were in no sense Canadians. They were the product of what some poet has described as "Time and the Ocean and a Westering Star." For four centuries they had drawn sailors to their inhospitable coasts because of the miraculous draught of fishes that could be taken off their continental shelf. Except for the appropriately named county of Avalon, a rich and smiling countryside linked to the main island by the slenderest of isthmuses, Newfoundland was largely a land of Cain, an empty waste that possessed healthy verdure only along its northern and western escarpments. But in a hundred coves and inlets, fishermen, battered and blown by the sea, could find shelter for their craft and landing places for their catch.

Thus it came about that of Newfoundland's population of one hundred fifty thousand at the dawn of the railway age in 1865, half lived in the bountiful but limited expanses of Avalon and virtually all others were scattered in handfuls among the many fishing villages that were known as the outports. These tiny settlements had no roads linking them, nor any regular connections by sea. They were, and many still are, huddles of cottages around little coves, with racks on the beaches and hillsides for the drying of fish and the mending of nets and with a homing beacon on high ground. Their inhabitants were tough and fearless afloat or ashore; their social proclivities owed much to alcohol, and their imports of spirituous liquors at the beginning of this century were the highest per capita in the world. Newfoundlanders were of mixed blood, but with the British strain predominant, and their language was, and is, a treasure trove of bygone words and usages to which they have added in a manner unique among English-speaking races. Their everyday vocabulary is salted with expressions that retain the simplicity, the power and the beauty of other centuries and their place names might have been selected by a congress of poets. On their maps may be seen Bare Need, Blow Me Down, Come-by-Chance, Gaff Topsails, Garnish, Haystack, Heart's Content, Heart's Delight, Heart's Desire, Heart's Ease, Ireland's Eye, Juniper Stump, Leading Tickles, Little Seldom, Open Hall, Old Shop, Sop's Arm, and Spread Eagle.

First Try at a Railway

For more than three centuries, therefore, Newfoundland was less a place of abode than an anchorage. Nevertheless in the grip of a romantic dream, Sandford Fleming in 1865 considered it as a site for a railway. He included it in his All-Red Route, whereon the citizens of the Empire might traverse the world and be served unfailingly by railways on land and ships upon the seas and always under the Union Jack. He even made a survey of sorts with estimates of mileages and quantities of material to be shifted, but it was not until 1880 that Premier Sir William Whiteway sought to relieve the long winter isolation of the ice-bound outports of the northern coast by a railway linking St. John's with Notre Dame Bay. He was able to interest an American syndicate, which in 1881 began to build out of Avalon. After skirting the innumerable inlets of the east coast, the route turned west beyond Lake Gander and into the valley of the Exploits River. Thereafter it swung due north to a terminal at Hall's Bay, one of the principal inlets of Notre Dame Bay.

It was narrow gauge (3'6") and was destined to be thrown down rather than built. The Americans soon found that they had taken on more than they had bargained for. After two years they relinquished the project to the British bondholders who had provided the capital. In place of the Notre Dame Bay project, these backers agreed to build a line to Harbour Grace, the second port of the island, eighty-six miles from St. John's on the western shore of Conception Bay. This section was completed in 1884. HMS *Bacchante* happened to be in harbor at the time, and one of its midshipmen drove the last spike. He afterward became His Majesty King George V.

Enter the Reids

For some years the trains joggled and jounced over this bit of line from which a branch twenty-six miles in length eventually was built to Placentia on the western coast of Avalon. The railway project thus became the sole possession of this county, a situation that sat ill on the other half of Newfoundland's population. The Notre Dame project never really died, but each year when it was broached, the Colonial Office in London in almost as many words asked the Newfoundland government what it proposed to use for money to pay for it.

Then in 1889, fate took a hand and presented the colony with perhaps the only man in the world who would satisfy its needs. Robert Gillespie Reid was a Scot who had begun life as a stonemason's apprentice and who, before he was fifty, had made his first million as a bridge builder in the United States and Canada. He was a bold and farsighted man of affairs, and he viewed the virgin wilderness of Newfoundland as an empty space to be fructified for generations to come. He had three stalwart sons with him, and in June 1890, he accepted an almost unbelievable contract. He would build the Notre Dame Bay Railway, 262 miles from point of junction with the Placentia spur, within five years under a forfeit of $250,000 for failure, at a price of $15,600 per mile, to be paid in the bonds of the colony. On such terms Newfoundland scarcely could lose.

By autumn of that year, the work was under way. It was all hand labor, and there were more wheelbarrows than carts. After the first thirty-five miles, the gracious Avalon landscape ended, and the contractors were faced with solid rock through which a roadbed was hewn at a cost of more than twice their price. Some fifteen hundred men were employed; they were given rolls of tar paper to build tiny shacks, and the contractors sold them food. Everything else they found for themselves. They baked their bread in iron pots before open fires, and they used their round-top shovels as frying pans. They worked ten hours a day for six days a week at a wage of a dollar a day. They were quite satisfied, for they had come for the most part from lonely settlements, and the company of their fellows in a common task was deemed rewarding.

A New Direction

By the end of 1892, seventy-five miles of line had been completed, and railhead was on the westerning swing to the north of Lake Gander. Reid's engineers had scouted ahead and had returned to render good report of the route northward to Norris Arm and thence into the valley of the Exploits River, but they had brought back a poor opinion of the last section to Hall's Bay; it crossed desolate waste, a veritable blasted heath. They thought a better purpose would be served by continuing on to the west, to tap the heavily afforested Strait of Belle Isle coast, terminating the line at Port aux Basques, the point nearest to Canada.

Newfoundlanders had every reason to be pleased with the Reids, so they accepted this recommendation, adding a startling condition to it. The contractors must consent to undertake the operation of the railway at their own expense for a period of ten years after completion, providing their own rolling stock and adhering to time tables and rate schedules prescribed by the government. For this service they would receive 5,000 acres of land for every mile built or operated. The government bought the Harbour Grace line from its British owners and gave it to the Reids as sop to the bargain.

This agreement was accepted by the contractors in the face of strong protests by their advisors. Their engineers were aghast at such a gamble, for they were losing heavily on the present work, and the new contract lengthened the line by upward of 300 miles. It seemed sheer effrontery to embark on such a long shot at such a time, for in the United States the cycle of prosperity had run its course, and a depression with attendant panics was in the making. In Canada a series of do-nothing ministries had soured a considerable proportion of the population with confederation, and the movement for continental union was at its height; American organizers were preaching this solution in the English-speaking provinces. Newfoundland, with its unstable economy, already was in desperate straits; its official historian wrote:

> The bitterest partisan war was waged at home, in the press, in the courts, and in the Legislature. Public credit was impaired abroad; a truncated Parliament and a make-shift ministry were collecting duties without warrant of law under the cover of a warship's guns. Timid investors were unloading the Colony's securities at a paralyzing discount in London. Midway through the interior Reid was trying to

carry out his self-appointed task, distracted by reports that the political warfare behind him was threatening at times to bring down the whole financial fabric of the Colony. At the end of 1894 the memorable Bank Crash proved to be the climax of the Colony's troubles. Local banks went to pieces, many mercantile firms closed their doors forever. Thousands were reduced to beggary, panic swept the island to its farthest shore and the Colony had to pawn its securities at 50 cents on the dollar to meet the interest due in London and thereby avert bankruptcy.[1]

In this extremity, the Reids were at their best. They rallied their Canadian and British associates to the support of their Newfoundland venture, and they worked on. By the end of 1893, they were beyond Grand Falls, (Mile 276) and were approaching Badger, where they would take off across the Gaff Topsails plateau, sixty miles of obdurate, naked terrain, to Howley (Mile 357) and so to the crossing of Grand Lake. In the following year, railhead had passed Corner Brook in the Humber forests. There were still 250 miles to traverse, and it took two years to build across the southern badlands between the Long Range Mountains and the sea. In June, 1898, the first train left St. John's for Port aux Basques.

A New Contract

The Reids had borne the heat and burden of the day. It was estimated that they had lost $6 million on the construction of the railway. In addition, they had bought the St. John's dry dock, and had built a street railway and a power station for that city. The Newfoundland government was more than willing to leave the railway project and all that pertained to it in the Reids' hands, and in March 1898, a new contract was negotiated to this end. The Reids undertook to extend their period of management of the railway from ten to fifty years. Thereafter it would become their property, in return for a payment of $1 million, which was to be made immediately. They also would undertake the management of the coastal shipping service and would provide eight additional vessels in return for an annual subsidy of $91,180. They would take over the Newfoundland telegraph service in 1904, at the expiry of an existing contract. In return for these various commitments, they would be entitled to an additional 5,000 acres of Crown land for every mile built or operated; but half of their 1893 grant would revert to the Newfoundland government, which would leave them with about 6,430 square miles of land in all.

Newfoundland Railway: The "Newfie Bullet."

This new contract became a political issue. It was opposed by a minority of Newfoundlanders on the grounds that it constituted a concession to greedy capitalists. (In point of fact, it provided a line of escape for the Newfoundland government from a situation that well might have bankrupted it.) The Reids already were developing their land holdings, exporting lumber from their mills; they had induced the Harmsworth brothers, afterward to be known to fame as Lord Northcliffe and Lord Rothermere, to join them in what was destined to be the Anglo-Newfoundland Development Company, today one of the great hydroelectric and paper-making organizations of the world. A little later, by pledging their western forest reserves, they became in similar fashion partners of Bowaters, a strong English company, in the establishment of a paper mill at Corner Brook. In 1903, they offered the government the opportunity to participate in the establishment of a number of new branch lines, flour mills, cold storage plants and hotels. But by then, the politicians had muddled the project, and the rank and file of Newfoundlanders wanted nothing more than to be assured that the Reids would continue to operate the railway and the coastal shipping services at their own expense for the allotted span of their contract. In 1901, the contractors had been obliged to accept a government demand for the return of the railway after its fifty years operational contract had expired, together with the telegraph system and a portion of the early land grants.

The Reids accepted this shabby treatment philosophically. They had come to Newfoundland not only to make money but also to pull a hope-less colony out of the slough of bankruptcy and to set its feet on firm ground. They had known from the beginning that the railway would be an expensive instrument in convincing Newfoundlanders and outsiders alike of the potential of the colony. In the first ten years of the new century, they lost $1.2 million on their operational contract. Yet when, in 1909, the Newfoundland legislature wanted more railways built, the Reids accepted a proposal to construct and thereafter to operate an additional 374 miles of branch lines. For this construction they were awarded a fee of $15,000 a mile. Their actual costs came to $26,400 a mile, and thus another $4,263,600 went down the drain. But they had picked up another 1,496,000 acres of Crown land on the deal, and they believed that the transaction eventually would prove rewarding to them.

The Impact of War

Then came the First World War. Newfoundlanders hastened to prove that the Elizabethans lived not only in their vocabulary but also in their hearts. If you drive up the Amiens-Douai road in Picardy, you will come suddenly upon a great, plunging stag in bronze, standing high above the countryside. This is Beaumont Hamel, and here, in the opening days of the Battle of the Somme, the Newfoundland Regiment was almost com-pletely destroyed. God rest gallant men.

During the war, losses on the Newfoundland Railway rose to $200,000 a year. There was not sufficient traffic to warrant its operation. During the winter, the driving snows, particularly on the Gaff Topsails plateau, made it all but impossible to keep the line open. By 1923, the operational contract had cost the Reids another $6 million, and they were nearing the end of their resources. Whereupon the government can-celed the agreement and paid the contractors $2 million for their inter-ests. This was the end of the Reid chapter. The merits and demerits of their Newfoundland ventures will be argued for many years to come, but no critic can impugn their courage and their vision.

Thereafter devoted civil servants battled as manfully as the Reids with the recalcitrant property. The rates that would have made it pay never would have been acceptable to shippers who also were voters. A minute from the manager's office at the beginning of 1925 declared that to earn enough to buy a bottle of ink the railway must carry a ton of freight for five miles, or a lantern for thirty-five miles, or a pound of waste for six miles, or a gallon of engine oil for twenty miles. Until such time as

Newfoundland development had caught up with the times, the railway was an unwarranted extravagance.

The Crunch of the Depression

By 1929, the railway staff had risen to two thousand employees and work was in hand to improve portions of the line. Some new rolling stock also was at point of order. Then came the impact of the world depression, when money went to ground and standards of living collapsed. In Newfoundland, the scattered communities remained hungry and unshod, and the railway took a fearful beating. With the growth of dirt roads, every man who owned or could borrow a motor car went into the transport business, and at sea, every fishing vessel became a common carrier. In February 1932, the railway management announced that in the previous year, motor vehicles had cut its volume of freight by more than half, carrying 490,000 tons as against 320,000 tons on the railway, which also had lost 27,000 passengers to road transport. Fifty-seven railway stations had not earned enough to pay their upkeep. Canadian railways had been hard hit, but they were earning seven times more per passenger-mile and sixteen times more per ton-mile than the Newfoundland Railway.

By 1933, the colony was within touching distance of bankruptcy. A joint committee of British, Canadian and local representatives reported that they could see no solution but a virtual admission of insolvency. They recommended that responsible government be suspended and administration entrusted to a committee with instructions to compound with Newfoundland's creditors and to secure funds wherever available for essential services. On May 18, 1934, this drastic measure went into effect, and the colony passed under the management of a commission consisting of three prominent Britons and the same number of Newfoundlanders.

Transformation by the War

For the next two years, this able group managed to keep most of the wheels turning. In 1936, the depression began to break, but by then an even greater shadow obscured the future, for the Nazi regime in Germany was openly exhibiting its preparations for an era of conquest. The pitiful failure of the major powers to limit German encroachments on her weaker neighbors did nothing to delay the coming of The Day, and in September 1939, the British Empire and Commonwealth were at war once more.

As before, the Newfoundlanders responded generously to the call of their blood. On this occasion, the war proved to be an almost unmixed blessing for them. The growth of air power had put a premium on their geographical location, and the German submarine campaign made the island the mid-way station in the protection of North Atlantic traffic. The rally of the United States to Britain's support resulted in the first Lend-Lease transaction; in January 1941, a detachment of United States troops arrived to garrison certain Newfoundland ports. In August of that year, Argentia was the scene of the memorable meeting of President Roosevelt and Prime Minister Churchill. Then came the climactic event in the second week of December: Japanese aggression enlisted the United States with Great Britain and her Commonwealth under the banner of a common cause.

There followed the richest years in Newfoundland's history. The island became the sentry box of the North Atlantic traffic. Troops flowed in, bringing money in quantities that had never been seen before. The railway and its sea services actually approached prosperity. In the four years of war, freight traffic nearly doubled to more than 700,000 tons annually; whereas formerly the Newfoundland Railway had pared pennies to remain in operation, it now had a wealth of everything it needed, much of it supplied for next to nothing by the United States. A network of cables and telephone lines tied the colony together; it enjoyed a degree of activity, a wealth of expenditure, that it may never see again.

The war ended. The seas became safe. The soldiers went home, but not all of them; the United States Air Force still occupies a station at Stephenville, on the southwestern coast. Traffic diminished, but it never reverted to its former starvation levels. For four years, Newfoundlanders had been incorporated in another world, and they would not return willingly to their meager yesterdays. It therefore was natural that they should think of permanent incorporation in a larger political, economic and social entity. There were two schools of thought: one still wished the colony to go it alone, and the other thought that it should join the Canadian Confederation. The latter cause was championed by Joey Smallwood, a newspaper editor who spoke as he wrote, with a bite in his words. His harangues probably carried the day. In a referendum on April 1, 1949, Newfoundland by a hairbreadth elected to become the tenth province of Canada. Concurrently the Newfoundland Railway became an element of Canadian National Railways.

It was rumored that Canadian National executives considered the day of takeover to be significant. It was an unpromising property. S. W. Fairweather, who had been dispatched to examine it in the previous year, could do no better in his report than to praise it with faint damns. Its 705 miles of narrow-gauge tracks ran for the most part through an uninhabited wilderness; its takeover included a fleet of small merchant vessels that served a host of outports; it had never earned its keep. Its freight traffic in 1947 had fallen to 94,470,537 ton-miles, which was one-seventh of the traffic in its best war years. Its cost of operation was $5.76 per running mile, as against earnings of $4.64 over the same distance; its net operational deficit for that year was $1,335,351.40. Under Newfoundland ownership, the annual wage bill for 4,169 employees came to $7.4 million; when they became eligible for Canadian National rates of pay they would receive an increase of 33 percent to $9,791,094. There therefore were incentives for both parties to the takeover; for the Canadian National to seek out and create more traffic, for Newfoundland employees to labor more diligently at their tasks.

25

Over the Hump

         The Newfoundland Railway takeover was the last important transaction of President R. C. Vaughan's period of office. On October 11, 1949, he retired, amid a chorus of praise for his assiduous and courageous administration. He was succeeded by one who on his own admission knew nothing at all about railways. Nevertheless, viewed from two decades later, there are grounds for the assumption that if there had been no Donald Gordon, it would have been necessary for Canadian National Railways to have invented him. At the close of the 1940s, the company's debts were mounting, its freight volumes were diminishing, its passenger traffic appeared to be doomed. The old controversy as to the wisdom and justice of competition between a private corporation and a public utility still simmered; to many Canadians, the participation of government in business appeared to be an unnecessary and unfair intrusion. Sectionalism, stilled by the war, was reviving, and local attitudes prevailed in politics. In such a situation, Canadian National Railways needed a champion, tough and resolute, prepared to take on its adversaries on their own grounds.

Background

         That was what it got. Donald Gordon, born in Scotland in 1901, had arrived in Canada at fourteen years of age and had taken the first job offering, at $6 a week. Within two years, he had joined a bank. At thirty he had reached managerial rank. In 1935, on the formation of the Bank of Canada, he became its secretary. Three years later, as its deputy governor, his signature grew familiar on Canadian currency.

After the fall of France in 1940, Canada organized for battle to the end. Among the first tightenings of the official belt was the creation of the War Prices and Trade Board, which established an almost authoritarian control over Canadian commerce and industry. It set prices, selected sources of supply, instituted rationing and on occasion took over control of distribution. It introduced hitherto undreamed-of austerities—half a pound of sugar a week, no nylon or silk stockings at all. Its chairman and the man above all others who made it work was Donald Gordon.

For five years, Canadians endured restrictions bordering on hardship. A world of plenty existed beyond their southern boundary but it largely was closed to them. There were few complaints, for all thinking Canadians knew that they must give without stint to the war effort. Gordon decided what the nation might have and what it must do without. Each year he covered many thousand miles, counseling and cheering his subordinates; he had six hundred local committees, of which more than a hundred were exclusively composed of housewives. They often waited for his arrival with black words and even anger in their hearts, but he seldom left except amid cheers and laughter. He had a certain amount of the ham actor, the Rory O'Moore, about him; in a handful of back-chat exchanges he could win the day. On occasion, he was stern and peremptory, but more often he was sentimental and even emotional. He based his demands on a single plea—that the civilians at home should exhibit the same fortitude as their kinsmen on the battlefields. Out of office hours, he was free and easy; with a glass in his hand and a song on his lips he could charm all into one company. He sang well, with a rolling baritone.

In the six years of the Second World War, the prices of controlled commodities in Canada only increased on an average of 3 percent per annum, as against treble that amount in the four years of the First World War and far below those of other combatant nations. No single Canadian matched Gordon in inspiring community effort. The Honorable Lionel Chevrier, then Minister of Railways, on one occasion said of him:

> He was given the job of building a complicated structure of price ceilings, supply controls and rationing machinery almost overnight. United States officials, who followed the same path a year or two later, made no secret of the fact that their policy and organization were patterned on the Donald Gordon plan. He was one of the first

few men to rule as a price czar and to return to his peacetime work with the plaudits of commerce and industry on one side and of the consuming public on the other ringing in his ears.[1]

When victory was assured, he was given the task of dismantling the structure he had brought into being. This entailed no simple reversion to the usages of the past; the Canadian economy during the period of the conflict had taken on stature; it was caught in the flood of world changes. Donald Gordon therefore made no rigid plans; he permitted commerce and industry to seek normal levels. Thereafter he went back to banking. By 1949, he was Canadian representative on the International Bank for Reconstruction and Development, afterward to be known as the World Bank. It was there that the call came to him from Canadian National Railways.

A Fresh Challenge

There are reasons to believe that he received the summons gladly. He recognized, as did few, the momentous changes imminent in the future. He was certain that if Canada was to survive as an economic and social entity its traffic must continue to move on an east-west axis. In order to attain this end Canadian National Railways must keep abreast if not ahead

Central Vermont Railroad: White River Junction Station.

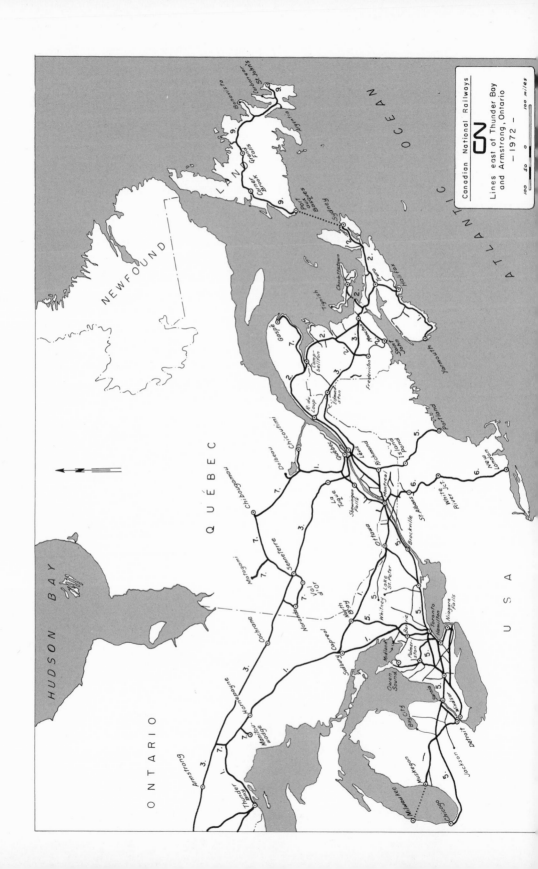

Canadian National Railways

CN

Lines east of Thunder Bay
and Armstrong, Ontario
– 1972 –

100   50   0   100 miles

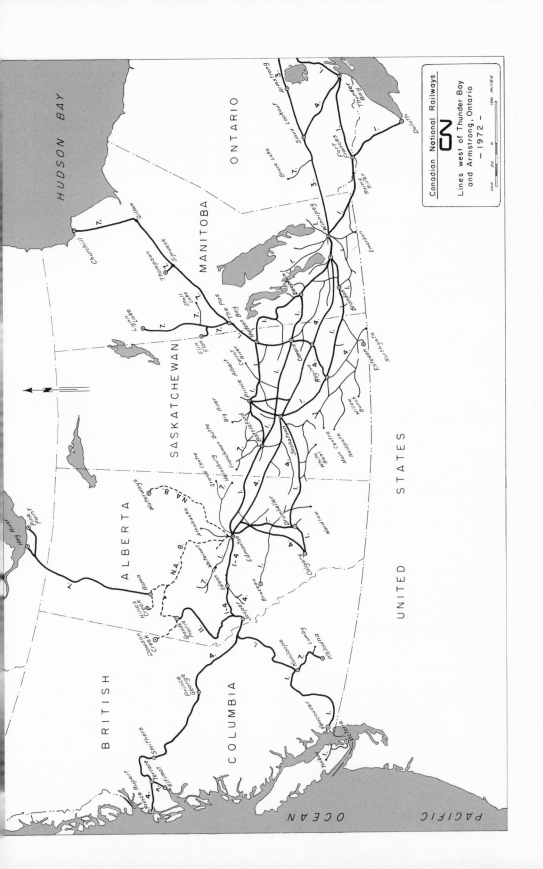

Canadian National Railways

CN

Lines west of Thunder Bay
and Armstrong, Ontario
- 1972 -

100   50   0   100   miles

of American practice. Out of his wartime experiences there had been born an unique appreciation of the Canadian character. He was confident that if Canadians trusted their leaders they would keep step with whatever passed for progress in the unpredictable years ahead.

Gordon's appointment received a mixed reception. Those favorable to him based their views on his wartime achievements; those critical dwelt on his shortcomings—that he had never been a railwayman and that he had been a banker. In his first press interview, given within twenty-four hours of his appointment, he was inclined to agree with both friends and enemies, but he voiced his determination to regard caution as a dispensable virtue. In fifteen years of war and depression, he had seen all too many Canadian problems left to settle themselves, with dire effects on everybody. He admitted that he had a great deal to learn and he declared that his first venture would be a voyage of discovery on which he would listen intently and say as little as possible. He would set out with certain preconceived opinions but as he encountered new evidence he reserved the right to change them without apology.

In his first message to his staff, he defined the relationship that he desired:

> You have a right to expect of me that I show leadership, imagination and energy in the development and betterment of the system. You also have a right to expect me to be jealous of your welfare in all respects. For my part I must remind you that no leader can be better than the men and women of the organization that he serves. I expect your continued cooperation in the interests of our system. Working together, we can develop an efficient and loyal organization that cannot fail to produce results in which we can take pride. In that task we not only will have the satisfaction of our immediate job well done but we shall gain the exciting and satisfying experience of playing a vital role in the country in which we live.[2]

A Series of Catastrophes

As if to put the new leader to the test, the first months of his administration were haunted by a series of operational catastrophes. The winter of 1949–1950 was of unparalleled severity, and one misadventure succeeded another. Serious trouble really had begun in the previous July, when the western section of the trestle of the Central Vermont Railroad, 1,650 feet in length across Mississquoi Bay, had been destroyed by fire. Most of the piles had been burned to the waters edge, which either necessitated replacements driven through forty feet of water into holding depths on the bottom of the bay or else recapping those that remained undamaged below its surface. Either task was tricky enough in fine weather, but that summer Lake Champlain chose to be boisterous, so that the reconstruction of the trestle claimed every ounce of courage, strength and skill that the repair crews could muster. They worked continuously in fourteen-hour shifts, disdainful of risks and difficulties. In thirty-six days the line was open for traffic.

On the prairies, January 1950 proved a savage month, with wild gales and bitter cold, often well below zero. Daily, at the cost of frozen fingers, ears and toes, the crews of scores of trains were obliged to deal with jammed journal boxes, wheels frozen to icy rails, congealed oil systems, fractured drawbars and other low-temperature damage. Blizzards beat brutally against the lurching rolling stock, while their locomotives crashed through cuts piled high with drifting snow. To keep the lines open was a labor of giants; even as the snow plows cleared the rails, fresh falls clogged the tracks behind them.

In British Columbia, the weather was milder but even more treacherous. Nightly freezes alternated with daily thaws so that great bodies of snow perched precariously on the mountainsides until their weight overcame their inertia; then huge slides would sweep down from the crests, stripping the slopes bare and filling the valley bottoms. On January 19, 1950, a series of such avalanches crashed into the Fraser Canyon for thirty miles between Yale and Boston Bar. The laboring plows punched fifteen troughs through slides in which rocks and trees were intermingled with snow and ice. Trains could make only short distances before being halted anew; passengers were obliged to detrain and walk to the nearest villages, following guide ropes. Freezing rains alternated with heavy snowfalls, and the drifts sometimes stood a hundred feet in height across the tracks. It was a fortnight before the line was cleared, and for every hour of that time Canadian National crews kept up the fight. An observer wrote:

> You see men walk away from a rotary with every nerve tingling from the vibrations of the revolving blades, their faces wet from steam, their nostrils distended from the fumes of the hot oil, their clothes drenched from the condensation of the snow thrown from the great arc of the rotarys. You peer into the faces of the shovellers as they grab a sandwich and coffee or puff a cigarette before plunging into their work anew. It is their skill and muscles that pry loose the machines locked in the slides. The squint of their eyes comes from the driving snow, the stoop in their backs from the strain of lifting endless scoops, hour after hour, of ice and wet snow.[3]

In February, the Atlantic coast bore the brunt of the winter gales. Trains in many instances were marooned for days. Then came spring, with surging rivers overflowing their banks, washing out substructures and submerging long stretches of tracks. The Red River, which drains 100,000 square miles of Manitoba, ran wild. It compelled Canadian National Railways to dike their station and yards in Winnipeg and to evacuate more than 3,000 farmers and 150 carloads of stock from the Letellier area between Winnipeg and Emerson, where eighteen miles of line were completely destroyed and where on a small island, marooned amid the floods, a passenger train continued to house and feed escaping countryfolk, sometimes serving 2,000 meals in a day. Canadian National Railways brought in 590 hospital cases and pending the repair of the line carried 100,000 passengers by roundabout routes and shuttle services to and from their homes and destinations.

Finally, there came fires. On May 6, half the thriving town of Rimouski, 180 miles downstream from Quebec City, was destroyed, the remainder being saved in large party by the railwaymen, who improvised communications with the outside world and operated a continuous service on the railway bridge after the highway bridges had been destroyed. At Cabano, on the Temiscouata branch, similar fires swept in from the countryside. As at Rimouski, the railwaymen were responsible for saving much of the village.

The First Major Decision

It took a banker's eye no more than a first glimpse to realize the key problem of Canadian National Railways. As it stood, it was not earning enough to pay its way, and in order to make it competitive and attractive to shippers and travelers, it must pull itself up by its bootstraps and achieve higher standards of service. This would involve thumping expenditures—a billion, perhaps two billions, of outlay. Scarcely a fraction of this sum could be derived from higher fares, for railway rates already were undercut by road transport on much of its traffic. Nor would there be any point in seeking further government assistance; such requests would merely reawaken the old controversy of whether a publicly owned railway had any right to exist. Gordon therefore had no choice of strategy: he must spend and spend fulsomely to create what was required of a railway in the new era. Dieselization had been an object lesson; its advantages had been proved; there was no sane course but to complete it as rapidly as possible. There were a dozen other possibilities in the air—modernized rolling stock, improved communications, better services to the shippers and travelers, exploitations of new markets. These circumstances made Gordon's task a great gamble, but in his view, Canada deserved it. He ceased to be a banker and became a speculator in a venture that, on the face of it, seemed to have most of the cards stacked against it.

The Money Side

The overhanging burden of two billions of funded debt had been discussed *ad nauseam* and to many Canadians, it seemed that the publicly owned railway either must live with or die from it. But in March 1950, the time-honored subject came up once more before the Royal Commission on Transportation of the House of Commons and Gordon seized the opportunity to speak in a banker's terms, as one who knew the inmost secrets of money. He began with a terse statement of case:

> The Canadian National is the largest transportation system in the world. It is Canada's largest employer of labour, with over 111,000 employees. It is the largest single consumer of Canadian products. In the previous year it has passed the half-billion mark in earnings, with a net operating revenue of rather better than four percent: but because of its legacy of inherited indebtedness its balance sheet shows a deficit of approximately ten times its operational surplus.[4]

Much of this indebtedness, he pointed out succinctly, arose out of bad bookkeeping. On the takeover of bankrupt and half-finished railway systems in 1917–1922, it would have been better business for the federal government to have accepted all such liabilities and to have given the new system a fresh start. Instead, it had saddled Canadian National Railways with a billion and a half dollars in discharge of the debts of its constituents. Until some remedial action was taken, the systems would remain in garnishee to their creditors for debts that it had not contracted. On the threshold of the unpredictable postwar era, therefore, Gordon appealed for summary action to relieve Canadian National Railways of the burden of these monstrous charges, which kept it in perennial deficit, with consequent loss of confidence by the Canadian public.

Meanwhile, he proposed to continue to manage the system as though such relief would be forthcoming. S. W. Fairweather's estimate of the costs of modernization ($630 million) was in every way justified. Three-quarters of the system's locomotives were over thirty years of age. Nearly all the other equipment of the railway was crying out for replacement. Gordon from his first day in office refused to be shackled by inherited deficits. His job was to organize, modernize and operate a Canadian government service to the advantage of both the shipper and the taxpayer.

It was a bold undertaking, for in the early 1950s, the postwar tide of inflation was still making, with higher costs of operation, dwindling value of money and ever-growing competition from other forms of transportation. Gordon had every excuse to delay major changes until the advent of a stabilized economy, but that was not his mode. Like Lord Herbert of Cherbury, in moments of challenge he preferred to plunge downstairs in his shirt tail, sword in hand.

A Welcome Surprise

By 1951, Canadian National Railways was spending at the rate of a thousand dollars a minute. The increase in rates was a fleabite beside the additional expenses; the system carried three tons of freight for a mile in order to earn the cost of a typewriter ribbon. But, somewhat belatedly, there came a glad surprise. Gordon's representations before the Sessional Committee in 1950 had borne fruit, for on July 5, 1952, the Canadian National Railways Revision Act passed the House of Commons. It cut the company's funded indebtedness of $1,472,780,808 in half by transferring 50 percent of it into 4 percent Canadian National preferred stock, which ceased to be a fixed charge and on which the railway only paid dividends out of clear surpluses. The remaining portion, consisting of $615,107,035 outstanding to private investors and $121,187,270 in government loans, remained a charge on the company, but a ten-year moratorium was granted on $100 million of government indebtedness. Therefore for nine years the federal government undertook to buy additional preferred stock representing portions of the remaining inherited debt, the amount of such purchase to be determined by the operational surplus of the year in question.

This revision relieved Canadian National Railways of payments of $22,154,956 annually in interest charges, together with other lesser benefits. Its effect was galvanic: it permitted the company to go to the money markets for its immediate requirements. Donald Gordon was exultant; in a booklet for employees he wrote, "This is the break that we have been looking for. . . . Hereafter our financial record will speak for itself. . . . We have nothing to hide behind or to stand in our way. . . . Our teamwork will tell the world that we know our jobs and will show results. Now let us get on with it."

The Voyage of Discovery

In April 1950, the president had set off on his tour of the system, which with occasional intervals continued for the remainder of that year.

His first point of call was in Vermont, where he received a warm welcome; that state had not forgotten the prompt assistance rendered by Canadian National Railways during the devastating 1927 floods. Passing on into the Middle West, he encountered equal friendship and cooperation in Michigan, where the Grand Trunk Railway never had been forgotten; indeed, there the legends and the old name clings to it. In Chicago, fifteen railway presidents were among the guests at the dinner tendered in Gordon's honor. At his stops in Ontario, he reiterated that he had come to learn and to listen; breaking into his broadest Scots at one luncheon, he pronounced himself to be "a chiel among ye, takin' notes." In the West, at his receptions at Saskatoon, Edmonton, Calgary, Vancouver, Victoria and Prince Rupert, he maintained the grass roots approach. He wanted to be told, not to tell; but to leading questions, he gave straightforward and unequivocal answers. At Winnipeg he frankly confessed his ignorance:

> Long before I had an inkling that I was to become associated with Canadian National Railways I thought that I knew a lot about it. But daily as I move across the system I find myself astonished at the unfolding scope and magnitude of its operations. I find that I must be in unequal parts a real estate broker, an engineer, an economist, a motion picture producer, an architect, an electrician, a lawyer, a mechanic, a publicist, an aviation specialist, a bridge builder, a medical man, a foregin trade expert, a hotel manager and on occasion, a father confessor and a philosopher. I never know whether the next piece of paper on my desk may deal with the affairs of immigrants from Copenhagen or with lights for bunkhouses, or the importation of bananas from the West Indies, or of wool from Australia, coal from the United States, or with new lines designed to open up the empty expanses of Canada. All these and many other things are my daily concern and I cannot do my job properly if I am not familiar with them.[5]

He was obliged to postpone his tour of Newfoundland until the following year, but here as elsewhere he left warm memories behind him. His inspection of the Newfoundland Railways was of the most searching nature; he pried into every nook and cranny. It was noticeable that in his frequent addresses, he invariably used the first person plural in speaking of the local system; whatever its shortcomings, it was to be regarded as a full member of the Canadian National family. Its needs would not be obliged to await their turn; already equipment to the value of more than $3 million was on order for Newfoundland, and there was more to come.

Donald Gordon, president,
Canadian National Railways,
1950–66.

Labor Trouble

In the midst of his tour of western Canada, Gordon was obliged to return to Ottawa, where a serious labor situation confronted him. The family concept that he had espoused as the ideal worker-management relationship had not found favor with most of his unions, which had adopted the American attitudes of staking their claims whenever the best occasion offered. In September 1949, the Board of Railway Commissioners had authorized an increase of 8 percent in frieght rates. When this became effective, fifteen Canadian branches of American unions and two all-Canadian groups hastened to claim a portion of the increased revenue. Their demands included an additional 10 percent in hourly pay and a decrease in weekly working time as a fringe benefit.*

* Some of the unions had made more or less similar demands in June 1949, and their action may have provided the impetus of the larger movement in the following year.

The negotiations with the unions had been conducted jointly by both railway systems, but Gordon quickly became the storm center of the dispute. The railways counteroffer more or less met the workers' demands, but at the cost of certain stipulations that the unions refused to consider. The conciliation boards appointed by the Federal Government recommended more pay and shorter working hours but rejected other union demands, whereupon strike notices were given for August 23, 1950. In the course of this controversy, Gordon was denounced as a dictator, a Canadian Pacific hireling, an enemy of the working class. A dozen unions passed resolutions calling for his dismissal; in the House of Commons, the leader of the western farmers group declared that Gordon had lost the confidence of the workers and that his usefulness was ended.

To such charges, Prime Minister St. Laurent reacted strongly. He made it clear that Gordon had his confidence, and he urged the labor leaders to arrive at an agreement before the federal government was compelled to intervene. Negotiations continued in the first three weeks of August in a highly charged atmosphere, halfway between bartering and brawling. Eventually one hundred twenty thousand Canadian railwaymen downed tools, and from coast to coast, rail transport was suspended. The Prime Minister immediately summoned Parliament; on August 29, a bill was rushed through the House making it compulsory for the men to return to work within forty-eight hours. Concurrently, an arbitrator was appointed with instructions to recommend not more than the unions sought nor less than the system offered. Should either party refuse acceptance of his findings, the government would restore essential services on its own terms.

This bold but statesmanlike intervention, unparalleled in Canadian labor disputes, was accepted, despite last minute endeavors by two of the strongest Canadian nonrailway unions, with over a million members, to secure its rejection. The settlement cost Canadian National Railways about $15 million annually, but in the opinion of most Canadians, it was cheap at that price. With the issue decided, it quickly became plain that the abuse of Gordon had been tactical rather than sincere. Frank Hall, the union leader, declared, "The President is a hard but just man." Gordon reorganized the Personnel Department, endowing it with new functions, so that any matters concerning employment might be discussed at any time. Soon afterward, he solidified employee support by introducing an improved pension plan, which provided higher rates in event of disablement or demise and which enabled employees to increment their pensions through deductions from their pay, on which compound interest would be contributed by the company. The trouble was not over: late in 1952, two of the unions adopted an intransigent attitude and refused to bargain save on their own terms. However, they lacked general support, and when they set the day of strike—February 3, 1953—the Prime Minister declared that under no circumstances would he tolerate a repetition of what had happened in 1950. Faced with this direct challenge, twenty-two thousand men returned to work on receipt of a 12 percent pay raise. Thereafter there were occasional clashes between management and labor, generally generated by concessions elsewhere on the continent; but usually an amicable atmosphere prevailed. If Gordon's hope of a happy family was not fully realized, it was perhaps because, like everything else, family relationships had changed in this strange new world.

A Royal Visit

In October 1951, Canada was honored by a royal visit—the first in twelve years. At this time there had been little diminution on the part of Canadians as a whole of their loyalty to the Crown. During a month-long stay, Princess Elizabeth and her husband, the Duke of Edinburgh, were received with rejoicings in thirty-five centers of the Dominion. The official reception—a splendid event—was held in the Chateau Laurier. At the conclusion of the tour, a special letter of thanks from the Princess for the

Unit train of grain hoppers on the prairies.

Unit train of coal cars in the Rockies.

services of Canadian National Railways was conveyed by Prime Minister St. Laurent to President Gordon.

This tour marked the last official appearance of Walter Thompson. Indeed, he came out of retirement to participate in it. In October 1950, after thirty-six years service, he had relinquished his post as head of public relations. He had been seen off in a deluge of tributes, for there was scarcely a newspaper office in the English-speaking world in which he was not at home. At his farewell dinner, the Prime Minister of Canada headed the list of distinguished guests. Affectionate good-byes flowed in from the ends of the earth. Perhaps the telegram from the Archbishop of Canterbury best summarized them: "Thompson is one of the few people in the world who should be endowed with immortality, since he could deal forever with jobs that no one else could do half so well." One of the photo-

Royal visitors: H.R.H. Princess Elizabeth clambers up to take the throttle during her 1951 tour of Canada.

graphs of the tour showed the Princess clambering with some apprehension into the cab of the locomotive, to take a turn at the throttle of the royal train; nearby and anxiously watching stood Walter Thompson, ready if necessary to provide a boost to the royal person. Within a matter of months, the Princess was Queen, on the death of His Majesty King George VI on February 6, 1952.

The Buildup of Rolling Stock Begins

In the matter of heavy expenditures on rolling stock, the sum available was not enough to repair the erosion of fifteen lost years, to say nothing of catching up with the present; yet to win through, Canadian National Railways without delay must anticipate the needs of tomorrow. Gordon had no choice but to gamble, and with the hearty support of the federal government, he set about with gusto on his task of renewals.

H.R.H. Princess Elizabeth and her husband, the Duke of
Edinburgh, touring Canada in 1951 by Canadian National Railways.

In 1951, he declared for complete Dieselization within five years.
This would cost roughly $500 million—a serious sum at a time when Ca-
nadian National Railways was just beginning to break even on its operational revenues and expenses. But by then it was plain that the Diesel was
cheaper than the steam locomotive; it could draw three times the load of
the latter at greater speeds and lesser costs of upkeep. It possessed one
unsolved problem—how to keep passenger coaches warm in winter. An
English inventor, however, put the engineers on the way to success with a
rough-and-ready device in which steam was created by dripping water
over white hot tubes. Thereafter it was but a step to constructing Diesels
with generators of sufficient capacity to keep the longest passenger trains
comfortable at the lowest temperature.

Another of the great advantages of the Diesel was its light maintenance. It spent one-eighth of the time of the steam locomotives in the
roundhouses. It needed special servicing, however, and it became neces-

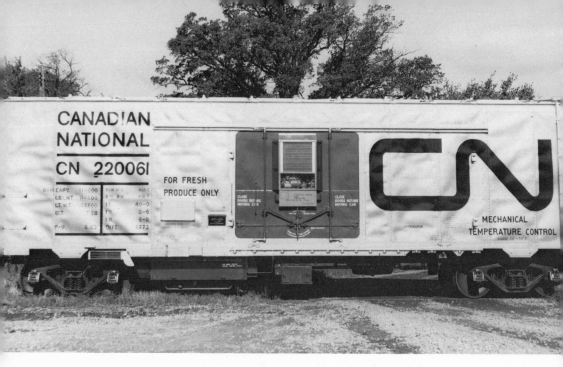

TOP: Car with mechanical temperature control for perishable freight.

BOTTOM: Express container car.

TOP: Hopper for dry bulk freight.

BOTTOM: Piggybacks.

Newsprint car.

sary at Pointe St. Charles (Montreal), Campbellton in New Brunswick, Fort William and Transcona (Winnipeg) in western Canada, to reconstruct or to modify the railway workshops.

Early in 1950, a triple unit Diesel made the run from Montreal to Winnipeg (1,358 miles) and returned the same night. By the close of 1951, Diesels were operating on all sections of the system. In the following year, Prince Edward Island went over entirely to Diesels, and in January 1953, the first narrow-gauge Diesels took up duties in Newfoundland. In April 1954, the Super-Continental, the crack trans-Canada express train hauled by Diesels, cut off fifteen hours on its run of 2,930 miles from Montreal to Vancouver.

A Diesel School of Instruction was established on Prince Edward Island. A stripped demonstration Diesel took to the rails and traversed the system in order that all railway workers might become familiar with it. Its mastery demanded knowledge and efficiency far in advance of anything previously required of railwaymen. An observer who visited the Diesel school declared on his return that Canadian National Railways had adopted the tough training methods of the postwar military schools. "It is like a Guards brigade," he declared. The satisfaction that workers obtained from improvements in their crafts brought rewards of pride, to say nothing of additional pay. Intensive training bred a new atmosphere and a new attitude toward the tasks in hand.

Improved Freight Services

The adoption of locomotives that ran farther and faster naturally reacted on rolling stock requirements. The outbreak of war in Korea in June 1950, with Canada pledged as an ally of the Western powers, accentuated the demand for freight cars, which were still in short supply for local services. Without hesitation, Gordon placed large orders for deliveries over the ensuing years. In December 1951, he announced that the company's intake during that year had been 5,205 freight cars of various types and that there were another thousand such units on order. Among those delivered were five hundred drop-end gondola cars for loose cargo; others soon expected were rail-borne trailers, in which shippers could load up to 6,000 pounds of freight in wheeled vehicles, to be transported on flatcars and towed, when unloaded, to their destinations. This was the beginning

Turbo train in Toronto yard.

of the modern piggyback service, destined to play a substantial role in the future. Other new types included refrigerator cars with underslung Diesel engines that kept the contents at required temperatures. Self-propelled coaches and switch engines for yard and terminal services also arrived early in 1953.

These improvements brought profit in their train. In 1950, Canadian National Railways was able to report 40 percent more ton-miles of freight with 13 percent less rolling stock than twenty years before. In sponsoring these extensive changes, involving heavy additional outlays, Gordon never asked himself if he could afford them; his question always was if he could afford not to change. Without progress he could see no survival.

A Second Look at the Passenger Traffic

With regard to passenger traffic, Gordon had been compelled to change his mind. During his first voyages of discovery, he had declared on more than one occasion that aircraft sooner or later would write *finis* to passenger trains; that the advent of the jet engine might prove the *coup de grâce*. Passengers supplied less than one-tenth of the total revenue of Canadian National Railways; it was seasonable and unpredictable traffic, and on two of its principal services, commuter trains and dining cars, it was almost impossible to make a profit. Everywhere except on continental runs its appeal was low; for instance, in 1951, passenger cars on Canadian National lines averaged only 183 miles per day with an occupancy of only thirteen passengers per mile. The replacement cost of a transcontinental passenger train was over $2 million, and it required an operating staff of more than twenty per train.

To aggravate the problem, the present passenger rolling stock was prewar, and heavy replacement expenditures in the immediate future were unavoidable. Passenger coaches presented a special problem. Should Canadian National Railways follow the Canadian Pacific lead and restock with the attractive but expensive "dome" cars? Or be content with the ordinary type at half the cost? Gordon chose to be frugal, and in 1953, he placed an order for 263 of the ordinary passenger coaches at a cost of upward of $50 million. Each contained eighty rotating seats with reclining backs, the bodies supported by coil springs of a strength never before used in Canada, together with thermostatically controlled air conditioning and heating. The order also included the first dinettes, providing cheaper meals than the ordinary dining cars, which customarily served less than 8 percent of all passengers.

"Super-Continental" fast passenger train crossing the Athabaska River.

When called to account, Gordon's explanation was simple. In his plans to reduce or discontinue passenger services, one factor, that of prestige, had been overlooked:

> We had reached the decision to discontinue during the winter months on transcontinental train service, so that we would have only one train daily during the period when the traffic normally falls off. We found that the word immediately got around in western Canada that we did not have a "super-duper" service any more. Cancellation of reservations began to appear. We also found a general reaction in respect to the prestige of the railway. Its impact on our freight service was much greater than we had expected. We saw that our analysis of what might be called the psychological effects of our cancellation had not been good. I happened to be in western Canada when I learned at first hand of the effects of our action. When I got back I called together the Board of Directors who decided that we should not

hesitate to admit an error of judgment. We felt that it was in the best interests of Canadian National Railways that our decision should be reversed. When we did continue the double service that winter we obtained quite satisfactory results. The loss was not as great as we thought it would be.[6]

This was the turn of the tide for the passenger trade. The company had decided to stick to it and, wherever possible, to improve it. A Department of Tours was created to stimulate group holiday travel. Early in 1953, a Museum Train took to the rails to celebrate the centenary of the Toronto, Simcoe and Lake Huron Railroad, the first line to be built in Upper Canada. It consisted entirely of primitives; one of the three loco-

Museum train with wood- and coal-burning locomotives, 1953.

motives went back to 1872 and a passenger car to 1859. The coaches were crammed with appointments and fixtures that told the story of travel in those far-off days. In six months of chugging about eastern Canada and the United States, it drew 463,118 visitors to pay tribute to the railways of yesterday.

By 1952, the number of revenue passengers had climbed to 18,832,-815—an increase of 25 percent in two years. This gain represented better service but with the major problems unsolved—commuter services still involved heavy losses, and the substantial influx of immigrants, anticipated as aftermath of the Second World War, failed to materialize. Nevertheless, the Passenger Department persevered; transcontinental services such

as the Ocean Limited, from Halifax to Montreal, and the Super-Continental, from Montreal to Vancouver, were Dieselized, with remarkable saving of travel time. Medical cars, dental cars and "schools on wheels" provided community services in the bleak, thinly inhabited areas. When a community demanded additional aid, the request was appraised less on its cost than on its yield to those in need.

These changes would have been of little avail if train crews had not been taught how to put them to best use. A number of courses were instituted to train craftsmen employees in the new methods, and in June 1953, a six-week course was established at Bishops University at Lennoxville for managers who would organize and supervise the trainees. This staff college course afterward became a permanent fixture in the Canadian National Railways training program.

The Awakening of the North

Every time that Donald Gordon scanned the map of Canada his eyes dwelt on the sub-Arctic area—the million square miles of emptiness between Hudson Bay and the Yukon, between the cereal zone of the open prairies and the Arctic seas. Almost every week there came tidings that its future was in the making; that Kipling's "everlasting whisper" soon would take the tones of command:

> Something hidden. Go and find it. Go and look behind
> the ranges.
> Lost and waiting for you. Go.

On the other side of the North Pole, the Russians were thrusting to the utmost limits of their lands. The first of the Siberian cities with its foundations on permafrost was under construction. Such developments must follow in Canada in due course, and Canadian National Railways could not afford to be less than a pioneer.

It no longer was necessary to paddle or track up the rivers, to blaze a way through the endless scrub, to follow trappers' trails or to pick a path gingerly over the soupy muskeg. Aircraft fitted with floats could land on a thousand lakes, depositing and picking up prospectors and mining engineers. But when the finds had been sampled and the mineralized areas had been demarcated, there remained a major step in converting a waste area into a viable property. It must have a railway to bring out the yields.

Canadian National Railways, by virtue of its possession of the most northerly transcontinental system, naturally was in the best position to serve the needs of the new discoveries. It will be remembered that even before the completion of the Hudson Bay Railway in 1929, plans were afoot for a line to service the Flin Flon and Sherridon areas, to the north of The Pas. In the succeeding twenty years, Flin Flon had grown to a town of ten thousand inhabitants, and mineral finds were multiplying in its area. The original railway from The Pas was extended northward for nearly two hundred miles to Lynn Lake, this section being opened for traffic in November 9, 1953. Other branches soon were under construction eastward from the Lynn Lake line to the Chisel Lake and Optic Lake areas, a distance of fifty-two miles, and from Sipiwisk to Thompson, thirty-one miles. On the completion of those feeders, the Hudson Bay Railway was promoted into a separate division with jurisdiction over all branches in its area.

Concurrently a line 161 miles in length was being built from the Beattyville spur in western Quebec to the new mining district of Chibougamau in the western Laurentians. It afterward was extended east-

The barren lands—the Canadian Arctic.

ward to a junction at St. Felicien on the Lake St. John line, thus bringing that field two hundred miles nearer to tidewater. Other mining short lines built during the same period ran from Bartibog on the main line in central New Brunswick to Heath Steele, a distance of thirty-three miles, and twenty-four miles from the Canadian National main line southward to Manitouwadge, on the shores of Lake Superior. In British Columbia, the Aluminium Company of Canada was building a huge smelter to process imported bauxite at Kitimat, at the head of a deep fjord eighty-six miles to the southeast of Prince Rupert. In May 1952, construction began on a branch from Kitimat to link up with the Canadian National main line at Terrace. This section, forty-six miles in length, was opened on July 30, 1955.

Donald Gordon, however, was not disposed to build a railway to the back of beyond simply because someone owned a mine there. If such a branch was built for a particular customer, he asked a traffic guarantee that would enable Canadian National Railways to recover the capital cost of the line over a reasonable period. If such guarantee was not forthcoming, it was up to the federal or provincial governments to decide whether or not the line should be built and what subsidy should be paid toward its costs of construction. In either case, Canadian National Railways would build and operate the branch.

In the first five years of the Gordon regime, approximately $75 million was invested in branch lines, a circumstance that did not escape the notice of the politicians. In 1951, before the Sessional Committee of the House of Commons, Gordon was censured on the grounds that he was building new lines for the mining industry while on the prairies he was abandoning farmers' trackage, which had been built in the early decades of the century, during the frenzied Grand Trunk–Canadian Northern competition. In response to this charge, the president stood by the Fair-weather thesis that the prime purpose of Canadian National Railways was to serve Canadian communities, but it likewise was its duty to prove that a government-owned railway could be operated at a profit. These were twin necessities. As for surplus agricultural trackage, he said this:

> We do not like abandoning lines. It is a confession of failure. We seek out every possible way to rehabilitate the line and keep it going; we make efforts to get new industries and everything of that kind. We sometimes degrade the service, attaching a passenger car to a mixed train and run a service three times a week instead of every day. Before applying for permission to abandonment no less than

Intercolonial Railway: Causeway from Nova Scotia to Cape Breton Island,
opened August 13, 1955.

eleven circumstances must be satisfied to back the application. Compassionate claims were not enough to keep them open.[7]

Additional trackage acquired during this period was the Quebec Railway, Light and Power Company, 25 miles of line that linked company operations between Quebec City and Nairn Falls on the north bank of the St. Lawrence River, and the New London Northern Railroad Company, 121 miles between Brattleboro and New London, already under lease to the Central Vermont Railroad. The decision to build a causeway across the strait of Canso necessitated the construction of fourteen miles of tracks between the former ports of Mulgrave and Port Tupper.

Improved Revenues

There had been a steady increase in earnings since the end of the Second World War, but increasing operational costs and inherited indebtedness had continued to impose perennial deficits. In 1952, revenues of

$675,216,415 were the highest on record: despite heavy extraneous charges, Canadian National Railways for the first peace year since 1928 showed an overall surplus. It was a moment for rejoicing. In the following year, there likewise was a surplus, due in large part to greater earnings in the Express and Communications Departments. In 1954, however, freight traffic, which accounted for 78 percent of all revenues, fell off by about 10 percent, reinstating an overall deficit of $28,758,098. That this was in no sense due to operational deficiencies was evident from the gross ton-miles per hour figures, which were higher than ever before. Instead, the loss came from exceptional expenditures on right of way, including a costly tie-replacement and rail-laying program, together with heavy damage in mid-October from Hurricane "Hazel," which for a week dislocated all traffic in central Ontario. In the following two years, healthy surpluses were forthcoming despite high levels of expenditures.

Progress in the Air

From 1950 onward, railwaymen observed with envious eyes the progress of air transport. The new medium seemed to be carrying all before it—not only in the matter of passengers but as a growing encroachment upon freight traffic. Year by year, Trans-Canada Airlines expanded —in mileage flown, in earnings and perhaps most important of all, in the public eye. There was the same subconscious sense of adventure in travel in the air as in a motor car thirty-five years before; as someone put it, "a feeling of accomplishment with a kick in it." It was part of the mode and the mood of the times.

As in the case of Canadian National Railways, Trans-Canada Airlines had been fortunate in finding a leader who knew how to lead. Gordon R. McGregòr, born in Montreal in 1901, was over thirty when he first took to the air, but within three years he was acclaimed as the best amateur pilot in Canada. On the outbreak of the Second World War, he immediately enlisted, and in the following six years, he served as a fighter pilot in the Battle of Britain and in the European theater, rising to command the Second Canadian Fighter Squadron before appointment as director of the Air Staff, Royal Canadian Force Headquarters (Overseas). He was demobilized as a group captain; in addition to receiving the Officer of the Order of the British Empire and the Distinguished Flying Cross, he had been decorated by the governments of France, the Netherlands and Czechoslovakia. He joined Trans-Canada Airlines in 1945 as general traffic manager, and in 1948 he was appointed president.

Air Canada jetliner, 1970.
(COURTESY OF AIR CANADA, LTD.)

His first instruction was the brusque advice of C. D. Howe, Minister of Transport, "You keep out of the taxpayer's pocket and I'll keep out of your hair."

As has been previously reported, he began with an infant airline. In his first three years as president, his passenger traffic tripled. He was aware that no air service could be better than its machines, and he was resolved from the first that Trans-Canada Airlines would not be stampeded into making purchases it could not afford nor into establishing routes that would not pay. In the period 1945–1950, his passenger business had increased by 32 percent, and the mileage flown had doubled nearly every year. By 1950, in addition to local services, he had opened a trans-Atlantic route to Britain. Its early deficit was converted to a surplus in the following year, in which Trans-Canada carried 930,691 passengers. Both express and mails were making substantial contributions to earnings. Trans-Canada also undertook the maintenance of military aircraft in

western Canada, expanded its local routes whenever there was a possibility of meeting expenses, and gave particular attention to the improvement of landing strips and airports.

By 1953, McGregor knew what he wanted in aircraft, and deliveries
began in the following year. There were a few long-range Super-Constel-
lations for trans-Canadian and foreign routes, but his work horse for
medium loads and short runs, such as would build up the local traffic,
was the Vickers Viscount—undoubtedly one of the handiest and most
economical planes ever to take to the air. For years, it provided the
bulk of his fleet. In 1954, he also ordered a number of Bristol Freighters,
for his eyes were on the north, where, for the time being at least, the
plane must be the agent of exploration and early development.

By 1955, there was a daily return flight from Montreal to Vancouver, fourteen flights daily from Montreal to Toronto, a service to
Mexico and growing short-haul services to almost every part of Canada.
Trans-Canada Airlines now was the ninth largest airline in the world.
The records that Canadians had made above the battlefields were being
sustained in full by the steady growth of the peacetime services. The
company now had a capacity of twenty-six hundred seats daily—more
than double the number of five years before. Canadian traditionalists
(and there were plenty of them) to whom no government enterprise ever
could end in anything but failure, usually changed the subject when
Trans-Canada Airlines came into the conversation.

A Change for the Better

While Canadian National Railways could not show progress commensurate with that of its air associate, it too was on the march. In 1955,
its passenger traffic was the highest on record, as was its gross ton-miles
per freight-train hour. The opening of the St. Lawrence Seaway now
promised to be less damaging than had been feared, and initial developments on the Saskatchewan potash fields suggested that they in time might
yield a bulk freight second only to grain in importance. But above all
else, railway employees were being taught to earn their increased pay by
better service. In addition to the staff training course, there were eleven
major employee training programs under way, each with the consent and
full support of the unions. Almost to the last man, the 119,430 employees
were being made ready for the railway of tomorrow.

The president's leadership and the devotion of his colleagues, had
changed the picture and had led Gordon, early in 1955, to announce that

Canadian National Railways was "over the hump." As evidence, he pointed out that it had liquidated half its inheritance of debts and obsolescence; it had met the new technological challenges and was profiting by them. The transformation of Canada into a continental entity was almost complete. It had been urbanized; in 1939, one out of every three Canadians lived in the countryside; in 1955, the proportion had shrunk to one in eight. Of Canadian imports, 70 percent now came from the United States; Canada bought as much American goods as Europe and Latin America combined. The emerging question was, could the ten provinces, half of them sparsely inhabited, strewn over three thousand miles from sea to sea, stand the strain? Could they find enough common interests to weld them together and so perpetuate an east-west confederation? It was a moot question but Donald Gordon and Canadian National Railways meant to have a damn good shot at doing it.

26

Wider Still and Wider

It would be pleasant to accept Donald Gordon's declaration of 1955 that Canadian National Railways was "over the hump" and (to change the metaphor) that thereafter all would be plain sailing. But such belief would be fiction and not fact. The changes wrought by the new technologies often ran wild and brought neither security nor finality to the problems of the Western World. Discards were as plentiful as discoveries. The impact of mass communications media affected every level of activity, and the pace of living quickened; from the chalet to the shanty to the Arctic igloo, the volume of information (or misinformation) mounted monthly, with ever-increasing political, economic and social impact. The emergence of new nations with more enthusiasm than skill in the routines of administration, the feverish quest of national economies for growth and power at the expense of community services, the unending social competition for preferment through possessions, bred an atmosphere of instability, fear and envy that led in many parts of the world to confrontations, disputes and even to violence.

It always has taken some time for one set of intellectual attitudes to succeed another, and the second half of the twentieth century was no exception. The changes wrought by the profusion of what passed for knowledge could not have been consummated without serious impact on men's minds. To many thoughtful people, it seemed as though their subconscious selves had become almost as deceitful as their conscious selves; that in logging their seas of consciousness they never touched bottom; the fear grew in many that there was no bottom. Take, for instance, the impact of mass advertising. When a customer was confronted with merchandise that the billboards and the newspapers and radio and television had endowed with overwhelming allurements, no thought process, conscious or subconscious, decided the matter; reason had relinquished its throne, and the deal was closed by what James Branch Cabell once called "the patrimony of the five senses." In many respects, the human psyche seemed to have lost its bearings: the ids were hopping as nimbly as fleas from impulse to impulse. There were multitudinous snarl-ups, of both thought and action, which could not be accounted for on any more sensible grounds than that built-in perversity that our grandparents described as "cussedness." There seemed to be no accounting for the increasing obliquity of human behavior, unless one accepted the reason once given by H. G. Wells, that man had descended from the wrong ape.

Canada was fortunate in escaping the extreme impact of this period, but she had sustained a considerable degree of damage. A Commonwealth had emerged out of the liquidation of the British Empire, but it had replaced a well-mannered club with a casual pub, where wayfarers did not mind spending an hour now and then if someone else bought the drinks. The economic associations of the British group of nations had diminished, and Canada had lost a good deal of her stake in her former Imperial relationships. It had affected her attitudes; when she played host to the Commonwealth Conference in 1958, a modest British proposal for the strengthening of trade ties received such a cool reception that one observer declared the Canadian Minister of Finance had behaved as though the British delegate had taken liberties with his person.

For better or for worse, the axis of Canadian interest now was almost entirely altered from east-west to north-south. This strengthening of the continental ties boded no good for Canadian National Railways, partly because of the loss of overseas traffic but more particularly in the loosening bonds between the Canadian provinces and in the mounting pressure of the Canadian railway unions for equality of treatment with their United States affiliates. The minor but irritating emergence of the Quebec separatist movement was reflected in similar if lesser tendencies in some of the other provinces. They had begun to think in local rather than in federal terms—a development that made the administration of 25,000 miles of railway between British Columbia and Newfoundland increasingly difficult.

During the nineteen-fifties, the fluctuating economy of the United States was communicated in growing degree to analogous Canadian enterprises. Canadian National Railways had good years in which revenues mounted, mainly because of bulk exports. In 1956, for instance, the company for the first time in eleven years had a substantial surplus after all liabilities had been met. That year, it was deemed possible to raise the general level of freight rates by 6 percent; whereupon, with the certainty of night following day, the unions demanded an increase in wages of 15 percent across the board. In 1957, there occurred an abrupt fall in traffic with increased operating expenses; in the next year, the operational results were the worst since the depths of the depression in the 1930s. The federal government was obliged to come to the aid of Canadian National Railways with a substantial loan in order to avoid the curtailment of the modernization program that had been placed in train during President Gordon's first five years in office. One of the few stimulating events of the year was the visit of Her Majesty Queen Elizabeth II and Prince Philip to share, with President Eisenhower, in the ceremonies attendant on the opening of the St. Lawrence Seaway. Thereafter the royal couple traveled for 1,500 miles on Canadian National Railways in their visits to various communities. In 1959, there was a slight improvement in the volume of traffic, but a request for rate adjustments drew the reply that none would be forthcoming pending the report of a Royal Commission soon to be appointed.

Changes in the Sessional Committee

During his first eight years in office, President Gordon had sedulously nursed his relations with the Sessional Committee, which comprised his major link with the rank and file of the members of the Canadian government. He had built up an atmosphere of confidence, indeed, almost of affection, with these official examiners: he had answered questions with authority, straightforwardly; if they were inspired by political coggery, he would deal with them tersely, or on occasion, jocularly. He seldom reverted to his distinctive rough-and-tumble repartee; Instead, he frequently drew applause by the brevity and clarity of his reports. On one occasion a committee member enthusiastically declared him to be the greatest man in Canada. When his officers were questioned as to the origins of his abilities, they said that when once on the job, he never stopped working; he took his files home and even to bed with him. Among the outstanding gadflies of successive Sessional Committees was

Jean François Pouliot, member for Temiscouata County, whose small railway recently had been taken over by Canadian National Railways. Each year he had approached the Parliamentary investigators with a burden of complaints out of which he hoped to shape political advantage; yet after one encounter with Gordon, he made a staggering admission. "If you say so, I will take it as true." On some occasions, when questions plainly revealed their political bias, Gordon gave his humor its head, reducing his colleagues to helpless laughter.

In June 1957, for the first time in twenty-two years, a Conservative government was elected. It will be remembered that in a previous term of office, it had made an end to Sir Henry Thornton. Its return to power suggested that Gordon's management might be the object of official criticism. Any newly elected government is conscious of the necessity of differing from its predecessor; in the same way, members of Parliament, freshly in power and having bowed before the Throne for the first time, realize the value of attitudes or behavior that distinguish them from the herd and that give their constituents reason to esteem them.

John G. Diefenbaker's Conservative administration, after its long sojourn in Opposition, naturally was anxious to put itself on the map. Its first session lasted for nine months. Its members were busy as bees; Royal Commissions sprang up like trilliums in the Canadian forests in spring. They undertook a dozen difficult investigations—the Canadian motor car industry, the Canadian press, Canadian advertising, provincial administrative methods and other key subjects that not only could be improved to the honor and glory of Canada but also might suitably impress the electorate.

In such a wide investigation of federal affairs, Canadian National Railways certainly could not be overlooked. Gordon had been in office for eight years, and he had spent upward of $2 billion in endeavors to make the system popular and profitable. Yet on the whole, its annual returns had been disappointing. There had been increases in freight traffic, but little or nothing in passengers, and the general financial condition of the system had not improved to any appreciable extent. The number of employees had not increased, but their wage bill was 50 percent greater than before Gordon took over, which gave grounds for the argument that the system was doing better for its personnel than for its owners, the Canadian people. Such a premise naturally appealed to the new administration, which forty years before had had the principle of public ownership of railways thrust upon its party entirely against its will. The annual reports for the late 1950s emphasized the grave situation arising out of higher costs and inadequate revenues. The 1958 report declared, "Our record for the year illustrates the vulnerability of Canadian National Railways to the shifts and challenges of a highly competitive transportation market." The first sentence of the 1959 report summarized the results of that year as "most disappointing." Such admissions touched chords in political memories.

Technical Improvements

Gordon and his able and hard-working staff were fully aware of these discouraging circumstances, but they were not prepared to wait for better times to intervene. They strove to effect improvements by lowering costs and by increasing sales; in some directions, they had already accomplished much. The system now was almost completely Dieselized, which solved its power problem. The overdue improvements in maintenance of way were well advanced; improved maintenance equipment had cut the cost of track upkeep; flame hardening had made rail ends less susceptible to damage; special lubricators relieved tensions on curves. Specialization of rolling stock had continued; more than 40 percent of the old general-purpose freight cars had been replaced by improved equipment.

This progress, however was only the beginning of an overall change. The principal contribution of the twentieth century to economic progress had been automation, whereby machines not only took over the work of a man's hands but also did a considerable portion of his thinking for him. Peter B. Wilson, chief of operational research of Canadian National Railways, in a paper delivered at Northwestern University, gave explicit reasons for the soaring costs of railway operations. Every workman was tied to the tempo of his tools; their capacity set the limits of his production. Two out of every three cents earned by a railway went to its employees, who could only execute their set tasks to the limits of their strength and mobility. Under the existing organization, the pace of railway movement of freight traffic was almost unbelievably slow. Freight cars averaged two hours' movement in every twenty-four, the remainder being spent standing in yards, in loading, unloading and awaiting fresh consignments. Even when actively employed, they were only in motion for fifteen out of every hundred minutes. For most of their lives, therefore, they stood waiting for work.

Adoption of Improved Mobility Devices

New auxiliaries, however, solved many problems. Hump yards, in which freight cars were assembled and sorted by remote control, were designed to speed up dispatch on fresh assignments. By means of punch cards the location and status of every piece of equipment were recorded in data centers. Thus every movement of cargo was integrated into the general panorama of operation.

In 1958, construction of Canadian National hump yards began at four divisional points. Moncton was first to be opened, in 1961. It contained nineteen miles of tracks, with a capacity for the reception of 5,062 cars and the dispatch of 3,500 cars a day. It lessened by 75 percent the time wasted in awaiting employment. In the following year, the Montreal hump yard was completed. It covered 834 acres, with capacity of receiving and dispatching 7,000 cars daily. It included a YMCA hostel

Montreal hump yards.

for the use of train crews during stopovers. In 1962, the Symington hump yard in Winnipeg took over the duties of four of the old-type yards. In Toronto, work began on a similar project that would have a capacity of 10,500 cars, of which 6,000 could be processed daily. It involved the building of sixty-four miles of access tracks.

A Major Organizational Development

These improvements were accompanied by a major reorganization of operations. It was quite all right to save money by innovations, but the prime necessity was to earn more by keeping rolling stock busy. In the first eight years of the Gordon regime, freight-revenue ton-miles had increased only by about 10 percent, and passenger-revenue miles actually had decreased. There were more goods and more people on the move in Canada than ever before, yet the train, subconsciously perhaps, was becoming in many minds a relic of yesterday, to be employed only in case of necessity. Since prices now were loaded with advertising and other extraneous charges, costs of delivery had become minor items, and there was no logical reason for not using railways to a greater extent. But amid the hurry and scurry of the new era, with slogans and appeals shouting at the consumer from every roadside billboard, from every newspaper and over the air, the railway had slipped out of the limelight. It had been relegated to the limbo of old-fashioned services. Donald Gordon's chief problem, therefore, was to restore its significance. He had not forgotten, as related earlier, how the cancellation of a deluxe passenger service had cost him freight traffic in western Canada. His necessity now was to reinstate the railway as a current device—indeed, to sell it anew. It no longer could wait for business to come to it.

By 1960, there were piles and files with suggestions of improvements. Leading business consultants came in to digest them and to make recommendations. The plan eventually accepted involved a major decentralization of administration responsibilities. Local representatives were entrusted with new duties and routines were adopted which instituted the "Line and Staff" system, with the man in the field as the "Line," undertaking many services that previously had been administered by "Staff"— that is to say, Head Office. The existing structure of management, which previously had consisted of three regions, ten districts and thirty-one divisions, all subject to centralized control, was abolished, to be replaced by five regions and eighteen management areas, to whom nearly all functions, barring matters of general policy, were entrusted. Chief among the duties transferred was the responsibility for sales. The Traffic Department at Head Office was renamed the Sales Department, and the men in the field, who formerly functioned only as general staff, now became salesmen as well. Thereafter they would be expected to deal with all matters that would increase the utility and attractiveness of the railway as a common carrier. As set out in the *1960 Annual Report,* they would be expected to advise Head Office on such matters as rates and tariff-making techniques and on the value of specialized types of equipment. They also must be prepared to forecast traffic volumes, to set sales objectives and to plan market surveys.

The Change of Face

Concurrently, the company undertook to repackage itself in more striking containers. A corporate trademark was adopted in the form of the elision of the letters CN into an attractive monogram that swam endlessly forward, as a symbol of the manner in which Canadian National Railways covered its territory. This identification went on everything— stations, rolling stock, motor vehicles, credit cards and company forms. It would be accompanied by visual designs in a range of colors, not only to distinguish various types of equipment but also to catch the eye of Canadians and remind them of the great property that they possessed.

In the following year, incentive freight rates were introduced on a wide range of merchandise. In 1962, there came a further refinement of the sales campaign in the form of the Master Agency Plan. Because of the vast distances traversed and the huge number of way stations and flag stops that received only occasional shipments, it had been decided to quicken the traffic by entrusting documentation, pick-up and delivery of such freights to certain terminals, whence they would be conveyed to and from their minor destinations by road vehicles. The first trial area chosen was around Moncton, where thirty-three stops were eliminated. Twelve of them served off-line communities, which were provided with telephone connections with the Moncton terminal. When traffic was routed in this fashion, it became possible to close eight stations. The second installation was around Edmonton, where a somewhat different situation prevailed because of the pick-ups of grain from the countryside elevators and because of the innate fear of the prairie farmers of the loss of their branch line services. But here, too, it was soon discovered that a telephone call into the Edmonton terminal involved less difficulty and more speedy action, and so the former way station customers took to it gladly. As a shipper from a small community put it in a letter, "It has given us the equivalent of a personal shopping service."

Gordon Under Fire

None of these improvements, nor the extra traffic they generated, was sufficient to assure Canadian National Railways of an unfailing operational surplus. The company was by no means unique in this respect; the 1950s had proved a difficult period for almost all North American railways. As is not unusual in service organizations, the early popularity of the Gordon regime gradually diminished when miracles were not forthcoming. The changed attitude of the Sessional Committees, the questions asked in the House of Commons, the private and not-so-private opinions of individual members of the government seemed to many to be shaping toward the selection of a scapegoat, with perhaps the reenactment of the tragedy of Sir Henry Thornton.

Those who held such opinions did not know their man. Gordon was a born leader and a bonny fighter; after ten years' service, he knew a great deal more about railways, their potentials and their necessities, than any politician. He had assembled a magnificent staff about him— men who had been inspired by his vision and his courage and who gave him support and advice that allowed him to meet his critics without fear or favor. So when in 1959 a Canadian government for the thirty-second time adopted the device of a Royal Commission to investigate and to recommend in railway matters, it was confronted by a cadre of officials highly competent to explain why the publicly owned system had not yet been able to show a profit. The Royal Commission was headed by W. A. MacPherson, a distinguished western jurist; his instructions led directly to the prickliest of all railway problems, that of freight rates. The huge area of Canada, its uneven distribution of population, the duplication of branch lines on the prairies, the growing competition of highways, the discriminatory agreements that dated back to the era of parochial patronage, together with a round dozen other exceptions to the general rule, had made the Canadian railway rates structure an agglomeration of individual instances, with logical determinations usually conspicuous by their absence. They included locally inspired concessions, such as the Crows Nest Pass cutrates to assist in the export of prairie grains through Pacific ports, similar reductions granted to attract traffic to the Maritime Provinces ports and rates that had been set to overcome the disadvantage of the thousand miles of empty wilderness to the north of the Great

Lakes. These and other exceptions made a crazy quilt of the Canadian rates structure and had created a condition in which it was next to impossible for much of the Canadian system to earn its keep. President Gordon in 1957, while giving evidence before a committee of inquiry, had revealed that one-quarter of the trackage of Canadian National Railways barely earned its operational expenses, contributing nothing to overhead or other charges. Another 30 percent earned no better than a marginal surplus. Thus less than half of the railway was obliged to shoulder the cost of the thousand and one items essential to the construction and maintenance of the system. It therefore seemed only sensible that when transportation projects originated in local rather than in national needs, part, at least, of the outlays involved or the losses sustained should be charges on the public purse.

Such a startling proposal gave the politicians and the press a field day. In many instances they reacted in accordance with views that they had inherited and that bore little resemblance to contemporary realities. Naturally, the House of Commons Railway Committee became the cockpit of the encounters, and the standards of in-fighting were little, if any, higher than in Sir Henry Thornton's day. Gordon and his men met their adversaries head on. In 1959, the president's term of office had expired and the government had taken no immediate steps to renew it. This circumstance naturally encouraged the critics, but they encountered no passive targets. On one occasion Gordon closed out a seemingly endless session with the challenge, "If you have come to the conclusion that we are not an efficient management, for God's sake tell us so and fire the lot of us."[1] In the course of what passed for cross-examination, he and his colleagues endured such picayune accusations as the wrongful issuance of parliamentary passes and whether or not the company had paid for the president's kerosene at his summer cottage at Lustre Lake. Eventually Gordon took twenty-five minutes to tell the committee exactly what he thought of them. The following excerpt was typical:

> There has been a stream of irresponsible, uninformed, hostile and malicious statements in the House of Commons, naturally carried by the press and over radio and television, all seeking to disparage Canadian National management. This is designed to disturb the morale of our employees, which is the ultimate aim of a campaign against anyone charged with duties that call for action or for decisions which effect changes in old-established methods and customs. [Such investigations] are easily avoided by those content to drift along in the customary complacency of inertia.[2]

A *Cheering Report*

After more than a year of hearings, the MacPherson Commission had rendered a comprehensive and positive report. It had been impressed by the evidence that Canadian National Railways from its origin had been obliged to assume liabilities that were not of its making. One of the commission's first recommendations was that burdens which had been imposed on railways for reasons of public policy should be removed and their liability assumed by the state. Also, that the operation of railways in low-density traffic areas either should be accepted as a public charge or that the railways should be allowed to abandon them. In cases of doubt, fourteen conditions were laid down by which to decide whether the railway company or the state should assume responsibility.

These recommendations were accepted by the government and went into effect immediately. In 1960, subsidy payments to the amount of $36.3 million were disbursed in fulfillment of the MacPherson recommendations. In the following year, the amount almost doubled to $66.7 million. Roughly two-thirds of such subsidies went to Canadian National Railways. In 1964, these grants reached their peak at $103.3 million. Such payments also included losses on marine services arising out of agreements between the federal authority and the provinces.

Trouble from Another Quarter

Gordon had every reason to be satisfied with such determinations. His forthright rebuttals of the charges ventilated against him before the political committees had done him no harm; indeed, they rallied public opinion behind him. Two of his strongest unions, with whom his relations often had been strained, entered vigorous protests over the campaign against him. His troubles, however, were not over. The French Canadians were on the march; after two centuries of comparative isolation and contentment with their lot they had awakened to the recognition that there was more to living than their way of life made possible. All of a sudden they were demanding that their race and tongue should receive greater consideration from the English-speaking majority. They took no heed of time; they wanted to hurry the clock along and they were not overly fastidious about the means they used to attain their ends.

In November 1962, a member of the Sessional Committee asked Gordon why Canadian National Railways did not employ more French Canadians. He responded that they comprised 13 percent of his overall staff and 23 percent of all employed university graduates. These proportions were reasonable in relation to the railway mileage of Quebec and to the proportion of French Canadians in the population. But perhaps unwisely he capped his statement with the declaration, "As long as I am President there is not going to be a promotion or an appointment simply because the man is a French-Canadian." The French-language newspapers seized upon this statement as illustrative of Anglo-Saxon arrogance. Three nights later a small group of students burned an effigy of Gordon in front of the Queen Elizabeth Hotel. There was no particular disturbance, and on November 30, the president issued a further statement to the effect that there had never been any discrimination against French Canadians. Indeed, he was always on the lookout for those who had the requisite capacity for the available appointments.

Probably nothing more would have been heard of the matter if the French-Canadian press had not continued to snap at Gordon's heels. On December 12, several thousand students, reinforced by the usual raggle-taggle, marched on Canadian National Headquarters. They endeavored to force their way into the Queen Elizabeth Hotel but desisted when they encountered police. A flag was torn from its masthead, wrapped around another effigy of Gordon and hoisted flaming to the peak. There was a great deal of milling about but little damage to railway property.

Gordon had dispatched an officer to invite representatives on the students into his office. He told this delegation that he favored bilingualism in all railway services in French-speaking areas. Language would never be a bar to promotion if a candidate knew his job. From then onward, every effort was made to provide French-language railway literature and time-tables. Company officers were instructed whenever possible to meet the French-Canadian demand for the use of their tongue in their own province.

A Change of Government

In the spring of 1963, a federal election had ejected the Conservative administration, and the Liberal Party, which had always been the paramount federal party in Quebec, returned to power with a strong array of supporters, some of whom, at least, were anxious to continue the feud with Canadian National Railways and its allegedly unaccommodating president. A binational virus was spreading, and the extremists who demanded separation from Canada were getting a hearing. Among the early worries of the new Prime Minister, the Right Honorable Lester B. Pearson, was a demand by a minority of his French-Canadian members, supported by at least two members of his cabinet, for a change in the management of Canadian National Railways. What was sought was French-Canadian recognition at the top—an English-origin president and a French-origin chairman, or something of that sort. The proposal troubled the Prime Minister sufficiently for him to delay the reappointment of Gordon for several months. In September, as the result of an interview, Pearson asked the president for a written reply to the charges against him. On September 14, Gordon bluntly denied that at any time had he disparaged the French Canadians. He denounced such statements as downright lies, and he challenged his critics to cite a single instance on which he had exhibited favoritism on ethnic grounds.

On receipt of this assurance, the Prime Minister on October 2 invited Gordon to serve another term. The president accepted but declared that the tasks of rehabilitation were all but complete and that as soon as he was certain that he had done as much as he could to modernize the system, he would like to be relieved of his duties. The Prime Minister expressed his appreciation of Gordon's services and declared his agreement with "your concern about the completion of certain work to re-organize and strengthen the railway." In reply the president declared "My work should be finished in about a year and a half, in which case I will with good conscience, ask to be released."*

It will be noted that neither correspondent specified the nature of tasks still to be fulfilled. The decentralization of management, the development of an aggressive sales policy, the conversion from steam to Diesel, the replacement of obsolete rolling stock by specialist carriers, the purchase of trucking companies for road transport, the development of piggyback and container traffic, the construction of hump yards, the tremendous growth of communications, the modernization of the hotel chain, the introduction of automation and data processing, the highly developed training programs for employees, the acceptance by the federal government of numerous politically inspired responsibilities of the company—such tasks were virtually completed. What, then, were the additional enterprises that the president hoped to conclude if given a further eighteen months in office?

Gordon was known to be interested, if only mildly, in an organizational structure that was beginning to emerge in the more highly sophis-

---

* This exchange of correspondence was immediately published.

ticated economies of the Western World. The new technologies were creating radical demands for change, sometimes at enormous expense. Such developments might prove dangerous even to the strongest enterprise that was dependent on a single product or group of products. In some cases, therefore, there had been moves to diversify investments so that in event of sudden and expensive changes, there might be revenues available from disparate sources to cushion the shocks. Thus, a steel mill might buy a biscuit factory, which in turn might own a group of lingerie shops. The common denominator of such unusual associations would be their sensitivity to public demand, so that in times of stress some constituent might be able to expand its output and lend support to the other components of the amalgamation. The gullibility of consumers in a society in which possessions were paramount might constitute a form of insurance.

Another development that may have been in Gordon's thoughts was the backlash to the overwhelming success of the motor car, which had beaten down the bounds of distance. By the 1960s, the annual mileage traversed by the Canadian citizen was at least forty times greater than it had been forty years before. There now were signs, however, of resistance againtst the hordes of vehicles that cluttered the highways and clogged the streets. The motor car had become a hallucinatory adjunct to full living, almost as essential as breath, but a few percipient organizations had begun to count its costs. The Wittauch investigation, conducted by a high official of the Federal Savings and Loan Association of Chicago, declared that the expense of traveling by motor car in a modern city was twenty-five times greater than the cost of walking, three times the cost of travel by bus, twice as much as by train and $63 more per year than the use of taxicabs over the same distance. But these costs were only the beginning of the community charges against individual private transport. When such fixed outlays as the wear and tear of streets, policing and other indirect motor car charges were added, the Chicago motorist who earned $8,000 a year was spending 6.5 percent of his total income on local transportation, and he was losing eight hours more per week of his leisure time than if he had adopted other methods of conveyance. A similar investigation by the New Haven Railroad revealed that it cost approximately $1,500 a year to commute to downtown New York by motor car, as against $262.80 by subway. The Bay City Transit complex of San Francisco placed the costs of urban motor car travel at from three to four times that of other forms of transportation. There therefore was encouragement for railways to persevere in the passenger traffic and to endeavor to reassert their former preeminence as carriers of bodies as well as merchandise.

Neither of these developments promised to play any immediate role

in the progress of Canadian National Railways. What Gordon was thinking about was a major change, to be achieved through recapitalization.
He wanted a final and climactic repetition of what he had obtained in the
Capital Revision Act of 1952 and in the recommendations of the Mac-
Pherson Commission seven years later. He sought to end, once and for
all, the inherited encumbrances of Canadian National Railways. He saw
the past thirteen years as something in the nature of life in an arena, in
which he had power rather to worry his problems than to kill or cure
them. What he now sought was an opening for a matador's stroke.

It was a brave dream, but it took too little account of too many
things, time included.

A Fresh Passenger Campaign

After the Second World War, the company's passenger traffic had
fallen steadily. For upward of fifteen years, it continued to dwindle, not
only in numbers but also in earnings, and a larger percentage—approximately half—consisted of short-haul commuters, whose custom never had
been remunerative. But salesmanship was working well in the case of
freight, and as alternative to abandonments, Canadian National Railways
deemed it worthwhile to attempt to obtain passenger business in the
modern manner, by the advertisement of special inducements and opportunities.

In 1961, the program of incentive fares was broadened, and substantial discounts were inauguarated for group travelers. Special terms were
offered to long-distance passengers, and the conversion of a portion of
the dining car fleet into cafeteria cars was expedited. On May 1, 1962, the
experimental Red, White and Blue Plan went into effect in eastern Canada. It offered three levels of fare—Bargain, Economy and Standard—the
lowest of which would apply to those months of the year and days of the
week on which passenger travel traditionally was thin. The idea caught on,
and before the end of the year, studies were under way for its extension
to western Canada. Its early success led to its adoption in 1963 by the
Grand Trunk Western lines; it was said to have been the first experiment
of its kind in the United States. Other travel features adopted in this year
were the Car-Go-Rail, whereby travelers took their motor cars with them,
and a Charge-a-Trip credit plan. The effect of these concessions were
apparent in 1964 when the number of passengers increased by 14 percent
over the preceding year.

In 1965, heavy increases in passenger traffic and in passenger reve-

The last steam locomotive, 6218, retired in 1971.

nues testified to the success of the Red, White and Blue Plan. Not only had numbers increased; unit passenger revenues also were well above average. General progress continued in 1966, with the heaviest earnings per passenger-mile in many years. Improvements were so constant that the company was encouraged to introduce new fast services, such as the Rapido between Montreal and Toronto and between Montreal and Quebec City. Turbo trains now were in the offing, with the promise of hitherto unknown speeds in areas of dense population. Canadian National Railways arranged with United Aircraft of Canada for a lease-maintenance contract on turbo trains that included an option for outright purchase when the new designs had been proved.

As might have been expected because of the World Exposition in Montreal, passenger travel in 1967 broke all records. Canadian National Railways carried 18 million passengers for greater distances than every before. New commuter services, sponsored by the province of Ontario, came into operation. Entertainment cars were introduced on the denser runs, agreements were negotiated with bus and airline companies for interline ticketing of passengers. In Newfoundland, bus routes were sponsored that proved immediately successful; in its first year in that province, the Road Cruiser Service carried roughly twice as many passengers as the trains.

In 1969, the passenger train emerged in a new role—that of a Tower of Silence, a place of soundproof seclusion. The oil companies were intent on executing a joint lease of millions of acres of Arctic lands and the first necessity was to conduct the preliminary negotiations in a location where no electronic listener-in stood the slightest chance of picking up clues. So a Canadian National Railway train of fourteen passenger cars was hired, at a reputed rental of $10,000 a day, to shuttle continuously between Edmonton and Calgary, void of contracts with the outside world. For five days this mechanical eremite plied its solitary courses, evoking wonder and speculation. With all decisions reached, its passengers flew off to Alaska.

Dawn of a New Day

Despite these gains, the passenger problem had not been solved. At the end of the 1960s, the motor car still held 85 percent of the Canadian passenger traffic; of the remainder, the railway's share was only 3 percent. This situation did not discourage but stimulated the Passenger Section of Canadian National Railways; in the poet's phrase, it was baffled to fight better. It was bad business to continue to operate the crack Super-Continental at a loss of nearly a million dollars a month, but it was not feasible to discontinue it; the government and the Canadian communities alike were anxious to decrease rather than to increase the endless columns of motor vehicles on the highways. The first Canadian-built turbo train units were disappointing, partly because of errors in design and partly because the impact of the extremes of the Canadian climate had been underestimated. The greatest density of passenger traffic in Canada was to be found in the Quebec City–Windsor corridor (715 miles), and here radical experiments got under way, in new types of equipment, in the composition of trains and in the nature of services. (Approximately 70 percent of the present loss was incurred in providing sleeping and dining car accommodations.) To avoid expensive roadbed outlays, a lightweight train was being designed, that was expected to attain a speed of 110 miles an hour. On the existing trackage, air-cushioned coaches derived from the British hovercraft also were under experiment. Canadian National Railways were in the position to command considerable official support for such developments from the recently formed Department of Urban Affairs and from the federal Transport Development Agency. One thing was certain; to solve the passenger problem, the company was not tied to any traditional method of transportation. It was prepared to consider radical innovations in order to preserve and increase its take in the carriage of travelers. The ever-growing urge of western peoples to see what is beyond the horizon was a challenge that the railways dare not ignore.

Improvements in the Hotel Chain

Travelers need more than more trains. They require accommodations, entertainment and communication facilities. Canadian National Railways had inherited Chateau Laurier in Ottawa from the Grand Trunk Railway; it had become a hotel of worldwide reputation. Others acquired in various transactions were the Hotel Vancouver, owned by the company, but operated conjointly with the Canadian Pacific Railway; the MacDonald in Edmonton; the Prince Edward at Brandon; the Fort Garry in Winnipeg; the Prince Arthur in Thunder Bay; the Nova Scotian at Halifax; and, last to arrive, the Newfoundland at St. John's. The company likewise had built the Bessborough in Saskatoon and the Charlottetown in the capital of Prince Edward Island. In addition, it had owned three country lodges —Jasper Park at the gateway to the Rockies, Minaki in the Lake of the Woods countryside and Pictou Lodge in Nova Scotia.

On July 5, 1952, the main lodge at Jasper Park, together with kitchens, dining rooms and business offices, was destroyed by fire. The lodge at that time had five hundred fifty guests. The incident became a worldwide press story because of the courage and ingenuity of the employees: waitresses with doused blankets lay on the thatched roofs of the cottages, and a Canadian National employee gave his life in endeavors to halt the flames.

Jasper Park Lodge from the Athabaska River.

Macdonald Hotel, Edmonton.

Within a matter of hours, essential services had been restored, and by the following morning, cafeterias were serving all guests.

This splendid behavior may have played some part in President Gordon's decision not only to repair the damage without delay but also to expand Jasper into an outstanding resort. It was one of the few places in the world where primitive and sophisticated communities tolerated each other; nearly every species of native wildlife could be identified and studied within walking distance of the cottages. The accommodations of the lodge was increased by approximately 40 percent but preserved in every detail the atmosphere of a community in the wild. When the 1953 season opened, there were twelve thousand advance bookings. Almost without exception, every visitor had become an advertiser. Jasper retains its reputation to this day.

It has become necessary, on the takeover of the Newfoundland Hotel in 1949, to rebuild it in order to bring it up to modern standards. Next to receive attention was the Macdonald in Edmonton, which, after thirty-five years needed to catch up with the growth of the Alberta capital. A wing sixteen stories in height more than doubled its accommodation. In 1963, Canadian National Railways had purchased the Canadian Pacific interest in the Hotel Vancouver; over the years the company had expended $9 million on its enlargement and improvements. During the same period its hotels at Brandon, Thunder Bay and Charlottetown and the two eastern lodges had been sold or closed.

The Montreal Venture

The trend of the times, and particularly the growing importance of the convention trade, plainly indicated the choice of Montreal as a site for a major investment. That city was well behind other Canadian centers in accommodation facilities, with only three hundred rooms per hundred thousand inhabitants. Yet 62 percent of the entire population of Canada and 52 million Americans lived within 500 miles of that city. The lures of Paris were part of the American legend, and in Quebec a renaissance of the "French Fact" was in progress. The sparkle of French attitudes as exemplified in their culture, to say nothing of that nation's naughty niceties, undoubtedly should prove a lure to travelers.

In August 1953, President Gordon announced that Canadian National Railways would build a hotel fronting on Dorchester Street, contiguous both to the Montreal railway station and the new company headquarters, which soon was to be placed in work. It would be twenty stories in height, with accommodations for two thousand guests. Its estimated cost was $20 million. When work began in 1954, the plans called for 1,216 guest rooms, many of the studio type, with public rooms that would accommodate twenty-five hundred diners at banquets and an auditorium with four thousand seats for assemblies. It would be one of the great hotels of the world.

Shortly before construction began, Gordon was visited by a representative of the Hilton Corporation, an organization that controlled twenty-five large hotels in the United States, with interests in many other parts of the world. In addition to the properties it owned, it sought management contracts, and it had been eyeing Montreal for some time. Other hotel groups also made approaches, but the Hilton possessed a key attraction, since it could recruit customers through other members of its chain. In July 1954, Gordon advised the Minister of Transport of his conversations with the Hilton representatives and that he had decided to continue them. In December, an agreement was reached whereby Hilton would take over the management of the Montreal hotel on behalf of Canadian National Railways and would undertake not to compete with that company's hotels elsewhere in Canada. Such contract offered marked advantages to both parties, particularly in connection with the convention traffic.

Queen Elizabeth Hotel, Montreal.

The name chosen for the new hotel was the Queen Elizabeth. This choice sat ill with some of the local patriots, but Gordon stood stoutly to his guns. He pointed out that more than 90 percent of the guests drawn to Montreal would be English-speaking and that Americans, particularly of the nearby New England states, were impressed by royalist or old English associations. His views prevailed, and Her Majesty the Queen graciously extended her patronage to the new venture.

The Grand Opening

The Queen Elizabeth was opened on April 16, 1958. For two days, revelry reigned. Special trains brought in throngs from the United States, with the emphasis on the newsworthy—Hollywood and theatrical celebrities, newspaper and periodical feature writers, political and other public figures, with a generous proportion of the latter from Ottawa and from the provincial capitals. They came into an almost bewildering array, to gaze and to exclaim. By the use of disappearing walls any of the service floors

could be transformed to fit any occasion; the Grand Salon, of 7,000
square feet, could be expanded to 18,000 square feet by adding the adjoining compartments. The Convention Hall, normally of 50,000 square
feet, was flanked by five banquet halls, eleven private dining rooms and
four display galleries, all of which could become part of the central salon
if required. There was a complete floor of sample rooms, a stage, orches-
tra stands and a profusion of cocktail lounges. It was a characteristic setting for business discussions in the new manner, with as many distrac-
tions as possible.

The Beaver Club

In 1785, the Beaver Club had been formed by factors of the North
West Company and other fur traders wintering in Montreal. For forty
years, it had been the scene of their revels, and they had evolved a ritual
in which toasts, choruses and costumes were the concomitants of a celebration based on their lives in the forests and on the rivers. After the
North West Company merger with the Hudson Bay Company in 1824, the
club disbanded, but in 1958, it was reconstituted with every appointment
and all the rites of old times. One of the Queen Elizabeth's dining rooms
was bedecked with the furnishings of yesterday—the heavy furs, the
great medallions, the candelabra, basketry, silverware and old weapons.

On all but one night in the year it was a seemly and decorous restaurant but on the evening of the annual dinner of the Beaver Club, it
went mad. Members were in costume—top hats, tail coats, frilled shirt
fronts with heavy stocks, snuffboxes and demijohns in hand. All night the
rafters rang: the Honorary Wintering Partners, as the members called
themselves, smoked the pipe of peace, bawled the old *chansons*, ranged
themselves on the floor as canoe crews with walking sticks as paddles and
punctuated their strokes with war whoops. None bore himself more dili-
gently and well in his role than Donald Gordon. In the transactions of the
club, he is recorded as a principal participant, famous for his retorts, his
roaring songs, his toasts and his utter immersion in the gambols of the
past.

Canadian National Hotels never were large earners, but they usually
showed credit balances. In some years, the Queen Elizabeth did exceptionally well, but its profits often were consumed by the necessity of improvements and rehabilitations elsewhere. In 1962, a special Hilton survey
led to a plan for a general renovation over five years for all company
hotels. In the following year, there occurred a small loss on their opera-

The Beaver Club: Donald Gordon (CENTER, SEATED) in song.
(COURTESY OF BUSINESS & INDUSTRIAL PHOTOGRAPHERS LTD., MONTREAL)

tions, which was more than repaired in 1964. The growth of Place Ville-Marie in Montreal (which will be described shortly) had first damaged and then improved the returns from the Queen Elizabeth, which had opened new restaurants in the premises of the complex. In 1967, the revenues of the hotels increased sharply, due in large part to the World Exposition at Montreal. The introduction in 1969 of winter sports at Jasper Lodge promised to give that resort continuous employment throughout the year.

Freight Keeps Pace with Passenger Progress

The improvements already noted in freight routines through the introduction of the hump yards and the Line and Staff organization were the fruits of earlier efforts during the discouraging 1950s, when freight yields varied unpredictably from year to year and when heavy capital expenditures seldom earned commensurate returns. Even before the 1960 reorganization had been effected, plans were in train to profit by it. Two years earlier, a System Freight Sales program had been introduced. It was followed by Marketing and Distribution seminars for senior personnel in order that any innovations might benefit from the guidance by expertly trained managers. In 1963, a Customers Research Service was inaugurated. Fast freight services like the Trans-Canada Highballer cut time of deliveries and costs of operation. Incentive carload lot rates were introduced to meet trucking competition and piggyback services multiplied. Such competitive improvements became plain in the returns for 1963, which showed the highest carriage of freight in Canadian National history. Two years later, the freight load once again surpassed all previous records with 101,051,792,000 gross ton-miles.

By now most Canadian National areas on the prairies were in full production, and their large wheat export shipments were handled in a manner which drew hearty commendation from the Canadian Grain Board. Very welcome increases in the movement of manufactured goods to western Canada also were recorded. The growing demands of Japan for raw materials substantially increased freights to the Pacific ports.

In 1967, for the first time in seven years, Canadian National freights showed no gain. This falling-off was in keeping with the continental trend. In that year, however, Canadian National Railways made its first experiment with containers, both in import and export shipments. In 1968, despite a grain handlers strike during the principal shipping months, the company's freight traffic increased materially, due in part to the introduction of the Cargo-Flo system, which in effect applied the Master Agency Plan to bulk commodities, loading and unloading them by pressure in and out of specialized hoppers. In the period 1955–1969, freights of Canadian National increased in volume by more than 50 percent, and its annual earnings in that period rose from $643,900,000 to $1,113,400,000.

Road Transport

Canadian National Railways freight policy was based on the simple assumption that anything that could be carried economically either in whole or in part by rail should be borne by that medium; but when, because of disadvantage of position or other reasons, rail carriage became too expensive or too slow, the company would complete deliveries by road in their own vehicles. Over the years a growing number of truck companies had been purchased and Canadian National Transportation

Limited had been organized to administer the trucking services, which played an ever-increasing role in express and less-than-carload freight movements. In 1960, shortage of road vehicles led to the purchase of four additional trucking companies, together with an option on a fifth, which was exercised soon afterward.

In January 1961, the Canadian National Department of Highways was formed to correlate all road transport activities. Two additional Ontario trucking firms were purchased, giving the company an investment of $11.9 million in road conveyances. These trucking units were earning their keep, but their benefits went far beyond their immediate profits because of the savings they effected on revenues formerly lost on traffic lines and because of the ability they gave Canadian National Railways to compete with other road services, not only in cost but also in rapidity of deliveries.

In 1963, a new express service was established as an extension of the Master Agency Plan. It provided low-cost, flexible deliveries through coordination of rail, piggyback and road transport. It was well received by shippers and soon spread across the system. At principal sources, such as Montreal, Toronto and Hamilton, special terminals were installed to handle this traffic. By now, containerization had come ashore and was multiplying its services. In 1965, Canadian National Railways placed orders for an additional 400 fifty-ton piggybacks and for eighty-four containers, together with flatcars to carry them. This traffic grew rapidly and entered the import-export field. By 1970, there were 1,115 such units in operation, some of them insulated for hot and cold cargo, with a tanker division for fluid freights. In that year, the express services earned $116 million, or about 9 percent of the total gross revenues of the system.

Communications—A Great Advance

The exploitation of new communications techniques provides a particularly significant page in the progress of Canadian National Railways. The electric telegraph, transmitting by a series of dots and dashes, had been invented in the 1830s by Morse in the United States and Wheatstone in Great Britain. Within the next decade, it had been applied extensively to railway communications. Before the end of the century, the telephone had come into common usage as a valuable auxiliary of the telegraph.*

---

* Morse has been but lately numbered with the dead. In 1970, Canadian National Railways had 13,884 miles of telegraph wires in service to 730 destinations. Most of them were on branch lines or to isolated locations. Other media now have taken over virtually all of them.

After the First World War, long-distance telephone multiplied its capacity by means of carrier current devices, by which a number of messages or conversations could be transmitted concurrently over a single wire. But by then, Marconi had harnessed the electromagnetic waves in wireless telegraphy; as has been previously recorded, by 1923, Canadian National Railways were transmitting radio programs to their passenger trains. The Second World War gave enormous impetus to improved communications facilities, and before the end of that struggle, Canadian National Railways had space to sell on its network of circuits and was leasing its lines to such other users as broadcasting, meteorological and teletype services.

In the late 1940s, the telephone became a full partner in railway communications, with combined services between many centers. In 1952, telegraphic messages were channeled for the first time over frequency modulation radio. Teletype had been introduced in 1920, and in 1950, it became a regular Canadian National Railways service. In 1951, the company's telegraph offices began to be equipped for the transmission and reception of messages in facsimile. This process at first was used solely for interdepartmental correspondence, but afterward, in the form of Deskfax, it was made available to major customers. Concurrently, radio facilities were introduced whereby trains in motion never were out of touch with operational controls, nor their locomotives with attendant cabooses. Hot-box detectors were installed at strategic points in the trackage for radio report of abnormal temperatures in the bearings or journal boxes of the rolling stock.

On the entry of Newfoundland into Confederation, the new province possessed a single radio link with Canada through a service between New Waterford in Nova Scotia and Table Mountain, in the extreme southwest corner of the island. When this proved inadequate to meet the needs of the growing traffic, Canadian National Railways in 1957 built a 600-channel microwave circuit, equipped to handle a television network, between Sydney in Cape Breton and St. John's.

At company headquarters in Montreal, electronic calculators had been installed in the accounting offices. By 1950, the traffic was so heavy that it became necessary to create, a new department, with seventeen control boards and 250 miles of wire on its operations floor, providing a capacity of eighty-three thousand messages daily. In the following year, punch card machines, which had been employed on miscellaneous duties previously, were enrolled in an integrated data registration system, so that every move of every train in operation could be traced instantaneously.

Teleprinters and data-flow machines took over the processing of waybills and other standard documentation.

An Imposing Partnership

In 1947, the Canadian Pacific Railway and Canadian National Railways had agreed to pool their revenues on private wire operations in certain highly competitive areas. Thus began Canadian National–Canadian Pacific Communications. The association proved profitable, and it gradually expanded until it covered all communications facilities in such areas. In 1961, it became a nationwide service, and it grew necessary to build a new microwave network 3,375 miles in length, from Montreal to Vancouver. The western section of 1,425 miles, from Melville to the Pacific port, was built by Canadian National Railways. It consisted of thirty-nine stations, of which two were perched on peaks of the Rockies that could only be reached by aerial tramways. This service, opened on May 11, 1964, provided six hundred channels that could be used for either voice, telegraph, telephone, or facsimile or adapted for any other type of transmission.

Out of the standing agreement with the Canadian Pacific for cooperation wherever feasible, a variety of joint communications enterprises emerged. In 1955, the two companies provided Canadian Broadcasting Corporation with a French-language microwave circuit between Montreal and Quebec City, afterward to be extended to other centers. Two years later, telex services under joint sponsorship were established in twenty-one Canadian cities. In 1967, the combined services of the two railways systems were enlarged by the introduction of the Broadband Exchange Service, with a potential transmission of fifty-one thousand words a minute. It was aimed at capturing machine-to-machine communications. It could be used with tape, punch cards, and facsimile, as well as the simpler methods of transmission.

The agreement between the two systems did not cover Newfoundland or the Arctic areas. There Canadian National Railways operated independently. In its individual capacity, it undertook to provide connections with Alaska through the construction of a microwave circuit from Grande Prairie in northern Alberta to the Alaska boundary. It consisted of forty-two stations, on an average of thirty miles apart. It also provided microwave connections with the Pine Tree Radar Line and the Sago-Bomarc Missile System, with the United States defense installations in the Arctic and with the United States Air Base at Stephenville in Newfoundland.

Radical Extensions

Canadian National telephone installations led the way in the opening up of the Arctic; communications were the first of its services to break the isolation of that vast area. Within the boundaries of Alberta, the provincially controlled systems monopolized the telephone services, but throughout the 1.3 million square miles of the North West Territories, Canadian National Telecommunications was the forerunner in almost every area. It bought up a number of small exchanges, and it extended Alberta provincial telephone lines northward beyond the sixtieth parallel. It also purchased the Yukon Telephone Company and enlarged its field of operations. In 1961, it moved into the Great Slave Lake area, and by means of both radio and landline, provided such formerly isolated settlements as Hay, Pine Point, Fort Resolution, Fort Smith, Fort Providence and Yellowknife with connections with the outside world. In 1966, it built a pole line far into the north along the Mackenzie river to Inuvik, where it installed a dial service for one hundred subscribers. In the same year, it opened an exchange at Gander in Newfoundland, which provided telephone facilities for thirty-five communities in that area. Here, there and everywhere it served as watchman calling a new day; in 1962, two years before the arrival of Canadian National rails at Great Slave Lake, an American visitor wrote:

> The Canadian north is one surprise after another. A land of brave men and brave women; of Eskimos whose carvings adorn museums; of fur trappers who know Ravel from Rabelais. Yet the biggest surprise of all is the Canadian National Railways which runs trains for 365 days in the year in places where no railroad should run.[3]

The Branch Lines

Canadian National Railways had not hesitated to continue its branch lines program, particularly as a vast northern area was seeking communications with the outside world. It was manifestly impossible to allow mining towns in the high latitudes to await natural growth. The opening of an Arctic mine necessitated the prior construction of a more or less complete settlement—homes, schools, hospitals, water and electric power services, as well as groceries, hardware shops, drugstores and a hotel of sorts. When the mining companies contracted for the construction of a railway, therefore, they usually undertook at the same time to lay out a town site and to provide essential services prior to the development of the property. Thus the newly arrived railway would be assured of the traffic of a growing population in addition to the output of the mine.

The Great Slave Lake Line

Perhaps the most spectacular of the Arctic ventures was the railway to Pine Point, which would serve a highly mineralized area along the southern shore of Great Slave Lake, a full 400 miles beyond the most northering branch of Northern Alberta Railways. Already there was a scattered population of farmers and lumbermen in this area, who brought in about 30,000 tons of supplies annually by means of river boats during the four or five months on which the main Arctic streams—the Athabaska, the Peace, the Slave and the Mackenzie—were open. The favorite route of such freight had been by Northern Alberta Railways to Waterways, on the Athabaska river 300 miles north of Edmonton, where it was loaded into steamers that moved north, to be transfered to other craft beyond the portage at Lake Chipweyan for carriage down the Peace and Slave rivers and, when necessary, to destinations on the Mackenzie River, the main artery of Arctic territory. Such routing was costly and made return cargoes of bulk commodities virtually impossible.

Early surveys had selected two routes into this great wilderness. A line directly north from Waterways would be the shortest, but it traversed less accommodating terrain. Moreover, the whooping crane stood in its way. The only sanctuary in the world of this rare bird lay in the northwest corner of Wood Buffalo Park, and a Waterways extension would pass through it. The Audubon Society therefore made vigorous protests and a takeoff from Northern Alberta Railways 225 miles further west was selected in its stead. Its point of departure was at Roma, beyond Peace River Crossing and 310 miles to the northwest of Edmonton. The route chosen ran due north to Hay River on Great Slave Lake, thence along the foreshore of that expanse to the mineralized area at Pine Point, a distance of 377 miles in all. It roughly followed the upper Mackenzie River Valley and traversed a huge tract of land that, despite its high latitude, was protected by mountain ranges to the west and, as a consequence, enjoyed a climate only a little more severe than the open prairies to the south of the bushland. Over half of the area traversed by this route therefore possessed agricultural potential.

During the 1950s, Consolidated Mining and Smelting Company, one of the larger Canadian mineral organizations, expressed its interest in the

Pine Point area. In 1959, a Royal Commission reported favorably on it, and the Alberta provincial government offered to pay for the construction of the line, the cost being estimated at $86.25 million. In 1961, a Canadian National survey reported few serious obstacles, and the company undertook to build and to operate the railway, under the provisos that it should be completed within four years and that it would be guaranteed a minimum freight of 215,000 tons of mineral concentrates annually.

Modern construction methods—lining up.

A number of machines were developed by Canadian National Railways to minimize hand labor on savage terrain and increase the efficiency of tracklaying equipment, thus easing the impact of the climate on the construction crews. There was little muskeg or other morass; most of the streams to be bridged were narrow, with convenient rocky approaches; an exception was the Meikle River, which required a bridge 2,000 feet in length. As the steel advanced, the population of the countryside increased perceptibly, and grain elevators soon began to go up at the larger settlements. In October 1964, when the crossing out of Alberta into the North West Territories was celebrated, steel laying was well ahead of schedule. The track was ready in the following spring, and the first shipments of ore left Pine Point in November 1964, a full year ahead of the contract date.

Before the line was finished, the province of Alberta had approached Canadian National Railways anew, offering a similar contract for the construction of a railway one hundred miles in length northward from Solo-

New methods—automatic spike driving.

Pine Point, Arctic mining town. Open work mine pits are visible at the top of the picture.

mon, near Jasper, into the foothills of the Rockies, where large coal deposits and timber stands awaited exploitation. This line, named the Alberta Resources Railway, was completed in 1969 and placed under Canadian National management.

Other Branch Lines

Meanwhile, similar construction was under way elsewhere. In 1961, work began on sixty-five miles of line northward from the Chibougamau branch to the Lake Metagami area, where substantial zinc and copper finds were being developed. This line was opened in October 1963. In the preceding year an extension of twenty-three miles was placed in work in Alberta to permit the shipment of sulphur from the Windfall gas fields. The great Saskatchewan potash body now was fully proved, and services to handle shipments had been extended to the Yarbo region. Near Bathurst in New Brunswick, a spur fifteen miles in length afforded entry to a lead and copper development.

In 1966, work began on three branch lines, with a total trackage of ninety-five miles. One was designed to serve an iron ore deposit on Bruce Lake in Ontario, another a copper mine, also in Ontario. The third secured an outlet for a potash plant at Guernsey in Saskatchewan.

All were completed in 1968. Among other new construction were branches to a pulp mill at Fort Saskatchewan in Alberta and to a fertilizer complex at Redwater in the same province. A line sixty miles in length also was built to serve other sulphur recovery plants in the Woodfall area.

There is no reason to believe that these individual ventures will not continue and that in due course they will be linked into a new system in the sub-Arctic areas.

Newfoundland Hastens to Catch Up

In the fifteen years since Newfoundland entered Confederation and Canadian National Railways assumed control of its railway, changes have been continuous, with a view to complete integration in the national system. Mile for mile, there had been greater expenditures and more improvements than in any other Canadian area, for the Newfoundland line on its takeover was a railway of yesterday. The first major alteration had been in the roadbed, which was raised in the northern marshes to facilitate the clearances of the heavy winter snowfalls. Thereafter stretches of track that formerly had been closed for weeks at a time were cleared as soon as the snowmobile patrols reported the blockages.

As in Canada, steam had become a thing of the past. Diesel locomotives had been introduced, together with fourteen hundred pieces of new rolling stock, much of it of a specialist nature, designed to handle such freights as fish, woodpulp and iron ore. A new yard had been built at Corner Brook, and the existing St. John's installations had been enlarged. A number of new branch lines had been constructed to provide requisite services for the island's expanding industries.

The coastal fleet had been increased by 50 percent through the addition of seven new vessels. The old and slow connections with Canada had ended with the entry into service of MV *William Carson*, the world's largest icebreaking automobile ferry. With a capacity of five hundred passengers and one hundred twenty motor cars, it cut down the time of the crossing to Canada to six hours and provided a daily service. Its freight space had been containerized, with a consequent increase in the movements of frozen foods across the Cabot Strait.

In these improvements, Canadian National Railways had invested over $80 million in order to bring its new property into line with Canadian continental standards. As mentioned in an earlier chapter, the wage bill of the Newfoundland Railway had tripled since 1949, by increases of local pay to continental levels. Training had been on the same scale as on the mainland, and Newfoundlanders no longer were confined to their home stations but were to be found in employment in the other provinces. Canadian National Railways, therefore, had exercised a benignant influence not only on the local services but also on the living standards of its Newfoundland employees.

Trans-Canada Airlines

Although the Canadian National Railways air offspring is now virtually an independent operation, it is perhaps permissible to round off its story. Year by year, Trans-Canada Airlines grew, compiling new records of miles flown, of passengers borne, of freight carried. Within five years, the service opened to New York in 1946 had more than tripled its traffic, and the early deficits on the trans-Atlantic service were being reduced annually, with daily return flights to Britain. As has been previously recorded, the air services were able to intervene effectively in the rescue operations of the Red River floods. There were fourteen daily flights between Montreal and Toronto, and in 1947, an operational profit emerged for the first time.

By then, improvements in fleet and in ground installations had begun to effect economies in various directions, and under the vigorous and far-seeing leadership of President G. R. McGregor (OBE, DFC), the company marched from strength to strength. In 1952, three Constellations were ordered for the long range service, as well as twelve Vickers Viscounts and three Bristol Air Freighters. All proved to be splendid choices: the Constellations set the standards of the long-range services, the Viscounts became and remained for many years the work horses of the short runs, the Air Freighters were the first specialist planes for freight traffic to be put in service in North America. With these additions, Trans-Canada became the world's ninth largest airline. It offered twenty-six hundred seats daily, adding long-distance routes to Florida and Mexico to serve the increasing exodus of Canadians during the winter months.

In 1957, the first Douglas DC8s, with an air speed of 550 miles per hour, were acquired, together with a further fleet of Viscounts and its refinement, the Vanguard. By 1959, Trans-Canada annual earnings had soared to $120,554,768, with fourteen transcontinental flights daily and eighteen transatlantic flights weekly. Flying time had been cut on the Toronto-Vancouver route to four hours and on Montreal-London to six hours. By 1960, the fleet consisted of seven DC8s, forty-nine Viscounts and Vanguards, twenty-one Super-Constellations and twenty-one North Stars, the latter a Canadian-built adaptation that proved worthy of its company.

Air travel now was commonplace, and the introduction of economy class seating temporarily ate into the earnings of the fleet. In 1962, a sales agreement with British Overseas Airways Corporation led to a partnership on routes traversed by both airlines, with arrangements for cooperation on other services. The Rolls-Royce Dart engine now was being adopted as replacement on many aircraft; it gave forty-two hundred hours flying time between overhauls.

In 1963, Trans-Canada Airlines carried 3,883,590 passengers. In that year also, the company placed an order valued at $24 million with the Douglas company for DC9s. By 1965, operations showed a healthy profit of $6,830,156, with five all-freight services weekly traversing the Trans-Canada runs. On January 1 of that year, in conformity with European practice, Trans-Canada Airlines was renamed Air Canada.

In 1966, it showed its thirteenth profit in sixteen years. It now possessed three transborder routes—Toronto-Los Angeles, Montreal-Chicago and Montreal-Toronto-Miami. It also had opened a weekly service to Moscow via Copenhagen and had entered an option for four of the 1,500-mile-an-hour Anglo-French Concordes, if and when this controversial aircraft became available.

Because of the World Exposition at Montreal, 1967 proved a tremendous year for Air Canada. It carried 6,393,124 passengers, with an equally large increase in freight; it also provided a wide range of services in connection with the Exposition. It likewise continued to spread its wings abroad, and in 1968, it again became the partner of British Overseas Airways Corporation in the construction of terminal headquarters at New York, at a cost of $20 million.

Throughout the 1960s, Canadian manufacturers of aircraft parts and accessories greatly increased their sales to American manufacturers. It would seem to be only a matter of time until Air Canada should be able to order at least some of its aircraft at home.

Decline of Shipping Interests

As has been noted in an earlier chapter, Canadian National Railways, as partner in the Canada–West Indies Trade Agreement, built and operated the *Lady* fleet of small liners between Canada and the Commonwealth Caribbean colonies. They sustained two services—in the east, to the Leeward and Windward islands, Barbados, Trinidad and British Guiana; in the west, to Bermuda, the Bahamas, Jamaica and British Honduras. Except during the Second World War and immediately after it, neither service proved profitable, and the destruction of three of the *Lady* ships in naval operations effectively crippled the fleet. In 1952, the Canadian government gave notice that it would not replace the lost ships, and it released the Caribbean colonies from the subsidies that they contributed under their trade agreement with Canada. For five more years, however, services continued with charter ships at Canadian National Railways expense. But as the seasons passed, the volume of traffic increased sufficiently to attract private lines into the trade, and the survivors of the government services could not compete with them. In 1957, when a strike occurred on Canadian lake services, the crews on the West Indian run demanded commensurate treatment, whereupon President Gordon seized

Electronic hump yard scale, one of many machines developed by Canadian National Railways Department of Research and Development.

the opportunity to cut his losses and canceled the West Indian services. The remaining ships, by now well worn, were tied up in Canadian ports until sold to foreign companies, most of them going to Cuba.

Thereafter the company's marine interests were largely confined to the Maritime Provinces and Newfoundland. In 1953, modern ferries were introduced between North Sydney and Port aux Basques in Newfoundland and between Yarmouth and Bar Harbour in Maine. In 1961, new car ferries also were provided for the Lake Michigan services of the Grand Trunk Western Railroad. In 1965, the Newfoundland service was augmented by a passenger-auto carrier and a container ship. It became necessary to hire additional charters to cope with the growing traffic.

On the Pacific coast, the well-weathered *Prince George* continued with its summer excursions to Alaska, and the Aqua-Train from Prince Rupert made weekly trips to Alaska ports. In 1967, the Newfoundland coastal fleet was reinforced by two new vessels. The Prince Edward Island ferry service now required four ships on its regular runs. In 1969, three new ships joined the Newfoundland flotilla. Ferries began to ply between Ontario and Michigan at Sarnia. Tug and barge operations increased sharply on Lake Okanagan, as did the ferry service between Nova Scotia and Maine. The Canadian National Marine Services, therefore, still was doing what was expected of it.

Research and Development

The evolution of the Department of Research and Development out of its humble origin in 1923 as the Bureau of Railway Economics was in keeping with the times. That bureau, with R. A. C. Henry in control, was entrusted with the analysis of such economic problems as impinged on the operation of railways. But when in 1930, at the height of the depression, S. W. Fairweather took control, that brilliant officer immediately widened its scope, in recognition that mobility was the very pulsebeat of the and that anything that affected the health of the national economy sooner or later must be the concern of the railways. The role of the Department of Research and Development, therefore, became that of medical consultant—to recommend, to warn, to analyze and to prescribe—whenever changes altered the progress of the nation.

At the end of the Second World War, Canadian National Railways was well to the fore in a wide range of research; indeed, it was one of the few railways in the world to possess its own facilities for testing materials and for undertaking other types of primary investigation. The quickening technological developments of the postwar period found it particularly well situated to make expert evaluations of the multitude of new machines, materials and methods on offer. The appointment in 1957 of Dr. O. M. Solandt (OBE, DSC, MD), a distinguished Canadian scientist who had been employed on important assignments both in Great Britain and at home, as vice-president in charge of Research and Development, constituted significant evidence of the importance attached to current developments and to the determination of Canadian National Railways to keep up with, if not ahead of, the times.

As the years passed, with major reorganizations of management and services, the tasks of the Department of Research and Development multiplied. In 1963, it added a new laboratory for the purpose of extending the scope of its evaluations. This became known as the Technical Research Center, and in addition to routine duties, it was entrusted with such diverse and elaborate studies as soil mechanics, track materials and structures, equipment design, lubrication and fuel investigations, corrosion control and low-temperature operational problems. A special car was equipped with electronic devices for the study of trackage under various loadings and movements. This machine eventually was patented in eleven foreign countries. An electronic scale also was devised for weighing freight cars in motion.

A particularly successful project was an investigation of damage in transit by abrasion due to contact with the walls of the freight carriers during the inevitable oscillations of the train's motions. A new coating was devised that reduced claims by 50 percent over those incurred by former paints or dressings. Pneumatic pressure hoppers were developed for loading and unloading certain freights; they materially cut the cost of former operations. A Customers' Research Service was empowered to investigate any complaint that could be attributed justly to present railway operational methods or equipment.

In 1966, Research and Development was engaged in a widespread inquiry into the problem of balance in freight and passenger cars. This was in anticipation of the introduction of the new high-speed turbo trains. In this year also there were experiments with hydraulic "end of car" draft gears; the reports of this device aroused deep interest among other railways. Recommendations of economies in the handling of bulk commodities in loading, unloading and storage, also proved of deep interest to railway communities everywhere.

In 1967, Canadian National was host to the Second International Symposium on Cybernetics in Railways. More than two hundred dele-

Current competitors (FROM LEFT): British 4472, Canadian steam 6218, Canadian Diesel 2302, Turbo Diesel 1970.

gates from the great railways of the world were in attendance and some
forty technical papers, including a number of Canadian National Railways officers, were discussed and digested. As aftermath to this honor, the
Technical Research Branch learned that it had qualified for a federal
government grant for its assistance to industry. During the year, four
patents were granted on auxiliary devices developed by the department,
and all were destined to earn fees and royalties in Canada and abroad.

Research never stands still, and the ambit of Department of Research
and Development investigations constantly widened until it reached well
beyond the immediate concerns of the day and provided valuable indications of what tomorrow might bring. By 1968, pollution was a subject of
anxiety throughout the world, and methods to combat the contamination
of air and water were added to the list of Research and Development
tasks in hand. But the department had not in any degree neglected its
primary duties. A device for detecting abnormalities in Diesel locomotives and a computer designed to record trackage variations were among
the items patented and placed on sale toward the close of the 1960s.

Thus the record ran, year after year. Any prospects of improving
transportation facilities or the standards of community service were
deemed to be within the province of the Department of Research and
Development.

Technology for the World at Large

Since 1945, Canadian National Railways has designed and constructed more mileage than any other railroad in the Western World. Such
activity did not go unnoticed abroad, and many requests were received
for advice and assistance from the new nations that were struggling to
catch up with the times. On March 28, 1968, an International Consulting
Division was formed to offer the fruits of Canadian National Railways
experience abroad. The service was launched with an assignment in
Turkey in July of that year, to be followed almost immediately with a
request for assistance to Argentina. Early in 1969, there followed a commission to examine and make recommendations on the Jamaican Railway. By then, the division was committed to its first major assignment
in the form of a study and report on the Korean National Railroad, an
appointment that was obtained in competition with five other foreign
firms. No less than seventeen technicians from Canadian National Railways participated in this task. Thereafter other offers came thick and
fast. By the end of 1970, the division had completed sixteen contracts

abroad, in areas as diverse as Australia, Botswana (formerly the British protectorate of Bechuanaland, which lies astride the railway that Cecil Rhodes began to build, more than seventy years ago, as the first leg of the Cape to Cairo Railroad), Brazil, Ceylon, Chile, Camaroons, Congo-Ocean Railway (in the former French Congo), as well as varying assignments in Mexico, Nigeria, Pakistan and the former British East Africa group of new nations. These enterprises showed a profit on Canadian National Railways outlays, but their real value lay in the advertisement abroad of Canadian skills and talents and the consequent enhancement of the Canadian image in the far parts of the earth. At the close of 1970, the International Consulting Division had nine foreign contracts in work.

Forty Years of Motion Pictures

It will be remembered that as early as 1923, Canadian National Railways was dispatching radio programs to moving trains. This initiative undoubtedly led to the production of the company's first motion pictures. The talented group contributing to the inception of this enterprise included Merrill Dennison, afterward historian of the Bank of Montreal, Courtenay Ryly Cooper, a well-known American feature writer, and particularly Sir Tyrone Guthrie, who made an invaluable contribution to Canadian culture by his role in the foundation of the Stratford Shakespearean Theatre.

The first company motion picture on record, entitled *One Perfect Day*, was produced in 1927. By 1931, the railway catalogue listed forty-seven films available for exhibitors. The great Canadian outdoors provided the subject matter of most of them; fifteen films were devoted entirely to fishing excursions, others to hunting and to winter sports, but there also were "scenics," with producer Bill Robinson strapped on the cowcatcher of a locomotive or bouncing high in the prow of a canoe as it catapulted through rapids. Film libraries were established at a score of passenger departments in Canada and the United States and afterward in Great Britain, Australia and New Zealand. With the advent of television, these films acquired new audiences, and by 1960, they had achieved a quality that made them acceptable for general exhibition.

By then, the intricacy of many of the railway-sponsored productions had compelled the Photographic Section to order films, in part at least, from professional producers. Nevertheless approximately half of the footage continued to be company-made. Sometimes considerable cooperation prevailed; for instance, in the 1965 feature *The Railrodder*, starring

Canadian National Railways motion pictures: Buster Keaton in *The Railrodder*.

Buster Keaton, the National Film Board made the film, with Canadian National Railways providing all settings and properties. The first company cartoon film, made in 1971, dealt with containerization. In that year, there were twenty-eight Canadian National films on offer, which it was estimated would obtain eighteen thousand screenings before audiences approximating 1.5 million viewers. There would be in addition approximately six hundred theatrical bookings in Canada and abroad. Two Canadian National Railways films had won awards at United States industrial film festivals.

During the 1960s, film became a major device in teaching railway employees their jobs. Almost any railway operation could be explained expertly on the screen. In 1969, a section of the public relations department was entrusted with the production of videotapes designed to convey increased knowledge of operational routines so that every employee could become familiar with basic details that until recent years had been the province only of the specialists.

At the World Exposition

The World Exposition of 1967, staged on the shores and islands of the St. Lawrence in the midst of the city of Montreal, was designed to illustrate in every possible particular the theme of "Man and His World." Nowhere was this concept better exemplified than in the magnificent pavilion of Canadian National Railways. There a series of huge exhibit cells, arranged in a geometrical pattern, portrayed diverse and diverting expositions of Time and Motion, perhaps the two predominating factors in the growth of mankind. The static exhibits depicted how time, from the earliest ages, has served man and has shaped his functional progress. In an adjoining theater, a huge screen portrayed the impacts and exploitations of motion, from a crawling baby to breathtaking free-fall sky-diving. One observer described this panorama as "tender, powerful and exciting." This pavilion, at a cost of $1.3 million, was conspicuous, amid an array of outstanding exhibits, in its portrayal of the impact of natural circumstances on the progress of the human species.

Real Estate Operations

The passage of the years had brought unexpected dividends to Canadian National Railways. The early lines embodied in its system had been built into the centers of the Canadian towns or else the towns had grown up around the railway yards and stations. In either event, when the urbanization of Canada went into high gear after the Second World War, the railways found themselves with considerable property whose earning power would be enhanced if it were used for other than railway purposes. It was this circumstance that put Canadian National Railways into the real estate business.

Montreal was a classic instance of the existing situation. There Canadian National Railways had inherited with the Mackenzie and Mann estate twenty-two acres of land around the southern portals of the Mount Royal tunnel. The old city, built along the ridge between the St. Lawrence River and the St. Pierre Rivulet, could not possibly retain its status as the center of Montreal, for that city was growing like a bad weed, particularly northward over the crown of the St. Lawrence escarpment and up the easy slopes of Mount Royal. The Mackenzie and Mann inheritance lay directly in the path of this progress, and during the 1950s, the company had begun to put part of this holding to more profitable employment. The International Aviation Transport Building went up on its northeast corner: company headquarters, seventeen stories high, rose on its southwest corner beside the enlarged station, against whose rear stood the great bulk of the Queen Elizabeth Hotel, fronting on Dorchester Street. But on the opposite side of that street lay six more or less empty acres that clamored for attention. There were buildings of sorts on parts of them, but its strategic location made it an inevitable site for a major development.

President Gordon had received inquiries concerning the availability of this land, but nothing of a concrete nature occurred until Bill Zeckendorff came to town. He was advance man and principal persuader of Webb and Knapp, who specialized in the construction of huge urban complexes, which often were small towns set cosily in the midst of great cities. He told Gordon what he wanted to do, and he intrigued the president sufficiently to induce him to visit New York for a closer look at Webb and Knapp. Thereafter negotiations were placed in train. Zeckendorff, in his lusty, gusty autobiography, gives details of what followed, together with pen pictures of his Montreal colleagues. Gordon, he said, led the Canadian group. He was the only man whom Zeckendorff had ever encountered who could outdrink him. James Muir, president of the Royal Bank of Canada, was a tough man; a few generations back he would have been chieftain of a lawless Scottish clan. Jean Drapeau, mayor of Montreal, was a clear-headed, agile negotiator. Lazarus Phillips, outstanding lawyer and leader of the Jewish community, was a percipient and farsighted advisor.

A Great Structure

Out of the gestation of this group came Place Ville-Marie, a complex such as Canada had never known. Its main structure would be a cruciform skyscraper forty stories in height. (In order to preserve its lead over rivals, it eventually ended with forty-seven stories.) The building would provide 1.6 million square feet of office space, but its principal property would be underground, where a network of three miles of subway passages, many of them lined with shops, would afford access to a metro and two railway stations, ten office buildings, twenty-two hundred hotel rooms, thirty-six restaurants, four cinemas, four thousand parking spaces and eventually to Place Bonaventure, a great exhibition and shopping hall of 2 million square feet covering the entrances of Canadian National tracks as they approached the station over the rooftop levels of the streets below.

Place Ville-Marie was completed in 1962 and Place Bonaventure in 1967. Because of their size and intricacy they became in a trice not only the center of Montreal but also the outstanding instance of correlated construction in all Canada. In 1964, an office building of twenty-eight stories sprang up between the Queen Elizabeth Hotel and the Aviation Building, thus closing the last gap in the solid frontage of Canadian National holdings on Dorchester Street.

Canadian National Railways complex, Montreal.

Toronto Also in the Field

By then, there was an even greater project in the offing. In December 1968, Canadian National Railways and the Canadian Pacific Railway announced their partnership, in Toronto, in Metro Centre, whose magnitude put everything accomplished to date into the shade. The property concerned consisted of 190 acres of railway land between Yonge and Bathurst streets, in the heart of the city, and the project included the construction of a new passenger terminal that would integrate rail, commuter, bus and air depots, with the addition of a communications broadcasting complex, convention halls and trade centers. Its cost was estimated at $1 billion, and it would take fifteen years to complete it.

In addition to this combined project, Canadian National Railways in the same year placed in work an individual enterprise on eight acres of its land at the junction of Main and Danforth streets in southeastern Toronto. Here $15 million was invested in Main Center, whose principal components are three high-rise towers containing eleven hundred apartments for low-income occupants, together with surrounding shopping, recreation and parking facilities. This project was due for completion in 1971.

Progress Elsewhere

In 1960, negotiations began in Moncton for the conversion of twenty-five acres of railway land in the center of the town into a modern business complex. The construction would include a new station, as well as a terminal and a staff office building. By the following year, the project was in full swing; it transformed the Moncton downtown area with an array of new shops, office buildings, restaurants and auxiliary enterprises. A similar project on a smaller scale had been placed in work at Campbellton in northern New Brunswick and at London in southern Ontario.

In mid-1963, twenty-four acres of railway land became available for redevelopment in the heart of Saskatoon, through the decision to remove all railways installations across the Saskatchewan River to the Chappell suburb on the southwestern outskirts of the city. The land freed by this move proved ground space for a centennial auditorium and for Midtown Plaza, which would comprise a twelve-story office building, two department stores and a range of small shops, involving in all a private investment of $15 million.

In other cities, without involving the evacuation of railway installations, it was found possible to increase the community value of railway
property by additional developments. As an example, in Edmonton construction began in 1964 on a twenty-five-story office building, which, in
addition to other tenants, housed the railway station and the company
offices. It was the tallest building at that time on the Canadian prairies.
In 1967, similar work began on company land in the rear of Hotel Vancouver, where a five-hundred-car parking garage was topped by a four-
teen-story office building.

Industrial Promotions

It was not only in the cities that Canadian National Railways turned
its land holdings to good account. The rapid industrialization of the period had led to constantly increasing inquiries for additional properties.
The extraction of mineral products in Canada tripled in little more than a
decade to a value of $6 billion annually, and the incessantly mounting
demand for mineral byproducts in the United States brought hundreds of
new factories into production throughout Canada. A section of the Department of Research and Development undertook to assist prospective
customers in choosing their sites. In 1960, more than four hundred new
factories chose to build beside Canadian National lines. They required
in all forty-one miles of spurs, sidings and other industrial trackage. It
became necessary to plan industrial parks in which factories could group
to advantage; in the construction of such areas, Canadian National Railways participated. In 1961, no less than 708 industrial enterprises selected properties contiguous to the company's lines, and 201 of them
required sidings or other auxiliary services. In the period 1960–1969
4,005 industrial ventures chose sites adjacent to Canadian National Railway lines, creating a substantial volume of new traffic. In eighteen Canadian and American cities, research and development offices now proffer
advice and assistance; their efforts are reinforced by an international
advertising campaign that draws inquiries from faraway places. In
1970, eleven new industrial parks were opened and five hundred additional business establishments selected sites beside Canadian National
tracks.

Labor Relations

Canadian National Railways labor relations in postwar years faithfully reflected the sociological fluctuations of this higglety-pigglety period. The company was still something of a family, but its ties were honored as much in the breach as in the observance. Communications media incessantly fostered social ambitions which only money, and more money, could satisfy. There was scarcely a year in which wage increases were not presented, and almost inevitably the employer compromised in the face, if not of demands, of subsequent threats. That such confrontations seldom resulted in an open break, as was sought by a militant minority of the workers, bespoke the presence of cool heads and common sense on both sides.

In 1956, payrolls amounted to 60.2 percent of total railway operating expenditures. Over the next three years, a number of agreements were negotiated that, in all, cost the company an additional $40 million annually. In the autumn of 1957, the nonoperating employees, seventy-seven thousand strong, demanded additional benefits that would have raised their wages by $75 million over the next three years. A settlement was reached in 1959 which awarded increases of 10 percent over the next four years. At the same time, other employees, probably because of a similar increase of twenty-five cents an hour in the United States, demanded equal treatment but were held to a modest advance.

Fewer Jobs Now Available

A new factor now supervened. Technology was taking an increasing toll of the number of jobs available. In 1956, the total company strength stood at 126,859 employees. By 1960, it had fallen to 104,375 staff of all ranks. In the following year, employment dropped below the hundred thousand mark. The bitter controversy over the removal of firemen from Diesels had been prelude to many similar adjustments of labor force throughout the system. The company realized the predicaments of its workers and increased its training programs, with a view not only to fitting as many as possible into new jobs but also to upgrading the skills of those who remained in their former employments. During 1960, 3,560 railwaymen attended training courses with a view to permitting them to hold their old jobs or to prepare them for new ones. No outside labor was hired if a present employee was available.

In 1961, after long negotiations, all express, cartage and freight handling staff were combined in a union twenty thousand strong. As a result of various representations, increases of pay averaging sixteen cents an hour were granted. This was not considered sufficient, in large part because scarcely a week passed without report of a new increase or strike on American railways. Negotiations in Canada, however, remained on a friendly level, with the majority of the staff appreciating the efforts of the company to keep them in employment. In that year, no less than forty-eight thousand employees applied for retraining courses, a considerable number taking more than one course. Increases of pay in 1960 and 1961 averaged fourteen cents an hour, and during this period, the employees accepted many changes in work rules necessitated by altered routines.

Throughout 1962, negotiations continued with such goodwill that the report of a conciliation board was accepted unanimously by management and by fifteen unions representing sixty thousand employees. Minor increases of pay were granted, in some instances in contracts covering as much as five years. In all, 178 collective agreements were negotiated by thirty-five unions, representing eighty-eight thousand seven hundred employees. There were sixty-two thousand enrollments for special training, and by means of bulletins, news letters and films, employees were kept abreast of current developments and changes. The company made no secret of the fact that its employees on its Grand Trunk Western group and the Central Vermont lines were better paid than corresponding Canadian ranks because of the rulings of a United States presidential commission; but the Canadian railway unions were less given to threats and ultimatums than their American colleagues, and they found management more approachable and understanding. Canadian National Railways gave modest advances whenever possible. In 1964, there were two increases, of 5 percent and five cents an hour that covered most employees.

Establishment of Office of Arbitration

On July 1, 1965, a Railway Office of Arbitration was established for the first time in Canada. Many of the larger unions immediately announced their intention of accepting its decisions. On the same date, the Canadian Labour (Standards) Code became effective. It set minimum wages, working hours, vacations and holidays for all employees covered by federal legislation. These two enactments did much to stabilize employer-employee relations, which were further improved by a series of joint labor-management investigations of railway problems. As instances, management and unions joined in a study of problems arising out of the closing of the London car shops, the handling of traffic from Cape Breton to Newfoundland across Cabot Strait and an inspection and report on bunkhouse facilities everywhere across Canada.

There Were Still Clashes

These cooperative measures, while highly satisfactory, did not always avert clashes. Dieselization imposed swifter and longer runs, with consequent changes of terminals. In October 1964, the company dispensed with some terminals in northern Ontario and in Alberta, inaugurating longer run-throughs. There was an immediate outcry and resistance by the trainmen and the Prime Minister appointed an Industrial Inquiry Commission. It was nearly a year before its report was tabled, but it recommended that impending changes in routines should be discussed with the unions involved—a sensible finding that proved satisfactory to nearly everyone.

In the autumn of 1965, strong union groups, representing 64,912 employees, demanded substantial increases of wages, together with important fringe benefits. Five months of negotiations and the efforts of four conciliation boards failed to break the deadlock, and in August, the workers, for the first time in fourteen years, walked off their jobs. As in 1952, Parliament acted swiftly. On September 1, at an Emergency Session, it ordered resumption of operations immediately. An 18 percent wage increase was authorized, phased over two years, with compulsory arbitration should mediation fail. The result of such arbitration was the award in 1967 of 24 percent increases in pay over a period of three years.

More Protection for Employees

By 1968, the working staff had been reduced to 85,240 employees and every effort was made to find alternate employment either within or outside the company for those whom the changes had made redundant. Benefits to laid-off employees were increased, a Voluntary Early Retirement Plan went into effect and the company established a Centennial Scholarship Plan for dependants of employees and pensioners. At the end of that year renewed negotiations over pay led to awards by the Office of Arbitration of a small addition to wages for the next two years. A public relations course had been introduced to provide supervisors who would explain the workings of the system to all ranks and familiarize them with

Cartoon entitled "His Last Run" from *The Montreal Star,* December 29, 1966.
(COURTESY OF *The Montreal Star*)

the problems of management in a nationwide railway structure. They
would be able to speak in down-to-earth language of the relationship of all
employees to each other and to the common task. Above all else, they
would seek to preserve the family atmosphere and to treat all members
alike. This course, purely voluntary, drew more than twelve hundred members of the company to its sessions in its first two years.

The Pension Fund

The company pension fund is a story in itself. It is the family savings,
kept first under a brick in the fireplace, then in a stocking, then in a bank,
growing steadily and ever improving its terms of subscription and payout.
There were major changes in its procedures in 1935, 1952, 1959 and 1962,
but all were designed ultimately to improve the lot of the pensioners. In
1960, the company became an individual subscriber and paid up its
whack each year, instead of charging itself annually with the outlays of
the preceding year. By then, the fund had assets of $708,145,711. On

January 1, 1961, additional flexibility was sanctioned: thereafter any employee with fifteen years' service who had reached the age of sixty might become eligible for pension. In 1962, the subscription rate was slightly increased, and a higher return was stipulated accordingly. At this time the annual payouts were about twice the interest earned each year on the pension fund investments. In addition to ordinary pensions, Canadian National Railways in 1964 found $6.9 million for welfare projects, which included medical care, life insurance and other benefits for its employees. By 1966, the total assets of the fund had mounted to $1,261,818,658, with charges against it, including regular pensions, payments on termination of service, subscriptions to other federal, provincial and United States retirement funds, amounting to $55.4 million. On December 31, 1968, the total pension reserve fund stood at $1,414,744,356. In that year it had received subscriptions from employees, from the company and from earnings on investments totaling $107,185,269, and it had disbursed $53,500,000 to 34,768 pensioners.

Gordon Goes

On December 31, 1966, Donald Gordon retired. The Prime Minister led the chorus of acclaim and regret. He described Gordon as a truly great Canadian, "skillful in controversy, eloquent in debate, steadfast in his missions, a boon companion in his off-duty hours. The nation has enlisted too few of his calibre. Gordon leaves in the hearts of those who had the privilege of working with him the indelible impression that the Company has had at its head a man whose name is already part of the history of our country, a man who has become a legend in his own lifetime." Perhaps his crowning achievement was the proof that a publicly owned utility could be managed just as well and would be of equal value to the community as a private enterprise. That there had been errors and lacks in the conduct of Canadian National Railways was plain for all to see, but it was equally plain that the blame in such instances rested less on Gordon's shoulders than on those of the people of Canada, whom he faithfully represented on every occasion.

His legacy to Canada was a proud property. Canadian National Railways possessed more than 35,000 miles of tracks, with its network of services operating in all ten provinces of Canada, in the North West Territories and in twelve of the United States. Its gross revenues exceeded a billion dollars annually, its inherited indebtedness from its components had been reduced from a staggering sum to a mere 2.2 percent of its annual revenues. At a time when railways were facing mortal challenges from other carriers, it had more than held its own, with earnings that mounted year by year. It had conformed to or had improved upon every technological advance; its skills in operations, in management, in research, in anticipating the trends of tomorrow, had been recognized and had brought it handsome commissions from abroad. It had put the stamp of authority on those who served it.

Donald Gordon was succeeded as president by his faithful adjutant, Norman John MacMillan, who was born at Bracebridge, Ontario, in 1909 and had joined the Canadian National Railways in the 1930s as solicitor in the Winnipeg office. He rose steadily, becoming a vice-president in 1949. In 1956, he was appointed the president's second-in-command as executive vice-president. For ten years thereafter, he proved a courageous and efficient chief of staff, not only carrying out orders but on occasion improving on them. During the Second World War, he was loaned to the Canadian government as one of the organizers of the Commonwealth Air Training Plan, to whose sixty-five schools and airfields thousands of volunteers from all parts of the world flocked to be trained for battle in the skies. On return to civilian employment, he quickly earned his laurels in his reorganization of the Law Department of Canadian National Railways. He exhibited astonishing mastery of detail, and an admirer wrote, "he talks of roadbeds and tracks with the familiarity of a section hand . . . his unflappable temperament is equal to any challenge. He seems to have a built-in governing mechanism which . . . is revealed in his manner of speaking—down to earth simplicity, couched in full, carefully-phrased sentences."

Under such leadership, the passing of Gordon did not signalize the end of an era so much as its amplification to meet whatever challenges lay ahead. Canadians retain, to a greater degree than their cousins and neighbors, a commendable caution concerning the New Thing. They prefer to wait and see how it works elsewhere. But with MacMillan at the helm, the delay in arriving at decisions will not be overlong; nevertheless he will retain his respect for the lesson learned yesterday. He undoubtedly subscribes to the dictum of Sir Henry Thornton, voiced half a century ago, that "there could be no prouder title than 'servant of a common cause.'" He will see that in Canadian National Railways, the family atmosphere and the pride in public service lives on. This residue of loyalty and of community of outlook is no mean possession in a century so palpably poised between yesterday and tomorrow.

Appendix

DETAILS OF CONSTITUENTS OF CANADIAN NATIONAL RAILWAYS

The principal groups comprising this system entered as follows:

National Transcontinental (origin)	1915
Canadian Northern	1917
Grand Trunk	1918
Intercolonial	1919
Newfoundland	1949

	LENGTH	OPENED
NEWFOUNDLAND		
Newfoundland Railway:		
St. John's—Port aux Basques	547 miles	1884–1910
Four branch lines	249 miles	1884–1910
PRINCE EDWARD ISLAND		
Prince Edward Island Railway:		
Charlottetown—Tignish	115 miles	1874
Five branch lines	182 miles	1904–12
NOVA SCOTIA		
Intercolonial Railway group		
Nova Scotia Railway:		
Halifax—Truro—Pictou	165 miles	1858–67
Oxford Junction—Pictou	67 miles	1890
Eastern Extension Railway:		
New Glasgow—Canso	80 miles	1879
Cape Breton Main Line:		
Canso—Sydney	100 miles	1890

	LENGTH	OPENED
Cape Breton Railway Extension Company		
Hawkesbury—St. Peters	31 miles	1903
Musquodoboit Railway		
Halifax—Deans Corners	69 miles	1915
Intercolonial Railway:		
Truro—Amherst	85 miles	1872
Mackenzie and Mann, afterward the		
Canadian Northern group:		
Central Railway of Nova Scotia	72 miles	1890
Halifax and Southwestern Railway	185 miles	1904–1905
Inverness Railway	60 miles	1901
Middleton and Victoria Beach Railway	39 miles	1907
Liverpool and Milton Railway	5 miles	1907

NEW BRUNSWICK

Intercolonial Railway group

	LENGTH	OPENED
European and North American Railway:		
Saint John—Shediac	111 miles	1860
Intercolonial Railway (main line):		
Amherst—Riviere du Loup	423 miles	1876
National Transcontinental Railway (main line):		
Moncton—Riviere Bleue	276 miles	1907–11
International Railway Company of		
New Brunswick		
Campbellton—St. Leonard	111 miles	1898–1910
New Brunswick and Prince Edward		
Island Railway		
Sackville—Cape Tormentine	36 miles	1882–86
Albert Railway:		
Salisbury—Albert	45 miles	1874–76
Elgin and Havelock Railway:		
Peticodiac—Havelock	28 miles	1885
Saint Martins Railway (abandoned 1940):		
Hampton—St. Martins	29 miles	1878
Buctouche and Moncton Railway		
Moncton—Buctouche	32 miles	1887
Kent Northern Railway:		
Kent Junction—Richibucto	26 miles	1883
Canada Eastern Railway:		
Fredericton—Loggieville	150 miles	1887
Intercolonial Railway:		
Miramichi—Indian Town	15 miles	1887

	LENGTH	OPENED
York and Carleton Railway:		
Cross Creek—Ryan Creek	10 miles	1909
Caraquet and Gulf Shore Railway:		
Gloucester Junction—Sheila	73 miles	1895–1911
St. John and Quebec Railway:		
Saint John—Grand Falls	158 miles	1912–19
Canadian National Railways construction (after 1922):		
Bartiborg—Heath Steele	33 miles	1953
Bathurst spur	15 miles	1963
QUEBEC		
Intercolonial Railway:		
Riviere du Loup—Levis	115 miles	1879
National Transcontinental Railway (transcontinental line):		
Riviere Bleue—Ontario boundary	651 miles	1912
Grand Trunk Railway Group:		
Montreal—Ontario boundary	48 miles	1856
Quebec—Richmond	100 miles	1852
Montreal—Richmond—Island Pond	158 miles	1852
Montreal—St. John—Rouses Point	51 miles	1863
St. John—Waterloo	43 miles	1883
Brosseau—Valleyfield	81 miles	1893
Montreal—Moers	38 miles	1852
Montreal—Lachine	9 miles	1847
Montreal—Farnham—Stanbridge	62 miles	1877–82
Ste. Martine—Valleyfield	19 miles	1888
Southern Counties (electric)— abandoned in 1956	41 miles	1923
Canadian Northern Railway group:		
Quebec—Chicoutimi	227 miles	1912
Chambord—St. Felicien	18 miles	1917
Linton—La Tuque	40 miles	1907
Great Northern Railway of Canada	308 miles	1903
Montfort Colonization Railway	31 miles	1903
Canadian National Railways purchases 1919–51		
Matapedia—Gaspe	202 miles	1893–1912
Drummond County Railway	130 miles	1898
Sorel—Iberville	60 miles	1895
Temiscouata Railway	113 miles	1889–90
Quebec—Murray Bay	87 miles	1888–1912

	LENGTH	OPENED
Canadian National Railway construction after 1922:		
Beattyville—Chibougamau	161 miles	1953
Extension to St. Felicien	150 miles	1953
Metagami spur	65 miles	1954
Noranda—Rouyn Loop Line	145 miles	1928–37

NEW ENGLAND STATES

These railways passed into the control of the
Grand Trunk Railway group in 1898:

Atlantic and St. Lawrence Railroad:		
Island Pond—Portland	158 miles	1852
Central Vermont Railway:		
Windsor—Rouses Point	158 miles	1851
Sullivan County Railroad:		
Windsor—Bellows Falls	25 miles	1849
Vermont Valley Railroad:		
Bellows Falls—Brattleboro	23 miles	1865
Rutland Railroad:		
Brattleboro—Millers Falls	26 miles	1865
New London Northern Railroad:		
Millers Falls—New London	100 miles	1871
St. Albans—Richford	28 miles	1874
Essex Junction—Burlington	8 miles	1860
Fonda Junction—Highgate	11 miles	1851
Highgate—Farnham	28 miles	1851

ONTARIO

National Transcontinental Railway main line:		
Quebec to Manitoba boundaries	956 miles	
Canadian Northern Railway main line:		
Toronto to Manitoba boundary	1171 miles	
Grand Trunk Railway group:		
Toronto—Quebec boundary	294 miles	1856
Toronto—Sarnia	179 miles	1859
Midland Railway group, taken over by the Grand Trunk group in 1884:		
Toronto and Nipissing Railway	78 miles	1871–72
Lake Simcoe Junction Railway	26 miles	1877

	LENGTH	OPENED
Port Whitby and Port Perry Railway:		
Whitby—Port Perry	19 miles	1871
Port Perry—Lindsay	26 miles	1877
Victoria Railway	35 miles	
Belleville and North Hastings Railway	22 miles	1878
Grand Junction Railway:		
Belleville—Peterborough	64 miles	1878–79
Toronto and Ottawa Railway (in part)	30 miles	1882–83
Midland Railway of Canada	45 miles	
Port Hope, Lindsay and Beaverton Railway:		
Port Hope—Lindsay (South Junction)	42 miles	1857
Northern Railway group, taken over by the		
Grand Trunk Railway group in 1888:		
North Simcoe Railway:		
Colwell—Penetanguishene	34 miles	1878
Toronto, Simcoe and Muskoka Junction Railway:		
Barrie—Gravenhurst	42 miles	1875
Northern and Pacific Junction Railway:		
Gravenhurst—Callendar	111 miles	1886
Hamilton and Northwestern Railway:		
Port Dover—Collingwood—Allandale	150 miles	1875
North Grey Railway:		
Collingwood—Meaford	22 miles	1872
Great Western Railway group, taken over by the		
Grand Trunk Railway in 1882:		
Main line: Toronto—Windsor	228 miles	1855
London—Sarnia	78 miles	1858
Hamilton—Niagara Falls	43 miles	1853
Canada Air Line Railway:		
Fort Erie—Glencoe	198 miles	1873
London and Port Stanley Railway	25 miles	1856
Brantford, Norfolk and Port Burwell Railway:		
Tillsonburg—Brantford	50 miles	1878
Wellington, Grey and Bruce Railway:		
Guelph—Southampton	102 miles	1871
Palmerston—Kincardine	67 miles	1874
London, Huron and Bruce Railway:		
London—Wingham	74 miles	1875
Welland Railway:		
Port Dalhousie—Port Colborne	25 miles	1859

	LENGTH	OPENED
Grand Trunk, Georgian Bay and Lake Erie Railway:		
Port Dover—Wiarton	198 miles	1876–82
Buffalo and Lake Huron Railway:		
Fort Erie—Goderich	160 miles	1864
Mackenzie and Mann—Canadian Northern group		
Toronto—Capreol	335 miles	1908
Toronto—Ottawa	219 miles	1913
Ottawa—Manitoba boundary (transcontinental line)	929 miles	1917
Hawkesbury—Ottawa	57 miles	1917
Irondale, Bancroft and Ottawa Railway:		
Irondale—Bancroft	46 miles	1909
Central Ontario Railway	156 miles	1910
Brockville, Westport and North Western Railway	45 miles	1910
Bay of Quinte Railway	85 miles	1909
Canadian National Railways construction after 1922:		
Manitouage—Lake Superior	24 miles	1953
Amesdale—Bruce Lake	66 miles	1969
Longlac—Nakina	30 miles	1923

	LENGTH	ACQUIRED
MICHIGAN		
These railways passed into the Grand Trunk Railway control as per dates given. These dates are *not* openings.		
Chicago and State Line Railway:		
Elsdon—Chicago	34 miles	1880
Chicago, Detroit and Canada Grand Trunk Junction Railroad:		
Port Huron—Detroit	60 miles	1860
Chicago and Lake Huron Railroad:		
Port Huron—Flint	66 miles	1878
Peninsular Railway (Michigan):		
Lansing—Indiana boundary	109 miles	1878
Peninsular Railroad (Indiana):		
Indiana boundary—Valparaiso	55 miles	1878
Chicago and Northeastern Railroad:		
Flint—Lansing	47 miles	1878
Valparaiso—Elsdon (built)	34 miles	1879

	LENGTH	ACQUIRED
Toledo, Saginaw and Muskegon Railway:		
Ashely—Muskegon	96 miles	1888
Cincinnati, Saginaw and Mackinaw Railroad:		
Duran—Bay City	64 miles	1890
Detroit and Grand Haven Railroad (obtained in		
the Great Western Railway merger)	1911 miles	1858
Michigan Air Line Railway:		
Richmond—Jackson	106 miles	1877

	LENGTH	OPENED
MANITOBA		
Main lines:		
National Transcontinental Railway:		
Ontario boundary—Winnipeg (end of line)	100 miles	1913
Grand Trunk Pacific Railway:		
Winnipeg—Saskatchewan boundary		
(beginning of line)	204 miles	1907
Canadian Northern Railway:		
Ontario boundary—Winnipeg—Kamsack	589 miles	1905–14
Canadian Northern Railway group		
Southern Manitoba:		
Gladstone—Winnipegosis	125 miles	1897
Port Arthur—Winnipeg	438 miles	1902
Sifton—Hudson Bay Junction	186 miles	1900
Dauphin—Grandview	29 miles	1902
Winnipeg—Emerson	66 miles	1901
Morris—Brandon	145 miles	1901
Winnipeg—Portage la Prairie	51 miles	1901
Hartney Junction—Hartney	51 miles	1901
Carman Junction—Carman	44 miles	1901
Beaver—Gladstone	18 miles	1901
Muir—Neepawa	34 miles	1902
Portage la Prairie—Delta	15 miles	1902
Oakland—Beaver	20 miles	1902
Carman—Learys	20 miles	1903
Neepawa—McCreay's Junction	37 miles	1903
Rossburn—Clanwilliam	20 miles	1903
Carberry Junction—Brandon	52 miles	1905
Learys—Somerset	15 miles	1905
Hartney—Virden	37 miles	1905
Dauphin—Westgate	171 miles	
Emerson—South Junction	71 miles	1907
Adelpha—Deloraine	28 miles	1914

	LENGTH	OPENED
Between the lake chains:		
Moore—Gypsumville	149 miles	1905
Grosse Isle—Hodgson	109 miles	
Steep Rock spur	12 miles	1914
West of Lake Manitoba:		
Oakland—Amaranth	46 miles	1907–13
East of Lake Winnipeg:		
Winnipeg—Victoria Beach	75 miles	1909–16
Beginning of the Hudson Bay Railway:		
Hudson Bay Junction—The Pas	88 miles	1910
Canadian National Railways construction		
since 1922		
Hudson Bay Railway:		
The Pas—Churchill	510 miles	1927
Sherridon branch	40 miles	1930
Rose du Lac branch	34 miles	1930
Flin Flon Railway	87 miles	1930
Pine Falls—Beaconia	19 miles	1926
Sipiwisk—Thompson	31 miles	1957
SASKATCHEWAN		
Main lines		
Grand Trunk Pacific Railway:		
Manitoba—Alberta boundary	416 miles	1905–1908
Canadian Northern Railway:		
Manitoba—Alberta boundary	366 miles	1905
Canadian Northern Railway branch lines		
Qu'Appelle, Long Lake and		
Saskatchewan Railway	249 miles	1906
Hudson Bay Junction—Saskatchewan	129 miles	1907
Swan River—Sturgis—Canora	94 miles	1908–15
Russell—Yorkton (and feeders)	155 miles	1910–15
Hallboro—Beulah	74 miles	1911
Maryfield—Bengough—Moose Jaw—Estevan	371 miles	1911–15
Saskatoon—Alsask	170 miles	1908–11
Delisle—Eston	124 miles	1908–11
Hudson Bay Junction—Prince Albert	161 miles	1909
Prince Albert—Shellbrook—Big River	79 miles	1910–11
Prince Albert—Watrous	111 miles	
Shellbrook—Turtleford	107 miles	1911–14
North Battleford—Edam	38 miles	1914
Dalmeny—Laird	28 miles	1910
Prince Albert—Frenchman Butte	193 miles	1910

	LENGTH	OPENED
Canadian National Railways construction since *takeover of Canadian Northern Railway, 1917*		
St. Brieux—Humboldt	32 miles	1920
Eston—Alsask	63 miles	1920
Aberdeen—Melfort	88 miles	1930
Bengough—Willowbunch	28 miles	
Central Butte—Dunblane	38 miles	1926
Eston—White Bear	35 miles	1937
Hudson Bay Junction—Reserve	69 miles	1930
Kelvington branch	42 miles	1921
Kindersley—Glidden	16 miles	1929
Gravelbourg Extension	31 miles	1922
Loverna branch	50 miles	1925
Mower branch	49 miles	1930
Neidpath branch	31 miles	1937
Peebles Extension	22 miles	1924
Prince Albert—Paddockwood	24 miles	1925
Radville—Weyburn	23 miles	1928
Shellbrook—Westerley	75 miles	1929
Spruce Lake branch	29 miles	1929
Turtleford branch	91 miles	1928
Unity—Bodo	51 miles	1931
Willowbrook—Parkerview Extension	22 miles	1928
North Battleford—Lloydminster	84 miles	1905
Lynn Lake Extension	144 miles	1955
Chisel Lake—Optic Lake	59 miles	1960

ALBERTA

Main lines

Grand Trunk Pacific Railway:		
Artland—Jasper	470 miles	1905–12
Canadian Northern Railway:		
Lloydminster—Lucerne	329 miles	1905–15

Note: From Edmonton to Yellowhead Pass the two main lines sometimes ran
beside each other. During World War I (1914–18) the demand for rails
for the fighting front led to the dismantling of 103 miles of Canadian
National tracks and the use of Grand Trunk Pacific trackage by both
systems thereafter—which reduced that company's mileage on this
sector to 329 miles.

	LENGTH	OPENED
Canadian Northern Railway branch lines		
Vegreville—Drumheller	173 miles	1911
Alsask—Munson	222 miles	1911
Drumheller—Calgary	85 miles	1914
Warden—Brazeau	173 miles	1914
Edmonton—Athabaska Landing	74 miles	1914
Morinville—Stony Plain	41 miles	1906
Peace River Junction—Sangudo	44 miles	1914
Edmonton—Alliance	100 miles	1916
Hanna—Cessford	47 miles	1917
Canadian National Railways construction		
after 1922		
Sangudo—Whitecourt	44 miles	1921
Acadia Valley branch	25 miles	1926
Hanna—Warden	62 miles	1926
Rosedale—Trefoil	26 miles	1929
St. Paul Extension	40 miles	1929
Whitecourt—Windfall	88 miles	1968
Great Slave Lake Railway	377 miles	1964

Northern Alberta Railways is jointly owned and operated by Canadian National Railways and Canadian Pacific Railway. Its branches are:

Edmonton—Waterways	299 miles	1923
Edmonton—McLennan—Dawson Creek	489 miles	1931
McLennan—Peace River—Hines Creek	114 miles	1930
Belvedere—Barrhead	27 miles	1927

BRITISH COLUMBIA
Main lines
Grand Trunk Pacific Railway:

Jasper—Prince Rupert	720 miles	1914

Canadian Northern Railway:

Lucerne—Port Mann	529 miles	1915–16

Branches:

Port Mann—Steveston	12 miles	1913
Port Mann—Vancouver	15 miles	1915

Canadian National Railways construction
after 1922

Kamloops—Penticton	152 miles	1925 et seq.
Victoria—Youbou	83 miles	1928
Lulu Island branch	16 miles	1932
Terrace—Kitimat	40 miles	1955

Notes

Chapter 1

1. Thomas Need, *Letters of 1830*.

Chapter 3

1. Stuart Ball Holbrook, *The Story of American Railroads* (New York: Crown Publishing Company, 1947), p. 73.
2. William Lawson Grant, *The Tribune of Nova Scotia* (Toronto: Glasgow Brook & Company, 1922), p. 100.
3. J. A. Chisholm, editor, *Speeches and Public Lectures of Joseph Howe* (Halifax Chronicle Publishing Company, 1909), Vol. II, p. 169.
4. A. R. M. Lower, *Colony to Nation* (Toronto: Longmans Green Company, 1946), p. 246.
5. O. D. Skelton, *The Railway Builders* (Toronto: Glasgow Brook and Company, 1916), p. 54.
6. Donald Creighton, *John A. MacDonald—The Young Politician* (Toronto: The Macmillan Company of Canada, 1952), p. 198.

Chapter 4

1. Thomas Storrow Brown, *The Grand Trunk Railway of Canada* (his letterbook, 1864), p. 11.
2. O. D. Skelton, *Life and Times of Alexander Tilloch Galt* (Toronto: Oxford Press, 1920), p. 73.
3. Sir Edmund Grimani Hornby, *An Autobiography* (London: Constable & Company, 1929), p. 91.
4. Donald Creighton, *John A. Macdonald—The Young Politician* (Toronto: The Macmillan Company of Canada, 1952), p. 250.
5. James Hodges, *Construction of the Great Victoria Bridge in Canada* (London: John Weale, 1860), p. 33.
6. A. W. Currie, *The Grand Trunk Railway of Canada* (Toronto: University of Toronto Press, 1957), pp. 98–99.

Chapter 5

1. Adam Shortt and Arthur G. Doughty, *Canada and Its Provinces* (Toronto: Glasgow Brook and Company, 1917), Vol. XIII, p. 131.
2. Sandford Fleming, *The Intercolonial* (Montreal: Dawson Brothers, 1876), p. 159.
3. *Ibid.*, p. 94.
4. Intercolonial Letterbooks, Public Archives, Ottawa. The Intercolonial Letter-books are not indexed. This extract is taken from an 1872 entry in which a cautious clerk has blotted out the names.
5. Pottinger Papers, Intercolonial Letterbooks, Public Archives, Ottawa. The Pottinger Papers are unindexed.
6. *Ibid.*
7. The writer was Sir Charles Tupper. Intercolonial Letterbooks, Public Archives, Ottawa.
8. Samuel O. Dunn, *Journal of Political Economy* (June 1916), p. 5.

Chapter 6

1. E. W. Guillet, *Cobourg: 1798–1848* (Oshawa: Goodfellow Printing Company, 1948), p. 17.

Chapter 7

1. G. P. de T. Glazebrook, *A History of Transportation in Canada* (Toronto: Ryerson Press, 1938), p. 298.

Chapter 8

1. Conference of six writers, *Eighty Years of Progress in British North America* (Toronto: L. Stebbins, 1863), p. 255.
2. J. M. Copeland, *The Trail of the Swinging Lanterns* (Toronto: privately printed, 1918), p. 112.
3. Myles Pennington, *Railways and Other Ways* (Toronto: Williamson and Company, 1894), p. 113.
4. A. W. Currie. *The Grand Trunk Railway of Canada* (Toronto: University of Toronto Press, 1951), p. 178.

Chapter 9

1. Donald Creighton, *Dominion of the North* (Toronto: The Macmillan Company of Canada, 1957), p. 64.

Chapter 10

1. D. B. Hanna, *Trains of Recollection* (Toronto: The Macmillan Company of Canada, 1924).
2. *Ibid.*, p. 85.
3. *Ibid.*, p. 172.
4. J. W. Davidson, "The Canadian Northern Railway," *Queen's University Quarterly* (Autumn 1906), Vol. 14, p. 108.

Chapter 11

1. Joseph Schull, *Laurier* (Toronto: The Macmillan Company of Canada, 1965), p. 424.
2. Laurier Papers, Public Archives, Ottawa.

Chapter 12

1. William Hard, "Spiking Down an Empire," *Everybody's Magazine* (November 1909).
2. A letter from C. A. Buchanan to the historian.
3. This description, written by Henry Horwood and dated February 1909, is taken from a book of clippings, which affords no other clue as to its origin.
4. William Hard, *op. cit.*

Chapter 13

1. *The Rubaiyat of Omar Khayyam*, first (nonliteral) translation by Edward FitzGerald, 1859.

Chapter 14

1. *The Railway Age Gazette* (June 22, 1917).

Chapter 15

1. *Robert Laird Borden: His Memoirs*, two vols. (Toronto: The Macmillan Company of Canada, 1938), Vol. II, p. 60.

Chapter 16

1. *Report of Lynch-Staunton-Gutelius Royal Commission*, February 12, 1914.
2. Drayton-Ackworth Royal Commission, April 1917.
3. *Proceedings of House of Commons*, Public Archives of Canada.

Chapter 17

1. Press interview in Montreal, September 20, 1922.

Chapter 18

1. Dafoe Papers, Canada Public Archives, Ottawa (not yet indexed).
2. Personal letter to Martha Watriss, June 10, 1924.
3. *Ibid.,* December 23, 1925.
4. Address to Montreal Chamber of Commerce, March 14, 1923.

Chapter 19

1. Dafoe Papers, Canada Public Archives, Ottawa.
2. Howard A. Fleming, *Canada's Arctic Outlet* (Berkeley: University of California Press, 1957), p. 163.
3. Public address, Ottawa banquet, August 14, 1927.
4. Leonard D. Myers, *Twenty-Three Skidoo* (Toronto: Kingswood House, 1958), pp. 173–174.
5. From the correspondence of Mrs. Henry James (formerly Lady Thornton).
6. Luncheon address, Toronto Board of Trade, July 16, 1928.

Chapter 20

1. A personal letter to the historian from Mrs. Henry James (formerly Lady Thornton).
2. Sir Henry Thornton's correspondence, Department of Transport, Ottawa.
3. Records of Sessional Committee, House of Commons, Public Archives, 1931.
4. D'Arcey Marsh, *The Tragedy of Sir Henry Thornton* (Toronto: The Macmillan Company of Canada, 1935), pp. 198–199.
5. R. J. Manion, *Life is an Adventure* (Toronto: Ryerson Press, 1938), p. 309.
6. From a letter in the possession of Mrs. Henry James (formerly Lady Thornton).
7. Dafoe Papers, Canada Public Archives, Ottawa.

Chapter 21

1. Ralph Allan, *Ordeal by Fire* (Toronto: Doubleday Canada, 1961), p. 198.

Chapter 22

1. *Canadian National Magazine* (December 1943), pp. 8–9.
2. *Ibid.*
3. Historian's Report No. 5, Director of History, Canadian Force Headquarters.

Chapter 23

1. John C. Noel, "Behind the Steamship Screen," *Canadian National Magazine* (May 1948), pp. 8–9.
2. Homer S. Reilley, *Fifteen Years of Progress* (Montreal: Department of Research and Development, Canadian National Railways, 1964), pp. 1–2.

Chapter 24

1. The Honorable J. R. Smallwood, afterward Premier of Newfoundland, compiled *The Book of Newfoundland*, 2 vols., upon behalf of the Newfoundland Government in 1937. This quotation is from Vol. II, pp. 263–264.

Chapter 25

1. *Canadian National Magazine* (November 1949), p. 12.
2. *Ibid.* (January 1950), p. 3.
3. Jack Lynch, "Railwaymen Battle Great Snowslides," *Canadian National Magazine* (March 1950), p. 18.
4. *Royal Committee on Transportation*, Appendix A, p. 60.
5. Speech given at Chamber of Commerce Luncheon, Winnipeg, May 4, 1950.
6. *Sessional Committee Reports, 1953*, p. 79.
7. *Sessional Committee Reports, 1951*, p. 120.

Chapter 26

1. *Canada Commons Railway Committee Report, 1959*, p. 369.
2. *Canada Commons Railway Committee Report, 1961*, p. 291.
3. Allan Sellers, "North to the Bay," *New York World-Telegram and The Sun*. Quoted in *Keeping Track* (April 1962), p. 17.

Bibliography

Legislation

(Note: When no other present-day source is given, read Canadian National Railways Library, Company Headquarters, Lagauchetiere Street, Montreal.)

Great Britain. *An Act to Re-unite the Provinces of Upper and Lower Canada, and for the Government of Canada.* 3–4 Vic., 1840, ch. 35. *Province of Canada Statutes,* 1841–43.

Canada. *An Act to provide for affording the Guarantee of the Province to the Bonds of Railway Companies on certain conditions, and for rendering assistance in the construction in the Halifax and Quebec Railway.* 12 Vic., 1849, ch. 29. *Province of Canada Statutes,* 1849.

Canada. *An Act respecting the construction of a National Transcontinental Railway.* 3 Edw. VIII, ch. 71. *Statutes of Canada,* 1903.

Canada. *An Act providing for the acquisition by His Majesty of the capital stock of the Canadian Northern Railway Company.* 7–8 Geo. V, ch. 24. *Statutes of Canada,* 1917.

Canada. Board of Arbitration of the Grand Trunk Railway Company of Canada. *Arbitration Proceedings,* 1918–22 (71 vols.). Ottawa: Public Archives.

Reports

Canada. Department of Railways and Canals. *Annual Report,* 1878/79–1935/36. Ottawa: King's Printer.

Canada. Department of Transport/Ministère des Transports. *Annual Report/Rapport Annuel,* 1936/37–1970/71. Ottawa: Queen's Printer.

Canada. Parliament. House. Select Standing Committee on Railways and Shipping. *Minutes of Proceedings and Evidence,* 1921–45. Ottawa: King's Printer.

Canada. Parliament. House. Sessional Committee on Railways, Airlines and
    Shipping. *Minutes of Proceedings and Evidence*, 1958–64. Ottawa:
    Queen's Printer.
Canada. Parliament. House. Sessional Committee on Railways and Shipping.
    Minutes of Proceedings and Evidence, 1946–57. Ottawa: Queen's
    Printer.
Canada. Parliament. House. Standing Committee on Transport and Communi-
    cations/Parlement. Chambre des Communes. Comité permanent des
    transports et des communications. *Minutes of Proceedings and Evi-
    dence/Procès-verbaux et témoignages*, 1967–69/1970. Ottawa: Queen's
    Printer.
Canada. Royal Commission on Railways. *Report*. Alexander T. Galt, chairman.
    Ottawa: MacLean, Roger Co., 1888.
Canada. Royal Commission on Transportation, 1903. *Report*. Robert Reford,
    chairman. Ottawa: King's Printer, 1906.
Canada. Royal Commission to Inquire into Railways and Transportation in
    Canada, 1917. *Report*. Alfred Holland Smith, chairman. Ottawa: King's
    Printer, 1917.
Canada. Royal Commission on Railways and Transportation, 1931–32. *Report*.
    Sir Lyman Duff, chairman. Ottawa: King's Printer, 1932.
Canada. Royal Commission on Transportation, 1951. *Report*. W. F. A. Turgeon,
    chairman. Ottawa: King's Printer, 1951.
Canada. Royal Commission on Agreed Charges. *Report*. W. F. A. Turgeon,
    chairman. Ottawa: Queen's Printer, 1955.
Canada. Royal Commission on Transportation, 1961–62. *Report*. 3 vols. M. A.
    MacPherson, chairman. Ottawa: Queen's Printer, 1961–62.
Canadian National Railways. *Annual Report*, 1923–70. Montreal.
Coverdale and Colpitts, Inc. *Report on the Canadian Northern Railway System*.
    New York: 1917.
Durham, John George Lambton, 1st Earl of. *Report on the Affairs of British
    North America, 1841*. Ottawa: Public Archives.
Grand Trunk Railway Company of Canada. *Annual Report*, 1854–1922.
    Montreal.
Neilly, Homer B. *Fifteen Years of Progress, 1950–64*. Montreal: Canadian
    National Railways. Research and Development Department. Develop-
    ment Planning Branch, 1964.

Books

Official Catalogue, *Statutory History of Steam and Electric Railways of Canada,
    1837–1937*. Compiled by Robert Dorman for Department of Transport.
Allen, Ralph. *Ordeal by Fire: Canada 1910–1945*. Canadian History Series,
    vol. 5. Toronto: Doubleday, 1961.

Borden, Henry, ed. *Robert Laird Borden: His Memoirs.* 2 vols. Toronto: Macmillan, 1938.

Brown, Thomas Storrow. *A History of the Grand Trunk Railway of Canada,* compiled from public documents. Quebec: Hunter, Rose, 1864.

Bryant, Sir Arthur. *Age of Elegance, 1812–1822.* Toronto: Collins, 1950.

———. *English Saga, 1840–1940.* London: Collins, 1940.

Careless, J. M. S., and Brown, R. Craig, eds. *The Canadians 1867–1967.* Toronto: Macmillan, 1967.

Chisholm, Joseph A., ed. *Speeches and Public Letters of Hon. Joseph Howe.* Halifax: Halifax Chronicle Publishing Co., 1909.

Copeland, John Morison. *The Trail of the Swinging Lanterns: A Racy, Railroading Review of Transportation Matters, Methods and Men.* Toronto: Addison and Mainprice, 1918.

Creighton, Donald. *Dominion of the North: A History of Canada.* Toronto: Macmillan, 1957.

———. *John A. Macdonald, the Young Politician.* Toronto: Macmillan, 1952.

Currie, Archibald William. *The Grand Trunk Railway of Canada.* Toronto: University of Toronto Press, 1957.

Fleming, Howard A. *Canada's Arctic Outlet: A History of the Hudson Bay Railway.* Berkeley and Los Angeles: University of California Press, 1957.

Fleming, Sir Sandford. *The Intercolonial: A Historical Sketch of the Inception, Location, Construction and Completion of the Line of Railway Uniting the Inland and Atlantic Provinces of the Dominion.* Montreal: Dawson Bros., 1876.

Fournier, Leslie Thomas. *Railway Nationalization in Canada.* Toronto: Macmillan, 1935.

Gibbon, John Murray. *Steel of Empire: The Romantic History of the Canadian Pacific, the Northwest Passage of Today.* Toronto: McClelland and Stewart, 1935.

Glazebrook, George Parkin de Pwenebroke. *A History of Transportation in Canada.* Toronto: Ryerson Press, 1938.

Grant, William Lawson. *The Tribune of Nova Scotia: A Chronicle of Joseph Howe. Chronicles of Canada,* vol. 26. Toronto: Glasgow, Brook, 1922.

Guillet, Edwin C. *Cobourg 1798–1948.* Oshawa: Goodfellow Printing, 1948.

Hanna, D. B. *Trains of Recollection: Drawn from Fifty Years of Railway Service in Scotland and Canada.* Toronto: Macmillan, 1924.

Harvey, D. C., ed. *The Heart of Howe: Selections from His Letters and Speeches.* Toronto: Oxford University Press, 1939.

Hind, H. Y., Keefer, T. C., and others. *Eighty Years of Progress of British North America.* Toronto: Stebbins, 1863.

Hodges, James. *Construction of the Great Victoria Bridge in Canada.* London: J. Weale, 1860.

Holbrook, Stewart Hall. *The Story of American Railroads.* New York: Crown, 1947.

Hornby, Sir Edmund Grimani. *Sir Edmund Hornby: An Autobiography*. London: Constable and Co., 1929.

Lovett, H. *Canada and the Grand Trunk, 1829–1924*. Montreal: 1924.

Lower, Arthur Reginald Marsden. *Canadians in the Making: A Social History of Canada*. Toronto: Longmans, Green, 1958.

———. *Colony to Nation: A History of Canada*. Toronto: Longmans, Green, 1946.

Manion, R. J. *Life Is an Adventure*. Toronto: Ryerson, 1936.

Marsh, D'Arcy. *The Tragedy of Henry Thornton*. Toronto: Macmillan, 1935.

Meyers, Leonard W. *Twenty-three Skidoo*. Toronto: British Book Service, 1958.

Pennington, Myles. *Railways and Other Ways: Being Reminiscences of Canal and Railway Life During a Period of 67 Years with Characteristic Sketches of Canal and Railway Men, Early Tram Roads and Railways, Steamboats and Ocean Steamships, the Electric Telegraph and Atlantic Cable, Canada and Its Railways, Trade and Commerce*. Toronto: Williamson, 1894.

Schull, Joseph. *Laurier: The First Canadian*. Toronto: Macmillan, 1965.

Shortt, Adam, and Doughty, Arthur G., eds. *Canada and Its Provinces: A History of the Canadian People and Their Institutions*. 23 vols. Toronto: Glasgow, Brook, 1914–17.

Skelton, Oscar Douglas. *Life and Times of Sir Alexander Tilloch Galt*. Toronto: Oxford University Press, 1920.

———. *The Railway Builders: A Chronicle of Overland Highways*. Chronicles of Canada, vol. 32. Toronto: Glasgow, Brook, 1916, 1922.

Smallwood, Joseph, ed. *The Book of Newfoundland*. 2 vols. St. John's, 1937.

Stevens, George Roy. *Canadian National Railways*. Vol. 1: *Sixty Years of Trial and Error 1836–1896*. Toronto: Clarke, Irwin, 1960.

———. *Canadian National Railways*. Vol. 2: *Towards the Inevitable 1896–1922*. Toronto: Clarke, Irwin, 1962.

Trollope, Frances Milton. *Domestic Manners of the Americans*, edited by Donald Smalley. New York: Knopf, 1949.

Trout, J. M., and Trout, Edward. *The Railways of Canada for 1870–1*. Toronto: Monetary Times, 1871.

Wade, Mason. *The French Canadians 1760–1945*. Toronto: Macmillan, 1955.

Magazines

Canadian Government Railways Employees Magazine, 1915–April 1919.

Canadian National Railways Employees Magazine, 1919–December 1921. Montreal.

Canadian National Railways Magazine, 1922–October 1937. Montreal.

Canadian National Magazine, 1937–57. Montreal.

Keeping Track, 1958–   . Montreal.

Clark, J. M. Review of *The Regulation of Railways*, by Samuel O. Dunn. *Journal of Political Economy*, XXVII, November 1919, pp. 802–804.

Davidson, James W. "The Canadian Northern Railway." *Queen's Quarterly*, XIV, October 1906.

Hard, W. "Spiking Down an Empire, Canada's New, Farthest North Transcontinental Railway." *Everybody's Magazine*, November 1909, pp. 633–45.

Newspapers

Brantford Daily Courier, 1855 et seq. Brantford, Ontario.

Brantford Expositor, 1855 et seq. Brantford, Ontario.

Calgary Eye-Opener, 1907 et seq. Calgary, Alberta.

The Empire, 1912. Prince Rupert, British Columbia.

Manitoba Free Press, 1897 et seq. Winnipeg, Manitoba.

Montreal Gazette, 1778–1970. Montreal.

The Montreal Star, 1912 et seq. Montreal.

New York World, 1890 et seq. New York.

New York Herald, July 1961. New York.

The Times (London), 1874 et seq. London.

Toronto Star, 1932. Toronto.

Witness, 1870 et seq. Montreal.

Index

Index

Abbott, J. C. C., 13
Abegweit, SS, 401
Aberhart, William, 364
Accommodation, SS, 6
Ackworth, W. H., 275
Act of Union (1841), 20n
advertising, impact of, 449
Air Canada, 394, 482. *See also* Trans-Canada Airlines
Air Transport Board, 393
air travel, impact of, 371–72
Alberta, 362
Alberta Resources Railway, 479
Albion (locomotive), 14, 15
Albion Railway, 14
Allan, Sir Hugh, 70, 71, 89, 108, 139
Allport, James, 66
All-Red Route, 196, 406
Aluminum Company of Canada, 442
Anderson, James, 79
Anglo-Newfoundland Development Company, 410
Annual Report, 1960, 455
Armour, Philip D., 191
Armstrong, Charles Newhouse, 247, 248, 249
Army Service Corps, 35
Aronivici, Arnold, 320, 346
Ashburton Award, 25
Ashfield, Lord, 352, 356
Asiatic cholera, 8, 52
Associated British Chambers of Commerce, 82
Athenia (ship), 389
Atholstan, Lord. *See* Graham, Hugh
Atlantic and Pacific Transit and Telegraph Company, 60
Atlantic and St. Lawrence Railroad, 21
Audubon Society, 476

automobile, impact of, 304–305, 323–24, 370, 399–401
aviation, expansion of, 401–402

Bacchante, HMS, 406
Bank of Canada, 381, 416
Bank Crash (1894), 409
Bank of Montreal, 7, 46, 74, 139, 140, 141, 143, 282
Bank of Upper Canada, 46
Barcelona Traction Company, 182
Baring, Thomas, 36, 38, 42, 46, 60, 66
Baring Brothers, 34, 41, 45, 55, 57, 65, 66, 77, 79, 121, 130
Beatty, E. W. (president, Canadian Pacific Railway), 315, 324, 342, 349, 352, 354, 355, 356, 367, 371
Beaumont Hamel, 411
Beaver Club, 469
Bellerose, G. E., 381
Belleville and North Hastings Railway, 122
Bennett, Richard Bedford (Prime Minister), 287, 346, 347, 357, 359, 363, 367
Bishop, Billy, 291
Black, W. A., 322, 365
Blackwell, E. T., 54, 56
Blair, A. G., 105, 245, 246
Boeing Aircraft Company, 393
Bold, James, 113
Booth group, 252
Borden, Sir Robert L., 202, 207, 213, 228, 246, 272, 273, 275, 277, 285, 287–88, 293, 294, 301, 310, 335
Bowater Paper Company, 410
Bradshaw's Railway Manual, Shareholders Guide and Directory (1916), 290

brakes, 156
Brantford *Courier, The*, 129
Brantford *Expositor, The*, 129, 130
Brassey, Thomas, 43, 44
Brazilian Traction group, 181
bridges and culverts, 152
British Columbia, 362
British Columbia Electric Railway, 183
British Empire Trust Company, 183
British North America Act (1867), 90
British North American Association, 81
British Overseas Airways Corporation, 482
Broadband Exchange Service, 474
Bromley, J., 358
Brooks, C. E., 318, 319, 330
Brotherhood of Locomotive Engineers and Conductors, 158
Brown, George, 47, 49, 54, 56, 70, 83
Brown, Roy, 291
Brown, S. T., 251
Brown, Thomas Storrow, 31, 39
Brunel, Alfred, 124
Brydges, C. J., 60, 62, 99
Brydges, Thomas, 70
Buchanan, Isaac, 128
Buffalo and Brantford Joint Stock Railroad, 129
Buffalo and Lake Huron Railway, 64
Bulwer-Lytton, Sir Edward, 81

Cabell, James Branch, 449
Calgary Eye Opener, 227n, 241, 299, 316, 347. *See* Bob Edwards
Camden and Amboy Railroad, 151
Camsell, Charles, 240
Canada (in general), 1–7
  during the Depression, 361–64
  in the 1850s, 108
  Laurier's influence on, 163
  Marquis wheat impact, 165
  original settlements in, 4–5
  prairie colonization, 224
  Rebellion of 1837, 29
  post World War I, 291
  during World War II, 378–96
Canada Atlantic Railway, 246
Canada Company, 3, 20, 128
Canada Southern Railway, 111
Canada–West Indies Trade Agreement, 374, 483
Canadian Airways Limited, 371, 372

Canadian Bank of Commerce, 188, 194, 279, 288
Canadian Corps, 269
Canadian Expeditionary Force, 383
Canadian Government Geological Survey, 240
Canadian Government Merchant Marine, 339, 374, 375, 401
Canadian Government Railways, 219
Canadian Labour (Standards) Code, 497
Canadian Main Line, 35, 36, 39, 142
Canadian National–Canadian Pacific Communications, 474
Canadian National Department of Highways, 472
Canadian National Exhibition, 400
Canadian National Hotels, 469
Canadian National Magazine, 388, 400
Canadian National Marine Services, 484
Canadian National Railways, 14, 17, 98, 116, 153, 185, 240, 244, 262, 280, 301, 305
  American properties, 332–33
  Arctic services, 474
  aviation and, 371–72
  Bennett administration, 346–47
  branch lines, 475–80
  British Treasury transfer, 380–81
  Bureau of Statistics, 376
  Canadian Pacific and, 324, 339–42, 367, 474. *See also* Canadian Pacific Railway
  communications, 331, 472–74
  community services, 329, 440
  corporate trademark, 454
  debt relieved, 424
  during Depression, 348–49, 362–66
  Dieselization, 331–32
  Express Department, 376
  equipment improvement, 376
  freight services, 335, 470–71
  hotels and ships, 339–40, 465–67
  Howe Ministry of Transport, 367
  immigration and, 321–23
  industrial promotions, 495
  labor relations, 496–500
  mobility devices improvement, 453
  Montreal investments, 467–69
  motion picture production, 489–91
  Newfoundland Railway takeover, 403
  passenger services, 336–39, 363, 370
  radio broadcasting, 326–29

problems and solutions, 311–12
real estate operations, 491–93
Research and Development Department, 484–88
road transport and, 369–70, 471–72
rolling stock buildup, 430
St. Lawrence Seaway project, 404
steamship business, 339, 372–75, 483–84
socio-economic changes, 323–24, 342–43
technical innovations, 452
Thornton administration, 350–60
Toronto and, 332, 494
Vermont flood repair, 332–33
"Whisper of Death" attack, 315–16
World Exposition display, 491
World War II and, 380–403
worldwide technology and, 488–89
Canadian National Railways Revision Act, 424
Canadian National Telecommunications, 475
Canadian National Transportation Limited, 471–72
Canadian Northern Ontario Railway, 241
Canadian Northern Railway, 291. See also Mackenzie and Mann partnership
Canadian Northern Railway Company, 280. See also Canadian National Railways
Canadian Pacific Railway, 127, 148, 171, 173, 177, 191, 193, 200, 202, 205, 219, 222, 250, 259, 260, 277, 295, 314, 354, 357, 427
aviation, 353, 372
Beatty and, 349, 367, 368
Bennett and, 347
Booths, feud with, 252
Canadian National Railways and, 339–42, 356
early history, 138–39
Eastern expansion, 119
election, 1891, 146
financing, 142–44
Grand Trunk Railway and, 140, 143–45, 191–92
hotels, 339–40
in Maine, 270
in Manitoba, 165–67, 169

Manitoba monopoly, 183–84
Metro Centre partnership, 494
ocean services, 339
Qu'Appelle, Long Lake and Saskatchewan Railway, 186–87
Oriental labor, 258
Saskatchewan invasion, 340–42
Shaughnessy presidency, 306
strike of 1910, 283
Thornton, relationship with, 316–17
in Vancouver, 262–63
Western monopoly, 180
wire operations, 474
Canadian Radio Broadcasting Corporation, 329
Canadian Railway Loan Act (1867), 90
Canadian Railways Overseas Corps, 267
Canadian Railway Troops, 269
Canatco (ship), 392
Cape Breton, 24
Capreol, Frederick Chase, 30, 31, 33, 124
Capital Revision Act (1952), 462
Cargo-Flo system, 471
Car-Go-Rail, 462
Carillon and Grenville Railway, 13
Carnegie, Andrew, 202
Cartier, George Etienne, 23, 81
Cassels, Sir Walter, 296, 297
Cayley, Thomas, 47
Centralized Traffic Control, 386
Central Vermont Railroad, 131, 134, 191, 283, 332–33, 370, 388, 420, 443
Chamberlin, Edson J., 282, 284–85, 286, 287, 289–90, 293
Champlain and St. Lawrence Railroad, 9
Chandler, Edward Barron, 87, 88
Chapman, H. C., 56
Charge-a-Trip, 462
Chateau Laurier Hotel, 344, 357, 428, 465
Chevrier, Hon. Lionel, 394
Chiang Kai-shek, Madame, 387
Chicago, 35–36, 109
Chicago and Lake Huron Railroad, 111
Chicago and Northern Railroad, 111
Chicago, Milwaukee and St. Paul Railway, 140
Chicago World's Fair (1893), 14, 147
Childers, Hon. H. E. C., 118, 119
Church, Colonel, 196
Churchill, Sir Winston, 380, 387, 413

Cincinnati, Saginaw and Mackinaw Railway, 116
Civil War, American, 57–58, 69, 81, 151
Cobourg Rail Road Company, 120
Cochrane, Francis, 272, 273, 275, 287
Coleman, D. C., 397
Commonwealth Air Training Plan, 393, 501
communications, railway, 472–74
computerization, railway, 473–74
Consolidated Mining and Smelting Company, 476–77
containerization, 471, 472
Cooke, Jay, 69
Cooper, Courtenay Ryly, 489
Cooper, Theodore, 217, 218
Co-Operative Commonwealth Federation, 364
Cornwallis (ship), 392
couplings, 157
Coverdale and Colpits, 275, 276, 277, 279
Cox, George A., 121, 123, 124, 194, 197
Credit Valley Railway, 142, 172
Crerar, Peter, 14
Crimean War, 45, 77
Crow's Nest Pass, 169–70
culverts, bridges and, 152
Cumberland, Frederick, 124, 125, 126

Dafoe, J. A., 313
Daimler, Gottlieb, 303
Danforth, Asa, 3
Delaware and Hudson Railroad, 352
Dennison, Merrill, 489
Depew, Chauncey, 135
Depression, Great (1929), 361–68
Detroit, Grand Haven and Milwaukee Railway, 116
D Day, 391
Dickens, Charles, 12, 104, 129
Diefenbaker, John G., 451
Dieselization, 331–32, 399
Disraeli, Benjamin, 81
Dorchester (locomotive), 9, 10
Douglas, Maj. C. H., 364
Dougall, John, 49
Drapeau, Jean, 492
Drayton, Sir Henry Lumley, 273, 275, 294
Drumheller mines, 254

Duff, Justice Lyman, 352, 353, 356, 358, 359
Dufferin, Lord, 97
Duke of Edinburgh, Philip, 428, 450
Dunn, Samuel, 102
Dunning, C. A., 337, 338–39, 348
Dunsmuir coal properties, 264
Durham Report, 48

Edward, Prince, 24
Edwards, Bob, 227, 241, 299, 316, 347. See *Calgary Eye Opener*
Eisenhower, Dwight D., 450
Elgin, Lord, 22
Elgin, Earl of, 40
Elizabeth II, 428, 430, 450
Emerald, HMS, 381
Empire, The, 335–36
employment, railroad
  protection, 498–500
  technology and, 496–97
Empress liners, 195
Enclosure Acts, 4
Erie Railroad, 60
Europe, Battle of, 387
European and North American Railway, 25, 79
Everybody's Magazine, 216

Fairweather, Starr W., 318, 319, 355, 356, 358, 360, 368, 396, 400, 413, 423, 484
Federal Savings and Loan Association (Chicago), 461
"Feed Britain" campaign, 302
Fenian Brotherhood, 84
Ferrier, James, 12
Financial Times, 145
Financial World, 400
First Canadian Division, 275
Firth of Forth Bridge, 152, 217
Fisk, Jim, 69
Flavelle, Sir Joseph, 296, 306, 307, 313, 352
Fleming, Sir Sandford, 25, 31, 84, 85, 86, 87, 88, 90, 92, 93, 124, 140, 150, 164, 186, 195, 209, 406
Foley, Welch and Stewart, 232, 268
Ford, Henry, 303
Franklin, Benjamin, 108
freight cars, 154–55, 470–71
French Canada, 458–59
Fulton, Robert, 6

Galsworthy, John, 126
Galt, Alexander Tilloch, 20, 21, 22, 23, 28, 37, 38, 39, 40, 54, 55, 65, 81, 83
Gaston, George W., 320
General Motors Corporation, 324, 399
George, David Lloyd (Prime Minister), 165
George IV, 14
George V, 406
George VI, 378, 430
Georgian Bay and Wellington Railway, 128
Girouard, Sir Percy, 267
Gladstone, William Ewart, 83
Globe, The, 83
Glyn, George Carr, 42, 46, 53, 57, 60, 66
Glyn Mills and Company, 28, 34, 41, 45, 57, 65, 66, 74, 121
Gooderham, William, 123
Gordon, Donald, 352, 415, 416, 417, 420, 422, 423, 424, 426, 427, 429, 436, 440, 442, 447, 448, 450, 452, 454, 456-58, 460, 483, 492, 500-501
Gore Loyalists, 28
Gosford, Earl of, 10
Gould, Jay, 69
Graham, George P., 300
Graham, Hugh (Lord Atholstan), 206, 315
Grand Junction Railroad, 39, 122
Grand Trunk Acquisition Act (1919), 295
Grand Trunk Act (1857), 66
Grand Trunk Arrangements Act (1862), 59, 61
Grand Trunk Pacific Railway, 219, 258, 259, 270, 275, 277, 278, 281, 283, 285, 287, 291
  branch lines, 225-26
  colonization formula, 224-25
  construction, 221, 229
  indebtedness, 1912, 288
  lakehead line, 214
  governmental takeover, 296
  political difficulties, 227-28
  terminals changed, 228
Grand Trunk Pacific Town and Development Company, 224
Grand Trunk Railway, 84, 106, 118, 119, 140, 141, 142, 145, 147, 151, 154, 177, 200, 250, 252, 258, 425
  early development, 34-74

as British property, 281
equipment improvements, 189-91
expansion, summary of, 134-36
governmental takeover, 296
Hays administration, 281-300
in Michigan, 115
Midland takeover, 124
Ontario acquisitions, 120-24, 128-30
property assessment, 1917, 282
Rivers-Wilson and Hays administration, 148
Royal Commission report, 286
traffic growth, 108
Transcontinental and, 144
Vermont takeover, 130-34
Grand Trunk Western Railroad, 191, 192, 196, 388
Gray, Col. Francis D., 119
Great Britain
  Ashburton Award, 25
  Battle of Britain, 382
  Civil War in United States, attitudes toward, 82
  "mania," railway, 18-20, 22, 34, 42
Great Eastern Railway, 307, 308, 317, 320
Great Northern Railway, 250, 263
Great Slave Lake Line, 476-77
Great Western Railroad, 16, 28, 29, 37, 38, 54, 60, 110, 116, 118, 119, 129, 148
Great Western Suspension Bridge (Niagara River), 63
Grey, Earl, 335
Grey, Sir Edward, 274
Guthrie, Sir Tyrone, 489
Gzowski, Casimir, and Company, 30, 38, 50, 55

Hackett, John, 349
Halifax Disaster, 271
Halifax Railway, 75
Hall, Capt. Basil, 3
Hamilton and Northwestern Railway, 121, 127
Hamilton, Lord Claude, 308
Hanna, David Blythe, 177, 178, 182, 186, 242, 301, 307, 310
Hard, William, 216, 230
Harmsworth Brothers, 410
Hays, Charles Melville, 148, 190, 191,

192, 193, 194, 195, 196, 197, 199,
   204, 205, 282, 283, 284, 286, 297
Heygate, William Unwin, 113, 114
Henry, R. A. C., 318, 484
Hickson, Sir Joseph, 70, 74, 107, 115,
   119, 120, 124, 127, 128, 145, 146,
   147, 189
Hill, James J., 139, 140, 167, 187
Hilton Corporation, 467
Hincks, Francis, 22, 23, 28, 29, 33, 34,
   35, 36–37, 38, 41, 47, 75, 80, 82,
   120, 124, 128
Hitler, Adolf, 377, 380, 384
Hobson, Joseph, 136
Hodges, James, 50, 52
Holbrook, Stuart Ball, 20
Holt, Herbert, 172, 173
Holton, Luther, 61
Hornby, Sir Edmund Grimani, 48, 53–
   54, 103
Horne-Payne, Robert Montgomery, 183,
   185, 188, 241, 242, 254, 259, 273,
   274, 302
hotel chains, railroad, 465–69
Hotel Vancouver, 340
Houston, John, 235
Howe, Charles Decatur, 367, 368, 372,
   393, 445
Howe, Joseph, 24, 25, 26, 35, 47, 76,
   77, 79, 82, 88
Howland, W. P., 83
Hudson, George, 19, 28
Hudson Bay Railway, 174, 176, 330,
   334, 337, 341, 353, 441
Hudson River Railroad, 110
Hudson's Bay Company, 60, 138, 185, 469
Hummell, L. V., 319
hump yards, 453–54
Hungerford, S. J., 302, 355, 358, 363,
   375, 383, 393, 401

Illinois Central Railway, 140
Imperial Guarantee (1851), 75, 76, 80,
   82
industrial promotions, 495
Industrial Workers of the World, 250
Intercolonial Railway, 144, 199, 202,
   206, 209, 219, 243, 245, 252
   construction and completion, 75–105
   Grand Trunk acquisition, 112
   western extension, 246
   World War I, 270–71

International Bank for Reconstruction
   and Development, 417
International Contract Company, 87
International Prime Meridian Confer-
   ence, 85
Interstate Commerce Commission, 115
Irondale and Bancroft Railway, 252

Jackson, Andrew, 8
Jackson, William Mather, 38, 122
Jamaican Railway, 488
James Bay Railway, 240
Jameson, Anna, 27
Jasper Park Lodge, 344, 356, 465–66
Jenkins, Edward, 70, 71
Johnson, Elisha, 27
Johnson, Philip G., 372, 392
Journal of Political Economy, 102

Keefer, Thomas Coltrin, 29, 50
Kelly, Howard, 293, 295
King, William Lyon Mackenzie (Prime
   Minister), 3, 283, 299, 306, 310,
   325, 336, 337, 348, 367, 393, 398
Korean National Railroad, 488
Korean War, 435

labor relations, railroad, 397–99, 496
Lady fleet, 373, 374–75, 401, 483
Lady Drake, 392
Lady Hawkins, 392
Lady Nelson, 392
Lady Rodney, 392
Lady Somers, 392
Lake Simcoe Junction Railway, 124
Lash, G. H., 383, 397
Lash, Zebulon Aston, 182, 183, 198, 263,
   280, 302
Laurie, James, 77, 206
Laurier, Sir Wilfred, 105, 163, 164, 181,
   193, 194, 196, 198, 200, 201, 202,
   203, 204, 209, 227, 228, 246, 297,
   334
Lazard Frères, 274
Leacock, Stephen, 86, 312
Leonard, Col. R. W., 213
Lind, Jenny, 31
Livesay, James, 87
locomotives, 152–54
London (Ontario), 15–17
London and Gore Railway, 15–16, 27.
   See also Great Western Railroad

London and Northwestern Railway, 151
London and Port Stanley Railway, 15, 17
Long Island Railroad, 307
Loree, L. F., 352

McAdoo Award, 302
McBride, Richard, 257, 258
Macdonald, Sir John A., 53, 59, 70, 86, 90, 94, 96, 139, 145, 146, 160, 162, 227
Macdonald, Sandfield, 59
Macdonald Hotel, 466
M'Ewen, Alexander, 68
McGibbon, Peter, 350, 351, 357
McGill, Peter, 7, 8, 9, 21
McGregor, Gordon R., 444, 446, 481
McIntyre, Duncan, 148
Mackenzie, Alexander, 70, 73, 74, 89, 94, 97, 99, 138, 139
Mackenzie, William, 171. *See also* Mackenzie and Mann partnership
Mackenzie, William Lyon, 3
Mackenzie and Mann partnership, 297, 334
  Alberta coal fields, 254
  Arctic ventures, 254, 256
  branch line coup, 180
  Canadian Northern Ontario and, 241
  Canadian Northern Railway and, 179, 185–86, 187–88, 264, 280
  Canadian Pacific monopoly and, 180
  Credit Valley Railway, 172
  East-West linkup, 1914, 252
  financial disaster, 1911–17, 272–80
  foreign ventures, 181–82
  grand design, 242–43
  Hanna joins, 177
  Horne-Payne joins, 183
  Hudson Bay dispute, 174–75
  Icelanders' branch lines, 174
  James Bay Railway acquisition, 240–41
  knighthoods, 251
  labor troubles, 260, 262
  Lash, Z. A., joins, 182–83
  Maritime ventures, 243–47
  Manitoba Railway and Canal Company acquisition, 176
  Manitoba expansion, 1910, 253
  Manitoba land grant campaign, 183–85
  Montreal entry, 250–51
  mineral interests, 239–40
  Northern Alberta Railways, 256
  Ontario acquisitions, 252–53
  Pacific terminals, 262–63
  panic, 1907, 241–42
  prairie difficulties, 241
  Qu'Appelle, Long Lake and Saskatchewan Railroad, 173, 186–87
  Quebec ventures, 247–51
  resignation, 280
  Royal Commission, 275–78
  Western difficulties, 1910, 258–59
  Western lines, first, 179
  Western prospects, 238–39
  World War I, 274
  Yellowhead Pass, 259
McKinley tariff, 144, 161
McLachlin, Donald W., 335–36
McLuhan, Marshall, 403
MacMillan, Norman John, 501
MacPherson, W. A., 456
MacNab, Sir Allen, 23, 27, 28, 29, 30
Macoun, John, 164
Maine Legislature, 21
Malcolm, James, 344
Mania, the British railway, 18–20, 22, 34, 42
"Manifest Destiny," 108
Manion, R. J., 347, 348, 350, 353, 354, 357
Manitoba, 362
Manitoba Free Press, The, 166, 313, 336, 353, 358
Manitoba Railway and Canal Company, 176
Mann, Donald, 171. *See also* Mackenzie and Mann partnership
Marconi, 473
Maritime Provinces, 3, 24, 75–76, 362
Marquis wheat, 165, 341
Master Agency Plan, 471, 472
Master Car Builders List, 155
Meighen, Arthur (Prime Minister), 287, 293, 294, 296, 306, 313
Meredith, Sir William, 280
Merritt, William Hamilton, 130
Metcalf, Maynard, 400
Metis, revolt of the, 144n
Metro Centre (Toronto), 494
Mexican Light, Heat and Power Company, 182

Michigan Air Line Railway, 116
Michigan Central Railroad, 37, 111, 118
Midland Railway, 66, 121, 124
Miller, Alexander, 12
Milner, Lord, 282
Milwaukee (locomotive), 58
mining, branch lines and, 478–80
Mohawk and Hudson Railroad, 7
Molson, John, 6, 9, 21
Monck, Viscount, 83
Montreal, railroad investments in, 467–69
Montreal (Daily) Star, The, 206, 236, 315, 323, 499
Montreal Gazette, The, 315
Montreal Tunnel and Terminal Company, 251
Montreal World Exposition (1967), 463, 491
Montstephen, Lord. *See* Stephen, George
Morgan, Pierpont, 148, 185
Morse, Frank W., 210, 215, 227, 282, 297
Morse, Samuel F. B., 157, 472
Morton Rose and Company, 140, 141
motion picture, railroad, 489–91
Muir, James, 492
Muir, Ramsey, 177
Murray, Charles, 352

Napier, Hon. William, 47
Napoleonic Wars, 239
National Railways Revision Act, 424
National Transcontinental Railway, 200, 207, 249, 252, 278, 283, 284, 334
    construction, 208–37
    Eastern Division, 246, 248, 250
National Transcontinental Railway Act, 202, 203, 206, 209
New Brunswick, 24, 79–80
Newfoundland, 24, 480–81
Newfoundland Hotel, 466
Newfoundland Railway, 404, 411, 412, 413, 414, 481
Newfoundland Regiment, 411
New Haven Railroad, 461
New London Northern Railroad Company, 443
New York Central Railroad, 64, 110, 111, 118, 129, 135, 147, 275
New York Herald, 58

New York, New Haven and Hartford Railroad, 284
New York World, The, 161
Niagara River Bridge, 63, 64, 66, 152, 191
Nipissing Central Railroad, 252
Noel, John C., 400
Northcliffe, Lord, 410
Northern Alberta Railways, 256, 342, 476
Northern Pacific Railway, 180, 184
Northern Railway, 125, 126, 127, 157
North Grey Railway, 126
North Shore Railway, 71
North Simcoe, Railway, 126
North Star (airplane), 401
North West Company, 469
Notre Dame Bay Railway, 407
Nova Scotia, 24
Nova Scotian, The, 25, 79
Nova Scotia Railway Company, 76, 78
    short lines, 76–78, 244–45

Oberon (locomotive), 117
Ocean Limited service, 440
Old Families (Quebec), 247, 248
Olympic, HMT, 271
O'Moore, Rory, 416
Ontario, 362
Ontario Agricultural College, 109
Ontario Short Lines, 252–53
Ontario, Simcoe and Huron Union Railroad, 39, 84
"On to the Bay" Association, 337
Overseas Railway Construction Corps, 268

Paish, Sir George, 275
Palmer, Alfred, 337
Panic of 1873, 69, 108, 118, 121, 131
Papineau, Louis Joseph, 10
passenger service
    business campaigns, 462–64
    cars, 155–56
    traffic, 471
Pearl Harbor, 384
Pearson, Lester B., 460
Pearson, S. F., 181
Peninsular Railway (Indiana), 114
Peninsular Railway (Michigan), 114
Pennsylvania Railroad, 307, 319
pension fund, 499–500

Peoples Pacific Railroad, 184n
Perham, Josiah, 184n
Perley, Sir George, 279, 287, 294
personnel, behavior of railway, 157–59
Peto, Brassey, Jackson and Betts, 36, 37, 41, 42, 44, 45, 50, 53, 76, 79, 150
Philadelphia and Reading Railroad, 147
Philip, Duke of Edinburgh, 428, 450
Phillips, Lazarus, 492
Philosophy of Railroads, 29
Phippen, F. H., 280
Pierce, Jason B., 7, 8, 9, 21
Pine Tree Radar Line, 474
Place Ville-Marie (Montreal), 470, 492–93
Poor, John A., 20, 21, 23, 25, 37, 83
Pope, J. C., 94
Port Hope, Lindsay and Beaverton Railway, 121. *See also* Midland Railway
Port Huron and Lake Michigan Railroad, 113
Potter, Richard, 64–65, 66, 67, 68, 70, 74, 138
Pottinger, David, 99, 100, 101, 105, 245
Pouliot, Jean François, 451
"Prairies First" policy, 240
Price, Joseph, 148, 189, 190
Prince David (ship), 375, 389, 390, 391, 392
Prince Edward Island, 24
Prince Edward Island Railway, 94–98
Prince George (ship), 401, 484
Prince Henry (ship), 375, 389, 390, 391, 392
Prince liners, 373, 375, 401
Prince Robert (ship), 375, 389, 391, 392
Prince Rupert (city), 234–35
Princess Victoria (ferry), 10
Price-Green, Charles, 240
Prophetic Bible Institute, 364

Qu'Appelle, Long Lake and Saskatchewan Railroad, 173, 186
Quebec, 362
Quebec Bridge, 217–19
Quebec and Lake St. John Railway, 248, 249
Quebec Railway, Light and Power Company, 443
Quebec separatist movement, 449
Queen Elizabeth Hotel, 468–69
Queens University Quarterly, 185

radio broadcasting, railroads and, 326–27, 328
railroad development, 149–59
  advertising, 403
  automobile and, 399–401
  brakes, 156
  bridges and culverts, 152
  community services, 329–30
  construction methods, 477–78
  corporate trademark, 455
  couplings, 157
  employment and, 496–97
  expansion, improvements, innovations, 330–32
  labor relations and, 397–99
  mobility devices, 453
  organization and, 454–55
  passenger campaigns, 462–64
  personnel behavior, 157–59
  rails, 151–52
  railway terminology, 159
  research, 484–85, 488
  roadbed and superstructure, 150
  road transport, 369–70
  rolling stock, 152–56
  service improvements, 399
  signals, 157
  sites, choice of, 150
  social pressures on, 396
  socio-economic factors (1920s), 342–43
  technical improvements (1950s), 452–54
  post World War I, 303–306
Railrodder, The (film), 489–90
rails, 150–52
Railway Association of Canada, 397
Railway Builders, The, 28
Railway Committee of the Privy Council, 176
Railway Guarantee Act (1849), 29, 31, 34, 36
Railways Staff College, 376
railway strike (1910), 283
railway terminology, 159
Ralston, Col. J. L., 383
real estate operations, 491–93
Red Cross, 388
Red, White and Blue Plan, 462, 463
Reid, J. D., 301
Reid, Robert Gillespie, 407, 408, 409, 410, 411

Rhodes, Cecil, 489
Ridout, Thomas G., 46
Riel, Louis, 143
Rivers-Wilson, Sir Charles, 148, 189, 190, 191, 192, 193, 194, 196, 197, 198, 199, 201, 203, 204, 206, 215, 226, 282, 283, 289, 297
roadbed and superstructure, 150
Road Cruiser Service, 463
road transport, impact of, 369–70, 471–72
Robert Stephenson and Company, 10
Robinson, Bill, 489
rolling stock, 152–56
    freight cars, 154–55
    locomotives, 152–54
    passenger cars, 155–56
Roosevelt, Franklin Delano (U.S. President), 366, 387, 413
Roosevelt, Theodore, 228
Rose, Sir John, 96
Ross, Alexander Mackenzie, 57
Ross, James, 172, 173, 174, 175
Ross, John, 42
Rothermore, Lord, 410
Royal Air Force, 291, 371
Royal Bank of Canada, 492
Royal Canadian Air Force, 393
Royal Canadian Mounted Police, 381
Ruel, Gerard, 302, 355, 358

Sago-Bomarc Missile System, 474
St. Laurent, Louis Stephen (Prime Minister), 427, 429
St. Lawrence and Atlantic Railroad, 21, 23
St. Lawrence Bridge, 152
St. Lawrence Seaway, 404, 446, 450
St. Paul, Minneapolis and Manitoba Railroad, 139
Samuels, Sir Herbert, 360
Samson (locomotive), 14, 15
Saskatchewan, 362, 363
Saunder, Charles, 165
Saunder, James, 165
Saunder, Percy, 165
Schreiber, Collingwood, 99, 102, 245
Schull, Joseph, 202
Seargeant, Lewis, 70, 115, 146, 148, 204
Seymour, Hezekiah K., 31
Shanley, Walter, 56, 121

Shaughnessy, Sir Thomas (Lord), 145, 146, 186, 192, 207, 306
Shea, George A., 381
shipping, 373, 483–84
Shopcrafts Cooperative Plan, 325
Sicotte, L. V., 83
Sifton, Clifford, 164, 169, 199, 202
    settlement plan, 167, 175, 179, 184, 323
signals, 157
Simcoe, George Graves, 2
Simpson, Sir George, 2
Skelton, O. D., 28, 41
Smallwood, J. H. "Joey" (Premier), 413
Smith, A. H., 275, 277
Smith, Donald (Lord Strathcona), 138, 139, 140, 143, 145
Smith, John, 131
Smith, Marcus, 92
Smithers, Alfred M., 282, 285, 288, 293, 294, 297
Social Credit, 364
Solandt, O. M., 485
Somme, Battle of the, 411
South African War, 163, 198
South Wales Railway, 70
Spitfire planes, 382
Statute of Westminster (1926), 291
steamship service, 401
Stearman biplane, 368
Steep Rock ore body, 240
Stefansson, Vilhjalmur, 336
Stephen, George, 138, 139, 140, 141, 142, 143, 145, 146, 188
Stephenson, George, 6, 151
Stephenson, Robert, 50
Stevens, R. L., 151
Stewart, Gen. J. W., 221, 268, 269, 308
Stratford and Huron Railway, 128
Stratford Shakespearean Theatre, 489
Strathcona, Lord. See Smith, Donald
Sun Life Assurance Company, 381
Super-Continental service, 434, 440
superstructure, roadbed and, 150
Swiftsure (ship), 6
Swift, Wagstaff and Company, Solicitors, 39
Swinyard, Thomas, 97, 98
Sydenham, Lord, 22
Sykes, James, 13
Symington, H. J., 393
System Freight Sales program, 471

Taft, William Howard, 296, 297, 298
Talbot, Col. Thomas, 15, 29
Thomas, J. H., 308, 309, 329, 359
Thomas Cook and Son, 354
Thompson, Walter, 318, 378, 383, 387, 427
Thornton, Sir Henry, 148, 307–308, 309, 311–21, 322–44, 346, 347, 348, 349, 350, 351, 352, 353, 354, 356, 358, 359, 360, 371
Thornton, Lady, 347, 357
Tilley, Leonard, 82, 90
Times (London), *The*, 71, 147
Titanic disaster, 284
Toledo, Ann Arbor and North Michigan Railway, 116
Toledo, Saginaw and Muskegon Railway, 116
Toronto Globe, 49, 50, 147
Toronto Metro Centre, 494
Toronto and Nipissing Railway, 123–24
Toronto, Simcoe and Lake Huron Railway, 30–31, 32, 33, 124, 438
Toronto, Simcoe and Muskoka Junction Railway, 126
Toronto Star, 358
Toronto Telegram, The, 313
Trans-Canada Airlines Limited, 372, 393, 394, 401, 402, 444, 481–82
Trans-Canada Highballer, 471
Trans-Canada Railway, 196
Treasure transfer, British, 380–81
Trent affair, 58, 82, 83
Trollope, Anthony, 157
tunnels
  Kicking Horse Canyon, 150
  Mount Royal, 250–51
  New Westminster–Vancouver, 264
  St. Clair, 136
Tupper, Sir Charles, 77, 80, 81, 86, 88, 99, 140, 141, 142, 145, 147
Tyler, Sir Henry Whatley, 63, 64, 74, 106, 107, 108, 111, 112, 113, 114, 115, 116, 119, 124, 127, 141, 142, 144, 146, 148, 189, 227, 289
Tyrell brothers, 164

unions, labor, 158–59
United Aircraft of Canada, 463
United Empire Loyalists, 3, 24
United States, 69
  Ashburton Award, 25

Civil War, 57–58, 69, 81, 151
fishing conventions dispute, 144
McAdoo Award, 302
Manifest Destiny, 108
panic of 1873 impact, 69, 108, 118, 121, 131
War of 1812, 16, 35
World War I, 292

Vancouver Island (ship), 390
Vanderbilt, Cornelius, 69, 109–10
Vanderbilt, William, 110, 111, 112, 114, 135
Van Horne, Sir William Cornelius, 140, 142, 143, 144, 145, 177, 180, 192
Vankoughnet, P. M., 82
Vansittart, Admiral, 128
Vaughan, R. C., 302, 377, 383, 389, 401, 404, 415
Vickers Viscount (aircraft), 446
Victoria Bridge, 50–53, 158, 191
Victoria, Queen, 24, 163
Victoria Railway, 123, 171
Victory Loan campaign, 388

War of 1812, 35
War Prices and Trade Board, 416
Watkin, Edward, 57, 58, 59, 60, 62, 64, 66, 81
Watson Watt, Robin, 382
Webb, Beatrice, 64, 74
Webb, Sydney, 64
Webb and Knapp, 492
Webster, J. C., 353
Welland Railway, 130
Wellesley, Sir Arthur (Lord Wellington), 35, 161
Wellington, Grey and Bruce Railway, 118
Wells, H. G., 449
Welsh, Paddy, 221
White, Sir Thomas, 287, 293, 295
William, Prince, 24
Winnipeg Great Northern Railway, 176
Winnipegosis Railway, 179
Weser (ship), 390
Western Canada Wheat Pool, 367
Western Union Telegraph Company, 344
Westinghouse air brake, 156
Whitby and Port Perry Extension Railway, 122
White, Thomas, 272, 273, 275

Whiteway, Sir William, 406
William Carson, MV, 480
Wilson, Sir Henry, 309
Wilson, Peter B., 452
"Whisper of Death" campaign, 315–16
Witness, The, 49, 50
Wittauch investigation, 461
Wolverton, Lord. *See* Glyn, George Carr
Woodstock, Lake Erie Railway and Harbour Company, 128

Woodsworth, J. S., 364
World Bank, 417
World War I, 281, 303
World War II, 377, 379–94

Young, Sir Charles, 113, 114
Yukon Telephone Company, 475

Zeckendorff, Bill, 492